Advance praise for
Boy with the Bullhorn

"Ron Goldberg's *Boy with the Bullhorn* is something special. It's not just the story of ACT UP and his coming of age with the organization but a bearing witness to a tragedy that took the lives of so many of his, our, friends, way, way before their time. In deep detail, Ron tells the story of how a nation abandoned a generation of young men and women, left them to die, and ignored and how they fought back to survive. But even with footnotes galore, beyond the history what comes shining through this narrative is the beating heart of ACT UP, the sorrow, the anger, the joy, and, yes, humor of those moments, because Ron personified so much of who we were in those days long ago. And this is more than a testament, a valedictory; it is a challenge to a new generation to take up the struggle. In showing how a small group of committed individuals changed the world, most of them terribly young, Ron provides hope that the challenges we face now, from COVID-19 to climate change, are not just fate, things to which we must just surrender but things that we can and must act up and fight back against. I can hear Ron's voice in these pages, full of passion, full of hope, sassy and funny, cajoling us, urging us on once again. Pick up that bullhorn. Let's go."

—**Gregg Gonsalves**, Yale School of Public Health

"What a lively, richly textured history of ACT UP New York, a coalition of people who, united in anger, fought to the death to save our lives, and the lives of our comrades, lovers, and friends. Moving with ease between the personal and the political, Ron Goldberg captures the sights and sounds of the early years of the AIDS crisis and of the activist response to it. In this book, The Boy with the Bullhorn shows himself a gifted and generous movement griot."

—**Kendall Thomas**, Nash Professor of Law, Columbia University

"In *Boy with the Bullhorn*, Ron Goldberg offers extraordinary insight into the collective draw of ACT UP, how AIDS activism opened our hearts to care for the most vulnerable among us, and how a mix of queer activists, undaunted by the stigma of AIDS, challenged the multiple structural violences of the U.S. healthcare and welfare systems. Combining a coming-of-age narrative with a meticulously documented social history of his years in ACT UP New York from 1987 to 1995, Goldberg uses his caustic, campy 'chant queen' voice to serve up a theatrical recounting of ACT UP's creative expressions of civil disobedience. The real fierceness of Goldberg's narrative lies in his insistent position as historical witness to the sexist, racist, and anti-gay government response to the AIDS crisis, exploding the reader's perception of who we were as activists, the political changes we accomplished, and how through ACT UP we became the fullest and best expression of ourselves."

—**Debra Levine**, Director of Studies in Theater, Dance & Media, Harvard University

"Ron Goldberg's passion ignites every page of this powerful, fiery memoir. 'Inspiring' might seem too trite a word to describe such a rich offering, but that's exactly what this memoir is. It *inspires* in the deepest sense of that verb, giving breath and life to history that continues to ripple out into our continuing organizing work. Those who need a good mix of rage, humor, and hope to keep them acting up will find plenty here to push, provoke, and empower."

—**Micah Bucey**, author of *The Book of Tiny Prayer*

"As the first fifteen years, 1981 to 1996, of the global AIDS crisis drift further from memory and evermore into the past, there has been an urgent need for survivors of that period to tell their stories, document the losses, share the strategies that helped activists overcome government and medical neglect of the pandemic, and convey the complex array of emotions—not always of grief, often of joy in community and personal agency—that characterized the era for people who lived through it and with it and in spite of it. I can hardly imagine a better narrator of that story than Ron Goldberg. Anyone who went to an ACT UP meeting or demonstration between 1987 and 1995 knew him as an organizer, street activist, and composer of ingenious chants. His audacity, theatricality, political acuity, and profound commitment to the AIDS and LGBTQ communities typified the best qualities of ACT UP New York and are everywhere in evidence in *Boy with the Bullhorn*, a book that shows us not just how to survive a crisis, but how to become ourselves in the midst of it."

—**John Weir**, author of *The Irreversible Decline of Eddie Socket* and *What I Did Wrong*

Boy with the Bullhorn

BOY WITH THE BULLHORN

BULLHORN

A Memoir and History
of ACT UP New York

Ron Goldberg

**EMPIRE
STATE
EDITIONS**

AN IMPRINT OF FORDHAM UNIVERSITY PRESS
NEW YORK   2022

Visit us online at www.fordhampress.com/empire-state-editions.

Library of Congress Cataloging-in-Publication Data available online at https://catalog.loc.gov.

Printed in the United States of America

24 23 22   5 4 3 2 1

First edition

for

Bradley Ball, Gary Clare, Spencer Cox, David B. Feinberg,
Mark Fotopoulos, Robert Garcia, Jon Greenberg,
Michael Irwin, David E. Kirschenbaum, Tim Kivel,
Tony Malliaris, Aldyn McKean, Michael Morrissey,
Howie Pope, Tim Powers, Bob Rafsky, Mark Roberts,
David Roche, Vito Russo, Lee Schy,
Kevin Smith, David Wayne

and

David Serko

CONTENTS

PREFACE

LET ME SAY at the outset, I blame Larry Kramer.

I'd first started working on this book back in 1994, as I was beginning to drift out of ACT UP. It was an attempt to get my bearings and make sense of just what the hell I'd been through over the last seven years.

I pored over my files, summarizing original documents, including fact sheets, teach-in guides, meeting notes, newsletters and committee digests, flyers, posters, letters to the Floor, and other materials, as well as press clippings, news articles, and my own journal entries and writings. But after a few years' work, I put my notes away. The task was too overwhelming, and it was time, I thought, to move on.

Instead of writing the book, I concentrated on fleshing out an ACT UP timeline I'd constructed to help me maintain a basic chronology of events, both inside the organization and externally. I saw it as a pared-down way to capture the density of our days—not just our zaps and actions, but internal events, AIDS-related news and milestones, as well as the ever-mounting deaths of friends and comrades. Then in 2008, as I contemplated my upcoming fiftieth birthday, I started thinking about what was important to me and realized I needed to dive back in and write this book.

A few weeks later, I came home from my family seder on the first night of Passover to a message from Larry Kramer on my answering machine. (I have no idea how he got my phone number and was shocked he even remembered who I was.) "Ron Goldberg," he thundered. "This is Larry Kramer.

Where is your timeline? You said in your Oral History interview that you had a timeline of ACT UP demonstrations—where is it? Call me back!"

Well, when gay Moses comes down from Mt. Sinai demanding your tablets, what can you do? I called him back. I told him I'd send him the timeline, but also that I'd returned to writing my book. "Good," he said. "Let me know when I can see it."

I sent Larry the first few chapters, which he generously critiqued, and he soon became a booster, both personally and professionally as I continued to write and tried to find a publisher.

Sadly, he died before I could tell him that I'd sold my manuscript—though given the somewhat biblical underpinnings of our relationship, I'm guessing he knows.

Boy with the Bullhorn is a history of ACT UP/New York, the original and largest chapter of the AIDS Coalition to Unleash Power, from 1987 to 1995, and a memoir of my coming of age as an activist on the front lines of the AIDS epidemic. It uses my story—the activist education of a well-intentioned, if somewhat naïve, nice gay Jewish theater queen—to navigate the larger history of ACT UP, the grassroots AIDS activist organization that confronted politicians, scientists, pharmaceutical companies, religious leaders, the media, and an often-uncaring public, to change the course of the AIDS epidemic. Combining personal accounts and behind-the-scenes details with diligent documentation and research, it provides an intimate look into how activist strategies are developed and deployed as well as a snapshot of life in New York City during the darkest days of the AIDS epidemic.

From my first ACT UP meeting in June 1987, ACT UP quickly took over my life. For the next eight years, I chaired committees, planned protests, led teach-ins, and facilitated our Monday night meetings. I visited friends in hospitals, attended far too many AIDS memorials, and participated in over a hundred zaps and demonstrations, where I came to be known as ACT UP's unofficial "Chant Queen"—the boy with the bullhorn, leading and writing chants for many of our major actions.

It was the hardest, most intense, most rewarding, most joyous, and most devastating time of my life.

Even from my earliest days in the organization, I was keenly aware that I was taking part in history and had a responsibility to record what was happening and pass it on to future generations. I say this with great humility. No one person can tell the history of ACT UP. To begin with, which history and which ACT UP? At its peak, ACT UP had close to 150 chapters worldwide. In early 1991, ACT UP/New York alone had close to five hundred people attending our weekly Monday night meetings, as well as forty-five separate committees, caucuses, and affinity groups working on myriad actions, projects, and issues. While I may have been in several of the "rooms where it happened," I was by no means in all of them.

I have, however, tried to honor the work of other activists, including not only our celebrated treatment activists, but also those who fought to change the AIDS definition, created AIDS housing, conducted needle exchanges, advocated for national health care, and distributed safe sex information, and others. I've also tried to acknowledge the work of ACT UP's Women's, Latina/o Activist, Majority Action (People of Color), Asian and Pacific Islander (API), and PISD (People with Immune Deficiency Syndrome) committees and caucuses, recognizing both their struggles and their achievements, as well as their impact on my political awareness and understanding of the AIDS crisis. While my account of their efforts is limited by the nature of my own activist experiences—and let's face it, as a cisgender gay white male with health insurance living in New York City, my perspective on ACT UP and the AIDS crisis is hardly universal—I've tried to at least leave some breadcrumbs for others to follow.

I've also made an effort to be clear about the events where I was present and those where I was not. Throughout the book, and particularly on those occasions where I've gone outside of my own experiences, I've relied on my own extensive archive of original ACT UP documents, contemporaneous news articles, and other published material, as well as the invaluable ACT UP Oral Histories and activist videos, to help flesh out actions and events, as well as the background stories of some of the key activists involved.

I've done my best to give an honest appraisal of the organization, highlighting our failures as well as our successes and discussing at length some of the controversies and bad behavior that eventually ripped the group apart. I've tried to be equally truthful about my own experiences and shortcomings. If, in my attempt to untangle some of this history, I've made it seem as though events always flowed logically or that we were forever sure of our direction and the eventual outcome of our efforts, please know this was not the case. We were operating amidst the "fog of war," if you'll forgive the military metaphor, and often way out of our depth.

Most importantly, what I hope I've been able to capture is the evanescent spirit of ACT UP and the exhilarating adrenaline rush of activism—the anger, grief, and desperation, but also the joy, camaraderie, and sexy, campy playfulness. Although this book chronicles a dark and painful time in my life, there was also a lot of light and laughter.

This is a story of ordinary people doing extraordinary things. The AIDS crisis was a crucible that forced many of us to open our eyes, find our voice, and discover the courage to "act up" when our communities and lives were being threatened. We were young, smart, and terrified, often making it up as we went along. With the help of more experienced activists, we taught ourselves how to navigate the intricacies of drug research as well as the byzantine structures of government bureaucracies. We learned the strategies of civil disobedience and explored how systemic injustice helped transform AIDS from a medical crisis into a political one.

They say activism can only happen when there's hope. And yes, sometimes it's hard to feel that hope when faced by a world that seems to embrace and celebrate cruelty. It's been shocking to see how many of the issues and prejudices that helped create the AIDS crisis in the '80s and '90s have returned with a vengeance, sometimes with new names but all fed by the same cynical fearmongering and the corrosive power of racism, sexism, and homophobia.

But this, too, is an important function of activism: to call out the evils of society and bring them to the surface to shrivel in the light of day. To create what Dr. King called a "tension that is necessary for growth."[1]

It is *my* hope that these stories will inspire current and future generations to keep stoking that tension; to become activists and find their voice, discover their power, and make change happen for generations to come.

AIDS is really a test of us, as a people. When future generations ask what we did in this crisis, we're going to have to tell them that we were out here today. And we have to leave the legacy to those generations of people who will come after us.

—Vito Russo

Find the human in yourself by finding the citizen in yourself, the activist, the hero in yourself.

—Tony Kushner

Part I

BECOMING AN ACTIVIST

Chapter 1

▟▟

Awakening

June 30, 1987

Seven minutes to twelve.

I stole another glance at the flyer hidden in my backpack—the pink triangle and the shouted headline, "Silence = Death."

I returned to my spreadsheet, checking the receipts against the invoice for business expenses, but it was no use. Why did I have to work at a place with a time clock?

Six minutes to twelve.

I'd first read about ACT UP, the AIDS Coalition to Unleash Power, in the *New York Native,* our biweekly gay tabloid—how they'd stopped rush hour traffic on Wall Street and gotten arrested outside the post office on Tax Day. I'd seen them in action, heckling Mayor Ed Koch at the annual AIDS Walk and marching at the Gay Pride Parade. They were bold, angry, and—unlike the other AIDS groups—dedicated to confrontation, not caregiving. More importantly, their actions produced results. Just weeks after their first protest, the Food and Drug Administration (FDA) announced plans to speed access to potentially lifesaving AIDS drugs.

Five minutes to twelve. *Fuck it!*

I grabbed my bag and ran out of the office.

I dashed across World Trade Center Plaza and up Church Street, cut over to Broadway, past City Hall, and on to Federal Plaza, where ACT UP was holding its big lunchtime rally and demonstration.

But where were the people? There were only fifty, sixty, tops.

I slowly circled to the back of the crowd, searching for a shady spot on the sidelines where I could safely split the difference between bystander and attendee. I loosened my tie, dug out my shiny new "Silence = Death" button, and nervously pinned it to my shirt, reminding myself I was only going to watch. I wasn't going to *do* anything.

My plans soon changed, however, when a curly-haired activist in a tight T-shirt and cutoff jeans bounded over with a dazzling smile and muscular armful of posters.

Did I want to hold a sign?

"Sure," I croaked, and he handed me a foam core poster and asked me to move up and join the rest of the demonstration.

I smiled, but he was gone. I looked down at the sign—**"Release the Drugs!"** It seemed harmless enough. I took a deep breath and then one small step forward.

As a Jewish kid growing up in Great Neck, Long Island, in the 1960s and '70s, World War II and the Holocaust were part of my DNA. My dad had flown as a navigator in a B-24 bomber over Germany, and while my family was lucky, we had friends who'd lost relatives in the camps. I learned about Hitler and the war against the Jews in school, solemnly read Elie Wiesel's *Night*, and had nightmares after watching the grisly concentration camp footage of *Night and Fog*. When I was ten, my grandmother mistakenly took me to see the musical *Cabaret* on Broadway thinking it was a revival of *Carousel*, jump-starting my theatrical ambitions and a lifelong fascination with the seductive death throes of Weimar Germany.

Since then, I've tried to understand how people could have blinded themselves to the evil that was gathering around them and wondered how I'd have acted had I been alive in Europe at that time. Would I have stayed or fled? Joined the underground resistance or just fought to survive? Would I have behaved nobly?

How would I have reacted at a time when my country, my community, my beliefs, and my life were under attack?

I'm not sure when I first realized I might be gay, though I remember having strong feelings at a very young age about Bobby Sherman in *Here Come the Brides.* And while I had a wonderful girlfriend in high school—and Tina, if you're reading this, I apologize—I also fooled around with guys. I had my first serious gay relationship during my sophomore year in college, and officially came out that summer while performing in a production of *The Boyfriend* (my life has never been subtle).

After graduating college in 1980, I moved to New York City to pursue an acting career. I attended my first Gay Pride the following June, and one month later made my first pilgrimage to Fire Island, a magical place where I didn't have to worry about ogling the boys on the beach, blasting show tunes from my boom box, or returning the interested stares of attractive strangers.

Back in the city, I sandwiched my social life in between acting classes, auditions, and restaurant shifts, hitting the bars with friends on weekends or late nights after work. I went to the theater as often as I could, earned points toward my "Gay Card" attending campy double features at the Regency, and occasionally, with the help of the requisite medications, danced the night and early morning away at the Flamingo or Twelve West, or, when someone managed to snag a membership card, the Saint.

And every so often, when the stars magically aligned, I'd meet someone and go back to his place or mine.

Although I was aware of gay politics, I didn't consider myself "political." I may have bought copies of the *Native,* but I probably spent more time scouring the personal ads than I did reading the articles. (Remind me to tell you about the ex-boyfriend I once found gracing the cover in his underwear!) And when news began to appear about a mysterious "gay cancer" invading the community,* I was more concerned than worried. It seemed confined to mostly "older" gays—the A-List, *Dancer from the Dance* types, with their fast-lane "Four Ds" lifestyle of disco, drugs, dick, and dish[1]—and while I may have visited that world, I wasn't part of it. I *knew* the names of all the men *I* had sex with.

Well, most of them.

In March 1983, the *Native* ran a front-page article by Larry Kramer titled "1,112 and Counting."[2] Larry was a controversial figure in the gay community,

---

*The first article about the disease, by Lawrence Mass, MD, "Disease Rumors Largely Unfounded," in the *New York Native,* May 16–31, 1981, was published more than six weeks before the *New York Times* article by Lawrence K. Altman, "Rare Cancer Found in 41 Homosexuals," July 3, 1981, which is regularly cited as the first article about AIDS.

known for his antisex attitudes and alarmist rants about AIDS—and this one was a doozy. "If this article doesn't scare the shit out of you," he began, "we're in real trouble."

He went on to describe a rising tsunami, a cataclysm brought on by a homophobic government and an indifferent medical establishment. Young men were dying horrible deaths—drowning in their beds, unable to breathe; eaten alive by cancerous lesions that scarred their bodies, limbs, and faces; and wasting away with exotic diseases previously found only in pets and livestock. Doctors were clueless about what was killing their patients and how to stop it, while a paralyzed gay community ricocheted between panic and denial.

It scared me plenty.

So, like many other gay men, I reluctantly threw out my poppers and scaled back my already limited number of sexual encounters. Later, as the routes of viral transmission became clearer, I further restricted my sexual behavior, devoutly following the safe sex credo of "on me, not in me," and committed myself to years of mutual nonoxynol-9–based masturbation and rubbing.*

My political activity, such as it was, consisted of reading articles, rounding up friends to attend AIDS benefits, and cater-waitering at AIDS fundraising events. I cheered from the rafters of Madison Square Garden when eighteen thousand gay men and their supporters gathered for the sold-out circus benefit for Gay Men's Health Crisis (GMHC), fell in love with Lou Liberatore as he fielded questions on an AIDS hotline in Broadway's *As Is*, and frantically combed the newspapers for any information I could find about this terrible new disease.

In June 1985, I saw Larry Kramer's play *The Normal Heart*. It was a bulletin from the front, a whistleblower's account of a hidden war happening just outside the door. Walking into the theater was like stumbling into a secret bunker. The walls were covered with the names of the dead and the evidence of their murder, with columns of weekly death totals juxtaposed against the meager ledger of government funding for AIDS research, services, and education.[3]

---

*In the early years of the crisis, it was thought the spermicide nonoxynol-9 also possessed antimicrobial properties that could kill HIV. Later research revealed the lubricant instead induced inflammation and ulceration of the vaginal and anal tissues, resulting in an increased risk of HIV transmission. "Nonoxynol-9 Ineffective in Preventing HIV Infection," World Health Organization, June 28, 2002, https://www.who.int/news/item/28-06-2002-nonoxynol-9-ineffective-in-preventing-hiv-infection.

Printed on a separate wall of the theater was a lengthy passage from *American Jewry during the Holocaust,* a report explaining how Jewish organizations of the 1930s and '40s faced two choices as they tried to persuade the US government to rescue the Jews of Europe: they could either work quietly behind the scenes to convince the administration to take action or publicly pressure the government by embarrassing Roosevelt and rallying public opinion. The American Jewish Committee opted for quiet cooperation and spent years fruitlessly knocking on doors. They were still knocking when the war ended.[4]

The play begins in July 1981, with three frightened young men waiting to see the doctor. Another young man comes out of the examining room, his face covered with hideous purple spots, and announces, "I'm her twenty-eighth case and sixteen of them are dead."[5] The next two and a half hours were like a spiraling nightmare from which there was no hope of waking. When it was over, I couldn't move or speak. I'm not even sure I applauded.

All of us—my friends and I, anyone who was gay and living in New York—were living under a pervasive cloud of dread. It wasn't necessarily a front-of-your-mind kind of thing; we still showed up at work, watched TV, and went to the movies. We shopped and ate and hung out with our friends. But there was a low threatening hum in the background of everything we did. Was that a bruise or a lesion? A chest cold or pneumonia? You could be fine one day and gasping for breath the next, your life suddenly measured in months, if not weeks. And if you listened to the politicians or read the newspapers, you knew how much they hated us. "The poor homosexuals," sayeth Pat Buchanan, "they have declared war upon nature, and now nature is exacting an awful retribution."[6]

So, I tithed money to the cause, went to AIDS benefits, and added "politically involved" to my list of desirable attributes for potential boyfriends. I briefly considered becoming a GMHC "buddy"—delivering meals to people with AIDS (PWAs), running errands, and taking them to doctors' appointments—but I didn't have that kind of courage. I knew I wasn't strong enough to become friends with someone I knew was dying. Instead, I gave more money, loudly bellyached about Ronald Reagan, and searched for some other way to get involved.

By the beginning of 1987, 16,301 Americans had died and another million were estimated to be infected with HIV,* the virus most scientists had agreed was the cause of AIDS. Six years after the first cases were reported,

---

*The cumulative AIDS caseload total for 1986 was 29,003, with 9,182 reported in New York State and 8,415 in New York City. "AIDS Weekly Surveillance Report," CDC, December 29,

President Reagan had barely even said the word "AIDS,"* while William F. Buckley's shocking *New York Times* op-ed proposing the tattooing of all people with HIV—gay men on their buttocks and intravenous drug users on their forearms[7]—looked less and less outrageous, as legislators and community boards debated mandatory HIV testing and the forced quarantine of people with AIDS.

In New York City, neighborhoods were emptying and familiar faces disappearing. If you listened closely, you could hear the whispered stories of gay men being thrown out of their homes or left to die unattended in hospital hallways. And all the while, our bachelor mayor maintained an uncharacteristic silence.

I was twenty-eight years old and unsure of my HIV status. I was scared, angry, and more than a little freaked out. And I was looking for *something*— something I could do, yes, but also something inside of me. How would I respond? How would I measure up? What would I do now that my community, my friends, and possibly my life were under attack?

ACT UP formed in March 1987, shortly after Larry Kramer delivered yet another of his incendiary speeches, this time at the Lesbian and Gay Community Services Center on Thirteenth Street.† Before AIDS, Larry had

---

1986, https://www.cdc.gov/hiv/pdf/library/reports/surveillance/cdc-hiv-surveillance-report
-1986.pdf.

*Reagan first acknowledged the disease in September 1985, when his Hollywood friend Rock Hudson became ill. In February 1986, Reagan ordered Surgeon General C. Everett Koop to prepare a "major report" on AIDS and claimed finding a cure for the disease was "one of our highest public health priorities," while simultaneously cutting the AIDS research budget by 22 percent. (Bernard Weinraub, "Reagan Orders AIDS Report," *New York Times*, February 6, 1986, https://www.nytimes.com/1986/02/06/us/reagan-orders-aids-report-giving-high-priority-to-work-for-cure.html?searchResultPosition=10.) Reagan would not utter the word AIDS again until April 1987, when, in an April Fool's Day speech, he called AIDS "Public Enemy No. 1," despite advocating for only a modest federal role in AIDS education because, he asked, "After all, when it comes to preventing AIDS, don't medicine and morality teach the same lessons?" Gerald M. Boyd, "Reagan Urges Abstinence for Young to Avoid AIDS," *New York Times*, April 2, 1987.

†The Community Center, as it was commonly known, changed its full name in 2001 to the Lesbian, Gay, Bisexual & Transgender Community Center. "Center History," Lesbian, Gay,

beèn a successful film executive, producer, and screenwriter. He'd been nominated for an Oscar for his adaptation of *Women in Love*, though perhaps the less said about his screenplay for the musical version of *Lost Horizon* the better.* In 1982, at the beginning of the epidemic, Larry helped found GMHC, the world's first and largest AIDS organization. He was pushed out a little over a year later, when the agency's board, tired of his tirades and bad behavior, called his bluff and accepted his threatened resignation.

Battered but unbowed, Larry wrote *The Normal Heart*, partly as payback, but also as a cri de coeur against the complacency, cowardice, and homophobia that had allowed AIDS to metastasize into a crisis. He continued making speeches and writing letters and articles excoriating everyone within earshot: politicians, scientists, and pharmaceutical companies for their bigotry, greed, and ineptitude; the media—especially the *New York Times*—for its myopia, prejudice, and smug liberal self-righteousness; and the gay community for tolerating ineffective leadership and supporting overly timid organizations like GMHC that focused on providing AIDS services—services that should have been provided by our government—rather than taking on a more activist role. He screamed it was time for gay men to grow up, start organizing politically, and stop thinking with our cocks.

Unfortunately, Larry was a less than ideal messenger. In the late 1970s, he'd·written *Faggots*, a brutal satire about the lives and sexual habits of the same A-List Fire Island crowd that had become the epidemic's first victims. Larry was branded a sexual puritan and a traitor to the community, a reputation that allowed his early warnings about the connection between sex and AIDS to be waved away as the dangerous I-told-you-so ravings of a self-loathing fanatic.

But his was not the only voice challenging gay men to wake up and change our sexual habits. In November 1982, Michael Callen and Richard Berkowitz, two gay men with AIDS, published their article "We Know Who We Are,"[8] which linked the disease to "excessive promiscuity" or "multiple sexual contracts [*sic*] with partners who are having multiple sexual contacts." Six

---

Bisexual & Transgender Community Center, viewed March 22, 2022, https://gaycenter.org /about/history/.

*According to Larry, it was the money he made from that notorious flop, invested wisely by his brother, that gave him the financial security to pursue his activism. Charles McNulty, "'Larry Kramer in Love & Anger': At 80, the Film's Subject Reveals a Complex Heart," *Los Angeles Times*, June 26, 2015, https://www.latimes.com/entertainment/arts/la-ca-cm-larry -kramer-20150628-column.html.

months later, Callen and Berkowitz published *How to Have Sex in an Epidemic: One Approach*,[9] which pioneered the concept of safe sex.*

People with AIDS had begun organizing as early as 1983, when a group including Callen and Berkowitz drafted "The Denver Principles," enumerating the rights of people who were living, not dying, with AIDS. It said PWAs should be treated as whole people, not just victims of a disease, and must be allowed to participate as equal partners in all levels of decision-making about their health and the priorities of the organizations that cared for them. These same principles would be echoed in the mission statements of the many PWA support, service, and information-sharing organizations that would soon spring up around the country.

By 1985, there were even some early stirrings of more radical grassroots street activism. In San Francisco, two HIV-positive men, Steven Russell and Frank Bert, chained themselves to the doors of the Federal Building, beginning a ten-year ARC/AIDS Vigil† to protest government inaction and demand increased funding and leadership. In New York, Vito Russo and Marty Robinson, two veterans of the earlier Gay Activist Alliance (GAA) and future founders of ACT UP, joined other community activists to found the Gay and Lesbian Alliance Against Defamation, or GLAAD, in response to the panic and homophobia being spread by the sensationalized AIDS coverage found in the mainstream media.‡

Marty Robinson was a trip—a real throwback to the stoned-out power-to-the-people politics of gay liberation. But while his speech may have been littered with the *"baby*s," *"man*s," and *"brothers and sisters"* of the 1960s, his political acumen was sharp as ever. Under the banner of GLAAD's Swift & Terrible Retribution Committee, Marty revived many of the confrontational in-your-face tactics he'd pioneered with GAA some fifteen years earlier. Increasingly dissatisfied with GLAAD's "Star Board" and their

---

*At the 1982 Gay Pride celebration in San Francisco, the Sisters of Perpetual Indulgence had handed out an earlier "safe sex" pamphlet, "Play Fair," but it was focused on protecting against STDs in general rather than AIDS specifically. Larry Maas, "Creative Sex, Creative Medicine," *New York Native*, July 19–August 1, 1982.

†ARC or AIDS-Related Complex was an early designation for people who had tested HIV-positive and who displayed a set of less severe clinically defined symptoms, such as chronically swollen glands.

‡The group was originally called the Gay and Lesbian Anti-defamation League but was forced to change its name when the original (Jewish) Anti-defamation League threatened them with a lawsuit, claiming to have copyrighted the phrase. "GLAAD," Wikipedia, viewed December 30, 2019, https://en.wikipedia.org/wiki/GLAAD.

top-down approach, Marty and the other Swift & Terrible members soon left GLAAD and joined the Coalition for Lesbian and Gay Rights, where they led a series of unauthorized yet wildly successful demonstrations in the summer of 1986 protesting the Supreme Court's *Hardwick* decision upholding the legality of state sodomy laws. Later that summer, they decided to start their own group, and the Lavender Hill Mob* was born.[10]

The Mob wasn't afraid of anybody. Cardinal O'Connor, Senator Al D'Amato, and Chief Justice Burger were all early targets of the Mob's wrath. In November 1986, they hit the *New York Times* over a particularly reprehensible editorial titled "Don't Panic, Yet, Over AIDS,"[11] which argued since AIDS was only happening to homosexuals (who were taking care of themselves) and intravenous drug users (who just needed more drug treatment slots), there was no reason for the "general public" to worry about the disease at all. Despite the protest, the *Times* would continue to publish variations on this same editorial for the next five years.

In February 1987, the Mob took their outrageous tactics to the Centers for Disease Control† in Atlanta. Donning the striped uniform of concentration camp victims—including the pink triangles used to identify "sexual deviants"—the Mob disrupted a CDC-sponsored conference on HIV testing. They spoke out at forums, demanding the government "Test Drugs, Not People," and shut down the final plenary session, denouncing the conference as an attempt by the Reagan administration to secure scientific legitimacy for its politically driven policies of testing and quarantine.

At the same time, hundreds of mysterious black posters with a bright pink triangle and the stark phrase "Silence = Death"‡ began to appear on scaffoldings and abandoned buildings all over New York City. At the bottom of the poster, in small print, the message continued:

> Why is Reagan silent about AIDS? What is really going on at the Center for Disease Control [*sic*], the Federal Drug Administration [*sic*], and the Vatican? Gays and lesbians are not expendable . . . Use

---

*Early Mob members included Bill Bahlman, Sara Belcher, Jean Elizabeth Glass, Michael Hirsch, David Z. Kirschenbaum, Buddy Noro, Michael Perelman, Eric Perez, Michael Petrelis, Marty Robinson, Rand Snyder, and Henry Yeager. Author conversation with Bill Bahlman, December 7, 2021.

†Now "Centers for Disease Control and Prevention," but this was the correct nomenclature at the time.

‡Note: "Silence = Death" with spaces before and after the equal sign, as per Avram Finkelstein, *After Silence* (Berkeley: University of California Press, 2018).

your power . . . Vote . . . Boycott . . . Defend yourselves . . . Turn anger, fear, grief into action.*

No one knew the origins of this poster—no group or individual had stepped forward to claim credit—but we all knew what it meant. It was an alarm, a secret coded message alerting us to a growing AIDS resistance movement. And even if no formal group had yet been organized, it was inevitable that one soon would be.

The posters were the work of a group of six friends—Avram Finkelstein, Brian Howard, Oliver Johnston, Charles Kreloff, Chris Lione, and Jorge Socarrás[12]—artists and graphic designers who had been meeting as an informal support group to talk about AIDS and to help one another cope with the mounting deaths of their friends and lovers. They were angry about the government's lack of response to the AIDS crisis and wanted to spur the community into taking political action. They'd designed the poster and had copies printed and sniped† across the city at their own expense, not knowing what, if anything, would come from their efforts.

All these groups, along with members of the activist video collective Testing the Limits‡ (which had recently formed to document and raise consciousness about the emerging wave of AIDS activism), as well as representatives from most of the city's AIDS and gay rights organizations, were in attendance at the Lesbian and Gay Community Services Center on March 10, 1987, when Larry Kramer stepped up to the microphone.

---

*For such an iconic image, the original poster contained several errors, beginning with the pink triangle, which was based on the symbol used by the Nazis to denote "sexual deviance" and later adopted as a gay rights symbol. While the creators had intentionally modified the color to a fuchsia, they'd unknowingly flipped the direction of the triangle to point up, not down. They decided to own the error—something we'd do all the time in ACT UP—saying it, too, was intentional, as a way of reclaiming a symbol of violence and turning it into one of empowerment. (Theodore Kerr, "How Six NYC Activists Changed History with 'Silence = Death,'" *Village Voice,* June 20, 2017, https://www.villagevoice.com/2017/06/20/how-six-nyc-activists-changed -history-with-silence-death/.) In addition, the text mistakenly referred to the CDC as the "Center" for Disease Control and the Food and Drug Administration as the "Federal" Drug Administration. Finkelstein, *After Silence,* 45–48.

†The term refers to the "snipers," the local family-owned companies that made "arrangements" to professionally wheatpaste commercial posters on construction sites, which were "otherwise illegal to use." Finkelstein, *After Silence,* 41.

‡The original members of the Testing the Limits collective were Gregg Bordowitz, Jean Carlomusto, Sandra Elgear, Robyn Hutt, Hilery Joy Kipnis, and David Meieran. Roger Hallas, *Reframing Bodies: AIDS, Bearing Witness, and the Queer Moving Image* (Durham, NC: Duke University Press, 2009), 268.

Larry was a last-minute substitute for Nora Ephron, who'd originally been scheduled as part of the Community Center's monthly speaker's forum. Given the short lead time, he must have burned a hole through his address book, as 250 people packed the third-floor auditorium to hear him speak.[13]

He began by quoting "1,112 and Counting," his article from four years earlier, and updating the total of AIDS cases to a staggering 32,000, with 10,000 in the New York area alone.* He then asked two-thirds of the room to stand up. "At the rate we are going," he warned, "you could be dead in less than five years."[14] After rattling off some more frightening statistics and complaining about the incompetence of the FDA and National Institutes of Health (NIH) and the lack of accountability from our elected officials, Larry threw down the gauntlet. "We can no longer afford to operate in separate and individual cocoons," he argued. "We must immediately rethink the structure of our community, and that is why I have invited you here tonight."[15]

Larry had hoped that by bringing all these different parties together, they could figure out a way to better coordinate their efforts. The most likely solution, he thought, would be to resurrect the old AIDS Network, a "breakfast group" of community leaders that had regularly met in the early days of the crisis to work out strategies and actions around AIDS issues.[16] Or maybe, if there was enough interest, they could start a new organization, one focused solely on the kind of confrontational political action and advocacy sorely missing from the current roster of gay and AIDS organizations.

Two days later, more than 350 people[17] crowded the Community Center's first-floor assembly hall[18] to continue the discussion, and a new ad hoc protest group was formed.

The initial floor fights were over procedure—whoever controls the process, controls the agenda—and there were already years of mistrust between many of the participants. The street activists were worried the mainstreamers were going to turn the group into yet another too-timid, top-down, board-driven organization, while the mainstream leaders were concerned a reckless

---

*According to the *New York Native* of March 9, 1987, the CDC caseload as of February 23, 1987, was 31,096, of which 8,761 cases were reported in New York City, with a national total of approximately 17,851 deaths, or 57 percent of the total cases, so Larry's figures hold. Of course, the *Native* called it "Cases of Tertiary Syphilis" [!], but that's a story for a later time.

group of unfocused street activists would alienate friends and potential allies and destroy whatever tentative progress had already been achieved. Once a compromise was reached—meeting facilitators would alternate between the two factions, with both sides having equal input in the meeting agenda—the group began identifying issues and potential targets.

Many felt the priority should be "experimental drugs," a broad category that included everything from speeding up access to experimental AIDS treatments caught in the FDA's lethargic drug approval process to lowering the cost of the one newly approved AIDS drug, AZT. AIDS education; access to housing, health care, and drug treatment programs; women with AIDS; and the pursuit of antidiscrimination laws and HIV confidentiality protections were other subjects deemed worthy of the new group's attention. Looking at the racial makeup of the overwhelmingly White room, the attendees also acknowledged the need to diversify membership to include all the different communities affected by the disease.[19]

After much debate, the group selected Wall Street and the New York Stock Exchange as the site of their first demonstration. The theme for the protest would be "no more business as usual"—not for the FDA, which continued to ignore promising new AIDS drugs while rushing the toxic and inadequately tested AZT to market; not for Burroughs Wellcome, AZT's manufacturer, which had priced the drug at a record $10,000 per year; and not for the NIH, whose placebo-controlled drug trials continued to jeopardize the lives of the patients they tried to cure. Not for New York's Mayor Ed Koch and Governor Mario Cuomo, both of whom refused to appropriate the necessary funds for AIDS services. And especially not for President Ronald Reagan, who, despite the deaths of almost twenty thousand Americans, had still not made a single AIDS policy speech.

To underline the urgency of their demands, the activists planned to block traffic around Wall Street in an act of nonviolent civil disobedience, culminating in a mass arrest.

But the fledgling group still needed a name. GMHC's Tim Sweeney suggested the businesslike "AIDS Coalition of New York," but that sounded too stodgy and mainstream. The room wanted something edgier, something that reflected the group's more radical nature and the tactics of direct action. After admitting his strange habit of collecting names and making up acronyms, Steve Bohrer* suggested the **A**IDS **C**oalition **t**o **U**nleash **P**ower, or

---

*Sometimes spelled Steev Bohrer.

ACT UP. Despite concerns it sounded more like a toothpaste than an activist group,[20] the new name was approved.

At 7 a.m. on Tuesday, March 24, ACT UP burst into life.

Several hundred demonstrators marched in front of Trinity Church at the foot of Wall Street, holding handmade signs and greeting startled workers with fact sheets headlined "AIDS and Death, AIDS and $$$" and shouts of *"NO! MORE! Business as Usual."* They chanted and cheered, blew whistles, and hung FDA Commissioner Frank Young in effigy. Then, at 8 a.m., seventeen protesters stepped off the sidewalk and sat down in the middle of Broadway and a new, more militant AIDS activist movement was born.

Much as they'd hoped, the demonstration made national news. And when, two weeks later, the FDA announced it would begin to streamline its drug approval process, the media credited ACT UP for helping force the change in policy.

The group returned to the streets on April 15, when it tried to hijack the annual Tax Day media circus at the city's main post office, demanding the collected tax dollars be spent on AIDS. And in early June, the group traveled down to Washington, DC, to take part in a coalition demonstration with other AIDS and gay rights organizations outside the White House. Even though ACT UP served primarily as backdrop for the negotiated arrest of sixty-four gay leaders and notables, the activists still managed to grab the spotlight, serenading D.C.'s yellow-gloved police force with the chant, *"Your GLOVES don't MATCH your SHOES! You'll SEE it ON the NEWS!"**

Later that same day, ACT UP staged its own demonstration outside the Washington Hilton, where the Third International AIDS Conference was being held. While they were protesting, men claiming to be government health officials approached the group's bus drivers to warn them about the "danger of their cargo" and advised them to fumigate the buses when they returned home.[21] Larry Kramer, Marty Robinson, and several others stayed

---

*For many years, police insisted on wearing protective gloves when dealing with AIDS activists and gay groups out of a misplaced fear of contracting HIV from touching potentially infected protesters. It was a dehumanizing practice that revealed how the police and others truly viewed us—as biohazards rather than people.

on in DC to attend the conference, booing President Reagan and Vice President Bush when they called for mandatory HIV testing in their first AIDS-related speeches.

I stumbled into ACT UP two weeks later, on June 15. I was attending a meeting at the Community Center for volunteers for the October March on Washington for Lesbian and Gay Rights. I'd been looking for a way to become more politically involved, and it seemed an easy place to start. I was surprised by the low turnout, as was the overwhelmed lead organizer, who made a rambling and desperate presentation highlighting all the daunting work that lay ahead. After an uninspiring hour, I volunteered to help leaflet at the upcoming Gay Pride parade but held off making any further commitments.

As our meeting was breaking up, another group started to gather next door.

I'd read about ACT UP in the *Native* and been impressed by the group's chutzpah, as well as their notable good looks and campy sense of humor. But as they began to fill up the large assembly hall, I noticed something else—a sudden surge of energy, like an electric charge bouncing around the room. I decided to stand in the doorway and hang around for a few minutes to see what all the excitement was about.

The meeting quickly descended into a pitched battle over the group's participation in the upcoming Pride parade. Someone at the front of the room was reporting back on the previous week's proposal that ACT UP march with an AIDS Concentration Camp Float to dramatize the dangers of the mandatory HIV testing and quarantine policies being promoted by members of the Reagan administration and other right-wing politicians.* Even as his report was greeted with a mighty whoop of approval, a hand shot up and a man stood to complain about the use of holocaust imagery. Wasn't it too over-the-top? Didn't it blur the issue? Another hand, and someone suggested the theme be changed to a graveyard, with the group carrying coffins down Fifth Avenue. "Yes," added an angry third speaker,

---

*Only the day before, during an appearance on *Face the Nation*, Senator Jesse Helms, who was sponsoring a bill calling for mandatory HIV testing, proposed quarantining people who tested positive for HIV.

"coffins would bring the message home to 'younger gays' who haven't yet experienced the death of friends and loved ones. AIDS is about people dying." "No," countered an impassioned redhead, "AIDS activism is supposed to be about empowerment and people living, not dying from AIDS."

And round and round it went. After much shouting, someone pointed out that even empty coffins were awfully heavy and besides, the flatbed truck had already been rented. The question was called, a vote taken, and the AIDS Concentration Camp won the day.

The room was hot and uncomfortable, and the vibe more than a little intimidating. People were yelling about issues I didn't fully understand and displaying cultural and political sensitivities I hadn't even begun to contemplate, and yet there was something undeniably exciting going on in that room. These were smart, passionate men and women committed to fighting back, to moving beyond the overwhelming panic and despair, and actually *doing* something to bring about an end to this terrible epidemic.

No one who saw the ACT UP contingent on Pride Sunday was likely to forget it. In contrast to the colorful contingents of drag queens, marching bands, and hot disco bunnies dancing atop bar floats, ACT UP had, in fact, created a concentration camp tableau on the back of a truck, complete with barbed wire, a miniature watchtower, and cowering PWAs—men, women, and children—surrounded by guards in yellow gloves and Reagan masks. Marching behind them was a small army of ACT UP members in their black "Silence = Death" T-shirts, chanting and handing out flyers announcing a "Massive AIDS Demonstration and Rally" two days later at Federal Plaza.*

But I was not marching with them. Not yet. Instead, I was having my own march, boldly cruising the parade route, handing out leaflets for the March on Washington, inviting everyone to come on down to attend the "big party" Ron and Nancy were throwing in mid-October. I felt powerful and sexy; the epitome of "out and proud."

---

*There remains to this day a great debate about whether Pride is a march or a parade; it seems to vary by year and sometimes even by contingent. To ACT UP, it was a march. Heritage of Pride (HOP), the group that organized Pride, was initially anxious about ACT UP's plans, only to turn around and honor ACT UP with its Best March Contingent award months later.

I bought a "Silence = Death" button later that afternoon and vowed to check out the ACT UP demonstration on Tuesday.

June 30, 1987: Federal Plaza

It was hot in the sun, and I was starting to sweat through my work clothes. I was also feeling very visible standing there holding my "**Release the Drugs**" sign. I looked around at the other protesters and tried to absorb some of their swagger. These were definitely not the usual aging gay-activist-hippie types. These guys were young and cute.

I listened absentmindedly to the speakers, cheering and booing when everyone else did, doing my best to blend in. And then I saw him. He looked to be about my age, standing alone in the crowd and holding up a handwritten sign: "**LIVING** with AIDS 2 yrs 2 mos + counting NO THANKS TO YOU MR. REAGAN."

I'd never met anyone with AIDS. I had seen people I assumed were sick—they were thin and weak and looked days away from dying. But this guy looked fine. More than fine. Sexy even, like he still went to the gym.

I tried not to stare, but I kept looking back at him, trying to figure him out; trying to understand why someone who didn't look sick would willingly hold up a sign in the middle of Manhattan announcing he had AIDS.

I tagged along with the group after the rally was over, marching around Foley Square and then over to the federal courthouse, where some of the demonstrators were planning to get arrested. I'd been nervous about leaving the protection of the park but felt my fear lifting as we paraded through downtown. When we reached the courthouse, I found myself standing inches away from the guy with the sign. Up close, I noticed he was beginning to sweat through a heavy layer of makeup and that there, on his nose and chin, were the threatening shadows of two KS lesions.

While each of the diseases associated with AIDS had their own unique cruelties, Kaposi's sarcoma (KS) was the one I feared most. Those splotchy purple bruises were not just disfiguring (and deadly), they were a shaming "scarlet letter" that marked you as diseased, announcing to everyone that you had AIDS, that you were gay, and that you probably got it from being fucked. (There was even a joke going around at the time, "What's the hardest part of having AIDS? Convincing your parents that you're Haitian.")* Just the idea of KS completely terrified me.

But there I was, face-to-face with someone who had KS, and even though he was wearing makeup to hide his lesions, he wasn't ashamed of having AIDS, he proclaimed it to the world. And instead of quietly withering away in some sickbed, he was getting arrested on the courthouse steps with thirty other guys who I guess might also be sick, shouting that their lives and the lives of gay men had value and demanding the government take action to help them.

Rushing back to the office, I removed my "Silence = Death" button from my shirt and stuffed it back into my knapsack. It felt wrong and cowardly, but I was afraid to let anyone know I'd been to an AIDS demonstration—*what if they thought I was sick?* And even if people didn't make the connection between "Silence = Death" and AIDS, there was still the button's bright pink triangle branding me as gay, and I suddenly didn't see why I had to broadcast that fact to everyone in the street.

Up until that moment, I'd thought of myself as living fully "out and proud." But I'd discovered there was a great deal of distance between being out in your personal life, or even at work, and wearing it like a yellow star on your shirt. Or standing with a sign in the middle of downtown Manhattan shouting that your life as a gay man was worth fighting for.

Two days later, on July 2, I woke up to the news that Michael Bennett, the director-choreographer of *A Chorus Line*, had died of AIDS.

I'd first seen *A Chorus Line* twelve years earlier, almost to the day, when I was sixteen years old. When it moved to Broadway, I saw it again and again, paying five dollars a pop for standing room tickets. "Don't tell me Broadway's dying," says one young dancer, "I just got here!" That was me, and *A Chorus Line* was the story of my life. Or at least what I thought my life was going to be.

All day long at work, I stared at my word processing screen, trying to figure out why I was taking Bennett's death so badly. I'd admired him, of

---

*At the time, the disease was believed to be restricted to only the "Four Hs"—homos, heroin users, hemophiliacs, and Haitians.

course, and had hoped to work with him one day, but this felt more personal. Like I'd lost a friend.

That night, I ran to see *A Chorus Line* again, hoping to make some sense of my feelings. Watching the show for the first time as an adult, I discovered, even more than show business, *A Chorus Line* was about the struggles of adolescence—about growing up and fitting in, about being creative and needing to be seen, about acceptance and, to a remarkable degree, coming to terms with your sexuality. Three of the male dancers talk candidly about being gay, and their sexual experiences are treated as unexceptional and in the same spirit as the straight stories.* All the gay characters are presented without excuse or comment as equal members of the larger theatrical community. What a gift for a teenager struggling with his sexuality back in 1975.

I'd always known the theater would be my home; a safe place where I'd be accepted, valued, and protected, no matter who I was or what I turned out to be. But that was no longer true. The theater couldn't protect us—not me, not Michael Bennett, not those three gay dancers, none of us.

MICHAEL BENNETT (1943–1987)
May his memory be for a blessing.

Not that my theatrical career was going particularly well anyway.

While I'd done some summer stock, had studied acting with Uta Hagen, and had even earned my Equity Card touring the South with a Jewish Children's Theater troupe—*Shalom, y'all*—I was having trouble getting to the next level. Despite consistently being called back to audition for the Broadway and touring productions of the three biographical Neil Simon plays,† I still hadn't landed an agent. I'd recently done a staged reading of *The Survivor*, about a band of teenagers who'd taken part in the Warsaw Ghetto uprising (*foreshadowing?*), but plans for a transfer Off-Broadway had fallen through. Though no longer waiting tables, I was now working odd hours as an office temp—with some cater-waitering on the side—to pay my rent as well as tuition for my full complement of singing lessons, dance classes, acting courses, and audition workshops.

---

*Okay, all except for the one monologue about dancing in drag shows, but at least that was the dramatic highlight!

†*Brighton Beach Memoirs, Biloxi Blues*, and *Broadway Bound*.

The past spring, as a challenge, I'd taken an Acting Shakespeare course led by a visiting actor-director of a certain age from South Africa. He was old school, both in his approach to the work and in his personal style. There was something very "dear boy" about him—a slightly seedy, perfumed quality, complete with cravats and cigarette holders. He was also vaguely closeted, with one of those "open secret" marriage/partnerships with his leading lady. Although he was very nice and quite encouraging, I didn't completely respect him or trust his opinion.

We'd been working on audition pieces, when he suggested I have a go at Bushy from *Richard II*. Bushy is a scheming courtier, full of flattery and insinuations. As an exercise in "going for it," I decided to play him as an over-the-top, hissing, sibilant fop.

I knew it was effective—I could feel the crackle in the room—and every-one insisted that I *must* use it for our upcoming class audition for the New York Shakespeare Festival. But instead of being elated, I felt sick to my stomach. I'd dredged up this hateful caricature from some dark place, filled with an anger and self-loathing I didn't know I had. It scared me, and it felt wrong to go forward with such an offensive performance.

I'd always wanted to work at the Shakespeare Festival. They did the kind of challenging and important theater I wanted to be doing, and more than anything, I wanted to be a part of its vibrant artistic community. And there, in the same theater where I'd seen *The Normal Heart*, and just upstairs from where I first saw *A Chorus Line*, I auditioned with this hateful, mincing, faggoty performance. I felt dirty and ashamed.

Then, just as I began to attend ACT UP meetings in early July, I landed the lead role in a staged reading of a play written by someone with "TV connections," about a Jewish boy (me) who's ashamed of being Jewish, pre-ferring instead to hang around Spanish Harlem and act like a Puerto Rican homeboy. His mother believes it was her refusal to have him circumcised that's responsible for his current cultural confusion. To repair the damage, she hires a Latina hooker to seduce and circumcise him, in the hopes of returning him to his tribe and his senses.

Both it and I were terrible.

I was quickly losing faith in the one thing I'd always known about myself—that I was going to be an actor. I'd always felt most comfortable, most sure of myself onstage, and trusted acting would help me organize and make sense of my life. Suddenly, I wasn't so sure. But if I wasn't an actor, who was I, anyway?

Chapter 2

First Steps

FRANK JUMP WAS a beanpole of a guy, an imp with a great sense of camp and boundless energy—the perfect chair for ACT UP's Zap Committee. Zaps were small, tightly focused, sometimes prankish, direct-action protests. They could be phone or fax zaps, a lunchtime picket or unannounced "office visit," or maybe a disruption of a public meeting, fundraiser, or rally. Whatever the target or tactic, zaps were proposed at ACT UP's weekly Monday night meeting and then developed and executed with the assistance of Frank and his committee within the space of a week by anyone interested in participating. The larger group, or "the Floor," would approve the zap in concept, and then get out of the way.

In early August, Frank announced Northwest Orient Airlines had quietly enacted a policy prohibiting people with AIDS—as well as people they *believed* to be infected with HIV—from traveling on their planes. The airline had recently refused to allow a man with AIDS to board a flight home for medical treatment, stranding him in China and forcing his family to pay $40,000 to have him airlifted back to the US.[1] After the usual snorts of outrage, Frank led a small band of volunteers to the back of the room to plan a response.

The next day, the zappers flooded the airline with bogus reservations, booking hundreds of thousands of dollars in expensive round-trip tickets, only to call back the following morning to cancel their reservations while complaining angrily about the airline's outrageous behavior toward "that gay man with AIDS" and vowing to "never fly Northwest Orient again."[2] That afternoon, the same handful of activists staged a lunchtime picket at North-west's Park Avenue headquarters. The zap was picked up by the media and became a major source of embarrassment for the airline. Bolstered by additional actions on the West Coast and the threat of a lawsuit, Northwest soon changed its policy. It was the first time I saw, firsthand, how a small group of people could make a difference.

Throughout July, I found myself unexpectedly resenting rehearsals for interfering with my nascent activism. So even as I bravely battled forced theatrical circumcision, I still managed to squeeze in a couple of ACT UP meetings and a few hours on the picket line outside Sloan Kettering Hospital during ACT UP's four-day, ninety-six-hour vigil protesting the failure of the government's $47 million AIDS drug-testing program.* But I knew I wanted to get more involved.

I've never been good at lurking around the edges of things; I get too nervous and become paralyzed. That's why I try to raise my hand and speak on the first day of class and get out on the dance floor as soon as possible. Better to commit and make the leap in a quick burst of bravado than sweat it out waiting for the perfect moment. But here, there was no music and I had neither the activist credentials nor a sufficient understanding of the issues to speak up at Monday night meetings. To make that leap, I needed to join a committee.

At the time, there were six committees to choose from: Fundraising, Issues, Logistics, Media, Outreach, and Zaps. I knew nothing about raising money or doing media or public relations. I didn't understand drug treatment and development, which appeared to be the focus of the Issues Committee, and Zaps felt way too scary and confrontational. Logistics, which was respon-sible for planning ACT UP's larger actions, seemed the best fit. I'd learn how to organize a demonstration—which honestly didn't seem too different from putting on a show—and the Logistics chair, Michael Savino, was cute

---

*Sloan Kettering was one of nineteen designated AIDS Treatment Evaluation Units (ATEUs) created to test promising new AIDS treatments. But after thirteen months, only 844 people had been enrolled in ATEU trials nationwide and over 92 percent of those patients were enrolled in studies involving AZT, the one treatment already approved by the FDA. Meanwhile, with over 5,000 New Yorkers living with AIDS, the four local ATEUs had enrolled only 149 patients.

and far less intimidating than some of the other committee heads. So, when Michael asked for new members to help plan an upcoming protest against President Reagan's AIDS commission, I quickly volunteered.

Reagan had announced the creation of the Presidential Commission on the Human Immunodeficiency Virus Epidemic in late June. It would be his administration's first and only attempt to develop a comprehensive response to the AIDS crisis. The commission's mandate was extremely broad—everything from AIDS prevention, medical research, and treatment options to social and economic policy and legal protections—and the president had promised to fill the panel with "distinguished individuals" with experience in all the relevant disciplines.[3]

Instead, he'd stuffed his AIDS commission with a collection of right-wing extremists and crazies: people like Dr. Theresa Crenshaw, a San Diego sex therapist who believed AIDS could be transmitted through mosquitoes, household pets, and food handlers, and warned against using public toilets and swimming in public pools. Crenshaw had also been a strong supporter of California's Proposition 64, Lyndon LaRouche's failed 1986 AIDS quarantine initiative—"the right legislation sponsored by the wrong group,"[4] she explained—and had successfully campaigned to have children with HIV barred from her local public school. Illinois state representative Penny Pullen, another prize appointee, had accused homosexuals of engaging in "blood terrorism"—deliberately donating infected blood in order to increase public support for AIDS—and was the proud sponsor of some of the country's most aggressive mandatory AIDS testing legislation.

Richard DeVos—yes, father-in-law of Betsy—was the founder and president of Amway, though his most pertinent credential was being the single largest individual contributor to Reagan's 1980 presidential campaign. Though "unsure" about whether AIDS could be transmitted casually, DeVos sure knew what he felt about homosexuals: "I hear a lot of people talk about gay rights," he proclaimed, "but I don't hear anybody talking about gay responsibilities."[5] Dr. Cory SerVaas was the editor and publisher of the *Saturday Evening Post* and the host of a regular medical segment on Pat Robertson's *700 Club* program on the Christian Broadcasting Network. She also ran her own mobile AIDS testing center, where she ignored all standard HIV counseling and confidentiality recommendations, storing the names of people who got tested on her office computers and sending them their results by mail. A lunchtime zap of her New York offices would spawn one of my favorite ACT UP chants: *"CORY SERvaas/MAKES US NERVaas/ WITH her MObile TESTing SERVaas!"*⁕

Also named to the commission was John Cardinal O'Connor. For years, O'Connor had led the fight against New York's gay antidiscrimination law and had recently banned the gay Catholic group Dignity from holding services on church property. The cardinal was also a vocal opponent of AIDS education in schools and refused to allow condoms or safe sex information in any of the diocese's many Catholic hospitals. When challenged about his fiercely antigay and, in the case of AIDS, medically dangerous positions, the cardinal and his defenders inevitably trotted out his oft-repeated claim of personally ministering to PWAs in diocese hospitals, as if tending to the sick somehow absolved him of responsibility for the pain and damage he inflicted on the rest of the community. It was also a fabrication. Prior to his appointment to the commission, the cardinal had visited St. Clare's AIDS ward only once, and then for less than an hour.[6] A second hasty and well-publicized visit was quickly arranged for July. The other appointees, though less outrageous by comparison, were equally political in nature.

Notably missing from Reagan's commission was anyone with firsthand experience with AIDS. Even commission chair Dr. W. Eugene Mayberry, who at least was chief executive of the Mayo Clinic, was forced to admit he was "no AIDS expert."[7] When confronted about the panel's lack of promised expertise, the White House reversed itself, insisting it had wanted "a group of distinguished Americans who reflect the views of ordinary people."[8]

Ironically, the panel's most controversial appointee turned out to be the one member who might have been considered an expert.

Dr. Frank Lilly was chairman of the Genetics Department at Albert Einstein Medical Center in New York City, had served on the original National Academy of Sciences (NAS) AIDS panel in 1986,† and was an early board member of GMHC. But since Dr. Lilly was also gay, his appointment unleashed a firestorm of criticism from conservatives who screeched that the administration was kowtowing to "special interest groups" and sending

---

⁕Sadly, not one of mine. Kudos, Jon Nalley!

†The National Academy of Sciences (NAS) is a "private, non-profit society of distinguished scholars," first established by Congress in 1863 and "charged with providing independent, objective advice to the nation on matters related to science and technology." "Mission," National Academy of Sciences, viewed March 25, 2022, http://www.nasonline.org/about-nas/mission/.

an unacceptable message to this country's "impressionable youth that homo-sexuality is simply an alternative lifestyle."[9]

In a fitting coda to this madness, the commission's executive director, Linda Sheaffer—who also professed no professional background in AIDS—was not hired until late August, giving her a scant three weeks to get the commission's administrative function up and running before the first hearing.

About the same amount of time we had to pull together our demonstration.

On a hot Wednesday night, the Logistics Committee—a mix of a dozen ACT UP veterans and newbies, including one guy I swear I recognized from a Marlboro ad*—met in Michael Savino's small Upper West Side apartment to discuss tactics, themes, and visuals for our upcoming demonstration.

At first, we thought we'd attack the panel directly, ridiculing them as a "Mickey Mouse Commission," but after having second thoughts about the credibility of AIDS activists in mouse-ear hats, we concluded the commission was a distraction and our real target should be the Reagan administration's murderous do-nothing policies. The president had already ignored a joint report from the NAS and the Institute of Medicine,† recommendations from the Public Health Service, and advice from his own surgeon general. Everyone already knew what needed to be done. This bogus new commission was just another waste of time and an excuse to avoid taking action.

To help dramatize our message, we decided to have a "Grim Reaper" figure in a dark robe and Reagan mask pop up alongside our picket every thirty minutes ringing a loud bell to announce another new AIDS death.‡

---

*Tom McBride was an actor and model. He died of an AIDS-related brain disease, in 1995—*May his memory be for a blessing*—and was the subject of the documentary *Life and Death on the A-List*. And it was Winston cigarettes, not Marlboro.

†The Institute of Medicine (IOM) was founded under the NAS charter in 1970, changing its name to the National Academy of Medicine in 2015. "Academy History," viewed March 25, 2022, http://www.nasonline.org/about-nas/history/.

‡We used the "one AIDS death every half hour" calculation as gospel, though I don't know that we actually did the math. I imagine it was extrapolated from the current monthly rate of AIDS deaths, though whether these were CDC's statistics or a potentially suspect "Larry fact," I cannot say. (We were never quite sure about Larry's figures, as he was prone to hyperbole and

At the same time, we still felt it important to undermine the commission itself, which we assumed would be used by the administration to legitimize specious and medically disproved theories about transmissibility and promote dangerous policies like mandatory testing and quarantine. We needed to let them know ACT UP was watching and would hold them accountable for their actions. We also knew if we could get the media to cover our protest, it not only would impact the story on the first day of hearings but could help shape the coverage and public perception of the commission for months to come.

Thanks to a scathing article in the *Washington Post*[10] and a threatened lawsuit from the American Civil Liberties Union (ACLU) and the Public Citizen Health Research Group,* the administration had already been forced to defend its indefensible commission. In his opening statement before the commission, Secretary of Health and Human Services Dr. Otis Bowen whined that "the constant criticism that this government is not doing enough is unfair and unwarranted," adding, "to criticize is counterproductive and mean-spirited."[11]

Sadly for Dr. Bowen, things were about to get a lot meaner.

September 9, 1987: ACT UP Meets the AIDS Commission

Our buses, carrying members of ACT UP and the Addiction Anonymous Hotline, arrived in DC around noon. We quickly set up our picket, circling the sidewalk in front of the National Press Club holding handmade signs and distributing fact sheets charging the Reagan administration with complicity in the AIDS-related deaths of 25,000 Americans and the 12,000 more who would die before the commission delivered its final report. "As far as they're concerned—the right kind of people aren't dying YET!"[12]

---

his numbers often seemed too outrageous to be true. But in fact-checking for this book, I've found his numbers mostly hold up, even if his projections turned out to be wide of the mark.)

*The lawsuit, *National Association of People with AIDS v. Reagan*, was filed on October 14, 1987, and alleged the AIDS commission did not meet the Federal Advisory Committee Act (FACA) requirements that advisory committee membership be "fairly balanced in terms of the points of view represented" and that it "lacks representatives of groups most affected by its work." (Statement of Rosslyn S. Kleeman, Senior Associate Director, General Government Division, before the Committee on Governmental Affairs, United States Senate, December 3, 1987, 6 citing *National Association of People with AIDS v. Reagan*), chrome-extension:// efaidnbmnnnibpcajpcglclefindmkaj/viewer.html?pdfurl=https%3A%2F%2Ffiles.eric.ed.gov% 2Ffulltext%2FED293031.pdf&clen=230882.) The case was dismissed on July 13, 1988.

Rather than wait for the commission's recommendations, we provided our own list of actions that "MUST BE DONE NOW," including establishing a "congressionally-appointed commission . . . to cut through red tape and direct national policy"; implementing "massive" public AIDS education programs ("Congress has allocated the money—use it!"); publicizing the use of prophylactic treatments to prevent opportunistic infections; expanding research on possible causes beyond HIV and drugs other than AZT; and passing federal antidiscrimination legislation to protect the jobs, homes, and health care of people with AIDS.[13]

And every thirty minutes, our relentless Grim Reaper danced about ringing his bell and celebrating another American dead from AIDS.

Despite efforts to reach out to local gay and AIDS organizations, only a handful of DC activists showed up to support our demonstration. One surprising recruit was my younger brother Rick, who picked up a sign and marched around with us for an hour during his lunch break. Although straight and working as an associate at a Washington-based law firm, Rick didn't seem worried about showing up on local TV or even being mistakenly identified as gay or HIV-positive. It was a generous and courageous gesture I didn't fully appreciate at the time.

Later, after we shut down our picket, Eric, our cute Grim Reaper, and I went inside to catch the last half hour of public comment and testimony. What surprised me most was how unimpressive it all was. There was almost no stage setup and few symbols of authority—just a group of haggard, shell-shocked commissioners schlumped behind two rows of blue cloth–covered folding tables, surrounded by a loud and hostile peanut gallery.

As we walked in, Amy Ashworth, from National Federation of Parents and Friends of Lesbians and Gays (PFLAG), was lecturing the commission about the challenges faced by PWAs and their families. When Chairman Mayberry attempted to express his condolences for the recent death of her son, Tucker, Ashworth quickly shut him down. "No, don't tell me you're sorry. Do something. Words can do nothing."[14] The room exploded in cheers.

Several ACT UP members also gave testimony, including PWA bomb-thrower-in-residence, Michael Petrelis, who urged the commissioners to do their job quickly or he "may not be around to see the implementation of any of [their] recommendations."[15] Rebecca Cole quizzed the panel on their knowledge of AIDS, asking them many of the same questions she fielded every day at her job at the National AIDS Hotline. If they didn't know the answers, she snapped, "You don't know enough to sit on the Commission."[16]

Bill Bahlman, Marty Robinson, and Henry Yeager spoke as well, though as members of the Lavender Hill Mob, a separate identity they maintained for another year as a hedge against ACT UP's taking a more conservative turn. Bill outlined the problems with the federal drug-testing program and asked the commission to ensure that people who were already infected with HIV were not forgotten and "dismissed as expendable."[17] Marty, extemporizing in his usual fashion, addressed the stigmatization of PWAs and the damage done by the continued categorization of AIDS as a "gay disease";[18] while Henry dismantled the right-wing argument for mandatory testing by pointing out the fallibility of the current HIV test, the lack of discrimination safeguards for people who test positive, and the prodigious waste of resources and funding that would be required to carry out the testing of predominantly healthy populations.[19]

Everyone took a deep breath when Larry stepped up to the microphone—the panel visibly stiffening in anticipation of the expected onslaught—but he surprised us by taking a sadder, more rueful tone. After running through the by now familiar list of bureaucratic missteps, willful ignorance, and sheer ineptitude that had plagued the research establishment's response to AIDS, Larry begged the commissioners to work with the gay community; to use our bodies and hard-won expertise as a resource to help find treatments and a cure for this terrible disease. "Quite frankly," he confessed, "we think many of you would as soon see us dead. But sometimes the challenge makes the man or woman. . . . We pray this will be one of those rare and precious God-inspired occasions."[20] Then, staring directly at Cardinal O'Connor, Larry concluded his testimony with a brief and provocative list of religious figures long rumored to be gay, including Joan of Arc, King James, and several popes and cardinals.

Listening to the public testimony and follow-up questions from the commissioners, what became shockingly clear was that we—the PWAs, activists, and members of the community—really *were* the experts. It wasn't just rhetoric. And while this knowledge would make it easier for me to challenge other so-called authorities in the future, it also scared the shit out of me. If *I* knew more than the people in charge, we were in real trouble.

As we'd hoped, our presence at the hearings helped frame the narrative for the national press. The majority of next-day stories focused on the histories of the more controversial members of the commission and the contentious atmosphere surrounding the hearings. The one notable exception was the

New York Times, which centered their front-page story on Surgeon General C. Everett Koop's testimony denouncing "doctors who shunned AIDS patients,"[21] relegating any discussion of AIDS activists or the controversy surrounding the commission to later paragraphs.

The *Times*'s coverage of the commission, and AIDS in general, would prove remarkably inconsistent. The very next day, they published a follow-up story about skeptical commission members questioning the government's rose-colored testimony. "'If everyone is doing' what they say they are doing," wondered William Walsh, "'I don't see how anyone is sick.'" And yet, the title of the article was "AIDS Panel Marvels at Government's Efforts."[22]

Despite the confusion at the *Times*, the controversy we'd helped ignite quickly took its toll. By mid-October, Chairman Mayberry was gone, replaced by Adm. James B. Watkins, who promised to right the ship and "bring all our prima donnas, including me, into a nice, neat, unified package."[23] Also departing was Executive Director Sheaffer and Vice Chair Woodrow Myers Jr. However, the panel would soon gain some much-needed expertise in IV drug issues and public health with the addition of Dr. Beny J. Primm, president of the Urban Resources Institute and president and executive director of the Brooklyn-based Addiction Research and Treatment Corporation; and Kristine Gebbie, assistant director for health at the Department of Human Resources and administrator of the Oregon State Health Division.

With our help, the commission, which had been established to shield the White House from criticism over its handling of the AIDS crisis, had instead become a lightning rod drawing attention to the administration's willful disregard, inaction, and incompetence.

As if the imploding AIDS commission wasn't a big enough black eye for the administration, October also brought the publication of *And the Band Played On* by *San Francisco Chronicle* reporter Randy Shilts. The book, the first detailed account of the AIDS crisis, was a 600-page indictment; an infuriating history of an epidemic that "was allowed to happen by an array of institutions, all of which failed to perform their appropriate tasks to safeguard the public health."[24]

The media, however, chose to focus instead on the tawdry story of "Patient Zero," a false narrative about a gay Canadian flight attendant named Gaëtan

Dugas who was, in the words of the screaming *New York Post* headline, "The Man Who Gave Us AIDS." In 2016, Shilts's publisher admitted they'd intentionally pushed the "Patient Zero" story to raise publicity for the book. Dugas was not "Patient Zero," but rather "Patient O," so designated to indicate that unlike the other members of the so-called California cluster of AIDS cases documented by the CDC, he was from "Outside-of California."[25] Regardless of its veracity, the story of a gay man whose unrepentant and relentless promiscuity had spread the AIDS virus across the entire United States helped promote book sales and became a convenient proof point for right-wing moralists and ideologues.

It also dovetailed nicely with the needs of the Reagan administration, which desperately needed to change the topic from its own malfeasance, given the fallout from its failing commission and the expected bad publicity from the upcoming March on Washington for Lesbian and Gay Rights, scheduled for mid-October.

AIDS was not supposed to be the primary focus of the 1987 march. It would be a key issue, of course, but mostly in terms of how the epidemic was being used by the community's enemies to further their agenda of "hatred, fear and bigotry."[26] Money for AIDS and an end to AIDS discrimination ranked a lowly fifth of seven official demands, and protest organizers had balked at ACT UP's suggestion that perhaps they could add the phrase "and Action on AIDS" to the March's official title.

We had a hard time understanding their priorities. "What good are rights, if you're dead?" we asked.[27] Gay men accounted for almost 75 percent of the country's total AIDS caseload.[28] If we couldn't get our own community to make AIDS a priority, what hope did we have of convincing the government?

We debated organizing an additional AIDS-specific action, but our weekend calendar was already jam-packed with demonstrations and conferences. We tried to pressure the organizers to add an AIDS activist—Larry Kramer, for instance—to the rally program, but this unwittingly put us into competition with PWA groups who were likewise lobbying for a PWA speaker.

In the end, we needn't have worried. Regardless of the order of demands or the list of speakers, AIDS would dominate the 1987 March on Washington, and AIDS activism would be its great legacy.

October 11, 1987: The March on Washington

About two hundred of us marched behind our **"Silence = Death"** banner, a small shock troop in matching T-shirts. We held our freshly mounted signs high above our heads—the stark black **"Silence = Death"** and our new **"AIDSGATE"** poster featuring a black silk-screened photo of President Reagan set aglow with hot pink rat's eyes, stamped on a bilious chartreuse background. Small teams of activists carried hinged, double-sided poster "snakes" that rippled through our group like angry Chinese dragons, as our powerful chants echoed down the corridors of official Washington.

Breaking out of the crowd, I ran up ahead, planting myself in the middle of Pennsylvania Avenue, and watched as this incredible force came marching toward me. For years, our community had been battered by this brutal disease and the vicious homophobia that allowed it to thrive. Because no one else would, we cared for our own, looking after the sick and helping our friends die. But now, here we were, a brave new Queer Army ready to fight like hell for the living. I was so proud of us, and so proud to be a part of it and not just watching from the sidelines.

Later, when we were stopped at a corner, I turned to a group of people standing silently on the sidewalk and started chanting, *"We'll NEVER Be SILENT AGAIN! We'll NEVER Be SILENT AGAIN!"* At first, they looked startled and stared back at me wondering, I guess, if I was yelling at them or accusing them of something. But then they got it. "We" meant all of us, and the time had come for us to stand up and speak out "loud and proud" for our rights. And they began to join me, until the whole corner was joyfully chanting and grabbing for our fact sheets.

This would happen again and again all afternoon.

By the time we arrived at the Mall, Jesse Jackson was speaking and the rally was well under way. ACT UP didn't much care for rallies and speeches anyway, but *wow*, it was impressive. Half a million people!* Had there ever, in the whole history of humankind, been so many lesbians and gay men gathered together in one place?†

---

*The National Parks Department, as is their policy, would lowball their estimate of the crowd to a ridiculous 200,000.

†While there were, no doubt, bisexuals, transgender and nonbinary folx, and others present, for historical accuracy, I am using the nomenclature of the time. No disrespect intended. I will start using the more inclusive "queer" at the point when the term became more widely used in activist circles.

Sitting quietly, directly behind us, was the Names Project Memorial AIDS Quilt.

None of us had seen the Quilt before. It, too, was making its national debut. Twenty-five thousand panels, each just three feet by six feet—the size of a small grave[29]—but stitched together, measuring the length of two football fields. Twenty-five thousand lives lost and memorialized, not including the hundreds of new names being inscribed in pen and magic marker on the empty spaces and blank panels dotting its expanse.

Standing together at the edge of the Quilt, Eric and I silently took each other's hand.

I'd been doggedly pursuing Eric ever since we first met planning the AIDS commission demonstration. He had twinkling brown eyes, a killer smile, and a rumbly low seductive voice that went right through me. There was also a slight sense of damage about Eric, a mysterious darkness I couldn't quite figure out. Although he hadn't been tested, he had chronically swollen glands from a recent bout of Epstein-Barr. I assumed he was Positive, just as I assumed I was Negative, and understood that taking care of him would be part of the bargain of our budding relationship.

Stepping into the Quilt, the scale of it immediately shifted from the enormity of the epidemic to the tragedy of each individual life lost. The air grew heavy, and the sounds of the rally faded away. Grief and sorrow took on physical proportions. And when Eric began to sob, I wrapped my arms around him and pulled him close, vowing silently to protect him through whatever battles might lie ahead.

The following morning, Eric and I were greeted by a feverish knot of ACT UPpers smoking, swearing, and warning us to stay away if we valued our sanity. "Agitate, Educate, Organize!," our daylong "mobilizing and planning meeting for AIDS activists,"[30] had been taken over by activists from the Los Angeles–based Lavender Left, who'd fashioned the day's agenda around their proposed week of national AIDS actions. They'd even preselected each of the day's themes, covering a worthy list of issues and populations, but bizarrely omitting anything about AIDS in the gay community.[31]

Rather than wait for an unlikely consensus, we joined my friends Neal, Tim, and Doug at the Lincoln Memorial. Neal was my best friend, the cornerstone of my social life ever since college, and his comfortable New York apartment, located just a block from mine, my de facto living room. But while Tim and I were good friends, connecting over a love of movies, disco divas, and, perhaps unexpectedly, the New York Mets, not to mention our common career paths—acting, with an emphasis on waiting tables—I always felt like I was failing him; falling short of being the best friends we once portrayed in a college play. With my attention focused on Eric and ACT UP, it was much the same that weekend.

That afternoon, the memorial—the site of the historic 1963 March on Washington and Dr. King's famous "I Have a Dream" speech—was overrun with lesbians and gay men.* Just one day after our own civil rights march, I read the words of the Gettysburg Address and Lincoln's Second Inaugural and thought about how we were now a part of this nation's history; the latest in a long line of people fighting for justice.

But something else was happening. Everywhere I looked, I saw people wearing the familiar black and pink of a "Silence = Death" button or T-shirt. Not just my New York colleagues, but strangers from all over the country. In a matter of days, it was as if we'd gone from two hundred ACT UP members to several thousand. No one said it out loud, but I could see it in the eyes of my friends; the gob-smacking recognition that we were on the verge of becoming something much bigger than we'd ever imagined.

ACT UP had arrived at just the right moment. The community was ready to rise up, and we were perfectly positioned to ride the wave. We might've gone to Washington a small fierce band of local AIDS activists, but we were coming back a Movement.

---

*Like many in ACT UP, I had been galvanized by the civil rights documentary *Eyes on the Prize*, which had been shown on PBS earlier in the year. While AIDS activism would incorporate many of the lessons and tactics of that earlier movement, like the use of nonviolent civil disobedience and the targeting of actions directly at sites of injustice including those not usually considered to be political (e.g., the FDA, drug company offices, etc.), our actions added a more theatrical component, expanding on some of the zap tactics of the gay liberation movement. Also, with occasional exceptions like needle exchange, our actions were less about fighting unjust laws than about drawing attention to a lack of response or sense of urgency on the part of our targets. Nor did we ever suffer the level of police or public violence visited on our predecessors in the civil rights movement as a consequence of our actions.

I returned home Monday night just in time to tune in to Ted Koppel and his *Nightline* news program. Coming off the weekend's big march, the topic, not surprisingly, was "Gay Rights." But instead of a conversation about the march and its similarities to past civil rights demonstrations, or the arc of justice and the inevitable road to equality, it was just a bunch of straight old White guys debating whether gay people deserved to have any rights at all—as if there was a question!

Two days later, as the Senate was preparing to vote on a bipartisan appropriations bill, which included an uncontroversial $310 million designated for AIDS education, Senator Jesse Helms stood up and, brandishing a couple of GMHC safe sex comic books, proclaimed, "If the American people saw these books, they would be on the verge of revolt."[32]

"We've got to call a spade a spade," he declared, "and a perverted human being a perverted human being."[33] After reading aloud from the sexually explicit pamphlets—none of which were produced with federal money— Helms introduced an amendment prohibiting the use of federal funds for any materials or activities that would "promote, encourage, or condone sexual activity outside a sexually monogamous marriage (including homosexual sexual activities) or the use of illegal intravenous drugs."[34]

Though Helms was eventually persuaded to drop the word "condone," as well as the reference to sexual activity outside of marriage, the final amendment still required all federally funded AIDS educational materials to stress sexual abstinence, and explicitly forbade the funding of materials that "promote or encourage, directly or indirectly, homosexual sexual activities."[35] In other words, the government would not pay for the creation, printing, or distribution of any information that might actually save the lives of the people most in danger of contracting the disease.

And it passed the Senate 96 to 2.

Only two senators voted against the amendment: Daniel Patrick Moynihan (D-NY) and Lowell Weicker (R-CT). Not Ted Kennedy. Not John Kerry. Not Cranston, Biden, Bradley, or Gore. None of our other so-called friends in the Senate.*

---

*A similar bill would later pass the House by a vote of 358 to 47.

Three days after half a million lesbian and gay citizens marched on Washington, three days after the Quilt was spread at the foot of the Capitol, and one day after over eight hundred demonstrators were arrested on the steps of the Supreme Court protesting the *Hardwick* sodomy ruling, the US Senate said, *"Fuck you. You're only faggots."*

I felt like I'd run full speed into a brick wall. How was this even possible? And then I got it.

Larry was right. In the eyes of most Americans, our rights were negotiable and our lives expendable. We were, truly, on our own. We were going to have to yell, scream, and ratchet up the pressure on anyone whose action or inaction prolonged this epidemic, until "doing the right thing" became their only option.

No more "Nice Jewish Boy." The social contract had been broken.

It was time to get arrested.

October 20, 1987: The United Nations

Grasshopper, here's a riddle: If you hold a demonstration, but no one sees it, covers it, or hears about it, has there been a demonstration?

The United Nations was holding its first General Assembly session on AIDS, and ACT UP was going to "hold our government accountable in front of the world"[36] by organizing a big civil disobedience action at its headquarters.

Unfortunately, the UN is a notoriously bad place for a demonstration. Due to security concerns, no protests are allowed to occur on or in front of the UN campus. Instead, demonstrators are shunted across the street to Dag Hammarskjöld Plaza and an isolated little park located about a block and a half away. As there were no stores or apartments on this stretch of First Avenue, just an entrance ramp to the Midtown Tunnel, there was little pedestrian traffic, and the park itself was cramped, its meandering paths bordered with trees and shrubs that successfully shielded it from the street.*

And did you notice the date of our action? October 20, 1987. The day after the "Black Monday" stock market crash, the largest one-day decline in stock market history.[37] Every reporter in New York was downtown on Wall Street, interviewing despondent stockbrokers. To make matters worse, we'd negotiated the arrest in advance with the police, who'd taken the precaution of rerouting all vehicular traffic two blocks south of our action.

---

*The Park has since been renovated but remains inhospitable to protesters.

There we were, all dressed up in our "Silence = Death" T-shirts, marching in deformed circles, dodging trees and shrubs, and yelling slogans to no one at all. When the designated hour arrived, we exited the park and headed onto First Avenue. Eric and I, having decided to consecrate our ACT UP relationship by getting arrested together, grabbed hands and ran into the street, plopping ourselves down beside a big banner declaring **"We Won't Move Till You Do."** And there we sat, pumping our fists in the air, screaming *"ACT UP! Fight BACK! FIGHT AIDS!"* while staring down an empty avenue, with nary a car nor pedestrian in sight.

After indulging us for about ten minutes, the police sauntered over and announced that anyone remaining in the street would be arrested. We gripped one another tightly, waiting for our brave moment of defiance. Instead, they just tapped us on the shoulder and walked us to the waiting police bus. They didn't even bother handcuffing us!

The day's only drama was provided by a few of our members who, fresh from their arrests at the Supreme Court, went the noncooperation route and had to be dragged onto the bus. We were then driven to the local station house and given desk summonses for charges that would eventually be dropped. The whole thing took less than half an hour.

It would be the last time ACT UP prenegotiated a large civil disobedience demonstration with the police.*

---

*We would also, shortly thereafter, stop requesting demonstration permits from the police. Although there were occasions when we'd notify the police and get permits—usually to protect PWAs and others who might be at higher risk for being locked up or badly handled—we knew the parameters of what constituted a "legal picket," and those did not require permits. This gave us greater flexibility in executing our actions and greater leverage in any necessary on-site negotiations. While we lost a fair number of bullhorns in the early days—a sound permit is generally required for their use—the police soon relented when they realized that it was better for them if we could keep our protests organized. This was, however, pre-9/11; the police were not as militarized as they are now, and we were largely a White, well-organized, and politically well-connected group.

Chapter 3

Welcome to ACT UP

EVERY MONDAY NIGHT at 7:30, the first-floor assembly hall at the Lesbian and Gay Community Services Center was "packed with short-haired muscle boys and power dykes, stockbrokers in suits and carpenters in flannel, writers, actors, graphic designers, college students, and, *hmmm—who's that?*"[1]

The room was long and narrow, studded by thin support columns that separated the punched-tin ceiling from the green-gray checkerboard linoleum-tiled floor below. A couple hundred drab gray metal folding chairs, mostly filled, were spread across the room in three sections, six to ten rows deep, with just enough space along the back and side walls for standing and schmoozing. There was an information table in the back stacked with flyers and fact sheets, and a merchandise table in the front, larded with buttons and T-shirts.

It was a dingy, badly lit, institutional space in desperate need of a paint job—and the most exciting place in town.

> Welcome to ACT UP, The AIDS Coalition to Unleash Power. We are a diverse, non-partisan group of individuals united in anger and committed to direct action to end the AIDS crisis. We protest and demonstrate; we meet with government and public health officials; we research and distribute the latest medical information; we are not silent.[2]

Monday nights were the beating heart of ACT UP—our Forum and Town Hall. Meetings were "long, loud, and loaded with process; everyone had input—and god knows everyone had an opinion—yet, week after week, zaps were planned, strategies discussed, and information imparted."[3] While most of the day-to-day work might have been carried out by our committees and caucuses, the general membership—"the Floor" of our weekly meetings— was ACT UP's main deliberative body.

Meetings were led by a rotating team of Floor-elected facilitators who, armed with little but their wits and "a loose interpretation of *Robert's Rules of Order*,"[4] were responsible for keeping the meeting on track and on time, encouraging debate, focusing discussion, and shepherding the group through an intense and always overstuffed agenda.

First up, after any ACT UP–related announcements, was "Life Saving Information," a broad category that embraced everything from treatment reports to PWA housing and support services—any information that could arguably prolong the life of someone living with AIDS—followed, inevitably, by the week's death announcements—usually, one or two a week—dutifully commemorated by three cheerless rounds of *"ACT UP! Fight Back! Fight AIDS!"* Then, after an awkward silence, it was on to the rest of the agenda: a rowdy mix of zap proposals, action updates, committee reports, volunteer requests, administrative amendments, and general announcements.

To ensure Monday nights weren't completely bogged down in process, we'd created a Coordinating Committee to "streamline the administrative functioning of the group without usurping the power and energy residing in the body as a whole."[5] Thanks to ACT UP's deep distrust of authority— even that of our own making—Coordinating was expressly forbidden by our "Working Document" from deciding policy. All its recommendations and actions were subject to review and scrutiny by the Floor.

Coordinating comprised a single representative from each of the major committees, the number expanding or contracting as new committees were formed and disbanded, and four elected members—a secretary (later administrator), treasurer, and two "at-large" reps. Its key responsibilities were to review and authorize expenditures over $500 (later $1,000); edit and sign off on all public-facing ACT UP literature, including all flyers, posters, newsletters, and fundraising materials; and promote and facilitate communication between committees.

Coordinating Committee meetings were open; anyone could attend and participate in discussions, but only the committee's members could vote. To further limit its powers, Coordinating, unlike our general meeting, was required to operate by consensus; any issues that couldn't be resolved by the committee would return to the proposing group for further tweaking or be brought before the Floor for discussion and final vote.

While Monday night meetings could be maddening, filled with circular discussions and endless pontification, they could also turn quite thrilling, when someone—Bob Rafsky, Gregg Bordowitz, or Maxine Wolfe, among countless others—would capture the moment or articulate, as if for the first time, some profound and instantly recognizable truth. Every week, I learned something new, not just about science and semiotics, but also about myself and my relationship to the world. And if I didn't immediately grasp the nuances of each issue or intuit which course of action might be best, I knew if I listened long enough, I'd be able to figure it out. It remains, without question, the smartest room I've ever been in.

Even at its most frustrating, there was always an undeniable energy and churn to our meetings, with dozens of side conversations taking place at the margins of the room or over cigarettes in the courtyard. Monday nights were also a time to socialize; a chance to gossip, flirt, and commiserate. And then there was the cruising. Not that anyone regarded ACT UP *exclusively* as a dating service, but even if they came for the boys (or girls), it's not why they stayed. It was our passion that was sexy, our commitment to doing the work, saving lives, and changing the world. Getting laid was simply a bonus.

When the meeting was over, usually just before 11, several dozens of us would reconvene over at Woody's for a couple of beers and a late-night snack. Woody's was the best place to find out what was really going on in ACT UP. No matter the intensity of the day's arguments, you'd find us all laughing and flirting around a makeshift, hydra-headed banquet table in the back. It's where problems were aired and proposals floated, stories told, and gossip shared. Where we first pieced together the "ACT UP Food Chain," diagramming who'd slept with whom; and where Bradley Ball and I would choke with laughter as we madly sang our way through *The ACT UP Songbook*.

Bradley was ACT UP's elected secretary and unofficial headmistress; think Maggie Smith as Miss Jean Brodie. ("*Gif me an activist at an imprrrresionable age, and he's mine firrr life!*") An autodidact with a bone-dry wit, he'd somehow managed the neat trick of being both off-putting and beloved.

Bradley had been one of the unaffiliated masses who'd somehow found their way to the Community Center that fateful night to hear Larry's speech. Two days later, when the new group began to brainstorm issues and demonstration targets, he volunteered to write down the suggestions on a big sketchpad. When the meeting was over, Bradley was literally left holding the pad. So, he ripped off the pages, typed up the notes, and distributed copies at the next meeting.[6] He'd been taking notes ever since.

Our friendship was predicated, at least initially, on our ability to keep up with one another's show queen references. Sitting at Woody's, we'd often laugh ourselves breathless, careening from show to show. "*Evita!*" he'd shout, and we'd be off singing, "Don't Cry for Me, Tony Fauci." Little Orphan Annie would arrive at the big city hospital and belt, "A-Z-T! What is it about you," while Larry Kramer, taking the Paul Lynde role in *Bye Bye Birdie*, would wax poetic about his upcoming appearance on "Phil Donahue! Phil Donahue! I'm going to be on Phil Donahue!" *Guys and Dolls* naturally became *Guys and Guys*, with Miss Adelaide lamenting her series of Opportunistic Infections, and Nicely-Nicely Johnson touting the latest new AIDS treatments ("I got the drug right here. It's called acyclovir. And though it's used for herpes I have no fear . . ."). When particularly inspired, I'd expand these snippets into full-length parodies, which we'd then perform at ACT UP parties and talent shows.

We'd all stay at Woody's through last call, only to reassemble on the sidewalk, still talking, shouting, and laughing. Even though we'd been together for hours and would probably see one another again in a matter of days (if that long), we'd cling together, glowing in each other's company and hating to say good night.

In the fall of 1987, New Museum curator Bill Olander contacted his friend and Testing the Limits video-activist David Mcieran, to ask if ACT UP might want to create an installation for the museum's storefront window.[7] There'd be no restrictions, and ACT UP could use the street-level space, located on Broadway just south of Houston, for ten weeks, from mid-November to mid-January.

David approached Avram Finkelstein, who was one of the people who'd created the "**Silence = Death**" poster, to see if he'd be interested in the project. An artist and red diaper baby, Avram had both politics and aesthetics—the perfect ACT UP combination. He was also one of the group's early leaders, having been elected, along with Eric Sawyer, ACT UP's first at-large members. Calm and focused, with a Talmudic ability to sort through a variety of options and opinions, Avram was an old soul and one of the first people in ACT UP whose opinion I learned to seek out and value.

Over fifty ACT UP members would contribute to the final project—type-setters, photographers, artists, and lighting designers, as well as laymen, pitching-in with exacto knives, hammers, chisels, and supplies.[8] They called the exhibit "Let the Record Show . . ." and it was a powerful *"J'Accuse"* against the individuals, groups, and corporations who'd used the AIDS epidemic to further their own agendas.

Against a photomural backdrop of the Nuremberg Trials, the activists created their own AIDS tribunal, the docket filled with enlarged cutout photographs of six "AIDS criminals" illuminated one by one under a harsh interrogation light, their damning words cast for eternity in cement. There was Jesse Helms, announcing, "The logical outcome of testing is a quarantine of those infected"; and the AIDS commission's Cory SerVaas proclaiming, "It is patriotic to have the AIDS test and be negative." William F. Buckley Jr. made the cut with his heinous tattoo proposal, as did Jerry Falwell, with his assertion that "AIDS is God's judgment of a society that does not live by His rules." An anonymous surgeon, hiding behind his surgical mask, announced, "We used to hate faggots on an emotional level. Now we have a good reason"; while, last but not least, President Reagan's words and actions were represented by an eloquent ". . ." The fateful tallies of their crimes flickered across a running LED display, with each damning fact and statistic preceded by the words, "Let the Record Show . . ." And above it all, hanging in judgment, was a ghostly neon "**Silence = Death**" sign.[9]

Eric and I didn't have a chance to see the window until we passed by late one cold night just after New Year's. It was incredibly powerful, like a silent scream on an empty street, even more so for our being the only witnesses, the sole survivors in a postapocalyptic New York.

When the exhibit finally closed, Avram and a number of the volunteers formed an activist art collective to continue making public works—posters, billboards, T-shirts, and stickers—to "inspire collective action and change public perception and governmental policy on AIDS."[10] They called them-selves Gran Fury, after the Plymouth squad car used by city police, and their work would grace our demonstrations and promote our issues in public spaces, arts festivals, and museums, for the next seven years.*

---

*The membership of Gran Fury remained open and fluid until 1989, when the group was closed to new members. The core, post-1989 Gran Fury included Richard Elovich, Avram Finkelstein, Tom Kalin, John Lindell, Loring McAlpin, Marlene McCarty, Donald Moffett, Michael Nesline, Mark Simpson, and Robert Vasquez. Earlier, pre-1989 members included

January 15, 1988: Just Say "No" to *Cosmo*

The January cover of *Cosmopolitan* magazine promised tips on "What Makes Marriage Work," a feature on the "Taming of Nick Nolte," an "All-New 1988 Bedside Astrologer," and a tantalizing excerpt from the memoir of Lana Turner's daughter, Cheryl Crane, titled "When I Killed My Mother's Lover." It was another life-and-death story, however, that attracted the attention of ACT UP's newly formed Women's Caucus. There, in a white box, right next to the viciously teased coiffure of Cindy Crawford, was the headline: "A Doctor Tells Why Most Women Are Safe from AIDS."[11]

The article, written by Dr. Robert Gould, ignored both science and medicine in its effort to reassure the young, sexually active readers of *Cosmo* there was "almost no danger of contracting AIDS through ordinary sexual intercourse."[12] Waving away CDC statistics showing 26 percent of all women diagnosed with AIDS had contracted the disease from unprotected vaginal intercourse, Gould insisted all 1,074 of these women were lying about their sexual conduct and had contracted the disease from anal sex. He similarly dismissed the explosion of heterosexually transmitted AIDS in Africa, explaining that "many men in Africa take their women in a brutal way, so that some heterosexual activity regarded as normal by them would be closer to rape by our standards."[13]

Ignoring, if you can, the unbelievable racism of this last claim and the inherent sexism in the rest of his argument, the article, with its casual inaccuracies, out-of-date statistics, and best-case scenarios, was endangering the lives of hundreds of thousands of women.

The time had come for ACT UP to take up the fight for women's lives.

The women of ACT UP, though comparatively few in number, played a highly active role in the organization. Maria Maggenti, a writer and budding filmmaker, was a Monday night facilitator and a member of the Outreach Committee. Rebecca Cole, who'd testified at the AIDS commission hearings

Steven Barker, Leonard Bruno, Richard Deagle, Mark Harrington, Todd Haynes, Amy Heard, John Keenen, Terry Riley, Don Ruddy, Neil Spisak, and Anthony Viti. *Gran Fury: Read My Lips,* Exhibition Guide, Acknowledgements, exhibit curated by Gran Fury and Michael Cohen, New York University, Steinhardt Gallery, January–March 2012 (New York: 80SWE Press, 2011).

and was the first to alert the group to the exclusion of women from experimental drug trials, was a mainstay of our Issues Committee and was a newly elected at-large representative. Dr. Iris Long would educate the group on research issues and drug development and mentor many of ACT UP's future treatment activist leaders. Jean Carlomusto was a videographer at GMHC and a member of the Testing the Limits collective. And there were many others—Marion Banzhaf, Jamie Bauer, Jean Elizabeth Glass, Debra Levine, Margaret McCarthy, Gerri Wells—who'd take on major roles heading committees, facilitating meetings, leading civil disobedience trainings, and becoming leaders and prominent voices in the organization.

And then there's Max.

A self-described "bisexual, Trotskyist, anarchist, Reichian, lesbian-feminist," Maxine Wolfe had always felt "on the periphery of the periphery" during her many years of political work. Frustrated by the "sexism and homophobia of the male-identified left . . . the homophobia of the women's movement . . . [and] the inability of lesbians to organize around or even figure out what their issues were," she found, in ACT UP, a home where ideology did not rule; where members were willing to learn and expand their political awareness, and power truly came from the ground up. It was also a place where, despite the overwhelming number of gay men, she could be "a lesbian, a woman, and an activist" without having to leave any of these identities at the door.[14]

Though her long wavy brown hair and wardrobe of jeans, peasant shirts, and sandals gave her a mellow "aging hippie" vibe, Max was Brooklyn tough. A professor of psychology at CUNY, she was smart and plainspoken; she quickly became one of ACT UP's unofficial leaders, tirelessly championing the expansion of our agenda to embrace issues affecting women, people of color, and all the communities affected by AIDS.

There was, however, a lot of testosterone in the room, and the ACT UP women—lesbian, straight, and bi—felt they needed to establish a safe space away from the boys, where they could connect with one another as women and try to figure out their role in ACT UP and AIDS activism. What started with a series of informal "dyke dinners" quickly led to the formation of the Women's Caucus in late December, and shortly thereafter, their first demonstration outside the offices of *Cosmopolitan* magazine.

When they first tried to meet with the magazine to discuss the article and argue for a retraction, the editors stonewalled, claiming the piece was "thoroughly researched" and that *Cosmo* was "not responsible for the content of each individual article that is printed."[15] Any falsehoods or misrepresentations, they argued, were the sole responsibility of the author, and they suggested the women contact Dr. Gould directly, handing them his phone number.

The activists called the good doctor and arranged a meeting, bringing along a video camera to capture the interview. With tape rolling, Gould paraded his ignorance of biology and women's bodies, and repeated his outrageous statement that the women who claimed to have contracted the disease through vaginal intercourse were all "liars."* With neither the doctor nor the magazine willing to issue a retraction, it was time for a little street agitation.

On a brutally cold January day, two hundred demonstrators, both women and men, braved single-digit temperatures for a lunchtime protest outside the Hearst Building. Our fact sheet, headlined "Don't Go to Bed with *Cosmo*," explained the dangers of Gould's article and asked readers to boycott the magazine, advertisers to withdraw their ads, and everyone else to call the editors to "voice their outrage."[16] While the rest of us picketed in chilly circles, Maxine and a small group of women attempted to enter the building, only to be rebuffed by security, who'd been tipped off to the demonstration by a "Page Six" item warning Hearst employees to "go to lunch early" if they wanted to avoid a crowd of "angry homosexuals" coming to protest at their offices.[17]

Unable to directly confront the corporate bosses at Hearst, we left our police pen and marched *v-e-e-e-r-y s-l-o-o-o-w-l-y* over to the *Cosmo* offices, loitering at every intersection, and tying up traffic all along Fifty-Seventh Street. Finding the doors closed to us once again, we turned and slowly crept back to the Hearst Building. The cops, tired of tracking us hither and yon, tried to shut things down by arresting two of our members† and impounding our bullhorn. But they had miscalculated. Instead of cowing us into submission, they'd only stoked our anger, shifting its target from the offices twenty floors above us to the officers directly in front of us. We swarmed the police van demanding our friends' release and warning any further provocation would likely result in a messy mass arrest. The police

---

*Shockingly, Gould was a professor of psychiatry, obstetrics, and gynecology at New York Medical College, as well as the chair of the committee on gay and lesbian rights and chair of the committee on AIDS for the New York County branch of the American Psychiatric Association. But despite Gould's titles, as Ed Sikov pointed out in his Media Watch column in the January 25, 1988, *New York Native*, "Gould's theory," in this case that HIV is not transmissible through "ordinary sexual intercourse" [quoting Gould], "always seems to come before his evidence; when the evidence doesn't fit the theory, he simply plays with it until it does."

†Gerri Wells, who was just coming from the bedside of her brother, Easton, who was dying from AIDS; and Actions cochair Alan Klein.

soon released our friends with desk summonses, and we gladly adjourned to warmer environs.

But the campaign against *Cosmo* was only just beginning. The controversy had proved irresistible for the media, particularly the woman-friendly afternoon talk shows like *People Are Talking*, which invited the protesters to appear as part of the audience for a program featuring Dr. Gould, promising they'd be able to challenge him on air. But when their questions were ignored, two of the activists* stormed the stage demanding the voices of women with AIDS and their advocates be heard.[18] When other programs withdrew their invitations, the fight was taken up by others, notably AmFAR's† Dr. Mathilde Krim, who spoke out against the article when she appeared on *Nightline* opposite Dr. Gould and *Cosmo* editor Helen Gurley Brown.[19]

Prevented from telling their story in the mainstream media, Maria Maggenti and Jean Carlomusto produced the video *Doctors, Liars and Women: AIDS Activists Say No to Cosmo*, which quickly became a resource for women with HIV and an organizing tool for other activists.

Eric

When we first started dating, Eric commented that I seemed to need a lot of physical attention; I liked being hugged and held and stroked. (Unlike, I suppose, his psychotic cats.) So, when he began pulling back from the physical part of our relationship, I figured we were heading into a rough patch. Nonetheless, when a water main break forced him to abandon his apartment shortly after the *Cosmo* demonstration, I invited him to stay with me until things returned to normal.

But after three chilly nights in a narrow bed without so much as a cuddle, I told him we needed to have "a talk." He sighed and suggested perhaps what we needed instead was a "time out" to "reevaluate our relationship." He confessed that, although he felt badly about it, he just wasn't feeling what I seemed to be feeling. "I kept waiting to fall in love with you," he said.

After I stuffed my heart back into my chest, I asked him how long this had been going on, and he said pretty much from the beginning. Evidently, I'd spun our relationship into some gay activist fantasy, a New Queer Cinema

---

*Denise Ribble from the Community Health Project and Chris Norwood from the National Women's Health Network.

†The organization now calls itself amfAR, the Foundation for AIDS Research, which better reflects its current mission and international focus. I will be using instead the contemporaneous name and branded spelling: AmFAR, the American Foundation for AIDS Research.

version of *Les Misérables*. Moments I thought romantic were now revealed to be "nice, but forced." And maybe I'd pushed things a little fast, but we were on the barricades and time was precious. (OK. *Les Miz* point taken.)

I ended January hurt, angry, sad, and alone. What better time to become cochair of the Actions Committee?

"Actions" was the new name for the Logistics Committee; the change occurring as its role shifted from facilitating Floor-mandated demonstrations to developing actions for Floor input and approval.

My cochair was Alan Klein, a cute, funny, prematurely balding, preter-naturally ballsy Jewish kid from Long Island. Alan and his equally young boyfriend, Karl Soehnlein, had met at Ithaca College and were now both core members of ACT UP.* A study in contrasts, Karl was blond, bird-like, and a writer; Alan was dark-haired, puppyish, and a talker. In the cross-gender version of *ACT UP—The Movie*, they would be played by Shelley Long and Rhea Perlman, respectively. (And I, by Bette Midler!)

Alan and I connected on the *kishka* level. With little provocation, the two of us would slip into Jewish *alte kaker* dialect—think Mel Brooks's 2,000-year-old man, with a *bissel* Miami Beach, and a touch Myron Cohen. I called him "Klein," he called me "Goldboig," and our relationship was (and remains) affectionately fraternal.

Alan had a confidence and fearlessness I admired. Though smart and full of ideas, he also had a tendency to shoot from the hip, while I was more cautious and attuned to the temperature in the room. When Alan would get carried away at committee meetings or presenting to the Floor, I'd walk him back a few steps, reframing his ideas to build the necessary consensus. We were a good team; I kept him grounded, and he pushed me beyond my comfort zone.

As Actions was notorious for burnout—we were averaging at least a demo a week if you included zaps, which often relied on committee resources, and that's on top of the weekly complement of Monday night, committee, and Coordinating Committee meetings—we begged Michael Miles to soldier on as our Coordinating rep. Alan would run the demonstrations, handling

---

*Karl was chair of the Outreach Committee and would later become a Monday night facilitator.

the nuts-and-bolts logistics and the on-site coordination of our actions, while I'd run the committee—facilitating our Friday night meetings, coordinating all the various pre-action activities, and acting as the public face of Actions—working the Floor on Monday nights, speaking on behalf of the committee, and schmoozing and recruiting new members.

For our first big action, the committee was charged with planning a demonstration to "welcome" Reagan's AIDS commission back to New York for three days of hearings, February 18–20.

Our efforts were complicated by growing complaints that our demos were too reactive—always responding to someone else's agenda instead of setting our own—and the general boredom with marching around in circles yelling. (We suspected the media was getting tired of it, too.) There were also logistical concerns, as the hearing site on Park Avenue South would become dark and untrafficked shortly after 5 p.m., when our demonstration was scheduled to begin. Additionally, thanks to Bill Bahlman's dogged attendance at every commission hearing, the panel was already well-versed in our "drugs into bodies" message, so there'd be little to gain from yelling at them in the street.

Huddled together in our small, white-tiled meeting room at the Community Center,* our committee feverishly brainstormed new tactics and strategies until we finally came up with what we all agreed was a scathingly brilliant idea. What if, instead of making the commission the subject of the demonstration, we used it as a hook for a self-defined action focused on the lack of access to experimental AIDS treatments? We could start with a picket in front of the hearings, but then march somewhere nearby where we knew we'd have a fresh audience—say, Union Square!—where we could stage a more outreach-oriented action. For a visual, everyone could bring empty pill bottles—or maybe fill them with pennies so they'd rattle!—which would also emphasize the high cost of drugs. And we could label them with the names of forty promising AIDS drugs—and then leave them in a pile!—creating this big mountain of bottles and unavailable treatments—and then surround it with a barricade of red tape!

Perfect!

We were so excited by our proposal that the entire committee came up to the front of the room to present the action to the Floor the following Monday.

---

*I'd insisted we meet at the Community Center rather than at someone's apartment, as it was a convenient "neutral" space, where everyone would be equally comfortable (or in this case, uncomfortable).

And it died.

Although people expressed appreciation that we'd listened to the Floor's criticisms and tried to do something new, a vocal minority couldn't understand why we weren't just zapping the commission. The Floor argued for twenty minutes, with Alan and I frantically trying to explain why our proposal was so fabulous, until the motion was mercifully called. Although the demonstration was approved, it was by only the slimmest of margins, accompanied by a loud chorus of "boos."

Despite our "victory," we knew we had to rethink the proposal. It wasn't enough for the Floor to approve an action just because they appreciated all our hard work; we needed their enthusiastic support. We also wanted to send a strong message that under our leadership, Actions was not going to be dictating demonstrations to the Floor—something that had remained a concern ever since the committee's responsibilities had first expanded—but rather creating and facilitating actions on the Floor's behalf. We had to show we were responsive to their criticisms.

That Friday, our demoralized committee reluctantly hammered out a new, less adventurous proposal and quickly adjourned to Woody's. The following Monday, Alan and I returned to the Floor, and with as much enthusiasm as we could muster, explained that we'd listened to their concerns and wanted to withdraw the previously approved action and instead propose a simple rush hour picket demonstration directly targeting the commission. The room erupted in cheers and our new action passed by acclamation.

Three hundred people showed up for our AIDS commission demo, and it was about as loud and enthusiastic a demonstration as I can recall. Fifteen protesters, led by members of the newly formed Metropolitan Health Association (MHA) affinity group,* hopped from corner to corner, playing cat-and-mouse with the police, until they plopped themselves down in the middle of the intersection just in time for a live feed at the top of the six o'clock news.

We'd learned an important lesson—even the most brilliant demonstration won't work unless people feel inspired to show up. If the AIDS commission action was a success, it was because it was the Floor's action, not ours.

---

*Metropolitan Health Association (MHA) was the name a group of activists, including Ortez Alderson, Gregg Bordowitz, Neil Broome, Steven Cordova, Michael Frisch, Tim Landers, Bill Monaghan, and SPREE, used to bluff their way into a meeting with NYC health commissioner Stephen Joseph on December 10, 1987, to confront him about his recent proposals for mandatory AIDS testing and potential quarantine for prostitutes and drug users and the contact tracing of sexual partners of all people with HIV.

■■■

There was, perhaps, another explanation for the sudden jolt of passion at the demonstration. Two days earlier, we'd received the incomprehensible news that Steve Webb had killed himself.

Steve had been a member of ACT UP's inner circle—"*L'Ancien Régime*," as Bradley put it—acting as our de facto treasurer, and coauthor with Stephen Gendin of the "Working Document" that governed the way ACT UP functioned. Steve was also a hunk, the early prototype for the buff Chelsea Boy of the 1990s, and his dazzling physical appearance and apparent good health made his suicide all the more difficult to understand. Our meetings were chock full of people fighting for their lives, and the idea that someone who was fortunate enough to be healthy—and beautiful—would turn around and kill himself seemed a rebuke to everything we were fighting for.[*]

Steve's memorial was held on Saturday afternoon, February 20, two days after our demonstration. Although I didn't know Steve particularly well, it was a death in the family, so I attended. It would be my first of many such memorials.

It wasn't held in a church or chapel, but in a bare, medium-sized room on the second floor of the Community Center. It might as well have been underwater. Everything felt slowed down and muffled. People who two days earlier were bursting with energy, were now red-eyed, pale, and barely able to stand. Bradley, just out of the hospital, was crumpled in a chair. Maria was perched on a windowsill, her head resting on her knees. Alan had his arm around Karl, who was sniffling and wiping away tears. Others were clumped in small groups, talking in flat hushed tones. It felt unnatural seeing these strong, young, joyful people so devastated by grief.

There would be no service. Chairs were arranged in a broken circle, several rows deep, and people just stood up wherever they were and talked. Steve's closest friends spoke first, most memorably Avram, who had, until recently, been Steve's lover. Always thin, Avram looked gaunt, his deep-set eyes disappearing under his dark and heavy brow. He spoke quietly, voice drained of emotion, about how Steve had been driven out of his home as a teenager, arriving in New York with little more than his corn-fed good looks.

---

[*] As it turned out, Steve was HIV-positive, but asymptomatic. However, this was not common knowledge, as people didn't generally share their serostatus with the larger group at the time.

Even as an adult, Steve had often felt that was all he had going for him—the only thing of value he had to offer.[20]

He told us how Steve had learned to use his looks to make ends meet and how, along the way, he'd overcome a bad cocaine habit. ACT UP, said Avram, was both a home and an escape for Steve, who was proud of his work with the group and happy to be appreciated for his mind and spirit, and not just his body.[21]

Over the past couple of months, however, his relationship with ACT UP had soured. He'd become disillusioned by the endless process and constant in-fighting and had begun to distance himself from the group. While trying to find work as a freelance journalist, he was getting increasingly anxious about falling back into his former life.[22]

Then Avram spoke about Steve's funeral and how little his estranged family seemed to know him; how Steve's gayness went unmentioned and his relationship with Avram unrecognized.[23] Avram believed Steve's death was the result of the same homophobia that was allowing people to die from AIDS; a homophobia that judged our lives to be of little value and our relationships beneath recognition.[24]

Slowly, others in the room began to speak; often of Steve's physical beauty, but also of his spirit and the hard work he'd put into ACT UP, helping us to become a powerful and thriving organization. Then Mark Fotopoulos, the man with the handwritten "Living with AIDS" sign, told a story about how he'd met Steve on Fire Island, long before AIDS and ACT UP, and as with most stories about Steve, he remarked on how beautiful he was. So, when Mark showed up at his first ACT UP meeting last summer, he assumed Steve wouldn't remember him. Beauty only remembers beauty.

But Steve recognized him immediately and asked how he was doing. And as Mark told him of his diagnosis and confessed how self-conscious he felt about his KS lesions, particularly now that he was wearing short sleeves, Steve reached out and gently began stroking the lesions on Mark's arms. "I mean, to touch me at that time," Mark said, his voice cracking. "I will never forget him for that."[25]

At the end of the memorial, they played a tape of Steve singing one of his own compositions. An angelic tenor voice filled the room. I hadn't even known he could sing.

STEVE WEBB (1958–1988)
May his memory be for a blessing.

Chapter 4

We Are Family

MARCH 24, 1988, would mark the one-year anniversary of ACT UP. Though the federal response to the epidemic remained anemic, ACT UP had only grown stronger and more committed than ever to "taking direct action to bring about an end to the AIDS crisis."

And what better way to celebrate our birthday than to return to Wall Street, the site of our first demonstration, to flex our muscles, show off our street smarts, and test-drive some new tactics? While Actions would oversee "Wall Street II," we enlisted the entire organization to help make it a success. Issues researched our fact sheet and compiled demands, Media drafted press releases and mailed media packets, and Outreach arranged speaking opportunities with other organizations and coordinated our street awareness campaign with leaflets and posters. To plaster those posters in the streets, we deployed a group of frisky twenty-somethings we called "Charlie's Angels."

Charlie Franchino, our Outreach chair, had a knack for recruiting sweet, attractive young men to volunteer for his committee. Sexy and self-assured, Charlie was in his early thirties and, as befits a chiropractor, very good with his hands. Several nights a week, Charlie sent his Angels and their crews out into the streets with stacks of posters and buckets of homemade wheatpaste. Though wheatpasting was illegal, the police usually left us alone. Nonetheless, the threat remained. If caught, the individuals involved—and the group responsible—could be subject to fines of up to $250 per offense.*

We always wheatpasted in groups. While one Angel played lookout, the rest of the team hurriedly slapped flyers onto whatever flat surface was available. In a matter of days, the Angels would paper their way across Manhattan and into Brooklyn, returning week after week to replace posters that had been torn down or plastered over.

This endless series of ever-changing street messages was crucial for spreading the word about our upcoming protests and helped educate the public about our issues. Sometimes, the posters were actions in themselves, deliberate provocations to promote a community-wide sense of militancy around AIDS and the need for a political response.

To communicate our message internally, we activated the ACT UP Phone Tree, a kind of exponential alert system, whereby five people called another five people, who each called another five people, and so on. At least, that was the theory. But given our fluid membership and fluctuations in health, we opted for a flat system, "more like crabgrass than a tree," according to Bradley Ball, who was responsible for maintaining the forty-two discrete phone lists. And every Monday night, Alan Klein and I staged a mini–pep rally, updating the Floor on our plans, displaying posters, whipping up enthusiasm, and recruiting volunteers for our civil disobedience (CD) action.

While we were planning a large legal picket—*"our biggest ever!"*—the main event would be a series of coordinated nonviolent CD actions and arrests. We encouraged everyone to sign up for CD training, promoting it as an ACT UP rite of passage and a way for members to "up the ante" on their commitment to the group and AIDS activism. Led by our own CD-experienced trainers,† the sessions were long and intense, equal parts consciousness-raising, skill-development, and team-building exercise. They

---

*It is still unlawful for any person without authorization to "paste, post, paint, print or nail any handbill, poster, notice, sign or advertisement upon any curb, gutter, flagstone, tree, lamppost, awning post, telegraph pole, telephone pole, public utility pole, public garbage bin, bus shelter" and a half dozen other places. While the cost of an infraction is now capped at $150, another provision regarding the posting of stickers and decals has penalties running as high as $500. Under both provisions, each handbill, poster, sticker, etc., is considered a separate violation. "Posting and Graffiti Laws," viewed March 23, 2022, https://www1.nyc.gov/assets /dsny/site/resources/streets-and-sidewalks-laws/posting-graffiti-laws.

†Our main CD trainers included Jamie Bauer, Gregg Bordowitz, Steven Cordova, BC Craig, Alexis Danzig, Mike Frisch, Jean Elizabeth Glass, John Kelly, and Brian Zabcik. Together, they were responsible for training hundreds of activists.

not only prepared us for getting arrested but also gave us a common language and taught us how to work together and take care of one another in the streets.

Civil disobedience is grounded in the philosophy of nonviolence, which is based on love, dignity, a respect for the humanity of all human beings, including one's enemies, and the unshakable belief that *everyone* is capable of change. During our five-hour trainings, we reviewed the history of nonviolent civil disobedience—from Thoreau and Gandhi to Martin Luther King; pored over copies of Gene Sharp's list of 198 different nonviolent actions;[1] and discussed the strategies of the movements that preceded us, making connections between their struggles and our own, and claiming our place in the continuum of American history.

We talked about "affinity groups," the self-selected collections of likeminded individuals who came together to carry out a specific action or actions and were the basic organizing unit of our CD demonstrations. Operating by consensus, to ensure every member had an equal voice in the group's decisions, affinity groups were self-contained units, responsible for every aspect of their chosen action. Because of their small size and autonomous structure, they could organize quickly and carry out covert, targeted actions without sign-off from the Floor. However, in the case of Wall Street II and other major actions, they'd be expected to coordinate their activities with our head marshals and work within the given framework of the larger demonstration.

To prepare ourselves for arrest, we conducted role-playing exercises, acting out arrest scenarios, practicing consensus decision-making skills, coaching each other on passive resistance techniques, and trying out "cooperation" and "noncooperation" strategies upon arrest. But whatever the scenario, violence—whether against police, spectators, or other demonstrators—was strictly prohibited. We similarly warned against bringing weapons, or objects that might be construed as weapons, to our demonstrations and asked participants to refrain from any activity that might endanger the rest of the group. Acts of "property alteration," such as graffiti or flag burning, were to be performed openly and at a safe distance from the rest of the demonstration to prevent putting other protesters at risk.

As a further precaution, we always staffed our demonstrations with trained marshals and legal observers. The marshals' job was to facilitate the demonstration; help participants carry out their actions; streamline communication between the protesters and the head marshals; and defuse any potentially dangerous situations by acting as buffers between protesters, police, and an often-hostile public. Legal observers stood outside the demonstration, monitoring and taking notes on interactions between the police and the protesters from a safe distance.

Despite these precautions, we could never truly guarantee the safety of anyone who participated in our demonstrations. However, to ensure everyone arrested would at least be followed as they made their way through the system, we always put a support structure in place, including designated affinity group members and volunteer lawyers who'd wait outside the precinct houses to see that our rights were protected and to advocate for our safe and speedy release.

For the day's final exercise, each participant would share their feelings about the upcoming action, their reasons for joining ACT UP, and why they were willing to risk arrest. Often, it was the first time we'd hear about someone's HIV status, the people whose lives they were fighting for, or the friends, lovers, or family members they'd lost. Despite the endless hours we spent with one another, most of us were relative strangers. All we knew was what we saw at meetings or demonstrations. In this moment, we got the chance to see each other more fully, helping us forge deep bonds of trust, friendship, and community. It's why, no matter how scary the police or frightening the action, I always felt safe in the streets with ACT UP.

March 24, 1988: Wall Street II

"Attention! Attention! The AIDS Crisis is over—you can all go home! . . . Just kidding! Marshals!"

It was 6:30 in the morning—too early for my cool John Lennon sunglasses, but I wore them anyway; they gave my dazed and panicked expression a little *don't-fuck-with-me* attitude. Alan, my cochair and the comedian with the bullhorn, would be running the day's demonstration, coordinating the waves of civil disobedience and handling any interactions or on-site police negotiations with CD trainer extraordinaire Jamie Bauer.*

Though we were the same age, Jamie had a history of street activism that dated back to the 1980 Women's Pentagon Action.† They'd first come to ACT UP in the spring of 1987 to recruit members for the October Supreme Court CD protest, then stayed to marshal our first Wall Street action. Over

---

*Jamie is the name they adopted upon their transition to nonbinary several decades after their work with ACT UP.

†Jamie had also long been active in the struggle for lesbian and gay rights, including heading up GLAAD's Swift & Terrible Retribution Committee, and, when the GLAAD board refused to support their actions, moved with the group to the Coalition for Lesbian and Gay Rights (CLGR).

the years, Jamie would facilitate Monday night meetings, organize and marshal countless demonstrations, and train a generation of activists in civil disobedience. Jamie's negotiation strategy was simple:

> We have a right to free speech and freedom of assembly, and we don't have to ask permission for it. And if you want to arrest us for it, that's your business, but we're not going to ask your permission. And if you don't grant us permission, we're going to do it anyway.[2]

As about twenty of us huddled together in front of Trinity Church, knotting one another's hot pink marshal armbands, support coordinators checked in CD participants on the opposite corner, collecting emergency numbers and writing down drug regimens.

With only minutes to spare, Frank Smithson's truck, stacked with our posters and boxes of freshly printed fact sheets, screeched up to the corner. An artist with a flirty Southern charm, Frank was one of ACT UP's resident rogues, who could talk his way into or out of anything. Frank apologized for being late, admitting he'd overslept after a late-night prank removing certain unattended police stanchions and sawhorses. As Frank batted his eyes, I looked around and realized there wasn't a single police barricade in sight.

"WHAT do we WANT? A CURE for AIDS! WHEN do we WANT IT? NOW!"

At 7 a.m., hundreds of protesters hoisted their placards and marched in loud and angry circles on the sidewalk in front of Trinity Church. Leafleteers spread out to the surrounding corners distributing our message to the gathering crowd—"We are here on behalf of the 25,000 Americans living with this disease, and out of respect for the 32,000 lost to it. WE WILL NOT GO QUIETLY. WE ARE NOT GOING AWAY"[3]—while members of Gran Fury littered the ground with phony money stamped with accusatory messages: "FUCK YOUR PROFITEERING. People are dying while you play business."[4]

Reporters pointed their cameras and flipped open spiral notepads. "The only place we can raise these demands is on the street," explained Jamie. "The government is letting people die."[5] "We have to fight for ourselves," argued Ortez Alderson. "We have no choice but to go to jail."[6] Photographers clustered around Mark Fotopoulos and his mother with their matching signs: "<u>LIVING</u> With AIDS 2 yrs. *11* mos. + counting! No Thanks to You Mr. Reagan" and "<u>LOVING</u> A SON <u>LIVING</u> with AIDS."[7]

And as the church bells sounded eight o'clock, the TV trucks raised their towers, ready to broadcast our demonstration live to America.

"Act UUUUP! Fight BAAAACK! FIGHT AIDS!"

Twenty-five protesters linked arms and charged into the street. Spreading themselves out across the width of Broadway, they sat down to an eruption of whistles, cheers, and car horns, before disappearing under a crush of cops, cameras, and microphones. But as the minutes ticked by—and much to our surprise—the police made no effort to move or arrest the protesters. Did they think they could wait us out, that we'd get bored and go away? Fat chance!

"Whose Streets? OUR Streets!"

After almost thirty minutes—and with traffic backed up for ten blocks— the police finally relented and began dragging the demonstrators onto an empty police bus, until the street was cleared. But just as the bus began to pull away, a second wave of demonstrators bolted out of the crowd and hurled themselves down in its path.

"How many MORE Have to Die? How many MORE . . ."

The police, angered by the unexpected turn of events, lumbered off the bus, badge numbers now covered in black tape, and began pulling the protesters by their hair and jerking them to their feet by their jacket collars.*

"SHAME! SHAME! SHAME!"

At a far corner, Michael Petrelis and Neil Broome stepped off the curb, unfurled a small American flag and attempted to set it on fire. Flag burning was a hot political issue that spring, and the two had argued it would be a great hook for the media and the perfect symbol of our anger at the government's negligence. Though the Floor had vetoed their proposal, rightly fearing it would distract from our issues, they were told they could still burn the flag if they wanted, provided they distanced themselves from the rest of the demonstration. But as soon as they took out their lighters, Michael and Neil were tackled by police, who rewarded them with a couple of swift kicks before yanking them to their feet, grabbing them by the neck, and hurling them face-first onto the steps of the departing police bus.[8]

To regain control of the situation, the police quietly dispatched a group of officers a few blocks uptown to detour traffic away from our demonstration. We countered by secretly sending a third wave of protesters around the

---

*Thirteen protesters filed complaints against the police for their actions at Wall Street II. When the initial investigation by the Civilian Complaint Review Board (CCRB) failed to find evidence of police misconduct, protests from gay activists and the Anti-Violence Project convinced the CCRB to reopen the case. After further review, they would finally recommend disciplinary action against one officer, NYPD Sgt. James Wagner, for having "punched" Stephen Gendin and used "excessive force" against Marion Banzhaf. Complaints against four other police were dismissed. John Hammond, "Civilian Complaint Review Board Prefers Charges," *New York Native*, March 26, 1990.

corner to Rector Street, where they blocked all the cops' freshly detoured traffic. By the time the police discovered our deception and loaded "Wave 3" onto a second bus, our fourth and final wave of protesters burst through the picket line back on Broadway, shouting *"AIDS KILLS WOMEN! STOP the RED TAPE!"* and draping themselves and the intersection accordingly in rolls of red tape.

After the final group had been hauled away, I grabbed Alan's bullhorn and called the troops together for a short and enthusiastic send-off.

"WE'LL Be BACK! And WE'LL BE STRONGER!"

While the demo might be over, we still had to deal with the aftermath. Instead of processing everybody at one station house, the police had scattered our members across several precincts, splintering affinity groups and shredding our support network. As a further challenge, they announced they were putting everyone "through the system": booking them and then shipping them off to "The Tombs" to be held overnight while awaiting arraignment.

Since we had no way of knowing who'd been taken where, we'd be unable to track our members and could possibly lose them in the system for hours, if not days. And while extended jail time is never pleasant, it could prove lethal for our HIV-positive members, who'd be unable to take their medications while risking exposure to TB and the other infectious diseases rampant in the city's jails.

We quickly improvised a new support system, transforming a donated apartment into Support Central and recruiting additional members to cover the various precinct houses. Alan handed me the master list of all the arrestees and told me to head to the Thirteenth Precinct, where we believed the majority of our members had been taken. I grabbed a cute marshal I'd been eyeing—*why not?*—jumped in a cab, and raced uptown. When we arrived, we found the police bus still parked outside the station house, filled with our arrested comrades laughing and singing songs like on some big gay high school field trip. And when the police finally marched the glee club off the bus and into the precinct house, I marched in right behind them, barely noticing the little sign posted at the top of the stairs: "**No Unauthorized Personnel Allowed**."

Swooping around the detention area like some half-crazed activist Auntie Mame, I camped my way from cell-to-cell—*"Darling, those bars are you!"*—kissing everyone as I checked them off my support list. Before long, an astonished senior officer inquired just-what-the-hell-I-thought-I-was-doing and ordered me thrown out of the station house. But before I could be dragged outside, I was stopped by another officer who looked me up and down and sneered, "Let's put him through the system—teach 'im a lesson." I was then hauled off to the back of the precinct house and locked in a small holding cell.

It was my first time in jail, and I was pretty freaked out. Not only had I been separated from the rest of the group; no one knew I'd been arrested. If the police decided to move me or take me out the back of the station house, no one would have any idea what had happened to me. I was now a prime candidate for "getting lost in the system." And if that weren't bad enough, my reckless stupidity had endangered the rest of the group, for there in my coat pocket was the only copy of our master support list.

To calm myself, I thought back to my CD training and after calculating the risks and benefits of noncooperation, I decided to cooperate like crazy. I was friendly and talkative, treating my arresting officer with love and dignity, respecting his humanity, and recognizing his capacity for change. My one slight feint toward principled resistance came when I refused to divulge my HIV status (not that I knew it anyway). I even gave him a copy of our fact sheet.

My charm offensive must have worked, because Police Officer Perez, bless his heart, took pity on me, and instead of fingerprinting me alone in my cell, paraded me out to the front desk where I could be seen by my colleagues.

Thanks to some timely calls from sympathetic city council members and the mayor's gay liaison, the police were persuaded not to put us through the system after all. Once I was released, I joined our lawyer, Joan Gibbs, and my fellow activists outside the precinct house. We waited all afternoon, cheering each arrestee as they emerged from jail, offering them juice and snacks, and swapping stories until everyone was free.[*]

---

[*]Of the 96 arrestees who chose to go to trial, 81 defendants, including me, had their charges "dismissed in the interest of justice" on August 5. The other 15, who had previous arrest records either for the Stephen Joseph zaps, the February 18 AIDS commission demo, or the later June 28 zap of KOWA Pharmaceuticals (which occurred after Wall Street II, but before our August hearing), had to go through additional hearings, though they would receive ACDs (Adjournments

███

Three days later, ACT UP threw itself a more traditional celebration. There was no fundraising or Robert's Rules of Order; just dancing, drinking, and, oh yes, a talent show.

Longtime PWA activist Michael Callen and his group, the Flirtations, sang their a cappella version of "Mr. Sandman"—"Mr. Sandman, won't you believe, (*bung-bung-bung-bung*) We want a Superman like Christopher Reeve. Give him two legs, like Greg Louganis, but make him public about his gayness."[9] I did my imitation of Julie Andrews singing the Tracy Chapman Songbook (don't ask), and Bradley ended the program with his version of "Rose's Turn." ("I did it for you, Steve. It wasn't for me, Larry. And if it wasn't for me, then where would you be, Coordinating Committee!")

For the evening's grand finale, Bradley called everyone back onstage and led the crowd in a breathtakingly arch rendition of "Getting to Know You." Much to my delight, everyone spontaneously picked up the movie's cross-armed handshake choreography, proving conclusively that underneath the leather jacket of the most jaded East Village activist beats the heart of a Musical Theater Queen. I couldn't have been happier.

The whole week—the demonstration and the party that evening—was like falling in love, not with a person, but with a group. ACT UP was more than just a remarkably effective activist organization; it was the community I'd always been looking for.

███

And then David got sick.

███

David

I'd fallen in love with David Serko the minute I met him, almost ten years earlier, when we were both students at SUNY Binghamton. David wasn't exactly handsome—he had a long face and an almost beakish nose—and

in Contemplation of Dismissal), whereby their records would be closed in six months if they had no further arrests during that time.

yet he was devastatingly attractive. More than his dancer's body or his mischievous twinkle, there was an ease about David, a remarkable sense of confidence and a comfortableness with who he was that was completely intoxicating. He was also more fun than anyone I'd ever met.

A cross between Huck Finn and Lucy Ricardo, David could make a simple trip to the mall a wild and campy adventure. He loved musicals and old movies and could quote *Mary Tyler Moore Show* episodes at will. Within hours of meeting, we were finishing each other's sentences. And, like me, David loved to dance. It was a connection I'd never had with anyone before or since.

In college, we'd had an intense romantic friendship. We hung out between classes, downed pizza and beer after rehearsals, and on weekends, went dancing with friends at Lenny's, the local gay bar. During school breaks, David and I would head into New York City to take dance classes and catch the hot new musical. After the show, we'd go to one of the popular actors' hangouts, Jimmy Ray's or Ted Hook's, and watch the Broadway performers come in for their postshow meal, just like we knew we'd be doing in a few short years. Early on, I'd tried to push things a bit further, but, alas, the sex produced more giggles than passion—at least on his side. I was completely smitten.

After college, we both moved to the city to pursue acting careers. We remained close—taking dance classes together, barhopping on "girls' nights out," and even slinging sushi at the same Upper West Side restaurant. But as the '80s wore on, our careers and relationships took us in different directions. Though our connection was strong, we began drifting apart, becoming old friends rather than good ones.

ACT UP, I assumed, would be a further path away from David. He'd never been particularly political and, to be honest, I hadn't encouraged my friends to join. I didn't want to feel responsible for them, or maybe I was afraid of what they might say about my new activist self—or, more likely, what they might reveal about my old self to my new activist friends. Whatever the reason, I jealously guarded my ACT UP friendships and experiences and kept them apart from the rest of my life.

To my delight and surprise, David became the exception to the rule. From his first ACT UP meeting in early 1988, David became the door between my two lives. ACT UP recharged our relationship, giving us a powerful new connection. But when David got sick just days after getting arrested at Wall Street II, I was caught completely off guard. I hadn't even known he was Positive.

David had received his test results just days before the demonstration, telling only his older brother, Peter, and best friend, Tim. When follow-up blood tests showed a low T-cell count, indicating a damaged immune system, his doctor put him on a regimen of AZT and Bactrim, the latter a prophylactic or preventive treatment against the most common AIDS-related opportunistic infection, *Pneumocystis carinii* pneumonia or PCP.

Even after David told me he was Positive—a conversation which to this day I can't recall—I still didn't connect his current illness with AIDS. He insisted it was just a bug, and I was more than happy to agree with him. I assumed David would remain Positive but asymptomatic, like many of our other activist friends. Alarm bells didn't go off until a week later, when David, who was never a complainer, mentioned he was still feeling sick and hadn't been getting much sleep. To cheer him up—and to check up on him without seeming overly concerned—I gathered a few of our old gang to head over to his apartment for pizza and videos.

When I arrived, David was wrapped in a blanket, ashen and spiking a 104° fever. He looked terrible. Our friends looked even worse. It was our circle's first brush with AIDS, and while everyone tried to carry on as if nothing was wrong, no one knew what to do or say. With David alternately sweating and shivering on the couch, not even *The Women* could lift his spirits.

After pushing everyone else out the door, David and I switched into activist mode and tried to figure out whether he was actually sick or just having a bad reaction to his new medications. Since his fevers and chills sounded like they could be an allergic reaction to Bactrim, we agreed he would skip his next round of pills and see if his fever broke. I'd stay with him overnight, just in case his fever spiked and he needed to go to the hospital.

I sat up on the couch with David most of the night, his head in my lap and his body swathed in blankets. As he tried to sleep, I thought about how he'd blossomed over the last few years, not only working himself into a beautiful, athletic body, but also maturing into a handsome and effortlessly charming man. I thought back to the many times I'd been envious of his confidence, of his ease and grace, and though I knew better, wondered if they were partly to blame for his being sick. I was, I suppose, looking for some difference that would explain why David was sick and not me.

But most of all, I was surprised to discover how calm I was. I guess because it was David—of all people, David—there was no choice, no decision to be made. I'd just have to step up and do whatever had to be done.

I think I was also, in a strange way, relieved. The shoe had finally dropped. AIDS had invaded my innermost circle. And while I certainly didn't want David to be sick, part of me thought, okay, maybe this will be it—as if David's illness was the price we had to pay for the rest of us staying well. It didn't make any sense, but nothing about AIDS made any sense. For fuck-sake, we were all still in our twenties.

Somehow, both David and I managed to catch a few hours' sleep, and by the time I rushed off to work the following morning, his fever had broken. His doctor took him off Bactrim, as we'd suggested, switching him instead to the experimental aerosolized pentamidine, and everything soon returned to our new normal, with David HIV-positive, but asymptomatic.

I didn't say anything at the office about David or what had happened the night before. There was no way of wedging AIDS into a casual conversation around the coffee machine; it belonged to a separate reality. So, I just went about my work and, not surprisingly, the subject of AIDS never came up.

Part II

EXPANDING THE AGENDA

▚

Chapter 5

ACT NOW
and the Nine Days of Rain

ACT NOW, OR the AIDS Coalition To Network, Organize and Win, was the lovechild born of October's "Agitate, Educate, Organize!" conference, a nationwide network of over sixty activist organizations, devoted to "protests, lobbying efforts, civil disobedience demonstrations, and community organizing."[1] For its first action, ACT NOW had proposed an ambitious nine-day orgy of protests and demonstrations called "Spring AIDS Action '88,"* with each day dedicated to a different AIDS-related issue.

ACT UP/NY didn't much like taking marching orders from anyone, especially other activists. We were all for coalitions, as long as everyone agreed to be led by us. At the same time, we wanted the freedom to go out and do our own thing without being answerable to anyone else. Hell, we didn't even think we should have to add "/NY" to our name. We were ACT UP, The Original—the brains, brawn, and bank account of the movement. It was up to the rest of the groups to differentiate themselves from us!

I guess you could say we were having control issues.

----

*Though some refer to these actions as the "Nine Days of Rage," I can find no contemporaneous use of that title. The ACT UP meeting notes referred to it as the "ACT NOW Actions," and our flyers and fact sheets used "Spring AIDS Action '88" or similar. Though it would make sense for "Nine Days of Rain" to evolve as a play on "Nine Days of Rage," I think it was the reverse, with people unintentionally creating the latter title after the fact, turning "Nine Days of Rain" into an easy pun on an originally fierce title, rather than just humorous commentary on a soggy stretch of weather.

Nonetheless, we did have some legitimate questions about the ACT NOW proposal, beginning with the idea of nine straight days of actions. We already had a full slate of demonstrations in the works, and while there was no law saying we had to do all nine days—other groups seemed content to focus on only a few—we were ACT UP (/NY), the *mightiest* of all the ACT UPs, and if there were nine days of actions, we'd damn well do all nine.

This wasn't just a case of New York arrogance. Despite our ongoing arguments about organizational priorities, we had committees working on most of the issues being targeted. Indeed, the Floor complained there wasn't a day devoted specifically to intravenous drug use and AIDS. (In a fleeting moment of sanity, we suggested that, rather than add a tenth day, ACT NOW could change one of the existing days to "AIDS and Substance Abuse," with the stipulation that even if they didn't adopt our proposal, we'd do it anyway.)

But it was about more than issues; it was about who we were. Several of the days focused on the impact of AIDS on specific communities—gay people, women, IV drug users, people of color—and ACT UP comprised all these groups. How could we fight for the lives of only some of our members?

For reasons known only to him, Michael Miles volunteered to coordinate the entire nine days of actions. Michael (*The Lady*) Miles was a gangly Texan, with a mighty twang, a highly developed sense of style, and a fierce dedication to detail. A movie set designer and decorator, Michael had headed up our March on Washington subcommittee and designed our fabulous hinged poster "snakes," coming to the Floor with miniaturized reproductions of our "**Silence = Death**" and "**AIDSGATE**" posters mounted on toothpicks and fastened with matching colored tape. He'd quickly assumed a leadership role within the Logistics Committee, becoming committee cochair, with Dan Butler and Tony Siebert, when the group changed its name to Actions.

But sometime during the lead-up to the nine days, Michael took a vacation someplace tropical and came back a bottle blonde, with Carmen Miranda fruit-basket earrings and a brash new attitude to match. Michael was not just more flamboyant; he was positively unbridled. He began speaking his mind and making decisions on behalf of ACT UP, ACT NOW, and our committee without discussion or prior approval, triggering all kinds of tripwires and leading to his eventual departure from the group. For the short term, however, we just kept smoothing things over as his tireless leadership remained essential to our success.

We decided to treat each day as a separate individual action, with its own leader and team, and assigned each of ACT UP's committees a specific role. Some, like Outreach and the Women's Caucus, would handle a specific day of action, while others, like Issues and Media, supported the entire campaign, providing fact sheets and publicity, respectively. In addition to overseeing the entire production, Actions was responsible for the big opening and closing day demonstrations.

To further boost participation, we divided the Floor one Monday night into nine separate mini-Actions meetings, so each team could staff up and assign tasks and responsibilities. This proved a boon not just for the nine days of actions but for the entire organization, pulling people into the orbit of our committees and educating the full membership about the process of planning and executing demonstrations. As a result, we ended the nine days a much stronger and more nimble organization—even if it was hell getting there.

April 29–May 7, 1988: The Nine Days of Rain

Day One: AIDS and Homophobia

To kick off Spring AIDS Action '88, we organized a celebratory "Take Back the Night" march up Christopher Street, the symbolic heart of the gay community, ending with a rally and sex-positive kiss-in at Sheridan Square, across from the site of the original Stonewall Inn. We envisioned the demonstration as a call to arms and a chance to reach out to our community in a fun and nonthreatening way.

Gran Fury designed two eye-catching posters—one featuring a World War II–era photograph of two male sailors kissing in a tight passionate embrace,* and the other, a vintage theatrical photo of two women clasping hands, looking soulfully into each other's eyes—each with the phrase "Read My Lips" stamped across the image.[2] While everyone loved the men's poster, the women rightly protested that their image was meek and sexless. Properly chastened, the artists withdrew the poster, replacing it with another using a vintage image of two women kissing. A later T-shirt featured a sexy

---

*It turned out to be an image from a 1950s gay porn magazine of two sailors who were real-life lovers, cropped to hide the fact that they were naked (and erect) below the waist. Avram Finkelstein, *After Silence: A History of AIDS through Its Images* (Berkeley: University of California Press, 2018), 100.

contemporary photo of two women of color (ACT UP members and artists Lola Flash and Julie Tolentino) in a playful lip-lock.

But despite our posters, pink helium-filled balloons, and shouts of *"OUT of the BARS and INTO the STREETS!"* we had little luck luring the Friday night crowd off their barstools. While I'm sure the rain didn't help, many of the bars refused to even allow us to come inside and leaflet. When we arrived at Sheridan Square for our rally, the area's largest gay bar, the Monster, bolted its doors and closed its shutters to ensure no one could see the kiss-in taking place just outside its windows. Was the management worried about the competition: that the bar might lose customers to the free action outside? Or was it the larger threat: that any reminder of the ongoing crisis might lose the bar its customers for good?

Why We Kiss.

WE KISS in an aggressive demonstration of affection. We kiss to protest the cruel and painful bigotry that affects the lives of lesbians and gay men. We kiss so that all who see us will be forced to confront their homophobia. We kiss to challenge repressive conventions that prohibit displays of love between persons of the same sex. We kiss as an affirmation of our feelings, our desires, ourselves.[3]

First, I kissed Michael. Then David. Then Frank. Then Michael and Michael—*um, tongue!*—and Tom and Robert and Allan—*mmmmm . . .* TONY!—then Eric and Peter and Steven and Dan. Then pecks for the girls, for Maria and Ellen, and Jean and for Jamie, then back to the boys, back to Alan and Karl and Ch*aaaaa*rlie and Michael and Jeff (*huh! Jeff!*), and David and Duncan and Andrew and Brian, and where were those cute humpy boys dressed in black . . . ?*

Later, after drying off and applying some much-needed ChapStick, David Serko and I made our way over to the ACT UP fundraiser at Tracks, a dance club on the far west side of Chelsea. Not having been there in several years, we were surprised to discover Friday nights now hosted a predominantly

---

*Apologies for all the Michaels and Davids. Sometimes it felt like half of ACT UP was named Michael or David.

Black and Latino crowd. Although I'd been to places where I'd been in the minority before—as a man, a gay man, a Jew, and even as a White man—I'd never been part of a White minority in a gay environment. And while it wasn't uncomfortable—unlike, for instance, my one brief visit to the Mineshaft—it was definitely unfamiliar; like being at a wedding and finding yourself seated with the other side of the family. I don't think I'd ever fully registered just how racially divided our community was, or how segregated my own social life had become.

But the music was great, the vibe hot and friendly, and there was some *serious* dancing going on. I'd *never* seen anything like some of the moves I saw on that dance floor. I tried to keep up, but these guys were way out of my league. It wasn't until I saw *Paris Is Burning* two years later that I realized those stylized moves had come from the uptown ballroom culture and were called "voguing."

Day Two: AIDS and PWAs

Early the following morning, at the request of ACT UP/New Jersey, I joined thirty other hungover activists on a bus to Newark's University Hospital. Although located in the county with the state's largest reported AIDS caseload, the hospital had somehow failed to enroll a single patient in its federally sponsored AIDS trials.[4] We picketed the hospital's empty parking lot for a damp ninety minutes, with nary a car, bus, or ambulance in sight. Nonetheless, we managed to score some local coverage, putting the plight of PWAs and the failures of the New Jersey AIDS trial centers onto the front page of the local Sunday papers.

Day Three: AIDS and People of Color

On Sunday morning, ACT UP went to church.

Although the church wielded great power and influence within communities of color and had a long history of advocating for civil rights and social justice issues, the stigma against homosexuality and drug use was so strong that it had largely remained silent about the AIDS crisis, despite the great damage the disease was inflicting on its flock.

Blacks and Hispanics made up 55 percent of New York's PWA population and 38 percent of the PWA population nationwide. One out of every sixty-one babies born in New York City was born with AIDS or HIV antibodies, the vast majority of whom were children of color.[5]

Armed with an endorsement from the Reverend Jesse Jackson, the Outreach Committee had sent letters to the pastors of over one hundred community churches, encouraging them to talk with their congregations about AIDS. They provided suggestions for activities to increase awareness about the disease, everything from sermon topics to fellowship programs, and from special offerings for local AIDS service groups to letter-writing campaigns targeting local congressmen and city officials.

That Sunday, ACT UP members held a "A Day of Remembrance and Solidarity," attending church services, setting up information tables, and handing out flyers on 125th Street and Lenox Avenue. Some, like Kendall Thomas, participated in church-sponsored dialogues where congregants acknowledged, often for the first time, their own illness or the illness of family members.[6]

The action had a particular resonance for Kendall, who had grown up in "a very fundamentalist Christian family," but one that understood Christian theology within the African American context "as a theology of liberation." The protests he participated in as a child, "marching with all these other Black folks, from the predominantly Black part of town, down to the courthouse, or being on picket lines at grocery stores in the neighborhood, where Black people couldn't get jobs . . . [were] explained in terms of God's will that people who were oppressed not be oppressed." He saw his work with ACT UP in a similar light.[7]

Kendall and other Black and Latino members would soon realize the need to create a space within ACT UP where they could generate a critique around issues of racial power and privilege in relation to the AIDS crisis and the provision of health care. They wanted to develop "actions that involved coalition with groups that weren't likely to come to the Monday night meetings," while also acting "as a kind of conscience of ACT UP on these issues."[8]

ACT UP's Majority Action Subcommittee would hold its first meeting on May 11.

Day Four: AIDS and Substance Abuse

Gregg Bordowitz was the point person for Monday's action, a soggy noontime rally and demonstration at City Hall Park highlighting the relationship between AIDS and substance abuse. A budding film and video maker, Gregg was a major ACT UP heartthrob—young, dark, brilliant, and charismatic. Gregg was also HIV-positive, a fact he announced on the Floor one Monday night shortly after receiving his test results, shocking several former sexual and romantic partners, both men and women, who were present in the room.

To me, he was like a figure out of an Odets play—the "doomed," Jewish, left-wing, bohemian intellectual. (Even now, I swoon.) Gregg talked fast and fearlessly, and could riff on Marx, Foucault, and feminism with great alacrity, punctuated by an occasional and delightfully unexpected self-deprecating giggle. He also sported the most spectacular set of sideburns in all of AIDS activism.

When Gregg presented the action to the Floor, he also came out as a recovering alcoholic and addict. I was stunned. It had never occurred to me that some of the people in the room might be Positive due to drug use. I assumed that since everyone there was gay—another incorrect assumption—the main risk for infection was unprotected sex. Gregg's point, an obvious one in retrospect, was that the categories of gay and drug user were not mutually exclusive and that substance abuse of any kind, whether with drugs or alcohol, could lead to unsafe sex. "Who are the fags and who are the junkies?" he would ask.[9] These categories were fictions used to divide us. Almost 9 percent of the city's cases of AIDS among IV drug users were gay men.

Until Gregg had spoken, the issue of drug use within ACT UP was deeply closeted. While everyone gave lip service to the importance of drug treatment on demand, we'd never discussed it with any urgency.

Intravenous drug users (IVDUs) were the fastest-growing population for HIV infection. Of the city's estimated 250,000 IVDUs, 60 percent had been exposed to HIV, up 10 percent from three years before. They accounted for 70 percent of all AIDS patients in city hospitals and 53 percent of the city's AIDS deaths. Approximately 80 percent of women infected with HIV were either drug users themselves or the sexual partners of drug users, and 82 percent of all children with AIDS had an IVDU as a parent.[10]

As part of our coalition-building effort, the day's demonstration was cosponsored by ADAPT, the Association for Drug Abuse Prevention and Treatment, the leading nongovernmental organization working with drug users in New York City. In addition to the usual demands for expanded drug treatment programs—unbelievably, no new programs had opened in the city since 1972—ADAPT also argued for the decriminalization of drug paraphernalia and the implementation of needle exchange and clean needle education programs. Needle exchange was a controversial street outreach program that encouraged drug users to return their used needles for clean ones, lessening the risk of infection by removing dirty works from the street. The exchange also served as a point of contact for disseminating health and AIDS education information and, ideally, for encouraging enrollment in drug treatment programs.

While many individuals in ACT UP supported needle exchange, we'd never discussed the issue in any depth and couldn't reach a quick consensus about supporting it as a group. As a result, we had to withhold our endorsement of ADAPT's demands and, embarrassingly, remove our name from the back of the fact sheet.

Day Five: AIDS and Prisons

For Tuesday's demo, protesting the medical and civil rights abuses faced by prisoners with HIV/AIDS, our Prisons Subcommittee led us back uptown to 125th Street for a drizzly march and rally outside the offices of the New York State Department of Corrections.

Prisoners with AIDS survived only one-third as long as PWAs on the outside, to an average age of only thirty-four years old.[11] Over 737 inmates had already died from AIDS in New York State prison facilities, and as much as 25 percent of the inmate population was thought to be HIV-positive.[12] Inmates diagnosed with HIV/AIDS were routinely segregated from the rest of the prison population and given no access to recreation, education, or work-release programs. Prisoners who became too sick to be treated in prison were removed to civilian wards where they were often shackled to their beds, sometimes for months on end. And despite the prevalence of drug use and sex between prisoners, the state refused to provide them with safe sex information, or to distribute condoms anywhere in the prison system.[13]

Day Six: Women and AIDS

Wednesday would also be about condoms and AIDS education. And dental dams, safe sex, and baseball.

The Women's Caucus had ambitiously planned a full day of actions, beginning with an early morning outreach effort outside nine city high schools across all five boroughs, distributing explicit safe sex and AIDS information, as well as condoms, dental dams, spermicidal jellies, and lubricants.

Then, as now, teenage sexuality was a hot-button issue, with AIDS education providing a flashpoint for many of the city's more reactionary elements, including the Catholic Church. The issue had proved so controversial that seven years into the epidemic, the city had yet to implement a coherent AIDS and safe sex curriculum in public schools.

Now, imagine this information being provided in schoolyards by a bunch of queers.

For many people, any interaction between gay people and school-age children was regarded as suspect, an opportunity for predatory sexual abuse and "gay recruiting." Though there were many out teachers in the city school system—we had at least a dozen of them in ACT UP alone—memories were still fresh of the failed 1978 Briggs Initiative that would have outlawed homosexuals and their allies from teaching in California public schools. Any discussion of AIDS or safe sex, and certainly anything involving gay sexuality, was highly charged and potentially job threatening.

Indeed, the activists had no idea if they'd be allowed onto school property, let alone to interact with students, or how those students might react to receiving information from such an obviously gay source. Would the activists be welcomed or attacked? Embraced or arrested? (And would it be raining?)

They needn't have worried. The sun was out, and the kids were starved for information, whatever the source. More than a few teachers and principals also confided they, too, were glad *someone* was finally talking to their students about AIDS.

But teenagers were just one segment of the population that needed to be educated. As was the case with birth control, most heterosexual safe sex messages targeted women as the responsible parties for having condoms and enforcing safe sex. (It remains one of the great ironies of American health policy that while women are regularly held responsible for the well-being of everyone else, they are not considered responsible or rational enough to make decisions about their own bodies and lives.) While we all supported female sexual empowerment, the caucus thought it only fair to shift some of the responsibility back onto men.

To help disseminate this message, Gran Fury came up with an attention-grabbing poster featuring an enlarged (I'm assuming) photograph of an erect penis, with the headline "SEXISM REARS ITS UNPROTECTED HEAD" and the tagline "MEN: Use Condoms Or Beat It." While the poster had a relatively small (ahem) run, the tagline soon caught on and was replicated—sans phallus—on T-shirts, stickers, and buttons by several groups, including GMHC.[14]

While the posters were fun, our goal was to deliver this message to straight men directly. And where better than at a baseball game?

When the women first came to the Floor with their proposal for an action at Shea Stadium, we all applauded their chutzpah and creativity. The idea of a group of lesbians and gay men invading a baseball stadium to lecture straight men on sexual responsibility took, well, balls. But underneath our bravado, many—all right, mostly the men—were worried about the potential for violence. I know I was.

I liked baseball. I was a longtime Mets fan and had gone to Shea Stadium many times with my dad and brother. But going to a ballgame as a gay man was particularly fraught—like high school gym class, but with beer. I always felt I had to butch it up a bit so I could pass and avoid any potential trouble. But if I was brave enough to get arrested at a demonstration, I guess I could risk going to a ballgame with ACT UP.

The evening's first action was possibly the most dangerous, as small groups of activists stationed themselves at each of the entrances and handed out flyers and condoms to the approaching crowd. I'm sure the humor of our flyers helped defuse some of the tension (as did the presence of stadium security).

AIDS IS NOT A BALL GAME!
MEN! DON'T ENDANGER THE WOMEN YOU LOVE.*

Here's the score:

Single: Only *one* woman has been included in government sponsored tests for new drugs for AIDS.

Double: Women diagnosed with AIDS die *twice* as fast as men.

Triple: The number of women with AIDS has *tripled* as a result of sexual contact with men in NYC since the 1984 World Series.

The Grand Slam: Most men still don't use condoms.

USE CONDOMS. NO GLOVE, NO LOVE!

*And if you can't be with the one you love, protect the one you're with.[15]

The Goddess was clearly with us, as it was a beautiful spring night, the lush green of the baseball field glowing in all its Technicolor radiance. ACT UP had reserved four hundred seats[16] across three sections in the middle reaches of the Upper Deck. I was seated in one of six rows stacked up along the third baseline. Across the way I could make out another six rows of activists in ACT UP regalia, and another eight in the center section. (Originally, we'd reserved only two sections, but as soon as word got out, requests came pouring in from every queer baseball fan in the movement.)

Each section was given two different sets of banners, each divided in thirds, so every line of our message would be two rows high and one row long. Maxine Wolfe and Debra Levine had snuck into the stadium when they first bought the tickets, scuttling over the empty seats with tape measures to scope out the correct dimensions.[17] Each message would be displayed twice—and only when the opposing team was at bat.

When the Astros stepped up to the plate in the top half of the third inning, we took our banners out of their numbered bags and stared across the stadium, eagerly waiting for the first message to appear. In a matter of seconds, "**DON'T BALK . . . AT . . . SAFER SEX**" was unfurled, and a high-pitched whoop drifted across the stadium. Then it was our turn.

Beginning from the top of our section on the right-hand aisle, our fifth row unraveled the first banner, deftly passing it along from person to person, over the metal railings that divided the sections. When it reached the aisle, everyone unfolded the banner, held on to the bottom flap and passed the top half to the sixth row above. This same action was then repeated by rows three and four, and then rows one and two until the message "**AIDS . . . KILLS . . . WOMEN**" was fully revealed.

The center section then completed the triptych with "**MEN! . . . USE . . . CONDOMS**." We kept our banners up, stomping, swaying, and cheering until the inning was over. Reversing the process, we then passed the banners back, closing and refolding until they were returned to their carefully numbered bags, and braced ourselves for the fallout. Would it be stadium security marching over to forbid us from displaying our banners, or some drunken troublemakers storming upstairs to avenge our desecration of the national pastime? But none arrived.

Neither did the hot dog or beer vendors, but at least there were no confrontations. Instead, we were swarmed by a neighboring group of high school girls from Queens, who thought what we were doing was cool and talked to us about problems with their school's AIDS education program. They returned to their seats—and their squeamish boyfriends—laden with *Silence = Death* buttons, fact sheets, and condoms.

When the fifth inning came, we repeated the process, this time with the messages: "**NO GLOVE! NO LOVE!**" "**STRIKE OUT AIDS**," and "**SILENCE = DEATH ACT UP**," the latter spread out across all eight rows of the center section.

Life was glorious in our Upper Deck oasis. We cheered for the Mets, sang "Take Me Out to the Ballgame," and when the organ began the BOOM-BOOM-CLAP refrain of "We Will Rock You," we improvised our own lyrics, singing "*We Wear, We Wear CONDOMS!*" Since we were official group ticket purchasers, we even got to cheer our own messages on the stadium's DiamondVision scoreboard: "*AIDS Coalition—ACT UP*"; "*National Women and AIDS Day Committee*"; and "*Strike Out AIDS*."

And to make it a perfect evening, the Mets won!

Day Seven: AIDS: A Worldwide Crisis

At the last minute, with little more than a week to spare, The Lady Miles asked me to take over the seventh day's action when the original coordinator flaked out. While the obvious target for a day with an international theme was the UN, we weren't going to make that mistake again. Rockefeller Center, with its high visibility, international imagery, and density of tourists, had already been selected as the protest site, and Michael assured me it could be a simple picket and leaflet demonstration.

The original plan had been to march down the long promenade of Rockefeller Plaza and circle around the skating rink, which was surrounded by flagpoles displaying a variety of international flags. Unfortunately, I discovered the entire plaza was private property and any sort of organized protest would be shut down immediately by police. We could organize the demo as a CD action, but it would be hard to rationalize the arrest. What would we be protesting—the high price of ice-skating?

Instead, I moved the action site a half block north to the public space at 630 Fifth Avenue, right in front of the famous statue of Atlas shouldering the world. We still had our Rockefeller Center location, plus a visual that echoed our call for the US to *shoulder* its responsibility in fighting the worldwide AIDS epidemic. But despite my best efforts—including a repurposed AIDS tote board* and a kick-ass fact sheet—we got clobbered by a torrential rainstorm and folded our umbrellas after an unfulfilling hour.

I returned home to my empty apartment drenched and deeply defeated. I'd worked so hard, organizing almost the entire demo myself—calling in last-minute favors, writing my own fucking fact sheet, begging people to show up—all for nothing. And when I came home, there was no one there for me. I missed Eric—or maybe just the idea of Eric—and I missed my life, the one I had before I stepped out of my bubble and took on the AIDS crisis. Before I felt responsible for changing the world—and before failing so miserably.

Day Eight: AIDS: Testing and Treatment

And on the eighth day, it rained even harder. The Issues Committee had chosen to focus its demonstration on pediatric AIDS and the plight of infants and children involved in the clinical trial for Intravenous Immunoglobulin (IVIG).

---

*Thanks, Steve Cohen.

There were serious problems with the IVIG protocol, beginning with its use of placebos. We believed it was unethical to use placebos in any drug trials involving life-threatening illnesses. What made it particularly egregious was the drug being tested was already available to patients who could pay for treatment. But for most of the children with pediatric AIDS, their only hope for getting proper medical care was to enroll in the trial and risk getting the placebo rather than the drug.

To make matters worse, the treatment (or nontreatment) was being delivered intravenously, requiring some of the younger children, who averaged only eighteen months of age, to be bound in restraints for hours at a time. In addition, the trial put the health of the children in the placebo group at risk, by subjecting them to potential infections both from the IV site and from the hospital environment while being immunosuppressed.

Alas, while the cause was worthy, the demonstration was a mess. Having chosen Grand Army Plaza on Fifth Avenue, just across the street from FAO Schwarz, the "toy store of millionaires,"[18] as its site, the committee had opted for a street theater approach, complete with a lengthy and complicated plot. I've always had an aversion to demonstrations that rely on narrative. Who's going to stick around for the entire show—especially in a downpour?

Day Nine: National Day of Protest

For the ninth and final day of action, AIDS activists from across the country would be marching on their respective state capitals to demand immediate action to end the AIDS crisis. For us, this meant a Saturday morning bus trip to Albany, where we would set up a small display of AIDS Quilt panels and then march to the State Capitol building for an afternoon rally.

When we pulled into Albany at 10 a.m., the sun was out, and Washington Park was abuzz with activity. But this didn't look like a typical activist crowd. Where were the leather jackets, "Silence = Death" buttons, and earrings? Where were the sideburns?

Unbeknownst to us, our demonstration coincided with Albany's annual Pinkster Fest, and the park was filled with families, food trucks, and several dozen arts and crafts booths. It was as if we'd parachuted into some alternate universe; several hundred bleary-eyed activists clad in black, wandering through the land of pastels and funnel cakes.

As we stumbled through the park looking for the AIDS Quilt display, we suddenly came upon a caravan of beauty queens, all decked out in prom dresses, sashes, and tiaras, sitting atop a procession of vintage convertibles. Everything stopped. We just stood and stared at them, as they slowly turned and stared at us. Seconds ticked by. Then Michael Nesline, who was at the front of our group, broke out in a big smile, raised his long right arm, and offered his best beauty pageant wave. We all raised our arms and did the same—our queens saluting their queens. And slowly, if warily, the Tulip Queen and her retinue waved back.

Just beyond the roadway, we found the small hedged-off garden where the forty-one Quilt panels had been laid out. The contrast between the two events couldn't have been starker. As America goes about its business, with its fairs and its picnics, we have deaths and memorials. It was a theme picked up by Vito Russo at our rally later that afternoon.

I first became aware of Vito shortly after I graduated college, when I discovered a copy of his book, *The Celluloid Closet*,[19] an analysis of Hollywood's representation of lesbians and gays in the movies, at the old Doubleday Bookstore on Fifth Avenue. Too nervous to buy it, I devoured it a chapter at a time over several visits. The author, I later discovered, was very much like his book—smart, funny, outspoken, and politically astute, though never sacrificing his humanity for the sake of ideology. Over the years, I searched out his columns in *The Advocate, Village Voice,* and *New York Native,* and watched him on public access as the host of *Our Time,* one of the first gay cable TV shows.*

A few years later, when Vito invited me to his apartment for a movie screening of the camp "Women in Prison" classic, *Caged,* he also showed clips from his personal collection of historical videos, including one from the 1973 Gay Pride rally in Washington Square Park, where Vito, as emcee, tried to negotiate a truce between the radical lesbians and the drag queens, who were arguing about whether drag denigrated women and the appropriateness of having drag performers at the rally, while legendary activist Sylvia Rivera berated the entire crowd for turning their backs on the street queens who'd sparked the riots that paved the way for gay liberation.[20] Each side took turns grabbing the microphone and hurling accusations at one another until Vito magically produced surprise guest Bette Midler, who calmed the crowd by singing "Friends."

Vito was a legendary activist as well. He'd been a leading figure in the Gay Activist Alliance, organizing their popular movie nights at the fabled GAA Firehouse; cofounded the Gay and Lesbian Alliance Against Defamation (GLAAD); led demonstrations against the dangerously homophobic movie

---

*In my favorite episode, Vito escorted Lily Tomlin, dressed as her character Judith Beasley—"I am not an actress. I am an ordinary housewife and person like yourself"—as she visited a number of gay bars delivering a conciliatory "Quiche of Peace" on behalf of the straight community.

Cruising; and, as a self-identified PWA, been one of the earliest and loudest voices fighting the government's murderous inaction about AIDS.

A founding member of ACT UP, Vito was, at the ripe old age of forty-two, also one of our wise elders, and his speech in Albany that afternoon was a brilliant distillation of our shared experiences as activists, PWAs, and members of the AIDS community.

Living with AIDS in this country is like living in The Twilight Zone. Living with AIDS is like living through a war which is happening only for those people who are in the trenches. Every time a shell explodes you look around to discover that you've lost more of your friends. But nobody else notices. It isn't happening to them. They're walking the streets as though we weren't living through some sort of nightmare. And only you can hear the screams of the people who are dying and their cries for help. No one else seems to be noticing.

And it's worse than a war, because during a war people are united in a shared experience. This war has not united us, it's divided us. It's separated those of us with AIDS and those of us who fight for people with AIDS from the rest of the population.

. . .

Someday, the AIDS crisis will be over. Remember that. And when that day comes—when that day has come and gone, there'll be people alive on this earth—gay people and straight people, men and women, black and white, who will hear the story that once there was a terrible disease in this country and all over the world, and that a brave group of people stood up and fought and, in some cases, gave their lives, so that other people might live and be free.

. . .

In a lot of ways, AIDS activists are like those doctors out there—they're so busy putting out fires and taking care of people on respirators, that they don't have the time to take care of all the sick people. We're so busy putting out fires right now, that we don't have the time to talk to each other and strategize and plan for the next wave, and the next day, and next month and the next week and the next year.

And, we're going to have to find the time to do that in the next few months. . . . And then, after we kick the shit out of this disease, we're all going to be alive to kick the shit out of this system, so that this never happens again.[21]

The day's other high point took place at the end of the rally, when Frank Jump got up to sing. Unlike most of the entertainment, which was of the well-intentioned "We are a gentle loving people" variety, Frank brought his boom box. Dance rhythms and guitar riffs poured out of his speakers as he began to rock and rap his song "Lilywhite Lies." And when Frank launched into the chorus, the New York contingent jumped up and began to dance.

The rest of the crowd didn't know what to make of us. According to our reputation, ACT UP was very serious, very political, and very angry. Dancing wouldn't seem to be part of our repertoire. But if ACT UP had only been about anger, we never would have lasted. There was hard work, grief, and anger, surely, but there was also great joy. To paraphrase Emma Goldman, "If I can't dance, it's not my revolution."

In ACT UP, we danced.

Chapter 6

Taking Actions

ACTIONS, WHETHER THE Actions Committee itself or simply planning and organizing demonstrations, would remain the primary focus of my activism, providing me with a simple and pragmatic framework for dealing with AIDS. It wasn't about finding the drugs, fixing the system, or answering the big questions—things I felt unqualified to do. In some ways, it wasn't even about AIDS. It was about translating ideas and demands into actions; figuring out how best to sell those actions to the Floor, the media, and the larger community; and then rallying the troops and putting on a show.

Along the way, I discovered hidden talents as a project manager and facilitator. I'd always thought of myself as more a synthesizer than an original thinker, and here I was able to tease out other people's ideas and help mold them into an exciting package. It was a good fit, and I flourished.

Another unexpected bonus of my chairmanship was the impact it had on my relationship with my parents.

I was one of the lucky ones. Granted, when I came out during my senior year of college, they received the news as if I were feeding them some bad-tasting medicine, but I suppose I was. I was telling them I was not who they thought I was or who they thought I was going to be, and their dreams for my future of marriage, kids, and family were not going to happen.* Nonetheless,

---

*Gay marriage was not on anyone's radar in 1980. It certainly wasn't anything I expected to happen in my lifetime, nor was it something I was interested in pursuing at the time. Same goes for kids, though I certainly love my nieces and nephews.

they told me they still loved me, even as they continued to suggest that maybe this was "only a phase" and warned I should be careful not to "close any doors."

Soon, and without any subsequent discussion, we settled into an uncomfortable truce. My gayness would be acknowledged, but not discussed—an early family version of "Don't ask, don't tell." For the next few years, our tacitly agreed-upon topics of conversation were my struggling acting career, my finances (or lack thereof), and my brother, sister, and other family news. Notably missing was any discussion of my friends or personal life. As a result, for several long years I was something of a stranger in their midst.

Occasionally, incidents from my "gay life" would explode into my parents' consciousness—a case of crabs when I was still living at home right after college, or the traumatic breakup of a torrid summer stock romance that happened the day before they came to visit—but these only added to the specter of unhappiness and depravity they suspected was the "gay lifestyle." Things hit bottom when I announced I was being treated to a trip to San Francisco—*San Francisco!*—by a friend with whom I'd been having a long-distance affair. My parents were appalled I'd accepted a free vacation from a relative stranger (I was having problems squaring it as well), and they tellingly forgot to wish me a safe trip.

It would take several years of hard work on all our parts—and a healthy dose of therapy on mine—to get our relationship functioning again. Much of this work took place on family vacations and involved intense discussions in hotels and restaurants across South Florida. Part of the problem was lack of context. When discussing my friends and day-to-day life became off-limits, all that remained to fill the void were the often lurid, and always unhappy, images of gay life provided by the media.

It fell to me to explain that not all gay bars were dark and sleazy, that my friends were the same nice boys they'd met when I was in college, and that regardless of being gay, I remained the same son they'd always known. I lived my life by the same beliefs and values they'd taught me, even if the circumstances of their application were sometimes different than they'd anticipated. In return, they shared their concerns about my unhappiness—present and future—and warned about the dangers and limitations of isolating myself in a "gay ghetto." I countered that it was only natural for me to seek out places where I could meet other gay people and be myself without having to look over my shoulder or censor my feelings.

I told them about an experience I'd had in summer stock, when, after a long day of rehearsal, the cast and crew went to our regular hangout for a couple of drinks. The place was empty except for us and maybe three or four other people. After a drink or two, I was pulled aside by the bartender who told me I was "making people uncomfortable" because I'd put my hand on my boyfriend's back. He then warned if I so much as touched my friend again, he'd throw me out of the bar.

Another time, as we sat on the beach, I pointed to a straight couple walking hand in hand along the water's edge and said if I wanted to do the same thing with someone I loved, I'd risk being harassed and called names, and maybe even physically attacked. At a minimum, I'd have to ignore everyone's clucking disapproval and comments about "flaunting my lifestyle." And all I wanted was a romantic walk on the beach, something most people, including my parents, did without a second thought.

Strangely, or maybe not, AIDS was not a major topic of discussion, even as it loomed threateningly over much of our conversation. We never talked much about sex anyway, but when the topic came up, I told them I was safe, without getting too specific. I'm sure they wanted to believe me, but they must have been terrified. I found out years later they'd quietly made arrangements so that if I got sick, there'd be money for my care, and I'd be able to move back home.

But it was ACT UP that changed my parents' view of my life as a gay man. They could see the effect that activism was having on me. I was enthusiastic, involved with interesting people, using my brain, and doing important work.

When I first became chair of Actions, I had a conversation with my mother about the responsibilities of running a committee. My mom was a formidable committee chair at Temple Sisterhood and at the local Senior Center, and much like her mother before her (and all the women in my family, across generations), she would, in short order, wind up running whatever organization she joined. After telling her about all the prep work I did before my weekly Actions meetings—the phone calls and cross-checking information, the schmoozing and behind-the-scenes politicking—she nodded sagely and said, "A good chairman is only surprised at a meeting on her birthday."

My involvement with ACT UP, rather than further isolating me in an unknown gay world, had instead made both it and me more comprehensible to them—just as it was making the world, and my place in it, more comprehensible to me.

May 16, 1988: Send in the Clowns

The US Commission on Civil Rights, once the proud defender of people's rights, had been transformed by the Reagan administration into a forum for reversing many of the antidiscrimination policies and programs of the last thirty years. Little wonder we were suspicious when the commission announced it was holding a series of hearings on AIDS and AIDS-related discrimination.

Our worst fears were confirmed when friends in Ted Kennedy's office slipped us a copy of the Civil Rights Commission's project proposal. Its ideologically driven agenda was apparent even in its mission statement:

> To gather information on the transmissibility of AIDS and the danger to the public health posed by AIDS; to gather information on allegations of discrimination against persons afflicted with AIDS; and to gather information with respect to the view that according civil rights protections to AIDS carriers jeopardizes the public health.[1]

Why would it be necessary for yet another commission to gather information on AIDS transmissibility? Hadn't those questions already been answered by the National Academy of Science panel, the CDC, and the surgeon general? And if the gathering of information on cases of AIDS discrimination seemed on point, give or take the use of the word "allegations," what about the final directive, which bluntly pitted "civil rights protections" for PWAs against the interests of "public health"? In every area, the proposal revealed a bias toward identifying opportunities to legally restrict the rights of PWAs, whether by employers wishing to screen job applicants for HIV, by landlords looking to deny them housing, or by school boards seeking to ban HIV-positive children from their schools.

And then there were the Bible quotes.

Noting that the "stigma" of AIDS was attributable not only to fears of transmission, but to the "often illegal and . . . morally proscribed"[2] behaviors responsible for transmitting the virus, the proposal was laden with gratuitous biblical citations condemning homosexuality. Not just the usual Leviticus 18:22: "You shall not lie with a male as one lies with a female; it is an abomination"; but Romans 1:26–27: "For this reason, God gave them over to degrading passions; for their women exchanged the natural function for that which is unnatural, and in the same way also the men abandoned the natural function of the women and burned in their desire towards one another, men with men committing indecent acts and receiving in their own persons the due penalty of their error"; and another chart-topper from Leviticus 20:13: "If there is a man who lies with a male as those who lie with a woman, both of them have committed a detestable act; they shall surely be put to death. Their blood guiltiness is upon them";[3] and several others.

Senators Ted Kennedy, Tom Harkin, Lowell Weicker, and Robert Stafford shared our concerns, and raised their own questions about the purpose and scope of the project. They argued that since the recent *Arline*[4] court decision, which indicated PWAs, people with HIV, and even people perceived as being HIV-positive were all covered by antidiscrimination protections, there was no need for the Civil Rights Commission to revisit the issue; it should, instead, monitor enforcement and give "Congress and the public a sense of the extent of the discrimination that exists and the effectiveness of efforts to redress such discrimination."[5]

In response, Chairman Clarence Pendleton Jr., a Black conservative who'd been appointed to the panel by President Reagan for his opposition to affirmative action, school integration, and other bulwarks of civil rights policy, questioned the senators' interpretation of *Arline* and defended the commission's investigation of medical and scientific issues as "vital to the determination of what civil rights protections should be accorded." Since "fear of contagion . . . is at the root of much AIDS-related discrimination," he continued, the Civil Rights Commission was the correct venue for determining whether those concerns were valid. "I hope you would agree that if Rosa Parks were forced to sit in the back of the bus today, you would rather have her complaint investigated by a civil rights body than by the U.S. Department of Transportation."[6]

Well, yes; but I wonder whether he would expect them to devote so much time to exploring how the rights of White businesses were negatively impacted by Ms. Parks's use of public transportation and to footnote theories of genetic inferiority and biblical quotes condoning slavery in the project proposal.

But despite the obviously partisan nature of the hearings, the Actions Committee was having a difficult time figuring out how best to respond.

An important clue magically appeared one evening, as I sorted through the stacks of "to be read" newspapers that littered my bedroom floor. Buried in the middle pages of a weeks-old *New York Times* was a small news service squib about a memorandum sent by William Bradford Reynolds, counselor to Attorney General Edwin Meese III, urging the Justice Department to "polarize the debate" on issues like AIDS, drugs, obscenity, and the death penalty. "We must not seek 'consensus,'" the memo said, "we must confront."[7]

"AIDS is not a civil rights or privacy issue," the memo continued, "but one of public health and safety." Therefore, the Justice Department should press lawsuits to counter "the privacy advocates who challenge AIDS testing." The memo advocated using public health laws, building codes, and health and safety rules to attack obscenity, and it urged confronting drug use with a "tough approach" that emphasized law enforcement and drug testing, as opposed to "the soft, easy way that emphasizes drug treatment and rehabilitation."[8]

I could barely believe what I was reading. Here, in their own words, was a road map of their intentions for their remaining nine months in office. There would be no moving them.

My discovery proved oddly liberating. If their only goal was to polarize the debate, there was no sense trying to reason with them. And if the hearings were just a charade, there was no point pretending to play along. Our course was clear. We'd have to blow the mother up.

But how?

The usual picket and CD would give the commission more credibility than it deserved, while testifying at the hearings ran the risk of legitimizing the obviously bogus exercise, allowing the commission to claim that all viewpoints were being represented. The more mainstream organizations had similar concerns, although, in the end, they felt compelled to testify, if only to ensure that the conservatives didn't present their case unchallenged.

We felt no such obligation. At our Friday meeting, we brainstormed what we would like to have happen at the hearings. We were thinking of pranks, releasing insects or marbles—something that would disrupt the meeting and challenge its very legitimacy—when someone sighed, "The whole thing is such a big fucking circus . . ."

We arrived in Washington just in time to set up a lunchtime picket with OUT (Oppression Under Target), a new activist group hastily organized by a recently relocated Michael Petrelis. While remaining a key member of ACT UP, Michael would often go off on his own, creating fly-by-night organizations to carry out actions or campaigns without any restrictions from the Floor. This worked to everyone's advantage, allowing ACT UP to share the credit when he was successful—everyone assumed he was part of ACT UP anyway—but also giving us plausible deniability whenever he inevitably went too far. In return, Michael could do pretty much whatever he wanted while using ACT UP as a resource for funding and, when necessary, additional recruits.

Everyone in DC was bug-eyed from the morning session, which had been far worse than anyone had anticipated. Chairman Pendleton had opened the hearings by attacking the commission's critics, reserving special derision for gay groups. "We've also been told a homosexual group plans to demonstrate in front of this building while we're holding our hearing. The truth is, homosexual groups are represented in this hearing, and I'm therefore having trouble understanding what all the moaning is about."[9]

It had gone quickly downhill from there.

When the lunch break was over, we slowly filtered into the hearing room, spreading ourselves across six or seven rows in the center section of the auditorium. The press, alerted by our Media Committee that *something* was going to happen, had set up a bank of cameras at the front of the auditorium and were practicing pivoting back and forth between the audience and the stage. At one o'clock, the commissioners filed in and took their seats onstage, eyeing us warily. We remained silent. Then, when the first speaker began his testimony, we reached into our bags and put on our clown masks—pink and translucent, and edged with a shock of orange synthetic hair, with big white ovals of eye makeup, thick arched eyebrows, and a bright red cherry nose.

The commissioners froze, their mouths hanging open. The press whirled around and charged at us, a blinding wall of photo flashes and camera lights. The speaker, noting the commotion, turned around and the color quickly drained from his face. We stared back at him blankly.

The hearing ground to a standstill.

After several moments, we silently took off our watches and held them up in front of us. *Time is running out.* Gripping the podium tightly, the speaker attempted to resume his testimony, his voice shaking. Swinging our watches, we began to make clicking sounds with our tongues: *"Tick . . . tock . . . tick . . . tock . . ."*

"You're wasting our time," shouted out one protester. "How many more have to die?" The camera lights blinked on again as Chairman Pendleton asked us for patience. "Were you patient twenty years ago?" came the reply.[10]

Next up was Dr. Alexander Langmuir, a retired CDC epidemiologist, who explained that while he "had no direct access to any special information,"[11] he had, according to his handout, used a statistical model based on the British Cattle Plague of 1865–66 to predict the trajectory of the AIDS crisis.[12] *"REA-gan's PA-nels Keep Debating. EIGHT YEARS LATER: We're still WA-A-A-I-TING!"* Pendleton asked us again for silence. We stood up and turned our backs in disgust.

It was Langmuir's belief that "since AIDS cases die within 2 to 3 years of diagnosis," the decline of new cases would occur naturally as more and more infected people die off.[13] Referring to his accompanying graph, he suggested there were indications that infection rates may have already begun to plateau. "There is," he asserted triumphantly, pointing to the lines charting the incidence of AIDS cases in homosexuals, "a constant curve towards bending over."[14]

Well, something about the phrase "bending over" inspired us, and with a giant *"Wheeeeee!"* we all bent over and showed the commission just what we thought of their "experts." The audience, the press, and even the commissioners burst out laughing, as Pendleton banged his gavel demanding order. After several more interruptions, Langmuir concluded his testimony by stating that based on his calculations, AIDS cases "will peak this year or next," and that in just two to three years, AIDS will become "a serious, but a manageable problem."[15]

The next speaker was yet another crackpot doctor who barely got started before Chairman Pendleton was forced to call for a break. As the commission retreated offstage, Mary Berry, a Carter-era appointee, smiled and shot us a big thumbs-up.

But the mood soon darkened, as police began to line the aisles around the auditorium. When the commission returned, Pendleton warned that any further interruptions would result in our arrest. We began to hum "America the Beautiful." More testimony. More shouted comments from the audience. And as the police grew increasingly antsy, I began to look for a way for us to leave the hearing room under our own steam. Finally, when the speaker announced that, in fact, "There is no AIDS epidemic,"[16] we stood up, pointed at the commission, and shouting *"Shame! Shame! Shame!"* marched out of the auditorium.

Though they'd be able to resume their hearings, the commission and its reputation never recovered, and their eventual recommendations went largely unremarked and ignored.

If we'd given the Commission on Civil Rights a hard time, the administration was having even less luck with its AIDS commission. This was no longer the same panel we'd protested back in September. In addition to the change in personnel, including the replacement of Chairman Mayberry with Admiral James D. Watkins, there had been a noticeable shift in the commission's perspective.

These changes had been reflected in the AIDS commission's interim reports.* When questioned about his own change of attitude, Admiral Watkins admitted he'd "learned a lot on a very steep learning curve," adding he felt much like the conservative Southern doctor who'd testified, "'the more that I'm in this fight against AIDS, the more I become a liberal.'"[17]

While newspaper editorial pages and mainstream AIDS organizations applauded the commission's evolution, right-wing conservatives were apoplectic at the unexpected turn. Rep. William E. Dannemeyer (R-CA), a senior member of the House subcommittee on Health and the Environment, warned "special interest groups" like homosexuals and civil libertarians were writing the AIDS commission reports, running roughshod over the recommendations and interests of the commission members who supported strong public health measures, like testing and name reporting.[18]

Perhaps he was right.

Since September, Bill Bahlman had attended every meeting and open hearing on ACT UP's behalf, testifying and providing the commissioners and their staff with fact sheets and information. According to Commissioner Burton Lee, ACT UP's presence had been "indispensable" in persuading the commission that "AIDS required a political solution as much as a medical one . . . and [in] continuing to bring pressure to bear in political circles."[19] But even as we acknowledged Bill's positive impact, we began to question whether sending him around the country to attend yet another hearing was the best use of ACT UP's modest funds. When, after much begging, the Issues Committee finally submitted a budget for Bill's attendance at the final eight AIDS commission meetings, the total was three times the amount in ACT UP's bank account.

Bill's efforts also seemed far closer to lobbying than direct action, feeding suspicions this was some sort of end-run to make Bill our de facto lobbyist. Bill and his Lavender Hill Mob confederates had long advocated ACT UP take on a lobbying role, proposing a Legislative Action Subcommittee to follow and draft legislation and develop relationships on Capitol Hill, but their proposals never gained much traction.

Was Bill's or ACT UP's presence necessary at these hearings, or was the commission just distracting theater, especially when there were many other important battles to fight?

---

*The Presidential Commission on the HIV Epidemic had issued a preliminary report to President Reagan on December 2, 1987, followed by a second report and series of recommendations on March 3, 1988.

Week after week, these arguments and others played out in the Coordinating Committee and on the Floor, as we tried to define the limits and priorities of the organization. Questions about Bill's expenses had already cost us a $3,500 loan from Larry Kramer, who'd promised to front the money to pay for our first direct mail fundraising campaign. When ACT UP voted to continue bankrolling Bill's trips over Larry's loudly voiced objections, he withdrew his financing, arguing that if we could afford Bill's plane fare and hotel, we didn't need his money. Although Larry still offered to write the cover letter for our mailer, we thought better of it and found another funding source and a different playwright (Harvey Fierstein).*

Not that ACT UP held any hard grudges against Larry. If not indispensable, Larry was irreplaceable and greatly venerated; so, whatever the disagreement, he was always welcomed back with open arms. But baby was learning how to walk on its own and would not be pushed around by anyone. Not even Larry.

As it turned out, we'd made the right decision about Bill Bahlman. When the AIDS commission delivered its final report in late June, it read far more like an ACT UP fact sheet than the administration's hoped-for defense of its policies. The report was also deeply critical of the federal response to the epidemic and the lack of leadership from the Reagan administration.†

Not surprisingly, the administration tried to bury the report. There was no Rose Garden ceremony or press conference in the White House Press Room, only a short twenty-minute closed-door briefing between the president and Admiral Watkins. Rather than speak publicly about the commission's

---

*The mailing, sent to 50,000 prospective donors, proved a great success, grossing close to $70,000, and was followed by a second mailing of the Fierstein letter to an additional 150,000 potential donors. According to Peter Staley, the two mailings brought in close to $300,000 gross (Peter Staley, *Never Silent: ACT UP and My Life in Activism* [Chicago: Chicago Review Press, 2022], 94), though Sean Strub suggests the total was probably closer to $200,000 (personal correspondence with author dated November 14, 2021); in either case an extraordinary amount. However, the success of the mailings soon raised concerns about ACT UP's tax status and its responsibility to share the wealth with other ACT UPs around the country. ACT UP would eventually agree to register with the IRS as a 501c(4) nonprofit social welfare group, which made contributions non-tax-deductible but allowed us to continue our political work.

†On the negative side, the report also included recommendations that doctors and health care personnel be required to report the names of all infected individuals to state health officials on a confidential basis for partner notification.

findings or take immediate action on any of its recommendations, Reagan requested that Dr. Donald Ian Macdonald, the White House drug policy adviser, review the report and produce a new summary plan.

Macdonald's ten-point plan would pointedly ignore the commission's confidentiality and antidiscrimination recommendations—"the key to the entire [commission] report," according to Admiral Watkins—and replace funding for drug treatment programs with a call for more "just say no" antidrug legislation. It also proposed wasting time with yet another round of conferences on AIDS and public health issues, while directing the FDA to immediately improve the procedures and accuracy of HIV blood tests.[20]

But despite the administration's best efforts, the commission's original recommendations would become the baseline for all future discussion about government action in the fight against AIDS. Both George Bush and Michael Dukakis would endorse them as part of their AIDS platforms during the 1988 presidential campaign, with Bush announcing his support for the federal antidiscrimination legislation as part of his effort to differentiate himself from the policies of the previous president.[21]

Even though our actions may not have done much to improve the day-to-day life of PWAs, we'd profoundly influenced the national dialogue around AIDS. Our early success in labeling the AIDS commission a partisan right-wing panel had given its eventual embrace of our agenda greater credibility, while the commission's imprimatur helped legitimize our demands and further burnished ACT UP's reputation.

June 26, 1988: Gay Pride

Ever since my first Gay Pride parade back in 1981, Pride Sunday had been one of my favorite days of the year. It was the one day I felt completely comfortable being out and gay in public; no holds barred. The one day I could put on my pink triangle pin, smile at sexy strangers, and dance in the streets.

This year would be different. For the past ten months, I'd been wearing a pink triangle every day and marching, not dancing, in the streets. And instead of smiling furtively at sexy strangers, I knew them.

Over the years, ACT UP would have several social hubs. There was Woody's and later Benny's Burritos for after-meeting margaritas; the East Village hangs—the Bar, Wonder Bar, and Crowbar; and the dance clubs—the World,

Mars, and Meat. But at least in the early years, if there was an ACT UP party, it was probably at Maria's.*

Maria Maggenti lived on East Tenth Street in Alphabet City, across from Tompkins Square Park at the height of its homeless-anarchist-drug dealer-drag queen heyday. I never remembered Maria's apartment number, and since there were no names on the downstairs buzzers, I'd keep pressing the buttons until someone buzzed me in. Then, it was just a matter of following the noise up a couple of flights and knocking on the door covered with ACT UP stickers.

We would gather at Maria's several times a year, for holiday and Pride parties, to celebrate demonstrations and commiserate after elections. There was, admittedly, a bit of a status issue around Maria's parties, with invitees sarcastically referred to as the "A-List" by those who felt left out. (If all this sounds like high school, you wouldn't be wrong.) We were, I guess, "the in crowd"—the movers and shakers, the ones who ran the meetings and committees and regularly spoke up on the Floor—and Maria was ACT UP's golden girl.

Maria's was always hot and crowded, her small three-room apartment awash in beer, cigarettes, and politics. There was a bathtub in the kitchen, which, when covered with an old wooden door, doubled as a bar, and in the far corner a tiny WC with a sign reminding the guys to please put the seat down when they were finished. Doubling back, there was a small book-lined hallway/second bedroom, which led to the brick-walled living room/bedroom overlooking the park.

On one particularly hot Saturday evening, Maria's was packed as usual, and as the night wore on it became increasingly hot and sultry in her un-air-conditioned apartment. Among the sweltering guests was a particularly attractive subset of ACT UP's notorious "Boys in Black." With their chiseled good looks and gym-toned bodies, they were a strutting advertisement for the healthful benefits of AIDS activism, and their powerfully sexualized outlaw style—think Marlon Brando in *The Wild One* with Doc Martens, political stickers, and a couple of extra earrings—quickly became the new

---

*By the early '90s, however, the best and hottest ACT UP parties were at the Warren Street loft shared by Gregg Bordowitz, Robert Garcia, Catherine Gund, Karen Ramspacher, Joycelyn Taylor, Deborah Thomas, and Storme Webber (among others), where there was room for dancing, access to the roof, and a real powerful, sexy dyke vibe. (According to Catherine, the Clit Club, started by Joycelyn and Julie Tolentino, came out of the loft. The club even used their home phone number so when you called the apartment, you'd hear the message, "Hello, you've reached the Clit Club.") Email between Catherine Gund and the author, April 17, 2022.

gay uniform; the perfect response to years of illness and an increasingly pathologized sexuality.

On a dare, the Boys—including David Serko, who, though not an East Village denizen, easily made the cut—left the party for a spontaneous swim in the park fountain. When they returned to the party fifteen minutes later in nothing but wet T-shirts and tighty-whities, conversations stopped and temperatures rose. Henceforth, in lust and admiration, we simply called them "the Swim Team."

While the Swim Team was definitely out of my league, it was standard ACT UP practice to always greet one another with a kiss, regardless of where you were or who else was around. Although I always assumed this act had some political significance, whether as a publicly defiant acknowledgment of our being gay or some implicit safe sex message, it was never really discussed or explained. Not that I was complaining. I always enjoyed that whenever I ran into one or more of the "team"—there never seemed to be less than three of them at a time—they would all come over and kiss me hello, much to the slack-jawed shock of my nonactivist friends.

I also discovered, contrary to my envious assumptions about really good-looking men, they were all lovely guys; kinda goofy really, in an endearing puppy-dog way. And, though I wouldn't discover this till later, many of them, like David, were also Positive and fighting for their own lives, as well as those of their friends and lovers. And goddess love them, they showed up, got arrested, volunteered for poster parties and wheatpasting duties, and were happy to use their good looks to help recruit new members.

But our best recruitment tool was always ACT UP in action, and no day gave us a better opportunity to make our case than Pride.

If the goal of the previous year's Concentration Camp float was to shock people into action, this year we wanted to politicize them and turn the Pride Parade back into a march. Using the New Museum "Let the Record Show . . ." display as our theme, we created a rogue's gallery of enemies, placed their photos and quotes on sandwich boards, mounted them on a series of litters, and carried them on our shoulders like something out of *Land of the Pharaohs* (though sadly minus the men in short skirts). We accused the government, through its willful indifference and inaction, of committing genocide against "expendable minorities," and declared our commitment to fighting back and bearing witness through direct action "because we believe it is no longer enough to quietly take care of ourselves."[22]

Unlike the year before, ACT UP was given pride of place at the front of the AIDS section, and we received a hero's welcome all the way down Fifth Avenue. By the time we reached Christopher Street, our contingent had grown to over several blocks long. More importantly, many who came off the sidewalks that afternoon would stay with us, participating in demonstrations, coming to Monday night meetings, joining committees and affinity groups, and contributing their time, talent, and enthusiasm.

We'd certainly need them, for the summer of 1988 would find ACT UP fighting on several fronts at the same time, and in multiple locations across the country.

Chapter 7

Summer Awakening

July 17–21, 1988: The Democratic Convention

IN MID-JULY, ACT UP sent forty-two activists down to Atlanta to draw attention to AIDS issues at the Democratic National Convention. Despite the deaths of almost 32,000 Americans, AIDS was still not a priority for the candidates in the 1988 presidential election. It was considered, at most, a minor parochial matter, a "gay issue" of little concern to the "general public." Republicans, when they referred to AIDS at all, used the disease as a convenient marker for all that was morally wrong with liberal America, while Democrats mouthed pro forma endorsements of whatever it was the AIDS commission recommended, before quickly changing the subject.

ACT UP had been following the campaign since November, when Clarke Taylor, a longtime journalist, organized our Election Subcommittee to monitor the candidates' positions and help them to develop AIDS position papers and talking points. Michael Petrelis, as was his wont, launched his own more confrontational campaign in February, bringing the Bailey House AIDS Quilt to New Hampshire for the first presidential primary,* and later to South

---

*Bailey House was founded in 1983 in a former gay luxury hotel at the foot of Christopher Street. It was the first and, at the time, only dedicated residence for homeless and indigent PWAs in the city. Michael, who lived in Bailey House, was joined in New Hampshire by fellow resident James Reed. It was James who'd first had the idea of making a Bailey House Quilt as a memorial for those residents who'd passed away and an advocacy tool for those still living with HIV/AIDS. James would die of a massive heart attack one week after returning from New

Carolina. The Actions Committee did its part, zapping campaign rallies and debates around the city and state during the New York primaries.

We'd had the most success with the Reverend Jesse Jackson, who had not only endorsed Spring AIDS Action '88 but also held a campaign rally at the Lesbian and Gay Community Services Center, a first for any major presidential candidate. While Jackson's open embrace of lesbian and gay rights along with his progressive agenda on AIDS and other issues made him the preferred candidate for a large portion of ACT UP and the gay community, it wasn't enough to tear the nomination away from Massachusetts governor Michael Dukakis. So as the Atlanta convention began, the conversation among gay politicos shifted from who was the better candidate to calibrating how far they could push Dukakis on our issues without damaging his chances for election—also known as "Do we go to the back of the bus, or throw ourselves under it?"

Just blocks away from the convention, ACT UP was involved in a different kind of power struggle.

To protest Georgia's Supreme Court–approved antisodomy law, ACT UP had organized a kiss-in on the sidewalk in front of the Atlanta convention headquarters at the Omni Hotel. The activists were careful to maintain a legal picket, keeping the two lines of kissing protesters moving steadily in opposite directions, pausing just long enough to exchange a quick smooch. Unfortunately, that wasn't good enough for the Atlanta police, who descended on the group in full riot gear and pushed them down the block into the "designated free speech area."[1] (*Insert your favorite George Orwell reference here.*)

Being New Yorkers, they were not so easily thwarted. As soon as the police withdrew, the activists slipped out of their pen and resumed their kiss-in in front of the Omni, where they were serenaded by a group of jeering punks yelling, *"FAGgots SUCK and DYKES LICK!"* A delighted ACT UP joyfully appropriated their chant and soon began shouting it between kisses, much to the confusion of the scowling skinheads.[2]

The police, however, were less than amused. Lining up in rows two and three deep, they raised their riot shields and charged the demonstrators, crushing them against the barricades. Activists, reporters, and bystanders were all indiscriminately swept up in the fray, and several people were injured as they attempted to flee the police attack.[3]

Hampshire. His panel has since been added to the Quilt. (Michael Petrelis, "James Reed," *New York Native*, March 14, 1988.) James Reed (1940–1988). *May his memory be for a blessing.*

At their post-action press conference, the activists pointed to the violent police response as emblematic of the very homophobia their protest was trying to address. They had obeyed the law and had been attacked only for kissing while gay. They demanded an apology from the police and from Mayor Andrew Young. To underline their point, the activists snuck into Atlanta City Hall the following day and took over an empty city council room, refusing to leave until the mayor agreed to their demands.

That evening, Mayor Young admitted his police force had overreacted to the kiss-in out of homophobia, but also blamed ACT UP for instigating the confrontation by "making an issue of lifestyles."[4] Unrepentant, the activists returned to the Omni the following afternoon to resume their kiss-in, only to be blocked once again by police.

Behind the scenes, local gay leaders grumbled that ACT UP was being unreasonable; they should have accepted the mayor's apology and moved on. These leaders preferred to follow the example of local civil rights groups, choosing negotiation over confrontation when dealing with City Hall. This in-your-face belligerence was simply "not the way they did things in Atlanta."[5]

Yet there was Mayor Young the next day, apologizing to ACT UP for his earlier apology; this time, sending his staff to accompany the activists back to the Omni to ensure they could complete their kiss-in. Instead of damaging their relationship with the mayor, local activists soon discovered ACT UP had opened a new avenue for dialogue between the community and city leaders. "Some conversations that needed to happen happened," explained one city official, "and this helped enlighten some of the officials concerned."[6] They were not the only ones so enlightened.

On August 1, ACT UP/Atlanta held its first meeting.

New York City was the epicenter of the US AIDS epidemic. With just 3 percent of the nation's population, New York was home to 24 percent of the country's PWAs.[7] After downplaying the crisis in its early years, Mayor Ed Koch was now caught flat-footed as he tried to cope with the city's exploding AIDS caseload. Local health services were already strained to the breaking point—almost everyone had a horror story about a loved one being rushed to the hospital only to spend days in a crowded hallway or emergency room waiting for an available bed—and the city had no plan for handling the surge in new cases. Although community organizations were doing their

best to make up for the city's shortcomings, funding levels remained appall-
ingly low, even as caseloads skyrocketed.

When the Koch administration finally released its long-awaited three-year
"Strategic Plan for AIDS," in May 1988, it was immediately savaged for
underestimating both the number of residents with HIV and the costs
associated with caring for them. Even the city's health commissioner, Stephen
Joseph, admitted the plan provided for only "minimum services" based on
"conservative" estimates of an AIDS caseload of only 200,000 people.[8]

New York's current projections were based on the understanding that
only 50 percent of people infected with HIV would progress to AIDS. It
was assumed, as with other diseases, that those who were infected but didn't
develop AIDS within a few years would never do so. But in June, a study
published in *Science* magazine found the chances of developing AIDS only
increased over time, and 99 percent of people infected with HIV would
eventually develop the full-blown disease.[9] This devastating news meant
the city's original estimate would have to be doubled, as would funding and
services.

So, imagine our surprise when on July 19, at a hastily organized press
conference, Commissioner Joseph unveiled the city's newest weapon in the
fight against AIDS.

Statistics.

Joseph had slashed the estimated number of city residents infected with
HIV in half and—*Poof!*—overnight, New York's HIV caseload dropped
back down from 400,000 to 200,000, leaving the city's Strategic Plan magically unaffected.

Joseph achieved his new totals by adjusting the caseload in only a single
population: gay and bisexual men. He based his new estimates on statistics
gleaned from a recent San Francisco study of HIV infection rates. Since
New York had recorded roughly twice the number of AIDS cases among
gay/bisexual men as San Francisco, the commissioner reasoned the city must
also have twice the number of gay/bisexual men infected with HIV. Therefore, if San Francisco estimated it had 27,000 gay/bi men infected with HIV,
New York must have roughly 50,000.[10] The resulting calculations cut the
city's estimated population of HIV-infected gay/bi men by 80 percent, from
250,000 to roughly 50,000, slicing citywide HIV projections in half and
rescuing the mayor's wobbly Strategic Plan.

Although these numbers were jaw-dropping on their face, they became
even more extraordinary the harder you looked at them. San Francisco had
estimated approximately half of its gay/bi male population was HIV-positive.
Applying those same extrapolations to New York, 50,000 infected gay/bi

men would mean the city had a gay/bi male population of only about 100,000 out of a population of over 7.2 million. That's less than 1 percent.[11]

Joseph's projections also depended on the false assumption that the demographics of the gay/bi populations of the two cities were identical. But while San Francisco's gay/bi population was almost exclusively White, middle-class, gay-identified, and geographically centralized, New York's was far more diverse racially, economically, and geographically. Many, including many men of color who made up close to a third of the city's population of men who had sex with men, did not identify as gay or have any connection with the organized gay community.[12]

Nor did this take into account the severe undercounting of IV drug–related AIDS deaths; the rampant misdiagnosis in the city's emergency rooms, where the majority of poor New Yorkers received their health care; and the intentional concealment of AIDS diagnoses due to the risk of social stigma and the potential loss of housing, employment, or insurance.[13] One more problem: the exceedingly narrow CDC AIDS definition included few of the opportunistic infections found in women, drug users, and people of color. Even city officials estimated that up to 50 percent of the city's HIV-related deaths went undiagnosed.[14]

Further stoking suspicion was the timing of the announcement at a surprise press conference while the mayor was conveniently out of the country, and on the same day State Comptroller Edward V. Regan was scheduled to release a scathing report criticizing the city's response to the epidemic. As GMHC's Richard Dunne quipped, "It reminds me of persons who do their income tax by figuring out how much they can afford to pay, then backing into deductions to make it come out right."[15]

Three days after Joseph's announcement, as the Actions Committee feverishly hammered out the details for an emergency demonstration to protest the new numbers, Charlie Franchino burst into our Friday night meeting with news that FDA commissioner Frank Young would be speaking at the Tenth National Lesbian and Gay Health Conference and AIDS Forum in Boston the following afternoon. Members who were already at the conference were planning a protest and had called down asking for reinforcements.

The FDA had been a major source of anger and frustration for PWAs and a target of ACT UP since our first demonstration. After seven years of the AIDS epidemic, the FDA had approved only one drug to treat HIV—the overpriced, highly toxic AZT—while over forty promising drugs languished in the testing and approval pipeline, stymied by the financial and ego-driven priorities of the NIH and the fossilized bureaucracy of the FDA.

Our Issues Committee had been studying the drug approval process for many months under the tutelage of Dr. Iris Long, a straight married fifty-three-year-old retired chemist from Queens with no gay friends and no previous history of political or community involvement. Iris was, however, fascinated by the science of the disease, and knew from her own experiences as a caretaker for her sick mother that people with AIDS needed informed and medically astute advocates.[16]

Although she'd previously worked at Sloan Kettering and other medical institutions doing research on a class of drugs in the same family as AZT, she preferred to volunteer with more community-oriented organizations, believing she would have a more direct impact. Not coincidentally, these organizations were also far more likely to accept the input of a soft-spoken, middle-aged woman.

Their loss was our gain. Iris found a perfect home in ACT UP's Issues Committee, where she quickly gathered a small group of acolytes, most without any previous scientific background, and began to teach them the basics of drug research and how to navigate the bureaucracies that tested drugs and approved them.

One of Iris's earliest and most prized students was Jim Eigo. With his ivory skin, dark serious features, and long black ponytail, Jim looked every inch the East Village poet and experimental playwright. Jim had wandered into ACT UP by mistake, sitting down in the wrong meeting room, but then stayed, finding it "the most vital group of people I'd ever sat among in my life."[17] Jim proved the perfect complement to Iris; where she was knowledgeable but unfocused and often inarticulate, Jim was a quick study, well organized, and a natural writer. Within weeks, he became Iris's "Guy Friday,"[18] drafting scientific papers and structuring her insights into coherent documents and presentations.

Along with Jim, Garry Kleinman, a Jersey-born hairdresser and DJ with a background in fine arts, and David Z. Kirschenbaum, an architect who'd originally studied biomedical engineering, were the core members of Iris's first study group. David Z—as he was known, to differentiate him from David E. Kirschenbaum, ACT UP's treasurer—had been working with Margaret McCarthy, a young Columbia law student, to submit Freedom of Information Act requests to find out details about the drugs being tested by the federal government through their AIDS Treatment Evaluation Units

(ATEUs). As this information was considered proprietary, there was no central registry of AIDS drug trials, leaving doctors and patients clueless about treatment opportunities and the trials woefully underenrolled.

Recognizing the value of their work, I'd tried to jump-start a joint Actions-Issues "ATEU Subcommittee" to help them develop actions to pressure the local units to release their data, improve trial recruitment efforts, and expand the range and number of drugs being tested. We soon realized, however, that zaps and street actions were not the best approach in this instance, and they turned to less confrontational strategies, combining Iris's expanding treatment work with David Z's copious data gathering to form the Treatment and Data Collection Subcommittee.

As one of their first projects, they developed the AIDS Treatment Registry (ATR), a "computerized database containing the most complete, accurate and up-to-date information available on both government and non-government sponsored trials of AIDS-related drug treatments and therapies underway in New York."[19] By the end of April, when ATR began to seek separate funding, they became ACT UP's first independent spin-off organization. Meanwhile, the subcommittee continued to add new members and would soon morph into one of ACT UP's most influential committees, Treatment and Data, or T+D.

July 23, 1988: The Boston Health Conference

With preparations for our New York action well underway, I grabbed an early morning ride with Charlie Franchino and Debra Levine and arrived in Boston to find the conference center abuzz with rumors about ACT UP's afternoon action. The conference organizers, though supportive of our demo, were nervous about the potential backlash from sponsors. We had similar worries about the conference attendees. This was not a typical ACT UP crowd; these were gay health professionals and PWAs and we had no idea how our gay sisters and brothers might react or how much they might know about the workings of the FDA.

Our protest played out in highly theatrical fashion—sort of like *Frank Young in Wonderland,* with the FDA commissioner as the March Hare standing trial on stage in his navy whites, surrounded by sign-wielding protesters, including a four-foot-long cartoon "Hand of God" pointing down at him with the word "SHAME" etched across its clenched fingers, while a dozen PWAs staged a die-in at his feet. But despite the surrounding drama, the stoic Dr. Young would soon win over the crowd with his announcement that the FDA would no longer interfere with the import of unapproved foreign drugs. "You can get it by mail," affirmed Young. "If it's for personal use under physician's care, it's not in excessive amounts and it's not being used for commercial purposes, then the product will not be intercepted."[20]

In response to the slow and tortured pace of FDA drug approval, PWAs in major cities had created a network of underground "buyers clubs," whereby doctors and patients could import promising yet unapproved over-the-counter drugs already available in other countries. Some clubs also imported pirated and generic versions of approved drugs like AZT, which they sold for $2,000 per year, only a quarter of the price charged by Burroughs Well-come, and pentamidine, which was smuggled in at a cost of roughly $30 per treatment, as opposed to the $90–$100 charged in the US.*

The FDA, which had the power to prohibit the manufacture, sale, and distribution of unapproved substances, largely winked at this practice, allowing the clubs to thrive. But the FDA's response was inconsistent, and a sudden raid or seizure of drugs at an airport or warehouse could affect availability across the entire network. The latest such incident involved dextran sulfate, a Japanese anticholesterol drug with rumored anti-HIV capabilities. The drug was safe—it had been an over-the-counter medication in Japan for more than twenty years—and relatively cheap, so when the NIH designated the drug as a "high priority" for testing in November 1987, demand skyrocketed as individuals and buyers clubs flocked to Japan to purchase the drug from local pharmacies.[21]

But in mid-April, the dextran pipeline suddenly shut down when Kowa Pharmaceuticals, which manufactured the preferred version of the drug, refused to sell it to American visitors. Whether due to a government directive or a case of corporate skittishness, PWAs around the country panicked, fearing the drug would soon be unavailable.

One of them was Peter Staley.

Boy-next-door cute, with big brown eyes and tightly curled brown hair, Peter couldn't tolerate AZT and had been taking dextran to try to keep his

---

*On March 6, 1989, New York's PWA Health Group would announce they'd be the first buyers club to import prescription drugs available in other countries but not yet available in the US. Gina Kolata, "Group Will Import Unapproved Drugs for Treating AIDS," *New York Times*, March 6, 1989.

HIV under control. Peter would soon become ACT UP's first media star, with the requisite looks, smarts, and charisma for the job. He also had the perfect story line.

A former Wall Street bond trader, Peter had been professionally closeted when he was diagnosed in 1985 with ARC, an early stage of HIV infection. His radicalizing moment came when he encountered ACT UP's first Wall Street demonstration on his way to work. Everyone on the intensely homophobic trading floor had an opinion about the AIDS protest, and when Peter's mentor loudly proclaimed, "They all deserve to die 'cause they took it up the butt,"[22] Peter could only nod and smile.

But when he got home, he saw the demonstration on the evening news and decided to go to his first ACT UP meeting the following week. Peter immediately lent his financial expertise to our Fundraising Committee and, over the years, would help bring hundreds of thousands of dollars into the organization. He would also get involved with the Issues Committee and later with T+D, and become a major player in ACT UP's "food chain" of sexual relationships.

Peter's most unlikely contribution, however, might be his introduction of hardware to the group's zap arsenal. Peter's actions always seemed to involve chains, handcuffs, smoke bombs, or power drills. The Kowa zap, his first, was no exception.

On June 28, 1988, Peter and ten other activists* stormed Kowa's New York office, chained themselves to the reception desk, and demanded to speak to the head of the company. That the New York branch of Kowa was a satellite office selling belts and handbags and not directly involved with the drug company was of no matter. Minutes later, a Japanese television crew, alerted in advance by our Media Committee, arrived to film the takeover for broadcast in Japan.

Within two weeks, the company reopened negotiations with US buyers clubs, and by the end of July, the deeply embarrassed Kowa announced a new policy allowing Americans to buy the drug from three designated pharmacies in Japan.[23] This conveniently coincided with Frank Young's announcement of the new FDA policy at the Boston health conference.

But ACT UP regarded the new policy as little more than a bone thrown by the commissioner to appease a potentially hostile crowd. The FDA had made promises to us before, but nothing had changed. We kept dying and it was still just business as usual.

---

*Neil Broome, Stephen Gendin, Mark Harrington, David Z. Kirschenbaum, Garry Kleinman, Bill Lent, Douglas Montgomery, Tim Powers, Marty Robinson, and Steve Zabel.

Back in New York the following Monday night, our meeting was wall-to-wall people. The mayor and his commissioner had crossed a serious line, and the community needed to send them a powerful message.

ACT UP wasn't afraid of the mayor or his prickly temperament. We didn't have to worry about losing our funding or damaging our relationship with City Hall. We'd already locked horns with the Koch administration, demonstrating on the steps of City Hall this past December to pressure the mayor to approve the "B-List" budget, which included funding for vitally important AIDS services; and just last month we'd surrounded City Hall with bedsheets to remind him of his pledge to provide a bed for every person with AIDS. We'd even disrupted his Gay Pride Proclamation ceremony, earning a public scolding from several so-called gay leaders, who accused ACT UP of being nothing more than "a band of screaming activists who seem bent on working against the causes of their own community."[24] Yet, little over a month later, when it was time for our community to rise up against the mayor, these same "leaders" were nowhere in sight.

But this wasn't just about the gay community. We were only the latest group to be made invisible by the policies of the Koch administration. While this sudden feeling of invisibility and powerlessness was relatively new to us, it was an everyday experience for New York's communities of color. We needed to make it clear we weren't just fighting to make sure gay lives were counted. It was about making sure all lives were equally valued and recognized.[25]

July 28, 1988: The Numbers Demonstration

A boisterous and angry crowd of three hundred demonstrators swarmed the New York City Department of Health, wearing special T-shirts designed by Richard Deagle proclaiming, "I DO ~~NOT~~ EXIST," and carrying signs like **"Doctor People, Not Numbers," "Don't Count Me Out,"** and **"I'll Count on Election Day."**[26] But our protest had begun hours earlier, when an affinity group made up of Metropolitan Health Association (MHA) and Wave 3 members snuck into the DOH offices demanding a meeting with Commissioner Joseph. The police, who dragged the twelve activists out of the building in handcuffs in the middle of our demonstration, processed them so quickly they were able to rejoin the protest as we surrounded City

Hall to the approving cheers of the homeless men and women encamped in their "Kochville" shantytown in City Hall Park.°

Moments before we were about to call the demonstration, who should step out of a black limousine, freshly returned from his overseas jaunt, but Mayor Koch. Everyone bolted the picket line and ran toward the car, pointing and shouting *"Shame! Shame! Shame!"* The mayor took one look at the approaching mob, ducked back into his limo, and sped away.

But as satisfying as the day had been, we knew it was only a first step. We had to come up with a long-term strategy for getting the city to withdraw the new numbers and develop a realistic plan to provide the necessary level of funding and services. Commissioner Joseph became our primary target, and we vowed we'd do everything in our power to force him to resign; even, we joked, if it meant climbing on a broomstick and skywriting *"Surrender Dorothy"* across the downtown sky.

Eric

Midway through the summer, after several months of drifting apart, Eric called to tell me he'd taken the HIV test. Even though I'd always assumed he was Positive, it was still a shock to hear him say the words out loud. I immediately saw his name spelled out in a golden script on a burgundy-colored quilt panel. The image was clear and startlingly vivid.

After I hung up the phone, I looked hard at the framed photo I had from the March on Washington. There were five of us in the photo, but Eric and I were the giddy center—happy, joyful, full of life. That's what I was fighting for, not some abstract political goal or ideology. I was fighting for us; for our lives and our future together. And even though I couldn't save "us," I hoped I could still save him.

August 13–18, 1988: The Republican Convention

Unlike at the Democratic convention in Atlanta, there were no "out" lesbian or gay delegates at the Republican convention in New Orleans. Even at the

---

°On June 1, 1988, a group of homeless people set up a camp in City Hall Park to protest the mayor's homeless policies. The camp remained in place for five months, growing to over a hundred people, until the city finally shut it down on November 1. Michel Marriott, "Belongings of Homeless Are Removed from Park," *New York Times,* November 2, 1989, http://www.nytimes.com/1988/11/02/nyregion/belongings-of-homeless-are-removed-from-park.html?mcubz=1.

reception held by a gay Republican group, none of the attendees dared identify themselves by name. The words "gay," "lesbian," "homosexual," "sexual orientation," and "sexual preference" were not included in the Republican platform,[27] nor was AIDS mentioned in any of the major televised speeches—though it was hard to mistake the meaning behind Pat Robertson's comment that "in the city of the Democratic Party, disease carriers are protected and the healthy are placed at great risk."[28] And while the Republican platform did offer a generic statement on AIDS, it included neither the antidiscrimination nor patient confidentiality policies endorsed by its candidate.

Once again, ACT UP ran afoul of the local gay politicos when, at the request of local activists, they heckled Democratic mayor Sidney J. Barthelmey at the week's first big gay-hosted event over his insufficient funding of AIDS services. While privately acknowledging the mayor's response to the community had often been "style over substance," they insisted that yelling at the mayor was—*everyone:*—not the New Orleans way.[29]

There were far fewer complaints when ACT UP ambushed Archbishop Philip Hannan with a kiss-in the following day, nor did it provoke a major police response. Unlike in Atlanta, the New Orleans police reaction to ACT UP would remain mostly low key, with few police in riot gear and little harassment of the protesters.

No, the biggest threat of violence would come from the delegates.

All week long, activists were pushed, punched, kicked, and spat at. When a group of protesters managed to sneak into the convention hall for an event welcoming President and Mrs. Reagan, they were set upon by a group of nasty young men in suits shouting, "Let's get the faggots" and "Queers go home." The violence quickly escalated, as delegates and campaign workers physically attacked the demonstrators until the police finally swooped in and rescued them.[30] "If the police hadn't been in there," admitted one Secret Service agent, "[the activists] would have been killed."[31]

However, according to "Barry Adams," the pseudonymous leader of the gay Republican group, it was the protesters who were at fault. "The president has a right to make his views known. There are limits to what is appropriate in lesbian and gay protests. Nancy Reagan's being honored at a luncheon. Are they going to picket that?"[32]

A similar confrontation took place on Tuesday, when ACT UP members infiltrated the crowd waiting to welcome George Bush as he steamed his way into New Orleans aboard a Mississippi riverboat. This time, the thugs from the Young Americans for Freedom spotted the activists even before they pulled out their signs. "They have no right to be here," proclaimed one

YAF member. "Those faggots are infecting our blood supply," charged another, "so we get sick and they get more money for their AIDS."[33]

But when the protesters began chanting, "*40,000 DEAD from AIDS! WHERE WAS GEORGE?*" it wasn't just the young Bush supporters who got their licks in. Older delegates pummeled activists, swatting them with umbrellas, calling them "AIDS scum," and shouting, "You deserve to die."[34] As one shaken ACT UP member confessed, "I've been called a 'fag' down here more times in three days than in the whole rest of my life. This town is full of Republicans and it's really not safe to walk here this week. . . . We've been on the news too many times. They know who we are."[35]

It was a feeling shared by ACT UP's Freedom Riders, a small group of activists, led by Frank Smithson and Neil Broome, who used the conventions as a springboard to tour the South "to increase awareness about the impact of AIDS in all communities, the connection between AIDS and homophobia, and the need for activism from the lesbian and gay community."[36]

They were an odd team, with Frank as easygoing as Neil was intense— intense verging on hysterical, earning him the affectionate nickname "Squeaky," after bizarre would-be presidential assassin Lynette "Squeaky" Fromme. A born outsider, Neil had spent his entire life being picked on—for being Jewish, being gay, being smart, being effeminate—but now that he was HIV-positive, he no longer gave a fuck.[37]

They were joined by gay reporter Rex Wockner and twenty-three-year-old Heidi Dorow. Heidi was a student on break from Hampshire College, having won a fellowship to "intern" with ACT UP for the summer.[38] Originally from a small town in Illinois, Heidi reminded me of Scout in *To Kill a Mocking-bird*—brave, confident, even-keeled, and naturally inquisitive.

Together, the Riders traveled in an old pickup truck through Alabama, Arkansas, Mississippi, Kentucky, and Tennessee, displaying the Bailey House AIDS Quilt, leading memorial services and teach-ins, visiting prison AIDS wards, speaking to local reporters and activists, and leaving newly formed ACT UPs in their wake.[39]

Their stories, particularly about the conditions they found in prison, were shocking, even when heard secondhand at Monday night meetings. PWAs were quarantined, sometimes on Death Row, with no access to AIDS information, services, or treatments, "eating off paper plates and with maggots all over [them] and [their] food."[40] They were forced to wear yellow gloves and masks, with plastic covering their legs; were prohibited from attending church services or participating in recreation activities; and were ineligible for early release programs or parole.

Equally shocking was the story the Riders told about their final stop in Arcadia, Florida, the former home of the Ray brothers: three elementary school students who had contracted HIV through contaminated blood products, and whose house was "mysteriously" destroyed by fire after they tried to return to class at their local school.

The night before the Riders' arrival, they received an anonymous tip, warning they'd be shot and killed if they dared show up in Arcadia. But when they contacted the FBI, the agency denied their request for assistance and told the Riders they were on their own.[41]

The following day, as if on cue, pickup trucks stacked with rifles and good ole boys shouting, "We're gonna kill you queers," circled the town square as the activists set up their picket on the DeSoto Courthouse steps.

The activists, their number now swollen to a mighty fifteen, including Gerri Wells from New York and members of two local Florida groups, We the People of Orlando and Swamp Rats of Dade County,[42] were safe under the watchful eye of the press, which had been alerted to the demonstration by Jay Blotcher and our Media Committee. But when the TV crews started to pack up their equipment, the activists took the hint and did the same, asking the police to escort them out of town.[43]

As their caravan approached the county line and the activists finally began to relax, until they noticed a dark black sedan pulling up alongside them. And when the stranger's tinted window slowly rolled down, the activists hit the floor and braced for the worst.

It was the FBI. They just wanted to let the activists know they'd arrested a group of men who'd been plotting to kill them.[44]

Something happened to those activists who'd ventured South that summer. They'd seen antigay hatred up close and experienced the violence on their own bodies. This wasn't Jesse Helms spewing venom on the floor of the Senate, but everyday Americans who thought nothing of pounding them with their fists, spitting at them, and wishing them dead.

It certainly made it harder to "act with love," as our CD training had taught us, or to believe our enemies were "capable of change." Over the coming months, our language and tone would grow more adversarial toward allies and enemies alike. It's one of the reasons I think our Actions Committee proposal to add "nonviolent" to the official ACT UP description was defeated. Not that anyone in the group was advocating violence—not once in our entire history would ACT UP, as a group, engage in violence—but there was growing sentiment that we should leave the option open or, at minimum, not let our enemies know it wasn't. Better to have them scared of us, or so the thinking went. While part of this was bad-boy macho posturing, I think it was also an honest reaction to the shocking realization about just how much we were hated out there.

And here.

On the evening of August 22, two gay men were attacked on the Upper West Side by a group of teenagers armed with bats and knives and shouting antigay epithets. One of the victims was stabbed twice in the back and suffered a collapsed lung. The attackers fled, and no weapons or suspects were ever found. On that same night, five other teenagers bludgeoned an unidentified gay man to death in Central Park. Sadly, these were not isolated incidents. According to the New York City Gay and Lesbian Anti-Violence Project, there had already been 309 bias-related assaults in the city during the first six months of 1988, a 36 percent increase from the previous year.[45]

On August 30, GLAAD held a nighttime rally and vigil on 103rd Street, the site of one of the attacks. Despite the presence of over one thousand demonstrators, the rally was a pretty torpid affair, with low-level politicians and gay politicos dispensing the usual trite sympathetic cant, until Maria Maggenti ignited the crowd by connecting the dots between the silence of public officials (like the absent mayor and police commissioner), the sanctimonious words of religious figures (see Cardinal O'Connor), and the "queer bashers who scream that 'AIDS is the cure.'"[46] With the activist fires finally lit, ACT UP led the crowd into the streets, shutting down Broadway for several hours, culminating in 105 arrests.

It was amazing to see how quickly ACT UP members sprang into action—stepping up to marshal, locking arms and marching into traffic to keep the cars from running over demonstrators, or scurrying about the seated protesters, explaining the risks of arrest and jotting down contact information. Since not everyone getting arrested was an ACT UP member or had gone through CD training, we did our best to explain arrest options and procedures and tried to team the first-timers up with more experienced activists who could look after them through the arrest process.

Our response was immediate and instinctual. This is how we took care of one another and of our community. No matter what others might think, ACT UP in action was love in the streets.

By the end of the summer, I'd been Actions chair for seven months. During that time, I'd organized more than a dozen demonstrations and participated in at least a dozen more. ACT UP had become the most important thing in my life and AIDS the prism through which I saw the world, the focus and fulcrum of all thought and conversation.

Mornings, over bagels and coffee, I'd scan the Obituaries—a.k.a. the "gay sports pages"—searching for familiar names and telltale euphemisms and elisions, usually a young man dying from "pneumonia" or a "long-term illness," survived only by parents, siblings, and loving nieces and nephews. At work, while temping at a conservative white-shoe law firm, I'd spend hours of company time planning actions, annexing fax machines for fax zaps, and commandeering copy machines to print flyers and fact sheets as part of ACT UP's "Xerox Anonymous" photocopying corps. After work, it was off to demos, committee meetings, poster parties, teach-ins, and CD trainings. And late at night, AIDS would invade my dreams, turning them into war-filled nightmares of dodging bullets, hiding in foxholes, and climbing over mountains of dead bodies.

So, at the end of August, I gladly turned over the reins of the Actions Committee to Brian Zabcik, who, along with Andrew Miller, as Coordinating rep, and Tim Powers, as head of Logistics, were part of the next wave of ACT UP leaders.

Not that the old wave ever left.

I'd still go to all the same meetings and demonstrations. Still scour the newspapers and have the same nightmares. I just wouldn't be in charge.

August 24, 1988: Lesbians for Bush

After our harsh reception in New Orleans, ACT UP was primed to return the favor when the Bushies and their cohorts visited New York. To ensure an appropriate welcome, one of our more resourceful members had secured an invitation to the kick-off reception for Bush's fall campaign at the posh headquarters of the Women's National Republican Club. Being a gentleman, he extended the invitation to the rest of ACT UP.

About two dozen of us took advantage of his offer, arriving at the well-appointed brownstone dressed in our best Republican drag. SPREE,° having shaved their mustache, showed up in a lovely black cocktail frock with elegant long gloves and sensible Barbara Bush pearls. As Ortez Alderson chivalrously took their arm,[47] the rest of us sorted ourselves into straight mixed-gender couples, clenched our jaws and sphincters, flashed our forged invitations, and drifted up the elegant marble staircase to the second-floor ballroom.

Nibbling on hors d'oeuvres and sipping glasses of wine, we exchanged pleasantries with other couples, stifling smiles when introduced to one another with assumed names, ersatz accents, and eccentric backstories. Poor Ortez was cornered by the only other Black man in the room, who carried on about "how much the Republicans are going to do for *us*."[48] Our charade continued unnoticed until a proud Park Avenue matron introduced "our wonderful New York Senator Alphonse D'Amato," at which point all hell broke loose.

Someone unrolled a big ACT UP banner and hoisted it high above his head, the women flashed their "Lesbians for Bush" buttons, and the rest of us pulled out our fact sheets and flung them into the air, chanting *"40,000 DEAD from AIDS! WHERE WAS GEORGE?"* It was like a scene out of a Marx Brothers movie, with papers flying, outraged Republicans trying to shout us down, and Margaret Dumont pounding away at the grand piano singing "God Bless America" as the cops lumbered up the stairs to drag us all outside.

One week later, this time costumed in khakis and Izod shirts, protesters disrupted vice presidential candidate Dan Quayle and his wife, Marilyn, at a Labor Day rally and photo op at the Statue of Liberty. Senator Quayle

---

°SPREE, interviewed by Sarah Schulman, October 16, 2004, 3. SPREE went by another name during their time in ACT UP. However, as they stated during their ACT UP Oral History interview, "Timmy became SPREE," so that's the name I will use here. Also, as I've been unable to contact them to confirm preferred pronouns, I will use the gender neutral "they/them/theirs."

(R-Indiana) was an acknowledged lightweight—young and attractive, but hardly ready to take over the reins of government—who'd been put on the ticket to boost Bush's still suspect conservative credentials. A disaster on AIDS issues, Quayle had backed all of the nefarious Helms amendments, opposed the use of federal funds to provide AZT for people who couldn't afford it, and voted five times to restrict funding for federal AIDS prevention efforts.[49]

Having secured a prime viewing spot at the front of the crowd, the protesters hoisted their "**AIDSGATE**" posters as soon as Quayle began speaking. The Republicans responded as expected, pushing and punching the activists, while Senator D'Amato displayed his usual innate sense of class and dignity, sticking out his tongue, flapping his limp wrists and arms, and shaking his ass at the protesters as the police escorted them away.[50]

There's an old saying, "Choose your enemies well, for you will surely become them." That was a fit description of the ongoing battle between ACT UP and Health Commissioner Stephen Joseph.

We were, in many ways, mirror images of one another—smart, dedicated, passionate, and proud of our reputations as tenacious street fighters. Sadly, we also shared a well-earned reputation for arrogance and self-righteousness which, when pushed, could cross the line into intolerance and aggressive bullying. Our interactions brought out the worst in both of us.

Our "Surrender Dorothy" campaign against the commissioner and his bogus statistics had begun calmly but aggressively with a series of weekly phone zaps of Joseph's office. Members of the newly christened Department of Health affinity group returned to the DOH offices the week after our initial protest, storming a conference room and demanding the commissioner meet with them to discuss the new estimates.* Joseph abruptly adjourned his meeting and pushed past the demonstrators, snarling, "I'm not going to

---

*Joseph would take the eleven arrested members to court in February 1989, the first time our members had been brought to trial for an ACT UP demonstration. (Andrew Miller, "ACT UP/NY Trespassing Trial Begins," *Gay Community News*, February 12–18, 1989.) The defendants, including Ortez Alderson, Jim Eigo, Jay Funk, Mark Harrington, Adam Hassuk, Bill Monaghan, Russell Pritchard, Steve Quester, Allan Robinson, David Robinson, and SPREE, were found guilty of one count each of criminal trespass in the third degree and were sentenced to community service.

talk to you when you tell me the terms of my talking to you."[51] He returned a few minutes later to wait for the police, staring silently as the demonstrators pelted him with questions. Or at least he did until Mark Harrington called him "a coward and a murderer," at which point Joseph lunged at the already handcuffed activist and had to be restrained by his staff.[52]

Two days later, ACT UP received an official invitation to meet with Joseph to discuss the new numbers, albeit on his terms. Even as we negotiated the conditions of the meeting, rumors surfaced of a secret new DOH memo outlining methods for further reducing the city's HIV infection estimates by another 95,000.[53] We responded by wheatpasting Gran Fury's crimson handprint posters accusing the mayor and his commissioner of having "blood on their hands" all over town.

The new numbers, when finally announced in mid-August, were both lower and higher than the July revisions. In order to mute some of the earlier criticism—and finesse a lack of solid epidemiology—Joseph's new estimates came within a range: between 149,000 and 226,000 infected, of which 46,000–70,000 were gay or bisexual men. These new figures did nothing to calm critics or assuage our anger.

Surrender Dorothy, which had by this time become a sort of hybrid subcommittee-cum-affinity group, redoubled their efforts and, with the help of a "donated" copy of Joseph's datebook, began zapping the commissioner wherever he went, ambushing him at meetings, luncheons, speeches, and town halls. True to form, the commissioner gave as good as he got, confronting the protesters, cursing, screaming, and threatening revenge. Remarkably, throughout these hostilities, ACT UP and Joseph continued to negotiate terms for our sit-down meeting. After receiving assurances it would "truly be a two-way discussion" and not just a lecture from the commissioner, we set the date for September 15.[54]

A few days before the meeting, reports of ACT UP–sponsored vandalism and phone threats at Joseph's Upper East Side home surfaced in the press. Although we denied the accusations—and truly, neither ACT UP nor any of our committees had ever officially endorsed such activities—no one doubted the actions had occurred or that members were responsible. And while the reports prompted a lengthy and heated Floor discussion about accountability, ACT UP was loathe to censure or place any official limit on affinity groups or personal behavior, except when it potentially endangered the safety of other members. Occasional excesses were considered the trade-off for empowerment, even when people were acting out more than ACTing UP, taking advantage of the anonymity of affinity groups and the protection afforded by our name to avoid accepting personal responsibility for their actions.

Predictably, Joseph was not so generous. Indeed, he began his meeting with our three representatives by drawing a clear line in the sand:

I think you [ACT UP] should do what you feel you need to do, and you will, and you can do all the legal things that you can do, around demonstrations and putting up your posters, and uh, etc. And we will see how that goes. You do what you need to do, and I'll need to do what I need to do. And that all is perfectly acceptable and, uh, perfectly appropriate. But I think I do want you to understand that should there be any further harassment of my wife, by telephone or otherwise, that you will need to be prepared to bear the consequences of your actions then. That has nothing to do with the other issues, which I consider perfectly appropriate. I just want that clear so that's understood, it's not a threat, it's just a statement.[55]

The meeting remained civil, if contentious, with Ortez Alderson, Jim Eigo, and Margaret McCarthy taking turns critiquing the city's epidemiology across the entire spectrum of categories of people with HIV, pointing out the anomalies between "real world evidence" and the city's "abstract projections," and highlighting the inconsistencies in the city's "patchwork epidemiology."[56] Joseph remained sullen and defensive throughout, repeatedly contradicting himself—one minute defending the city's AIDS plan for being based on caseload, not estimates; and the next claiming estimates, not caseload, provided the best baseline for policy—while rigidly maintaining his belief that no matter how flawed the new statistics might be, they were still better than the old ones.[57]

Although the meeting produced no agreements, at least it ended without incident. The day, alas, did not. That evening, as if to purposely destroy any lingering sense of goodwill and in direct defiance of Joseph's warning, Surrender Dorothy staged an action in front of the commissioner's home. Joseph was understandably furious and whatever détente might have been forged between the two parties was quickly forgotten.

The war was on.

Chapter 8

Seize Control of the FDA

FDA: US Food & Drug Administration, part of the PHS (Public Health Services). Glacial bureaucracy whose up-to-a-decade long delays in approving AIDS drugs for testing and treatment are responsible for the loss of thousands of lives.[1]

THE FOOD AND Drug Administration was not an obvious choice for a target—but it was a smart one. While other federal agencies were also derelict, only the FDA was *actively* preventing people with AIDS and HIV from getting access to the over forty promising drugs currently in the approval pipeline. The FDA's sins were sins of commission, not omission. More importantly, only the FDA had the power under current law to immediately make the changes necessary to meet our demands.

When Gregg Bordowitz first proposed the massive joint ACT UP/ACT NOW civil disobedience action, he framed it around the battle cry "Seize Control of the FDA." Despite the attractively menacing title, it was less about a physical occupation—though that, too, was part of the plan—than a call to imagine what a working FDA would look like and what it would take to make it a reality.[2]

But first, we had to understand how the FDA functioned and how the drug testing and approval process worked. We had to educate ourselves so we could develop and articulate a coherent critique of the agency and its policies and speak to the scientists and bureaucrats in their own language.

While our Treatment and Data Committee (T+D) may have gained a certain expertise, it was critical that their knowledge be shared across the entire organization.

Enter Mark Harrington. Pasty white and whippet thin with heavily gelled red hair, Mark reminded me of the cartoon character Tintin, if he'd been parachuted into the East Village and become a hyperarticulate, queer, coffeehouse hipster. Mark was dauntingly brilliant, with a cutting wit and a unique ability to grasp both the science of politics and the politics of science and distill both into a relatively comprehensible package.

The first indication of his abilities came in mid-July when, out of nowhere, he produced and distributed his "Glossary of AIDS Drug Trials, Testing & Treatment Issues,"[3] a sixty-page document defining every AIDS treatment term and piece of scientific jargon—each Latinate disease, polysyllabic drug, and maddening bureaucratic acronym—with a combination of laser-like clarity and withering sarcasm.

But to reimagine the FDA, we'd need more than just some deliciously snarky definitions.

Using the Glossary as a starting point, Mark and other members of T+D, including Jim Eigo, Margaret McCarthy, Stephen Spinella, and Rick Sugden, created the "FDA Action Handbook," a single-spaced thirty-two-page in-house guide and critique of the FDA and the entire drug approval process. It explained the history and mission of the agency and its place in the federal bureaucracy, identified the important players, and walked us through the sclerotic drug approval process, highlighting the "drug horror stories" that showed "how the FDA [had] betrayed its trust & intensified the AIDS crisis."[4]

To help get everyone up to speed, we organized a series of "teach-ins" led, not by the authors of the handbook or even by members of T+D, but by a group of "communicators"—familiar nonscientific Floor-types, including me and Robert Garcia, David Robinson, Maria Maggenti, Karl Soehnlein, and Robert Vasquez-Pacheco—who'd translate the scientific jargon into English, connecting the science with the politics, and hammering home our demands in what we hoped would be a more digestible form.

Science was not my forte. I'd opted out of Chemistry in high school and had fulfilled my college science requirement with a gut-course called The Physics of Photography. During T+D's floor presentations, all I'd hear after the first couple of sentences was the "waa-waa-waa" of Charlie Brown's teacher. It was much the same for most of ACT UP. But somehow, we'd all have to become expert in the ways of the FDA and its drug approval process—not just for ourselves, but to help explain the urgency of our demands to the general public.

And the press.

Despite some early success, ACT UP was still too small and insignificant to truly shake the FDA out of its complacency. We needed to find some way to amplify our voice and magnify our impact. To "Seize Control of the FDA," we'd first have to seize control of the media.

The FDA would be ACT UP's first truly media-driven demonstration. While we were good at communicating our message on-site, the FDA action would require more than just a press release and a collection of talking points. We needed to educate the media about the FDA and its role in the epidemic, distilling often complicated technical issues into easily understood demands. If we wanted them to help us move public opinion, we needed to frame our action not just as a one-day story about a bunch of activists getting arrested but as part of a larger ongoing life-and-death campaign.

Responsibility for this massive effort fell to ACT UP's new Media Committee chair, Michelangelo Signorile. Michelangelo (or Mike, as he was known in ACT UP), was a twenty-seven-year-old, Staten Island–born night-life journalist, a former column planter who'd helped PR firms get their clients mentioned in the gossip pages.[5] The Media Committee had, over the past year, become more professionalized, thanks in great part to Vito Russo, and particularly to former committee chairs Bob Rafsky and David Corkery. Bob was a vice president at Howard Rubenstein, the preeminent public relations firm in New York City, with a client list that included Donald Trump; while David had been a producer at *Good Morning America*. Both men were a little older by ACT UP standards—in their late thirties or early forties—and brought with them a great deal of experience and a wealth of media contacts. They trained the younger members and shifted the committee's focus from issuing press releases and monitoring media coverage to actively placing stories, developing relationships with reporters, and becoming an important information resource.

For his first major action, Michelangelo brought in his friend Chip Duckett, a former PR professional turned club party promoter. Previously, Chip had coordinated national publicity rollouts for cookbooks, and he adapted that same strategy to promote our FDA demonstration,[6] creating a national press tour, kind of like "'*Seize Control of the FDA.' Coming soon to a media outlet near you!*"

As a first step, the committee mailed out five hundred press kits introducing ACT UP to every newspaper and radio and TV station in each of the country's thirty-five major media markets. Each glossy black packet included a press release explaining the demonstration and its goals, a backgrounder on ACT UP and ACT NOW, and a collection of fact sheets and articles. To emphasize the human angle of the story and give it the requisite "Main Street" spin, each kit also included a tear-jerking cover letter talking about "families devastated by AIDS."[7]

But the true genius of the plan lay in how they pitched the demonstration as a local story. Thanks to our national ACT NOW network, we were able to provide each outlet with its own local hero—a plucky native son or daughter with AIDS, cut off from their lifesaving medications, bravely fighting for their lives against an unfeeling government bureaucracy. Chip organized a cadre of twenty "little publicists" to act as bookers, contacting local TV and radio shows across the country to secure interviews for local PWAs and activists, whom they then trained as spokespeople.[8]

From their "press office" in Michelangelo's East Village apartment, volunteers stuffed envelopes, organized media kits, and made hundreds of follow-up phone calls. Every week, they sent press releases repeating our mantra of "seizing control of the FDA" in a "massive civil disobedience" we promised would be "the largest demonstration since the storming of the Pentagon."[9] Was it hyperbole? Of course, but it didn't matter. We told them it was going to be big, and, by parroting our message, they would help make it big.

All this talk of "seizing control" was making the FDA nervous.

A few weeks after the Boston conference, and in response to a threatened lawsuit by Jay Lipner at Lambda Legal Defense and Education Fund, the FDA finally agreed to expand access to trimetrexate, a less toxic treatment for *Pneumocystis* pneumonia. The drug had been made available through the FDA's new treatment IND (Investigational New Drug) program, which was designed to make promising experimental drugs available to people with serious life-threatening illnesses immediately after small Phase I safety trials were completed.* Unfortunately, the FDA had so restricted eligibility—limiting it to only those patients who had experienced extreme life-threatening reactions to the two already approved treatments—that after six months only eighty-nine patients had received the drug.

Our campaign would receive an unexpected boost when Vice President Bush announced his own proposal for streamlining the agency's drug approval process. The "Bush Initiative" would allow drugs for desperately ill patients to go to market after completing an expanded Phase II trial, which would include more patients and, in addition to determining basic efficacy, collect data on potential side effects and dosage levels. Large-scale Phase III efficacy trials would be suspended completely, replaced by an extensive postmarketing surveillance study.

ACT UP viewed the proposal—and the sudden empathy of the vice president and his cheerleaders at the *Wall Street Journal* and Heritage Foundation—with great suspicion. We worried drug companies and their free-market cronies were using "compassion for PWAs" as an excuse to loosen regulations requiring drugs to show both safety *and* efficacy before reaching the market. Although we, too, wanted to speed potentially life-saving drugs to the people who needed them, we were aware of the shoddy history of postmarketing studies and worried PWAs and other seriously ill patients would never find out whether their expensive drugs finally worked.

The issue of access to AIDS treatments even made it into the presidential debates. When asked what the government should be doing to make AZT and other drugs available to people with AIDS, Governor Dukakis rightfully chastised the Reagan administration for its lack of leadership on "the single most important public health emergency we've had in our lifetime." But rather than outlining a more progressive AIDS policy and tying Bush to the administration's disastrous policies, Dukakis inexplicably added, "I think the Vice President and I are in general agreement on what we have to do."[10]

What could he have been thinking? Was he trying to position AIDS as an issue beyond politics, something about which all people of good conscience could agree? Maybe it was a defensive move, an attempt to inoculate himself from looking like a gay-loving liberal by implying that anything he would

---

*Clinical trials were traditionally broken into three phases: Phase I—small one-year studies to determine toxicity levels and safe-dose ranges; Phase II—larger trials to further assess safety and basic efficacy; and Phase III—large trials with several thousand subjects over several years focused on efficacy and dosage. Upon completion, the drug sponsor would present the data to the FDA, which would take two to three years to approve or reject the drug. The whole process would take up to eight years—fine for nasal spray, but not for people with life-threatening illnesses.

do about AIDS—and, by implication, The Gays—the vice president would do as well? Or was it just further proof neither candidate would show the necessary leadership to stop the dying?

The week before the action, ACT UP was summoned down to Rockville to meet with the FDA. Although a previous meeting in early September had proved a grave disappointment, this time, they'd meet with Commissioner Young and eleven staff members, including Ellen Cooper.*

Far more knowledgeable and outspoken than the commissioner, it was the unwavering Cooper, rather than the affable Young, who made the key decisions about the agency's AIDS treatment and drug approval policies. Though they were once again disappointed by the lack of progress, the activists knew they'd be back soon—this time, with several hundred of their closest friends.

October 8–11, 1988: FDA Weekend

The first day of our FDA weekend looked to be a washout. Scurrying over to the AIDS Quilt, which was also returning to Washington, I kept glancing up at the clouds, trying to wish away the raindrops. But just as I got to the Ellipse, as if on cue, shafts of bright sunlight pushed through the clouds like in some Cecil B. DeMille epic, and the vast expanse of the Quilt burst into dazzling color.

And oh my god, it was huge. The year before, there had been 1,920 panels; this year, there were 8,288. Still, it represented less than a quarter of all the AIDS/ARC-related deaths in the US.[11]

I scanned the crowd, looking for Robert Garcia and his red-and-black varsity jacket. Small, animated, with thick black hair and a wonderfully contagious smile, Robert was one of my favorite people in ACT UP. We'd quickly bonded as kindred spirits—there was little I enjoyed more than relaying chants with him across a picket line—and I knew if Robert raised his hand to talk at a meeting, I could take mine down.

The Names Project had agreed to let ACT UP leaflet for our upcoming demonstrations, but only if we promised to stay outside the Quilt, which

---

*Ortez Alderson, Jim Eigo, Mark Harrington, Margaret McCarthy, and Peter Staley attended the meeting. Mark Harrington, "AIDS Activists and People with AIDS: A Movement to Revolutionize Research and for Universal Access to Treatment," in *Tactical Biopolitics: Art, Activism, and Technoscience*, ed. Beatriz da Costa and Kavita Philip (Boston: MIT Press, 2010), 332.

was supposed to remain apolitical (or as apolitical as it could be sitting at the foot of the White House less than a month before the election). Despite my being an hour late, Robert greeted me with a big smile and warm hug before handing me a stack of flyers.

SHOW YOUR
ANGER TO THE
PEOPLE WHO
HELPED MAKE
THE QUILT
POSSIBLE: OUR
GOVERNMENT[12]

ACT UP had a complicated relationship with the Quilt, though it wasn't as bad as the rumors flying around Washington would suggest. We had no intention of ripping it up, pissing on it, or dousing it with fake blood. We fully understood the Quilt's value as a memorial and consciousness-raising tool, and many of us had our own friends and lovers memorialized in its panels. But the Quilt was a symbol of our community's grief, while our job was to be warriors, not mourners.

In a personal attempt to bridge the divide, I bought a button from a Names Project vendor—"The Quilt. See it and understand"—and pinned it to my denim jacket, right next to my "Silence = Death" button. But as I circled the Quilt, I found myself unable to leaflet. Instead, I stuffed the flyers into my backpack and stepped into the Quilt.

I turned right, then left, then right again, quickly skimming across its surface. My eyes darted from one set of panels to another, too afraid to focus; too afraid of whose name I might see. Finally, I stopped and forced myself to look down, vowing silently to read each panel and honor every stolen life. I calibrated the ages: 1954–1987 = 33; 1945–1985 = 40; 1958–1988 = 30. *That could be me.* 1965–1984 = 19. *Jesus.* I looked at the photos and mementos sewn onto the panels, and I thought of Eric . . . and Gregg and David and Tony and Tim. My future seemed filled with panels waiting to be sewn and stared at. And I felt myself being pulled down; lulled into an almost comforting sense of despair and powerlessness . . .

NO!

I pulled myself up as if out of a trance, took a deep breath, and marched out of the Quilt. And there, waiting to greet me, were Robert and Vito and Charles and Tom. And for a moment, we all stood there together, comrades-in-arms, staring at the big white house sitting silently just over the fence. Then I turned, looked back at the Quilt, and took out my flyers.

"Turn the power of the Quilt into action! Join the ACT UP demonstrations Monday and Tuesday of next week!"

At sundown, after the Quilt panels had been neatly folded and packed away for the night, the Names Project held a candlelight march from the Ellipse to the Lincoln Memorial. Despite concerns about what ACT UP might do, given our well-known aversion to silence, there was no formal action planned, though every now and then I'd see a small section ahead of me spring to life with muffled chants and candles punching upward in the nighttime sky.

As if by instinct, or maybe just by virtue of being pushy New Yorkers, I found the ACT UP contingent at the front of the crowd as it gathered around the Reflecting Pool for the rally. Frank Smithson did us one better, stretching out an ACT UP banner like a beacon on the steps of the Memorial, just behind the podium. It was clear from the list of speakers—mostly mothers of PWAs—that the focus would be more on the personal than the political. While Cleve Jones, the Names Project founder, was personally supportive of ACT UP, he couldn't risk compromising the Quilt's goodwill and tax-exempt status by officially endorsing our demonstration. He did his best, however, to give his speech an activist edge.

The quilt is a new monument. We bring it here with shocked sadness. Whoever the next President of the United States may be, by the time of his first State of the Union address, more Americans will have died from AIDS than in the Vietnam War. . . . We bear a burdensome truth that history will record. In the last quarter of the 20th century, in the richest, most powerful nation on earth, a deadly virus struck. This nation, which had the resources to respond to the virus, failed to do so. (*"Shame, shame, shame."*) This failure stems from ignorance in the Oval Office. (*"ACT UP! ACT UP!"*) We know how it can be done, we know who can do it. There is no conflict between love and logic. (*"Silence Equals Death! Silence Equals Death!"*)[13]

After the rally, I caught up with Frank and the rest of the gang, most particularly Jason, an adorable young modern dancer I'd been buzzing around for the past few weeks. That night, in the glow of our activism, our "hello" kiss had an added spark.

There was something liberating about ACT UP field trips. They released in me a sense of fearlessness that allowed me to stand up to authority, lean into my queerness, and more openly express my sexual side.

I smiled conspiratorially at Jason, grabbed his hand, and dashed through traffic across Pennsylvania Avenue and over to the White House, where, in defiance of Ron, Nancy, and Jesse Helms, we staged our own private, yet very public, late-night kiss-in.

There was, however, an unexpected hitch in my weekend plans.

I'd decided to give myself a small break by skipping the usual four-to-a-room activist housing and staying instead with my brother in his DC apartment. But as soon as I arrived, Rick informed me Great-Aunt Florrie had died that morning. Her funeral was scheduled for Sunday afternoon, and we needed to figure out our travel arrangements.

I'd like to say I was grief stricken and immediately agreed to return to New York, if not for me, at least for my grandmother, who had lost her youngest sister and closest friend. Instead, I was angry that my plans for the weekend—and if I'm being honest, for Jason—were being disrupted. While I admired my brother's sense of family obligation, I felt my place was with my ACT UP family at the FDA, rather than with my relatives. I kept waiting for the appropriate emotions to well up inside me, but I didn't feel all that sad. In fact, I resented having to pretend to feel badly about someone dying in their late eighties. It might be sad, but it was natural. People dying in their twenties and thirties was deeply wrong, and that's why I'd come to Washington. What could I do back in New York anyway? What could my presence possibly contribute?

I suspected, even then, that my argument was a little too easy and self-serving. Some years and many funerals later, I've come to understand it's not about what *I'm* feeling; it's about showing up and being there for the people I care about. In this case, my crisis of conscience was thankfully averted when my parents offered to pay for shuttle tickets, so Rick and I could fly back to Washington later that evening.

I rejoined the group Monday afternoon, just in time for the ACT NOW Health Care rally in front of the Health and Human Services (HHS) offices. Alas, it was not my idea of an empowering demonstration. It started with a group of kids from one of our regional affiliates singing "Be a Good Nazi" to the tune of "My Country 'Tis of Thee" ("Be a good Na-a-zi. Hate us we're not like thee. Just let us die.") and only got worse from there.[14]

The rally took the form of a mock trial against the usual suspects presided over by San Francisco sex-worker activist Carol Leigh, a.k.a. Scarlot Harlot from COYOTE (Call Off Your Old Tired Ethics), dressed in full red, white, and blue drag. Though Scarlot had her moments, it was activist amateur hour—a lot of flabby rhetoric and witless theatrics in front of an empty building. Despite everyone's good intentions—and an encore performance of Vito Russo's Albany speech—I found it embarrassing.

Things improved mightily that evening. Our pre-action meeting/pep rally at All Souls Church was packed to the rafters, with activists jammed into the pews, side bleachers, and even up in the choir balcony. We'd come from all over the country, from Miami to LA. Each group was introduced and celebrated with cheers, rising to a mad crescendo when Sylvia Ayres, a sixty-nine-year-old grandmother who'd taken part in the protests at the Democratic Convention, stood up to announce the Houston delegation.

To prepare us for the next day's media onslaught, Michelangelo introduced another of ACT UP's secret weapons, Ann Northrup. A former news producer, now gay youth educator at the Harvey Milk School, Ann was blessed with a caustic wit, a clarion voice, and an ability to speak only in declarative sentences. Stepping up to the microphone—not that she needed one—Ann tucked her sensibly bobbed hair behind her ears and began her lesson.

We do not talk *to* the media, she explained, but *through* the media. Reporters and their cameras were only vehicles for sending our message to our real audience—the general public, the pharmaceutical companies, and the people in charge. We communicate that message with our posters and fact sheets, but also by using easy-to-digest sound bites that could be quoted in the newspaper or spoken directly on camera. For example, if we were asked about the new "Bush Initiative," we shouldn't get caught up in the details. Just say, "It's a lie. It's a sham. And it won't work."

"It's a LIE! It's a SHAM! And it WON'T WORK!"

For the next half hour, affinity groups clustered in corners reviewing their plans. Smaller groups from different cities merged into larger units, while stragglers and the newly CD-trained—some as recently as that afternoon—were adopted into preexisting teams. I reported to the choir bay where Jean Elizabeth Glass ran us through our paces, ensuring all the marshals at tomorrow's demonstration would follow the same procedures.

For a grand finale, Bobby O'Malley and I came up and performed our dueling "FDA raps" (though admittedly, mine was more vaudeville than hip-hop):

> At last year's march
> We were one small group.
> Now we're coming back to Washington
> A national troop! Shouting:
> "Genocide!
> We won't allow!"
> The time has come to ACT UP! ACT NOW!
> **ACT UP! FIGHT BACK! FIGHT AIDS!**
> **ACT UP! FIGHT BACK! FIGHT AIDS!***

Still juiced from the meeting, and hungry besides, Jason and I made our way to Dupont Circle for some food and beer. The television above the bar was showing the local eleven o'clock news, and there, at the top of the show, was footage of police taping off the entrance to the FDA as they braced for what the reporter proclaimed would be "the largest demonstration since the takeover of the Pentagon."

October 11, 1988: Seize Control of the FDA

When I boarded the Red Line to Rockville at 6 a.m., the train was quiet, almost silent. Just the usual collection of groggy commuters in gender-appropriate shirts, ties, and dresses, heading to work. I searched the car for anyone wearing telltale black or a recognizable button—anything to indicate I wasn't the only person heading out to the FDA.

---

*For a much better example of an ACT UP rap, see Tony Malliaris's NIH rap from 1990, http://www.actupny.org/divatv/netcasts/malliaris_rap.html.

Thankfully, the demographics grew more encouraging the further we ventured into the Maryland suburbs. When we finally arrived at the Twinbrook station, hundreds of activists streamed out of every door, flooding the station platform, stickering all available surfaces, and relaying chants as we rode the long escalator down to the street.

Exiting the station, the first thing I saw was Richard Deagle being hauled into a police car for spray-painting "THE FDA HAS BLOO . . ." on the sidewalk. We tried to get him released, but as we were unwilling to transform the demo into a protest at the Metro stop, we let the police car go after a brief standoff—*sorry, Richard!*—and continued our march down the hill to the FDA.

There was something shockingly ordinary about FDA headquarters. Seventeen floors of boxy glass and chrome with a long, flat-roofed entryway, flanked by a series of glass doors and storefronts, including a bank, a dry cleaner, a hair salon, and, perhaps ironically, a drugstore. It looked like a cross between a suburban office building and a strip mall. There were smaller entrances and exits along the side and back—all of which I would get to know intimately over the next several hours—as well as a parking garage and large loading dock. The rest of the campus included three other buildings surrounded by parking lots and—*sigh*—a lot of hills.

The Media Committee had set up their press encampment in a parking lot atop one of those hills, directly across from the main building entrance. Each reporter was greeted and checked in by one of Chip's "little publicists," handed a shiny new press packet and a copy of the morning's *Washington Post*,[15] which featured a lengthy article about ACT UP,[15] and pointed to a welcome table larded with coffee and donuts.[16]

By 7 a.m., the stage was set and the actors—a thousand-plus demonstrators, several hundred police, and scores of reporters—were ready.

In the distance, we heard a chorus of *"ACT UP! Fight BACK! FIGHT AIDS!"* getting louder and louder as a column of a hundred activists came marching down the hill and pouring through the gates onto the FDA campus. The muddle of demonstrators standing about suddenly coagulated into a solid mass and advanced on the FDA and the thick wall of police protecting the building entrance. The noise was incredible: an explosion of shouts, air horns, sirens, and—*well, this was new*—police and news helicopters whirring above.

Behind the surging crowd, affinity groups huddled together to determine their morning strategies. The Delta Queens* broke first, joined by the

---

*The Delta Queens formed during the Atlanta and New Orleans conventions and comprised many of ACT UP's most visible and influential members, including Heidi Dorow, Avram

Atlanta-based DAR (Daughters of the American Revolution—though I'm guessing it was a different revolution). Darting around the police, they formed a protective circle around one of the empty flagpoles and hoisted our fighting colors: "**75,000 People with AIDS Fight Back**." The "seizing" had begun.[17]

A pack of activists charged forward, pushing the cops up against the windowed entryway until there was the sharp crash of broken glass. Everything stopped . . . but only for a second.

Everyone rushed to the sound. Locking arms, my fellow marshals and I inserted ourselves between the police and the protesters. Reporters pushed forward against us, cameras rolling, microphones at the ready, hoping to catch the moment when it would all spin out of control. But nobody wanted a riot, except maybe the press, so everyone took a breath and stepped back, revealing a single pane of broken glass.

What followed was a strange sort of activist vaudeville with Chip Duckett as emcee, introducing each affinity group action over the loudspeaker.

"Attention media: A die-in is about to occur in front of the main entrance—major photo opportunity."

As promised, the Tombstones lay down on the lawn, holding their cardboard namesakes above their heads; each one branded with a bloody handprint and inscribed with a different message: "**I Got the Placebo. R.I.P.**"; "**AZT Wasn't Enough**"; "**Dead: 'As a Person of Color, I Was Exempt from Drug Trials'**"; "**Because Women with AIDS Die Twice as Fast.**" Our very own AIDS cemetery; the anti-Quilt, angry and accusatory.

Another group circled the sidewalk with sandwich boards, hawking tabs of the still-unapproved dextran sulfate, while Boston's "Another United Fruit Company" handed out copies of their ingenious FDA drug development game, "Protocol."

> The drug companies are playing Monopoly; Reagan and Bush are playing What's My Line?; Respectable gays are playing The Newly-wed Game; Heterosexuals are playing Risk; While the press plays Trivial Pursuit. Let's Play Protocol.[18]

As if by magic, Peter Staley suddenly appeared atop the main entrance and began taping a series of ACT UP posters to the front of the building. In his black leather jacket and Mishima headband, he looked every inch the activist rock star, raising his arms in triumph as the crowd roared its approval.

Finkelstein, Maria Maggenti, Bill Monaghan, David Robinson, Karl Soehnlein, and Maxine Wolfe. The Delta Queens (later Costas) would become our longest-lasting affinity group.

"Attention media: The press conference will begin in five minutes in the parking lot."

On cue, the press turned and trudged back up the hill. Everyone else—Peter, the affinity groups, even the cops—stopped what they were doing until the press conference was over.

The Media Committee had designated three spokespeople, starting with Vito Russo, "the gutsy PWA." Behind him stood Mark Fotopoulos, holding his newly updated sign: "**Living with AIDS 3 yrs. 6 mos. and Counting!**"

> It takes eight months to test drugs in Europe. Why does it take five to seven years to test drugs here? I know there are drugs out there to save my life. I don't want a quilt with my name on it to be in front of the White House next year.[19]

> The side effect of AIDS is death. I would rather take my chances with the side effects of the drugs.[20]

John Thomas, from Dallas GUTS (Gay Urban Truth Squad), was up next, providing a softer, "we come in sorrow" message:

> I am here today—we are all here today—because we all have AIDS. Some of us have AIDS in our bloodstream. Some of us have AIDS in our minds. We look into the mirror and see a sore that won't go away, and we are fearful that we are going to be diagnosed. And we all have AIDS in our hearts. All of us have lost people we love.[21]

And then Ann Northrup bluntly slammed our message home:

> You think they're doing all they can? They're not. They're sitting on drugs that can save people's lives. Their message is very simple: "We're trying." They're not. They're lying. That is the message of ACT UP.[22]

At the conclusion of the speeches, Michelangelo pointed the media to a long line of activists, each holding a sign bearing the name of their state and hometown. The idea, a gift from fellow activist Urvashi Vaid, who'd used a similar strategy for the Supreme Court CD last year, was to give the regional press, most of whom had a dedicated national reporter in Washington, a local face and angle for the demonstration. As Mike later admitted, "It was the difference between getting the front page and getting buried in the paper, lost in the national section."[23]

Despite the cleverness of our visuals and the precision of our interviews and photo ops—or maybe because of it—things felt a little unreal down on the ground. The truth was, we'd already accomplished our goal; we'd seized control of the FDA and had done so before we'd even set foot in Rockville. The media were parroting our issues, the national conversation was starting to move in our direction, and the mere threat of our protest had forced the FDA to begin grappling with our demands. The demonstration was almost irrelevant, except we'd promised the press a show and now had to deliver one.

But after two and a half hours, the police had arrested only thirty-two people. Affinity groups, which had planned their actions assuming they'd be arrested after blocking an entrance or completing their die-in, were instead scrambling to figure out ways to force an arrest.

Members of the Majority Action Committee and Women's Caucus began a march around the campus with T-shirts and fliers that read:

WE RECOGNIZE THAT EVERY AIDS DEATH IS AN ACT OF RACIST, SEXIST AND HOMOPHOBIC VIOLENCE

WE [People of Color, whether we are Afro-American, Native American, Hispanic/Latino, or Asian, Women, Men, IV Drug Users, Partners of IV Drug Users, Lesbians, Gays, Straights, the Homeless, Prisoners and Children Affected by the AIDS Crisis]

DIE [16,634 of our lives lost according to the Centers for Disease Control. This is 42% of all the deaths. While . . .]

THEY [Ronald Reagan • George Bush • Michael Dukakis • National Institute of Health • Food and Drug Administration • The US Congress • The Congressional Black and Hispanic Caucus • Our National Media • Our National Minority Leaders]

DO [absolutely]

NOTHING![24]

Several other groups linked arms and charged the front entrance, only to march directly into, or rather onto, another group blocking the entryway with a sit-in. The press, hoping for hot footage, quickly followed suit, wedging themselves between the police and both sets of activists, stepping on the demonstrators and assaulting everyone with their cameras and microphones. In the ensuing commotion, there was another crash as a protester was bounced off a front window.

No one was hurt but, hallelujah, the police finally took out their plastic twist ties and began arresting people. "Please be careful!" "That's a friend of mine!" "Not too tight, please." We would shout these requests over and over to humanize the arrestees for the police and make it more difficult for them to treat our comrades harshly. When the waiting school bus was full and ready to leave, its path was blocked by a sudden and furious kiss-in. When the kiss-in turned into a sit-in, four arrestees popped open the top hatch of the bus and clambered onto the roof, and everything returned to a standstill.

With police refusing to respond to any of our provocations, the day morphed into an activist version of *They Shoot Horses, Don't They*, with Chip as Gig Young, rallying the remaining contestants to the next marathon activity.

"Attention media: An effigy of Ronald Reagan is being raised at the flagpole. Excellent photo op at the flagpole."

FDA employees, trapped in their offices, stared out their windows as Reagan's pants fell down to his ankles mid-hoist. We looked up at them and shouted, "Get back to work!" We blocked all the building's entrances and exits, transformed the Rite Aid sign into "Fite AIDS," and replaced Peter Staley with a go-go-boy from Rock 'n' Roll Fag Bar, who danced on the roof in a "Fuck Me Safe" T-shirt and black miniskirt.[25] Still no action from the police. As we stood around waiting for something, *anything*, to happen, Michael Nesline sidled up to me and, eyebrows arched, stage-whispered, "Who do you have to fuck around here to get arrested?"

It was rumored that three protesters had snuck into the main building through a dumpster, though no one knew where they were. Members of ACT UP/LA tried a more direct route, launching a brick through a ground-floor window, but the police grabbed them before they could crawl through.

Meanwhile, the protesters in the school bus were getting tired and needed their meds—and a bathroom—so the sit-in receded, the arrestees climbed back in and closed the hatch, and the bus slowly chugged off to a nearby high school gymnasium for processing.

By then, it was noon and time for a live update for the midday news programs. As soon as the camera lights blinked on, protesters began a loud and angry die-in in front of the main FDA entrance, and the police, finally picking up their cue, hauled them away.

"Eighty-one arrests. Yowza, yowza."

While everyone else was focused on this latest media frenzy, Mark Harrington, Jim Eigo, Jason, and other members of the ACT UP's Wave 3 affinity group quietly snuck up the hill and into the building that housed the FDA Ethics Center. Once inside, the activists "seized control" of a third-floor conference room and, declaring themselves "The New Center for Drugs and

Biologics," issued a series of edicts which, if implemented, would "alter the face of experimental medicine in this country."[26]

Unfortunately, their attempt to hold a press conference was thwarted by the arrival of federal police, who brought with them stiffer federal penalties.* Negotiations between the two parties continued for about a half hour, until the activists emerged from the building dressed in fresh white lab coats emblazoned with the NEW CENTER FOR DRUGS & BIOLOGICS logo.

"Attention media: Treatment press conference up the hill in front of Building 2."

By 2 p.m., the demonstration had hit the wall. We'd been seizing control for seven hours; everyone was getting tired and hungry, and things were turning a bit surreal. When Neil "Squeaky" Broome came staggering around the corner to report he'd just been threatened in the parking lot by a man with a chainsaw, we just looked at him blankly and nodded. Surrounded by cameras, Sylvia Ayres, the grandmother from Houston, pleaded, "as a mother, sixty-nine years old, who has no one but who loves all of these beautiful people . . . do something. Release these drugs. Help these young people! Let them live! Let them live, please . . ."[27] before collapsing to the ground and being dutifully arrested.

The plan had been to stay on-site until everyone who wanted had been arrested; but as both the temperature and our numbers began drifting downward, the press began packing up, and we worried that without their protection, the police might become increasingly hostile. Even the possibility of live coverage on the evening news hardly seemed worth the risk.

We called the demo at 4 p.m., with a total of 185 arrests.

My brother had scored two extra tickets to see Prince that evening, but sadly, there was not enough caffeine in the world to keep me and Jason awake. We both nodded off in the middle of the concert—I know, *unbelievable*—and could barely keep our eyes open long enough to watch the FDA footage on the eleven o'clock news.

When we awoke the next morning, Rick was gone, and the sun was streaming through the windows and onto our sofa bed. I was exhausted—my legs were dead weight, and I could hardly move—but all my muscles and

---

*Until then, the arrests had been handled by local Maryland police.

every inch of my skin was tingling. Just the feeling of the bed sheets sent an electric charge through my body. And then Jason rolled over and did something unexpected and extraordinary.

Was it "safe?" "Safer?" Who knew where it fell on the safe sex spectrum; but the feeling was glorious.

Having lived up to our part of the bargain, the media lived up to theirs. The FDA action was front-page news across the country. Articles appeared in thousands of newspapers, accompanied by remarkable information-packed photos—police in riot gear stepping through the Tombstone's die-in cemetery; a standoff between protesters and police; a young man in a "Person with AIDS" T-shirt being hauled away by a stern-faced cop—all with Peter's **Silence = Death** banner looming in the background.

On TV, the demonstration was featured nationally on all the major news programs, as well as the Spanish-language and cable networks feeding hundreds of local TV stations around the country. In Washington, the story dominated morning, noon, and evening broadcasts. All the 5 p.m. early news and interview shows were almost exclusively about the action and featured interviews with protesters and responses from FDA officials. And later in the evening, Peter appeared on CNN's *Crossfire*, memorably crossing swords with Pat Buchanan.

The demonstration was reported live on dozens of radio networks during the all-important morning drive time on both coasts, followed by numerous drop-ins and updates throughout the day. NPR covered us all weekend, beginning the Friday before the action and continuing with live coverage of both the Monday and the Tuesday demonstrations. The action was also carried internationally on the BBC, as well as on Italian, French, Dutch, Japanese, and Canadian TV networks and in stories and photographs that appeared in newspapers and magazines around the world.

The coverage in the New York papers, however, consisted of only captioned photos. *New York Newsday* used a shot by ACT UP's Tom McKitterick of a tote board noting the gruesome total of 42,476 AIDS deaths and headlined "One AIDS Death Every Hour," while the *Daily News* used the AP photo of the Tombstone cemetery. The *Times* photo, on the other hand, seemed purposely generic; it showed two cops arresting a single isolated, unidentifiable protester, with nothing to identify the issue, the location, or the people involved.[28]

Tellingly, one year after the FDA demonstration, another photo appeared in the *Times*, this time accompanying an article titled "How the AIDS Crisis Made Drug Regulators Speed Up."[29] It's a three-column shot from the FDA action, with a line of activists from the Seeing Red affinity group in bloodied white lab coats, hands clasped high above their heads, marching fearlessly toward a wall of police guarding an FDA entrance covered with ACT UP posters.[30] By then, the action had become a reference point, a visual short-hand for the struggle to release drugs for people with AIDS. In the space of a year, this was now the accepted image of people with AIDS—not alone and isolated, but powerful, angry, and united.

More importantly, cracks had begun to appear in the bureaucratic wall of the FDA. Politicians from the right and left joined AIDS activists—albeit for different reasons—in pushing for change. Just days after our demonstration, the FDA announced new procedures they claimed would reduce the average drug approval time by one-third to one-half. The new regulations, based on the Bush recommendations, would expand the scope and enroll-ment of Phase II studies and replace time-consuming Phase III efficacy testing with postmarketing studies. Upon closer inspection, however, it appeared none of these new procedures were mandatory, nor were any additional funds or staffing made available to implement the new program. In other words, a lie and a sham that won't work.

But then the researchers themselves began to come around.

In late November, the *Journal of the American Medical Association* published an editorial by Dr. Jere E. Goyen, a former head of the agency (1979–81), arguing the FDA should reexamine "all of the assumptions on which scientific requirements of the present system are based."[31] Rather than insisting upon double-blind placebo-controlled trials,* which the FDA held to be the "gold standard" for proving drug effectiveness, they should "consider alternative study designs that allow the patient maximum hope for cure and the opportunity for some control over his or her destiny."[32]

This was followed by stinging criticism from the head of the National Cancer Institute, Dr. Samuel Broder, who demanded the FDA allow investigators more flexibility in redesigning trials to include new informa-tion as knowledge develops—another of ACT UP's demands. Noting "those of us who treat patients speak a different language from those who make

---

*In these trials, patients are randomly assigned to a group receiving either the new drug or a placebo; neither the patient nor their doctor know who's assigned to which group. When the study is complete, scientists "un-blind" the groups and compare results. The problem for people with AIDS was that the difference between receiving the drug or the placebo could be life or death.

the rules,"[33] Broder asserted it was the doctors in the field who discovered most of the applications for drugs and how they were best used, and it was ridiculous to demand that drugs go through the full FDA approval process every time a new use or indication was discovered. He further demanded that insurance and Medicaid pay for the routine medical costs associated with drug trials and that the FDA drop its insistence on placebo trials, arguing, "Death as an endpoint is very difficult to defend."[34]

It would take another year for the walls to come down, but down they'd come.

The future on other fronts seemed less certain. According to a joint *Times/CBS* survey, while 75 percent of Americans had "a lot" or "some" sympathy for people with AIDS, that number shrunk to 36 percent if the PWAs were infected through gay sex and 26 percent if they were infected through illegal drug use.[35]

In Dallas, Judge Jack Hampton gave the eighteen-year-old murderer of two gay men a reduced sentence, explaining, "I put prostitutes and gays at about the same level, and I'd be hard put to give somebody life for killing a prostitute." And he added, "I don't care much for queers cruising the streets. I've got a teen-age boy."[36]

And on November 8, George Herbert Walker Bush was elected president.

Gathering at Maria's to drown our sorrows in booze and bitter cigarette smoke, it was hard to imagine how we'd survive four more years of the same deadly AIDS policies. The results were further proof of how little our lives mattered to our fellow citizens.

It was this desperate need for recognition—to have our lives seen and valued—that energized our ongoing battle with Stephen Joseph. Throughout the fall, our exchanges became even more heated and personal, with both parties engaging in escalating tit-for-tat reprisals, from Joseph's closure of gay movie houses as public health hazards to a series of unsanctioned phone threats made by ACT UP members to Joseph's home.

These attacks predictably put ACT UP under increased and unwelcome police surveillance. We began to recognize the undercover cops at our Monday night meetings and several ACT UP members received early morning visits from the department's elite major case squad. In response, our volunteer attorneys led a Monday night tutorial on our rights under police questioning and distributed a "Silence = Golden" handout instructing us on how to behave should the police show up unexpectedly at our door.

Hostilities came to a head shortly before Thanksgiving, when the commissioner was scheduled to participate in a forum at the Lesbian and Gay Community Services Center. What had been planned as a silent demonstration quickly devolved into a rancorous confrontation, as Joseph goaded the audience by deliberately refusing to acknowledge the impact of AIDS on the gay community or express any compassion for people who talked about their painful experiences with the disease and their frustrations with the city's health care system. Joseph was so infuriating, so openly contemptuous of everyone in the audience, that we lost it. I know I did. And I suppose that's what he wanted. He seemed to go out of his way to provoke us—and he was expert at it.

The forum came to its welcome end when Ortez Alderson stood up and asked the commissioner whether it wasn't "the essence of corruption" for the Department of Health to accept a $500,000 grant from the CDC to investigate its own underreporting of epidemiological data, and Joseph stormed out of the Community Center.[37]

But we would soon have other opportunities to confront the commissioner, and more importantly, his boss, Ed Koch. ACT UP was at the height of its powers. And no one, not the mayor, not the FDA, not the research establishment, not Burroughs Wellcome, not even the Catholic Church, was going to stand in our way.

Part III

CRASHING THROUGH

Chapter 9

Targeting City Hall

ON JANUARY 8, 1989, ACT UP took over the World.

The World was a huge dance club that had been carved out of a run-down theater and catering hall on the far edge of the East Village. A thumping hive of slumming artists, designers, club kids, neighborhood fags, drag queens, and banjee boys; it was where house music went after the demise of the Paradise Garage.[1]

The emcee for that evening's ACT UP benefit was none other than cable-TV porn star diva Robin Byrd. Byrd and her well-worn macramé bikini hosted a self-named public access talk show featuring gyrating strippers of both sexes, culminating in a dancing bump-and-grope fest to her tone-challenged recording of "Baby Let Me Bang Your Box." It was a trashy, sexy, only-in-New-York wonder, and like many, I tuned in regularly.

For entertainment, Byrd had brought a cadre of go-go boys and porn stars, including ACT UP members Jake Corbin and Joey Stefano, who spent the evening dancing on tables and swinging from lighting fixtures in one of the smaller party rooms. It was a wild night—a combination of (safe) sex club, dance party, and political rally—divinely decadent and defiantly alive.

And somehow, I was a part of it.

Growing up, I'd always fantasized about being in one of those places where "it" was happening; a magical moment when a certain someplace became the center of the universe. The movable feast of Paris in the '20s, midcentury modern Manhattan, or San Francisco during the Summer of

Love—those places that defined the world or a time, and when you looked back, it seemed that *everyone* was there.

That was ACT UP in 1989.

I don't know if we helped create the cultural moment or were simply swept up in it, but we saw our reflection cast back at us in the galleries of the New Museum and the holiday windows at Barneys;* in the dance music of Deee-Lite, Jimmy Somerville, Prince, and Madonna; at Wigstock and the drag shows at the Pyramid; and in the performance art at the Kitchen and P.S. 122. The line between art, politics, and queer life was growing increasingly thin, and no one walked that tightrope better—or with more style—than ACT UP.†

That I ever found myself there remains one of the wonders of my life.

Ed Koch had been mayor of New York since 1978. Initially celebrated as an ally of the gay community, he was now held in contempt for his murderous lack of response to the AIDS epidemic. Although ACT UP had taken on the mayor periodically, we'd focused primarily on national issues. Even as we protested the rejiggering of the city's AIDS caseload numbers, the target of our hostilities had been the health commissioner and not the mayor.

But with Koch facing a tough reelection battle, the time seemed right to set our sights on City Hall.

The city's AIDS crisis was not a single crisis, but rather a catastrophic collision of intersecting plagues and emergencies. Homelessness, drug addiction, poverty, and lack of health care combined with institutional homophobia, addictophobia, racism, and sexism helped create and perpetuate the AIDS crisis as surely as the lack of treatments.

By the 1980s, homelessness had become a national tragedy. Fed by a combination of stagnating wages—the result of a shift from an industrial economy into a service one—and the increase in households headed by women—half of whom lived below the poverty line—the spread of homelessness had accelerated under the brutal Social Darwinism of the Reagan

---

*Barneys' window designer Simon Doonan was another ACT UP member.

†On September 15, 1988, ACT UP was even given a "Special Citation" Bessie Award from the downtown *cognoscenti* for theatrical street demonstrations and our effort to focus attention on the AIDS crisis, and in 1990, we'd win an Obie for "Sustained Achievement."

administration. "You can't help those who simply will not be helped,"[2] shrugged the president, as he ruthlessly shredded the federal safety net and cut funding for public housing by 75 percent.

As with most urban plagues, the situation was even more desperate in New York City, where skyrocketing real estate values and city-subsidized "urban revitalization" programs had occasioned the loss of over 1 million apartments and 100,000 SRO (single-room occupancy) units in the past fifteen years. This disaster was further compounded by state policies that had released thousands of mentally ill patients from state-run institutions without providing the requisite funding for housing, care, and support services. By 1989, there were an estimated 70,000–90,000 homeless people in New York City, with more than half living on the streets.[3]

As a longtime New Yorker, I'd learned to look away from the men and women camped out in the doorways of my neighborhood and resented their often-smelly presence in the subway cars I took to work. Sure, I donated old coats to New York Cares and money to the Coalition for the Homeless, but if I was honest with myself, it was mostly to assuage my guilt—a way to fight homelessness, the *problem*, rather than see the homeless as *people*.

Once again, AIDS would force me to open my eyes.

It was estimated that between 5,000 and 8,000 of the city's homeless population had HIV-related illnesses. Within five years, the number would be closer to 30,000.[4] City streets were no place for anyone to live, especially not people with severely damaged immune systems, yet the Koch administration had set aside only 416 beds for homeless PWAs. The city's shelters and welfare hotels were little better. Overcrowded and dangerous, they were breeding grounds for TB, pneumonia, and other opportunistic infections. Although officially off-limits to people with AIDS and ARC,[5] as many as 2,800 people with HIV disease were resident in the city's homeless system. But whether in the streets or in shelters, the homeless were regularly denied access to PWA benefits and services because they lacked an established address or the requisite two forms of identification.

ACT UP had first addressed AIDS and homelessness in the spring of 1988, when Eric Sawyer organized A-Bomb, the AIDS Beds Or the Mayor's Butt affinity group. Leading-man handsome, Eric had come to the city in 1980, hoping to make money in real estate by renovating buildings and then living off the rental income so he could go into politics. But shortly after his lover died from AIDS in 1986, he befriended an ailing homeless Harlem neighbor and started to collect money to help him find a place to live. Soon Eric began exploring the possibility of buying and renovating empty SRO buildings and converting them into AIDS housing. His search for potential contacts and revenue sources eventually led him to Larry Kramer, who would later invite him to attend a speech he was giving at the Lesbian and Gay Community Services Center.[6]

Soon after organizing A-Bomb, Eric and Rich Jackman, an architect with similar interests, began scouring city tax records, looking for empty city-owned buildings that could be repurposed into AIDS housing units. The city showed little interest in the issue or their proposals until, on the eve of City Council hearings on the lack of AIDS housing, the Koch administration suddenly announced a new $25 million plan to provide eight hundred additional beds for PWAs in eight different sites across the city. Unfortunately, the facilities were too large, too expensive, and would take far too long to complete. They were also ill-suited to the needs of most homeless PWAs, as the city had selected a housing model designed for patients with acute end-stage illness rather than a more flexible facility that could provide the continuum of care they required.[7]

The entire proposal made little sense—until you looked at the financing. The Koch administration, which for years had subsidized the luxury housing market with tax breaks and abatements, had no interest in spending city money on AIDS housing. But if the city selected a *medical* housing model, Medicaid would step in and pay for 90 percent of the cost—a bargain for the city, if not for the PWAs they were supposed to serve.[8]

To highlight the city's woeful priorities, ACT UP had staged a Black Friday "Happy Trumpsgiving" protest in November 1988, at that monument to conspicuous consumption and greed, Trump Tower. Members of A-Bomb climbed to the top of the gaudy gold-and-pink marbled atrium and showered the holiday shoppers with flyers, while the Delta Queens lay down on bedsheets, blocking the building's entryway and chanting *"HOUSING for PEOPLE with AIDS! Not Tax Breaks for PEOPLE with MAIDS."**

Shortly thereafter, Eric and Rich formed the Housing Caucus, dedicated to promoting the development of medically appropriate housing for all people with HIV disease.† As there was no existing housing model that fully met

---

*The city had given Donald Trump $6,208,733 in tax abatements to build this gilded tribute to his own ego—enough to rehabilitate approximately 1,200 city-owned apartments for homeless PWAs. ACT UP fact sheet: "New York City Tricked Out of AIDS Care Trump Treated to Tax Abatements," [ca. October 31, 1989].

†The Housing Caucus would become a full ACT UP committee later that year. In 1990, four members—Keith D. Cylar, Charles King, Eric Sawyer, and Virginia Shubert—would branch off to create Housing Works, which provided actual housing for people with AIDS/HIV and would grow to become, at one point, the largest nongovernmental provider of housing in New York City.

the needs of PWAs, they created their own, a "Multi-Licensed Facility," which offered basic accommodations—private rooms and baths, a small refrigerator for medications, and a shared kitchen—and could provide additional services and health care as necessary, allowing PWAs to remain in one facility throughout the course of their illness.[9]

Looming over both the AIDS and the homelessness crises was the city's massive drug epidemic. An estimated 225,000 residents were at risk for HIV due to past or present drug-related behavior.* In the first six months of 1988 alone, incidence of AIDS among heterosexual men and women who use IV drugs had risen to 55 percent of all new cases and accounted for 40 percent of the cumulative total.[10]

Drug users, much like the homeless, had been robbed of their personhood and demonized as vectors of transmission or symbols of urban blight, rather than being seen as people with "the same rights to life, liberty and health as all other people and [whose] health should be provided for as aggressively as the health of their sexual partners and offspring."[11] There were still only 43,000 treatment slots in the city's addiction programs;[12] a number that had not changed since the mid-1970s. And as the crack cocaine epidemic tore through the city, over 80 percent of those slots remained reserved exclusively for heroin users, who still had to wait up to ten months to get into a treatment program. Meanwhile, only a handful of placements in drug residency programs were available for women with children.

The mayor blamed Albany, wrongly insisting the city had transferred all responsibility for drug treatment programs to the state before he took office.† Even so, he'd done little to advocate for more treatment slots, and his administration's ham-fisted, top-down approach had doomed his progressive needle exchange program, arousing fierce opposition from Black and Latino leaders, who were offended that Koch, who had long ignored their pleas for the most basic services, had, without consultation, funded a program that appeared to encourage the very behavior and lawlessness that were destroying their communities.

---

*The city's chronic undercounting of the AIDS caseload among IVDUs, combined with the exploding crack cocaine epidemic, make this estimate highly suspect.

† It was Koch who'd let the city's Addiction Services Agency go out of business during his first year as mayor and then limited funding to city-run methadone programs until they were eliminated in 1983. Lei Chou et al., "Target City Hall: An AIDS Activist's Guide to New York City in 1989," March 20, 1989, 29, citing Wayne Barrett, "Koch's Phony Drug War," *Village Voice*, March 14, 1989.

▟▟▟

When the members of the Majority Action Committee (MAC) chose their name, they did so deliberately,* to remind the group that despite their relatively small numbers within ACT UP, people of color comprised close to 60 percent of the city's AIDS caseload, including 85 percent of the reported cases among women and 91 percent of all children with AIDS.[13]

At age 37, Ortez Alderson was MAC's radical elder. Ortez had joined the Chicago Gay Liberation Front in 1969 at age seventeen and quickly became chair of the group's Black Caucus. In 1970, he was one of the "Pontiac Four," convicted of breaking into an Illinois draft board and destroying files, and spent close to a year in prison. Upon his release, Ortez became a leader in the Third World Gay Revolution and helped organize gay participation in the Black Panthers' 1971 Revolutionary People's Constitutional Convention.[14]

Not that I knew any of this at the time. I just knew Ortez was one fierce queen, afraid of nothing and no one, and when he spoke in his forceful rapid-fire manner, you damn well better listen.

Among MAC's toughest challenges was breaking the silence that existed around AIDS in the Black and Latino communities. As in White communities, there was not much sympathy for the populations most directly affected by the disease. Although gay men of color comprised almost one-third of the city's gay AIDS caseload, many in the community regarded homosexuality as a "white problem," a viewpoint gladly embraced by the church and greatly abetted by the media, who equated gay with White (and male). While grassroots organizations were doing their best to provide AIDS information and support services, the silence from community leaders was deafening. "Our so-called leaders are afraid they'll catch it or compromise

---

*Majority Action announced its intention to become a full committee on July 11, 1988. They did so as "Majority Action," though the committee was often called "Majority Actions." We were not particularly formal about such things. Also, as a full committee, membership was open to anyone interested in issues affecting communities of color. As a result, the subcommittee, and later committee, had a multiracial makeup, including Whites as well as Blacks, Latinas/os, and Asian/Pacific Islanders. Early committee members included Ortez Alderson, Keith Cylar, Jose Fidelino, Joe Franco, Robert Garcia, Elias Guerrero, Emily Gordon, Debra Levine, Ray Navarro, Allan Robinson, Robert Vasquez-Pacheco, and Dan Keith Williams.

their reputations if they help us," declared Ortez, "so we have to care for our own."[15]

One of the caucus's first actions had been at the 1988 CDC Conference on AIDS and People of Color. MAC members were shocked to discover the meeting was focused solely on AIDS education and prevention, rendering those already infected with HIV, whether gay men of color or intravenous drug users and their families, "invisible or seen only as vectors of transmission to the uninfected—then left for dead." [16] Not only did the activists demand a more comprehensive approach to future conferences, they also challenged the attendees to broaden the scope of their own activism, to "fight back, not just in the suites, but in the streets."[17]

> We must challenge, we must protest, demand a national health care policy, hand out safe sex information, distribute clean needle information, sit in our leaders' offices, and even go to jail if necessary, but do anything to politicize our communities around the AIDS crisis. To do less would be to play into the hands of those who speak of the "mainstream" as if we are not included in it.[18]

Ortez and Majority Action played a similar gadfly role within ACT UP, pushing us to see beyond the people and populations in the room, and reminding us—and not always gently—that our predominantly White, male, privileged experience was not a universal one. MAC, along with the Women's Caucus and other individual members with longer histories of activism, helped us see the connections between our issues and the struggles of other communities and develop a more robust framework for understanding the AIDS crisis.

This became increasingly important as the official narrative of the crisis began to shift. The new media story line, parroted by politicians of all stripes, was "the changing face of AIDS"—how it was no longer a gay (White male) disease, but a disease of Black and Latino IV drug users and their families.

Yes, Black was the new AIDS.

But AIDS had neither left the gay community—or rather, communities— nor only now suddenly appeared in communities of color. The disease had first been noticed among gay White middle-class men because we had access to health care, insurance, and private doctors. The AIDS definition was based on how HIV manifests in gay White bodies, further perpetuating the notion of AIDS as a "gay disease." But throughout this time, and earlier, people of color—gay men, women, IV drug users, their partners and children—were dying of undiagnosed HIV-related diseases, known on the street as "the dwindles" and "junkie pneumonia."*

However, the "New Face of AIDS" provided a convenient angle for the media, who never liked talking about gay sex anyway, and gave government officials a second chance to look as though they were taking decisive action, even if it was only shifting inadequate funding and resources from one community to another. For politicians like Ed Koch, who were primarily interested in staying in power, it provided an opportunity to drive a wedge into a potentially powerful progressive coalition by pitting the interests of the gay community against those of communities of color.

Koch was an old hand at "divide and conquer" tactics, with the previous summer's "numbers" controversy merely the most recent example. Fortunately, activists like Ray Navarro helped us see things in a larger context.

> We must recognize that the rise in homophobic violence (both AIDS-related and otherwise) has coincided with a rise in racist crimes, both locally and nationwide. The NYC that we are targeting [about AIDS] this March is also the city of Eleanor Bumpurs,† Howard Beach,‡ and Michael Stewart§ . . .
>
> . . . Together, [our] experiences have taught us that socially-constructed prejudices and legally-sanctioned discrimination in treating gay men infected with HIV have combined with increasing racism in NYC to create a system of very unequal distribution of rights to live.[19]

---

*Currently, it is believed the first documented AIDS death in this country was Robert R. (Rayford), a fifteen-year-old black teenager from St. Louis, who died in 1969 from a then inexplicable series of infections as the result of a collapsed immune system. Upon autopsy, it was discovered that he had Kaposi's sarcoma, and a battery of tests performed in 1987 on frozen blood and tissue samples revealed that he was infected with HIV. John Crewdson, "Case Shakes Theories of AIDS Origin," *Chicago Tribune*, October 25, 1987, http://articles. chicagotribune.com/1987-10-25/news/8703200167_1_aids-virus-kaposi-s-sarcoma-aids-origin.

† Eleanor Bumpurs was an elderly, mentally ill Black woman who was shot and killed by police on October 29, 1984, after she threatened them with a ten-inch kitchen knife as they attempted to evict her from her apartment.

‡ In December 1986, three Black men were attacked by a group of bat-wielding White teenagers when their car broke down in Howard Beach, Queens. One of the men was seriously injured, while another, Michael Griffith, was hit by a car and killed as he ran across the Belt Parkway in an attempt to flee his attackers.

§ Michael Stewart was a twenty-five-year-old Black art student and graffiti artist who was arrested and "allegedly" brutalized while in police custody by White transit police and later died, having never regained consciousness. Although all the officers involved were eventually acquitted, the case became a cause célèbre and the name Michael Stewart, like Eleanor Bumpurs, became shorthand for racially motivated police abuse and violence.

Ray was a young long-haired Chicano artist and filmmaker from California, and a founding member of Majority Action. A born teacher and community activist, Ray was one of several voices prodding us to take the longer view and recognize AIDS as a symptom of the larger underlying problems of poverty and lack of health care in communities of color.

It was estimated that roughly 24 percent of city residents, the majority of whom were people of color, were living in poverty. If you adjusted that number to reflect the ability to afford health care, the percentage jumped to 36 percent. Among children, the numbers were even worse, with 40 percent of children living in poverty and 54 percent defined as "medically poor." Many of the poorest neighborhoods—places like the South Bronx and Fort Greene, which were also among the hardest hit by AIDS—were federally designated Health Manpower Shortage Areas, as they lacked access to private doctors, clinics, nursing homes, and home-attendant programs. For these communities, emergency rooms were the primary source for health care, accounting for 51 percent of all hospital admissions, a figure that had jumped more than 30 percent in two years.[20]

PWAs who accessed health care through emergency rooms were usually diagnosed at a later stage of disease and received care only at the most acute stages of their illness. They received little or no prophylactic treatment for PCP or other opportunistic infections, no blood level monitoring or health maintenance assistance, and no real access to experimental drugs through clinical trials. Is it any wonder that people of color in New York lived an average of only six months after an AIDS diagnosis, while gay men with better access to health care were living three years or longer?

As Bruce C. Vladek, the president of the United Hospital Fund, admitted, "Whether or not you get adequate health care in New York is largely a function of your income and employment status."[21]

By early 1989, however, even those walls of privilege were beginning to crumble. Articles and editorials in the *Times* and—*gasp!*—even the *Wall Street Journal* warned of hospital overcrowding and lack of beds curtailing elective surgery and affecting the availability of ER services for heart attacks, strokes, and appendicitis. The wait for acute care beds for desperately ill patients had ballooned from four hours to four days,[22] while occupancy rates at both public and private city hospitals soared to over 95 percent.[23] Suddenly even the well-connected were stranded in hallways waiting for an empty bed.*

---

* Faced with declining occupancy rates and an increased emphasis on ambulatory care, New York State had cut over 8,000 city hospital beds in 1976. Ten years later, the city and state

The state of health care services had grown so grim that business leaders warned the mayor nothing less than "New York's standing as the center of finance and business [was] at stake." [24] Former deputy mayor John E. Zuccotti compared the risks the city was facing to those of the fiscal crisis of the 1970s. "More and more I hear people saying: 'What is happening with New York's health care? Are we going to be stepping over bodies, like Calcutta?'"[25]

So instead of returning to Wall Street for yet another largely symbolic anniversary action, ACT UP moved its demonstration a few blocks north to City Hall, to target the mayor and build a progressive coalition to fight for the lives of PWAs and the survival of our communities and our city.

In the run-up to the demonstration, ACT UP unleashed an unprecedented guerrilla advertising campaign, plastering thousands of promotional "Target City Hall" stickers, slipping Richard Deagle and Victor Mendolia's mock subway card ads of Mayor Koch asking "**10,000 New York City AIDS Deaths 'How'm I Doin'?**" onto local trains, and wheatpasting Ken Woodward's series of twelve stark black-and-white posters of "**Reasons to ACT UP at City Hall**" set above a row of silhouetted black tombstones:

Reason #2: 5,000 PEOPLE WITH AIDS DESERVE A BETTER PLACE TO LIVE THAN THE SIDEWALK YOU'RE STANDING ON.[26]

Reason #5: SINCE THE CITY CUT AIDS EDUCATION, MORE KIDS GET TO LEAVE SCHOOL EARLY.[27]

Reason #12: FOR MANY BLACKS AND LATINOS UNABLE TO AFFORD AIDS CARE THE COST OF LIVING IS TOO HIGH.[28]

To capitalize on widespread anti-Koch sentiment and expand our usual pool of protesters, we sent our wheatpasting crews uptown to Harlem and Fort Washington and across the river to Brooklyn and Queens. We bussed activists up to Albany to join the Health Care Workers Union when they protested Governor Cuomo's proposed budget cuts. And as the Swim Team made their rounds in Chelsea and the East Village, Scott Robbe roamed the dark city streets in his Jeep, projecting a "bat signal" of the Target City Hall logo onto blank billboards around the city, while Charlie's Angels leafleted the curious crowd.[29]

---

discovered it was much harder to add beds than cut them, particularly after Wall Street could no longer supply the needed revenue.

Once again, we ran a series of teach-ins to share our acquired knowledge, this time on the daunting range of AIDS issues affecting the city. The accompanying eighty-six-page "Target City Hall" handbook boasted twenty authors—a testament to both the breadth of the crisis and our growing expertise. Our demands were equally comprehensive *and affordable*, as we based them on the $41 million budget proposed by the Committee for AIDS Funding for 1989.*

Koch, meanwhile, was gearing up for the fight of his political life.

Faced with dwindling support from his former liberal base, as well as a slew of challengers running to his left, the mayor abandoned looking for votes in Manhattan and instead made a play for the more conservative Catholic voters of the outer boroughs. His "Hail Mary" was a book coauthored with John Cardinal O'Connor entitled *His Eminence and Hizzoner,* wherein the mayor wrote of his previously undisclosed discomfort with abortion-on-demand and newly minted support for both a constitutional amendment allowing prayer in public schools and tuition tax credits for parochial schools. Going further, Koch publicly questioned whether government was doing enough for the middle class, while suggesting the city was perhaps doing too much for the poor. "Their problems," he sighed, "are at such a profoundly deep level that government can't necessarily reach them, and when it tries, its efforts have only slight results."[30]

Ronald Reagan couldn't have said it better.

The cardinal, meanwhile, revealed no corresponding change of heart and remained unyielding in his opposition to abortion, gay rights, and the distribution of condoms and clean needles.

And if his sudden conversion on social issues wasn't enough, the mayor suddenly announced he was heterosexual.

Koch's sexuality had long been the subject of rumors and innuendo, dating back to his time as a bachelor congressman representing Greenwich Village. Most notoriously, he'd faced a nasty smear campaign during his 1977 run for mayor, responding to taunts of "Vote for Cuomo, not the Homo" by taking

---

*The $41 million was just one-sixth of the amount of the tax rebate given to Chase Manhattan for relocating to Brooklyn instead of New Jersey. Lei Chou et al., "Target City Hall," 2.

up a sudden public romance with Jewish beauty queen and former Consumer Affairs commissioner Bess Meyerson.*

Since then, Koch had refused to respond directly to any questions or allegations about his sexuality and, as recently as the previous week, declared the issue firmly closed. His unexpected pronouncement on a talk radio show—the first time he'd said flat out he was heterosexual—took everyone by surprise.

For us, the issue was not so much the mayor's sexuality as his administration's response to the AIDS epidemic. Larry Kramer, among others, had long charged it was the mayor's fear of being outed that had prevented him from forcefully responding to the AIDS crisis. True or not, Koch's disclosure shifted the focus of discussion from whether he'd ignored AIDS to whether he'd ignored it because he was afraid of being perceived as gay.

Koch was clearly off his game, and we did our best to keep him on the defensive. The following week, we ran a deliberately provocative full-page ad in the *Village Voice*, the Spanish-language daily *El Diario*, and the *City Sun*, a Brooklyn-based Black community paper, featuring a large photo of the mayor stuck among mounting rows of tombstones, with the headline: "What Does Koch Plan To Do About AIDS? Invest in Marble and Granite."[31] As we'd hoped, the ads themselves became a news story, garnering extensive local coverage.

Attempting to recover lost ground, Koch invited the press to join him as he visited AIDS patients at Goldwater Hospital. Much to our delight, he also directly addressed our upcoming demonstration by once again trying to deflect blame onto Governor Cuomo. "You know," he said, "a militant group called ACT UP plans to come down to City Hall next week to picket me. Why? Because they say I'm not doing enough [for AIDS sufferers]. I think they're picketing City Hall because you can do it for a dollar. It costs a lot more to picket in Albany or Washington."[32]

Don't worry, we'll get there. But first, City Hall.

---

*Flyers headlined "Vote for Cuomo, Not the Homo" had reportedly been distributed all over Queens by the Cuomo campaign as part of an unsuccessful effort to undermine Koch among Italian voters. The flyers would surface again in 1982 as part of a whispering campaign during Mario Cuomo's successful bid for governor. In both cases, it was assumed they were the work of Cuomo's son, Andrew, who was a key campaign aide in 1977 and campaign manager in 1982. Andrew Cuomo, who later became governor of New York himself, has always denied responsibility for the smear campaign.

March 27, 1989: A Chant Queen Is Born

Our Monday night pre-action meeting was standing room only and the Community Center was filled with the excitement of a final dress rehearsal for a big hit show.

After a lengthy roll call of affinity groups who'd be executing their own ancillary actions, Ellen Spiro announced the formation of DIVA TV— Damned Interfering Video Activists Television—a corps of ACT UP videographers* who'd be recording and archiving our demonstrations, ensuring our actions would be documented and our message heard, even when the mainstream press refused to cover us. DIVA TV would also monitor the police, making a record of all arrests and incidents of police misconduct and hopefully acting as a deterrent to any police violence.†

Ann Northrup then rallied the crowd with her latest installment of sound bites, setting the stage for Bob Rafsky. Already in his midforties, Bob was not just from a different generation, he was from a different time. Bob had been married until recently and had a young daughter. Although fifteen to twenty years older than most of our members, in terms of living as an out gay man, Bob was one of the youngest in the room. He was also one of our most gifted orators. We referred to him, half-jokingly, as "Bob 'Voice of the People' Rafsky" for his ability to inspire the Floor and send us bravely into battle.

Bob started off by reading a press clipping announcing the mayor's latest effort to "woo homosexual voters"—"Fat chance!" shouted a voice in the back—by establishing a new Office of Lesbian and Gay Affairs. This office would join similar offices "for communities with specialized needs: Gays, Blacks, Hispanics, and Asians."—"That's the majority of the city!" yelled someone else.

Bob continued reading. "Koch said he set up the new office to 'enhance an already strong relationship between my administration and gay and lesbian New Yorkers.'" "Now," said Bob, looking up from the article, his

---

*Original members of DIVA TV included Ray Navarro, Jean Carlomusto, Gregg Bordowitz, Bob Beck, Costa Pappas, Ellen Spiro, George Plagianos, Robert Kurilla, and Catherine Saalfield (now Gund). Catherine Saalfield, "On the Make: Activist Video Collectives," in *Queer Looks*, ed. Martha Gever, Pratibha Parmar, and John Greyson (New York: Routledge, 1993).

†House of Color, another activist video collective, would form in 1990, as a group of "Blacks, Latinos, Asians, who need to start a dialogue among ourselves." The group included Pamela Sneed, Robert Garcia, Julie Tolentino, Jocelyn Taylor, Wellington Love, Robert Mignott, and Jeff Nunokawa. Peter Boweres, "Collect Yourself," *OutWeek*, June 27, 1990.

voice cutting through the laughter and shouted comments of the crowd, "let us celebrate together tonight the end of the last day on which Ed Koch can tell himself that the communities that are being decimated by this epidemic are so weak and so divided among themselves that he can keep serving us this kind of bullshit! (The crowd began to cheer.) Tomorrow morning, he will begin to learn the truth!"[33]

Glory Hallelujah! Let the revival meeting begin!

Bounding up to the front of the room, I asked everyone to "take out their hymnals"—a double-sided chant sheet I'd typed up and distributed—and make with the incantations.[34]

I'd been leading chants at demonstrations ever since our first AIDS commission demo in 1987. I liked energizing the crowd and keeping people focused and on-message—and I was good at it. Here's what I learned:

The best chants are simple: easy to say and understand. They should include places to breathe and, if possible, a good beat or syncopation to keep it fun and propulsive. Call and response chants—either questions and answers or alternating phrases—keep the crowd involved and save vocal wear and tear. And don't forget to bring extra throat lozenges; you'll need them. Most critically, chants are distillations of your message—sound bites with rhythm—so make sure they're saying something important and shouted with power and emotion.

On the streets, chants helped bind ACT UP together, keeping our courage up and making us stronger and braver than we were individually. We needed the extra emotional padding—or at least I did—because what we were doing was scary. We never knew what was going to happen at a demonstration: a cop could be having a bad day; a passerby could turn violent; an affinity group could do something unexpected; or someone—a protester or a bystander—could suddenly lose it, changing everything in an instant. Even though we'd trained ourselves for the possibility of arrest and the risk of violence, it was impossible to prepare for the viciousness and hatred that sometimes came flying at us from our fellow citizens. Chants were our armor; and our emotion, anger, and passion created a buffer that helped protect us from the rest of the world.

Tonight, however, was about rallying the troops. I warmed up the room with a couple issue-specific chants. *"Just say NO is NOT ENOUGH! TEACH. SAFE. SEX!"* and *"HOUSING, NOT SHELTERS! AIDS. WON'T. WAIT!"** Then a sassy variation: *"C'MON Ed, honey—SPEND*

---

*When I noted that this chant format could be used for any number of issues, I was embarrassingly—but humorously—called out for creating a "token chant."

the MONEY! AIDS. WON'T. WAIT!" With a tip of the hat to recent headlines, we tried "*City AIDS care's Inef-FECtual, Thanks to KOCH, the HET'roSEXual!*" which, despite being a lousy chant, got a BIG reaction. (Sometimes, you just gotta have fun.)

We then attempted a musical chant to the tune of "Row, Row, Row Your Boat," which, we sang as a round.

Bury, bury, bury your head,
That's the Mayor's scheme.
No money, no care, no beds anywhere,
AIDS is but a dream!

"Save this for jail," I told them over the applause. "It will drive them CRAZY!"

Heading into the finale, we rocked the house with the rousing counter-point of "*HEALTH! CARE! IS a RIGHT! HEALTH Care IS a RIGHT! (Pump-UP the BUDget!*"), followed by a one-day-only special: "*ACT UP! Stand TALL! To-Morrow Morning at CITY HALL!*" Taking the cue, everyone stood up, clapping and cheering!

From that moment forward, no matter the actions planned, busts taken, fact sheets and fundraising letters written, or meetings, teach-ins, or trainings facilitated—I would be known first and foremost as ACT UP's Chant Queen (or, more elegantly, Chant-euse). While I initially resented it, feeling it reduced me to just a lightweight entertainer rather than a thoughtful and serious activist, I've since come to embrace the title and appreciate the warmth and genuine affection with which it was bestowed.

March 28, 1989: Target City Hall

The Koch administration had angered a lot of people, and almost all the offended constituencies were with us at City Hall the following morning. Over three thousand demonstrators snaked their way past the ever-tempting entrance to the Brooklyn Bridge, as our picket rapidly doubled, tripled, and quadrupled in size until it reached the southern tip of City Hall Park. We were joined by over five hundred cops in riot gear, pulled from every precinct in the city.

The festivities had begun in the early morning hours, when Gran Fury followed the newspaper trucks as they made their way around the city, then opened up the vending machines and replaced the front page of the *New York Times* with their own similarly formatted, four-page wraparound *New York Crimes*, featuring stories about the city's mishandling of the AIDS crisis.[35]

A few hours later, at 7:30 a.m., our demonstration officially kicked off when Peter Staley dropped a huge "**Silence = Death**" banner from the scaffolding atop the Municipal Building, just north of City Hall, as Wave 3, dressed in their white FDA lab coats, wended their way through the curious crowd, handing out palm cards with a sixteen-point "Health Care and AIDS Bill of Rights" printed in English and Spanish.

First in the streets was CHER!, an affinity group made up of the muscle boys of ACT UP's Swim Team and their leather-jacketed, red-lipsticked female counterparts. Though named in honor of the singer-actress-goddess whose picture graced their T-shirts, that didn't stop group members from earnestly explaining to reporters that "CHER!" was really an acronym for "Creative Homosexuals Enduring Reality," or "Commie Homos Engaged in Revolution," or even "Cathy Has Extra Rollers," whatever seemed to cross their minds.[36]

Once CHER! had blocked the Manhattan-bound entrance to the bridge, the other affinity groups began riffing off one another, alternating tactics and locations. Bored of Ed marched with their chalkboard messages decrying the lack of AIDS education in city schools. The Candelabras took Broadway on the east side of City Hall, allowing Seeing Red and Dada to sneak up around and over the police barricades onto City Hall property along the west side. While they were being chased down and arrested, an ad hoc group of business-suited activists and members of La Cocina paraded down the length of City Hall Park carrying signs plastered with copies of *Newsday*'s now infamous "**Koch 'I'm Heterosexual'**" headline, adding rejoinders like "**And I'm Melina Mercouri**," or, as in the sign held by SPREE, dressed in yet another stunning spring ensemble, "**And I'm Cary Grant**."

As the legal picket danced down the sidewalk in joyous block-long conga lines, the Boxtops, members of the Housing Caucus, dashed from the southern tip of the demonstration and set up a makeshift shantytown of cardboard boxes in the middle of the street. The police managed to scoop up only a few of the demonstrators before they were distracted by the Delta Queens, who'd taken over the intersection of Chamber and Center Streets several blocks north. Once the Queens were safely deposited in the waiting police vans, Wave 3 suddenly reemerged from the crowd to block their departure.[37] And everything was caught for posterity by our roving band of DIVA TV videographers.

We ended the morning with two hundred arrests, among them Gerri Wells, who was held for thirty hours on a false outstanding warrant claim.

Gerri, who was an ex-cop,* shrugged off the experience, bragging she'd spent the time leading safe sex teach-ins for her cellmates. But soon, we began to hear of other, more upsetting examples of police bad behavior.

More than two dozen ACT UP women had been subjected to strip searches at two of the police precincts. Having already been targeted with verbal abuse, the activists believed the searches were a deliberate effort to intimidate and humiliate them. They were also illegal.

According to city policy, strip searches were authorized only when an officer suspected an arrestee of carrying a concealed weapon or drugs. Many of the ACT UP women reported they'd never even been patted down or had their pockets searched. Instead, they'd been ordered to disrobe, squat, and bend over, so their body cavities could be searched for drugs. Even after the searches were completed, several of the activists were told they would not be released until they answered questions like "Do you belong to a gang? Do you have tattoos? Are you gay?"[38]

We were furious. I think a lot of the men felt deeply protective of the women in our group—even though many of them were far braver and had been arrested far more times than we had. While ACT UP would have stood by any of its members, there was an added sense of outrage because these women were fighting for *our* lives, even though it was far from clear we would have done the same had the situation been reversed. I think we would have stormed police headquarters had they asked us to, but the women had a better plan. They gave their story as an exclusive to the *New York Times*.[39] The story quickly went national, and the activists were booked for interviews on *Good Morning America* and other talk shows, where they used the interest in the more prurient details of the search to talk about the impact of AIDS on women.

Meanwhile, a preliminary inquiry by the police determined similar illegal searches of women prisoners had been going on for months. Although the police claimed they were the result of "overzealous" individual civilian staff members, it was soon apparent they'd been carried out routinely, primarily against poor women of color who lacked the standing or agency to object.[40]

The search story gave our action—and the accompanying demonstration footage—another week in the news cycle, delivering yet another black eye to the already reeling Koch administration. The story also gave lie once and for all to the charge that ACT UP was composed solely of gay White men.

---

*Gerri had worked in the Child Abuse unit up in Harlem and would often help out by negotiating with the "white shirts," the senior officers, at our demonstrations.

The women of ACT UP, always an integral part of our activism, would become even more prominent in the months to come.

As with many of the other men in the group, my understanding of the connection between so-called women's issues and AIDS had already been deepened, not just by the comments and contributions of the many ACT UP women, but also by the extraordinary "Women and AIDS" teach-in the Women's Caucus had organized in the run-up to Target City Hall.*

To be honest, I'd attended the teach-in mostly out of a sense of obligation and as a gesture of respect rather than out of any burning interest. I assumed it would be a rather narrow discussion of women's health issues—reproductive rights and the like—seasoned with a healthy dose of "isms." Instead, it was a political education, giving me the language to understand and articulate my evolving worldview and a political context for my activism.

I was not unaware of how sexism and racism affected our society. I knew, at least on an abstract level, that as a college-educated White male† I viewed the world from a place of privilege, even as I assumed that being a Jew and a gay man gave me some understanding of what it was like to be an outsider in society—not that it earned me an automatic "Get out of Racism and Sexism Free" card. But it wasn't until AIDS and the "brick wall" experiences of the Helms amendment(s), the city's AIDS numbers fiasco, and the recent election—moments when I felt suddenly invisible and stripped of my personhood—that I began to understand just how privileged I'd been (and continue to be).

---

*The teach-in handbook would be expanded into book form as *Women, AIDS & Activism*, which sought to "advance research by and about women in the AIDS crisis, provide information about women's particular needs, analyze the impact of AIDS on women's lives from a feminist perspective, and promote grassroots activism." The ACT UP/New York Women and AIDS Book Group, *Women, AIDS & Activism* (Boston: South End Press, 1990).

†While I would now add cisgender to this list, it was not a term in use at the time. (See Joanna McIntyre, "Explainer: What Does It Mean to Be 'Cisgender'?" The Conversation, September 18, 2018, http://theconversation.com/explainer-what-does-it-mean-to-be-cisgender-10315.) Coined in academic journals in the 1990s, it didn't gain cultural currency until 2007, after the publication of *Whipping Girl* by trans theorist Julia Serrano. Although ACT UP did have at least one out transgender member at the time, Kathy Ottersten, other members have since identified as nonbinary and trans.

Rather than clobbering us with judgments for current and past transgressions, these activists helped us—the well-meaning, but often politically naïve gay White men who attended the teach-in—to remove our blinders, check our assumptions, and see the deep roots of the attitudes and prejudices that exist in our institutions and culture, and in ourselves.

However tough the situation might be for gay HIV-positive men, women with HIV/AIDS were additionally burdened by the prejudices of a medical system and culture that considered all female functions, from menstruation through pregnancy and menopause, as inherently shameful, and valued women's lives only through their relationship to men. Once infected, women were regarded solely as "vectors of infection," endangering the lives of their children and their (presumed) male sex partners, without any health concerns of their own. Small wonder the few epidemiological studies of women and AIDS tracked either HIV transmission to newborns or the infection rates of sex workers.

Poor pregnant women were often coerced into taking the HIV test, not to determine their own health needs, but to discuss options for their unborn child. If they tested Positive, they were frequently counseled by doctors and health care providers to abort their pregnancy. This was not just ethically reprehensible, but also medically unnecessary. (Studies indicated the risk of perinatal transmission was only 20–40 percent, with the risk decidedly on the lower end if the mother was asymptomatic.)[41]

Similarly, because women were categorized as "potential child bearers," they were routinely prohibited from participating in experimental drug trials—often the only option for accessing treatment and vital AIDS and health care services—unless they first provided proof of contraception or, in an ugly echo of Southern "contraceptive" programs for people of color, agreed to undergo sterilization. The one drug trial where HIV-positive pregnant women were actively being recruited was a study monitoring the health of the baby, and not the mother.

As most women with HIV received their health care solely at times of crisis through clinics and emergency rooms where expensive blood work and diagnostic tests were rarely ordered, they were frequently misdiagnosed. Admittedly, doctors would have been hard-pressed to even consider an HIV-related diagnosis, given the shortcomings of the CDC's AIDS definition, which continued to reflect only those symptoms and diseases first found in gay men. The CDC's refusal to expand their definition to include gynecological indications not only resulted in the vast underreporting of women with HIV but was also a major reason they died at a far faster rate than men.

While the CDC would soon find itself in ACT UP's crosshairs, the spring provided us with a more immediate opportunity to make a direct connection between AIDS activism and women's health issues.

April 9, 1989: NOW March for Women's Lives

While there was never any issue about individual ACT UP members participating in the National Organization for Women's abortion rights march—members had previously participated in the 1987 "Bork Bork" demonstrations* as well as clinic defense efforts during the Operation Rescue actions in July 1988—there remained the question of whether ACT UP should attend as an "official presence." Would we run the risk of diluting our message if we strayed too far from our "AIDS only" focus?

It was a question that would come up regularly during discussions of endorsements or participation in a variety of protests and causes. We called ourselves nonpartisan, but there was little doubt most of the group supported a wide range of liberal-left causes. However, as the teach-in had made clear, the connection between AIDS activism and reproductive rights was fundamental, starting with the basic right of domain over one's body, whether for reproduction, sexual expression, or medical treatment. Further, the AIDS activist movement was predicated on the teachings of the women's health movement, which taught the necessity of becoming "expert" in matters relating to our health, learning about our bodies and how they function, finding alternative methods of accessing information and treatments, and demanding control over our treatment decisions.

The two movements also shared many of the same enemies. The forces aligned against abortion also preached AIDS as divine punishment for homosexuality. More fundamentally, the hatred of homosexuality was grounded in the revulsion against the perceived feminization of gay men, whether in manner or sexual activity, and the fear of truly autonomous women.

But beyond politics, the issues of reproductive rights were central to the lives of many of our members. As Maxine liked to point out, she'd come to

---

*This was the nickname for the protests over the nomination of arch-conservative Robert Bork to the Supreme Court by Ronald Reagan. In addition to being a vocal opponent of *Roe v. Wade* and a promoter of controversial legal theories considered far outside the mainstream of jurisprudence (at the time), Bork was most famous for being the Justice Department appointee who finally carried out Nixon's demand to fire the Watergate special prosecutor Archibald Cox after two attorneys general had refused and resigned, in what became known as the Saturday Night Massacre.

ACT UP as a woman and a lesbian and shouldn't have to leave those identities at the door to be an AIDS activist. Besides, being part of an activist
community—and a coalition—meant supporting things that are important
to other community members.

Although the Floor voted overwhelmingly to add our endorsement and
send an official contingent to the NOW demonstration, they left it up to the
Women's Caucus and those of us participating to determine how best to
present ourselves. While we wanted to maintain our identity as ACT UP
and AIDS activists, we needed to do so in a manner that was respectful of
the goals of the larger march, showing our support while highlighting the
connections between our issues. Alexis Danzig, who was organizing the
action, suggested another equally important mission: to march as a loud,
proud, and queer contingent.

There had been a long history of tension between the women's movement
and its lesbian members. Critics had often tried to discredit and marginalize
the early feminists by calling them "man-haters" and "mannish" radical
lesbians. (P.S.—They still do.) In response, NOW president Betty Friedan
warned of a growing "Lavender Menace" that threatened the potential
success of the entire movement and purged lesbian issues and pioneering
lesbian groups like the Daughters of Bilitis from NOW's First Congress to
Unite Women in 1969.*

Even as NOW and other feminist organizations came to officially endorse
lesbian rights, many of their lesbian members still felt the need to remain
closeted in their political lives so as not to harm the larger movement. By
marching as an openly queer group, we hoped to create a space where
women could openly be both pro-choice and queer, without dividing their
identities or allegiances.

As ACT UP's newly crowned Chant Queen, it was my job to come up
with some chants to express our dual identities. In a fit of early morning
giddiness, I came up with, "*MISS JOAN CRAWford Sure was Clever:
No More Wire Hangers—EVERRRRR!*"—but wisely decided to leave
that one on the bus. Instead, we used a chant that clearly articulated who
we were and what we stood for: "*ACT UP! WE'RE HERE! We're LOUD
and RUDE, Pro-CHOICE and QUEER!*" And judging from the scores
of women who leapt into the street to join us, we achieved our goal.

---

*A year later, a group of radical lesbian members famously zapped the Second NOW
Congress, taking over the meeting wearing purple "Lavender Menace" T-shirts and leading a
speak-out on lesbian issues.

A Different David

One evening, I received an unexpected call from my friend David Wayne, who was coming into town and asked if we could get together for lunch and maybe a matinee.

I'd met David just a few months before I joined ACT UP, when I was in LA, still touring with my Jewish Children's Theater troupe. Young, attractive, with tight pants and a new-wave mullet, David worked as an assistant at one of the smart synagogues in Bel Air where we were performing. We flirted, enjoyed a brief fling, and parted as friends.

I hadn't seen David in over two years, but from the moment I saw him, I knew. Even from across the street, I knew. He had "the look"—the big eyes and knifelike sharpness of his cheekbones. The skin pulled tight at the temples. I knew in an instant.

Of course, I said nothing. It was his news to share or not. So, we gave each other a big hug and chattered on about movies and theater, while I silently wondered if I'd need to look surprised if and when he told me.

Finally, as we waited for coffee, we stopped our tap dancing.

He confided he'd just come out of a bad couple of months, but now he was on AZT and aerosolized pentamidine and doing better. I nodded and held his hand and we talked about doctors and drug regimens, instead of the latest Sondheim musical, and I offered to send him any information he might need.

I saw David again briefly when I visited LA later that spring, but then we lost touch. I wouldn't even think about him again until a few years later when I received a letter from an unfamiliar California address.

Inside was a handwritten note from David's mother. She was writing, she said, to all of the names in David's address book. She apologized for the delay. But she just wanted to let us know her son, David, was gone.

DAVID WAYNE (196?–199?)
May his memory be for a blessing.

Chapter 10

Storming the Ivory Tower

June 4–9, 1989: The Montreal AIDS Conference

The International AIDS Conference had always been a "members-only" affair, a place where scientists and public health officials could hobnob with their fellow wizards while dining on the largesse of their pharmaceutical sponsors and basking in the unquestioning admiration of a doting press.[1] Though there'd been some minor disruptions at the 1987 conference in Washington, people with AIDS had been present mainly in the abstract: as numbers on a spreadsheet or footnotes in a scientific paper.

The Fifth International AIDS Conference in Montreal promised to be different.

The conference organizers, the venerable International AIDS Society, had expanded the meeting agenda beyond the traditional science-only forums to include a "social issues" track that would attempt to address patient care and the social, political, economic, and legal implications of the epidemic. The IAS had also, for the first time, made an effort to include doctors and organizations from Asia and Africa, which were rapidly becoming the new frontiers of the global pandemic. Nonetheless, the voices of people living with HIV/AIDS remained largely absent.

ACT UP was determined to be that voice. We spent $14,000 we didn't have to register twenty-eight activists to attend the conference. Jim Eigo, Mark Harrington, and Iris Long each won slots to give poster presentations—public displays of their research abstracts—on topics ranging from FDA reform and alternative models for clinical trials, to the enrollment figures of existing trials as uncovered by the AIDS Treatment Registry and the need for community-based pneumo-clinics to administer T-cell tests and dispense PCP prophylaxis.

As a cynical commentary on the intellectual bankruptcy of much of what passed for AIDS research, Mark had submitted an abstract entitled "Viral Dialectics in the Soul Music of Prince." When it inexplicably won a presentation slot, Mark had to race to come up with an actual paper defending his thesis of HIV-awareness and disease theory in the song catalogue of His Purpleness.

But our objectives went beyond merely observing and influencing research. The AIDS conference was the one time of the year when all the major media from around the world would focus their attention on AIDS. This was a chance for us not only to affect the coverage of the conference but to change the media's narrative of the AIDS epidemic worldwide.

Working with the Toronto-based AIDS Action Now!, we planned a week of eye-catching, media-friendly actions to "hijack the conference" and create an activist counternarrative to the congratulatory press releases issuing from the conference. To bolster our chances, we doubled down on our initial outlay and sent a second bus of activists up to Montreal to take part in a big opening day protest and the first few days of street actions.

It was a huge gamble, one that came close to bankrupting us, but we'd always been able to find the money before, and it seemed much too important an opportunity to pass up.

Granted, things didn't look too promising at the outset.

Our first demonstration at the Canadian border—where we'd planned to test rumors about PWAs being denied entry into Canada by announcing we all had AIDS—fizzled when our bus entered the country without incident, save the late realization that our bilingual T-shirts had misgendered the virus—it's "le SIDA," not "la SIDA"—causing a frantic scramble for sharpies and eyebrow pencils to correct the offending vowel.

Then, on the opening day of the conference, we found ourselves relegated to a remote and largely untrafficked side of the Palais des Congrès, far away from the main plaza entrance, the media, and conference attendees. Even with a crowd of three hundred protesters, including Canadian activists from AIDS Action Now! and Montreal's newly formed Réaction SIDA, it seemed unlikely anyone would notice we were there.

Out of deference to our hosts, and despite much grumbling up and down the picket line, we decided to stay put, politely marching on the sidewalk in discreet circles, until Alan Shaw dashed across the grass and grabbed the handle of an unattended fire door . . . *Click*.

And like Dorothy stepping into Oz, we marched through the open door and into the Technicolor world of the main exhibition hall.

"Not VICTIMS! Not PATIENTS! But PEOPLE LIVING with AIDS!"

We snaked through the endless rows of shiny trade booths plastered with photos of face-masked scientists and smiling doctors, past Burroughs Wellcome and Hoffmann-La Roche, past the three-dimensional HIV displays and the stacks of brochures hawking the latest new drug, past GMHC and AmFAR, past the bowls of condoms and the sexy safe sex posters in German and Swedish.

Then, just as we began circling back to the main entrance, I saw Billy Heekin and his "**Silence = Death**" sign slowly gliding up the escalator. I was so surprised it took me a few moments to register what had happened. Then I saw a few more posters floating upward. I turned and began pointing frantically at the escalator while shouting, *"ACT UP! FIGHT BACK! FIGHT AIDS! ACT UP! FIGHT BACK! FIGHT AIDS!"*

Everyone stopped, turned, and looked . . .

And with a huge roar, we surged toward the escalators, overwhelming the decorative pair of Mounties trying to block our way, and then headed up, miraculously up the escalator, down the aisles of the Grand Assembly Hall, and up onto the stage.

"The AIDS! CRISIS! KNOWS NO BORDERS! The AIDS! CRISIS! KNOWS NO BORDERS!"

Squinting through the glare of the stage lights, I was surprised to see the neatly attired crowd of doctors, nurses, scientists, and public health officials all standing and clapping, as if welcoming the arrival of the victorious home team. While we ran through our chant repertoire, our Canadian comrades negotiated with the conference organizers, demanding they turn on the microphones so we could properly address the crowd. Finally, Tim McCaskell of AIDS Action Now! stepped up to the podium.

"On behalf of people with AIDS from Canada and around the world, I would like to officially open this Fifth International Conference on AIDS!"

The entire hall burst into cheers.

Reluctant to give up the microphone, we sent Conyers Thompson up to read *The Montreal Manifesto,* our "Declaration of the Universal Rights and Needs of People Living with HIV Disease," in both English and French. The *Manifesto* was modeled after the 1983 Denver Principles, but rather than enumerating the rights of PWAs, it focused on the other side of the equation: the responsibilities of medical professionals, researchers, governments, and institutions for ensuring the health and well-being of people with HIV/AIDS.[2] Both documents, however, shared the central radical and animating idea, inherited from the women's health movement—that people with HIV/AIDS must be active participants in the decision-making that affects their lives and their bodies, whether determining their personal course of treatment or setting the priorities for AIDS research.

In exchange for getting the mic turned on, our Canadian colleagues had promised the organizers we'd leave the hall once we had addressed the conference and "made our point," so when Conyers finished his readings, we reluctantly filed offstage and began marching out of the auditorium to great applause.

I'd made it about halfway up the aisle when I heard a loud commotion behind me. I turned and saw my friends scrambling for seats in the empty VIP section. Suddenly, it was like musical chairs, with everyone running back down the aisles trying to grab a seat before the music ended.

The cheering stopped and an uneasy standoff began. The conference organizers were furious and refused to start the ceremonies until we left. They blamed the Canadian activists, who, in turn, were angry with us for breaking their agreement with the organizers, but still we refused to budge. "We're the VIPs!" yelled one activist. "I don't want to be a Quilt!" shouted another.

"WE Be-LONG HERE! WE Be-LONG HERE!"

And it dawned on me that this exactly was our point. We *did* belong here. We were not just some activist floor show there to give the proceedings a frisson of anger and urgency. *Fuck that.* Time was running out.

"START the CONFERENCE!"

Word filtered down that the president of Zambia was threatening to cancel his keynote speech due to our insulting behavior and concerns about his security. Canadian prime minister Brian Mulroney was likewise debating whether he would appear. But even as the minutes ticked by and the once supportive crowd turned against us, I realized I wasn't afraid. I trusted these people, my ACT UP comrades, and knew whatever happened and whatever the consequences, we were all in it together and I'd be fine.

As Jim, Mark, and Peter Staley took turns on the bullhorn announcing the upcoming press conference for ACT UP's *National AIDS Treatment Research Agenda*, the rest of us huddled together working toward our consensus decision: This was *our* conference. We'd come to demand our rightful place as people with HIV/AIDS and their advocates, and having won that place, we would not relinquish it.

Finally, after what felt like an endless stalemate, the organizers agreed. We could stay, as long as we were willing to shift a couple of rows back to create a security zone for the president of Zambia. We did so immediately. Then the lights dimmed, and the opening ceremonies began.

It was not at all what I expected.

First, a youth string ensemble came on stage and played two mournful pieces to remind us, I suppose, that this was a somber occasion and AIDS a serious disease. Next up, a short film about teenagers and AIDS entitled *At Risk*, which presented a world where only heterosexual teens were in danger. From the VIP section, we rewarded the film with a chorus of boos.

"What's missing from this picture?" "Homosexuals!"

And with that, any doubts I had about remaining inside the conference quickly vanished. But while our passionate commentary may have added a necessary note of reality to the proceedings, it also resulted in our worst moment of the conference, when a pocket of activists hissed Dame Nita Barrow, the UN representative from Barbados, for using the term "AIDS victim" when describing the tragic effects of AIDS and poverty on villages in the Caribbean.

Activists had been trying to persuade the media and public figures to stop using the phrase "AIDS victim," as it reduced people struggling to live with the disease to helpless victims and made the disease their defining feature. You'd have thought, however, we'd be able to practice a little cultural sensitivity of our own and, given her background and the importance of her message, overlook Dame Barrow's linguistic faux pas. Sadly, nuance was never our collective strong suit. I could only share despairing looks with my friends as Dame Barrow—who had no idea what she'd said to inspire such a negative response—bravely soldiered on.

Fortunately, Zambian president Kenneth Kaunda, who'd sadly lost his son to AIDS, managed to avoid the toxic phrase and ended the afternoon on an inspiring note, calling on the nations of the world "to divert our massive resource of dollars and rubles wasted on self-destruction through nuclear weapons to the more worthwhile destruction of AIDS."[3]

It had been a remarkable day. We'd accomplished even more than we'd dared hope. For once, our press release was not hyperbole; we *had* "altered these conferences forever."[4] But when we turned on the evening news to relive our triumph, we could only stare at the TV in disbelief as the newscaster read the litany of the day's events: prodemocracy protesters massacred in Tiananmen Square; Iran's Ayatollah Khomeini dead at the age of eighty-six; hundreds of Russians killed in a train explosion in Siberia; Poland holding its first democratic election; and then, finally, AIDS activists take over the International AIDS Conference.

The news from Tiananmen Square hit us all very hard. We'd identified with those brave Chinese students—not that our struggles were the same (nor our enemies, nor the consequences we faced), but we were inspired by their bravery. Even though they knew nothing of us, we felt united in a common struggle for justice, a global moment of hope and possibility. People everywhere were peaceably rising up to change the world—by year's end, the Berlin Wall would fall—yet, watching the footage of the tanks rolling into the square, it all suddenly felt hopeless.[*]

The following morning, I was jolted from my sleep by the shrill clanging of a school bell. Rather than springing for a hotel room, I'd taken the eight-dollar-a-night accommodations at the Collège Français, which, instead of the expected dorm, turned out to be an actual school where some of the larger classrooms had been tricked up with cots. What we hadn't known, having settled in over the weekend, was that school was still in session.

---

[*]The conference center was located next to Montreal's Chinatown district, and like many of our group, I drifted over there looking for some way to contribute. When a march was announced a few days later, organized by Chinese students studying in Montreal, we did what we could to help. We translated our **"Silence = Death"** posters into Mandarin and several other Chinese dialects and wore protest headbands with Chinese lettering. During the march, we also informally pitched in with marshalling the crowd, stopping traffic when necessary, and helping with chants (albeit in English).

While I staggered off to the school gym to take a shower, dodging the small children dashing all around me, my comrades were responding to a different alarm over at the Palais des Congrès, where our old nemesis, Stephen Joseph, was addressing the Morning Plenary. Although slated to offer "lessons" based on New York City's experience with the AIDS epidemic, we'd since learned he was planning to announce a new proposal to end the city's anonymous HIV testing policy and begin name reporting and contract tracing.[5]

Anonymous testing was a pillar of AIDS policy—a way to guarantee no one would be put on some list, lose their home or insurance, or be thrown into quarantine because they'd tested positive for HIV. Given the public stigma, the lack of antidiscrimination protections, and the continuing panic about the imagined dangers of AIDS transmission, the threat of name reporting could further drive the disease underground, increasing infection rates and preventing people from getting treatment.

With the doors of the Palais safely locked and guarded, only activists with official ID badges were allowed inside for the morning session. (Sadly, Richard Deagle's stack of counterfeit badges wouldn't arrive until later that afternoon.) Nonetheless, what began as a silent protest quickly became a verbal scuffle as the commissioner explained his tortured HIV statistics, rising to an angry crescendo as he tried to cast a rosy glow on the city's shameful AIDS record.[6]

Then it got worse.

Claiming recent advances in AIDS prophylaxis and treatment had made it imperative for public health policy to "shift towards a disease control approach to HIV infection along the lines of classic tuberculosis practices," Joseph proposed a series of radical policy changes, including the "reporting of seropositives, follow-up to assure adequate treatment, and more aggressive contact tracing."[7] Or at least that's what it said in his printed remarks, because certainly no one heard it inside the hall, where his comments were drowned out by a barrage of chants and catcalls.

The confrontation continued at the post-plenary press conference, where the commissioner was pelted with questions, many from ACT UP members and sympathizers attending the conference as journalists. While Joseph fiercely defended the city's ability to maintain the confidentiality of HIV records, he was forced to admit testing and contact tracing at the level proposed would take millions of dollars the city didn't have, and the added caseload would sink the city's already overburdened health care system. Nor could he explain how the city would pay for the promised treatments for the newly diagnosed. "It is cruel and almost a hoax to talk about the clinical advantages of knowing one's HIV status," charged Ron Johnson, the executive director of the city's Minority AIDS Task Force, "while at the same time knowing the realities of the public health care system which so many people in black and Latino communities are dependent upon."[8]

ACT UP was joined in its condemnation of Joseph's proposals by almost every major New York–based AIDS service and advocacy group, none of whom had been consulted prior to his announcement, including the New York City AIDS Task Force, which he chaired.[9] Upon his return to New York days later, Joseph would be greeted by hundreds of protesters marching outside his offices chanting, *"FIRST you DON'T EXIST! NOW You're ON His LIST!"* and demanding his resignation. Two weeks later, still reeling from continued pressure from a unified AIDS community, the mayor publicly disavowed Joseph's proposal.

Though I'd missed the morning fireworks, I scored a fake badge that afternoon and headed inside to attend some of the "social issues" panels. I was very aware of the discomfort my activist presence was causing, but I knew it was necessary—both as a threat and as a physical embodiment of the crisis. I pushed myself to speak up, challenging inaccurate statements and lofty academic theories that bore little resemblance to the realities of our lives, and was gratified my comments were often seconded by community doctors and health care providers who now had the space to share their own frontline experiences.

June 6, 1989: ACT UP's Treatment Agenda

On Tuesday afternoon, ACT UP unveiled its *National AIDS Treatment Research Agenda*. Tired of waiting for scientists, drug sponsors, and federal regulators to develop a comprehensive strategy, we'd come up with our own: a "set of guidelines for a sweeping revision to US AIDS research and regulatory priorities."[10]

Most drug trials focused almost exclusively on the interests of scientists and pharmaceutical companies—what was needed to get a drug approved—rather than on the needs of patients. Given the FDA's well-known preference for "clean data," this meant participants not only risked receiving placebos in place of medication but were also required to forgo prophylactic treatments for PCP and other opportunistic infections in order to keep the data "pure." This further allowed researchers to use death and disease progression as clinical "endpoints" to determine if a drug was working or not, regardless of whether other treatments might have saved the participant's life or prevented them from getting sick.

We argued that for PWAs, these trials were health care—the only way they could access the treatments and support services they needed to stay alive. Therefore, trials had to be designed "for the real world: prophylaxis permitted, placebos avoided, efficacy criteria and endpoints humane,"[11] and, most importantly, open to the entire range of people with HIV and AIDS.

Due to strict eligibility criteria, most trial participants were gay White men. Women were excluded due to fears about the potential impact on an unborn fetus and IV drug users because they were assumed to be unreliable research subjects. Poor people, though not explicitly excluded, were also eliminated due to "lifestyle variables" (e.g., inconsistent medical care, lack of stable housing, diet, or employment) that could complicate the desired "pure" trial results.

These exclusions were not just unethical, they were bad science. It's why no one knew AZT caused extreme anemia in IV drug users until the drug was already in the marketplace. Only by including these populations in their trials would researchers begin to understand how a drug worked in the real world and across the entire spectrum of potential users. As a bonus, it would also speed up enrollment by expanding the pool of potential participants.

To ensure the needs of patients were addressed, we demanded people with AIDS, HIV, and their advocates participate as equal partners in the design and execution of drug trials and in setting the priorities for AIDS treatment research. Only then could we create a "comprehensive, coordinated, compassionate drug development strategy that [ensured] all promising agents . . . are evaluated thoroughly and, if found effective, distributed rapidly."[12]

In addition to pointing out the failures of current AIDS research, we also provided solutions. These included, most importantly, Jim Eigo's "parallel track" proposal, which would allow people who were otherwise ineligible to participate in clinical trials to access promising new drugs as soon as they proved safe and minimally effective. This "treatment protocol" would run concurrently with Phase II clinical trials, but with far fewer restrictions—it would be "open label," meaning everyone would get the drug, and would expand eligibility criteria to ensure that anyone who might benefit from these new medications could have access to them.

Jim's proposal, which he first presented before a federal panel in early May,* had taken on added urgency with reports of two new promising

---

*On May 2, 1989, Jim, Mark Harrington, and Iris Long appeared before the National Committee to Review Current Procedures for Approval of New Drugs for Cancer and AIDS— a.k.a. the Lasagna Committee, named for its chair, Dr. Louis Lasagna.

antiviral treatments—ddI and ddC. As things stood, the people who most needed these new drugs—the more than 50 percent of PWAs who were either intolerant or no longer responsive to AZT—would likely be ineligible to participate in Phase II trials. Their only hope would be a program like parallel track.

The *Agenda* also included a list of "AIDS Clinical Research Priorities," starting with the "5 Drugs We Need Now"*—treatments that had been proven safe and demonstrated some degree of efficacy but were stalled in the drug approval process—and "7 Treatments We Want Tested Faster"†—drugs that were further behind in the pipeline but displayed early indications of effectiveness. More broadly, we proposed expanding antiviral research to include new approaches like protease and viral binding inhibitors, which attacked the virus at different stages in its life cycle, as well as the exploration of various immune-boosting therapies. Given over 80 percent of PWAs contracted one of the five major opportunistic infections,‡ we also demanded an increased emphasis on researching prophylactic treatments and outlined suggestions for well-designed, quickly executed studies that could make opportunistic infections rare within two years.

> AIDS advocates have identified the systematic problems afflicting the scientific and regulatory body politic. The point is to solve them. As citizens of this country, we have the right to demand that our government deploy its resources to save the most lives right now. Those with the power to redirect our nation's AIDS research effort must listen to and work with us. We will not rest until they do so.[13]

While a non-story for most of the press, the *Agenda* proved a revelation for many of the researchers—all the more so because it was produced, not by scientists, but by patients. Along with the requisite glow-in-the-dark

---

*These included the antiviral ddI; the antifungal fluconazole for treating cryptococcal meningitis; foscarnet, a non–bone marrow–suppressive treatment for CMV; EPO, which could fight HIV and AZT-related anemia; and GM-CSF, which reverses the bone marrow toxicity of AZT, DHPG, and cancer chemotherapy. ACT UP, *A National AIDS Treatment Research Agenda*, V International Conference on AIDS, Montreal, June 1989, 8–9.

†Including potential treatments for MAI (ansamycin) and cryptosporidiosis (diclazuril); two antiviral agents—hypericin, an herbal extract, and peptide T, a nontoxic sequence of amino acids; two second-generation CD4 drugs; and passive immunotherapy, where plasma rich in HIV antibodies is injected into people with AIDS. ACT UP, *A National AIDS Treatment Research Agenda*, 9–10.

‡*Pneumocysis carinii* pneumonia (PCP), cytomegalovirus (CMV), *Mycobacterium avium-intracellulare* (MAI), toxoplasmosis, and cryptococcal meningitis. ACT UP, *A National AIDS Treatment Agenda*, 11.

condoms and ACT UP's "Silence = Death" buttons, the *Agenda* quickly became one of the must-have souvenirs of the conference.

Receiving far less attention were issues concerning women and AIDS. "The greatest risk behaviour for women all over the world is unsafe sex with men," said Tracy Tief, a Toronto-based "former occasional sex worker," at our Wednesday protest against lesbian invisibility and the scapegoating of sex workers. "Do we call heterosexual men vectors of infection? Do we call for quarantine for men who don't wear condoms?"[14]

Also missing was any discussion about the possibility of woman-to-woman transmission. Controversial even within the lesbian community, the issue was largely dismissed, or worse, ridiculed by some like AIDS reporter Randy Shilts, who waved away concerns about lesbian transmissibility as "nothing more than political posturing."[15]

Certainly, the CDC didn't see any reason for concern, refusing to even keep statistics on woman-to-woman transmission, although such cases had already been documented.* Nor had they conducted any studies on cunnilingus as a method of HIV transmission or the presence of HIV in menstrual blood and vaginal secretions. Given the CDC's shoddy track record, however, their disinterest was hardly cause for comfort.

When conference security guards finally caught on to our fake-ID gambit, Tim Powers, who headed up our PISD (People with Immune System Disorders) Caucus, became point person in negotiations with conference president Ivan Head to improve PWA and community access to the conference.

Sweet, shy, and heavyset, with a distracted, often apologetic manner that reminded me of Ferdinand the Bull, Tim was an unlikely spokesperson. Yet,

---

*The CDC counted lesbians among the general population of women, whether they were infected through needles, unsafe sex with men, or an "unknown mechanism," which accounted for 8 percent of all cases of women with AIDS. ACT UP press release: "Background on the Centers for Disease Control," January 1990.

when his moment came, he proved a focused and fearless advocate for ACT UP and for the rights of PWAs. (He was also, for a brief time that summer, my roommate, sleeping in my living room on my wobbly foam sofa bed.) Not only did Tim get the conference to waive the $500 delegate fee for fifty people with AIDS, he also obtained promises for similar accommodations and additional PWA outreach and support efforts at future conferences.

But the conference was hardly all work and no play, not even for activists.

Every night after hours, the streets and bars of Le Village, Montreal's gay neighborhood, were packed with a combustible combination of French Canadian locals and horny conference attendees. While my friends and I managed to cruise most of the local bars, discos, and strip clubs, I let them venture into Montreal's still-thriving bathhouses on their own. This was no moral judgment on my part, but rather a matter of self-preservation.

Despite my long-standing curiosity, I'd never been to a bathhouse. Given my general exhaustion, not to mention my strong attraction to French (and French Canadian) men, I was also afraid of what I might do in such a tempting and unfamiliar environment. It was more than just the possibility of having unsafe sex, it was also about what I might discover and unlock in myself. What if I enjoyed it, loved the anonymity and abandon? What if I lost, or rather, gave up control and indulged my fantasies? Once I'd opened that door, would I be able to close it again? Would I even want to? And could I count on myself, in the heat of passion, to stay safe this time and the next and the next and the next?

For me, the risk was too high; so, I avoided the situation entirely. What I didn't know, taste, or experience, quite literally, wouldn't kill me.

Besides, I was still perfectly capable of getting in trouble with my clothes on.

On Wednesday night, the local activists threw a big party for ACT UP and the other visiting activist groups at *Club Foufones Electrique* (which translates as "Electric Asses"). It was a big, let-your-hair-down affair at this edgy "downtown" club, with a DJ, an outdoor patio, and *beaucoup* booze. While the early crowd was strictly activists and fellow travelers, more locals appeared as the evening progressed. Among the vanguard were two good-looking French Canadian men—one probably about my age, the other a few years younger—in business suits.

The older one—tall, dark black hair and moustache, effortlessly charming in the French manner—approached me first and, in perfect English, turned and introduced me to his younger friend, whose English was not so good, but who had other desirable qualities. For one, he was adorable. Smaller than his friend, compact and sinewy, with sandy brown hair and a sweet smile. Even better, he seemed totally infatuated with me.

The two of them took turns buying me drinks and passing me smokes. I tried to keep pace with them, but I'd been running on soggy croissants and coffee for days. It was intoxicating—all that attention, all that alcohol, all that French. Meanwhile, my young friend kept telling me, in his fractured, heavily accented English, how sexy I was. This, as anyone who's tried it can tell you, is my sucker punch. He tried to explain how new he was to all this—"I don't usually . . . you know, wiz men, but . . . unh . . . you are so . . . pwhhhh."

Things quickly accelerated. We left his friend and wandered out back to the darkened patio. I began to hint around about continuing our, um, conversation elsewhere. Since I was, by this time, sharing the floor of a hotel room with four or five other activists, it would have to be his place. He began to hesitate, waffling rather sweetly between his desire to continue and his wariness about being with a guy ("but you—pwhhhhh"). He explained—I think—that he lived just outside of Montreal with his family. I kept pressing. He said he would have to sneak me in tonight and sneak me out tomorrow morning. *Sounds hot—let's go! Vite! Vite!*

But alas, after a good half hour of back and forth, he apologized, gave me a terrific farewell kiss, got into his car, and left.

It remained for his dark and dashing friend to console me. He bought me another drink, allowed me some time to adjust to my new reality, and then played his hand. He knew what he wanted and went for it calmly, but directly. And while he was momentarily taken aback when I revealed my last name was Goldberg—he was, I believe, of French-Arab descent—the evening had progressed too far to let ancient blood rivalries impede our plans.

I arrived late for the next morning's plenary, where a coalition of AIDS advocacy groups led by David Barr, an ACT UP member who also worked as an attorney for Lambda Legal, was presenting a response to the HIV travel restrictions that had been put into place by the host nation of next year's AIDS conference, the U.S. of A.

The policy dated back to April 1986, when then–attorney general Ed Meese asked the Public Health Service to add AIDS to its list of "dangerous and contagious diseases." A year later, the PHS followed up with a White House–driven directive officially adding AIDS to the list, thereby denying entry to tourists infected with HIV and requiring the mandatory testing of all potential immigrants. Congress then codified this policy, thanks to yet another of Jesse Helms's always helpful amendments.

This left everyone wondering whether people with HIV would be allowed into the country to attend next year's conference in San Francisco. As if to prove the point, just days before this year's event, two HIV-positive individuals had been detained—one on his way to the conference, the other en route to San Francisco to participate in an experimental drug trial. And there were reports of other delegates who couldn't attend because they couldn't get the thirty-day HIV visa waiver in time.

David and his colleagues had gathered signatures throughout the week for their statement condemning HIV travel restrictions and demanding the IAS "seek assurances" from the US government that no one who wished to attend next year's conference would be denied entry because of their HIV status. And in a proposal approved by acclamation during the morning plenary session, they instructed the IAS to plan all future conferences "only in countries permitting entry of HIV infected travelers."[16]

That afternoon, Henry Yeager buttonholed me and asked that I join him at the annual IAS meeting to ensure the doors we'd forced open in Montreal remained open at next year's conference. Henry was one of our more senior members—a veteran activist who knew that diligence and perseverance were the keys to keeping bureaucracies and institutions honest. He was far less shocked than I when the IAS began blithely planning future conferences in countries and regions that still maintained HIV travel restrictions.*

When we pointed out that their plans were in direct conflict with the wishes expressed at the plenary, the IAS leaders patiently explained that since these countries would no doubt agree to waive their travel restrictions for the duration of the conference, there was no conflict; people with HIV would be able to attend. When we countered that while fine for conference attendees, this did nothing for PWAs who might want to visit when the conference wasn't in session or who lived under these restrictions, they

---

*These included Japan and the Bavarian region of Germany, as well as the US.

looked at us like we were crazy. They repeated their explanation, talking slowly and deliberately, as if we were children not yet old enough to understand grown-up rules. They simply could not fathom that they might have a responsibility to PWAs that extended beyond the conference.

It was the first time I witnessed the shortsightedness that frequently afflicted public officials, one which I'd see again and again—the idea that their responsibilities extended only as far as the people directly in front of them. That if they got those individuals in the room with them the requested drugs, services, or waiver, they'd fulfilled their obligation to the entire community.

As we were getting nowhere with our arguments, Henry proposed, and I seconded, a resolution using the exact language from the morning statement, "That the International AIDS Society will plan future International AIDS Conferences only in countries permitting entry of HIV infected travelers."[17] When we were told we couldn't make a motion unless we were IAS members, we both joined on the spot. Ballots were later mailed out to the entire membership, and when the votes were tabulated, the Yeager-Goldberg amendment passed decisively.

Although it was too late to change arrangements for next year's conference in San Francisco, the IAS was forced to move the 1992 conference from Boston to Amsterdam. The US would not host another AIDS conference until 2012, after President Barack Obama finally lifted the HIV travel restrictions.*

Not everyone was thrilled with our proposals, challenges, and interventions. Rumors swirled that many big-name scientists were debating whether to attend next year's conference. "I would like to choose who I interact with," sniffed HIV "discoverer" Dr. Robert Gallo. "We didn't expect this amount of diversity."[18] Right, countered Jim Eigo. "Nothing contaminates pure science quite like a live patient does."[19]

The scientists' carping was picked up and amplified by the press, many of whom, as science reporters, were not used to testy interactions and were put off by our "inappropriate" behavior. Leading the charge was ace AIDS reporter, Randy Shilts.

---

*XIX International AIDS Conference would take place in Washington, DC, July 22–27, 2012.

Expressing anger can give you a warm, fuzzy feeling inside, but this conference is not supposed to be a therapy session. It's supposed to help solve the problem posed by AIDS. It is not enough to be angry, if that anger is not paired with intelligence about its best tactical timing and its best strategic targets. Anger which does not produce results, anger that does not move us forward . . . that too is irrelevant.[20]

Shilts, for all his other skills and insights, never really understood ACT UP. While comfortable with narratives of individual heroes and villains, he neither trusted nor understood movements and communities. He also seemed confused that while we often staged actions with the media in mind, we were not seeking their approval but only using them to reach our real targets.

But even Shilts had to admit ACT UP had pushed the ball forward. So, while he grudgingly acknowledged our impact on AIDS funding or our ability to draw attention to treatment issues, he disapproved of the tactics that enabled us to do so. He seemed incapable of understanding our inside/outside, good cop/bad cop dynamic, or the synergy between what he perceived to be our unruly demonstrations and our more nuanced critiques of drug trials. He also failed to acknowledge what we already knew—these AIDS conferences had long since stopped being a venue for measured scientific inquiry and discourse. It was a stage, a media opportunity for scientists, government institutions, and drug companies. And now, for people with AIDS.

Each delegate, all the organizers, and every government official will remember that people with HIV disease demand to be included in the decisions that affect our lives. . . . From now until a cure is found, the voices of people who are living with HIV infection will be included.[21]

Chapter 11

Remember Stonewall
Was a Riot

FOR MOST OF America, "AIDS" and "gay" had become inextricably tied together. In much the same way, ACT UP was becoming synonymous with gay activism.

But "AIDS" and "gay" were not the same thing, nor had ACT UP ever claimed it was a gay organization or that AIDS was the only issue facing the gay community. However, there's no question it was *because* AIDS was first identified as a "gay disease"—literally, as Gay-Related Immune Deficiency (GRID)—that it was ignored and allowed to grow into a crisis. Or that the continuing perception of AIDS as something that happened only to gay men and other unpopular groups was why a health crisis had turned into a political one.

Which is why it was so important for ACT UP to fight AIDS not by hiding in some rhetorical closet as generic "Americans" but as out and proud gay people. The only way we could truly fight for our lives was by embracing and proclaiming the very identities for which we were being attacked—which, I would later discover, was much the same argument Hannah Arendt put forth about Jews wishing to fight anti-Semitism.*

But what did it mean to fight for our lives as gay Americans?

---

*"One truth that is unfamiliar to the Jewish people, though they are beginning to learn it, is that *you can only defend yourself as the person you are attacked as.* A person attacked as a Jew cannot defend himself as an Englishman or Frenchman. The world would only conclude that he is simply not defending himself." Hannah Arendt, *The Jewish Writings*, ed. Jerome Kohn and Ron H. Feldman (New York: Schocken Books, 2007), 137.

In anticipation of the upcoming twentieth anniversary of the Stonewall Riots, a number of us formed a small study group and set out to find our queer activist past.* We undertook this as a political act, an attempt to reclaim our hidden history—one neither taught in classrooms nor passed down around the kitchen table. We'd then share our discoveries through a series of teach-ins and by creating a handbook, *A His & Herstory of Queer Activism.*[1]

I was fascinated by the two major post-Stonewall gay liberation groups, the Gay Liberation Front (GLF) and the Gay Activist Alliance (GAA), and the ways in which ACT UP embodied aspects of both organizations. (The similarities would continue to reveal themselves over time, as the divisions that separated those two groups would soon appear in our own.)

While ACT UP, like GAA, may have organized around a single issue (AIDS and Gay Rights, respectively), our politics aspired to the broader-based intersectionality of GLF. We acknowledged the roles the linked oppressions of racism, sexism, and homophobia had played in the creation and escalation of the AIDS crisis and understood the connections between AIDS and the related epidemics of homelessness, drugs, and poverty. But critically, unlike GLF, we were not revolutionary. Our goal wasn't to tear down the system—at least not initially—but to make it work better.

Tactically, ACT UP followed much of the GAA model, most notably in our use of "zaps," which had been brought to us by veteran GAA members like Marty Robinson,† as well as our eager embrace of camp humor and ridicule as part of our political arsenal. I even discovered instances where our own demonstrations were eerily similar to those carried out by GAA, without having been aware of their provenance.

Though our identity-based caucuses and affinity groups may have resembled some of GLF's cells and consciousness-raising groups, we didn't look down on the sexualized "bar culture" but, like GAA, celebrated gay sexuality. Though we didn't have our own GAA Firehouse, we hung out in ACT UP–friendly bars and dance clubs and promoted sex positivity as part of our mission—not only as AIDS prevention work, but as a political act to combat a pervasive societal homophobia that equated gay life with death.

---

*Members of The Lesbian & Gay Activist History Project included Macky Alston, Walter Armstrong, Mark Bronnenberg, David Deitcher, Heidi Dorow, David Douglas, Peter Fleming, Robert Garcia, Ron Goldberg, Greg Lugliani, Maria Maggenti, Jon Nalley, and Polly Thistlethwaite.

†Other ACT UP members who were GAA veterans included Bill Bahlman, Jim Fouratt, Marc Rubin, and Vito Russo.

However, not everyone in the community was happy with ACT UP as the new face of gay activism.

Although almost everyone questioned the appropriateness of our tactics at some point, including me, there were certain members of the "gay establishment" who, while professing to approve of the idea of direct action, found us always too angry and confrontational, always targeting the wrong people at the wrong time. Such was our yearly interaction with Heritage of Pride (HOP), which organized the annual Gay Pride parade.

At ACT UP's first Pride in 1987, it was our Concentration Camp float that prompted their hand-wringing. In 1988, it was our zap of Mayor Koch during his annual Pride Month proclamation ceremony that sparked outrage.

While everyone agreed Koch was an appropriate target and AIDS an important issue, much was made of the timing of our demonstration, which coincided with the opening of a photo exhibit celebrating gay history at City Hall's Tweed Gallery. Typical was a letter from four self-anointed community leaders, calling us "a band of screaming activists who seem bent on working against the causes of their own community," and further wondering, "If AIDS is not a gay disease, as we so regularly protest, why does ACT UP choose to ruin a Gay Pride event?"[2]

Their suggestion that AIDS was an inappropriate topic at a gay event was, of course, absurd; but as their letter was sent not to ACT UP, but to the *Daily News, New York Post*, and the *Native*, it was clear we were not the real audience for their deliciously self-serving complaints. It was, instead, just another round in the ongoing gay political turf war over who was qualified to be the "legitimate" voice of the gay community—those working on the inside, or those in the streets.

For Vito Russo, the choice was obvious:

> All those good and polite little boys and girls who have been whining about how ACT UP trashed its own party and how this wasn't the time or the place to zap the mayor are not activists, they're a bunch of politically naive asswipes. . . .
>
> Activists do things that you're not supposed to do. Activists are not respectable. Activists are not gaycrats jockeying for a paid position on someone's staff next year. Activists are not dazzled by the crumbs off a table from a mayor who is allowing their friends to die. Activists are

not grateful for some rinky-dink exhibit which "allows" us to celebrate our history while our history is being systematically wiped out.[3]

Despite the name-calling, the zap did little long-term damage to our relationships with other gay organizations. ACT UP had already endorsed GLAAD's demonstration on the anniversary of the *Hardwick* Supreme Court decision, and we still carried out our June "sheet-in" budget demo at City Hall we'd organized at the behest of some of the same community leaders who had chastised us. But while ACT UP was frequently called upon by more mainstream groups to mobilize the troops and focus media attention on important issues, we were considered a dangerous substance—volatile and subject to unanticipated explosions—and best kept at a safe distance.

The one irreparable rift would be between ACT UP and the community's leading newspaper, the *New York Native*. Throughout the early days of the crisis, the *Native* had been the only consistent local media resource for AIDS information. It was where Larry Kramer first printed his incendiary columns and calls to action; where Michael Callen and Richard Berkowitz's landmark article "We Know Who We Are" first broached the idea that "excessive" sexual promiscuity might be behind the AIDS epidemic; and where information about the epidemiology and treatment of the disease was first shared.

The *Native* was also where I first read about ACT UP and, more than anything—more than the cute boys and the righteous anger in the streets—it was reading about Bradley Ball stepping onto the early morning bus to a Washington demo and dryly announcing "Hi, I'm Brad, and I'm your hostess," that first made me think maybe ACT UP was the group for me.[4]

But for the *Native*, attacking Koch at the Pride ceremony had crossed a line. The paper became increasingly critical of ACT UP, focusing on the growing tension between the group and the gay establishment, broadcasting the charges of anonymous critics who questioned our tactics and direction, and warning we'd better watch our step if we wished to continue to be financially supported by the community. Their opposition accelerated as we took on the mayor more directly; our coverage decreased in almost direct proportion to our activity against the mayor, to the point where the paper barely mentioned our Target City Hall demonstration.

And as the *Native* grew more politically conservative, it also became an outlier in its medical coverage. The paper was a major platform for AIDS deniers who declared "HIV" was not the cause of "AIDS"—putting both terms in quotation marks to underscore doubts about their legitimacy. They claimed AZT was poison and a tool for genocide, charging the government and research establishment with conspiring to wipe out the entire gay male population. Although many reasonable people continued to question whether HIV was the sole cause of AIDS and to debate the cost/benefit ratio of AZT, given its well-documented toxicity, the *Native*'s shocking headlines, poorly researched theories—most prominently that AIDS was a combination of syphilis and African swine fever—and refusal to print opposing viewpoints were putting people's lives in danger.

Matters came to a head in May 1989, when the combined political and medical bias of the paper, along with increasing editorial innuendo regarding ACT UP's finances, pushed the group to announce a boycott of the *Native*. The paper responded by publishing ACT UP's financial statements and urging mainstream papers to investigate us, claiming the money we raised was being spent on recreational drugs and that we had ties to right-wing wacko Lyndon LaRouche![5]

However, the *Native* soon faced a far more dangerous threat than our boycott. On June 26, 1989—just in time for Gay Pride—*OutWeek*, a new weekly lesbian and gay magazine, hit the newsstands. *OutWeek* was angry, campy, politically progressive, and aggressively queer. From its first issue, it announced itself as an unflinching advocate for gay rights and AIDS activism, and a deliberate corrective to the *Native*.

For members of ACT UP, *OutWeek* became required reading—and not just because the magazine was almost entirely written, edited, and designed by our members. Not only did it document our actions and demonstrations with unprecedented thoroughness, but its edgy and politically charged reporting reflected, and in some cases magnified, our activist mindset, earning it the reputation of being "ACT UP's *Pravda*." For the first time, I was reading a magazine for which I was the intended audience (*After Dark*, aside).* It was written by and for those of us who heard the bombs dropping.

OutWeek quickly moved to the center of queer life, often making news as well as reporting it, and, on more than one occasion, crossing over into the tightly guarded precincts of the straight media world. The *Native* never recovered. And even though it outlasted *OutWeek* by eight years,† it was never taken seriously again.

---

*After Dark (May 1968–January 1983) was an arts and entertainment magazine with a noticeably gay bent.

†*OutWeek* would last only a little over two years and 105 issues, from June 1989 to July 1991. Another magazine, *NYQ*, would attempt to take its place beginning in October 1991, with new owners and a broader embrace of the community (albeit with many of the same writers and contributors). Six months later, *NYQ* morphed into *QW* until November 1992, when it

There was, however, another strand of community-based criticism far more insidious than anything dreamed up in the *Native*. It impugned not just the integrity of ACT UP but the fundamental goals of AIDS activism, suggesting the entire AIDS activist movement was, at its core, antigay. Its leading proponent was Darrell Yates Rist, a former head of GLAAD and one of the self-serving "Fabulous Four" who had so harshly criticized our Koch Pride action. Following the example of that critique, Yates Rist published his broadside not in the *Native,* or some other community publication, but in the pages of *The Nation.*[6]

His thesis, at its most cogent, was that AIDS had overwhelmed the rest of the gay rights agenda and that more attention should be paid to other important issues, such as gay marriage, caring for gay youth, and antigay violence. No argument there. ACT UP had already participated in actions and demonstrations around all those issues.

But instead of championing more widespread activism, Yates Rist set up a false dichotomy, arguing gay rights and AIDS activism were incompatible and charging AIDS activists with parasitically sapping energy from "real" gay issues. He accused us of being motivated by a romance with death and promulgating a "fashionable hysteria" by ghoulishly carping on negative statistics, pointing to our response to Joseph's tricked-out AIDS caseload revisions and arguing that anyone who *really* cared about the community's well-being would have celebrated the lowered statistics, not protested them.

He ridiculed the men of ACT UP as "chic protestors" more concerned with being trendy than with creating real change and accused the women of getting involved with AIDS out of some warped "human need to partake in the drama of catastrophe." He then resuscitated the early-eighties argument that championing safe sex somehow made you antigay and accused us of equating sex with death—ignoring the fact ACT UP had been at the forefront of eroticizing safe sex—while complaining about the "coterie of cultish men" working out at his gym wearing activist T-shirts "as though sporting such gym wear was a courageous act."

I guess someone was not getting enough attention in the steam room.

---

stopped publication following the death of its publisher, William F. Chafin, on October 16, 1992, at age thirty-five. *May his memory be for a blessing.*

But while Yates Rist's article stirred up dust, his arguments gained little traction because in his anger and jealousy he couldn't see what was right in front of him. Rather than promoting a cult of death, ACT UP was very much about life; and rather than turning away from gay rights and the radical politics of gay liberation, ACT UP was a major step in their rebirth.

In fact, the baton of gay liberation—now *there's* an image—would officially and very publicly be passed to ACT UP during the Stonewall Anniversary celebrations, when gay historian Martin Duberman credited ACT UP with returning gay politics to its roots and the original radical goals of GLF.

> If we are ever fortunate enough to see the day when the AIDS plague is behind us, I think we will also see the dawn of a new gay movement which in fact harkens back in significant ways to the original movement of the Gay Liberation Front. Because what we are seeing among the legions of the young who make up ACT UP is once again gay men and lesbians acting in concert, welcoming and appreciating each other's differentness, and also welcoming minority people. Beyond that change in personnel, what ACT UP has discovered in the process of struggle is the full extent of entrenched privilege which characterizes our society. . . . Because of those insights gathered during ACT UP's struggles, I think we may yet see the birth of a new gay movement which is once more radically oriented.[7]

After that, I'm afraid we must have been insufferable. How it must have rankled the gay politicos who had spent years politely building contacts in the corridors of power to have these upstarts, these oh-so-fashionable Jane- and Johnny-come-latelys, not only grab the spotlight but be anointed as the heirs of gay liberation.

But the truth was on the ground, and regardless of how people felt, or how loudly they whined, ACT UP was, without question, on the cutting edge of gay politics.

Jeff

Late in June, I got an unexpected late-night call from an ex who was in town for a couple of days and asked if I'd like to meet him at his hotel for a drink.

Not surprisingly, our catch-up conversation quickly moved to the bedroom where, despite my activist credentials, we fell into our old pre-AIDS behavior, and I found myself unexpectedly having unprotected sex with him.

I froze for a moment; but when he urged me to continue, I did. And yes, he said he was HIV-negative, and I assumed I was, too, and yes, I pulled out before cumming, but still . . .

Walking to work the next morning, I kept replaying the moment, shocked at how easy it had been to lose myself in the heat of passion and ignore all the warnings and everything I knew about AIDS and safe sex. Yet another reason, I told myself, to avoid tempting situations where my dick might overrule my head.

June 24, 1989: In the Tradition . . .

Due to the big Stonewall 20 celebration, Pride weekend was going to shake out differently from previous years. Instead of holding the Pride Rally on Sunday, immediately following the march, the city had split the events, scheduling the rally for Saturday on the Great Lawn in Central Park, followed by the parade on Sunday. They claimed the change was necessary because of the expected large crowds—and who could complain about having a rally in Central Park versus some isolated street by the West Side Highway? However, by unlinking the two events, the city had also rather conveniently made Pride even less political than usual.

To ensure politics remained front and center, and to honor the spirit of Gay Liberation, we organized a Saturday morning march "In the Tradition of Stonewall," which would follow the original route of the first Christopher Street Liberation Day March—from the Stonewall Inn up Sixth Avenue to Central Park. We'd march without a permit and without negotiating in advance with the police. While ACT UP would be the lead contingent, marching behind a banner declaring "**In the Tradition: Lesbians & Gay Men Fighting Back**," we invited the entire community and encouraged everyone to bring their own props and banners. Gran Fury produced a commemorative sticker, a fabulous riff on the famous Robert Indiana "LOVE" poster from the sixties, which General Idea had replaced with "AIDS" in 1987; this one a shiny gold disco-ready "RIOT."

From its usual defensive crouch, Heritage of Pride assumed our march was a counterdemonstration designed to disrupt Saturday's rally and threaten the success of Sunday's parade. But our goal was to join the rally, not disrupt it—hell, after three years of petitioning, they'd finally given us a speaking slot. (It's certainly possible the city could've been pressuring HOP to try to get us to cancel our march—but that was never going to happen.)

Still, what were we going to do if the police tried to stop us from marching?

At our marshal meeting at the Tiffany Diner, just an hour before the march, I kept running through the most likely scenario: several hundred of us marching uptown until we're stopped by a wall of police blocking the street, unwilling to let us pass. We sit down and refuse to disperse, but the police wait us out until we lose energy and our numbers dwindle. And then the arrests begin.

As the other marshals discussed possible strategies, I took out my pen and began scribbling on my chant sheet.

By 10:30, a crowd had begun to gather in front of the Stonewall—or rather the Chinese restaurant and clothing store that stood in its place. The Radical Faeries had shown up with their wings, wands, and plumage, as had some of the veterans of Gay Liberation, including Sylvia Rivera and Marsha P. Johnson, who had been leading activists in GLF and later cofounded STAR (Street Transvestite Action Revolutionaries). I welcomed them and handed them our flyer:

WHY WE MARCH
FOR LESBIAN AND GAY LIBERATION

On June 29, 1969 at the Stonewall Rebellion, lesbians and gay men fought back against the regressive policies of New York City and the violent behavior of the New York City police. In June 1970 we marched for the first time to fight for our public existence.

Twenty years after Stonewall, we are still fighting! To be queer is to lead a life of protest against oppression. We are fighting against patriarchy and for diversity and self-determined gender roles . . .

NOW we march to make history again.

RIGHTS ARE GIVEN,
LIBERATION IS TAKEN!
COME OUT, WAY OUT!
ACT UP! FIGHT AIDS![8]

Shortly after 11 a.m., I raised my bullhorn and started the demonstration with the old "Gay Power" chant from 1969:

Gimme a G! —G! Gimme an A! —A! Gimme a Y! —Y!
What's That SPELL? —GAY POWER!

We sprinted east on Christopher and made the wide turn onto Sixth Avenue, our marshals spreading the crowd across the entire width of the street.

"1-3-5-9—LESbiANS are MIGH-ty FINE!"

But when we reached Fourteenth Street, we ran into a thick line of cops stretched across the avenue—exactly the standoff I'd been worried about. I looked down at my chant sheet, aimed my bullhorn at the crowd behind me, and shouted:

"ARREST US! Just TRY IT! ReMember STONEwall Was a RIOT!"

It took a couple of repetitions, but soon the new chant surged through the crowd. It was proud, sassy, and defiant—everything our march was about. You could almost feel everyone standing a couple of inches taller. After a short standoff, the police stepped aside, and with a mighty roar, we continued our march uptown.

"DYKES and FAGS are HERE to SAY: WE Have SAFE SEX EV'ry DAY!"

Marshal tag teams leapfrogged in front of one another, blocking traffic so we could proceed in safety. When we hit Twenty-First Street, a shirtless boy, still sopping wet from his shower, climbed out onto his fire escape to watch us. The crowd beckoned, *"OUT of the SHOWERS! INTO the STREETS!"* At Twenty-Eighth Street, we passed a flea market, and as the shoppers turned to look at us, we cheered, *"STOP SHOP-ping! START MAR-ching! AIDS. WON'T. WAIT!"* Crossing into Herald Square, the cry went up, *"Kiss-in!"* and we stopped in the middle of Thirty-Fourth Street, stalling multiple lanes of crisscrossing traffic; the blaring car horns and the stunned expressions on the tourists' faces only egged us on.

"HONK! If you LOVE QUEERS!"

At Forty-Sixth Street, a bunch of catcalling hardhats bravely booed us from scaffolding four stories above the street. We gave them our best beauty pageant waves and shouted, *"2-4-6-8: Are your GIRL-FRIENDS Really STRAIGHT?"* Nobody, no, nobody was going to rain on our . . . er, march. When we got to Radio City Music Hall, a line of marshals locked arms and blocked traffic with a synchronized high-kick routine chanting, *"2-4-6-8: HOW do you KNOW the Rock-ETTES ARE STRAIGHT?"* And when I finally ran out of steam on Central Park West, and the march went momentarily silent, a new chant welled up from the middle of the crowd as we approached the American Museum of Natural History: *"IT IS NO MYS-tery—WE ARE NAT'ral HIS-tory!"*

Reenergized, we marched onto the Great Lawn chanting gleefully. But HOP was so worried about a disruption that rather than welcoming our 1,000-plus marchers to the rally, they quickly brought on the Lesbian and Gay Big Apple Corps Marching Band to drown us out.

Even if our arrival had been made anticlimactic, we remained triumphant. We lay down on the grass and in each other's laps and began our very own Gay-In; sharing water, ice cream, and snacks, and listening to speakers like Allen Ginsburg, Barbara Smith, and Ginny Appuzo. We cheered Harvey Fierstein, who'd marched uptown with us, and screamed our approval when our own Tim Powers exhorted the crowd to "Join us or get the hell out of our way!" We sang along to old favorites—I'm always surprised how many fierce activists know all the words to "Where the Boys Are"—and when the disco divas took the stage, we all got up and boogie-oogie-oogied. It was all "Gimme an F!—Fabulous!" A little slice of Gay Lib heaven for those of us too young to have partaken the first time around.

Then at 2 p.m., Larry, Vito, Avram, and Eric got up and excused themselves from the party. There was a memorial to attend. Barry Gingell, Steve Webb's former roommate and the first Treatment Director at GMHC, had died. He was thirty-four years old.

BARRY GINGELL (1954–1989)
May his memory be for a blessing.

Lamenting the gay movement's trend toward mainstream conformity, the Radical Faeries had issued a call "for all radical, outsider, and countercultural Lesbian and Gay People"[9] to come to New York for the Stonewall anniversary. The Faeries had organized a week of actions ranging from a summer solstice celebration to a mock-funeral procession for Judy Garland*—"the gal whose death helped make it all possible"[10]—in an effort to "create a consciousness for a new, more radical culture that fucking loves diversity, and loves fucking diversely."[11] Their presence at our Saturday march was hardly surprising, given the weekend organizers, SPREE and Bru Dye, were both ACT UP

---

*According to the mythology, it was Judy Garland's funeral that afternoon in 1969 that made the Stonewall queens so emotional and ready to fight back against the police that evening.

members. The high point of the Faerie weekend, however, was going to be their theatrical reenactment of the Stonewall Riots on Saturday night.

Having had my fill of street activism for the day, I went instead to a party at Maria's. As always, there was beer in the fridge, chips and nibbles strewn across the door sitting atop her kitchen bathtub, windows open and fans whirring to little effect, along with way too many activists laughing, shouting, drinking, and smoking. Shortly after midnight, a rush of people burst into the apartment, breathless with tales of a near riot in Sheridan Square.

A big crowd had shown up to watch the Faerie reenactment in front of the Stonewall. After pelting each other with Styrofoam bricks—painted yellow (and not quite dry) in honor of Judy—the Faeries reprised the infamous Stonewall Girls kick-line *"We are the Stonewall girls! We wear our hair in curls! We wear no underwear! We show our pubic hair!"* until they were "attacked" by Faerie "cops" with balloon billy clubs.[12] Everyone was having a gay old time, until someone yelled, "Let's take Seventh Avenue," and off they went on a long march through the Village. They stopped at the Sixth Precinct Station on Tenth Street, demanding to know what the police were doing about a recent murder of two gay men down at the piers, and then took off for the Westside Highway before doubling back to Sheridan Square, blocking busy Saturday night traffic as they went, prompting some angry motorists to start running their cars into the crowd. When the police proved uninterested in providing protection for the marchers, some ACT UP members stepped up to marshal, several becoming victims themselves. By the end of the evening, five protesters were hospitalized and a red Chevy Cavalier, which had been chased down Christopher Street after crashing through the crowd, was destroyed.

The following morning, we woke up to the cover of the *New York Post* screaming "GAYS BASH BACK." Despite the *Post's* usual antigay slant and my own belief in nonviolence, it was a wonderful Pride present. Yes, please deliver the message to those young men who come to the Village and Chelsea looking for faggots to bash that the gays they stalk are not helpless targets. Gimme a G! GAY POWER!!

Sunday's parade was a joyride. After sweating through Saturday's march, we were able to just spread out and enjoy ourselves. We danced down Fifth Avenue, our entire contingent jumping up and punching the air, *"ACT U-U-U-P! Fight BACK! Fight AIDS!"* as Matt Ebert, Adam Smith, and the rest of the Swim Team darted in and out, their arms outstretched like human airplanes, tilting, swerving, and buzzing the crowd.

"LES-bi-ANS are HERE to SAY: We have GAY PRIDE EV'ry DAY!"
Our joy was contagious, and by the time we reached Washington Square Park and waved at Larry, watching us from his apartment balcony, our contingent was over five blocks long.
"ACT UP! WE'RE HERE! We're FIGHT-ing AIDS! We're PROUD and QUEER!"

Chapter 12

Parallel Tracks

WHEN SPIKE LEE'S *Do the Right Thing* opened in movie theaters at the end of June 1989, pundits and politicians worried the film, with its thumping "Fight the Power" soundtrack and depiction of a city boiling over with racial tensions, would incite rioting in the streets—as if Blacks and Latinos needed a movie to remind them of the continued existence of racism or the racist policies of the Koch administration.

When I saw the film, I was energized. I identified with the anger and frustrations of the film's Bed-Stuy residents, recognized many of their enemies as my own, and saw us as allies "fighting the power" in the streets. Not that our battles were the same, but wasn't AIDS an example of an issue where we could work across racial barriers? Hadn't we organized and marched together at City Hall against Mayor Koch? Although we might be coming from a different set of experiences, weren't we all arriving at the same conclusions about what needed to be done and what had to change?

And Priority #1 was electing a new mayor.

But would ACT UP be able to stay focused in our efforts to pressure the mayor and address city issues now that our big demonstration was over, or would we get distracted by the next shiny new controversy?

If ACT UP had left Montreal with the wind at its back, the breeze was particularly strong for Jim Eigo, Mark Harrington, and the T+D gang. Their *Treatment Research Agenda* had been received by many of the scientists and researchers with great interest, and their proposal for a "parallel track" expanding access to experimental drugs had been endorsed by no less an establishment figure than Tony Fauci of the National Institute of Allergy and Infectious Diseases (NIAID).[*]

Anthony Fauci was probably the most politically adept scientist in the entire country. Smart, affable, cute even, with a Noo Yawk accent that came and went (becoming decidedly more pronounced when trying to connect with activists), Fauci ping-ponged between friend and foe, protecting his researchers, pacifying activists, and placating his bosses in the White House.

Right now, he was our best friend.

Fauci had first discussed his support of parallel track in Montreal with Larry Kramer—not exactly the person to talk to if your goal is keeping a major AIDS policy shift under wraps. Another surprise convert was the FDA's Ellen Cooper, whom we'd previously targeted for her refusal to allow the approval of DHPG, a drug that had successfully suppressed cytomegalovirus (CMV)-related blindness and had already been distributed to over five thousand patients through the FDA's own expanded access program, because the drug manufacturer had not conducted a placebo-controlled trial to "prove" its effectiveness.[†]

Given her position and history, Cooper's endorsement was extremely important for reassuring drug companies their participation in the program would not endanger their chances of winning FDA approval.

Everyone agreed the ideal first candidate for parallel track was Bristol-Myers's new antiviral drug, ddI. An analog of AZT, dideoxyinosine (ddI) was "half as effective as AZT per unit volume, but ten times less toxic . . . provid[ing] a much bigger antiviral bang for the buck."[1] The drug was already in great demand, having received a glowing report from its Phase I trial, and there was a large population of PWAs who couldn't tolerate—or had grown resistant to—AZT and needed new antiviral therapy. These patients

---

[*] NIAID was one of, at the time, twelve constituent institutes of the National Institutes of Health (NIH) and the one most central to AIDS research, supporting everything from basic research and epidemiology studies to blood-screening tests, drug discovery and development, vaccine testing, and treatment studies. Most importantly, it administered the ACTG (AIDS Clinical Trial Group) program responsible for conducting the federally supported AIDS drug trials.

[†] After many months of mounting pressure from the community, including an ACT UP demonstration at an FDA hearing, the drug was finally approved on June 26, 1989.

would be unable to enroll in the upcoming Phase II trials comparing ddI to AZT, as they were neither AZT-naïve nor able to risk being randomized to the AZT "control" arm; but they'd be eager to try ddI under parallel track, where they'd be assured of getting the new drug.

Armed with news of Fauci's and Cooper's support, Larry, Jim, and Mark met with Bristol-Myers to make the case for the release of ddI on parallel track. Mark and Jim tried to allay the company's concerns about siphoning patients from their Phase II trials—now disappointingly delayed from July to September—promising that only people who couldn't qualify for the trial would be eligible for the new program. When Bristol refused to commit, Larry threatened them with the specter of an underground market flooded with bootleg ddI.[2]

Hours after their meeting, Fauci went public with the parallel track proposal. Two weeks later, Bristol officially came on board.

But T+D weren't the only ones keeping busy. In the space of two weeks in June, ACT UP joined a coalition of Brooklyn-based community groups protesting city budget cuts and lack of services at Kings County Hospital (June 17); zapped *Forbes* magazine over an article by Michael Fumento promoting his new book, *The Myth of Heterosexual AIDS* (June 20); staged a kiss-in and mock wedding at the New York City Marriage Bureau demanding official recognition of our relationships (June 23); demonstrated at the Department of Housing Preservation and Development over the lack of medical facilities and housing for PWAs (June 28); and led a coalition demonstration at City Hall pressuring the city council to boost the AIDS and health care budgets (June 29). And that doesn't even include the Stonewall 20 events (June 24–25).

In an unexpected development, gay relationships would become a campaign issue a few weeks later, when the New York Court of Appeals ruled gay couples should be considered "family" in the case of Miguel Braschi, who'd been threatened with eviction from the apartment he'd shared for over a decade with his recently deceased lover.[3] "The intended protection against sudden eviction should not rest on fictitious legal distinctions or genetic history," wrote Judge Vito Titone, "but instead should find its foundation in the reality of family life."

Although narrowly written to apply only to the city's rent-control regulations, the ruling established a new legal test for determining family relationships. "It is the totality of the relationship as evidenced by the dedication, caring and self-sacrifice of the parties which should, in the final analysis, control."[4]

Mayor Koch, who'd been trying to dance himself back into the good graces of New York's gay community, quickly announced a new policy giving unmarried city employees the same rights as married couples regarding hospital visitation and bereavement leave benefits. His Republican challenger, Rudy Giuliani, staked out the opposing position, reducing a humanitarian argument into a purely economic one. "At a time when the city needs more policemen and better health care, it is a mistake to offer expanded benefits for municipal workers."[5] This allowed Koch to accuse Giuliani of "gay bashing," even as the mayor still refused to extend health care and insurance benefits to the gay partners of city employees. Giuliani then began his own dance, explaining while he "supports full and complete legal rights and protection for everyone,"[6] he didn't agree with the *Braschi* definition of family, though he did agree with the ruling purely as a matter of tenants' rights.

Giuliani and Koch weren't the only ones tied into knots by *Braschi*. While the *New York Times* editorial page judged Koch's offer of bereavement leave "reasonable," so long as "any substantial economic benefits for such 'families' are a matter for collective bargaining"—*note, please, the quotation marks around "families"*—the *Times* editorial found the decision "humane," but "impractical"; an illustration of "how a warm heart can sometimes turn the law upside down."[7] The *Times* warned of the "unanticipated grief" of landlords turned into spies and the courts forced to question friends and sift through household bills to determine the true nature of the tenants' relationship. Surely, the *Times* added, "No legislature would ever contemplate taxing the courts so mercilessly." The paper was far less concerned with the grief of soon-to-be-displaced gay partners and other "family" members.

But as infuriating as the editorial was, it was merely the latest in a series of unbelievably callous, racist, and homophobic *Times* columns and editorials.

For as long as I can remember, the *New York Times* had been a part of my daily life. Growing up, it was delivered to our door every day. In elementary school, we bought our own student subscriptions and were taught how to fold the large broadsheets in half and half again, folding and unfolding the pages like the petals of an origami flower, never stretching it out to its full length—except for the Sunday Arts & Leisure section, where the full-page ads for Broadway shows were best appreciated spread across our kitchen floor. The *Times* was sacred text, the last word and ultimate authority.

I guess that's why their AIDS coverage made me so angry.

At first, the paper largely ignored the epidemic, publishing only seven stories in the first nineteen months of the crisis, by which time there were 983 cases. In contrast, the twenty-nine deaths from Legionnaire's disease merited sixty-two stories in two months, including eleven on the front page. AIDS did not get its eleventh front-page story until 1985, by which time there were more than 12,000 cases and 6,000 deaths.[8]

The *Times* was hardly alone in ignoring AIDS. According to the AP poll of editors and broadcasters, AIDS was not judged to be one of the year's top ten stories until 1985, when the Rock Hudson story broke.[9] Not one reporter had even thought to ask President Reagan about AIDS until Hudson was stricken with the disease.

Because AIDS was considered a "gay disease," the topic was judged to be of little interest to a "general readership." The *Times*'s executive editor, A. M. Rosenthal, had long made clear that stories about gays were inappropriate for his newspaper,[10] refusing to allow reporters to use the word "gay" except in instances when it was a part of the name of an organization or an attributed quote.* In all other cases, Rosenthal insisted the appropriate term was "homosexual." Despite years of pressure from the community, the *Times* would not officially lift its prohibition against the word "gay" until June 1987.

When the *Times* did cover AIDS, it was always as a medical or human-interest story, usually buried in the science or style sections, respectively, and receiving limited play in the rest of their pages. (Only the right-wing columnists of the *New York Post* seemed to grasp that AIDS was also a political story.) It rarely covered congressional hearings on AIDS issues or

---

*The *Times* had displayed similar recalcitrance in allowing the use of "Black" or "Ms." in their pages until many years after the words had achieved near-universal usage.

the various NIH or FDA advisory meetings, relying instead, if at all, on reprints of articles from the wire services. Reports on potential new treatments were often published only after the story had been covered elsewhere and were based on press releases rather than on any independent research or investigation of counterclaims by AIDS activists.

More importantly, because the *Times* was the "paper of record," the absence of consistent AIDS coverage and the lack of priority given to the epidemic in terms of story placement and resources echoed throughout the rest of the media, helping keep AIDS from becoming a national story.

Then there was the *Times* editorial page. Surely there is a special place in hell for the people responsible for those many clueless and hateful editorials. For ACT UP, the final provocation was the editorial "Why Make AIDS Worse Than It Is?"[11] Published just days after Pride, it suggested we ignore the recent "gloomy" report from the General Accounting Office warning that the government might have underestimated the future AIDS caseload by as much as one-third, and instead focus on the "possibility" that infection rates "seem to be leveling off [and] if so, the epidemic will peak and sooner than many of the forecasters expect." Why was the *Times* so optimistic? Because "the disease is still very largely confined to specific risk groups. Once all susceptible members are infected, the numbers of new victims will decline."

Ignoring the misinformation that pocked the rest of the editorial—e.g., the incubation period between infection and overt disease was eleven years, not five; the infection rate among IV drug users was skyrocketing, not stabilizing, and so on—the real message once again seemed to be that since the writers and presumed readers of the *Times* were safe, why all the yelling and screaming?

The editorial ended by chiding AIDS advocates for our habit of "accept[ing] good news badly" just because "steadily rising tolls are such a powerful argument for new resources." Just look how we reacted to Stephen Joseph and his reduced estimates! "The epidemic is terrifying enough without playing politics with the numbers."

It was bad enough when the *Times* was merely an impediment to our efforts to raise awareness and generate a commensurate response to the epidemic; but now that people were finally beginning to understand the urgency of the situation, the paper was actively fighting against us, saying everything's fine and under control.

ACT UP went into direct action mode, pasting "Buy Your Lies Here. *The New York Times* Reports Half the Truth About AIDS" decals on newsstands and covering the coin slots on the *Times*'s sidewalk newspaper boxes with

"*The New York Times* AIDS Reporting is OUT OF ORDER" stickers. We even held a demonstration in front of the Fifth Avenue brownstone of *Times* publisher Arthur "Punch" Sulzburger, then marched forty blocks south to the paper's Times Square headquarters.

But despite the large numbers of protesters and police, the high visibility of our targets, and the usual mountain of press releases sent out to all our regular media contacts prior to the demonstration, only two radio stations aired reports of the action, and only the *Village Voice* and *OutWeek* covered the event in print. There was no TV coverage, and no daily newspaper sent reporters or picked up the story, least of all, the *New York Times*.*

The Test

On July 13, 1989, at 1:15 p.m., I rolled up my sleeve and finally took The Test.

There was only one test for a gay man in 1989, the so-called AIDS Test. Despite the name, The Test wouldn't tell you if you had AIDS, only if you'd been exposed to HIV and developed antibodies to the virus. Further, it wasn't just one test, but two. The first, the ELISA, had been licensed in 1985, but it produced an unacceptable rate of false positives, so a second test, the Western Blot, was developed and licensed in 1987, to confirm any positive ELISA results. All this assumed HIV was, in fact, the cause of AIDS—a point widely accepted by 1989, but still contested in some activist corners.

I hadn't taken The Test before because I didn't see the point. My health was good—no night sweats, startling weight loss, or swollen glands—and the rest of my blood work was normal. And if it turned out I was Positive, there was, until recently, very little I could do.

Besides, I truly didn't think I was Positive. While I'd had an active sex life, I'd never been particularly adventurous. Most of the sex I had would be classified as *mostly* on the "safe" side; not that "mostly" was any sort of guarantee.

Even so, I didn't tell anyone I was getting tested.

I didn't want to worry about anyone else worrying about me or deal with well-meaning inquiries about how I was holding up while waiting the two weeks for the results to arrive. If I was Positive, I wanted to be able to process

---

*The irony doesn't escape me that despite my ranting against the *Times*, I cite it consistently throughout this book as an authoritative text. This is due, in part, to my personal archive of yellowing press clipping as well as easy access to the *Times*'s own online archives. But also, I guess, because old habits die hard.

it at my own speed and share the news in my own way. If I was Negative, I'd want to keep that private as well. I mean, how nice for me, but it wasn't the kind of news you announced. At least not in my circle.

Despite the best efforts of our health commissioner, The Test was still anonymous, so using my birth date as my ID number, I went for my appointment at the Chelsea clinic, doing my best to maintain a cheerful nonchalance throughout my pre-Test counseling session. Then it was just a quick make a fist, find a vein, tap, tap, tap, turn my head, an-n-n-n-n-n-n-n-n-d DONE. Call back in two weeks.

Fortunately, I'd developed an impressive ability to compartmentalize, so rather than spending the next fourteen days staring at the calendar, I grabbed a ride up to Provincetown, where the local ACT UP chapter was recruiting activists to help bolster their presence at their upcoming Pride celebration.

According to our hosts, P-Town was in deep denial. A tourist destination for both gays and straights, the town was reeling from a string of bad summers and was now doing its best to ignore the AIDS epidemic in hopes of avoiding further damage to local businesses during the tourist season.

Think *Jaws*, but with a virus instead of a shark.

Even after the deaths of over thirty residents and many others—both natives and visitors—living with some form of HIV-related illness, P-Town had little in the way of health care for PWAs and displayed a stubborn reluctance to fund necessary support services. There was also, reportedly, a growing gay-bashing problem that was being hushed up by the police to prevent further upset to the summer tourist trade.

Tensions had surfaced almost immediately between the local ACT UP and members of the town's "gay establishment," the merchants of the Provincetown Business Guild. When the activists proposed transforming the annual Pride commemoration from a solemn candlelight procession into a more lively and prideful political march, the Guild members didn't understand why this change was necessary and were suspicious of the activists' motives. As one member put it, "Very selfishly, I don't want you punks ruining this for the rest of us."[12]

Doesn't this just *scream* relaxing vacation?

To make matters worse, shortly after arriving in town, I discovered I'd contracted a case of crabs. The thing about me and crabs was I seemed to get them less from strange bed partners than from strange beds. (I hadn't had sex, but had been apartment sitting.) So, instead of enjoying a lovely late afternoon bike ride through the dunes, I scurried into town to secure a bottle of Kwell from the well-stocked local pharmacy. On the bright side, I reasoned crabs all but confirmed a negative test result—as if having HIV on top of Immaculate Crabs was somehow beyond the boundaries of cosmic justice.

In the meantime, there were meetings to attend, posters to design, and chant sheets to update. I also had a speech to write, as I'd been selected to speak on AIDS activism for the Pride Rally at Town Hall. And in a nod to the Stonewall twentieth anniversary, ACT UP's own gay icon, the legendary Rollerena, had been named honorary Grand Marshal of the Provincetown Pride celebration.

The self-described "Kentucky Bluegrass Belle of Three Counties," Rollerena had first emerged in all her splendor in the early '70s, attaining immortality later that decade on the dance floor of Studio 54. Too young to have seen her in her disco glory, I remember her instead as a vision skating down Christopher Street on many a sunny weekend afternoon, impeccably dressed in a long, white, twirly, high-necked gown, her hair twisted into a tasteful snood, her face powdered and adorned with pointy rhinestone glasses. Smiling and waving her magic wand, she blessed her subjects and dispensed goodwill, stopping every now and then to extend a lace-gloved hand so some attractive young swain could kneel and kiss her magical dingleberry ring.

But by the mid-'80s, Rollerena, like many of her fellow disco habitués, had vanished. No one knew where she was or who she might be once she hung up her skates. So, when a pale thin man with long frizzy brown hair first came to ACT UP, no one paid him much attention. Timid and soft-spoken, he became a regular face at meetings and demonstrations, but nothing more; just another good soldier ready to put his body on the line for AIDS activism.

But once her identity was revealed, Rollerena reemerged from her chrysalis, reborn as the Fairy Godmother of the AIDS activist movement. She appeared at ACT UP benefits, graced our recruitment posters—"Rollerena wants YOU!"—and regaled a whole new generation of queers with stories of her wayward youth, her exploits in the army, and her life in fabulous pre-AIDS New York.

The turnout for Sunday's Pride parade was estimated at anywhere from 600 to 1,000 people; huge for P-Town, and easily more than double the number at last year's event. Spectators lined the streets, loudly cheering and chanting, even joining in random "kiss-in" demonstrations. But as we got closer to the center of town and the crowd grew more heterosexual, the cheering stopped, the smiles froze, and people began to stare in silence. I turned to David Gipps, who was marching beside me, and said, half-laughing, "We are their worst nightmare."

We came to a stop in front of Town Hall, where we were scheduled to hold our rally. But having already transformed the procession into a parade, many of us wanted to turn it into a full-fledged march. We urged the crowd to continue down Commercial Street, past the bars and restaurants, to bring our message of Pride to the rest of our community.

"HOW FAR do we wanna GO?—ALL THE WAY!"

The police, however, were less than pleased with our sudden improvisation, and after a brief confrontation, we marched noisily into Town Hall.

Inside, everyone was buzzed and excited. Kate Clinton was the emcee—she's ALWAYS the emcee—and there were songs and speeches, and Holly Near herself sang "Over the Rainbow." I mean it was gay, gay, GAY!

For my speech, I'd decided to use the same biblical syllogism we'd used for Pride Sunday—"If not now, when? If not here, where? If not us, who?"—to make my case for becoming an activist. "Our communities," I began, "are under siege by an administration that refuses to take action on AIDS and a drug testing bureaucracy that fails to provide us with treatments."

> We are under attack from the courts, which seek to limit a women's right to choose and, in cases like *Bowers v. Hardwick*, our right to choose who we love. And we are regularly fag-bashed, not only in the streets, but in the United States Senate during their debates over AIDS appropriations and NEA funding,° and by the military when

---

° In June, the Corcoran Gallery in Washington, DC, withdrew an exhibit of Robert Mapplethorpe photos, citing complaints about its "obscene" and homoerotic content. The resulting controversy opened a long-simmering debate over censorship of the arts, the

they attempt to blame the deaths of 40 soldiers on the Battleship Iowa on the actions of a single depressed and jilted faggot.*

It's no wonder we come to places like Provincetown, a safe haven where we don't have to worry about being attacked or feel bad about being gay. And it's true; we act differently here. We relax; we're more open, more out, more ourselves. But why should we have to come all the way to the tip of Cape Cod, the very edge of the United States, to hold our lover's hand?

It was, in many ways, my Queer Bar Mitzvah Speech. I'd studied the sacred texts and learned our history, connected the lessons and struggles of previous generations to my own, and shared my conclusions with the congregation.

Today, I am a Rainbow Flag.

When the rally was over, I floated out of Town Hall on a cloud of empowerment. But as I drifted over to Spiritus Pizza for a celebratory slice and cruise, I was accosted by a stranger who started yelling about what "we" had done at the march. I had no idea what he was talking about, but boy, he sure was angry.

And he wasn't alone.

Arguments were breaking out up and down Commercial Street. It was like Jets versus Sharks in topsiders and polo shirts. When I finally got to Spiritus, I found the ACT UP gang huddled on the far side of the road, looking shell-shocked. People were screaming at us, accusing us of betraying the gay community and destroying the "delicate balance" of gay-straight relations. I had no idea what they were talking about. Then someone said something about "That Sign."

Oh, that.

Walter Armstrong, one of my Montreal roommates and a queer history project colleague, had marched in the parade with his own handmade sign that said "Legalize butt-fucking" on one side and "Legalize clit-licking" on the other. People were offended and horrified, and sadly that one sign seemed to blot out all the other messages and accomplishments of the evening.

---

definition of obscenity, and whether the government should have any role in funding the arts. This would come to a head the following year, with the "defunding" of the NEA Four (Karen Finley, John Fleck, Holly Hughes, and Tim Miller).

*On April 19, an explosion on the USS *Iowa* killed forty-seven crewmen. The navy tried to pin the blame on one of the sailors killed in the explosion, claiming he was suicidal over the end of an illicit love affair with another sailor. Subsequent investigations disproved the navy's claims, pointing instead to an accidental overram of powder bags.

Was it offensive? Sure. Would I have carried that sign myself? No. And perhaps, in retrospect, we should've discussed its appropriateness prior to the march. But ACT UP was all about letting individuals express themselves and, right or wrong, any attempt at censorship would have been against our ethos. And whatever my personal qualms, I could've easily made the argument the sign was only calling out the very acts forbidden by *Hardwick*, and by proudly and explicitly claiming a legal right to participate in these acts—and by using the same language that was used to taunt us—the sign was both reclaiming these terms and confronting the heart of the prejudice against us.

Or maybe it was just an immature prank done solely for shock value.

But, whatever the argument, was it something that would "set gay and straight relations back 40 years or more?"[13]

P-Town remained a battlefield for the next few days. Just wearing a "Silence = Death" button was enough to get your ear chewed off. Articles, editorials, and letters to the editor filled the local newspapers; everyone, it seemed, was mad about something—"the sign," the other signs, the number of people marching, the dykes on bikes, the chanting that "scared the children," the kiss-ins, the handing out of condoms. Even Rollerena was deemed by some to be an inappropriate presence. (I suppose P-Town preferred to see its drag queens only where there was a two-drink minimum.) One restaurant owner went so far as to harrumph that this kind of parade could take place "only in Provincetown."[14]

He should get out more.

The chief of police publicly accused the openly gay chaplain who'd helped organize the event of misleading the town when he applied for the parade permit, costing him his job. The chief further demanded all future groups requesting a permit adhere to an as-yet-to-be-determined "code of ethics," while advising the public to refrain from violence in response to the recent parade.[15] Meanwhile, the Business Guild wasted no time denouncing ACT UP and apologizing to anyone within hearing on behalf of the gay community.

We also had our supporters, the brave few who pointed out many of those same "offending words" or similar could be found on T-shirts and bumper stickers sold by the local souvenir shops; and wondered where all the outrage was when young men from the community began to die at an alarming rate, or when the *Hardwick* decision came down. But for the most part, the comments and letters revealed the surprising limit of Provincetown's celebrated "delicate balance" of tolerance.

It was, as they say, a learning moment. So, here's the quiz: Which is better—Tolerance, Respect, or Rights?

Tolerance alone is the weakest of the three and the most easily revoked. It's a social contract between unequal parties, with terms dictated by the more powerful partner.

Tolerance is better when combined with respect, which implies the other party considers you an equal or, even better, a possible threat; and the balance of power is held in check by the understanding that actions will have consequences.

Rights are best of all, because they mandate respect and at least a grudging tolerance, and are not dependent upon the approval of others. Rights must often be fought for, and while they are harder to win, they are also more difficult to take away. Nonetheless, they must be vigilantly guarded and defended.

Lesson learned, I returned to New York and soon thereafter received my Test results.

Negative.

While I was relieved, a small part of me felt strangely let down. Not that I wanted to be sick, but testing positive would have given me something definite to organize my life around. I'd be fighting for my life, first and foremost, with all other thoughts and aspirations pushed aside. Instead, I remained in limbo. I was going to live, which was great, but what was my future, now that I knew I'd have one? Was I still an actor? I hadn't auditioned for anything in a year and a half. But if I wasn't an actor—what was I?

Well, I knew I was an activist, at least for the short term—and ACT UP was the perfect place for the short term. There were no discussions of "the future" in ACT UP, there was only NOW! We were always in crisis mode, combating the newest outrage, tracking the hottest treatment, and planning the next action. How could we even talk about the future when so many of us might not be around to have one?

On July 20, Congressman Henry Waxman held a hearing to discuss the proposed parallel track program. Waxman, who represented the western districts of Los Angeles, was a staunch AIDS advocate but an equally strong defender of drug regulation. Parallel track, he warned, "could change ground rules on research, clinical care, markets, and insurance. It could also provide access to drugs—the good ones and the worthless ones—long before data are available. If it works, it could revolutionize drug development. If it fails, it could cripple AIDS research for some time."[16]

No pressure.

The program received an unexpected endorsement from the Bush administration, which expressed its interest in implementing the program not only for AIDS, but also for cancer and other diseases.[17] Even as we accepted their support, we recognized the administration was more concerned with what was good for drug companies than what was good for patients. But it was Jim Eigo who put the program in the proper perspective:

> I have friends, John and Peter and Lee and Murray and Brian. All have AIDS or ARC. None would be eligible for an AIDS clinical trial. None can take a demonstrably effective dose of AZT. Any more than my friend & gifted composer Louis could; & Louis just died. None of them should anymore be needlessly sacrificed to that strange and abstract god, clean data.[18]

In his testimony, FDA commissioner Young announced that owing to the lead time necessary to set up a new regulatory program, ddI would not be released under parallel track, but through an expanded version of the FDA's current treatment IND (Investigational New Drug) program. He went on to suggest that perhaps the better option would be to retool the existing program, rather than creating a whole new process—a proposal Jim immediately characterized as "the same old lemon with tail fins."[19]

At the hearing's conclusion, Jim was appointed, along with Martin Delaney from San Francisco's Project Inform,* as a community representative to the FDA advisory committee charged with preparing recommendations for the parallel track program. Jim was ACT UP's first representative on an official scientific panel. He wouldn't be our last.†

---

*Project Inform was a community-based AIDS advocacy organization focused on drug treatment and development issues.

†In September, Jim was named to the AIDS panel of the Institute of Medicine, and in October, Fauci and Dan Hoth, who was in charge of NIAID's AIDS Clinical Trial (ACTG) program, nominated him to sit on the AIDS Research Advisory Committee (ARAC), a congressionally mandated panel responsible for making recommendations to the NIH, NIAID, and the Division of AIDS. Recognizing the potential conflict of "being an ACT UP member and a government consultant at once," Jim brought his nomination to the group for discussion,

∎∎∎

For the next month, ACT UP worked feverishly to ensure the ddI expanded access program remained on track. With assistance from AmFAR, we also drafted a consensus statement, signed by seventeen community groups, endorsing our vision for a progressive parallel track program that would "offer the widest possible access to new drugs for people who lack other-than-experimental treatment options, and make it possible, at the same time, to proceed efficiently with drug licensing."[20]

Despite the impressive array of signatories and the backing of Fauci and Cooper, we felt it best for ACT UP to attend the final advisory meeting in force on August 17, to ensure the proposal did not get stalled or watered down at the last minute. Packing the hearing room, we stowed our signs and cheered when Jim and Martin Delaney presented the ACT UP/AmFAR consensus proposal. After Fauci finished his testimony defending parallel track, Larry Kramer cried out, "President Bush was right! You are our hero, Dr. Fauci!"[21]

But as the hours dragged on, there was little movement toward approval. Even after impassioned testimony from Mark Harrington and threats from Larry, who warned of activists sabotaging drug trials and "an uprising the likes of which you have never seen before or since the Vietnam War in this country,"[22] the meeting slid back into a general torpor as the panel waded deeper into the weeds of process and the endless discussion loop about whether the new program would negatively impact enrollment in clinical trials. In despair, we took off our watches and held them silently above our heads, wondering if, like the treatment IND program before it, parallel track would be talked and compromised into irrelevance. Suddenly, a single voice from the back of the room cut through the prattle.

"Would the panel accept a comment from the Floor?"[23]

I didn't even have to turn around.

Handsome, charismatic, and blessed with an actor's voice and presence, Aldyn McKean had panache. Also, balls. Aldyn had been an activist since his college days protesting the war in Vietnam and was another of ACT UP's

---

with the understanding he would withdraw if we felt his participation "would curtail rather than further [ACT UP's] mission." Coordinating, T+D, and the Floor all approved his nomination, and Jim served on ARAC for two years. ACT UP internal document: Jim Eigo, "Treatment & Data Update 100289," October 2, 1989.

fearless PWA warriors. While he may have asked the panel if they would "accept a comment," he wasn't waiting for a response.

> There is an extraordinary amount of consensus at this meeting that things need to be done. You are an Advisory Committee—ADVISE! Take a vote TODAY, before this meeting is over, on the proposal that Jim Eigo has put in front of you. If some of you have not read that proposal yet, take a minute and read it. If you have reservations about it, you need not say that it must be implemented word-for-word. You can say, "Some of us on this committee have reservations about this proposal, but we feel that this proposal provides the framework for activity that should be undertaken by the FDA IMMEDIATELY." And you have access to the people who can implement that proposal. Please do it. Thank you.[24]

And that seemed to do it. The panel almost immediately proceeded to a vote on parallel track based on the ACT UP proposal. Rather than wasting more time squabbling over the details, they agreed to form another high-level committee to create and refine policy for the new program, and once again nominated both Jim and Marty to participate as active voting members.

It was a stunning victory, and everyone knew who was responsible. "This is the way revolutions happen," said one scientist. "If people weren't sitting in at the FDA, and chaining themselves to the wall of Burroughs Wellcome Co., none of this would be happening," admitted another.[25]

About those chains.

Burroughs Wellcome had been the poster child for pharmaceutical greed ever since March 1987, when they announced the then record-breaking sum of $10,000 a year for their newly approved drug AZT. The price had shocked everyone, including the FDA, which had expedited approval of the drug, and the National Cancer Institute (NCI), which had discovered the drug on its shelves and carried out most of the early testing. Nonetheless, AZT became one of the fastest-selling drugs in history, with first-year sales of over $170 million.

Finally, in December 1987, after nine months of mounting pressure, Wellcome agreed to reduce the price by 20 percent, to a still outrageous

$8,000 per year. Just two months later, the company received yet another regulatory plum—a seventeen-year "use patent" giving them exclusive rights to manufacture the drug and control its price. By 1989, Wellcome's profits had doubled, and it was estimated sales of AZT could reach $1.2 billion, with over half that amount cleared as profit.[26] And still Wellcome refused to contemplate any further price reductions.

Then they met Peter Staley.

On January 23, 1989, Peter and Mark Harrington flew down to the company's US headquarters in North Carolina to demand Wellcome lower the price of AZT an additional 25 percent and provide full funding or free AZT to the federal government's assistance program.* Wellcome demurred, promising only to review their underutilized—and largely unadvertised—patient assistance program.

Three months later, Peter returned with his power drill.

Peter and his business-suited cohorts—Lee Arsenault, Blane Charles, and James McGrath—breezed past building security and headed to an unoccupied office on the third floor, where they sealed the door shut with steel plates and handcuffed themselves to a heavy chain they'd bolted into the opposing wall. "We won't let them tell us 'pay or die' any longer," said Peter in the ACT UP press release. "Either they knock down the cost or they knock down their own walls to get us out."[27]

The activists were charged with first-degree trespassing and injury to real property. Luckily, they were able to post the $20,000 bail, for had they not, Peter and Lee, who had been diagnosed with ARC and AIDS, respectively, would have been subject to North Carolina's punitive HIV policy and placed in isolation.

In late summer, Wellcome's fortunes improved dramatically when preliminary results of two separate early intervention trials indicated AZT delayed the onset of full-blown AIDS in people with ARC and moderately damaged immune systems, as well as in people who were HIV-positive but asymptomatic. These findings meant a potential tenfold increase in the market for AZT. Wellcome's stock prices jumped 32 percent,[28] once again raising questions about the cost of AZT and who was going to pay for it now that it might be of benefit to a half million Americans.

The *Times* took the company to task in a lead editorial entitled "AZT's Inhuman Cost,"[29] and other editorial boards and columnists joined the fray.

---

*Congress had ponied up $30 million in grants to allow state governments to supply AZT to PWAs who could not otherwise afford it, thereby guaranteeing the company additional sales at taxpayer expense.

On September 5, Burroughs Wellcome met with representatives from AIDS advocacy organizations for what they characterized as an opportunity to share information but continued to wave away demands for an immediate price reduction, claiming it would review the cost of AZT in due time.

Nine days later, time was up.

September 14, 1989: Sell Wellcome

At 9:25 a.m., Peter and six other activists in full stockbroker drag and with forged Bear Stearns badges strolled onto the floor of the New York Stock Exchange.[30] Peter led four of the activists up to a rarely used balcony overlooking the main trading floor, while the other two positioned themselves near the exits below.* As the clock ticked closer to opening, the activists on the balcony quietly chained themselves to the railing and waited.

At the sound of the opening bell, the activists dropped a huge "**Sell Wellcome**" banner over the side of the balcony and set off marine air horns, drowning out trading and stopping all transactions for the next five minutes—a historic first. The activists on the Floor whipped out their cameras and took photos as the angry crowd surged toward the balcony throwing wads of paper and shouting, "Mace the faggots!" The photographers then slipped outside and relayed their cameras to waiting ACT UP members, who ran them over to reporters at the Associated Press. The photographers then snuck back inside while the chained activists littered the trading floor with fake $100 bills stamped "Fuck your profiteering, we're dying while you play business." All seven activists were arrested.[31]

No doubt the police were caught off guard because they were busy preparing for our heavily publicized lunchtime demo outside the Exchange that afternoon, where over 1,500 activists, laden with air horns, whistles, and earplugs, swarmed noontime Wall Street demanding "**Free AZT**." Simultaneous demonstrations were also carried out in San Francisco and at Wellcome's international headquarters in London.

The protests were a public relations disaster for the company. The next morning, the *Wall Street Journal* carried a devastating front-page story warning that Wellcome's high-profile intransigence was putting the entire pharmaceutical industry at risk, noting that concerns about the high price of AZT had already forced changes to the formula for federal support for

---

*Gregg Bordowitz and Scott Robbe joined Peter and his fellow Wellcome veterans Lee Arsenault and James McGrath on the balcony, with Richard Elovich and Robert Hilferty positioned below.

corporate drug development and inspired the National Cancer Institute to include a "reasonable pricing" provision in its licensing agreements.[32]

The actions were covered around the country and in all the major New York dailies with the notable exception of—*guess who?*—the *New York Times*, which had similarly missed the earlier story of the North Carolina action. When they finally picked up the story two days later,[33] they discussed the inside action, but failed to quote any activists, refer to the lunchtime demo, or mention ACT UP.

Four days after our protests, Wellcome announced it would reduce the price of AZT by 25 percent, dropping the yearly cost from $8,000 to $6,000. But the new reductions did little to help the company deflect rising criticism over its pricing structure. Editorials called for Wellcome to open its books to public scrutiny, and several members of Congress began exploring the possibility of revoking the company's exclusive patent on AZT and nationalizing production in the interest of national security.

Nor did it satisfy ACT UP's demand for free AZT.

We knew, of course, that Wellcome wouldn't agree to free distribution of their prize drug, but that wasn't the point. When Peter and T+D first brought their proposal for the Stock Exchange demo to the Floor, their demands to Burroughs Wellcome included a "reasonable" drop in price of 20–30 percent: something achievable that wouldn't damage their credibility as honest brokers or their ability to negotiate. But as Maxine pointed out, it was not ACT UP's job to be reasonable or to negotiate. There were plenty of others who'd be willing to make the necessary compromises. Our role as activists was to keep pushing the envelope and advocating for what was actually needed by people with AIDS and HIV, and for most of those people, AZT would remain financially out of reach even at a 50 percent discount.

Unsatisfied by the new pricing, we moved directly on to the next phase of our campaign, a nationwide boycott of over-the-counter Wellcome products. In coordination with more than a dozen AIDS and patient advocacy groups around the country, we descended on drugstores, stickering Actifed, Sudafed, Neosporin, Empirin, and Polysporin with labels reading "AIDS Profiteer," and reached out to community doctors, sending them lists of comparable drugs and generic medications to recommend and prescribe to their patients.

Chapter 13

Heading Inside

THE MOOD AT Maria's the night of September 12, 1989, was unusually subdued. Instead of clustering in the kitchen, we were gathered around the small TV set in the living room quietly waiting for election returns.

It had been a long hot summer for the mayor. His campaign was floundering, the communities he'd angered were organizing against him, and even the people who liked him were tired of his showboating and confrontational manner. The final straw was his handling of the murder of sixteen-year-old Yusef Hawkins at the hands of an angry mob of young White men and teens in Bensonhurst, Brooklyn. Although he initially acknowledged the painful role racism had played in the attack, Koch switched sides the following week, blaming Black activists for stirring up racial tensions when their peaceful protest march was greeted by jeering White crowds.

Still, it was hard to believe Koch would lose. So, when David Dinkins was announced the winner of the Democratic primary, we were all a bit stunned. "I'm not used to my candidate winning," admitted Maxine Wolfe. Few of us were.

But whatever our personal political preferences, ACT UP was officially nonpartisan; we did not endorse candidates. Our job was to draw attention to "the silent issue of the 1989 Mayoral Elections," the city's AIDS crisis.[1] Working with Jamie Bauer and the Actions Committee, I helped organize "AIDS: Emergency '89: Break the Silence!," a series of actions highlighting the major AIDS issues facing our city.

Our first demonstration, "NYC AIDSCARE: A Crime Giuliani Never Investigated," targeted the opening of the Republican candidate's campaign headquarters. A former US district attorney, Rudy Giuliani had rarely talked about AIDS during his campaign. We thought it only right to help bring the candidate up to speed on the crisis and the actions required from the new mayor.

Our next demonstration, "Safe Sex > Ignorance: What Didn't Your Child Learn in School Today?," highlighted the lack of AIDS education in city schools. Though meagerly attended, this action at the Brooklyn offices of the NYC Board of Education would give birth to a new caucus, the Youth Brigade, later the Youth Education Life Line (YELL) Committee, dedicated to bringing explicit safe sex and AIDS education to students in city schools.

The final demo of the campaign, "Trick or Treat at Trump Tower: Trump Treated to Tax Abatements While NYC Tricked Out of AIDS Services," was a Halloween-themed action demanding the city prioritize the lives of its citizens over the pockets of its real estate contributors. Over a hundred protesters joined our lunchtime picket, waving paper Donald Trump face masks mounted on tongue depressors and chanting à la Bette Davis, "*Donald Trump: 'WHAT A DUMP!' AIDS Housing Now!*" An affinity group dropped a huge "**10,000 Homeless With AIDS**" banner from the building directly across Fifth Avenue, as the Delta Queens rode the golden escalators inside Trump Tower and sent leaflets cascading down the ten-story atrium onto the tourists below.

On Tuesday, November 7, David Dinkins was elected mayor of New York City. Five days later, Stephen Joseph announced his resignation as health commissioner. ACT UP had vanquished two of its major enemies and, realizing the dream of GAA almost twenty years earlier, won recognition of the lesbian and gay community as a formidable voting bloc. We'd earned our place at the table and now, with an ally as mayor, ACT UP would finally have a chance to contribute to the creation and implementation of the city's AIDS policies.

But it wasn't just ACT UP heading "inside." Many of our members were already working at various AIDS and gay organizations, and in late October, I became one of them, working part-time at one of the biggest and most glamorous of them all, the American Foundation for AIDS Research (AmFAR).

Although AmFAR had been cofounded by one of the earliest and best-known heroes of the AIDS epidemic, Dr. Mathilde Krim, it was far easier to describe it to civilians as "the Elizabeth Taylor charity." Taylor had first become involved with AIDS in 1984, as a major supporter of AIDS Project Los Angeles. She then joined the board of the Los Angeles–based National AIDS Research Foundation in 1985, and when that organization merged with Krim's New York–based AIDS Medical Foundation, she stayed on to become the new group's national chairman and the epidemic's star attraction.

But beyond its celebrity, AmFAR was also one of the good guys—lobbying for AIDS funding, fighting for antidiscrimination laws, promoting AIDS education and prevention efforts, and supporting the work of AIDS activists (and often the activists themselves).

Debra Levine, an ACT UP friend, had brought me on board to help prepare for an upcoming meeting of AmFAR's new Community-Based Clinical Trial (CBCT) network. Community-based research provided a faster and much-needed alternative to the more traditional university-based research centers, allowing private doctors and local clinics to band together to conduct efficacy trials on drugs of interest to the community, most notably treatments and prophylaxis for opportunistic infections, using protocols designed with patient input and featuring broad enrollment criteria.

Community-based research was a natural fit for AmFAR. Its predecessor organization had sponsored one of the first community-based trials back in 1984° and Krim was an early financial supporter of New York's Community Research Initiative (CRI) which, along with San Francisco's County Community Consortium, had, in a historic first, recently won FDA approval for aerosolized pentamidine as PCP prophylaxis based solely on data from their community-based studies. (That the drug was approved without requiring the use of a placebo-control group was another historic victory.)

°This was a trial led by Dr. Joseph Sonnabend, testing isoprinosine as a potential immunomodulator to improve immune response in people with HIV. Sonnabend was a pioneering AIDS researcher and community doctor who would become a founder of New York's CRI.

Based on this success and the enthusiastic reports of Reagan's AIDS commission, Congress had appropriated $6 million to NIAID to set up the Community Programs for Clinical Research on AIDS (CPCRA), a pilot program to seed community-based research centers across the country. To help kick-start the process, AmFAR had created their CBCT network to set up new trial centers and expand existing ones to make them more attractive to NIAID and other funding sources.

It was assumed the two networks would share many of the same members and resources and that their efforts would be complementary rather than competitive. NIAID would sponsor the larger trials through CPCRA, and AmFAR the smaller, more targeted research through CBCT. But when NIAID announced its grantees in early October, the New York CRI, along with several other AmFAR grantees, did not make the cut.

Many saw a conspiracy, claiming the rejection was payback for CRI's past criticism of NIAID, or that the "manifest homophobia" of review panel members had doomed not only the CRI proposal, but those of the other major gay-identified applicants.[2] Or maybe it was as simple as NIAID being more comfortable funding organizations that resembled their own—centers affiliated with local government agencies and university hospitals—rather than a grassroots network of loosely affiliated community-based doctors modeled after CRI.[3]

Whatever the cause, AmFAR shifted into crisis mode as it tried to shore up CRI and its other overlooked CBCT centers.

I would face my own crisis a few weeks later, when Debra was suddenly "disappeared" from AmFAR. I was never told the exact circumstances of her dismissal; I just came in one Monday, saw Debra's empty desk, and was promptly offered her job, but reconfigured so I'd be coordinating rather than managing the CBCT program. I'd work directly under the program's science adviser, Paul Corser, and we'd both report to David Corkery, who had taken over the prized CBCT portfolio.

David was another ACT UP comrade, a public relations whiz who'd chaired our Media Committee and helped train and professionalize our media team. While we both acknowledged this current position might not be the perfect fit, it would at least get me in the door. The one condition, however, was I couldn't tell anyone what had happened to Debra. So, I began my job at AmFAR under a cloud, completely unable to account for myself—a state of affairs that would continue for most of my tenure.

■■■

"*ACT UP! FIGHT BACK! FIGHT AIDS!*" ACT UP shocks the crowds at Gay Pride with a Concentration Camp float warning of the growing threats of mandatory AIDS testing and the quarantining of people with HIV. (June 28, 1987) (Photograph by Donna Binder)

"LIVING with AIDS 2 yrs. and 3 mos. + Counting!" One month after I first saw him at my first ACT UP demonstration, Mark Fotopoulos holds his updated sign as he protests the appointment of Cardinal O'Connor to President Reagan's AIDS commission. (July 26, 1987) (Photograph by Donna Binder)

What Ever Happened to Zaps? Bradley Ball and I sing our way through "ACT UP—The Musical!" (Photograph by Tom Keane)

Out and Proud! Enjoying Gay Pride in the mid-'80s with David Serko (*white tank top*), our college friend Howie (*left*), and one of David's many admirers. (Photographer unknown)

Send in the Clowns. When the Civil Rights Commission threatens to restrict the rights of People with AIDS (PWAs), ACT UP turns the hearings into a circus. (May 16, 1988) (Photograph by Tom McKitterick).

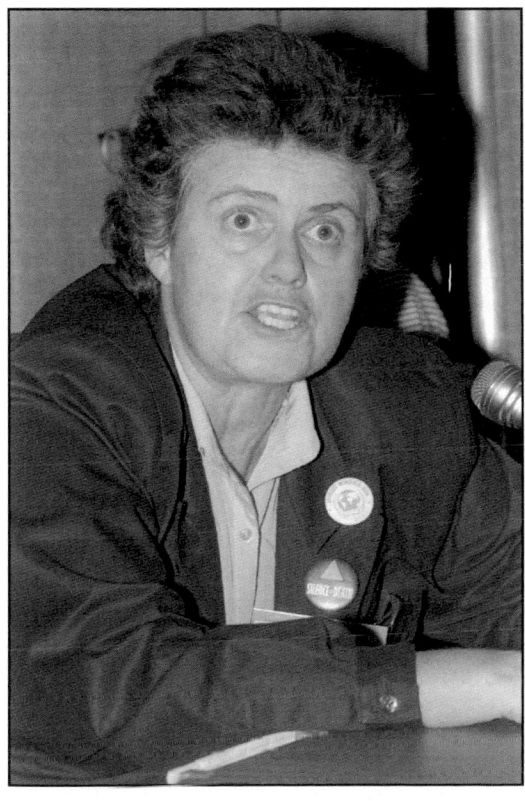

*"**Release the DRUGS!**"* Dr. Iris Long, who first explained the mysteries of the FDA and the drug testing and approval process to ACT UP. (Photograph by T. L. Litt)

*"**HEALTH! CARE! IS a RIGHT! HEALTH Care IS a RIGHT!**"* Robert Garcia leads chants in front of the Department of Health and Human Services (HHS) in Washington, DC, the day before our FDA action. (October 10, 1988) (Photograph by T. L. Litt)

*"**SEIZE CONTROL!**"* ACT UP and a nationwide network of AIDS activist organizations (ACT NOW) shut down the FDA in a daylong protest over the slow and tortured pace of the agency's drug approval process. (October 11, 1988) (Photograph by Donna Binder)

"WE DIE! THEY do NOTHING!" Ortez Alderson leads a joint affinity group of women and people of color protesting how IV-drug users, women, and people of color are regularly excluded from AIDS drug trials. (October 11, 1988) (Photograph by Donna Binder)

"NO! MORE! Business as Usual!" Mark Harrington, who quickly becomes one of ACT UP's leading treatment activists, on the ground at the FDA with his Wave 3 comrades. (October 11, 1988) (Photograph by Tom McKitterick)

"*City AIDS care's Inef-FECtual, Thanks to KOCH, the HET'roSEXual!*" SPREE and friends mock Mayor Ed Koch at ACT UP's "Target City Hall" demonstration. (March 28, 1989) (Photograph by T. L. Litt)

"*The WHOLE WORLD is WATCHING!*" Conyers Thompson (*center*) is surrounded by the press and activists Billy Heekin, Blane Charles, Tom Keane, Rolf Sjogren, and others as ACT UP storms the opening ceremonies of the International AIDS Conference in Montreal. (June 4, 1989) (Photograph by T. L. Litt)

Drugs into Bodies. Jim Eigo, Vito Russo, and Peter Staley present ACT UP's *AIDS Treatment Research Agenda* at the Montreal International AIDS Conference. (June 6, 1989) (Photograph by T. L. Litt)

"2-4-6-8: HOW do you KNOW the Rock-ETTES ARE STRAIGHT?" ACT UP celebrates "Stonewall 20" with a jubilant and unpermitted "In the Tradition of Stonewall" Pride March up Sixth Avenue to Central Park. (June 24, 1989) (Photograph by T. L. Litt)

"STOP THE CHURCH!" ACT UP's largest and most controversial demonstration, cosponsored by WHAM! (Women's Health Action Mobilization!), targets Cardinal O'Connor and the Catholic Church for their opposition to AIDS education, gay rights, and abortion. (December 10, 1989) (Photograph by T. L. Litt)

*"**Not VICTIMS! Not PATIENTS! But People LIVING with AIDS!**"* Ray Navarro celebrates Gay Pride surrounded by his mom (Pat Navarro), Kim Christensen, and his other ACT UP friends and caretakers. (June 24, 1990) (Photograph by T. L. Litt)

By Any Means Necessary. Gadfly/angry prophet/activist conscience/provocateur Larry Kramer during his Malcom X phase, at a protest marking the boycott of Miller Beer, corporate supporters of Senator Jesse Helms. (August 1990) (Photograph by Donna Binder)

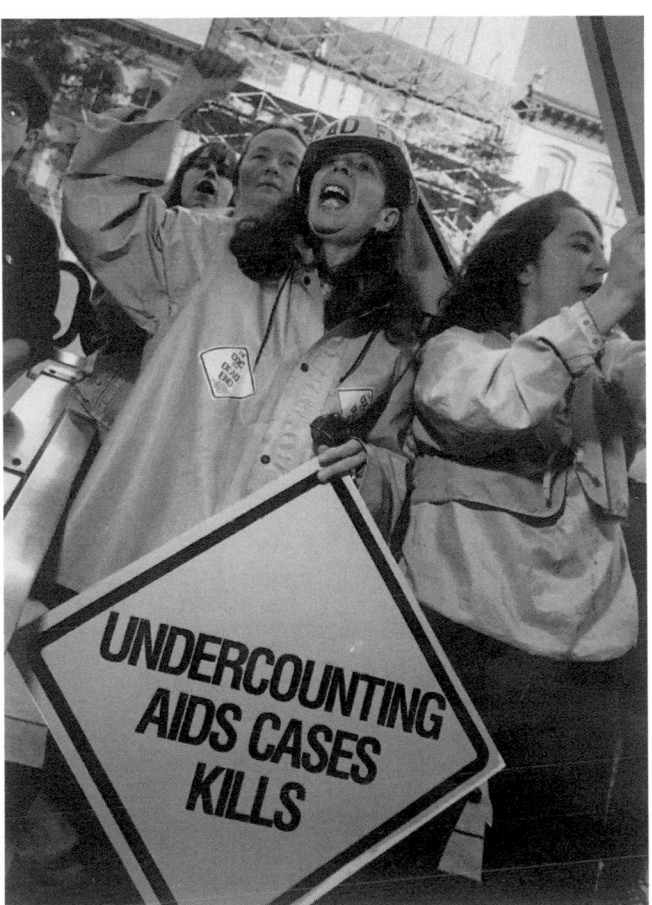

"The CDC is KILLING Me!"
Maxine Wolfe, who constantly pushed ACT UP to expand its agenda to address the needs of all people with AIDS, pickets the local CDC office demanding they expand the AIDS definition to include the HIV-related infections found in women. (May 21, 1991) (Photograph by Tom McKitterick)

Huracán SIDA. ACT UP's Latina/o Caucus travels to Puerto Rico for a monthlong series of protests and outreach efforts. (July–August 1990) (Photographer unknown, archive of Gonzalo Aburto)

Women Don't Get AIDS. They Just Die From It. Prison activist Katrina Haslip (*right*) is one of two dozen HIV-positive women protesting at HHS in support of a class action lawsuit by Terry McGovern (*center*) demanding Social Security benefits for women with HIV. (October 2, 1990) (Photograph by Donna Binder)

"DEAD ADDICTS DON'T Re-COVER!" Illith Rosenblum, Jane Auerbach, Richard Elovich, and Gay Wachman bring used hypodermic needles collected while conducting needle exchange to the NYC Department of Health as part of ACT UP's Day of Desperation. (January 23, 1991) (Photograph by Ellen Neipris)

"We're ALL Living With AIDS!" Marion Banzhaf, Loring McAlpin, Gregg Bordowitz, and Richard Elovich at Grand Central Terminal for the grand finale of ACT UP's Day of Desperation. (January 23, 1991) (Photograph by Tom McKitterick)

"*114,000 DEAD from AIDS! WHERE IS GEORGE?*" ACT UP launches its monthlong "Target Bush" campaign by descending on the Bush "ancestral home" in Kennebunkport, Maine. (September 1, 1991) (Photograph by Ellen Neipris)

"*We're HERE! We're QUEER! We're FA-A-A-BULOUS! (Get Used to It!)*" Little did I know after my "first date" with Joe Chiplock in Kennebunkport that we'd still be together thirty-plus years later. (Photographer unknown)

Bob "Voice of the People" Rafsky. Bob Rafsky mouthing off at a cop while getting arrested with Charles King at an AIDS housing demonstration. (Photograph by T. L. Litt)

What About AIDS? ACT UP's "AIDS Campaign '92" runs AIDS as a "candidate for national issue," successfully pressuring presidential candidates from both parties to talk about AIDS, even at the Democratic Convention. (July 14, 1992) (Photograph by T. L. Litt)

Living—not dying—with AIDS. Though physically weakened and now completely blind, David Serko (*right*) still lives his life. (Summer 1992) (Photograph by Joe Chiplock)

"***Bringing the DEAD to YOUR DOOR!***" David Robinson, holding the ashes of his lover, Warren Pierce, leads a group of mourners to the White House to throw their loved ones' remains on the White House Lawn. (October 11, 1992). (Photograph by Donna Binder)

"*Bringing the DEAD to YOUR DOOR!*" *Part II.* On election eve, ACT UP holds a political funeral for Mark Lowe Fisher, marching his open casket through the streets of the city to President Bush's campaign headquarters. (November 2, 1992) (Photograph by Tom McKitterick)

An Army of Lovers. I gasped when this photo of David Serko and Howie Pope unexpectedly popped up on my phone during the February 28, 2020, *New York Times* ACT UP photo shoot, twenty-five-plus years after they both had died. (June 29, 1991) (Photograph by Raymond Diskin Black)

"How Many MORE Have to DIE?" (Photograph by T. L. Litt)

"We'll NEVER be SILENT AGAIN!" A boy and his bullhorn. (Photograph by T. L. Litt)

In mid-November, NIAID and AmFAR sponsored the first joint meeting of the CBCT and CPCRA networks in Washington, DC. The goal was to ensure all the community-research centers were operating at the same professional level, regardless of their funding source or sponsorship, and had the necessary expertise to ensure clinical trials could be conducted seamlessly across both networks. In addition to Paul and me, David and Dr. Krim were coming down to DC to allay fears, smooth ruffled feathers, and ensure all the centers were able to move forward. But after a token appearance at the opening session, they all disappeared, leaving me as the sole AmFAR representative at the meeting.

I'd barely been introduced to any of these people and had been given no briefing on AmFAR's positions. Everyone was asking for Debra and wondering when they could speak to Paul or Dr. Krim, and I couldn't give them an answer. From the dais, Fauci and other NIAID officials asked for confirmations, commitments, and clarifications from AmFAR, and all I could do was mutter, "I don't know" or "I'm not sure." I was living a real-life version of the actor's nightmare, with no idea of my lines or what was expected of me.

Midway through the *second* day of this, I bolted from the meeting and fled to my room. I locked the door, turned off the lights, and rocked back and forth on the floor.

I'd been found out. I wasn't an "expert" on AIDS. I was a fake and a fraud—a man-child play-acting at being an activist. And now everyone knew it. But rocking and recriminations would only take me so far. I needed to find a more useful coping strategy.

Though not a religious man, I've always believed in the magical healing power of musical theater. As a child, many was the time I'd beat back the slings and arrows of outrageous fortune by slamming my bedroom door, cranking up my stereo, and belting "I'm the Greatest Star" along with Barbra Streisand. (And if you don't believe me, ask my brother and sister.)

Well, the Goddess of Musical Theater was once again looking out for me, for when I put on my headphones and hit "Play," my Walkman sputtered out the comforting sounds of Ben Vereen telling me that despite looking "frenzied and frazzled," I just needed to "take it easy" and "trust awhile," and I'd "pull through."[4] And after a few rewinds and a bunch of sing-alongs, I believed him. I could only do what I could do. If they thought it okay to leave me without any information or instruction, that was on them. And since I couldn't be expected to represent AmFAR, the best I could do was make a decent representation of myself.

And from that point on, I was Miss Congeniality—relaxed, funny, and charming. I didn't pretend to know where anyone was or what AmFAR's plans might be. I circulated, flirted, and introduced myself to everyone. And if someone had a question, I wrote it down and promised to relay it back to the bigwigs at AmFAR—assuming I ever saw them again.

Ben

Working at AmFAR, however, had other compensations.

There was the money—nothing extravagant, but it was steady and far more than I was used to. And then there was what it allowed me to do, like fly to LA for romantic weekends with my new long-distance . . . whatever, Ben.

I'd been introduced to Ben at an ACT UP meeting in early October by our mutual friend Tracey Litt. There was something vaguely bear-like about Ben, not in the current hairy-beefy way, but more like Yogi Bear—tall, a little goofy, with big paws. He was lovely.

We had a lot in common—both nice Jewish boys from New York, we shared a similar sense of humor and immediately understood one another's obscure theater and film references. Ben was working in a production office in LA, reading scripts and trying to break into the movie business, while I still imagined myself an actor, if one on a somewhat prolonged hiatus.

More significantly, we were both looking for a vacation from our current lives.

Ben was trying to get out of a relationship that had gone sour, while I was searching for at least a temporary respite from the world of AIDS. I was also envious of my actor friends, many of whom seemed to be proceeding quite nicely with their lives and careers without being burdened by my need to personally end the AIDS crisis. That two of my former acting-class colleagues had just landed major roles on hit TV series only added to my feelings of frustration. Hadn't I earned the right to be perfectly selfish for a while? Since when had the pursuit of personal happiness or a career become politically incorrect?

For nine days, Ben and I conducted our own little getaway affair. We went to the theater, to movies and museums. We enjoyed walks in the park, dinners in the Village, and sex at my apartment.

When Ben returned to LA, we started a long-distance romance, exchanging letters, phone calls, and the occasional mixtape. More and more, Ben and LA seemed like a viable alternative to my current AIDS-besotted life. Maybe I could move out there and get back to my acting. Maybe he could introduce me to some movie people or an agent. Maybe he was what I needed to get my life back on track.

David

Late that fall, I got a surprise call from David Serko. He'd been away, performing in regional theater and on tour in Europe, and we'd been out of touch. But now he was back in town for a day or two for some tests. He'd developed these strange abscesses on his arms and legs that wouldn't heal. No, they weren't KS, but they'd found something in those abscesses, though they weren't sure what. Otherwise, he felt fine and was going back out on tour.

David had always been a private person, at least with me. He never complained or volunteered information about himself, and as a result, I didn't spend too much time worrying about him. David always managed.

But this felt different. Nonetheless, David danced around the details when I asked. Nothing to worry about, he said. And because I desperately wanted to believe him, I did.

November 5–8, 1989: ACT UP at the ACTG

The researchers and principal investigators of NIAID's AIDS Clinical Trial Group (ACTG) program were *not* happy. Here they were at the top of their field, experts battling to solve one of the great riddles of modern medical science, only to have their professional expertise questioned, their livelihoods threatened, and their reputations tarnished by a bunch of scruffy, know-nothing street radicals and community activists—the very same ungrateful people whose lives they were trying to save.

The ACTG was NIAID's second attempt to create an AIDS research program. The first, the AIDS Trial Evaluation Unit (ATEU) initiative, had been established in 1985, but four months later, the unanticipated breakthrough success of AZT required the ATEU to shift focus almost entirely to large-scale Phase II AZT-based studies. By the end of 1987, NIAID was forced to acknowledge the program was a failure. The sudden scramble to carry out AZT trials had swamped the system and left it with neither the time nor the flexibility to correct problems or improve the efficiency of the massive program.[5] As reconfigured, the ACTG program would give researchers a bigger role in developing priorities and running studies in the belief that "investigator-initiated research" would produce better results in the long run.

And now their efforts were being disrupted yet again, not just by the street activists, but by NIAID director Tony Fauci. Not only had Fauci thrown his weight behind the parallel track proposal; he was trying to open their quarterly ACTG meetings to the prying eyes of these self-same, self-righteous community "experts."

Fauci had first invited members of T+D to attend the July ACTG meeting, but they agreed to wait at the request of ACTG chief Dan Hoth, who wanted some more time to prepare his researchers for the activists' arrival. When Hoth failed to follow through, T+D again confronted Fauci, who then invited, then disinvited, and then reinvited members to attend the November meeting.[6]

Any hope for a warm reception quickly vanished with Hoth's welcome remarks, which warned the startled scientists that the Visigoths of ACT UP had invaded the sacred citadel. "Against our will, they have sent four representatives who are here today. We did not invite them and we wish they were not here. Nonetheless, we did not wish to provoke a physical confrontation by attempting to secure their exit."[7] The four activists—Mark Harrington, Ken Fornataro, Rebecca Pringle Smith,* and Iris Long—were then informed that this was a "closed scientific meeting" and that they would be barred from attending two-thirds of the scheduled sessions, forbidden to speak, and prohibited from citing data without permission. Even Jim Eigo, who was attending as a member of the Institutes of Medicine panel charged with investigating the NIH and its response to AIDS, was "escorted bodily" out of a closed meeting of ddI investigators—a study Jim had helped set up.[8]

Despite their limited access, the activists still got an earful. The big news was the unveiling of the preliminary results of the two trials (ACTG 016 and 019), which claimed to show AZT delaying progression of disease in patients with early ARC and in asymptomatic seropositives. While the NIH had already announced these findings in mid-August, closer inspection of the data raised questions about the drug's purported effectiveness.†

We were not alone in our skepticism. British and French scientists found the results so inconclusive, they decided to continue their similar "Concorde"

---

*At the time, Rebecca was working at AmFAR as an assistant project manager, providing technical assistance to clinical research programs and staffing the Data Safety Monitoring Board. When moonlighting with ACT UP, she would often use the nom de guerre Cassandra Freedom-Jones, so she could speak to the media and provide additional scientific background about our proposals without running afoul of her superiors. The ruse was so convincing that Ms. Freedom-Jones was reputedly quoted in the New York Times.

†For instance, while 50 percent of those who were asymptomatic and progressed to AIDS had developed PCP, that number dropped to only 13 percent once participants were allowed to take PCP prophylaxis—raising the question of whether the prophylactic treatment was more effective in preventing progression to full-blown AIDS than AZT.

study to its originally planned conclusion in 1993, rather than shut it down based on the ACTG data.

But even as the ACTG continued to trumpet the questionable benefits of early intervention, they had yet to fully publicize the studies' other major finding—that low-dose AZT was equally effective and far less toxic than the current high-dose regimen. Instead of alerting doctors and sparing patients the brutal side effects of high-dose AZT, the researchers were busy sending out advisories to scare people away from the ddI expanded access program, which they blamed for the underenrollment of their clinical trials. They then poured their concerns and objections into the willing ear and keyboard of *New York Times* science writer Gina Kolata.

Though the list of science writers covering AIDS for the *Times* was hardly a noble one, Gina Kolata was in a class by herself. Admired for her ability to translate difficult science into headline-grabbing stories, her facility often came at a steep price. Earlier in the summer, in a rare front-page article,[9] Kolata had touted the results of an old and outdated study of alpha interferon, a drug that had since received a "Not Recommended" rating from the NIH. A month later, her article on the underground testing of Compound Q,[10] a Chinese cucumber extract that had shown great efficacy in the test tube against HIV, was likewise riddled with mistakes and inaccuracies.

Then in late November, at the urging of disgruntled ACTG researchers, Kolata focused her sights on parallel track and ddI. "Almost 20 times as many people have flocked to free distribution of the new drug ddI than have signed up for the clinical trial," she breathlessly reported, "leaving researchers in despair over whether they will ever be able to complete the formal study."[11] Never mind that 90 percent of the patients who'd "flocked" to the expanded access distribution were ineligible to enroll in the clinical trial, or that despite multiple delays, the clinical trials were enrolling at a faster rate than almost any other ACTG trial.

A month later, Kolata scored another dangerous front-page article touting bone marrow transplants in tandem with AZT as a potential cure for AIDS.[12] The article was based on the report of a single patient who had died a little over a month after the transplant, his autopsy apparently revealing an absence of the AIDS virus. Two days later, Kolata was forced to walk back her story in a second article[13] acknowledging the significant lack of data, including whether the tests performed could even identify HIV in an autopsy situation.*

With the *Times* apparently unwilling to take any action against Kolata, ACT UP began its own campaign, targeting the reporter with a raft of Christmas cards sent to her home and the *Times* offices bemoaning her lack of qualifications as an AIDS reporter. This was followed by another round of stickers for newsstands and newspaper boxes proclaiming: "Gina Kolata of *The New York Times* is the Worst AIDS Reporter in America."

However, in the odd-bedfellows world of AIDS activism, this didn't stop ACT UP and AmFAR from successfully petitioning Kolata to write an article about the FDA's delay in approving the lower-dose AZT regimen, which finally shamed Wellcome into submitting its data to the FDA.[14] The new dose regimen was announced three weeks later, on January 16.

But ACT UP had its own problems. We were broke. Despite being an all-volunteer organization with no hired staff, our expenses—including rent and utilities on our new ACT UP Workspace† and our storage unit, and a whopping Xerox bill at Village Copiers—ran to roughly $4,300/month, not including one-off costs for out-of-town actions and major demonstrations.

We'd always spent more money than we had, figuring we'd find some way to make up the difference. But by the end of October, our luck had run out. Our checkbook was locked away and no amount of T-shirt or button sales was going to bring in the necessary income.[15] We needed a fundraising miracle.

And we got one.

On Sunday, December 2, activists and art lovers gathered at the Lawrence A. Wien Center for Dance and Theater at 890 Broadway for the Auction for Action, a benefit for ACT UP. Produced by Sean Strub and Steve Petoniak,[16] and cochaired by David Hockney and Annie Leibovitz, the auction featured

---

*In 2019, a second patient was reportedly "cured" through a similar treatment, though questions remain about its viability as a treatment option.

†ACT UP had moved into its first Workspace, located on the Mezzanine Floor of the old Port Authority Building at 111 Eighth Avenue between Fifteenth and Sixteenth Streets (now the New York City home of Google), on May 1, 1989, thanks to a $10,000 grant from GMHC, which helped us pay off the first year's rent. The office was staffed completely by volunteers, as ACT UP had no paid staff.

paintings, photographs, sculptures, costumes, designer clothing, and more, from a who's who of the New York arts and culture scene: everyone from Keith Haring, Nan Goldin, Robert Mapplethorpe, and Andy Warhol to Ed Baynard, Judy Chicago, Francesco Clemente, Ross Bleckner, Robert Gober, Elizabeth Murray, Romare Bearden, Peter Max, Christo, and Robert Rauschenberg, as well as works by the cochairs and several of the ACT UP's in-house photographers. The auction brought in $335,000 and saved our necks.*

Just in time to have our heads handed to us.

---

*A second and even more successful "Auction for Action" was held the following year, netting us over $600,000.

Chapter 14

Stop the Church

THERE WAS NO question Cardinal O'Connor and the Catholic Church were legitimate targets for a demonstration. Since his appointment as bishop in 1984, O'Connor had aggressively attacked the gay community, successfully challenging Executive Order 50, which protected city workers from being fired because of their sexual orientation, and fighting subsequent attempts by the city council to legislatively restore the order once it had been struck down in court. The cardinal had also led the opposition to the city's gay rights law, arguing against the bill's antidiscrimination protections even as the church was explicitly exempted from its requirements.

In early 1987, the cardinal had literally closed the doors of the church to gay Catholics, expelling Dignity and other gay Catholic organizations from the diocese's church-owned properties, where they'd been holding their meetings and celebrating special masses for over a decade. The action was prompted by the publication of the Vatican's "Letter to the Bishops of the Catholic Church on the Pastoral Care of Homosexual Persons," which instructed the bishops to withdraw their support from "any organizations which seek to undermine the teaching of the church" on homosexuality. The letter, which was written by Cardinal Ratzinger, who later became Pope Benedict XVI, judged the mere inclination to homosexuality as "ordered toward an intrinsic moral evil" and suggested that while violence against homosexuals was "deplorable," it was to be expected when faced with legislation that condones or protects homosexual practices.[1]

The Catholic Church's stand on AIDS was hardly more enlightened: opposing all AIDS education efforts beyond affirming "abstinence outside of marriage and fidelity within marriage."[2] When the policy committee of the United States Catholic Conference had the temerity to suggest the church take a more realistic and less doctrinaire approach to AIDS prevention, such as providing information about condom use when dealing with non-Catholics,[3] they were publicly attacked by O'Connor for ignoring the purported failure rate of condoms and insufficiently emphasizing issues of sin and guilt, and were forced to withdraw the offending paper.[4]

The cardinal quickly became the Vatican's favorite emissary in America, forcefully espousing the preferred conservative line on social issues like AIDS, abortion, and homosexuality. "Good morality is good medicine," exclaimed O'Connor during his opening speech at the November 1989 Vatican conference on AIDS.[*] "Sometimes I believe the greatest damage done to persons with AIDS is done by those health-care professionals who refuse to confront the moral dimensions of sexual aberrations or drug abuse."[5] In his own remarks, Pope John Paul II slammed the door on any sanctioning of safe sex education or condom use, stating it was "morally illicit" to support prevention methods that violate "the authentically human sense of human sexuality."[6]

While the Catholic Church had long been involved in city politics, O'Connor had pushed past the previously accepted boundaries of church influence. He not only campaigned against gay rights and AIDS education, opposing the distribution of condoms and safe sex information in public schools and throughout the city, he demanded total fealty from liberal Catholic politicians, whom he threatened with excommunication over their stance on abortion rights. He'd endorsed the zealots of Operation Rescue and their often-violent antiabortion activities, urging all good Catholics to escalate their attacks on abortion rights and on women's health facilities, famously putting a "Help Wanted" ad in *Catholic New York* to recruit for the Sisters of Life, an order of nuns who would devote themselves full-time to legal, medical, and political opposition to abortion.[7]

Few institutions better illustrated the kinship between the issues of AIDS and reproductive rights than the church, and Stop the Church would provide our best opportunity yet to unite these two causes in the public imagination. The Women's Health Action Mobilization or WHAM!, a "non-partisan group

---

[*]The Fourth International Conference of the Pontifical Council for Pastoral Assistance to Health Care Workers. As in, "How should 'we' treat 'them,' the unmentionable 'lepers'?" The "othering" is palpable even in the title.

committed to demanding, securing and defending absolute reproductive freedom and quality health care for ALL women"[8] similarly dedicated to direct action, shared our vision and joined us as cosponsor.

The joint church working group proposed two concurrent demonstrations: a large legal protest outside the cathedral and a series of affinity group actions inside during Sunday Mass. As a matter of strategy, a number of us felt attacking O'Connor inside the cathedral was a bad idea. The cardinal had every right to say whatever he wanted from his pulpit; the church was his appropriate sphere, and confronting him where he had the greatest legitimacy seemed wrongheaded. Further, any controversy provoked by a demonstration inside the cathedral risked overwhelming our issues and could unintentionally shift sympathy to the cardinal.

For me, the more fundamental problem was the idea of invading a house of worship and disrupting a religious service. Maybe it was a Jewish thing, given the long history of attacks on Jewish synagogues and religious practices. (I couldn't help but notice many of those who shared my concerns were also Jewish.)

But the organizers, who were overwhelmingly Catholic, insisted it was the congregation, not the building, that constituted the real church. They walked us through the long history of demonstrations that had taken place inside St. Pat's, including a silent protest by a group of nuns who had lain down in the aisles to protest the church's policies toward women. Even more recently, the gay Catholic group Dignity had held monthly demonstrations inside the cathedral to protest their eviction from the church-owned spaces, including actions where members would stand or turn their backs on the cardinal during his homily, and wear signs like "Another Gay Catholic" or "I Don't Take Communion from Bigots."* These silent demonstrations, they promised, would be the model for their affinity actions.

Despite their explanations, I remained conflicted about the indoor demonstration. I felt there was something dishonest about it, a disconnect between our stated purpose and the action itself. Although we claimed to be protesting church interference with public health policy, the real motivation seemed to be the overwhelming—and completely understandable—sense of pain and betrayal felt by gay Catholics and their need to strike out at their church.

---

*After eleven members of Dignity were arrested inside the cathedral in December 1987, the diocese then obtained a court injunction prohibiting the protesters from interrupting or interfering with services or from picketing or demonstrating on the sidewalk outside the cathedral.

But as it *was* their church, I bowed to their judgment. The Floor likewise approved both actions with one major caveat—we strongly requested that the affinity group protests not actively interfere with the conducting of the religious service or include any screaming or violent behavior.

Taking into consideration concerns about the potential backlash, the organizers went to St. Patrick's the weekend before the action and handed out a low-key flyer formatted as a letter to parishioners, announcing the demonstration and asking for their "understanding and participation." It explained the reasons for our protest, reminding them, "The moral beliefs of the Catholic Church pertain only to its members. The doctrine of any one religion cannot be made into law without undermining our entire system of government. Religious freedom is dependent on a separation of church and state."[9]

We conducted a similar outreach effort to the police department, which had a strong and historic connection to the Catholic Church and St. Patrick's in particular; reaffirming our pledge to nonviolent protest and asking the police to respond in kind.

Nonetheless, many of us expected the worst. Although the action inside the cathedral would be more inflammatory, no cop was going to bash heads inside a church surrounded by nuns and priests. Outside on the street was another story. So, despite my deep misgivings about the action, there was never any question about showing up. Strong and experienced marshals were going to be essential for keeping everyone safe, and I felt it was my responsibility to take care of my friends in what could easily descend into a police riot.

December 10, 1989: St. Patrick's Cathedral

Dressed in my thermal underwear, two pairs of socks, a thick wool sweater, and my warmest winter parka, I joined the more than 4,500 protesters braving the cold in the barricaded police pens lining the west side of Fifth Avenue across from St. Patrick's. It was a massive turnout—far bigger than any of our demonstrations before or since. We were met by a grim-faced army of over 400 police, as well as a small cluster of maybe 100 counter-demonstrators standing in front of the famous Saks Fifth Avenue Christmas windows and holding their usual holiday collection of fetal photos, Bible quotes, and antigay slogans.

Given the stakes, the atmosphere outside the cathedral was oddly Halloween-like. There were lots of costumes—protesters sporting miters or wearing nun drag. Ray Navarro, recovered from his recent illness, was dressed like Jesus in a long flowing white robe and crown of thorns, interviewing demonstrators as a reporter from the "Fire and Brimstone Network." Protesters carried posters with cheeky messages like **"Curb Your Dogma,"** with its stick figure illustration of a priest sweeping up behind his dog, and **"Know Your Scumbags,"** which featured a comparison photo of the mitered cardinal side by side with a similarly shaped condom. Wave 3 paraded a twenty-foot-long condom stuffed with balloons they christened **"Condom O'Connor,"** while the crowd serenaded the counterprotesters with boisterous chants of *"Keep Your Rosaries Off My Ovaries"* and *"They Say, 'DON'T FUCK!' We Say, 'FUCK YOU!'"* Though I did my best to discourage the latter chant, as it automatically precluded any live TV or radio coverage, I suspect it was the most honest chant of the day.

Eventually, the crowd grew so large we could no longer move; any attempt to expand the pens or take the street in CD actions was quickly shut down by a wall of cops, who lifted the metal street stanchions to push us back onto the sidewalk. At the height of one of our shoving matches, a cab pulled up outside the cathedral, and out popped a half dozen activists in clown outfits and makeup. Calling themselves "Operation Ridiculous,"[10] they ran around the street in wild circles until the cops grabbed them and dragged them into the waiting police wagons.

Inside the cathedral, the tone was far more somber. Church officials had taken the unusual precaution of clearing the church after the 9 o'clock mass, bringing in police with bomb-sniffing dogs and checking the bags of everyone coming into the church for the 10:15 service. While there'd been no threats of bombs or violence, it helped establish their prepared narrative of "The Church under Siege." This was merely the first of the diocese's many media-savvy theatrics, which included filling the cathedral with sympathetic dignitaries like Mayor Koch and Police Commissioner Condon and stationing a dramatic wall of police along the front altar rail.

The protests inside the cathedral had been planned in private by the participating affinity groups, and the details remained unknown to the larger organization. As best we knew, it would be a silent action during the cardinal's homily, when the protesters would walk calmly and quietly into the center aisle of the cathedral and lie down in a symbolic die-in. While it was no doubt enough to get people arrested, it wasn't anything that hadn't been done in St. Patrick's before by other groups.

But as the activists began lying down in the aisles, Michael Petrelis stood up on a pew and started blowing his whistle and shouting, "Stop Killing Us!,"[11] at which point the dam broke and both parishioners and protesters began screaming. O'Connor stopped his homily and, as prearranged, had his comments distributed by a group of visiting seminarians. He then asked the churchgoers to stand and join him in reciting the Lord's Prayer, followed, at increasing volume, by several Hail Marys to try to drown out the shouts of protesters as they were carried out of the church.

Once things quieted down sufficiently, the cardinal returned to continue the Mass. Contrary to our agreement, the handful of activists who remained in the cathedral continued their disruptions. When, as the cardinal was conducting the sacred act of transubstantiation, a lone heckler shouted out, "O'Connor, you're a murderer," the cardinal retreated to his sacramental throne and sat, head in hands, ostensibly deep in prayer, as press cameras whirred and captured the image for the papers and evening news reports. Parishioners then stepped over the remaining protesters and moved to the altar to receive communion.

Among those parishioners was Tom Keane. The son of a Catholic school-teacher, Tom had joined ACT UP in 1987, while still attending Yale as an undergraduate. His actions at St. Patrick's would take on a life of their own, coming to define not only "Stop the Church" but, for much of the country, ACT UP itself.

Tom was a member of the Speaking in Tongues affinity group, which had planned to line up to receive communion, but then refuse it and say something in protest instead. But when it was Tom's turn, rather than refusing the offering, he put out his hand out of habit and received the consecrated wafer. Not knowing what to do, he crumpled it in his fingers, declaring, "Opposing safe sex is murder," as the pieces fell to the floor.[12] The police arrested him immediately, pulling him away from the altar as the priests dove to pick up the pieces of desecrated wafer.

Although Tom would later characterize his action as "a symbolic destruction of the body of Christ to signify the real destruction of human life by the Church's policies,"[13] it proved a gift to the cardinal and the reactionary forces of the church. Ignored were the 4,500 demonstrators protesting outside, the 110 arrests, and the legitimate issues of church overreach into the public sphere. Forgotten was O'Connor's support of Operation Rescue and the dangerous real-life repercussions of the church's "love the sinner, hate the sin" attitude toward the gay community. Instead, the cardinal was able to position himself as the defender of all religion and the victim of our intolerance, rather than the other way around.

"All hatred is terribly disturbing," he announced, but "I must preach what the church preaches, teach what the church teaches."[14] The congregation then broke into several minutes of applause, clapping again as O'Connor left the sanctuary and embraced his pal, Mayor Koch.

First set, the cardinal. Then the real match began.

The demonstration dominated the slow Sunday news cycle and was the top story on evening and late-night news broadcasts across the country. Monday morning, it was the cover story in the *Post*, the *Daily News*, and *Newsday*—the *Times* relegating its article to the Metro section—and received extensive coverage in the Spanish-language newspapers *El Diario*, *La Prensa*, and *La Nación*. Never had a demonstration of ours gotten more press or publicity. But unfortunately, we'd lost control of the narrative.

Immediately after the service, O'Connor held a press conference where the new story lines were drawn. The cardinal asserted he "was saddened but not really frightened"[15] by the demonstration, and while he supported the right to peaceful protest—forgetting, for the moment, the church's injunctions against Dignity—he left it to "the authorities" to determine whether our protest qualified as peaceful and what the appropriate legal consequences might be.* However, he was still stung enough by the protest to respond to some of our claims, trotting out the familiar church talking points and noting the church had provided more beds for AIDS patients than any other private organization. (He neglected to mention, however, how the influx of AIDS patients, compensated at a substantially higher rate by the state, had rescued many financially threatened Catholic hospitals from bankruptcy.)[16] He also claimed the church was the very first segment of society to respond to the epidemic—the gay community, I suppose, not qualifying in his eyes as a part of society.

It was left to soon-to-be-former Mayor Koch to execute the main pivot in the church's response. After questioning whether the demonstration was

---

*Out of the 110 arrests, six members would forgo the district attorney's offer of adjournment in exchange for three days' community service and would go to trial on October 31, 1990, as the "Safe Sex Six": Charles King, Ann Northrup, Kathy Ottersten, Rod Sorge, Sharon Tramutola, and Michael Wiggins. (A seventh arrestee, Dan Keith Williams, had his charges dismissed prior to trial due to lack of evidence.) The six were charged with criminal trespass, disorderly conduct, resisting arrest, and disruption of a religious service, and faced potential penalties of up to six months in jail. On January 4, 1991, the six were found guilty and given conditional discharges on the condition they perform 56–70 hours of community service.

a legitimate expression of free speech and seconding the idea we were attacking church teachings and not their undue influence in the public sphere, the mayor suggested the demonstration was an attempt to forcibly take away the right of Catholics to practice their religion, and that the perpetrators should be punished.[17] The cardinal would fully embrace this theme during his Monday press conference, where he proclaimed, in response to no known threat, "It would have to be over my dead body that the mass will not go on, that the word would not be preached orally or distributed in writing."[18] Of course, no one had threatened any such thing, but having given the cardinal an opportunity to paint himself as victim, rather than victimizer, he played it for all it was worth.

With great outward humility, the cardinal added he "felt very sad for the demonstrators. There was really so much hatred. . . . It's not that they hate me. That's not the important part. But I think that all hatred is destructive, and it primarily destroys the hater, not the person hated."[19] But given how the church's pronouncements about "hating the sin but loving the sinner" is used to condone the deaths of the gay "sinners"—whether from unprotected sex or antigay violence—the nuances of his position seem rather beside the point.

Naturally, the press ran with the "over my dead body" comment and the quote made the covers of two of the daily New York tabloids Tuesday morning. Virtually all the second-day coverage, masterfully orchestrated by the archdiocese, was pro-church, with little or no discussion of the issues that had prompted our protest. Tuesday also brought forth the odious scribblings of noted syndicated homophobes Ray Kerrison and Patrick Buchanan, as well as a slew of editorials, all of which condemned the actions inside the cathedral, though a few, including both the *Times* and *Newsday*, seemed okay with the actions outside the cathedral.

What surprised me most, however, was how shocked many ACT UP members were by the ferocity of the backlash and the almost universal condemnation of the demonstration. They also seemed stunned that so many of our allies, while generally supporting our goals and issues, had likewise denounced the action inside the cathedral.

Well, of course they did.

Even if, as individuals, they supported our action—and many community leaders and activists had participated in the demonstration outside the cathedral—organizationally, they had no choice but to distance themselves from the controversy because they were all, to some degree, dedicated to winning hearts and minds and garnering mainstream acceptance. We often berated these same groups for this very reason, priding ourselves in the purity of our actions and our ability to push the envelope and go it alone without needing anyone's approval. And now we were getting upset because they didn't have our back? They weren't supposed to. The whole point of playing "bad cop" is to allow the "good cop" to gain advantage by playing against you.

On Wednesday, ACT UP and WHAM! finally held their own press conference and tried to reframe the coverage. Refusing to apologize "for the actions of the 5,000 people who came on Sunday to protest Church actions that limit the rights of all Americans to make personal decisions in their own lives,"[20] we acknowledged the protest inside the cathedral was supposed to be a silent demonstration but characterized the ensuing actions as the "spontaneous and personal expressions of individuals,"[21] most of whom were Catholics protesting the policies of their own church. Unfortunately, neither this, nor the fact that most of the policies being challenged were matters of interpretation and not dogma, gained much traction.

In the end, ACT UP was beaten, but still defiant. As was our habit, we circled the wagons, claimed the reaction we received was exactly what we'd intended, and embraced Stop the Church as a brilliant success that had created a space for open discussion of the church as a political entity.

And maybe it was.

While it would be impossible to confirm a direct correlation, the church soon found itself on the losing end of several issues over the next few years. Only a week after the demonstration, an exposé of sexual abuse involving Father Bruce Ritter, the founder of Covenant House, the Catholic home for runaway teenagers, was published in the *Village Voice*.[22] The church also suffered a noticeable diminution of its local power base when Mayor Dinkins replaced friend-of-the-cardinal Koch. In short order, the church found itself embroiled in years of tough battles over AIDS education, condom distribution, and the teaching of the gay-friendly "Rainbow Curriculum" in the city's public schools. Even the church's contracts for publicly funded AIDS care facilities would come under increased scrutiny due to the diocese's unwillingness to provide clients with information about safe sex, birth control, and abortion, as required by state law.*

On the other hand, it certainly made life harder for the mainstream gay groups who were repeatedly asked to answer for our action, as if all gay people

---

* In May 1990, the state threatened to withhold $30 million in Medicaid funds if the church didn't sign a statement accepting state guidelines for the treatment of patients, including the provision of birth control, abortion counseling, and safe sex information. The eventual compromise, exempting the church from providing services but requiring them to refer patients to off-site providers, was challenged by a lawsuit from ACT UP and GMHC.

had taken over the cathedral and desecrated the wafer. O'Connor would continue to use it as a cudgel against gay Catholic groups to ensure, among other things, that the Ancient Order of Hibernians prohibit the Irish Lesbian and Gay Organization (ILGO) from marching in the annual St. Patrick's Day parade.* And whenever conservatives and the religious right wanted to whip up a frenzy of outrage, you could be sure footage from Stop the Church would be trotted out alongside photos of drag queens and men in leather marching in Gay Pride parades.

Not that I believe in self-censorship in order to avoid giving "ammunition" to our enemies to use against us. Our enemies will always find reasons to hate us, and it's pointless to waste time contorting ourselves into odd shapes to try to win their approval. But even now, I remain unclear about our goals for the demonstration. And regardless of precedent or the legitimacy of the cause, I still think what went on inside the church was wrong. I can't condone going into a place of worship and disrupting a religious service, period. Had the proposal been to demonstrate inside a Hasidic or ultraorthodox Jewish synagogue—groups that are equally misogynistic and homophobic, if not as influential—I'd have done all in my power to prevent it from happening.

But for better or worse, Stop the Church made ACT UP notorious, which probably had tactical benefits in the long run, prompting our targets to negotiate with us or with one of our more mainstream colleagues, rather than run the risk of provoking some radical god-knows-what response. It also no doubt increased police and undercover surveillance and infiltration of our group, which would soon have its own repercussions.

There was, however, a fundamental flaw in our effort to change church policy—if that's what we were trying to do. Whereas we were trying to save lives, the church was only interested in saving souls. As Monsignor Caffarra, the head of the John Paul II Institute for Studies of Matrimony and the Family and a consultant on moral theology to the Pope, explained, "From the church's point of view, saving a life is not the foremost value on a moral issue."[23] The church explicitly rejected the concept of the use of condoms as the "lesser evil" to prevent the "greater evil" of the spread of AIDS, because it believed "even the smallest moral wrong is so much greater than any physical wrong."[24]

---

*When ILGO was invited to march under a different banner with Mayor Dinkins in 1991, the entire contingent, including the mayor, was greeted with boos and pelted with bottles and beer cans. Dinkins would boycott the parade for the rest of his term in office. The policy finally changed in 2015, after NBC threatened to drop its coverage of the parade unless its LGBT employee group was given permission to march.

In other words, better dead than gay and having sex—safe or otherwise—period. Condoms and any sex outside of procreation were considered such an evil that even serodiscordant married couples were supposed to be celibate rather than use them, on penalty of death.

This concept remains completely foreign to me. In Jewish tradition, as I understand it, the saving of a life is the most important thing. All sorts of prohibitions can be cast aside if a life is at stake. But the church, at least under Pope John Paul II, didn't care about saving lives—except, of course, for the unborn. We therefore didn't share even the most basic point of agreement. And since we could only argue past one another, perhaps the better strategy would have been to take the issue to the public specifically in those terms; let them decide which was more important to public policy and public health—saving lives or saving "souls," as defined by one select religious organization.

There's an activist saying attributed to Bayard Rustin, "Don't waste your time on the 10 percent of the people who will never agree with you—concentrate on the 90 percent who are your potential allies." To which I'd add, while it's fine to send a message to the 10 percent holding you down, make sure you don't wind up alienating the other 90 percent in the process.

Two weeks later, on December 26, Costa Pappas—artist, videographer, activist, cofounder of DIVA TV, and member of the Delta Queens affinity group—died at age twenty-six.

COSTA PAPPAS (1963–1989)
May his memory be for a blessing.

Part IV

THE GORGEOUS MOSAIC

Chapter 15

The Myers Mess

ON THE FIRST day of the new decade,* David Dinkins, the son of a barber whose "ancestors were brought, chained and whipped in the hold of a slave ship,"[1] was sworn in as the 106th mayor of New York City.

In front of an estimated crowd of 12,000, including all four of New York's living former mayors, Governor Cuomo, Cardinal O'Connor (who had an ACT UP sticker affixed to his chair), Bishop Tutu, and the entire state Democratic establishment, Dinkins pledged to be "the Mayor of all the people of New York," a city he called "a gorgeous mosaic of race and religious faith, of national origin and sexual orientation," vowing to "renew the quest for social justice" and promising a government that belonged "not to any elite or any narrow interest" but rather "an open democracy that hears from diverse views and voices before it decides."[2]

It was an inspiring speech, articulating a vision for the city we'd fought for and so desperately needed. Not that we believed Dinkins would be able to deliver on all his promises, but he'd already acted in good faith by reaching out to community leaders to help prepare his new administration.

ACT UP's priority was the appointment of a new health commissioner. We looked forward to having an ally and advocate in the position, someone who recognized the urgency of the AIDS epidemic and would work with, and not against, the communities most affected by the disease. Although we didn't have our own representative on the search committee, we felt

---

*I know, 1990 is really the last year of the previous decade. Tough.

certain our interests would be well represented by AmFAR's Mathilde Krim and GMHC's Tim Sweeney.

It was Dr. Krim who first identified the likely nominee, Indiana health commissioner Dr. Woodrow Myers Jr. Myers was a member of the AmFAR board and had earned kudos for defending Ryan White, a young hemophiliac with AIDS, against local officials who had tried to prevent him from attending public school. As vice chair of Reagan's Presidential Commission on the HIV Epidemic, Myers had been one of its few moderate voices, but had resigned shortly after the first round of meetings, ostensibly in protest of the commission's lack of organization, though some argued he and Chairman Mayberry were chiefly responsible for the commission's lackluster start.[3]

Nonetheless, Myers was an attractive candidate. He was young, had degrees from Harvard and Stanford, and was considered an "up-and-comer" in public health circles. He was also, and not insignificantly, African American. Given the impact of the city's various health crises on communities of color—and the neglect by the previous administration—there was great symbolic value in appointing a Black commissioner. Myers quickly sailed through the review process, receiving the unanimous backing of the search committee and with it, the symbolic sign-off of all the necessary constituencies.

And then someone looked at his record.

Gabriel Rotello, *OutWeek's* editor in chief, was conducting a routine background check when he discovered that during Myers's tenure as Indiana's health commissioner, he had strongly supported mandatory name reporting and contact tracing of people testing positive for HIV. He'd also advocated for the closing of gay bars, bookstores, and movie theaters, and his department had quarantined people with HIV accused of having unsafe sex. Follow-up conversations with local organizations raised additional red flags about Myers's hostility to gay safe sex education, his unwillingness to secure funding for AIDS service organizations, and his opposition to appointing PWAs to policy boards.

When confronted by Rotello, Krim and Sweeney admitted they already knew about these issues but didn't see them as deal-breakers given Dinkins's position on these matters. Nonetheless, the two leaders recommended the mayor put the appointment on hold pending further investigation by outside counsel. Meanwhile Rotello, worried Myers might be appointed before he'd had the chance to publish his exposé in *OutWeek*, tipped the *Daily News* about his discovery,[4] and on January 10, the "Myers Mess" quickly became the first big crisis of the Dinkins administration.

In response to the growing controversy, Sweeney and Debra Fraser-Howze, from the Black Leadership Commission on AIDS (BLCOA),* called an emergency meeting of the search committee, inviting additional community representatives, including Mark Harrington, to join them. (Larry Kramer, who was not on the invite list, also managed to push his way in.) The meeting quickly divided along racial lines, with Fraser-Howze and several of her colleagues refusing to listen to charges against Myers from the Indiana groups or respond to a letter from the CDC questioning the candidate's management skills. They argued Myers was a done deal and the gay community should just relax and take a step back.[5]

Soon, more details began to surface about Myers's record. Not only had he been a staunch and vocal advocate for Indiana's odious Senate Bill 9, which required mandatory name reporting and included mechanisms for contact tracing and quarantine, but his department had also proposed giving health officers permission to conduct warrantless searches of the residences of people suspected of spreading AIDS. There were also reports of board of health employees confronting HIV-positive people in public places and threatening them with quarantine if they did not provide the names of their sexual contacts.[6]

When challenged by the search committee, Myers defended his record, claiming it had to be put in the context of conservative Indiana politics. He also stressed his loyalty to Dinkins and the mayor's views on anonymous testing and vowed to abide by New York law. Satisfied by his answers, the committee unanimously endorsed Myers's appointment.

Reaction from ACT UP was swift. While taking pains to praise Mayor Dinkins for including community input in the search process, both Larry and Mark were widely quoted castigating the search committee, and particularly Sweeney and Krim, for not researching Myers's record more thoroughly. They also blamed ACT UP for not having monitored the search more closely. "We fucked up," confessed Mark. "We trusted the wrong people."[7] But the controversy was far from over.

Rotello's *OutWeek* article[8] hit the newsstands Monday morning, January 15. That evening, our meeting was packed with angry community members demanding action. "We can't wait!" yelled Robert Garcia. "It's now or never."[9] After a series of fiery speeches, it was proposed ACT UP zap the

---

*The organization is now called the National Black Leadership Commission on Health, Inc., viewed April 4, 2022, https://nblch.org/about-us/history/.

mayor at Gracie Mansion that night, and again the following morning at City Hall.

But as the room cheered, members of Majority Action stood up and forcefully argued *against* the demonstrations. Acutely aware of the racial divisions surfacing as a result of the Myers controversy, they chastised ACT UP for assuming the mantle of the entire AIDS activist movement without first communicating with their committee and other like-minded activist organizations of color. (Though we'd often accused the media of making invisible the many women and people of color in ACT UP, we were frequently no better, failing to ask for their advice or perspective.)

While tensions between Black and Latino activists and the predominantly White AIDS organizations, including ACT UP, had been temporarily sublimated by a shared antipathy toward Mayor Koch, the Myers Mess, and particularly the way allegations had been made through the press and without prior conversation between all the concerned parties, had ripped open old wounds. In an attempt to rebuild bridges and create a more viable coalition against the Myers nomination, Majority Action proposed we delay our protests to allow the committee to work its connections and build additional support.

After a lengthy discussion, ACT UP voted to postpone the demonstrations, prompting a furious Larry Kramer to eviscerate the group for willingly marching ourselves into concentration camps.[10] As usual, Larry's kerosene was effectively, if wildly, thrown. A second vote was taken, and the meeting called so the group could storm Gracie Mansion, while the members of Majority Action stayed behind, debating whether they could continue to remain in the organization.[11]

Three days later, another bombshell dropped. In a front-page story with the screaming headline, "Lock Up Some AIDS Carriers," Myers told the *New York Post* he'd never promised the mayor he wouldn't advocate for quarantine and other isolation techniques.[12]

ACT UP held a press conference on the steps of City Hall demanding Myers be rejected. Soon thereafter, Sweeney and Krim, whose approval Dinkins stated was a prerequisite for Myers's appointment, withdrew their support for the embattled nominee. Among those joining them was Ron Johnson of the Minority Task Force on AIDS, alleviating concerns that opposition to Myers would fall strictly along racial lines.

Myers, meanwhile, contended the article was "a complete distortion of his position, and that he supports Mayor Dinkins on those issues 1,000 percent."[13] Myers still had some powerful supporters, including Fraser-Howze and James Dumpson of BLCOA, who chided, "It's about time that we recognized that we're asking the Mayor to appoint a commissioner of health, not a commissioner of AIDS."[14]

Despite our continued protests, Woodrow Myers Jr. was named New York City commissioner of health on Friday, January 19.

Completely obscured by the Myers controversy was the concurrent land-mark appointment of Dr. Billy E. Jones as the administration's commissioner of mental health. Jones, who was the medical director of Lincoln Medical and Mental Health Center in the Bronx, was the first openly gay commissioner in New York City history.

While Dinkins, GMHC, and other mainstream groups attempted to strike a note of reconciliation in their press statements, ACT UP charged the mayor with "betray[ing] the trust of the diverse communities which elected him," warning that any attempt to institute mandatory HIV testing, name reporting, contact tracing, or any detainment or quarantine programs would be met by "massive civil disobedience on a scale not seen since the height of the Vietnam War."[15] Larry went even further, proclaiming that having been "treated like shit," we were now in "a state of all-out war" with Dinkins. He reserved his greatest contempt, however, for Tim Sweeney and the other gays and lesbians on the transition and search committees. "GAYS SOLD OUT GAYS," he wrote, in his usual boldface caps, branding them and Krim as "quislings."[16]

But we'd played our hand badly. Once the controversy had spun out along racial lines—a narrative eagerly embraced by the press and abetted by our own shortsighted self-righteousness—the die was cast. The raw politics of the situation required Dinkins to appoint Myers and use it as a moment of character, standing up as his own man against the objections of one of his most vocal constituencies.

Although Majority Action publicly "disavow[ed] the actions of certain members of ACT UP" in the handling of the Myers nomination,[17] they decided to remain part of the group. They warned, however, of an "increasingly alarming pattern of culturally insensitive comments and actions" within the organization and took us to task for missing an opportunity to build alliances because "a few members of ACT UP chose to express their legitimate opposition in a manner that antagonized the communities of color involved in the decision process." Going forward, they proposed our "watch words for the 90's [sic] should be: INCLUSION, not EXCLUSION. VISIBILITY, not INVISIBILITY."[18]

And perhaps we should have added "Humility, not Arrogance." We needed to check our assumptions. As Ray Navarro reminded us, our priorities—even about something as important as the privacy of medical information and the confidentiality of HIV status—were not universal.

Privacy is not the first concern of a Black welfare mother, even one who may have AIDS. An unemployed or low income welfare mother is used to reporting every six weeks to the welfare office, where she has a "face-to-face" interview with a social worker, and is required to share the most intimate details about her personal life. Hundreds of thousands of poor people of color, and whites, have this kind of relationship with the government.

Within this framework, privacy, even with respect to mandatory name reporting and contact tracing for people with AIDS and HIV-related illness, has little meaning. The fear of job discrimination, losing one's apartment, or having one's insurance company discover one's HIV antibody status are largely middle-class anxieties, even within communities of color themselves. Poor people, and many Blacks and Latinos, have no privacy already. Possibly they never have.[19]

On January 5, Clarke Taylor, the former *Los Angeles Times* reporter who'd led our Presidential Election Subcommittee, died at age forty-six. Several months later, we received a check from Clarke's estate for $42,000. It was the largest single-donor contribution in ACT UP's history.[20]

CLARKE TAYLOR (1943–1990)
May his memory be for a blessing.

January 8–9, 1990: The CDC

The same weekend the Myers story first broke, forty activists flew to Atlanta to confront the Centers for Disease Control (CDC) over their dangerously narrow AIDS definition.

Ever since the first strange cases of KS and PCP were reported among clusters of gay men in New York and California, the CDC had been responsible for defining and tracking the disease, conducting epidemiological research, determining standards of care, and developing education and prevention programs. While the agency had been an abject failure in each of these roles, ACT UP, led by Maxine Wolfe and the members of the

Women's Action Committee,* had focused their attention on the deficiencies of the CDC's AIDS definition.

When the CDC announced its first surveillance definition† in 1982, it included an odd assortment of protozoal, bacterial, fungal, and viral opportunistic infections and lymphomas found in gay men with suppressed immune systems. Since then, the definition had undergone two major revisions, the first in 1985, which, thanks to the discovery of the "AIDS virus" included a positive test result for antibodies to LAV/HTLV-III (the original names of the respective French and American discoveries, later confirmed to be one and the same and renamed HIV) *plus* one of the CDC's designated AIDS-defining opportunistic infections.

This new definition also created a subset of individuals, like Peter Staley, who fell into the limbo category of AIDS-related Complex (ARC). These were people who had tested positive for the virus and displayed some signs of disease, such as chronically swollen glands or lowered or imbalanced T-cell counts, but did not have one of the CDC's AIDS-defining infections. This often left them ineligible for the services and financial support available to people with full-blown AIDS, even though many were desperately ill and might die before qualifying for an official AIDS diagnosis.

More substantive changes were made in 1987, when the CDC expanded the definition to include twenty-three AIDS-defining *conditions*, including HIV-wasting syndrome, HIV-dementia complex, and a broader range of malignancies. In addition, the CDC allowed for presumptive diagnoses of AIDS in people with HIV, giving drug users, as well as the poor and uninsured, who usually received their health care via emergency rooms without

---

*The Women's Action Committee (WAC) was formed in July 1989. Although the Women's Caucus initially rejected the idea of becoming a committee due to worries it would further ghettoize women's issues, they decided "it was better to be ghettoized than invisible and ignored." They hoped having an open committee and participating in the regular structure of ACT UP might "generate a broader concern among all the members of ACT UP around women and AIDS issues." Believing no one woman could be expected to represent all women, they successfully petitioned to have two representatives on the Coordinating Committee to offset the "sexism and power balance of the CC." The Women's Caucus would continue to meet informally, however, to provide a "woman-only space." Women's Caucus Report (July 17, 1989, ACT UP Weekly Report).

†The CDC had three classification systems to monitor HIV/AIDS, with the surveillance case definition the most important as it was used not only to track and report the disease caseload but also to set appropriate funding levels, establish criteria for participating in drug trials, and determine eligibility for social and medical benefits.

benefit of private doctors or access to expensive lab tests, a better chance of being correctly diagnosed at the first incidence of illness.

Not surprisingly, these new revisions not only increased the number of AIDS cases, but also shifted the demographics of the disease. Suddenly, IV drug users comprised 43 percent of the total caseload, up from 23 percent the previous year, with incidence among African Americans, Hispanics, and women all displaying significant increases as well.[21]

Still, the new definition fell short. Even the CDC admitted it would continue to undercount AIDS cases by approximately 40 percent.[22] The situation was particularly dire for women with HIV, almost half of whom, by the CDC's own estimates, died of conditions not included in the AIDS definition.[23] And yet, the CDC refused to expand the definition to include the gynecological infections and indicator diseases found in women with HIV. While acknowledging HPV, genital warts, and pelvic inflammatory disease could become debilitating or life-threatening when combined with HIV, the CDC preferred to keep women and their doctors ignorant of any potential danger rather than worry noninfected women or trust them to know the difference between an occasional outbreak and a chronic debilitating infection.* The result was a nasty Catch-22, where doctors didn't know to look for underlying HIV infection in women because they didn't know these diseases might be indicators of HIV because doctors weren't diagnosing women as being infected with HIV because the CDC was not alerting them to look for underlying HIV infection.

ACT UP's Women's Action Committee finally decided they'd had enough of their dawdling. It was time to pay a visit to CDC headquarters.

Actions began on Sunday afternoon with a "warm-up" demonstration hosted by ACT UP/Atlanta protesting Georgia's notorious sodomy law, upheld by the Supreme Court's 1986 *Hardwick* decision, which included a penalty for oral and anal sex of up to twenty years in prison—more than the punishment for armed assault or rape. (And for the record, sex with an animal would get you up to five years,[24] while sex with a corpse carried a maximum of ten.)[25]

The demonstration, which included a rally featuring speakers from the ACLU, NOW, and the National Gay and Lesbian Task Force (NGLTF), was the kick-off to a nationwide campaign to repeal the twenty-five remaining

---

*This paternalistic reasoning echoed the AMA's explanation for its opposition to including information about the potential deadly side effects of The Pill due to fear it might "confuse and alarm patients." Illith Rosenblum, Maxine Wolfe, et al., *The ACT UP Women's Caucus Women and AIDS Handbook*, March 1989, 35.

state sodomy laws.* Although rarely enforced, these laws criminalized our entire community and served as the legal foundation for discrimination against lesbians and gay men in all aspects of our lives—as pretext for removing our children from our homes, discharging us from the military, and revoking our professional licenses. And when it came to AIDS, their impact turned lethal, as states censored safer sex materials claiming they would "encourage" lawless behavior. Similar warnings were invoked to limit AIDS and safe sex education in prisons, schools, and state-run institutions around the country.

The next day, the action moved to the suburban campus of the CDC, where the Delta Queens, who'd renamed themselves the Costas in memory of member Costa Pappas, once again commandeered a flagpole and hoisted a banner, "**Cunnilingus Counts**," as other affinity groups played out their actions and scenarios. The Condams, named after the winning entry in the "Rename the Dental Dam Cuntest"—part of a campaign by the Women's Caucus to promote lesbian safe sex practices by renaming the six-by-six-inch latex square used by dentists during surgical procedures and by women wishing to have safe oral sex†—staged die-ins and chalked the outlines of bodies, inscribing them with the names of people who had died from AIDS, while the Awning Leapers once again lived up to their name, scaling the roof of the main building and hanging a "**CDC Kills**" banner.

Fifty protesters were arrested and carted off to DeKalb County Jail, the same jail where Martin Luther King had been held almost thirty years earlier.

New York seemed a little less magical when Keith Haring died on February 16. During my first years in New York, his joyful, quickly drawn, white-chalk graffiti designs had turned subway stations into instant art galleries. Though

---

*As of January 1990, sodomy was still prohibited in Alabama, Arizona, Florida, Georgia, Idaho, Kentucky, Louisiana, Maryland, Massachusetts, Michigan, Minnesota, Mississippi, North Carolina, Oklahoma, Rhode Island, South Carolina, Utah, and Virginia. In Arkansas, Kansas, Missouri, Montana, Nevada, Tennessee, and Texas, only same-sex sodomy was prohibited. Robb London, "Gay Groups Turn to State Courts to Win Rights," *New York Times*, information based on map from *New York Times*, December 21, 1990.

†Other entries included "sex shield," "labia leaf," "Venus veil," "bikini betweenie," "cunt cover," and "clit cape."

he'd since graduated to larger and more lucrative canvases, he kept to his roots as a remarkably accessible queer street artist, designing ads for GMHC, the AIDS hotline, and the annual Pride Parade.

I remember when I first spotted him at an ACT UP meeting. He was standing in the back of the room, trying not to draw any particular attention to himself, and I thought, *cool*, but also, *of course*. He seemed exactly the kind of guy who would be in ACT UP. (True confession: I once took advantage of my position as chant queen and broke a picket line so I could kiss him during a kiss-in demonstration in front of St. Vincent's Hospital.) And he not only donated his artwork, including his own ACT UP poster design, which we sold in poster, T-shirt, and button forms for years, but also authored one of our most successful fundraising letters and anonymously contributed thousands of dollars to help offset expenses for numerous demonstrations.

KEITH HARING (1958–1990)
May his memory be for a blessing.

In mid-February, with the Myers debacle barely behind us, ACT UP was once again forced to take a public stand against our new mayor, this time over his decision to shut down the city's failing needle exchange program.[26] Though the program was deeply flawed, we had come to actively embrace needle exchange as a key harm-reduction strategy, and had even started our own program handing out needles illegally in locations across the city.*

It was easy to see the parallels between the government's response to AIDS in the gay community and its similar disinterest in saving the lives of drug users and their families. Instead of arming people with the information they needed to protect themselves, it preferred, in both instances, to rely on "just say no" moralism and the threat—and in the case of drug use, the actual application—of laws that criminalized behavior and only further stigmatized an already despised population.[27]

---

*In New York State, possession of a syringe without a prescription was a felony. Instead of preventing drug use, as intended, the law had pushed it underground, forcing addicts into shooting galleries where they could rent and share works with multiple users, precipitating the spread of infectious diseases like hepatitis and HIV. Nina Reyes, "Needling the Queer Nation," *OutWeek*, June 27, 1990.

But whatever one's personal feelings about drug use, the penalty for addiction shouldn't be death. "What ought to be AIDS service and prevention during a health crisis," explained needle exchange activist Richard Elovich, "has become direct political action because the materials are made criminal or unfundable."[28]

Like Gregg Bordowitz, who had first personalized the issue of drug use in ACT UP, Richard was a White, Jewish, college-educated artist. Unlike Gregg, Richard had been a full-on junkie, an admission that once again forced me to confront my own assumptions and prejudices about addiction and the ever more porous boundaries between the various communities affected by the epidemic.

Having "bounc[ed] through methadone detox programs," Richard had all but given up on recovery until he got into a twenty-eight-day abstinence program. Borrowing $3,600, he'd bought a one-way ticket to Minnesota, and then stayed there for a year and a half, spending almost seven weeks in a four-week treatment program, followed by another five months at a halfway house with AA meetings.[29] By the time he began spearheading ACT UP's needle exchange efforts in February 1990,[30] Richard had been in recovery for over seven years. Still, he was adamant that there was no mixed message in his handing out clean needles. He wasn't condoning drug use, he explained, just responding to the fact that "dead addicts don't recover,"[31] and providing a living example of someone who'd fought through addiction and left it behind.

Every Saturday morning, Richard, Gregg, and the rest of their crew would head to Delancey Street on the Lower East Side and hand out needles, swapping clean-for-dirty, along with bleach kits, condoms, and a bilingual instruction sheet on how to clean syringes. Later, as the project expanded up to 125th Street and out to Mott Haven in the Bronx, they'd also hand out lists of service providers for HIV testing and counseling, drug treatment, and other health-related services.

Despite the committee's good intentions, a small covert operation passing out a couple hundred clean needles a week was never going to take the place of a robust city-run program. But given the fierce opposition from community leaders, it seemed unlikely they'd be able to convince the mayor to reverse himself and expand the program rather than shut it down.[32] They would need to take their case to a different court.

If the activists got arrested for distributing needles, they could go to trial and make the legal case for needle exchange as a medical necessity, pressuring the mayor to reinstate the program. But since the police had already turned a blind eye to their activities, the committee members had to figure out a way to force the police to arrest them. A press release to local media announcing their next illegal needle exchange seemed to do the trick, as the police immediately contacted Richard to negotiate an arrest scenario. "The police didn't want to be stuck with needles," Richard later explained. But in this instance, "it wasn't really about the arrest. It was about the court case."[33]

On the blustery morning of March 6, Richard, Gregg, and the designated committee members set up their table of injection paraphernalia and safe sex information under the watchful eye of local media, ACT UP's DIVA TV, and city police. To ensure none of their clients were mistakenly caught up in the arrest, the activists strung up a bright banner announcing the needle exchange, which they knew no addict would ever come near. "We had to tart that up a bit," Richard admitted, "because we didn't want to put any real drug user at risk."[34]

For similar reasons, they also changed the line-up of activists conducting the exchange.* "[I] had been through the system enough to know that you didn't just drag someone who was a person of color; you didn't just drag a drug user into this kind of demonstration . . . it was going to cost them a lot more than it would cost us"[35]—though that didn't stop Dan Keith Williams from participating.

Nor did it stop Kathy Ottersten who, as transgender, would potentially face very different obstacles upon arrest.† "That was very scary to me," they admitted. "I didn't know what with my . . . physical body and who I was, how I'd be treated. I figured that there was going to be a very tough time. But you roll with it." If not the only transgender member of ACT UP at the time, Kathy was certainly the most prominent, not only at demonstrations but also as a facilitator at our Monday night meetings.‡

As for the arrest, "It was all over in like ten minutes," remembers Gregg, "lots of press, lots of pictures. We handed over our sharps container, our

---

*The arrestees were Gregg Bordowitz, Cynthia Cochran, Richard Elovich, Debra Levine, Kathryn Ottersten, Monica Pearl, and Dan Keith Williams from ACT UP; and Velma Campbell, Phillip Flores, and Jon S. Parker from the National AIDS Brigade.

†Given their added risk, it's interesting to note that Dan and Kathy were the only ACT UP members who were defendants at both our Stop the Church and Needle Exchange trials.

‡Even though transgender issues were not a part of the discussion at ACT UP, as part of their work with the Gender Identity Project, Kathy would often invite people to meet them at our Monday night meetings, to dress as they wished and use their preferred name, to see how Kathy was welcomed and respected and to have the experience of being in a space where they'd feel safe presenting as who they were. Kathy Ottersten, interviewed by Sarah Schulman, ACT UP Oral History Project, December 28, 2017, 20.

few token containers of clean needles. Ten of us walked into the police vans, and that was it. Then we were in court for like a year."[36]

The defendants would be acquitted on June 25, 1991, after arguing that a medical emergency—the need to stop the escalating spread of HIV among IV drug users—necessitated their breaking the law by illegally possessing and distributing hypodermic needles to save lives. And surprisingly, one of the expert witnesses testifying on behalf of the defendants was none other than former New York City health commissioner Stephen Joseph.

Chapter 16

Time's Up, Mario!

WITH ED KOCH safely dispatched, it seemed both logical and necessary to shift our focus northward to the state government in Albany and Governor Mario Cuomo. For years, Governor Cuomo had balanced his budget on the lives of New York's PWAs, withholding funding for many of the AIDS services and programs we'd been demanding from the city, including the recommissioning of hospital beds and funding for new drug treatment programs.

But whereas Koch was easy to vilify—he was belligerent, impulsive, and condescending—Cuomo was empathetic and deliberate, often engaging his opponents in dialogue, safe in the knowledge his political and oratorical skills would make him the victor in almost any debate. The problem with Cuomo was the distance between his beautiful words and his disappointing actions.

When the governor finally unveiled his five-year plan to fight AIDS at a press conference held at St. Luke's-Roosevelt Hospital in February 1989, eight years after the first cases were reported in New York City, it was justly lauded for its vision and reach. But while it included some two hundred recommendations on everything from additional hospital beds and housing, to AIDS education and drug treatment programs, it lacked even a rough estimate of the projected costs. When challenged, the governor insisted releasing the cost estimates would be "counterproductive" because they would "create expectations that will not be useful [and] that might prove to have been wrong."[1]

Or could be used to hold the governor accountable.*

Nonetheless, he assured everyone his proposed 1989–90 AIDS budget of $195.5 million, while not ideal, would be enough to fund the first year of the plan. Then, in typical Cuomo fashion, he humbly acknowledged the budget shortfall.

> I want to say as clearly as I can, I am not putting into this plan this year nearly enough money to meet all these goals realistically—not at all . . . . There are not enough beds here. There is not enough for the drug programs, for treatment. There is not enough for hospices, not enough for housing. There's not enough money for nurses. I understand that.[2]

But while he could not currently provide the necessary financial support, he was "committing the political system" to the plan's implementation and promised the money would be there once he addressed the state's current budgetary crisis. He therefore asked AIDS activists and advocates to be patient, to hold off our protests in good faith, and to instead "remind us next year" of these promises, and then "goad us, plague us, march, hold up your signs and call us names."[3]

It was a masterful performance. He seemed so reasonable, so compassionate. He understood the issues and their urgency and had, Solomon-like, weighed the options and determined, regrettably, what must be done. Would it were otherwise.

Thankfully, Brent Nicholson Earle was at Cuomo's press conference to break the spell. "My friend, Len Calder, died in this hospital yesterday," Brent shouted. "He got great care, but it took four days to get him a bed. We need the money now. We need the beds now. We need the staff now. We cannot wait."[4]

But wait we did. And one year later, with little progress in the state's efforts, it was goading, plaguing, and marching time.

---

*It would take a Freedom of Information Act filing to finally reveal the plan's $1.6 billion price tag, with roughly 80 percent, or $1.268 billion, coming from state coffers. Catherine Woodard, "State 5-Year AIDS Care Plan Estimated Cost $1.6 Billion," *Newsday*, March 9, 1989.

On January 3, 1990, ten activists were arrested outside the State Assembly Chamber as the governor gave his State of the State address. But they were only a diversion. Inside the chamber, Gedalia Braverman sat in his tie and jacket, waiting for his moment. Midway through Cuomo's speech, as the governor began to discuss the state's response to AIDS, Gedalia stood up and bellowed, "Mario, you're missing the point. New York State AIDS care does not exist."[5] As the guards rushed to silence the intruder, Mario the Benevolent asked that the protester be allowed to speak. Gedalia accused the governor of being "all talk and no action" and blamed him for "an inadequate health care system, a lack of housing and services for homeless people with AIDS, and overcrowded and often inaccessible drug treatment programs."[6] And when the interloper was finally escorted out of the chamber, Mario the Empathetic commented, "You can argue with his timing or his taste, but you cannot argue with his sincerity."[7]

Several days later, the governor met for the first time with a coalition of AIDS activists, including representatives of ACT UP, who offered recommendations for new programs and pressed him to raise the AIDS budget for the coming year by $270 million. As always, Cuomo listened sympathetically before admitting, regretfully, that given the state's $1 billion shortfall, the activists were not going to be happy with this year's budget either.

He was right.

If the results of year one of Cuomo's five-year AIDS plan had been woefully inadequate, year two looked even worse. Despite an estimated 12,000 homeless New Yorkers living with AIDS, Cuomo's budget contained only $5 million for AIDS housing—enough for just 75 additional units. The governor had also short-changed the state's Rental Assistance Program, considered one of the most effective programs for preventing homelessness, by capping its budget at $3 million and maintaining inadequate individual subsidy levels.[8]

The situation in the state's hospitals and clinics was no better. Only 97 of the 1,075 new acute care beds approved for people with HIV-related illness since 1987 had been delivered.[9] Patients were stacked up for days in hospital emergency rooms waiting for a free bed, a practice that was not only dangerous but also illegal, as state law required a maximum wait of no more than eight hours.

Additional cuts were planned for the community-based organizations and clinics that provided PWHIV/AIDS with continuum of care services. These groups, whose caseloads had doubled in the past year, not only saved lives but saved the state money by allowing patients to remain in their homes and communities, providing them with treatment and support services *before* they required hospitalization.

Despite the lack of funds, the New York State Department of Health AIDS Institute had somehow been able to find money to begin a coercive program of "voluntary" testing of women as soon as they gave birth. While the professed goal was to draw women who might be HIV-positive and their children into early treatment—New York had 31 percent of the nation's pediatric AIDS cases[10]—the state had no such program in place, nor was funding being set aside to develop one.

Meanwhile, little to nothing was being done to relieve the catastrophic shortfall of drug treatment slots or alleviate the increasingly desperate situation in the state's prison system, where up to 17 percent of all male inmates and 20 percent of all female inmates were estimated to be HIV-positive.[11] Inmates with AIDS died twice as fast as patients of the same race, age, and IV drug history outside prison. Even though 95 percent of all infected inmates contracted HIV from IV drug use,[12] there were no system-wide drug treatment programs in place, nor were drug-using patients given access to clean needles or bleach for cleaning their works. The state also refused to provide prisoners with AIDS education or to allow the distribution of condoms, the latter purportedly due to worries they might be used as weapons or seen as sanctioning sex between prisoners. The Department of Corrections claimed condoms were unnecessary, since "no consensual sex occurred in prisons, anyway."[13]

Even as the State Department of Health had declared the prison system's AIDS care substandard, Cuomo had cut the Department of Corrections request for a $48 million increase in funding for medical care by over 80 percent. The cut's impact extended far beyond the prison walls, as roughly six hundred PWAs were released from prison every year into their already overburdened communities, with few provisions made for their care.[14]

On February 13, seventy-five ACT UP members from around the state returned to Albany for some more goading, plaguing, and marching. What they lacked in numbers, they made up for in boldness and theatricality.

The Mario Antoinettes, a Housing Committee* affinity group, paraded through the Empire State Plaza in gowns, wigs, and handheld Cuomo masks, passing out the cake crumbs of the governor's AIDS budget to amused bystanders.[15] Another group stormed the governor's office and chained

---

*The Housing Caucus became a full committee on October 23, 1989.

themselves to chairs and desks, demanding a meeting with Deputy Budget Director Paula Wilson;[16] while others marched through the hallways and corridors, chanting and carrying signs asking "**Am I Too Expensive to Keep Alive?**" and dropping to the floor in a series of die-ins.

All this was merely prelude to our upcoming anniversary demonstration.

In anticipation of another round of Cuomo's "but-we-have-no-money" chorus, we'd prepared a list of actions that could be taken by the governor and state legislature to save lives without spending a cent, including decriminalizing needle possession, distributing condoms in prisons, requiring doctors to accept Medicaid, and adding antidiscrimination language to insurance regulations. We further proposed the governor declare New York State an "AIDS Disaster Area," allowing him to demand relief funds from the federal government, which he could supplement with temporary state tax surcharges and special use bonds, like those used for previous state emergencies.

One week before the demonstration, we boldly laid out our intentions in a full-page ad in the *New York Times*, featuring the governor's directive to "remind us next year . . . ," declaring, "TIME'S UP. New York is an AIDS Disaster Area. We're Coming."

March 28, 1990: Albany, NY

And come we did, not just from New York City, but Ithaca, Rochester, Syracuse, Long Island, and more—one thousand activists from across the state descending on our state capital to goad, plague, and march.

As soon as we stepped off the bus, we spied a cluster of cameras, activists, and reporters at the foot of the Governor's Mansion. Sprinting over—you don't want to get between ACT UP and a camera—who should we find at the center of the scrum but Governor Cuomo. As always, the governor was impressive, bravely facing his enemies—I mean constituents—and engaging in spirited debate, with only a minimal security detail at his side as protection.

"What do you want?" asked Reasonable Mario, as if this were the first time he'd heard our demands. "Housing for homeless PWAs, legalized needle exchange, condoms in prisons . . . " rattled off Mark Aurigemma. "What else?" asked Mario the Concerned. "Increase treatment slots for women who use intravenous drugs, release health-care guidelines for people who test positive for HIV." "What else?" "Governor, isn't that enough?"[17]

"It's not just me," Mario the Just explained. What about the Republican Senate? "I asked you to prod the whole system."[18] And as Cuomo began his sorrowful song and dance, I looked at the cameras and realized he was going to co-opt our demonstration to tell the story of how Mario, Man of The People, had met with the protesters and sympathized with their plight, leaving us once again with nothing but words. I started yelling, "*PEOPLE are DYING! WHAT are <u>YOU</u> DOING? PEOPLE are DYING! WHAT are <u>YOU</u> DOING?*" Soon, everyone took up the chant and began dropping to the ground in an impromptu die-in.

Wishing to avoid front-page photos of him stepping over the bodies of AIDS activists, Cuomo made a hasty retreat back up the hill with us in hot pursuit, chanting, "*PROGRAMS, Not PROMISES! AIDS. WON'T. WAIT!*" and sealing the mansion gates shut with red tape.

Celebrating with a saucy "*YOU said, 'COME BACK in a YEAR: Time's UP, Mario! (snap) WE'RE HERE!*" we marched over to the Capitol building, arriving just as the Costas unfurled a large banner from a fourth-floor balcony: "**The Deaths of People with AIDS is a Capitol Crime.**"[19]*

Once inside, it was free-period—some activists stopped by their state legislators' offices, others hit Cuomo's offices on the second floor. One affinity group, protesting the conditions in state prisons, chained themselves to a desk in the governor's criminal justice office, while another set up camp outside the budget office, pinning up sheets with hand-painted windows and doors, hanging clotheslines, and plopping down on pillows and bedrolls.[20] The newly christened Action Tours affinity group ended their guided tour of the Capitol by climbing to the top of the grand staircase, dousing themselves with fake blood, and shouting, "*New York has blood on its hands!*"[21]

With chants of "*NO MORE Status Cuo-MO!*" and "*CUOMO MIra: DiNERO para SIDA!*" echoing through the halls, anxious staff members removed legislators' name plates from walls and locked their office doors,[22] while thirty activists laid siege to the third-floor Senate Chamber. Their sit-in would turn into a vigil when police delayed their arrests for five hours before violently hauling them off to jail.

---

*Only a day earlier, as a kind of activist *amuse bouche*, the Costas had disrupted a working session of the Republican-held New York State Senate, sounding air horns, unfurling banners, and raining down fake death certificates and money onto the senators from the Senate visitors' gallery, while a second group stormed the Senate Chamber and quickly read off ACT UP's list of demands. No one was arrested.

Media coverage was excellent, both upstate and down.* Cuomo got his expected moment of empathetic gravitas, but Mark's ability to hang tough with specific demands got equal play, as did the governor's noticeable deflation once we began to taunt him with our chants, which were also quoted extensively. Everyone played up Cuomo's invitation to "Come back next year," so our demonstration was viewed more as a chickens-coming-home-to-roost story than as another ill-tempered tantrum by those radical AIDS activists.

The day after our invasion of Albany, and fourteen months after he took office as president, George H. W. Bush made his first AIDS speech. "There is only one way to deal with an individual who is sick," the president told the National Leadership Coalition on AIDS, "With dignity, compassion, care, confidentiality, and without discrimination."[23] It was a lovely speech, albeit one delivered several years late. Meanwhile, Bush neither addressed the continuing immigration and travel ban nor promised any new funds for fighting and treating the disease. Instead, he claimed the US was already "on a wartime footing" with the epidemic, praising the efforts at the NIH and CDC and trumpeting his "unprecedented" budget of $3.5 billion to fight the disease.

But the president's numbers were seriously misleading. Over half the total went to Medicaid, Medicare, and other mandated health care expenditures, leaving only $1.7 billion for AIDS research, treatment, and education: just a 7 percent increase from the previous year and the smallest percentage increase in AIDS spending in five years.[24]

While the protesters outside the conference were to be expected, the president was startled to find himself heckled during his speech by Richard Deagle,[25] who had somehow managed to slip inside the conference despite his hippie-meets-leather-daddy appearance,† and then by Urvashi Vaid,

---

*In an interesting twist, harkening back to the days of police raids on gay bars, all eighty arrestees had their names, ages, and hometowns listed in the *Albany Times Union*. "An Army of AIDS Protesters," *Albany Times Union*, March 29, 1990.

†Richard had taken a bus with ten other activists directly from Albany and, having gotten to the venue early, grabbed a name badge from the stack and flashed it at the security guards when he later walked into the ballroom. Though how anyone could have mistaken him for Sandra Thurman remains a mystery. Richard Deagle, conversation with author, August 19, 2020.

executive director of the National Lesbian and Gay Task Force, who bravely stood up at her table just twenty feet from the podium and held up a sign that read: **"Talk is cheap. AIDS care isn't."** and shouted, "Mr. President, you don't understand. You're not doing enough. We need more than one speech every fourteen months. We need your leadership."[26]

And for the next year, perhaps lulled by the notion of Bush's professed "kinder-gentler" conservatism, we continued to ask, demand, and beg for his leadership, on the slim chance he might finally come through.

Chapter 17

Storm the NIH

BY THE SPRING of 1990, ACT UP had spent almost two years successfully targeting the Food and Drug Administration, but the FDA could only approve drugs once they'd been tested. The problem, it now appeared, lay further up the treatment pipeline, at the National Institutes of Health and its federally sponsored AIDS drug testing program, the AIDS Clinical Trial Group (ACTG).*

Despite three and a half years of trials and a quarter of a billion dollars in federal funds, the ACTG system had yet to yield a single new anti-AIDS drug, prophylactic treatment, or immune therapy. Of the fifteen "promising treatments" first identified in 1985, the ACTG had tested only eight.

It was time for an intervention.

Despite all the complaining about the activist presence at November's ACTG meeting, it appeared leadership had taken at least some of our criticisms seriously. In early January, the ACTG's Executive Committee had begun a comprehensive review of all forty protocols and concept sheets currently in

---

*While NIAID administers the ACTG program, NIH funds and oversees the program (and NIAID) and sets the larger US research agenda.

development, with the goal of better prioritizing the program's research efforts. Even more importantly, the NIH had convened a Patient Constituency Working Group (PCWG) as a first step in making good on Fauci's promise to integrate PWAs and members of the community into the ACTG system.

Despite instigating the concept of community involvement in ACTG, ACT UP was not invited to attend the first constituency group meeting.* We sent Mark Harrington anyway, and he crashed the proceedings along with Jesse Dobson from ACT UP/San Francisco. Mark and Jesse were later voted onto the working group and invited, along with the other members, to attend the next quarterly ACTG meeting in March.†

But even an official invitation couldn't guarantee a warm reception, as the community reps found themselves barred from attending many of the most important scientific sessions. Not that this stopped ACT UP, whose small band of uninvited observers spent most of their time getting thrown out of meetings. The presence of so many ACT UP members, however, raised concerns that ACT UP and its agenda would dominate the constituency group's efforts and swamp the voices of the other communities.

Our motives were further questioned when Mark distributed "A Critique of the AIDS Clinical Trials Group,"[1] his in-depth, no-holds-barred analysis of the entire ACTG system. While many of the demands were similar to those we'd formulated for the FDA, this time we were delivering them directly to the scientists conducting the research.

And this critique was personal. It attacked not only the ACTG system, but the scientists themselves, questioning their ethics and practices while articulating the unpleasant truth that research priorities were often driven by considerations beyond clinical need. Many of the scientists responsible for prioritizing the ACTG's research agenda had lucrative consultative agreements with the companies whose drugs they tested. In addition to possible financial incentives, there were also professional alliances that strongly influenced the types of research being conducted at the ACTG.

Larry Corey, Margaret Fischl, Martin Hirsch, Thomas Merigan, and Douglas Richman were five young, tightly connected infectious disease

---

*The NIH insisted the slight was unintentional, having assumed David Barr, who was attending on behalf of the Lambda Legal Defense and Education Fund, would also serve as our unofficial representative.

†The original members of the PCWG included David Barr (Lambda Legal Defense and Education Fund), Debra Fraser-Howze (Black Leadership Commission on AIDS—BLCOA), Pierre Ludington (American Association of Physicians for Human Rights—AAPHR), Chuck Mayer (National Association of People with AIDS—NAPWA), Mario Solis-Marich (AIDS Project LA—APLA), and Marie St. Cyr-Delpe (Women and AIDS Resource Network—WARN).

researchers with a shared background in virology and deep ties to Burroughs Wellcome. They were all members of the powerful Primary Infection Committee, which sponsored one-third of all ACTG trials and enrolled 70 percent of all patients thanks to the high priority rating given the trials by the ACTG Executive Committee, on which three of the five also served.

We called them "The Gang of Five."

Since their formative infectious disease experience had been primarily with herpes, they knew little of the medical lessons of TB, syphilis, and other infectious diseases, where overlapping toxicities and multidrug treatments were part of the standard of care. Nor were they likely to be familiar with the political issues raised in connection with those diseases involving quarantine, sanatoria, and mandatory testing.[2] This had a profound effect on the way ACTG designed protocols and approached potential treatment solutions. It also explained the heavy bias toward antiviral studies and frank disinterest in pursuing treatments and prophylaxis for opportunistic infections. Nowhere was this divide clearer than in the case of PCP, which remained the number one killer of people with AIDS.

While community doctors like Joseph Sonnabend had been using Bactrim for PCP prophylaxis since 1982, based on earlier studies showing the drug's effectiveness in young children, the ACTG didn't test the drug until 1987, when Margaret Fischl (a.k.a. the "Queen of AZT")[*] led an infamous trial that sacrificed the lives of twenty-eight of the thirty patients placed on placebo, in order to "prove" what doctors in the field already knew.[†]

The ACTG's record on trials for treatments of other opportunistic infections was not much better.

But even the best-designed trials were of little use if the results remained hidden from the doctors and patients who needed them.

Trial results were traditionally released through published articles in peer-reviewed medical journals. These journals often required researchers to remain silent about their discoveries until publication or risk withdrawal of the article. While we agreed that treatment information should be scientifically sound, the lag-time of six to eight months between discovery and publication was unconscionable in the case of AIDS and other life-threatening

---

[*] Fischl made her career investigating AZT, first as lead investigator of the original Phase II study and then by the "early-use" 002 trial, with fellow Gang of Five member Doug Richman.

[†] Of the 28 who died in the placebo arm, 16 developed PCP. While 18 patients in the Bactrim arm also died, none developed PCP. M. A. Fischl, G. M. Dickinson, and L. La Voie, "Safety and Efficacy of Sulfamethoxazole and Trimethoprim Chemoprophylaxis for Pneumocystis carinii Pneumonia in AIDS," *Journal of the American Medical Association* 259, no. 8 (February 26, 1988): 1185–89.

diseases. Although the journals claimed to have waived their insistence on prepublication *omerta*, most scientists continued to maintain their silence, wary of running afoul of these powerful editorial gatekeepers.

The NIH had attempted to speed the dissemination of information by issuing treatment press releases, but many doctors still preferred to wait until they could read the results for themselves in detailed journal articles. The press releases also had little impact on insurance companies, which refused to extend coverage for new treatments or alternate "off-label" use of already-approved drugs until the FDA gave its full approval. Nor had the NIH encouraged drug companies to make speedy data submission a priority to avoid delays like the five-month lag between the announcement of the success of low-dose AZT and its eventual approval.

None of this was a matter of evil intent, at least not on the part of the researchers, and our refusal to acknowledge this fact was later recognized as a major shortcoming of our critique. ACT UP was always quick to ascribe the worst motives to anyone we didn't agree with—not that our distrust wasn't in many cases justified. But perhaps my equanimity was the result of my own good fortune; I wasn't sick, so maybe I could afford to give people the benefit of the doubt. I might not have been so generous had my own life been at stake. Or maybe the harshness of our attack was simply the terms of engagement. We needed to be angry arrogant activists to face off against angry arrogant scientists.

And against incompetent reporters.

Just days after the March ACTG meeting, our old friend Gina Kolata penned a Sunday *Times* think-piece citing researchers, government officials, and others who "fear that the immediate gains made by Act-Up [*sic*] will come at the expense of long-term AIDS research and will alienate scientists or even drive them from the field."[3] The next day, Kolata followed up with a scurrilous front-page story suggesting activist demands for increased access to ddI had led to an "odd surge of deaths" among patients receiving the drug through the newly implemented expanded access program.[4]

While the quoted statistics were alarming—290 of the 8,000 patients taking ddI on expanded access had died, compared with only 2 of the 700 taking the drug in clinical trials—they were also misleading. Contrary to Kolata's narrative, most of the deaths in the expanded access program were the result of AIDS and not some dangerous and unmonitored side effect of the drug. Most expanded access patients were far sicker than those participating in the concurrent clinical trials, the severity of their illness being the reason they were excluded from clinical trials in the first place.

Kolata's article created a firestorm, generating angry letters to the editor, as well as a flurry of calls to doctors from panicked patients needing reassurance about the safety of the expanded access program and their now-suspect medication. Journalists on the AIDS beat, most prominently Marilyn Chase in the *Wall Street Journal*,[5] promptly dismantled the reasoning behind Kolata's article, and soon even the cited scientists backed away, accusing Kolata of misquoting them or at least misunderstanding their intent. When contacted directly by ACT UP, Kolata blamed the controversy on her editors and promised a follow-up article to "assuage the panic."[6]

But rather than correcting the mistakes of her article, Kolata's subsequent piece merely reported on the controversy she herself had manufactured.[7] The obligatory walk-back wouldn't happen until five days later, in an editorial titled "On AIDS, Compassion and Confusion,"[8] where the *Times* addressed the misunderstanding about the "surge of deaths" without acknowledging the paper's responsibility for the entire episode.

But Kolata's article not only wreaked havoc with the expanded access program, as the researchers had hoped; it also crippled enrollment efforts for their own trials, slowing down recruitment for months until confidence in the drug and the ACTG program could be restored.

May 21, 1990: Storm the NIH

Mark Harrington's ACTG critique was only the first step in ACT UP's campaign to change the NIH drug testing effort. Step two would be a massive demonstration along the lines of "Seize Control of the FDA."

While the buildup to "Storm the NIH" in many ways echoed our preparations for the FDA action, the NIH's response was tellingly different. Tony Fauci and his team took our protest and the potential media frenzy seriously, engaging in a preemptive PR campaign that included a point-by-point response to our demands and allegations issued just days before our demonstration.

What was most surprising weren't the NIH's various evasions and half-truths—those were to be expected. It was their claims to already be responding to our demands and their suggestions that our upcoming protest would endanger the current spirit of cooperation.[9] Rather than dismissing our arguments, their response acknowledged the legitimacy of our critique.

More than one thousand AIDS activists from over twenty states stormed the Bethesda campus of the National Institutes of Health. The demonstration had much the same carnival-like atmosphere as the FDA action, if operating at a higher pitch, complete with roaming affinity groups, impromptu grave-yards, blasting air horns—*One AIDS Death Every Twelve Minutes!*—and Peter Staley and his Power Tools igniting multicolored smoke canisters trailing red, purple, and yellow smoke from atop thirty-foot wooden poles.

Unlike the FDA, where we'd laid siege almost exclusively to the main building, the demonstration paraded across the NIH campus, navigating around—and sometimes through—temporary barricades and fences, leaving miles of red tape crisscrossing the bucolic NIH landscape. The police responded with startling violence—riding horses into peaceful crowds, rushing groups of demonstrators with billy clubs and Mace, and grabbing and hurling protesters to the ground. At least one attempt at further police mischief was thwarted when an intrepid DIVA TV activist filmed an officer putting illegal firecrackers into a demonstrator's bag.

While sixty protesters were being arrested on the NIH campus,[10] the Costas took over the offices of Dan Hoth in Rockville, four miles away, to protest the exclusion of women from most ACTG trials and the lack of a committee or working group dedicated to addressing the needs of women with AIDS.* Although Hoth, alas, was nowhere in sight, the Costas passed out their fact sheets, handing them to staff and stuffing them into file cabinets and mailboxes, and wrote their demands on his office whiteboard. They then tracked Hoth down at Fauci's office and called him there, warning they would not leave his office until he agreed to meet with them.[11] Unfortunately, the police arrived instead of Hoth, and all twenty-one activists were arrested.

On the same day ACT UP stormed the NIH and nine months after the FDA had first endorsed it as a concept, the official guidelines for the parallel track program were published in the *Federal Register.*†[12]

---

*Astonishingly, the current OB/GYN committee focused almost exclusively on perinatal trials and on mother-to-infant transmission.

†Although the regulations would normally become policy after a ninety-day period for public comment, parallel track would be delayed for almost two years, until April 15, 1992, allegedly due to concerns the policy would add to the budget deficit. Joe Evall and Richard Lynn, "Long-Awaited 'Parallel Track' Announced by Public Health Service," *QW*, May 10, 1992.

AmFAR

I'd planned to join my ACT UP comrades in Bethesda, but the day before the action, my boss, Paul Corser, told me I couldn't go to the demonstration because they were concerned my participation might jeopardize my working relationship with officials at NIH and NIAID.

As CBCT coordinator, my job was to be the community-friendly face of AmFAR and the conduit to Paul, the frequently inaccessible head of the Community-Based Clinical Trial program. Paul was painfully shy—to be honest, I think he would have been happier working in a lab, or perhaps dealing only with scientists and clinicians, but instead, he was charged with running a network of centers filled with all these *people*.

Not to mention dealing with me.

Though we were both gay and roughly the same age, we had almost nothing in common. We barely even spoke the same language. I hadn't taken a serious science course since high school, and Paul's idea of culture was the butter sculptures at the Minnesota State Fair.

I guess they hoped our skills would complement each other—I'd be Mr. Communication and keep things organized, while Paul concentrated on the science. I facilitated conference calls and ran meetings on "community concerns" that were of little interest to Paul or our mutual boss, David Corkery. I created agendas, typed up minutes, and wrote the monthly *CBCT Newsletter.* I made the doctors and community reps feel listened to. I charmed the women and flirted with the men. I even slept with a couple of the doctors, though admittedly that was more of a perk for me than a case of "taking one for AmFAR."

There were, however, two women I couldn't charm.

The team from AIDS Research Consortium of Atlanta—Principal Investigator Dr. Melanie Thompson and Executive Director Amy Morris—were smart, no-nonsense types, devoted to their patients and determined to have their center up and operational as quickly as possible. As an activist, I admired them, and if I'd been a PWA, I'd have wanted them to be my advocates. But they both realized early on that I was an empty pair of khakis—I neither knew the science nor had any real power—and was therefore a waste of their time.

And I couldn't blame them.

In truth, I was little more than an activist smiley-face; a friendly diversion to keep needy centers busy while the more important people were doing the "real work" behind the scenes. The smarter centers recognized this and, with varying degrees of politeness, dismissed or found ways to work around me. The others, the ones who liked and trusted me, I could do nothing for.

That's not to say I didn't have a lot to do. My work at AmFAR was so overwhelming I was forced to scale back my time with ACT UP. I was no longer involved with Actions or any of the other committees, and frequently came late to the Monday night meetings, if I got there at all. I'd been forced to cancel plans to go down to Atlanta for the January CDC demonstrations due to preparations for the quarterly CBCT/CPCRA meeting and had been similarly MIA from the local Woody Myers actions.

Even so, I was stunned when I was told that I couldn't go to the NIH demonstration. My membership in ACT UP was hardly a secret—it was the reason I was hired and the source of whatever credibility I still had. And it wasn't like I was negotiating with the NIH—not that they weren't used to negotiating with activists who participated in protests against them. Even more confusing, Spencer Cox, who was David's assistant, had been helping orchestrate ACT UP's media campaign with his boss's approval and assistance. Spencer, who was far better known by the folks at the NIH than I, was being allowed to attend the demonstration. Meanwhile, my paid position as a community activist was making it impossible for me to behave like one.

Thankfully, there was still one event that spring that made me feel that I was still a full-fledged member of ACT UP.

Alexis Danzig, Gregg Bordowitz, and other activist friends had decided to host a Queer Seder. The Seder is the ritual meal held at Passover, the Jewish holiday that celebrates our deliverance from slavery in Egypt. (You know, the story with Charlton Heston parting the Red Sea and Anne Baxter gurgling, "Oh, Moses, Moses, you stubborn, splendid, adorable fool!").[13] It's sort of a Jewish Thanksgiving. Growing up, it was one of my favorite holidays, as I always enjoyed the adults kibitzing around the table, not to mention the opportunity to show off when it was time to chant the Four Questions.

Even so, celebrating this holiday with my ACT UP family proved unexpectedly moving. So much of my life had required a certain compartmentalization, absenting parts of myself in order to fit in or get along with a minimum of conflict; acting one way with family, another at work, another with friends. There were, at least in my experience, few opportunities to be gay and Jewish, at least in the religious sense. I'd been to the gay synagogue a couple of times for High Holiday services in the early '80s, and while I found it in some ways astonishing—*who knew there were so many cute gay Jewish boys?*—welcoming, it was not. Services were held almost entirely in Hebrew and were far more Orthodox than I was used to. I found it forbidding, shaming even.°

This, however, felt *haimish*—like family. Several dozens of us gathered in Alexis's Brooklyn loft apartment, everyone bringing some dish they'd prepared at home or bought at Fairway or the special Kosher for Passover section of the local supermarket. Lubricated by wine and the smell of chicken soup, we folded ourselves around a makeshift banquet table, sitting on chairs, sofas, pillows, and bookcases, and shared our stories and traditions.

Before we began the service, someone told a story about a young lesbian who asked her rabbi about the place of lesbians in Judaism. The rabbi responded that a lesbian has as much place in Judaism as bread on a Seder plate. Bread is forbidden during the eight days of Passover, with tradition requiring that bread and all similarly leavened products be removed from the house—even so much as a crumb. The storyteller then slammed a plate with a slice of bread down onto the table, staking their claim and ours to the traditions of Judaism and the story of Passover.†

I was surprised to discover who knew the prayers and who didn't, who wore a yarmulke and who did not; but what was most remarkable was how relevant it all seemed. In retelling the story of the Jews' escape from Egypt, we could not help but hear echoes of our own queer stories of oppression and recognize the imperatives for *tzedakah* (charity/good deeds) and *tikkun olam* (repairing the world) found in the holiday Haggadah: to welcome the needy to our table and make the outcast welcome in our home; to reflect on our privilege by remembering when we, too, were slaves in Egypt; to recognize the humanity of even our enemies; and to remember that our celebration

---

°Things have changed substantially at Congregation Beit Simchat Torah, and though I'm still not a member (I know, I know), I've happily attended High Holiday services there for close to thirty years.

†There's a similar story about the place of women in Jewish religious life leading to the placement of an orange on the Seder plate, but a little research traces the story's origin back to the question of lesbianism. The bread was later switched to a tangerine and the symbolism broadened to one of lesbian and gay solidarity. As it made its way into the progressive mainstream, the story and symbol changed yet again, with the question now about the place of women as leaders of Jewish religious life, to which the male rabbi now answered, "As much place as an orange on the Seder plate." Anita Silvert, "The Real Story of the Orange on the Seder Plate," Jewish United Fund, March 22, 2012, https://www.juf.org/news/world.aspx?id=414773.

is lessened by the suffering inflicted by each one of our seemingly endless list of modern plagues.

Before we started the service, we went around the room and each one of us was asked to name something we were thankful for. Some were thankful for new relationships, for lovers and friends, others for sobriety, or for simply still being alive and healthy. Me, I was thankful for ACT UP, for finding and being welcomed into this incredible band of sisters and brothers, and for the opportunity it gave me to become the best possible version of myself.

Chapter 18

Inside or Out

IN EARLY MAY 1990, I took advantage of a slow Friday afternoon and snuck out of the office to see *Longtime Companion*,* the first mainstream film to address the AIDS crisis. The film focused on an extended family of mostly gay male friends as AIDS invaded their circle, from the earliest days of the epidemic to "present day." It was filled with situations and people I recognized—sometimes literally, like when Mark Fotopoulos popped up in a scene wearing his "Silence = Death" pin—or when, at the end, the three "survivors" were walking on the beach in their ACT UP buttons and T-shirts talking about getting arrested at next week's demonstration. It felt true—a story being told by people who were living through the same war and hearing the same bombs dropping as I did.

Not everyone agreed.

Several critics attacked the film for being too parochial and not addressing the larger crisis. In his review, "Manhattan's Privileged and the Plague of AIDS," *Times* critic Vincent Canby complained, "The movie ends as it begins, with the emphasis exclusively on the toll being taken in the white gay community. . . . It's as if the rest of America didn't exist."[1]

---

*The title of Norman René's 1989 film is taken from one of the more familiar obfuscations found in AIDS obituaries, when families or, in other cases, gatekeepers like the *New York Times*, refused to publish the word "lover" to designate a surviving partner.

While Canby may have professed concern over the missing IV drug users and people of color—which never seemed to bother him in a Woody Allen film—I suspect the real issue was the lack of straight people. Unlike the well-meaning *An Early Frost* or, later, *Philadelphia*, this wasn't a film about how a gay man's illness affected his straight family, friends, or coworkers. But to Canby and others, a story centering the experience of gay White men couldn't help but lack a certain depth. They dismissed the characters as trivial and the movie as merely an '80s update of *The Boys in the Band*, which it resembled only insofar as being about a group of gay male friends.°

Nor did the film please many of my comrades on the Left. Not only was it not angry or political enough, but the characters lived in the same privileged gay White male milieu they regularly criticized. (Gay White men don't get a lot of sympathy from the Left, as they enjoy the very real benefits—and often, the arrogance—of being White and male. As a result, there's a tendency to see them as "part of the problem" and to disregard their equally real challenges and experiences of discrimination.)

I found both sets of criticism deeply offensive. What they were saying was that the lives of gay White men—whether due to a lack of perceived gravitas or a surfeit of privilege—were somehow unworthy subjects for a film about a disease that was killing them by the thousands.

June 20–24, 1990: San Francisco AIDS Conference

What a difference a year makes.

If you wanted a snapshot of how the AIDS landscape had changed in the past year, at least in the scientific community, you couldn't do better than the International AIDS Conference in San Francisco. This year's conference incorporated many of our demands from Montreal, including 375 scholarships for people with HIV; rest areas, medical facilities, and welcome centers for attendees with health issues; and a speaking slot for ACT UP at the opening plenary. The same researchers who'd loudly complained about the intrusion of politics into their scientific conference now wore armbands and

---

°I could go on about the myopathy of straight White male reviewers and audiences, who somehow cannot connect or identify with characters that are not direct representations of themselves (something women, gays, and people of color have had to do since the beginning of film). *Thelma and Louise* would similarly get pilloried the following year for its lack of upstanding straight male characters.

spoke fervently about the dangerous and discriminatory policies of the Bush administration.

Even the Red Cross had become political.

Despite the adoption of the Yeager-Goldberg amendment requiring the International AIDS Society to hold conferences "only in countries permitting entry of HIV infected travelers,"[2] this year's event had been allowed to proceed despite the existing US travel ban. Then in November 1989, the League of Red Cross and Red Crescent Societies announced their withdrawal from the 1990 conference in protest of the ban,[3] setting the stage for a worldwide boycott. Instead of being shamed into reversing the policy, the Bush administration simply papered it over, creating a special ten-day visa to allow foreign visitors to attend the conference without having to declare their HIV status on their passports.[*]

It was widely assumed ACT UP would join the boycott, but the decision proved unexpectedly complicated. After three years of protests, we finally had the ear of the research establishment. Boycotting the conference would remove us from the conversation at a critical juncture and prevent us from making the case for our treatment agenda. Attending the conference, however, would mean crossing a picket line of our fellow activists and not only endorsing the conference, but supporting it financially. Our participation would also be a slap in the face to our own foreign nationals—activists whose lives were directly affected by these policies—and those whose lovers or partners were not US citizens.

In the midst of our deliberations, the Immigration and Naturalization Service (INS) inexplicably announced it would be enforcing the little-known and long-dormant Immigration and Nationality Act of 1952, which banned people "with psychopathic personality, or sexual deviation, or mental defect," including, specifically, homosexuals, from entering the country.[4] The INS claimed they were being forced to resurrect the policy by gay activists, who planned to challenge the law by declaring their homosexuality when they arrived in the US.[†]

---

[*] They'd still have to disclose their serostatus to the government to get the visa, however.

[†] The law instructed INS agents to refer all incoming aliens suspected of being homosexual to a Public Health Service officer for examination. If they were determined to be homosexual, the PHS officer would issue a certificate allowing the INS to bar said person from entering the country. Though seldom enforced, the policy had remained in place until 1979, when the American Psychological Association stopped listing homosexuality as a mental disorder, at which point the surgeon general instructed the PHS to stop issuing the certificates. The law was further neutered in 1983 when the Ninth Circuit ruled INS must obtain the

Whether it was malice or stupidity—a rogue ideological move by some rabid right-winger, or merely some bureaucratic functionary just following orders—the announcement further raised the pressure for us to take a stand and join the boycott.

Then Larry proposed his own response.

The ACTG system, he proclaimed, was "a sham, a shocking, sinful, sewer of ineptitude, run by idiots, nincompoops, quack doctors who should have their licenses revoked"; and the AIDS conference "a sick joke" and "about as 'International' as the Ku Klux Klan" thanks to the travel policies of "Uncle George's government." And that was just the preamble. "WE HAVE BEEN LINED UP IN FRONT OF A FIRING SQUAD AND IT IS CALLED AIDS . . . WE MUST RIOT! I AM CALLING FOR A FUCKING RIOT! . . . WE MUST RIOT IN SAN FRANCISCO!"[5]

ACT UP immediately distanced itself from Larry's call to violence. "Our policy is nonviolent, peaceful demonstrations," said media spokesperson Alan Beck. "We may be noisy, but we won't throw things or push people. We may stage sit-ins to stop proceedings, but we'll have nothing to do with [rioting]."[6] Though it was hardly the first time ACT UP had disagreed with Larry, it might've been the first time we'd issued so public a rebuke. Other groups quickly followed suit.

I've always wondered whether Larry believed everything he said or was just acting in his role as gadfly/angry prophet/activist conscience/provocateur (choose all that apply). This time, even Larry seemed a bit uncertain, one moment explaining all he wanted was a "massive disruption" and he wasn't really telling anyone "to burn the place down,"[7] and the next advocating for "an AIDS terrorist army, like the Irgun."[8] Adding a further wrinkle, Larry was, at the same time, angling for a speaking slot at the opening ceremonies.

In the end, both Larry's offer to speak and his "call to riot" were rejected, and ACT UP, heavily lobbied by T+D, decided it was more important to attend the conference and try to influence the future of AIDS research than to take the more politically expedient approach and join the boycott. So, while mainstream groups, like GMHC, stayed away in protest, we "radicals" sent over eighty activists to San Francisco* to attend the official conference

---

no-longer-issued certificate if it wished to exclude gay foreigners. Philip J. Hilts, "Agency to Use Dormant Law to Bar Homosexuals from U.S.," *New York Times*, March 3, 1990.

*This number includes both members who had their travel and hotel subsidized to some extent by ACT UP and those who paid their own way or were there under the aegis of another organization.

and participate in the outside "satellite" conferences and demonstrations.[9] Regardless of their formal assignment, everyone was expected to participate in events both inside and outside the conference, beginning with a kick-off demonstration at the INS offices scheduled for the day before the opening ceremony.

But even though I was already in San Francisco, I was not in the streets, but in a shirt and tie, sipping white wine and nibbling canapés.

AmFAR was hosting a big preconference soiree at Wolfgang Puck's exclusive Postrio restaurant. The room was an A-list mash-up of the AIDS demimonde—internationally renowned researchers and local community doctors, government officials and AIDS activists, philanthropists and PWAs. *Tutti AIDS* was there. (Even people who were boycotting the conference somehow made it to the reception.) And it wasn't for the fabulous food and open bar. It was for one reason only—to catch a glimpse of the evening's guest of honor, Miss Elizabeth Taylor.

"Elizabeth," as Spencer Cox and I used to call her in hushed tones—eyebrows raised, her name always in quotes—would be making her first public appearance in several months. Defying doctor's orders, she was coming directly from her sickbed to announce her new pet project, an international fund devoted to establishing partnerships between health agencies and local organizations that fight AIDS in Africa, Asia, and Latin America.

About an hour and a half past the appointed time, with the hors d'oeuvres gone but the wine still flowing, the lights dimmed, and *THERE SHE WAS!* Walking gingerly, she smiled beneficently at the crowd as cameras flashed and everyone began to cheer. She was frail, but stunning; lots of hair and eye makeup, and blessed with her own inner spotlight. Doctors, government officials, activists, everyone was standing on tiptoe, climbing on chairs, covering their mouths in shock and amazement. Spencer and I grabbed tightly onto each other's arms. We might as well have been dressed in bobby sox, clutching autograph books.

The room went silent as we waited for her to speak. She began in a tiny, little-girl whisper, pausing repeatedly for breath and emphasis. "When I whas . . . *sick* . . . and in . . . *hhhospital, I knhew . . . I* whould . . . re-*cover* . . ."

It was—and I mean this in the most complimentary way—a performance unlike any I had ever seen. I don't think anyone exhaled the entire time she was speaking. If she'd come down in a pink bubble, I don't think we could have been more in awe. And it wasn't just a gay thing. You should have seen Tony Fauci!

And while I can't speak for Fauci, I know for Spencer and me, and probably many others in the room, it was a singular and unexpected moment of validation. So many people still thought of us as dirty little faggots who deserved to die, and here was Elizabeth Taylor—Hollywood Goddess, American Royalty—talking to us as friends, comrades, and partners in the struggle. The most famous woman in the world, and she wasn't looking down at us, but joining hands with us. Layers of shame I had no idea I carried simply melted away. Suddenly, I was pounds lighter, inches taller.

I know it all sounds silly, but I have to tell you, it was remarkable.

June 20, 1990: AIDS Conference Opening Ceremonies

Less silly, though equally remarkable, were the events inside the Moscone Center the following afternoon. Politics were front and center at this year's opening ceremonies, where speaker after speaker railed against the Bush administration and its policies. Many, like conference chair John Ziegler, wore red armbands to protest the HIV travel ban and support the many who did not attend the meeting because of the US policy. Ziegler even asked the audience to stand for a moment of silence as a gesture of solidarity, adding, "A message to President Bush and to Congress from twelve thousand conference delegates to end AIDS discrimination cannot be ignored."[10]

Welcoming us to his city, Mayor Art Agnos reminded the crowd that when San Francisco suffered an earthquake just eight months earlier, the president and Congress quickly set aside 4 billion dollars to fix the damage and retrofit the city's infrastructure for the future. "Where," he asked, "is our retrofit for AIDS?"[11] Dr. June Osborn, chair of the US National Commission on AIDS,* added, "I would like to say how sorry I am, and how embarrassed as an American, that our country, whose tradition serves as a

---

*The second "AIDS commission," the US National Commission on AIDS, was established by Congress in November 1988, several months after the first commission had delivered its final report and disbanded. This commission would have greater longevity, if less impact, lasting until September 1993. Most notable were the diversity and qualifications of its fifteen members, who included a mix of medical and public health experts and "civilians" with direct experience in HIV/AIDS, including Belinda Mason, a journalist and PWA. The selection of its members was divided between the Senate and the House of Representatives, which each chose five members, and the president, who chose only two. The remaining three slots were designated for members of the president's cabinet. Bruce Lambert, "AIDS Panel to Organize

proud beacon for emerging democracies, should persist in such misguided and irrational current policy."[12]

Even Larry Kramer managed to get his two cents in, as part of a video compilation of interviews with PWAs. Dressed in a Malcolm X T-shirt, with the phrase "By Any Means Necessary" boldly printed on the front, Larry excoriated the audience for their complicity in prolonging the crisis. "You know what is going on and what is not going on, and yet you refuse to use your voices. You are conspirators in this plague, though you think you are heroes."[13]

Then, Peter Staley strode to the speaker's podium.

Peter was a last-minute substitute for Vito Russo, who'd originally been selected to fill the ACT UP slot but was too sick to make the trip. Dressed in black jeans and a "Silence = Death" T-shirt, Peter asked everyone to join him in "an act of activism." "Trust me," he told the wary crowd, "You'll enjoy this." He then invited all the AIDS activists attending the ceremony to come up and join him at the foot of the stage.[14]

And as all my friends jogged past me, I just stood there, frozen. Was I allowed to identify myself as an activist? I was attending the conference on behalf of AmFAR, not ACT UP—would I be betraying them if I joined my ACT UP colleagues while still wearing my AmFAR drag and ID badge? But as the last activists trickled into place, I darted down the aisle and threaded myself into one of the back rows, wrapping my arms around the shoulders of my T-shirted comrades.

Peter then invited the rest of the crowd, "all of you [who] were asked to stand earlier in silence . . . to stand up ACT UP-style"[15] and join in protest of the INS travel ban. Ten thousand delegates rose to their feet accompanied by tumultuous applause. With a photo of President Bush projected above him, Peter reminded the crowd the president had turned down several invitations to address the conference and was, instead, "at this very moment in North Carolina attending a fundraiser for the homophobic author of the INS barriers; that pig of the Senate known as Jesse Helms."[16] Peter then invited the entire room to join him in a chant. As it happened, it was one of mine: *"Three HUNdred THOUsand DEAD from AIDS—WHERE IS GEORGE?"* When we first used it, just over two years ago, it was "only" thirty-two thousand.

After the noise died down, Peter thanked the crowd—"You can all now consider yourselves members of ACT UP!"[17]—and continued his efforts to

after Delay of 7 Months," *New York Times*, July 31, 1989, https://www.nytimes.com/1989/07/31/us/aids-panel-to-organize-after-delay-of-7-months.html?searchResultPosition=2.

"bridge the widening gap" between AIDS activists and the scientific community:

> I do know that we have judged you at times unfairly. I believe that many of you care deeply about ending this crisis and that greed is not your motivation for fighting this disease.
>
> I also know that you have frequently judged us unfairly too. Yes, ACT UP has made mistakes, such as choosing an offensive tactic. Communion wafers come to mind. But let's be fair here . . . when we make mistakes, what's the fallout? Some people become offended and begin to hate ACT UP. Whereas when the government or scientific community makes a mistake, such as the now legendary delays in bringing aerosolized pentamidine to market, thousands of people can die. While at times we may offend you, remember as well that like you, ACT UP has succeeded in prolonging the lives of thousands of people living with HIV disease. . . . Can we all, before it's too late, begin to understand each other?[18]

At the conclusion of his speech, Peter raised his fist, and everyone stood and cheered. We started another loud round of chants and carried on until the lights dimmed and another selection of PWA interviews appeared on the projection screens. Not wishing to disrupt or silence their testimony, we all quietly returned to our seats, and I to the sidelines.

At the very moment Peter was christening our newly minted members of ACT UP, several hundred activists of longer standing were outside the Moscone Center attempting to storm the conference. Although the action was led by PWAs protesting their limited access to the conference and exclusion from trial and research design discussions,[19] the demonstration registered as largely symbolic, since so many activists were already inside.

The following day, three hundred activists took to the streets to "expose the crumbling 'San Francisco Model' of AIDS care."[20] Long considered the gold standard, San Francisco had developed "a coordinated, integrated system of inpatient hospital care, outpatient care, and community-based care"[21] that provided a continuum of medical, psychosocial, and support services to PWAs at all stages of illness. But by 1990, the system was on the verge of collapse due to an overreliance on community resources, including volunteers who were now facing their own health emergencies, and was ill-equipped to address the needs of an increasingly diverse and geographically diffuse group of patients.[22]

Another 150 activists were arrested at Friday's protest against the exclusion of women, children, and people of color from AIDS research, treatment, and services. "Women are undercounted, overlooked, misdiagnosed and underdiagnosed,"[23] trumpeted the fact sheet, which included demands for the CDC to expand its AIDS definition and the ACTG to design clinical trials examining the effects of AIDS drugs on women.[24] The women's group also confronted Dan Hoth directly in front of his peers during his plenary presentation, storming down the aisles and unfurling a large banner that read **"NIAID: FORM A WOMEN'S COMMITTEE NOW."**[*]

Not that I saw any of this firsthand.

I may have been at the conference, but I was nowhere near the action. Instead, I spent most of the week downstairs staffing the AmFAR booth in the carpeted climate-controlled silence of the pharmaceutical bazaar. Oh, sometimes I'd take a break and wander around the market floor picking up the occasional oddly colored condom or sexy European safe sex postcard, but mostly I stood sentry in my shirt and tie, passing out AmFAR goodies and explaining the activities of the CBCT network to anyone who wandered by.

"It's all here," touted the *San Francisco Examiner*, "How to design new research protocols, how to involve community-based doctors in research, how to get more of the new generation of drugs out of the labs and into the testing phase, why it's vital to get more women, including pregnant women, into the drug trials. The doctors are listening, not only because it's good politics but because it's wise research strategy as well."[25]

ACT UP's 1990 *AIDS Treatment Research Agenda* was more sophisticated than the previous year's version, or even the ACTG critique distributed by

---

[*]The women activists had been planning something more disruptive but were voted down when they brought their proposed action to the rest of the ACT UP attendees, including members of T+D and ACT UP/San Francisco, who were worried about the action endangering the ongoing dialogue between the treatment activists and the ACTG researchers. Linda Meredith, interviewed by Sarah Schulman, ACT UP Oral History Project, March 10, 2013, 36.

Mark Harrington a few months earlier. Less a political manifesto than a scientific one, this year's agenda was written in the language of scientists and researchers, addressing them as peers. While the tone remained aggressive, it was also more collegial, acknowledging that activists and scientists must learn to work together to develop the new drugs, methodologies, and approaches necessary to save the lives of PWAs.

After praising the early alliances that had led to the successful development of parallel track and the upcoming trials created in partnership with NIH statisticians,* the activists cautioned these were just the beginning of an emerging "new research order" that would put patients before profits. Trials would be designed to address real-world treatment issues like combination therapies and drug interactions—looking for the lowest effective dose rather than the highest nonlethal dose in order to lessen potential toxicities—and answer multiple treatment questions simultaneously. It meant an increased focus on treatments and prophylaxis for opportunistic infections, as well as studies to explore potential cofactors that might speed up disease progression, and including, in all cases, rational enrollment criteria to allow all people with HIV, from all demographic groups and at whatever stage of disease, to participate.

"History will record the names of those who assist in creating a more equitable, humane and efficient research system, and it will record the names of those who resist," they warned. "Either scientists will work with us in advocating for change, or they will be forced to step aside."[26]

The activists proposed major changes to the ACTG's structure and decision-making process, tying center funding to performance and democratizing the process for determining research priorities. Many of these proposals reflected the whispered complaints of frustrated researchers who had reached out to ACT UP after Mark's critique was circulated.

They also demanded greater accountability at the local level through the establishment of Community Advisory Boards at each ACTG site "to provide input on the relevance of studies, improvements in trial design, and advice on conducting outreach to the diverse affected communities."[27] The CABs, one of ACT UP's lasting contributions to the drug testing process, would also help improve communication between testing sites and their host hospitals and enhance participant services, including transportation subsidies, childcare, and ongoing health care once trials are completed.

---

*The studies were the MOPS (Multiple Opportunistic Infection Prophylaxis Study) and SOCA (Study of the Ocular Complications of AIDS).

The press conference announcing the *Agenda* was packed with scientists, researchers, and media, all scrambling to get copies of what everyone agreed was one of the most important papers of the conference. It was yet another instance of how successful our "treatment activists" had been in integrating themselves into the AIDS establishment. "The apparent divisions between us are not real,"[28] exclaimed conference organizer Paul Volberding at Saturday's big "United Call to Action" rally, a feel-good demonstration on the penultimate day of the conference; a chance for "a Noah's Ark of the AIDS world"[29] to join in a symbolic march and rally. "People ask me if there are any breakthroughs," declared conference chair John Ziegler. "This is the breakthrough. The breakthrough is that we're all in this together. Action equals life."[30]

June 24, 1990: Armageddon

"No More Words We Want Action." So read the fact sheet handed out by ACT UP members at Sunday's closing ceremonies.

> Thus far during this conference, ACT UP has made many points without disrupting the exchange of scientific information. However, today's scheduled speech by Secretary of Health and Human Services, Dr. Louis B. Sullivan, is not a scientific presentation. After 10 years of Bush/Reagan rhetoric on AIDS, we will no longer tolerate words without action. You will not hear Louis Sullivan today.[31]

And true to their word, no one did.

The protest against Sullivan, the highest-ranking Bush administration official to attend the conference, was widely expected. Indeed, the media had been salivating at the prospect all week. Conference organizers, anticipating the fracas, switched the program schedule so Sullivan would be the final speaker, in case order couldn't be restored. Even Sullivan knew what he was getting into. Prior to the conference, he'd received a letter signed by thirty-six organizations, ranging from activist groups to professional associations, critical of the country's immigration and travel policies and demanding much-needed leadership from the White House and HHS. And on the opening day of the conference, he'd preemptively accused activists of inappropriately trying to "turn a scientific conference into a political referendum."[32]

So, it was a great surprise to see him take his seat onstage with his fellow speakers at the beginning of the program, rather than waiting out of sight backstage. For his pains, the secretary was treated to multiple attacks on the US travel ban by IAS president Lars Kallings and WHO director-general Hiroshi Nakajima, as well as a speech by Tony Fauci that lauded the contribution of the very same activists who'd pledged to disrupt his speech.

All this paled, however, compared to the onslaught of boos, chants, whistles, and air horns that filled the hall as Sullivan was introduced. During the cacophony, a group of protesters raced to the foot of the stage and unfurled a banner that read, "**HE TALKS, WE DIE**."[33] According to Keith Cylar, the group, largely made up of members of Majority Action and the Latina/o Caucus, wanted to ensure the protest did not look racially motivated. (Perhaps we'd learned something from the Myers Mess after all.) "As a person of color and the highest-ranking black official in [the federal government], Sullivan should set the tone," Keith explained. "Blacks and Latinos are disproportionately represented in the epidemic. He should be out there strongly for us."[34] As hundreds of activists sprinted to the front of the hall, many audience members stood and turned their backs to the stage, as had been requested on the ACT UP fact sheet. Then, after a deafening eight minutes, Sullivan purposefully strode to the lectern and began his speech.

Or so it appeared.

Even with his microphone turned up full blast, no one inside the arena could hear him. His speech, according to the written transcript, was largely a defense of the Bush administration's AIDS policies combined with a collection of easily mouthed platitudes about "the need to work together." Although he included his personal criticism of a proposed amendment to the Americans with Disabilities Act that would permit employers to reassign food handlers infected with HIV, he made no mention of the travel ban, nor did he offer up any new policies or information from the administration.[35]

Unfortunately, as with our previous "drown them out" demos, our action threw audience sympathy to the speaker rather than our cause. In this case, the image of a dignified black man maintaining his composure while standing up to an angry ill-behaved mob—which sadly included some protesters throwing condom packets and crumpled fact sheets toward the stage—made a far stronger case for the Bush administration than anything Sullivan might have said in his speech.

We'd missed an opportunity to use the stature of the conference to our benefit. Instead of showing a unified response, we threw a tantrum. But the demonstration was never about winning hearts and minds or convincing anyone about anything. It was driven by the internal imperatives of ACT UP and the needs of the people protesting. There was no way we could allow a senior administration official to appear in San Francisco and talk about AIDS—on Gay Pride Sunday, no less—without a major display of anger. It also afforded the T+D gang, who'd been behaving like good boys and girls all week, a chance to show they hadn't been co-opted by Fauci and the research establishment. They were still angry and remained a threat.

Despite my own issues with the protest—strategic concerns aside, I don't think it's a good idea to shout people down, particularly when you're a group always demanding to be heard—I didn't feel I'd earned the right to voice my opposition. I hadn't attended the conference as an activist, so instead, I just stood at my chair with my back turned and waited for all the yelling to stop.

As expected, ACT UP was widely criticized for the Sullivan demonstration by conference leaders and delegates, though more on style than on substance. While some complained about lost opportunities, others worried the action would only cause the administration to further absent itself from the crisis and damage whatever working relationships currently existed. In fact, Sullivan would later say he'd never work with ACT UP and asked government officials to avoid all but "necessary and productive" dealings with the group.[36]

After a week of mostly positive press, the media got in a couple of punches as well, including a stunningly clueless editorial from the *New York Times,* which responded to the Sullivan action by clucking, "It's harder to think of a surer way for people with AIDS to alienate their best supporters." (Which would be who, exactly—the *Times* editorial board?) "What," they wondered, "could have caused such a pointless break-down in sense and civility? *It's not as if society had turned its back on AIDS and those whom it strikes*" (italics mine). And even if progress might be slow, "it's not now for want of effort or resources." Finding "little value" in our "disruptions," the *Times* reduced our actions to mere expressions of the belief that "it is better to rage than to do nothing," even as they conceded we'd *"probably* been effective in issues like speeding up the laborious Federal system of drug trials." But in the end, the Gray Lady sagely counseled that "if ACT UP's members would only keep their faith in education and hard lobbying and put down their bullhorns, they might find their rage surprisingly well understood, and effective when focused in the right way on the right targets."[37]

Contrast this with the editorial page of the *San Francisco Examiner*:

... ACT UP has learned that on this issue—as on many others—science and politics are inextricably entwined. They have brought political pressure to bear, and they have achieved results. . . . Never before have the constituents of a disease organized into such a potent political force. They have nothing to be ashamed of and nothing to apologize for.

Protest is rarely pleasant; it is frequently annoying to people who regard themselves as innocent, put-upon bystanders who may even be sympathetic to the goals of the protest. But it has been effective in the fight against AIDS, a fight that has been waged by hard-working and dedicated physicians, nurses, medical researchers and activists. They have all played important roles. . . . The frustration of those most affected [by AIDS] is palpable and understandable. They demand and deserve more from Bush than a slap in the face. Last week he could have shown them that he really cares. Instead, he turned away. We expect better.[38]

Chapter 19

Can the Center Hold?

ACT UP HAD become successful beyond its wildest dreams.

Monday night meetings were filled to bursting and our "diverse group of individuals" had grown markedly more diverse. There were more women and people of color, as well as activists with different goals, experiences, and political agendas—all of which was to the good.

But it also meant change.

Who were we now and what communities did we represent? What were our goals and who should speak for us? These were some of the questions that would roil the Floor for the summer of 1990 and beyond.

Case in point: Peter Staley.

Instead of returning in triumph from San Francisco, Peter was greeted with a barrage of criticism. Already suspect, thanks to his experience in the financial sector and his focus on fundraising—not that we had any qualms about spending the money he raised—Peter was accused of ACT UP apostasy for "apologizing" in his conference speech for the Stop the Church demonstration. That Peter had only conceded that crumbling a communion wafer was not the best idea was of no matter; publicly voicing any criticism of the group, however slight, was considered treasonous.

Peter had also recently signed a fundraising letter for the congressional campaign of ACT UP member Sean Strub. There was no issue with Sean's running—he was, in fact, the first HIV-positive person to do so—but he'd affixed "Silence = Death" stickers to the envelopes, making it seem like an

ACT UP mailing or at least an official endorsement.* Even though he knew nothing about the stickers, it was Peter who took most of the heat, as the combination of his raised profile and the fundraising letter suggested that he was setting himself up as our de facto spokesperson.

Our Media Committee had long promoted Peter as ACT UP's unofficial poster boy; articulate and mediagenic, with a personal story made for prime time and the front page of the *Wall Street Journal*.[1] But just because he fit their needs didn't mean he suited ours. If anything, ACT UP's notoriety and increased media access meant we had to be even more sensitive about who was representing us and whose stories we were telling.

All this, combined with Peter's often unthinking arrogance, made him a walking symbol of White male privilege and a target of nasty jealousy-tinged postings in "TITA" ("Tell It to ACT UP"), our weekly in-house gripe sheet.

A pet project of Bill Dobbs, "TITA" was made up of often anonymous messages, mash notes, and complaints collected in a box at every Monday night meeting and then collated, typed, and distributed by Bill the following week. Though he insisted "TITA" was merely a "'steam valve,' a means to facilitate change and communication" that functioned much like "a computer bulletin board, an open microphone, a marketplace of ideas,"[2] it more often served as an amplification system for people who had little to contribute beyond their own petty, poisonous, and ill-tempered divisiveness.

A second major controversy that summer involved a broadsheet titled "Queers Read This."

> How can I tell you. How can I convince you, brother, sister that your life is in danger. That every day you wake up alive, relatively happy, and a functioning human being, you are committing a rebellious act. You as an alive and functioning queer are a revolutionary. There is nothing on this planet that validates, protects or encourages your existence. It is a miracle you are standing here reading these words. You should by all rights be dead.[3]

Published anonymously and distributed by ACT UP members at New York Pride without the larger group's approval, *Queers Read This* included a series of essays confronting the continued apathy of the larger lesbian and

---

*That Sean's company, Strub/Collins, had conducted—and gotten paid for—our first mass mailing campaign had placed him on the "suspect" list as well, despite the large amount of money those mailings had brought in.

gay community in the face of AIDS and the fast-growing epidemic of antigay violence.

> Every day one of us is taken by the enemy. Whether it's an AIDS death due to homophobic government inaction or a lesbian bashing in an all-night diner (in a supposedly lesbian neighborhood), we are being systematically picked off and we will continue to be wiped out unless we realize that if they take one of us they must take all of us.

Why, it asked, had the gay community responded to the brutal gay-bashing murder of James Zappalorti* with only a single underattended demonstration, while people of color had repeatedly taken to the streets in large numbers to protest the killing of Yusef Hawkins? The broadsheet contended it was because the Black community understood "the bullet that hit Hawkins was meant for a black man, ANY black man . . . [while] most gays and lesbians think that the knife that punctured Zappalorti's heart was meant only for him."[4]

Bias-related crimes and incidents against gays and lesbians had gone up 122 percent nationwide between 1989 and 1990. In New York City during the same period, the number of antigay attacks had doubled.[5] Included among the victims were Alan Klein's lover Karl, who'd been attacked by lacrosse stick–wielding teens at the previous year's Wigstock celebration in Tompkins Square Park, along with Darren Jurmé Allumiér,† who not only suffered a fractured skull, scapula, and collarbone but was harassed by homophobic emergency room staff at St. Vincent's Hospital.[6] Kathy Ottersten was bashed in the head with a baseball bat;[7] Jim Provenzano had been punched in the face while wearing his "Read My Lips" T-shirt in front of Uncle Charlie's, a gay video bar in the Village;[8] while Liz Tracey and Sydney Pokorny had been chased by a car full of young men threatening and calling them "faggots,"[9] and many more of us had been on the receiving end of some taunt or physical provocation.

Our very personhood—our ability to live and love openly and simply be who we were—was under constant attack. What would it take, the anonymous writers wondered, for us to wake up as a community and rid ourselves

---

*In January 1990, James Zappalorti, an emotionally disturbed gay man, was followed home by two young men who called him "queer" and "faggot" before slashing his throat and stabbing him repeatedly in the chest with a five-inch folding knife. John Voelcker, "The Second Epidemic," *OutWeek*, July 11, 1990.

†Formerly known as Darren Britton in his ACT UP days. He changed his last name in 1996.

of the life-threatening illusion that America considered us as anything but "other"?

That April, Alan, Karl, Michelangelo Signorile, and Tom Blewitt had called a meeting to discuss the possibility of mobilizing around lesbian and gay issues. They were stunned when sixty people showed up. The following week, it was over a hundred, and Queer Nation was born.

While Queer Nation functioned differently than ACT UP, there was little question of its parentage, not only in terms of its membership but also its tactics and swagger.* Some accused the activists in Queer Nation of abandoning AIDS, calling it "ACT UP for Negatives," but that wasn't fair. While my loyalties remained with ACT UP, I understood both the need and the desire to fight for gay rights and queer visibility. Even ACT UP's own Gay Pride fact sheet had focused more on gay issues than on AIDS.

Not that anyone would remember our fact sheet. The only thing anyone could talk about was *Queers Read This,* and in particular, the full-page article with the incendiary title "I Hate Straights."

It wasn't really about hating straight people, but rather a pained and personal argument for the legitimacy of queer rage—a rage directed not just at the usual targets, but also at our friends and allies, who were unwilling or unable to accept the validity of our anger.

> The next time some straight person comes down on you for being angry tell them that until things change, you don't need any more evidence that the world turns at your expense. . . .Tell them "GO AWAY FROM ME, until YOU can change." Go away and try on a world without the brave, strong queers that is its backbone, that are its guts and brains and souls. Go tell them go away until they have spent a month walking hand in hand in public with someone of the same sex. After they survive that, then you'll hear what they have to say about queer anger. Otherwise, tell them to shut up and listen.[10]

Powerful stuff. But still, there was that title.

Did they know it was going to spark controversy? Of course, that was the point. The entire broadside was an act of provocation, an attempt to shake

---

*A second group, the Pink Panthers, led by ACT UP member Gerri Wells, would form that summer as a community patrol to deter gay bashers. After the group was successfully sued by MGM for copyright infringement, they changed their name to Outwatch (but kept their pink pawprint logo). AP, "Gay Group Can't Call Itself Pink Panthers," *New York Times,* October 5, 1991.

our community into consciousness, best understood as a polemic, a manifesto of Queer Nationalism harkening back to Gay Liberation (and to Black Nationalism and the feminist separatists[11]) and articles like Martha Shelley's seminal "Gay Is Good."

> Look out straights. Here comes the Gay Liberation Front, springing up like warts all over the bland face of Amerika, causing shudders of indigestion in the delicately balanced bowels of the movement.[12]

For weeks, the Floor engaged in heated debates over issues of inclusion and diversity—did ACT UP consider itself an AIDS organization or a gay organization and did it make sense to buy into that false dichotomy? Queer Nation had, to some extent, called the question; but you couldn't fight AIDS without fighting homophobia, nor could you fight for queer rights without fighting AIDS.

"ACT UP/NY is a queer group!" argued David Robinson, one of the article's authors, and one of ACT UP's most beloved members.*

> Every Monday night we are a queer room, and out on the street, when we're not doing a coalition demo, we are queer demonstrators. . . . We are not activists who happen to be queer; we are AIDS activists <u>because</u> we are queer: because after being despised all our lives for being dykes and faggots, we now have AIDS, which either kills us or leaves us to face a straight world that blames us for this disease and tries harder than ever to slam us back in the closet.[13]

Nor, he continued, would the absence of our handful of straight members, much as they might be missed as individuals, make any "essential difference" to the organization. "Straight people and other nonqueers who can work in a queer group should be welcome . . . [but] that doesn't mean they are needed." ACT UP would still remain a diverse coalition: a diverse coalition of queers.

In addition to our Majority Action and Women's Action Committees, ACT UP now boasted a Latina/o Caucus and an Asian and Pacific Islander (API)

---

*A lithe and lanky modern dancer, David was also one of ACT UP's earliest and best Monday night facilitators, leading meetings with a fair and open heart, an ear-to-ear smile, and a gender-queer sartorial style that included a rotating collection of long dangling earrings and short clingy pencil-skirts.

Caucus. Like the earlier groups, these caucuses served as think tanks and support, advocacy, and consciousness-raising groups: places where members could meet away from the still predominantly gay White male Floor, create their own analysis, and address issues of importance to their communities.

At the time, AIDS in the API community was to a large extent invisible. Although the CDC had recently given API their own category in monitoring incidence of AIDS and HIV infection, the city relegated them to a random pool with Native and Alaskan Americans, and the state to the undifferentiated category of "Others." As a result, there was little local funding for community services, only one community-based clinic in New York City targeting the API population, and only one Chinese speaker on the city's AIDS hotline.

Rather than organizing demonstrations, the API Caucus focused on AIDS education. "There was no culturally specific education targeting Asian Pacific Islanders in the tri-state area," remembers caucus member Ming-Yuen S. Ma.[14] "[It's] not just about translating brochures" (most of the API community could probably read English). "[It]'s about approaches—it's about mode of address, [and] who is doing the education."[15] So, the caucus did teach-ins with drag performers at Asian gay bars,[16] created language for brochures for other members of the community that talked in a more circumspect manner about sexuality and drug use—putting the information in the traditional red packets used for "lucky money" exchanged on Chinese or Lunar New Year[17]—and created curricula and safe sex information for presentations at schools and colleges.[18] "Education was an activist strategy."[19]

The Latina/o Caucus was an outgrowth of the Spanish Translation Committee ("El Groupo"), which had formed in late 1989 when ACT UP mandated that all posters and fact sheets must also be produced in Spanish. Early translation efforts, carried out mostly by well-meaning gringos with their textbook Spanish, were often stilted and lacked cultural sensitivity. Things would improve once native speakers like Moisés Agosto-Rosario joined the group.

A recent transplant from Puerto Rico, Moisés was getting his graduate degree in literature while working part-time as a literacy teacher in the South Bronx, teaching women to read and write in Spanish so they could qualify for English as a Second Language courses.[20] It should also be mentioned—if only for historical accuracy—that with his compact, muscular body, dark black hair, and shockingly bright blue eyes, Moisés was arguably the best-looking guy in ACT UP (which is reeeeaaally saying something).

When Moisés, who was HIV-positive, realized that very little of the vital AIDS information stacked on our back table was being made available to the Latino community, he began to translate the *Treatment and Data Digest* into Spanish. Joined by other native speakers, the group soon grew dissatisfied with functioning solely as a service committee and, with the encouragement and early leadership of ACT UP veterans Joe Franco and the Roberts, García and Vazquez-Pacheco, formed the Latina/o Caucus.* While they would continue to act as a conduit for information to their communities, they also began fighting for the myriad medical, social, and support services those communities required.

Nonetheless, many of us were surprised when they came to the Floor with a proposal for a monthlong campaign in Puerto Rico later that summer.

The situation for PWAs in Puerto Rico was dire. The island had the second-highest per capita incidence of AIDS in the US, higher even than New York City. San Juan had the thirteenth-highest AIDS caseload among all US cities, while the cities of Ponce and Caguas rated first and second for new AIDS cases among cities with populations under 500,000. As the majority of the HIV-positive population was poor and did not have sufficient insurance policies, they were dependent on a troubled and vastly underfunded public health service. Despite being required to serve over 63 percent of the island's population, Puerto Rico received only about one-tenth of the Medicaid funds given to full-fledged states: a block grant of only $79 million, or roughly $86 per patient. (Mississippi, our poorest state, received roughly $816 per patient.)[21]

Puerto Rico was unable to provide even routine care for most of its population, let alone expensive drugs like AZT or pentamidine—even though the latter was manufactured on the island. "When I tested positive to AIDS, I faced no alternative but to go live in the states to find treatment," Moisés admitted. "I had to pay the price of living in a country with a different climate, a different language and without my family."[22]

The caucus had learned that Puerto Rico would be hosting a series of AIDS-related events that summer. They proposed organizing two tentpole demonstrations, the first in late July at a conference on AIDS and Civil

---

*Members of the Latina/o Caucus included Gonzalo Aburto, Moisés Agosto-Rosario, Jesus Aguais, Marina Alvarez, Lydia Awadala, César Carrasco, Cathy Chang, Carlos Cordero, Rita Córdova, Steven Córdova, Mario de la Torriente, Joe Franco, Nelson Galarza, Pedro Galarza, Robert Garcia, Alfredo González, Héctor González, Elías Guerrero, Vic Hernández, Sam Larson, Dannette Lebron, Carlos Maldonado, Fernando Mariscal, Gilberto Martinez, Juan Méndez, Patricia Navarro, Cándido Negrón, Victor Parra, Jairito Pedraza, Mario Quiñones, Carmen Royster, Luis Salazar, Luis Santiago, José Santini, Héctor Seda, Robert Vazquez-Pacheco, Amador Vega, Andrew Velez, Luis Vera, and Walt Wilder. César Carrasco, interviewed by Sarah Schulman, ACT UP Oral History Project, March 9, 2014, 21–24.

Rights featuring none other than Louis Sullivan as its keynote speaker, and the second at another major conference scheduled for late August. They would use the intervening weeks to work with local activists to help strengthen AIDS activism and advocacy on the island.[23]

Though these were laudable ideas and targets, I was initially skeptical of the proposal, fearing people would treat it more as a vacation opportunity than as a sustained action. (I'd soon come to regard our junkets to the International AIDS Conferences in a similar light.) However, San Juan was far closer—and cheaper—than San Francisco, and given the tight, familial connection and frequently traveled *puente aéreo* or "air bridge," the flight corridor between Puerto Rico and New York City, the campaign could almost be regarded as a local action.

The rest of my concerns were quickly laid to rest by the mammoth efforts of the caucus members and their impact on the island, beginning with the protest against Louis Sullivan outside the conference on July 29.

Inside, in his keynote speech, Sullivan would bizarrely suggest the responsibility for "the tragedy of AIDS in Puerto Rico" lay not with a failed federal response but with a lack of will by the Puerto Rican people, "a certain fatalism, expressed by the Puerto Rican phrase '*Ay bandito!*' or, 'Isn't it terrible, but nothing can be done.'"[24] Having shifted blame to the ethnic character of Puerto Ricans, he then urged local businesses and organizations to step up and provide the necessary care and treatment, and to sponsor research.[25]

Pendejo!

One week later, ACT UP demonstrated at the International Conference on AIDS Education, where conference organizers not only had left education about AIDS treatments off their agenda but had insisted on conducting the conference solely in English. By the final day, activists had convinced over half the attendees to come outside and join their protest.[26]

Over the next two weeks, caucus members met with local AIDS activists and AIDS organizations, allaying fears about ACT UP steamrolling existing efforts or imposing its ideology and methods on the community. They visited hospices, hospitals, and clinics; appeared on TV; spoke at community forums; and canvassed the gay neighborhoods. Activists from our Needle Exchange Committee joined the newly formed ACT UP de Puerto Rico to visit Hogar Crea Las Americas, a drug-free treatment center for HIV-positive drug addicts, continuing on to the La Perla neighborhood in old San Juan, where they visited shooting galleries and conducted a needle exchange.

When the Second Big Think Tank AIDS Forum held its opening ceremony on August 22, the activists splashed themselves with stage blood and welcomed attendees with signs proclaiming, **"The Governor has blood on his hands**," demanding Governor Hernández Colón bring clinical trials to Puerto Rico.[27] Two days later, more than two hundred protesters, not just young activists, but mothers with children, older women, "everyday people, heterosexual people, who were willing to fight for the cause because they were being affected," marched to the governor's mansion.[28] On the way, the protesters stopped for a die-in on the steps of San Juan Cathedral to call out Cardinal Luis Aponte Martínez, a powerful opponent of safe sex education who'd recently pronounced condom use a worse sin than having AIDS (as if the disease itself was a sin).

The activists confronted the cardinal in person the following day, during a church-sponsored prayer procession and Mass for "AIDS victims." Dressed in black and wearing skeleton masks, the group marched behind their banner, **"Activistas Contra SIDA ACT UP**," and stopped directly in front of the stage where the cardinal would be holding Mass. Despite threats from police, the protesters held their ground, remaining a silent but visible rebuke until the cardinal began his homily, at which point they turned their backs and marched proudly out of the park.[29]

The Puerto Rico Huracán SIDA campaign was a triumph, empowering activists in both Puerto Rico and New York, and the caucus soon became a magnet for gay activists from across Latin America, as well as a major player on the Floor of ACT UP.

It might seem odd that ACT UP's PWAs and HIV-positive members also felt they needed a separate caucus to advocate for their concerns; but for a group founded on the principles of PWA empowerment, ACT UP was surprisingly tone deaf to the needs of our own PWAs.

While we'd always had a fair number of PWA members, as well as others with swollen glands and middling T-cells who knew they were infected, most would disappear once their health began to deteriorate. However, the advent of experimental prophylaxis and treatments meant many could remain active longer, and it behooved us to make sure they could continue to participate for as long as possible. Three years into our existence, we were finally being forced to consider rest spaces at our demonstrations, as well as access to doctors, wheelchairs, food, and water, so everyone could take part in our actions, regardless of their health status.

But for the PISD (People with Immune System Disorders) Caucus, there was an even more pressing issue. It was time, they argued, for ACT UP to leave the Lesbian and Gay Community Services Center. Our meetings were overcrowded, overlong, and, in the summer, quite literally overheated, with people standing two and three deep for several hours without benefit of water or air-conditioning. There were no ramps or elevators, nor any other accommodations for people with disabilities. And despite changes we'd made to the order of the agenda and the physical meeting space, it remained difficult for people in diminished health to attend, let alone make it through our Monday night meetings. We needed to find a more practical and welcoming space.

I didn't want to leave the Community Center. I loved the energy and intimacy of the room and felt it was important to maintain our presence in the heart of the gay community. I also liked that we were just one of many events there on Monday nights, and that people might stumble upon us, much as I did, while attending another meeting. PISD and its supporters argued this sentimental attachment was "a perfect example of the ableism which is rampant in this organization."[30] They were understandably angry that the active participation of PWAs, on whose behalf the movement was founded, was considered less important than the ambience of the room or the symbolic message of being rooted at the Community Center. It was as if, once diagnosed, their contributions were no longer valued.

And so that summer, with regrets and great misgivings, we moved to the Great Hall at Cooper Union.

July 24, 1990: Bush at the Waldorf

Having missed the opportunity to confront George Bush at the AIDS Conference, ACT UP pulled out all the stops when the president came to town for a Republican fundraising dinner in late July. Over seven hundred demonstrators, including members from WHAM! and NOW, marched from the steps of the New York Public Library to the Waldorf Astoria Hotel in a stomping New Orleans–style funeral procession protesting the president's AIDS policies and antiabortion efforts. Activists wore white skull masks, carried black cardboard coffins, hoisted signs, and shouldered a huge five-foot wire hanger dripping with stage blood, while marching to the boisterous sounds of a hot jazz band.[31]

Although the marchers were held behind barricades a block away from the hotel, affinity groups were already inside the Waldorf, waiting to spring into action. First, a window on the second floor flew open and a banner—"**ONE**

AIDS DEATH EVERY TEN MINUTES"—appeared,[32] followed by a flurry of fake one- and twenty-dollar bills with "ACT UP, Fight Back" and "Bush has blood on his hands" printed on the back. Soon, a second set of windows opened, this time on the fourth floor, and an even bigger banner appeared: "**READ OUR LIPS: AIDS ACTION NOW.**"[33]

While building security was busy with the banner drops, the Costas, dressed in full master-of-the-universe drag—"imagine Heidi Dorow in heels and a skirt" and Avram "in an Armani suit, clean-shaven, hair slicked back like fucking Michael Douglas in *Wall Street,* and a copy of Fortune held under the crook of his arm"[34]—gathered in the hotel conference room they'd rented for their fictional "Future Global Ventures: Profiting from America's Global Dominance" seminar.

The Costas had planned to storm the Bush fundraiser, but as the elevators were no longer stopping on the event floor, they ran up a back staircase and managed to find an open door on the "safe side" of the security screens, right down the hall from the dinner. Capitalizing on their good fortune, they marched down the hallway chanting and holding their George Bush "**Serial Killer**" signs. When stopped by Secret Service, they dropped to the floor and continued their disruption, as the press swirled around them.[35]

Meanwhile, several floors below, a fourth affinity group, made up of members of the Housing Committee, milled around the hotel lobby covered in fake blood before handcuffing themselves together in a circle around the famous Waldorf clock.

Thirty-five activists were arrested, most for criminal trespass inside the hotel. While waiting for their comrades outside the Seventh Precinct House, ten activists were doused by a plastic bag filled with water that was "mysteriously" pitched out of the station's third-floor window.[36]

Encouraged by the uproar over our protest against Louis Sullivan in San Francisco and our continued badgering of the president, the AIDS backlash crowd escalated their complaints against the increased funding and "special status" afforded to HIV/AIDS. But whether it was conservatives like Charles Krauthammer huffing that AIDS was "the most privileged disease in America";[37] or Mona Charen, detecting a "veiled accusation" of the "slanderous" notion of government complicity in the "tragedy of AIDS" in the display of the AIDS Quilt on the DC Mall;[38] or so-called liberals like Pete Hamill, decrying the "paranoid oratory of gay radicals" and their "self-pitying aura of victimhood,"[39] what they all shared was a profound desire for us to just shut-the-fuck-up and go away.

While willing to concede that AIDS was terrible—they weren't *monsters* after all—they resented being confronted with the reality of our lives, and worse, being pressured to feel sympathy for us, particularly for something they felt was the result of a nasty and immoral act we should all just stop doing, or at least have the decency to stop talking about. Perhaps worst of all, they were angry to find themselves forced to defend their responses to the epidemic and gay people in general and have their assumptions about being decent, caring people questioned.

The bible of the backlash crowd was *The Myth of Heterosexual AIDS*, written by Michael Fumento, who two years earlier had drafted the Civil Rights Commission's rancid AIDS project proposal.[40] Fumento argued the kind-hearted folks of America had been hoodwinked by the gay community and their handmaidens in the AIDS-industrial complex into believing AIDS was everyone's problem when it was not; and having done so, cashed in. "By the late 1980s," he claimed, "the pink triangle was used like an American Express Platinum Card, as a means of getting special privileges available only to the bearer."[41] While he admired our moxie, he contended it made no sense to continue to invest in AIDS research since by the time current research yielded any useful treatments, there'd be no one left to cure. Better to stop funding AIDS altogether and put all that money and attention into cancer and heart disease—diseases that affect all Americans.*

Tellingly, most of these pundits discussed AIDS only as a gay disease. The other affected communities were not even worth mentioning, except as a straw man in their insidious argument that by advocating for research into cures and treatments, activists had privileged the lives of already infected gay men "at the expense of educating Americans who remain at risk—primarily the black and Hispanics of the inner cities of the East." And, even better, that we'd found willing accomplices in conservative politicians who, while blanching at the prospect of supporting "safe sex" education, found AIDS research to be "politically neutral."[42] It was a line of reasoning that wasn't just absurd; it was obscene.

---

*For the record, the entire annual NIH budget, for all diseases combined, was $7.6 billion, compared to the annual budgets for two largely discredited military systems, the "Star Wars" Strategic Defense Initiative and the "Stealth" B-2 bomber, costing $3.8 billion and $4.3 billion, respectively. John S. James, "New Threats to AIDS Research Funding," *AIDS Treatment News*, no. 9, February 16, 1990.

Although the argument was paper-thin, it wasn't something Tony Fauci and the scientists at NIH wanted to hear at a time when federal funding for AIDS research was coming up for renewal.[43] This, possibly more than anything, explained the change of heart at NIH and the warm welcome that greeted ACT UP and community activists at the July ACTG meeting.

Among his myriad other skills, Fauci was a smart and agile politician, who no doubt realized that as a mobilized constituency with a powerful megaphone, the AIDS community could be a valuable ally in his upcoming budget battle. He apparently also made it clear to his researchers that it would be far better for them, and for the ACTG, if we all presented a united front when it was time to testify before Congress.

So, it was the same Dan Hoth who'd previously fought so bitterly against our presence who now welcomed us with open arms. Fauci, doubling down on his promise to include activists and community representatives at every level of ACTG, exhorted the researchers to take up our *Treatment Research Agenda* proposals for small-scale studies focusing on treatments for opportunistic infections. He even acknowledged the ACTG's poor record in addressing women with HIV/AIDS, announcing that the current OB/GYN Working Group's portfolio would be expanded to include women's health issues.

Further acceding to activist demands, Fauci, Hoth, and several of their colleagues sat down with members of ACT UP's Women's Action Committee, including Maxine Wolfe and Heidi Dorow, in late July to discuss plans for a NIAID-sponsored public meeting on Women and AIDS.* According to Maxine, the activists attended the meeting with three goals: "1) to confront Fauci and Hoth with their criminal negligence and ignorance concerning women with HIV/AIDS; 2) to inform them about what we have learned from women with HIV/AIDS and from women who work with them on a day-to-day basis; and 3) to give them a list of minimum demands based on our understanding of the situation."[44]

The meeting did not go well.

Although there were some points of agreement, Fauci appeared remarkably uninformed about how women with HIV/AIDS were being treated in

---

*In addition to Maxine and Heidi, the meeting was attended by Garance Franke-Ruta and Risa Dennenberg from ACT UP/NY and Linda Meredith, Melinda Daniels, and Laurie Specher of ACT UP/DC.

his own trials—calling it "totally crazy" that pregnant women were being given drugs only to assess the effects on their fetus while their own health was not being monitored. "If the approach that we have in protocols now is inadvertently doing that," he admitted, "then it has to be re-addressed."[45]

The activists found Fauci "officious, sexist, and paternalistic," telling them the only reason they were even having the meeting was because of "the men in ACT UP, that is gay ACT UP."[46] Adding that "demonstrations don't get me," he further warned, "If you come in and threaten, I can guarantee you 100 percent, if you threaten you will get nothing, zero. If you demonstrate with nothing to back it up, you will get nothing."[47] The lack of trust, they responded, was mutual, and they categorically refused to limit their options.

There was something else Fauci probably didn't understand. Unlike Mark and the folks from T+D, the ACT UP women were not looking to be brought into the system, to work within the ACTG, or to become members of Fauci's newly proposed Women's Committee. They understood their role to be acting as advocates, using ACT UP's access to pry open the door for women with HIV/AIDS and the women who work with them.[48] If they eventually agreed to help Fauci organize the upcoming Women and AIDS Conference, it was only to ensure it would "have the right people, the right agenda, the right issues."[49]

Mark

In August, Mark Fotopoulos invited me to spend a weekend at his beach house on Fire Island. Despite our many similarities, I'd felt nervous about becoming friends with someone who, despite our best efforts, was probably dying. It was an intimate time and I didn't want to pretend a closeness we didn't have or make promises to be there in ways I couldn't fulfill.

It wasn't like I saw Mark regularly, even at ACT UP. His primary concern, quite appropriately, was his own health; so outside of Monday nights or demonstrations, where we each had our own specific role to play, there wasn't much opportunity to connect.

What finally solidified our friendship was a shared love of a four-performance Broadway flop called *Rags*.

The show, a musical about the struggles of Jewish immigrants on the Lower East Side of Manhattan during the early years of the twentieth century—think *Fiddler on the Roof* after they left Anatevka—was a real heartbreaker. It had undergone one of those infamous out-of-town tryouts with new writers, directors, and designers cycling in and out, fixing one problem only to unearth another. But sitting in the balcony watching the show's final performance, I caught glimpses of what could have been. There were, even then, moments of real beauty and power, along with a glorious score and wonderful cast, including Mark Fotopoulos.

I didn't know Mark at the time—*Rags* had opened and closed in August 1986—though I later discovered I'd previously picked him out of the chorus in another Broadway flop several years earlier. There had been something special about him, an extra zip and energy to his performance that marked him as someone to watch. I'd also been amused by his capsule biography, which read:

> MARK FOTOPOULOS . . . was almost cast in *Zorba, Baby, The Three Musketeers, On Your Toes, La Cage aux Folles, Forbidden Broadway* and *Cats*. But he was, respectively, too young, too old, too short, too late, too Greek, too versatile, and too intimidating. He is too delighted to be performing for you tonight.[50]

Although the cast album of *Rags* had been recorded four years earlier, it was tied up with legal problems and remained unreleased. So, it was with great excitement that Mark announced during my visit that he had a special treat for me. Sitting down in his darkened living room, Mark flipped on the stereo and the room was filled with a Copland-esque fanfare, followed by church bells and a mix of klezmer and ragtime, transporting me back not just to Mott Street in 1910 or the Mark Hellinger Theater in 1986, but to a different time of my life—when I was an actor, not an activist, and my life's ambition was to sing and dance on Broadway.

Then I looked over at Mark and wondered how many lives ago this must seem for him.

Mark had one other surprise for me that afternoon. Reaching into his knapsack, he pulled out a copy of his one-man play, *Mark Fotopoulos: Alive Performance*.[51] It was the story of his life as a PWA, told in monologue, song, and dance.

Mark had been diagnosed in April 1985, with "one lesion on my right arm, two on my left arm, one on my calf, one on my chin, and two on my nose," although, at the time, he didn't feel sick.[52] He was appearing in his first non-musical play, *The Loves of Anatol*—"No singing, no dancing, no dance belts!"[53] Although that production, too, was a flop, it had earned a dubious place in history as the play where John Simon, the loathsome drama critic for *New York* magazine, was heard to exclaim, "Homosexuals in the theater! My God, I can't wait until AIDS gets all of them!"[54]

Unbeknownst to Simon, AIDS had already made an appearance. Just two days before opening night, the actor who originally played Mark's role was rushed to the hospital with PCP. Mark, his understudy, wore the felled actor's costume, and now he too had been diagnosed with AIDS. "Oh, my God," yelled Mark in feigned horror, "it IS contagious!"[55]

To keep his panic in check, Mark went home and, like any good New Yorker in a time of crisis, ordered-in Chinese. And when his fortune cookie message said, "There is yet time enough for you to take a different path!"— Mark changed his life.[56]

While continuing to work in the theater, Mark slipped out of the gay fast lane, settled down with a nice Jewish architect named Robert, and began to volunteer at a gay help line. By the time I saw him with his "**Living with AIDS**" sign at Federal Plaza two years later, he was already considered a long-term survivor. Only 15 percent of the 14,603 people diagnosed with AIDS in the US by mid-1985 were still alive and active by 1988.[57] By 1990, those numbers were even smaller.

Though no one could pinpoint why people like Mark were surviving, they shared a number of characteristics. Along with a baseline of access to health care and a certain financial stability, they all shared a realistic yet positive attitude about their illness, accepting their AIDS diagnosis without viewing it as a death sentence. They were fighters who took personal responsibility for their health and were active participants in their own health care—able to alter their lifestyles and remove themselves from stressful situations—and be "altruistically involved with other persons with AIDS."[58]

This was Mark to a T.

By the time of my visit, Mark had pretty much retired from ACT UP. In 1989, shortly after being diagnosed with pulmonary KS, he took a self-healing workshop with Niro Asistent, herself a long-term survivor, who helped him "get in touch with the healer within."[59] He then underwent a successful course of chemotherapy that cleared not only his lungs of lesions but his face as well. Now on a macrobiotic diet, Mark, a former beach and disco bunny, was careful about getting too much sun, took afternoon naps, and waved off Tea Dance and the other touchstones of Fire Island social life. Instead, he'd sit in a darkened room, put on his headphones, and listen to the meditation tapes of Louise Hay, another New Age guru who, having purportedly healed herself of cancer, had shifted her attention to gay men and AIDS.

Hay described AIDS as a case of "dis-ease," whereby "a negative self-image, compounded by guilt and shame, make a person susceptible to disease." Hay offered meditations, affirmations, and visualizations as a way for people to "heal themselves," if not from the actual illness, then from its accompanying anger, anxieties, and fears. To combat the "chronic patterns of self-hate, guilt, self-criticism, resentments, and negative beliefs [that] raise the body's stress levels and weaken the immune system," Hay preached the gospel of love, forgiveness, and self-acceptance. "The key is to love and respect yourself. Affirm in the mirror, 'I love you enough to heal you.'"[60]

While many profited from her teachings—she clearly gave Mark a way to take some control over his illness and keep himself healthy and mentally (lowercase) positive—I was suspicious of New Age philosophy and spirituality in general. Certainly, a good attitude was important, and anything that could limit stress and anxiety, whether it was meditation or a trip to the gym, was obviously of great value. But I was wary of gurus, many of whom seemed to have a touch of flimflam about them.

I also felt there was something inherently dangerous about buying into Hay's belief system. Even though she counseled not to criticize or blame yourself, it stood to reason if you were in some way responsible for your disease, you must also somehow be at fault if you didn't get better. Maybe you didn't love yourself enough. Hay herself would regularly comment, "Some people would rather leave this planet than change."[61] Wasn't that blaming the victim? And wouldn't it just feed the self-loathing and despair you were trying to eliminate?

There were others I knew who took this New Age concept of AIDS one step further, regarding their illness as some sort of life lesson and ladder to enlightenment. None believed this more fervently than Jon Greenberg.

Jon was yet another of the beautiful, smart, and charismatic young men of ACT UP. Jon had left me speechless one Monday night when, in the middle of one of our hallway conversations, he said not only was he happy he had AIDS, but he wished everyone had it. He said this without any anger, and acknowledged he probably sounded a little crazy, but he viewed his illness as some great and wonderful journey, one from which he thought everyone he cared about could benefit.

Jon had tested positive for HIV in 1987 and had chosen to follow a holistic approach, using a combination of acupuncture, Chinese herbs, and vitamin supplements to maintain his health.[62] According to the tenets of Holism, disease is a state of imbalance within a system that includes the mind, body, and spirit. A holistic approach to AIDS meant looking for treatments to restore the body's natural immune system and prevent disease, rather than searching for the antiviral "silver bullet" that was the obsession of the research establishment.[63]

According to a survey by the Physicians Association for AIDS Care, over half of PWAs had turned to "alternative" or "complementary" therapies as part of their treatment regimen. Nonetheless, the medical establishment remained skeptical, if not downright antagonistic, toward their use. Doctors resisted prescribing them, the NIH refused to research them, the FDA rejected them, and insurance companies declined to pay for them.[64]

Part of the bias against alternative treatments was economic—they were usually developed by entities outside the pharmaceutical industry, often from natural substances and therefore unpatentable, offering little financial incentive for their development and distribution. But there were also scientific reasons why the NIH and ACTG were unwilling to pursue the testing of nontraditional products. It was difficult to measure the success of these treatments by standard quantitative methods. While most scientific trials required hard end points like death or progression to disease to determine whether a treatment was working, alternative and holistic practitioners considered improved quality of life as their measure of success. Unlike ACTG studies where all subjects are treated identically, holism requires you to treat each person individually, so studies of alternative therapies would have to be designed along broad-based principles that could be adapted to each participant. There was also less focus on "how" a treatment worked than on the fact of its working.[65]

Although several such treatments had been successfully developed and tested in other countries, the FDA and NIH refused to consider foreign data, thereby trapping most alternative therapies in limbo. Since they'd not been tested in the United States, they were not taken seriously as potential treatments; and because they were not taken seriously as potential treatments, they were not going to be tested in the US. Not coincidentally, this was the preferred outcome for many interested parties in the medical, insurance, and pharmaceutical industries.

In September 1988, Jon, Bob Lederer, and a handful of other ACT UP members had formed the Alternative + Holistic Treatments subcommittee of T+D. In just two years, A+H had grown from a small interest group with five or six activists to a robust committee of thirty, including "lay healers, nurses, acupuncturists, PWAs, HIV-positive people, traditional Chinese medical practitioners, homeopathic students, nutritionists, massage therapists, writers and herbalists,"[66] cutting across a range of political and health philosophies.*

---

*A second group, the New Alternative Treatment Action Working Group, would form in late May 1991 as a result of a schism between members who questioned whether HIV was the

A+H was dedicated to identifying potentially useful treatments and therapies and ensuring people with HIV/AIDS had access to the broadest possible range of health care and medical information. They'd successfully pushed T+D to expand ACT UP's treatment agenda to include demands for federal research into alternative treatments and fielded their own affinity group, the Non-Toxics, to carry out actions highlighting the NIH's reluctance to test nonpharmaceutical products.[67]

A+H had recently completed a successful six-month campaign to stop the NIH from funding an insurance industry–backed computerized database of alternative AIDS treatments, which the committee feared would function more as a blacklist to discourage the use of nonpharmaceutical agents and give insurance companies carte blanche to refuse reimbursements for potentially beneficial therapies. Members had also joined with cancer activists to form the AIDS and Cancer Freedom of Choice Task Force, a coalition of seven groups dedicated to coordinating lobbying and activism efforts which, in one of its earliest victories, had secured passage of a New York State law establishing a procedure for the licensing for non-MD acupuncturists.

A+H would also take the lead in organizing protests at September's "Quackery, Health Fraud and Misinformation" conference in Kansas City. The conference was part of a long-term propaganda campaign to discredit all alternative treatments by blurring the distinctions between worthwhile treatments and pseudo-scientific scams. The real goal, much like the aborted database, was to suppress competition for the AMA and Big Pharma, while giving insurance companies further permission to restrict their already miserly coverage.[68]

This issue cut to the heart of PWA empowerment and patient rights. "We don't think it's the government's business to restrict the options available to patients, especially of life-threatening illnesses for which there is no cure," Bob explained. "The so-called quack-busters are simply defending corporate interests against the competing system of medicine."[69] Jon put things more bluntly, "I'm here to fight for my right to choose what treatments I take for my body. I consider it murder if they want to deny me access."[70]

---

cause of AIDS and those, like Jon Greenberg and Bob Lederer, who wanted to focus instead on pushing alternative treatments through more rigorous clinical trials.

This sense of urgency was exactly what was missing from my job at AmFAR, which more and more had come to feel like my own private EST training, where, despite all my hard work, I still didn't "get it."

I was used to ACT UP, with its open debate and exchange of ideas. What did I know of the brutal behind-closed-doors world of not-for-profit office politics? I saw myself as an implementer and team player, but to be effective, I needed to be included in discussions so I could understand larger goals and strategies. Instead, I was continually kept in the dark. I don't know if it was because they didn't think I had anything to contribute or didn't care to hear what I might have to say. Or maybe they just questioned my loyalty, never thinking of me as an "AmFAR guy."

Whatever the case, I frequently found myself in situations where nothing was explained, but results were expected. I was executing tasks, but to little effect or purpose. What was worse, I knew it. Rather than contributing, I'd become part of the problem—just another ineffectual AIDS bureaucrat taking up valuable time, space, and money. Deeply frustrated and dissatisfied with my work, I began to grumble about wanting to leave AmFAR, and after a few weeks, AmFAR granted my wish.

There's a famous chapter—at least in my circle—of Ethel Merman's autobiography titled "My Marriage to Ernest Borgnine." What follows is a blank page.[71] That's pretty much how I feel about my contributions to fighting AIDS during my time at AmFAR. I left a defeated man, unsure of my abilities and apologizing for breathing.

It remains the most dispiriting job of my life—and I've been a waiter.

Ben

Throughout my time at AmFAR, Ben and I had been building a long-distance friendship with occasional benefits. I'd flown out for a romantic California Christmas, and he returned the favor with a swoon-worthy spring visit to New York. But as spring turned to summer, Ben grew increasingly unhappy in LA. More and more, New York seemed like the answer. Even so, we agreed "we" would not be the reason for his move. We'd never discussed the nature of our relationship, made no promises or commitments, and preferred to enjoy our time together without trying to define it. So when Ben moved back to New York in September, we picked up a cautious friendship. But after a few weeks of movies and dinners that were not quite dates, we gave in to the obvious.

Ben was quickly welcomed into my circle of non–ACT UP friends. This was not necessarily a given. We could be a tough group, not by intent (well not *always* by intent), but we had a particular sense of humor—fast, witty, and reference-laden—and not everyone was able to keep up or even get a word in. Ben, thankfully, was more than up to the task and forged an immediate connection with my best friend, Neal.

Neal had been my first openly gay friend. We'd quickly bonded during my first semester of college over a shared appreciation of the score of *70, Girls, 70,* and had remained best friends ever since. Even though I would not "officially" come out for another two years, Neal became my cultural guide in The Way of Gay. He knew the lingo and taught me all the required references—the movies, music, and performers. If my knowledge of musical theater is now held to be encyclopedic, it's because I learned from a master. Neal also believed in my talent, casting me in his original musicals at school, and later in the city, writing tailored material that highlighted my particular skills.

Neal was also the first in our circle to grab a foothold in New York, with his own apartment and a steady paycheck writing movie ad campaigns, while continuing to develop musical projects as a lyricist and composer. When I finally graduated and moved into my shared one-bedroom apartment on Fifty-Sixth Street, Neal's apartment just one block away became my living room. For years we hung out, smoked joints, watched *Dynasty* and old movies, and listened to obscure original cast recordings together. We shared our lives, our friends, our dreams and heartaches, and, in one complicated instance, a boyfriend. Neal was the center of my non–ACT UP social life and though not an activist in the ACT UP sense, he was always sympathetic and supportive of the cause.

Ben fit perfectly into my relationship with Neal. They had similar tastes and temperaments and shared an equally jaundiced view of the movie business. The three of us developed a smooth and easy rhythm, a nonstop back-and-forth that was always great fun. Eventually, I came to realize my relationship with Ben was probably at its best when the three of us were together, where we could ignore the pressures of coupledom and its intimacies. But for the time being, it provided a welcome respite from the continuing tensions and stresses of activist life.

Chapter 20

Bombs Are Dropping

FALL 1990 BEGAN on a promising note. Early reports from Bristol-Myers Squibb indicated ddI might prove a more effective drug than AZT in battling HIV,* and there was another promising antiviral on the horizon, Hoffmann-LaRoche's ddC.

Unfortunately, Roche, unlike Bristol-Myers, refused our entreaties to create an expanded access program for ddC. When, after months of empty promises, ACT UP and the AIDS community finally forced them to administer a compassionate use program,† they limited access to only those patients who could prove they had failed *both* AZT and ddI—a requirement that was far too restrictive given the still limited availability of ddI and the rapid emergence of AZT-resistant HIV.

But antivirals were not a cure; nor did they address the opportunistic infections that killed 90 percent of people with AIDS.[1]

---

*After twenty-one months, 80 percent of those patients who entered ddI trials with an AIDS diagnosis and 93 percent of those with ARC were still alive, with statistically significant T-cell count increases for 9–15 months. *Lancet* 36 (September 1, 1990): 526–29.

†Compassionate use (or expanded access) is an FDA program that makes drugs currently at some stage of the drug development process available to patients on a case-by-case basis. Doctors were required to fill out a detailed application for each patient, which the FDA then reviewed to determine approval. Most significantly, drug companies are not required to make their drug available under this program. ACT UP internal document: Jim Eigo, Mark Harrington, Margaret McCarthy, Stephen Spinella, and Rick Sugden, "FDA Action Handbook," September 12, 1988, 12.

Enter Garance Franke-Ruta.

Garance, who remarkably was still a teenager, had arrived at ACT UP fully formed. Like a premed honors student with a double major in fashion design, Garance could spew scientific jargon at a clip rivaled only by Mark Harrington, while garbed in her own unique downtown-futuristic-retro-thrift-shop style. Garance could go toe-to-toe with any of ACT UP's major thinkers and personalities, as well as any researcher, government bureaucrat, or pharmaceutical CEO, whatever their age or gender.

She was an astonishment.

It was Garance who first proposed Countdown 18 Months, an ambitious campaign that would use all the tactics in ACT UP's arsenal to "challenge both government and industry to find more effective treatments and prevention for the five deadliest opportunistic infections associated with AIDS within the next 18 months."[2]

Her co-conspirator was Derek Link, another fast study and fearless young activist. For Derek, it was as though AIDS activism had thrown a switch, changing him from a seemingly sweet, slight young man into a bold, angry, and confrontational one. He would mark his transformation by shaving his hair into a Mohawk, which he alternately dyed cotton candy pink or swimming pool blue, even as he attended meetings and conferences with pharmaceutical reps and government officials.

The young activists envisioned their campaign as an antidote to the "attitude of resignation and fatalism" that currently surrounded the epidemic.[3] They proposed nothing less than to create a "comprehensive program of targeted research"[4] to optimize standard-of-care for opportunistic infections; design and conduct trials to rapidly bring new drugs to market; and create interim guidelines for prophylaxis.[5]

The five infections targeted were PCP, still the number one killer of PWAs; cytomegalovirus (CMV), which caused blindness and/or diarrhea and severe wasting; toxoplasmosis, a type of encephalitis that affected the brain and nervous system; *Mycobacterium avium-intracellulare* (MAI), a systemic disease related to tuberculosis that caused chronic fevers, night sweats, chills, diarrhea, and wasting; and a host of interrelated fungal infections, including cryptococcal meningitis, histoplasmosis, and candidiasis or thrush (oral, vaginal, and esophageal).

Each infection was assigned to a designated "point person," who was responsible for coordinating all aspects of their specific campaign, including negotiations with all the major players from the FDA and NIH to drug company executives. It spoke to the growing strength of T+D that they were able to take on such an impressive project even as their key veterans were busy with their own high-profile projects.

Countdown 18 Months was greeted enthusiastically by researchers when the activists introduced it during the November ACTG meeting. One disappointed scientist even complained that her disease had been left off the Countdown hit list.[6] It received a less than welcome response from Tony Fauci, however, who objected to the eighteen-month time frame, insisting that it was unrealistic to expect scientific discovery to follow a specific schedule.

Much had changed at ACTG in the past year. Where once activists and community members had to dodge security guards, we now had our own committee, the Community Constituency Group (CCG), as well as official representation on all of the major ACTG committees.

The CCG—the group's third name in as many meetings—was still very much a work-in-progress, trying to define itself, its mission, and how to best represent all its various constituencies. There were many conflicts between members, not only regarding the needs of their communities, but also concerning the respective needs, goals, and processes of organizations representing them—what Mark Harrington referred to as "the battle of grassroots activists vs. Executive Directors."[7]

ACT UP was the 800-pound gorilla, the group with the largest representation at ACTG and the biggest megaphone. We'd established our own direct lines of communication with Fauci and the research establishment and were not beholden to the CCG for access or leverage. Not surprisingly, the other groups began to push back against our presumed leadership and favored status. If the CCG was the official voice of the community, they asked, why should ACT UP have special privileges? Maybe all the participating groups should have their own direct access to Fauci et al. And if we expected them to trust us to speak for the community, shouldn't we trust them to speak for us as well?

It was left to Larry Kramer to point out that for all its benefits, the CCG might just be a trap created to isolate community issues within a single committee. "This Committee," he warned, "has been set up to police ourselves. . . . We are all fighting for the same issues. We have witnessed mal-feasances here. Part of *every* meeting should be for the community; we shouldn't be fighting over turf."[8] Debra Fraser-Howze—no friend of ACT UP—concurred, asking the activists to wait and let CCG figure out how to respond as a group rather than have ACT UP become its de facto spokesperson. "When the history of this is written," she reminded them, "you're gonna be in the first paragraph. We're just coming up to speed. Let it happen."[9] "Things take time," counseled T+D's Ken Fornataro. "This is an experiment in communication. Try it. Then, don't just blow it up—go back and fix it."[10]

November 6, 1990: Spoiling Mario's Party

On election night, it was once again time to goad and plague our dear friend Mario Cuomo.

Just days before the election, St. Mario, who was cruising to reelection for a third term as governor, announced he was cutting over one-third of the state's $60 million contribution to New York City's $193 million AIDS budget. The cuts would come largely from monies dedicated to community-based organizations, support services for women and children, primary care, and drug treatment, with additional reductions of services to prisons and community health centers. The governor had also "reclaimed" an additional $7.5 million in unspent funds—money that had already been reappropriated for this year's AIDS budget—to help balance the state budget.[11]

Knowing Cuomo would want to time his acceptance speech to coincide with the 11 p.m. news broadcasts, we'd made sure to arrive at the Sheraton Hotel Ballroom by 10:30, in plenty of time to disrupt his televised coronation. But as the minutes ticked by, there was no sign of the governor. Perhaps he calculated it was better to forgo the live victory speech than risk the equally live, and potentially uncontrollable, confrontation with ACT UP.

When the governor finally appeared at 12:15 a.m.—long after the news programs were over and most of the viewing audience asleep—we greeted him with a raucous demonstration. Once again, Mario the True tried to engage us in a dialogue, asking if anyone from ACT UP wanted to talk to him, claiming he could not hear us when we were shouting. But we now knew even if Cuomo heard us, he never really listened—so we just kept on shouting.

November 12, 1990: Incoming

Something was wrong. You could tell the minute you walked into our Monday night meeting. Instead of the usual premeeting buzz, people were clumped together whispering and hugging in quiet corners. I already knew what had happened, having been on both ends of phone calls that began, "I have some bad news . . ."

Vito Russo was dead.

He'd died early Wednesday morning, November 7, "just a few hours after Jesse Helms was reelected," as Larry bitterly noted.[12]

I'd last seen Vito three months earlier, when I was visiting Mark Fotopoulos on Fire Island. I was in the harbor, sitting on the steps of the Pavilion, when I saw a frail old man dressed in long sleeves and a big floppy hat slowly hobbling into town on his cane. After a silent gasp, I bounded over to say hello.

He was still Vito—weak but determined. I told him how much I enjoyed his speech at the Gay Film Festival in June, and he regaled me with the tale of how his friends had smuggled him out of the hospital with a 104-degree fever and pneumonia so he could attend. Since then, he'd come down with PCP and they'd discovered KS in his lungs and bone marrow. Too sick to travel to San Francisco to make his speech at the AIDS Conference, Vito had instead watched what was to be his final Gay Pride parade from the balcony of Larry's Fifth Avenue apartment, "wav[ing] like Evita" to the passing ACT UP contingent, which serenaded him with shouts of "*Vito! Vito! Vito! We love you! We love you! We love you!*"[13]

With Vito's death, we'd lost a friend, hero, and role model. If AIDS could claim Vito Russo, what chance did the rest of us have?

We'd barely had time to absorb the news when there was a second announcement—Ray Navarro had died.

Even though Ray had been desperately ill for most of the year—first with tuberculosis and then with cryptococcal meningitis, which had robbed him of his strength, his eyesight, and most of his hearing—he'd remained a vivid presence at ACT UP meetings thanks to the efforts of his legion of friends who'd become Ray's own "Army of Lovers": taking shifts at the hospital, "sleeping in bed with him, cleaning his body, wiping his lips with glycerin, reading, singing and gossiping with him, fighting and negotiating with doctors in the hospital, and sneaking in an acupuncturist."[14]

Every week, Kim Christensen would come to the Floor and ask for volunteers to visit with Ray or to read *OutWeek* and other magazines and newspapers into a tape recorder so he could listen to them, while fellow artists Zoe Leonard and Aldo Hernández helped complete his artwork, acting as his eyes, legs, and hands.[15] Ray's mother, Patricia, flew in from California to join his caretaking circle and soon became a fixture at ACT UP meetings and demonstrations, not just as a proxy for Ray, but as an AIDS activist in her own right, remaining an ACT UP member in both New York and Los Angeles for several years after Ray's death.

Ray was a talented artist and writer, a visionary activist, and a kind and generous soul. His death at age twenty-six left another irreparable hole in the organization.

And then there was a third announcement.

Kevin Smith wasn't an ACT UP "star" like Vito or Ray. For many, I'm sure he was just another face in the room. But I'd known Kevin since the early '80s. He'd been a friend of a former boyfriend—the one whose naked photo I'd found on the front page of the *Native*; one that Kevin, a professional photographer, had taken.

Kevin and I had rediscovered each other in ACT UP, where he continued his photojournalism, snapping pictures of demonstrations, meetings, and conferences. He'd been diagnosed in September 1989 with cryptosporidium, an intestinal infection that starved his body by preventing it from properly digesting food. Even though he lived only a few blocks away, I'd no idea Kevin had been sick until I ran into him on Ninth Avenue over the summer and noticed the telltale tightness at his temples. It had been a bad spell, he confessed, but he'd come through it and was determined to continue his activism. But when his health failed again, Kevin returned home to California.

I hadn't even noticed he was gone.

As one of his last political acts, he wrote "An Open Love Letter to My Warrior Friends":

Thousands of years ago there was a warrior race in Greece in a place called Sparta. When they went into battle they were an army of lovers. An army of lovers can never be defeated. We still chant that when we go into battle against the federal government, the NIH and FDA, the Dinkins administration, President Bush and all the other disinterested people in positions of power who don't help us in our struggle to survive. Some are helping but not enough to make me think I won't die of this monster that is inside of me; this monster virus that floats through my blood and makes me suffer so much and has killed so many of my friends and lovers . . .

Keep on fighting. Fight for me. Fight for yourselves. Fight for all our lives. ACT UP. FIGHT BACK. FIGHT AIDS.[16]

Kevin died quietly in his sleep on Sunday, November 11. He was thirty-six.

That Wednesday, as we gathered, still shell-shocked, at Judson Memorial Church for Ray's memorial, Alan Klein came up to me. "Did you hear?" he asked. "Oliver Johnston died last night."

The sweet, dandyish Oliver had been a member of the Silence = Death Project and a founding member of ACT UP. And while we hadn't seen him at meetings in a while, his death added yet another note of unreality to an already incomprehensible week. But it was also an alarm. We'd entered the next phase of this brutal war. The bombs were now dropping directly overhead, and the casualties would be unimaginable.

VITO RUSSO (1946–1990)
RAY NAVARRO (1964–1990)
KEVIN SMITH (1954–1990)
OLIVER JOHNSTON (1952–1990)
May their memories be for a blessing.

Amidst all the death and dying, I attended the wedding of a college friend. It was a joyous occasion, as most weddings are, but I felt like a visitor from another planet. It wasn't just the usual "single gay guy at a wedding" thing, though, as celebrations of heterosexuality and family values, weddings always required a certain amount of compartmentalization.

No, what I was feeling that Sunday afternoon picking at my poached salmon was not just left out, but invisible. There was no place at this wedding, or in this whole workaday world, for what was happening to me and my friends. And with no real outlet—ACT UP was great for channeling anger but not much else—my emotions began bubbling up in unexpected places.

One night at the theater, I found myself choking back sobs in the middle of *Once on This Island*, a fable-like musical about a young peasant girl's ill-fated romance with a handsome prince she nurses back to health after he's injured in a terrible car crash. Perhaps it was the idea of kindness eventually being rewarded or love proving triumphant; or maybe it was just the notion of a benevolent universe where prayers are answered, the sick recover, and goodness prevails. Whatever it was, I suddenly felt this huge unwanted wave of emotion welling up in my chest and rising into my throat, and I began to panic.

I'm not a crier. I actually find it physically painful. I don't know if it comes from a general discomfort with public displays of emotion or the result of a too-well-learned childhood lesson to never let them see you crying, but I clamped down on those feelings a long time ago and do not let them out.

So, I shut my eyes tight, clenched my jaw, and wrapped my arms around my chest like a straitjacket and physically pushed those feelings back down into their hiding place, terrified of what might happen if they ever escaped.

While my work at AmFAR had prevented my attending the first CDC demonstration eleven months earlier, I felt no such obligation to my new temp job and gladly joined my comrades for their return visit in early December.

For the past year, the Women's Action Committee had been spearheading a campaign to draw attention to the dangerous and often deadly shortcomings of the CDC's AIDS definition. In early October, 130 demonstrators from the New York and DC ACT UPs had stormed the Department of Health and Human Services to protest the Social Security Administration's use of the CDC definition. We'd also helped file a class-action lawsuit charging the department and SSA with violating the Equal Protection guarantee of the Fifth Amendment by creating "two classifications of similarly situated persons disabled by HIV-related impairments—those who exhibit manifestations of HIV-infection enumerated by the Centers for Disease Control and those exhibiting other manifestations of HIV-infection."[17] By relying on the "underinclusive" CDC definition—one that specifically failed to acknowledge how AIDS manifests in women—to determine eligibility for insurance and disability benefits, the department had also discriminated against women as a class.

The lawsuit was the idea of Terry McGovern, a young lawyer with the Mobilization for Youth Legal Services HIV Project.* Terry had been working in poverty law as a housing lawyer but shifted her practice when she became aware of the dangerous intersection of poverty and AIDS. Since her colleagues were afraid or unwilling to take on AIDS cases, she established the HIV Project so she could focus exclusively on her AIDS advocacy work.[18]

Terry came to ACT UP hoping to enlist the group in organizing a demonstration to protest the treatment of a client who had been mercilessly harassed and threatened with eviction from public housing following the death of his lover. But when she heard the Women's Action Committee presentation on

---

*MFY Legal Services was the legal arm of Mobilization for Youth. It was renamed Mobilization for Justice in 2017.

the CDC, she immediately recognized the connection between the definition and the problems facing her other clients—HIV-positive women who were demonstrably ill but did not qualify for disability or AIDS services because they did not "officially" have AIDS.[19]

She soon joined forces with ACT UP, adding a second, legal front to our battle to get women with AIDS the treatment, benefits, and services they needed. The combination proved mutually beneficial. Terry gained not only the extra leverage of an army of street activists but also the assistance of a cadre of skilled volunteers to help her craft press releases, make connections to powerful allies in the AIDS world, and wade through the enormous paperwork required to successfully litigate a class-action suit against the US government. In return, the lawsuit gave the CDC street campaign additional teeth and, more importantly, helped introduce ACT UP to Terry's clients, women with HIV and AIDS who would become intimately involved in the group's efforts to not only change the AIDS definition but also force the NIH to focus on research and treatments for women with AIDS.

Among the women who joined the fight—or rather, whose fight we joined—was Katrina Haslip. Katrina had begun her AIDS activism while still an inmate at Bedford Hills Correctional Facility. Unhappy with how she and her fellow HIV-positive inmates were being treated by both prison guards and other inmates, she formed a peer education, support, and advocacy group called ACE or the AIDS Counseling and Education Program. On her release in 1990, she formed the sister program, ACE-OUT, to help former prisoners with HIV/AIDS adjust to life on the outside.[20]

Though still on parole, Katrina was one of two dozen HIV-positive women, including Phyllis Sharpe, Iris de la Cruz, and Lydia Awadala, who traveled down to Washington with ACT UP on October 2 to demonstrate and speak out in front of the HHS building. Many of these women were former prisoners or recovering drug addicts, and they all put themselves at great personal risk by sharing their stories and participating in our demonstrations.[21]

The following month, Katrina joined Maxine Wolfe and Tracy Morgan, a health educator with the Community Family Planning Council and volunteer at the Community Health Project,[22] as part of an activist contingent meeting with CDC officials to discuss demands for an expanded and more inclusive AIDS definition. Despite their entreaties, the CDC once again refused to add gynecological infections and indicator diseases to the definition, demanding additional layers of procedures and research not previously required for earlier changes to the definition.

If some of the CDC's justifications were blatantly sexist, others simply defied common sense. Why should a man or woman with HIV who develops candidiasis, a yeast infection of the mouth, be immediately classified as having AIDS, while a woman with HIV who develops a severe case of vaginal candidiasis be denied an AIDS diagnosis? Same disease, different orifice.[23]

Underlying all these delays and excuses was the political reality that any expansion of the definition would mean a substantial increase in the AIDS caseload, which would, in turn, increase pressure for more funding—something the White House had little interest in pursuing. But the CDC's neglect of women was institutional, extending beyond the AIDS definition to its studies and data collection. If the CDC claimed it didn't have sufficient epidemiological data on HIV in women to merit a change in definition, it was because the CDC had decided the data weren't worth collecting.

Dissatisfied with the progress of their negotiations, seven hundred activists[24] from over thirty states marched on CDC headquarters on December 3. The demonstration, which took place in a soaking rain, was led by over thirty HIV-positive women who shared the stories of their struggles with HIV and the bureaucracies that withheld their support and denied them their services due to the CDC's AIDS definition. "I have a file at the county hospital that's four inches thick," charged one HIV-positive woman, grabbing the bullhorn. "I'm not sick yet. I'm on fifteen medications. But I'm not sick yet. I've got $35,000 in medical bills, and I'm not sick yet."[25] "I'm twenty-eight years old and I'm dying. And no one gives a shit," roared Keri Duran,* a fierce dyke activist from ACT UP/Boston. "Get off your asses and do some research."[26]

About an hour into the protest, a group of over fifty activists, led by the Costas, slipped away from the demonstration, piled into waiting vans, and invaded the offices of the CDC's HIV director, Dr. Gary Noble. By day's end, a total of ninety-eight activists would be arrested at the two demonstrations.[27]

While the CDC action was widely praised, questions were raised in "TITA" about how the Costas had handled their affinity action. Although they'd expanded the number of CD participants from ten to fifty to include additional members from New York, Atlanta, and DC, the Costas had kept much of the decision-making to themselves, making unilateral decisions and withholding information from their newer recruits. This ran completely counter to the nonhierarchical consensus-driven process by which our affinity groups usually functioned.

The day before the demonstration, John Kelly and Jamie Bauer had asked me to help with support for the CD. They wanted to make sure they had

---

*Keri Duran (1962–1995). *May her memory be for a blessing.*

enough coverage, given the increased number of participants, and assumed there would be no issue with my coming aboard. I even participated in the group's pre-action meeting.

Instead, I wound up going through this weird initiation ritual with two other experienced activists who were also looking to join the affinity action. As we three "pledges" waited outside in the motel hallway, the Costas and their new associates met to decide our fate. Initially, we were all approved, with the more recent recruits voting overwhelmingly in favor of our inclusion. But after the vote, some of the Costas expressed concerns that a certain amount of trust had been built up within the affinity group—even though some had been members for less than a day—which could not be sustained if they expanded any further. A second vote was taken, and the offer withdrawn.

Although the rejection stung, I was also relieved. I'd been nervous about the CD and ambivalent about joining the action. I hadn't been arrested in over two years and hadn't felt like a full-time ACT UP member since I started working at AmFAR a year earlier.

What I suspect happened was the core group had grown increasingly uncomfortable with all the new people involved and didn't want to further jeopardize the action's success. Control queens will be control queens. It wasn't personal.

For me, what was more troubling was how the Costas, many of whom had helped plan the main CDC demonstration, had abandoned it—and us—to carry out their affinity action, taking fifty of the most experienced activists with them. The rest of us were left facing riot police and various potential arrest scenarios—a situation that was particularly dangerous for the women with AIDS we'd sponsored and encouraged to join us. I'd always understood that as an organizer, I had a responsibility to the people who had shown up to demonstrate and, much as a captain doesn't abandon their ship, an organizer doesn't leave their protest until the demonstration is over and everyone has safely left the site. It seemed an unexpected misjudgment; an odd blind spot on the part of activists for whom I otherwise had only the deepest respect.

A little more than two weeks later, we gathered in the Great Hall at Cooper Union for Vito Russo's memorial service. There were performances by members of the Gay Men's Chorus and Baby Jane Dexter, and, as was only appropriate, film clips: Judy, of course, and Vito's beloved Thelma Ritter. There was a scene from *Caged*, the movie I'd first watched in Vito's apartment two years earlier, and Ethel Waters singing "His Eye on the Sparrow" from *Member of the Wedding* as a tribute to Vito's lover Jeffrey Sevcik, who had died from AIDS in 1986.*

There were eulogies by his good friends Arnie Kantrowitz, Larry Mass, and Jan Oxenberg, and from gay scholar Martin Duberman, who helped put Vito's accomplishments in historical perspective; but the one everyone remembers—given, or so he claimed, with the permission of the deceased— was the lacerating speech delivered by an angry and unforgiving Larry Kramer. "Lar," Vito once explained. "We're both cranky and angry. Nobody understands that cranky and angry for us is the same as big tits for Jane Russell, or Judy singing 'Over the Rainbow.'"[28]

That afternoon, Larry didn't stint on either emotion. He gave it to all of us—friends, politicians, activists, and even Vito's family—with both barrels. "We killed Vito," raged Larry. "As sure as any virus killed him, we killed him. Everyone in this room killed him. Twenty-five million people outside this room killed him. Vito was killed by twenty-five million gay men and lesbians who for ten long years of this plague have refused to get our act together."[29]

"There are no more than five thousand gay men and lesbians fighting to keep us alive in this entire country," he thundered; "even those of us who are fighting are not fighting hard enough." Larry condemned our community leaders as "cowards, or weak tokens, or idiots" and called the gay community "the most leaderless twenty-five million history has ever produced. . . . [If] Moses or Jesus or Joan of Arc came along to lead us, we'd shit all over them and throw them out."

He then challenged us—everyone who mourned Vito or said they loved him—to "go out and emulate him. Do what he did. Get your hands dirty. Fight in his memory. If you don't know what I'm talking about, learn."

Some people were furious. Others sat in numbed silence. I don't know what I felt. Chastened? Not that I believed I'd personally killed Vito, but maybe I—we—had let him down by not fighting hard enough.

At the end of the service, I joined a crowd of ACT UP members huddled around Larry. Was it a gesture of support or camaraderie? Were we protecting him or seeking succor? Whatever else it might have been, I think Larry had articulated what many of us secretly feared—maybe we *were* to

---

*Jeffrey was also the subject of the clip shown from *Common Threads*, a documentary about the AIDS Quilt that had featured Vito as one of its protagonists.

blame. If only we'd tried harder or worked smarter, somehow Vito and Ray and Oliver and Kevin, and all of those who'd died—or whose death was yet to come—would have been saved.

And on the following day, December 21, our fierce comrade, Ortez Alderson, died in Chicago at age thirty-eight.[30]

ORTEZ ALDERSON (1952–1990)
May his memory be for a blessing.

Part V

DAYS OF DESPERATION

Chapter 21

Desperate Measures

CRISES AREN'T SUPPOSED to last ten years. But by 1991, that's where we were. And as we entered this new phase of our struggle, the next generation of PWAs, the ones who'd been lucky enough to survive until AZT and aero-solized pentamidine, my friends and comrades, were getting sick and dying. Larry was right. For all our efforts, we hadn't stopped the virus or even slowed it down. Five thousand people were not enough to end the AIDS crisis. But what could we do?

The answer, at least according to Larry, was to scream even louder.

He'd come to ACT UP the past October with another of his *WHERE-ARE-WE-GOING-WHAT-IS-THE-PROBLEM-WITH-ACT-UP-WE-ARE-LOSING-OUR-RADICAL-EDGE* jeremiads. We must shut down the entire city, he raged, block every bridge and tunnel to proclaim our anger and demonstrate our power. Despite its lack of practicality or focus, Larry's proposal was overwhelmingly approved.

But while Larry was great at rousing the troops, he had little experience or interest in planning an action. And since those most easily roused were usually the last ones you'd want organizing a demonstration, Jamie Bauer and I volunteered to form a committee to flesh out a solid proposal.

The result was Day of Desperation: a daylong campaign of actions, zaps, and mass demonstrations fanning out across the city, targeting government offices and agencies, corporations and insurance companies, religious insti-tutions, service organizations, the media, and the public at large. For one day, we would make AIDS everybody's problem. For one day, everyone would hear the bombs dropping.

We'd selected January 23, to coincide with President Bush's State of the Union address, but even though the White House rescheduled the speech, our date proved fortuitous, for in the early morning hours of January 17, 1991, the United States launched Operation Desert Storm. Every night for the next week, a sleepless nation stayed up into the wee hours of the morning watching infrared images of bombs and antiaircraft missiles exploding in real time over Baghdad like some old-school video game. Ratings for both CNN and the president soared.

We quickly added "Money for AIDS, Not for War!" as a theme for our demonstration, arguing if the government could afford to spend billions of dollars to protect the interests of oil companies, they could find the money to combat a disease that was killing hundreds of thousands of its citizens. As a result, Day of Desperation would become the nation's first large post-invasion antiwar demonstration, and AIDS the stand-in for all the important domestic issues pushed aside so the Bush administration could pursue its unnecessary interventionist war.

January 22, 1991: *Erev* Desperation

Jewish holidays traditionally begin at sunset the night before the day of celebration. So it was with Day of Desperation. But instead of lighting candles, we lit up the airwaves.

A somber Dan Rather had only just begun intoning his live *CBS Evening News* broadcast when three activists from the Action Tours affinity group leapt in front of the cameras shouting, *"AIDS is news! Fight AIDS, not Arabs! Money for AIDS!"* Although the disruption may have lasted just a few seconds, with only the bobbing head of John Weir making it on camera before cutting to commercial—*Dayenu*, it was enough.

In a delirious display of media schadenfreude, the other networks gleefully broadcast the footage at the top of their news programs, accompanied by reports of a similar disruption at the PBS studios of the *MacNeil/Lehrer NewsHour* by the Bloody Marys affinity group, and a third thwarted attempt by a second group of Action Tours members over at NBC.* These takeovers, warned the otherwise delighted news anchors, were just the first in what

---

*Peter Jennings was given a pass at ABC thanks to his comparatively supportive AIDS coverage.

promised to be a day of provocative actions and protests planned by the radical AIDS activist group ACT UP.*

Media coverage: done and DONE!

January 23, 1991: Day of Desperation

Roughly twelve hours later, some 1,500 protesters gathered in the frigid cold in front of Federal Hall on Wall Street for our kickoff march through downtown Manhattan, delivering coffins with "AIDS Won't Wait" and *"El SIDA No Espera"* splashed across their lids in blood red to seven worthy targets.

First stop, the New York Stock Exchange (*"**DRUGS for PEOPLE! NOT for PROFIT!**"*). Then on to the World Trade Center and the offices of our AIDS-budget-freezing governor (*"**Cuo-Mo MIra! DiNEro para SIDA!**"*). A quick jog to Worth Street and the offices of the NYC Health and Hospitals Corporation (HHC) (*"**HOSpital EmERGency! CITY Health Care's KILLING ME!**"*), then the Federal Building (*"**HEALTH Care, not WAR Fare—AIDS. WON'T. WAIT!**"*), and over to the NYC Department of Health (*"**DEAD ADDicts DON'T ReCOVER!**"*), where Richard Elovich, Illith Rosenblum, and Gay Wachman from our Needle Exchange Committee attempted to deliver water cooler jugs filled with several hundred used needles they'd safely removed from the streets. Rather than accept delivery, Woody Myers had the activists arrested.[1]

Then it was over to the Department of Housing Preservation and Development (*"**HOUSING, not SHELTERS!**"*), before our final stop at City Hall to thank Mayor Dinkins for a year of broken promises (*"**HIS-to-RY WILL Re-CALL: NOTHING CAME from CITY HALL!**"*).

While our committee was responsible for Day of Desperation's opening and closing demonstrations, we gave the rest of the day over to ACT UP's other committees and affinity groups.† At noon, members of our Housing

---

*There was another action later that evening when eight Costas were arrested trying to hang two banners in the St. Paul's Chapel cemetery on lower Broadway. That action did not get any press coverage.

†Special shout-out to Victor Mendolia, who monitored the day's actions from the ACT UP Workspace, handling reports from the field, questions from the press, and the usual collection of bomb threats and angry messages from the public.

Committee joined a lunchtime march and demonstration in Harlem organized by the formerly homeless residents of Emmaus House. The seventy-five protesters, some with their faces painted as death masks, sang, chanted, and carried eight handmade coffins, each commemorating the life of an Emmaus community member who'd died from AIDS, and two smaller baby-size coffins to remind everyone that "in Harlem, AIDS is a family disease."[2] When they reached the State Office Building Plaza, eighteen protesters sat down in the busy intersection at 125th Street and Adam Clayton Powell Jr. Boulevard and were arrested as part of a planned CD action.

A little further uptown, Grito Latino, an affinity group made up of members of our Latina/o Caucus, laid siege to the offices of Bronx borough president Fernando Ferrer, presenting him with a *la negligencia*,[3] "Certificate of Negligence," for his handling of the AIDS crisis. Flustered by the video camera recording the confrontation, Ferrer was unable to answer even the most rudimentary questions about the disease and its impact on his borough, which had the largest concentration of PWAs in the country.[4]

Invigorated by their lunchtime foray, Grito Latino traveled downtown to the tony SoHo offices of the Hispanic AIDS Forum. HAF's location, miles away from the community it claimed to serve, was an apt metaphor for the organization itself. Despite five years and an annual budget of close to $1 million, HAF had provided little in the way of services, even as AIDS became the leading cause of death among Latino/a men and women ages twenty-five to forty-four in New York City.[5]

While Grito Latino took on HAF, Jon Greenberg and thirteen members of the Alternative + Holistic Committee paid a house call to Dr. Emilio Carrillo, president of the city's Health and Hospitals Corporation. Much to their surprise, Carrillo not only met with them, but agreed to implement several of their demands, including expanding access to acupuncture as a therapy option for IV drug users battling addiction and creating an advisory committee to help devise an immune-enhancing diet for people with HIV/AIDS in all HHC hospitals.[6]

The Bloody Marys, having regrouped from the previous evening's takeover of the *MacNeil/Lehrer NewsHour*, decided to "jolt the corporate workhorses from their mindless routine" by making a special lunchtime delivery to the Citicorp Center, depositing a pile of bloody bones and entrails in the center of the building's food court, accompanied by a message about the toll of the AIDS crisis, adapted from Dalton Trumbo's antiwar novel, *Johnny Got His Gun*:

94,770 DEAD MEN, WOMEN AND CHILDREN = 7,290 TONS OF BONE AND FLESH, 315,000 POUNDS OF BRAIN MATTER,

98,550 GALLONS OF BLOOD AND 4,264,650 YEARS OF LIFE THAT WILL NEVER BE LIVED.[7]

Later that afternoon, the Marys delivered a similar message and offal offering to the tourists gathering at the TKTS booth in Times Square.

Meanwhile, Karin Timour led her Vigilant Insurance Tactical Operation affinity group (the VITOs, in honor of Vito Russo) on a tour of the Madison Avenue offices of some of the country's largest insurance companies. Karin had already discovered how a small handful of demonstrators could put the fear of god into an insurance company—last year, it had taken only six protesters to convince Blue Cross/Blue Shield to cap out-of-pocket expenses in their open enrollment insurance program. Today, she returned with a cool dozen, hand-delivering a consumer "Bill of Rights," and distributing fact sheets listing the following big "Six Lies" insurance companies told the public about AIDS:

AIDS is an immensely costly illness; AIDS will bankrupt insurers; the government will take care of PWAs without insurance; insurance companies are paying their fair share in the epidemic; insurers treat people with AIDS fairly; and you can live without health insurance.[8]

Fittingly, the VITOs finished their rounds with a press conference held in the lobby of the Health Insurance Association of America, while the terrified staff barricaded themselves inside their offices.

Grand Central Terminal

After a long day of protests in subfreezing weather, we knew we'd need a warm indoor location for our closing demonstration; someplace dramatic where we could create a major disruption guaranteeing media coverage and providing us with an appropriately grand finale. Despite having no direct or even symbolic connection to the AIDS crisis, Grand Central Terminal— with its cavernous main hall, balustrade balconies, and grand marble stair-case*—fulfilled our requirements brilliantly. (*And, oh my god, THE ACOUSTICS . . . Coustics . . . coustics!*)

But much of what made Grand Central attractive also made it a challenge logistically. It would be easy for us to get lost in the rush hour chaos of such a vast and densely crowded open space; and the lack of sidewalks, stanchions,

---

*A second staircase at the east end would be added as part of the four-year $200 million renovation completed in 1998. Tara George, "A Grander Central," *Daily News,* September 30, 1998, https://www.newspapers.com/clip/26076040/a_grander_central/.

or other natural demarcations would make it difficult to create a separate safe space for a legal protest.

Our solution was the "Affinity 500," a campaign to enlist 500 activists willing to get arrested as part of our spectacular closing CD action. While we'd need to act together as a unit to maintain some sort of cohesion, we encouraged everyone to organize as smaller affinity groups for communication and support purposes, and to give everyone a little autonomy within the larger structure.

But even as we gathered at Grand Central, there remained a lot of unknowns. Although 463 activists had pledged to join us, we had no way of knowing how many would show. Or how many more might be inspired to join us, thanks to the oft-repeated warnings from radio and TV news desks about "major rush hour delays expected at Grand Central" due to our demonstration. Besides, with everyone bundled up in their winter coats and hats, it was nearly impossible to separate the protesters from the commuters.

My affinity group, the Desperatoes, had decided to purposely set ourselves apart by donning smocks with the hand-painted message "**WE ARE ALL LIVING WITH AIDS**," forcing those who took the statement literally to confront the possibility of interacting directly with someone who had AIDS, while also making the larger point that AIDS affects everyone.

Just before five p.m., a shock of pink and red helium-filled balloons came streaming through the glass doors and down the grand staircase. I assumed it was another one of those bizarre juxtapositions where the rest of America is celebrating a birthday while we fight for our lives—until I spied Heidi and Avram in the middle of the throng.

When they arrived at the center of the hall, the Costas released their balloons, unfurling a huge parachute cloth banner with the message, "**Money For AIDS, Not For War**." They held on to the bottom of the banner until it grew taut, then let it go. The balloons and banner floated dreamlike up to the terminal's high-vaulted, star-encrusted ceiling, like a magic curtain slowly rising on our demonstration. It was a perfect moment, a breathtaking *coup de théâtre*. I didn't know whether to scream or cry. I chose the former.

"Act UP! Fight BACK! FIGHT AIDS!"

The next forty-five minutes was barely controlled chaos. A group of protesters laid siege to the information kiosk, stickering and papering over its windows, grabbing handfuls of color-coded Metro-North timetables and throwing them into the air like confetti. Across the way, a group of musicians began beating conga drums and blowing whistles, adding their rhythms to the cacophony of shouts and chants echoing throughout the terminal. The escalators to the balcony stopped moving, the grand staircase turned into a giant viewing stand, and traffic on the floor congealed into a single throbbing mass.

At the sound of an air horn, we all dropped to the ground for the first of several die-ins. When it sounded again, we got up and moved to our next location; shuffling from one corner of the hall to the next, like an angry AIDS Mardi Gras parade, tossing our stickers and fact sheets like party favors, blocking commuters, and stretching ribbons of red tape across departure gates, until it was time for the next die-in.

As we crept to our next destination, the Featurettes affinity group scampered across the roofs of the now-shuttered ticket booths and draped a huge banner across the massive departure board. Commuters looking for the next scheduled train to New Rochelle would instead see a new timetable: "**One AIDS Death Every 8 Minutes**."

Heated arguments began breaking out between the commuters, furious at being prevented from getting home, and the protesters accusing them of complicity in the deaths of hundreds of thousands of their fellow citizens. Though the demonstration had no official marshals, we did our best to intercede, but after almost an hour of frustrating, ear-splitting gridlock, even the most sympathetic bystanders had had enough.

Once again, we'd been so focused on a scenario for mass arrest we hadn't thought out what we'd do if those arrests never came. We hadn't investigated the logistics or legal ramifications of sitting down on the tracks, nor had we discussed alternatives like marching to St. Patrick's or regrouping at Penn Station. After a quick meeting with the affinity group reps, we sounded an air horn and marched out of Grand Central and into the middle of Forty-Second Street for an hours-long die-in. A total of 263 people were arrested, some for the second time in twenty-four hours, for a one-day total of 313 arrests.

The following Monday, we faced a lot of criticism from members who found the Grand Central protest and CD finale better theater than politics. "When we engage in civil disobedience, we do so to achieve change," counseled Aldyn McKean. "[Arrests] are the means to an end, not the end itself."[9]

And he was right.

Nevertheless, I defended our decision as our best available option at the time. We'd based the entire action on the premise of getting arrested and had made no allowances for other contingencies. And while the dynamics of the day required we find some resolution, some way to channel all that pent-up anger and energy, we also had a responsibility to the people we'd recruited not to put them into a situation where their safety might be compromised by the sudden "inspiration" of one of our more volatile members.

By planting ourselves in front of Grand Central, we remained strong and unified as a group. The arrest was also an important marker for our newer members, who could now be counted on to take a more aggressive role in the organization and in planning and participating in future actions. And whatever its other merits, there's no denying the action made a handsome addition to the ACT UP promotional reel.

More importantly, we'd achieved our other goals, punching through the all-war-all-the-time news cycle, reawakening consciousness about AIDS as a nationally important issue, and further burnishing ACT UP's reputation as one of the country's leading dissident voices. Close to eight hundred people attended our next Monday night meeting, followed by phone calls from college groups and others seeking to organize antiwar demonstrations asking for trainings and logistical assistance.

The action also helped us internally. We had, if only for a moment, pushed ACT UP out of its funk, reenergized the Floor, and empowered committees that had previously been working in the shadows. We'd also trained 125 new activists in civil disobedience, and shown that, at least in the streets, ACT UP was still a force to be reckoned with.

Alas, our heightened profile also led to greater scrutiny from law enforcement. On February 5, three activists were arrested for spray-painting "O'Connor Spreads Death" on the sidewalk in front of the Cardinal's residence. One of the activists, Scott Sensenig, was beaten by six cops who called him "faggot" and "cocksucker,"[10] while the two women, Dolly Meiran and Cristiane San Miguel, were taunted by leering officers who said they wanted to videotape them having sex together and then jerk off to the video.[11]

When ACT UP gathered outside the precinct house the following Monday night to protest their treatment, the police violently attacked the crowd. An officer grabbed one of our peacekeeping marshals—a cherubic, blond-haired, former seminarian named Chris Hennelly—and took a two-fisted whack at his head with his nightstick. As Chris lay writhing on the ground, other officers joined in, mercilessly beating and kicking him. According to his medical records, Chris received at least eight blows to his head, as well as injuries to his neck, back, and extremities.[12] After crawling into the station house for protection, Chris was held in police custody for nearly twenty-four hours and charged with assaulting an officer and resisting arrest. Upon his release, Chris was hospitalized for six days, suffering from hearing loss, seizures, blurred vision, and dizziness.[13] He remains on disability to this day.*

Around the same time, several ACT UP women were targeted by a sinister harassment campaign bearing notable similarities to the FBI COINTELPRO efforts to disrupt and destabilize earlier dissident groups. In a modern updating, the tactics now included uninitiated three-way calls, serial hang-ups, recordings from other members' phone machines, unsolicited connections to gay sex lines, and threatening "I'm going to kick your fucking dyke ass" phone messages that soon escalated to instances of cut phone lines and anonymous warnings made to people's parents and employers. One woman, a recovering addict, had a needle and a packet of white powder deposited on her doorstep. Another found bullet holes in her window, and a third, a swastika made of "Silence = Death" stickers pasted to her door.[14]

We'd always assumed ACT UP was under surveillance, a suspicion confirmed when *OutWeek* reporter—and former Action Committee co-chair—Duncan Osborne received eleven pages of FBI telexes in response to his Freedom of Information Act request.[15] Two years later, a second FOIA request would yield a report of seventy-eight documents held in FBI offices across the country, the first being a memo dated September 1988 suggesting ACT UP had, rather incredibly, teamed up with a group of skinheads to foment the Tompkins Square Riots.[16] A subsequent 1994 request by the Center for Constitutional Rights would uncover almost two hundred pages of files in the FBI's New York office alone.[17]

While we may never know the extent to which ACT UP was targeted or even infiltrated, there's little question these activities helped ratchet up tensions within the organization, most notably between members of Women's Action Committee and Treatment and Data Committee. Resentments over access and differences in tactics that had been building since the San

---

*The charges against Chris would eventually be dismissed, the judge noting that not only were the accusing officers nowhere near him, but "It is hard to conceive of what resistance the defendant could have put up while being surrounded and beaten by the police. . . . The act of crawling away from such an onslaught can hardly be considered resisting arrest." James Barron, "Judge Denounces 'Lawless' Beating by Police at Rally," *New York Times*, October 1, 1991.

Francisco AIDS Conference had exploded on the Floor in late December after the long-awaited NIAID-sponsored conference on Women and AIDS.

The women activists had originally envisioned the conference, NIAID's first on the topic, as an opportunity for the community to educate the government about the real-life issues facing women with HIV. At the urging of the Latina/o Caucus, ACT UP had sponsored fifteen women with HIV to attend and share their experiences. Instead, attendees were treated to "an 'AIDS 101' lecture" from Tony Fauci, a presentation on treatments from Dan Hoth, "who began by saying he had no information about possible clinical treatments for women since NIAID had not researched any,"[18] and a presentation by James Curran, the chief of the CDC's HIV/AIDS Division, who refused to admit any problems with the CDC's AIDS definition. The HIV-positive women were shunted to a single "Living with HIV" panel, or at least they were until they took over the second day's morning plenary.[19]

Both Hoth and Fauci were openly contemptuous of the ACT UP women—Hoth referring to them as the "*junta*"[20]—and waved away their *Treatment and Research Agenda for Women with HIV Infection*, in stark contrast to the respectful manner with which they now engaged with the T+D "boys."* It's little wonder the activists reacted bitterly when, on the last day of the conference, they discovered Mark Harrington was in town—not to lend his support, but to attend a private dinner with Fauci. Many of the women felt personally betrayed; none more vocally than Tracy Morgan.

> I would like to know why, after Evil Anthony Fauci treated all the women at the Women and HIV Conference like dirt, Mark Harrington got to have dinner with "The Big Guy" that same evening? I find this revolting. In ACT UP are we merely acting as individuals or are we working together? What did the two of them meet to talk about—women and HIV? Certainly not. We must stop these private meeting[s] and commit ourselves to acting publicly, where we reach more people with our message . . . I think we've got to get our shit together and not perpetuate the syndrome of good boys versus bad girls. I resent the lack of thought behind the planning of this secret tete a tete.[21]

A cofounder of WHAM!, Tracy had joined ACT UP shortly after working on the Stop the Church action, bringing with her a school-taught feminism

---

*It's important to remember here and elsewhere that these are oversimplifications. Women were members of T+D, and men, including several who were HIV-positive, were equally involved with the women's NIH and CDC campaigns.

radicalized by her experiences in the women's reproductive rights movement. Convinced the movement's failures were directly related to its growing dependence on "insider" politics,[22] she now worried ACT UP was heading down the same destructive path.

> I do not believe that we gain anything at all by sitting on government committees, by meeting informally for coffee or a meal with government officials . . . by making casual phone calls or attending parties with these people. For three years, we have proved to them our extreme intelligence. Now that we've got their respect, it's time to show them our anger.[23]

.Tracy seemed unaware of how hard we, and T+D in particular, had fought—how much anger they'd both displayed and engendered—to earn that relatively recent and grudging respect. Like many of our newer, more politically grounded members, she appeared frustrated that ACT UP's organizing principles were more practical than ideological, and that both demonstrations and meetings with officials were considered crucial direct-action strategies for our stated goal of ending the AIDS crisis. Lacking our shared history, she viewed our inside-outside strategy as oppositional, rather than complimentary, and quickly grew suspicious of members who were pursuing less confrontational avenues of engagement.

When David Byar, the National Cancer Institute statistician who had invited Mark to that misbegotten dinner, sent an open letter to the Floor defending the idea of meeting with adversaries as "not collaborating with the enemy—but simply opening up a very useful and often productive dialogue,"[24] he was ridiculed by Tracy, who redistributed his letter the following week with her own annotations. Unfortunately, the underlined passages, outraged exclamation points, and snotty remarks in the margins only undercut her argument, making it read less like a cogent critique and more like the angry ranting of a bratty high school student. Nor was she helped by her choice of target.

David Byar was a highly respected statistician and member of the research establishment who was, himself, a PWA. Impressed by ACT UP's first *National Treatment Research Agenda,* Byar had become an important ally, arguing for an overhaul of how AIDS trials were being conducted and a reprioritization of the treatments being studied. He was also the guiding force behind three community-based AIDS research studies that attempted to address issues of vital importance to both activists and PWAs—a radically designed alpha-interferon trial, a multi-drug prophylaxis study, and AmFAR's observational database.

But Byar was only an ancillary target. Ditto the NIH, NIAID, and even the CDC. For Tracy, and for an increasingly vocal faction within ACT UP, the real enemy was T+D. In their view, T+D's attempts to tinker with and reform the system were at best misguided, because they failed to address the root causes of the epidemic, which were systemic and institutional.

Even more problematic was the growing coziness between certain members of T+D and Fauci, Hoth, and other powers that be. "Talking to [government officials] is collaborating w/the enemy when the same people from ACT UP do all the talking," Tracy argued.[25] Familiarity risked compromise and corruption, undercutting our outsiders' ability to remain "unwieldy, nerve-wracking, undeniably a force to be reckoned with."[26] Better to rotate people out of their "insider" positions. Expertise was overrated. "We do not have to understand precise details of the ACTG and NIAID in order to criticize them with fervor."[27] Better to remain an "elusive" and "scary element, one that cannot be tamed, named, or held down. We do not become members of the system that is killing us. We remain outside of it, able to affect it with our mass power."[28]

Though I disagreed with her priorities—of course there were profound institutional and systemic issues, but was it more important to remain outside the system or get potentially lifesaving drugs to more people?—Tracy and her cohorts raised some important points. While T+D may have worked hard to get their place at the table, they weren't exactly reaching back to bring the rest of us along with them. Nor did the committee's more visible members lend their "star power" to help with other issues. There were also legitimate concerns about a general lack of communication and coordination between T+D and other committees doing related work, particularly the Women's Action Committee.

It was quite another thing, however, to question Mark's loyalty to ACT UP, or to accuse him of not just consorting with the enemy but selling us out for a little Christmas punch. Things soon grew so heated that even Jim Eigo—as selfless, hardworking, and pure of heart as anyone in ACT UP—was trashed in "TITA" as a "flashy activist" speaking from a "tenuous position" of male privilege, who, along with Mark, should "get a real job, a real agenda and some hands-on experience" with AIDS, as opposed to operating from his cushy position "on boards or major decision-making bodies of the U.S. government or other corporations."[29]

Even though I'd always been put off by Mark's brusque manner and the general erudition of T+D members, I still trusted them. I had no issue with their becoming friendly with Fauci or anyone else, as I understood their goals and respected their efforts. Besides, I didn't see Fauci or the other researchers as mortal enemies, and I recognized the importance of building relationships with the people whose help you needed to accomplish your goals.

In an effort to work through the growing hostilities, Maxine and Larry hosted a four-hour "Strategy Brunch" back at the Community Center, featuring presentations by Tracy, Mark, Bill Dobbs, and Jay Lipner highlighting their differing views on ACT UP's relationship to the NIH, NIAID, and the ACTG system, followed by an open discussion by the larger group. The conversation would expand ten days later at a "Whither ACT UP?" Town Hall, one of our "semi-regular, semi-excruciating bouts of soul searching,"[30] where we'd gather to discuss everything from goals and strategies to meeting procedures and process—all those things we never seemed to have time for on Monday nights. Though these meetings rarely resulted in any major breakthroughs or changes, they did succeed in lowering the general temperature.

At least temporarily.

But the question was being called and lines were being drawn. Were you an outsider or an insider? Fighting for the privileged or for the people? Politically pure or co-opted?

Whose side were you on?

David

In early February, David Serko briefly checked into Room 816 in Lenox Hill Hospital to undergo a biopsy for his still mysterious lesions. Later diagnosed as *cutaneous Mycobacterium haemophilum*, a rare ulcerous skin lesion related to MAI occurring in people with severely depressed immune systems,* treatment remained a challenge, as doctors first tried freezing and then cutting them away until, months later, thanks to the ACT UP information network and the drug underground, David went on clarithromycin, an unapproved experimental drug that dissolved the lesions, leaving him with only angry-looking scars.[31]

---

* David would be one of thirteen patients whose cases were used to define the characteristics of the infection in immunocompromised patients. Walter L. Straus et al., "Clinical and Epidemiological Characteristics of *Mycobacterium haemophilum*, an Emerging Pathogen in Immunocompromised Patients," *Annals of Internal Medicine* 120, no. 2 (January 15, 1994): 118–25.

Two weeks after his biopsy, David and I had plans to go to Michael Morrissey's annual Valentine's Day party. Michael reminded me of a grown-up version of Wendy's brother John in *Peter Pan*, fighting AIDS in his top hat, umbrella, and pajamas. I loved the twinkling sense of mischief that lurked beneath his otherwise buttoned-down WASP exterior. Every year, Michael would send out a meticulously crafted invitation referencing a movie starring his favorite screen actress, Audrey Hepburn. My personal favorite was the engraved invitation he sent from the Wright-Dobie Boarding School run by Hepburn and Shirley MacLaine in *The Children's Hour*.

But when I called David that afternoon, he told me he didn't think he was going to make it to the party. The vision in his right eye was starting to get a bit cloudy around the edges, so he was going to the Emergency Room at Lenox Hill to have it checked out. I asked if he wanted company, but he coolly brushed aside my offer, insisting he was fine and would go by himself. I didn't push, as I wanted to respect his autonomy and, frankly, was looking forward to Michael's party.

Still, it didn't feel right. When I called Ben to tell him what had happened, he immediately, and to his great credit, answered, "But you're going to the hospital anyway, *right*?" and everything snapped into focus. No matter how casually David may have mentioned this latest incident—or how easily he'd handled everything else about his serostatus thus far—this was serious. I hopped on the subway and met a surprised but grateful David in the hospital waiting room. His usual calm bravado was gone, and he seemed more fragile than I'd remembered. He was scared. So was I. We did our best to pretend that everything was fine, and this was nothing out of the ordinary—but we already knew what the doctor would tell us.

David had CMV.

Cytomegalovirus is a common virus; most adults are exposed to CMV by the time they reach forty. Once contracted, it usually remains dormant in the body for life, held in check by a healthy immune system. But for people who are immunocompromised, CMV is extremely dangerous, gathering in the eyes, lungs, esophagus, or intestine and producing a variety of lethal symptoms.

David's manifestation was CMV retinitis. Beginning with spots and "floaters," the virus attacks the retina, moving stealthily from the periphery to the center of the eye, leading to inevitable blindness. For now, only the right eye was infected. But even with treatment, the disease would eventually progress, dimming the light in one eye and then the other—unless it killed him first.

What no one said, perhaps because they didn't have to, was the CMV diagnosis also meant David officially had AIDS. The clock was now ticking.

The two of us stumbled out of Lenox Hill and headed someplace, I don't remember where, for dinner, or, more accurately, a couple of drinks that bled into dinner. I don't remember what we talked about. Small stuff, I imagine. Chatter.

I'm sure we talked briefly, if matter-of-factly, about treatment options, of which there was but one: DHPG, a drug ACT UP had helped push to FDA approval just two years earlier. But even that was not a simple solution. DHPG interacted badly with AZT—both drugs suppressed bone marrow production—so David would first need to switch his antiviral treatment from AZT to ddI or maybe ddC, both of which were still unapproved. Also, DHPG was administered intravenously, requiring the implantation of a catheter, usually in the chest. Meanwhile, no one knew how DHPG might interact with any of the other medications David was taking and was, at best, a stopgap treatment and not a cure.

What I do remember, however, were the silences—highly unusual for us, but what was there to say? For those few hours, we were the only two people in David's life who knew he had AIDS and would eventually lose his eyesight . . . and probably his life.

Two weeks later, David threw a get-together dinner at his apartment in Washington Heights so his close friends and parents could meet and take stock of one another before there were any more hospital visits or nasty surprises.

I'd first met David's parents when he and I were in college. I was fond of them, and they were always quite lovely to me, but it had been over ten years since we had last seen each other, and the circumstances were now far different. I wondered if they'd be bitter or angry or blame me in some way for David's illness. But despite the lurking terrors, David and his parents made it easy, and we all played along, skimming the surface with gently forced good humor, and only the occasional silence to give the game away.

There was, however, one moment when the mask slipped. David's dad stood up with his mom to give a little speech. He looked like the man David was never going to grow old enough to become. They had the same nose, the same chin, the same smile. David, he explained, had decided to stay in New York, and they'd agreed this was best. The city was his home, where his life and friends were, and where he could get the best possible care. He then graciously offered a toast to David's devoted friends.

And as we raised our glasses, David's mother added, in a quiet, broken voice, "Take care of my baby . . ."

Chapter 22

Splitting Differences

ACCORDING TO STUDIES, 80 percent of New York City high school students had had sex by the time they were nineteen.[1] One in six sexually active teenagers contracted STDs each year.[2] And since over one-fifth of the AIDS caseload comprised people between the ages of twenty and twenty-nine, most were probably infected while still in their teens.[3] But despite the desperate need to teach students about safe sex, condom use, and harm reduction, the city AIDS curriculum had been held hostage by the Catholic Church and other reactionary forces who demanded schools teach "just say no" and emphasize abstinence.

YELL (Youth Education Life Line)* had been founded shortly after our Election '89 Board of Ed demonstration by two teachers, Jeffrey Fennelly and Eric Epstein.[4] Frustrated by the city's inadequate, and frankly life-threatening, AIDS education program, YELL set out to ensure city high school students were given "comprehensive, accurate, and up-to-date information about HIV, AIDS, and AIDS prevention."[5]

Once a week, throughout the winter and spring of 1990, YELL members stationed themselves outside city high schools, talking to students and distributing condoms and safe sex information. Realizing their GMHC-published AIDS prevention pamphlets did not speak to the real-world needs of their school-aged audience, they created "AIDS: What YOU Need to

*Originally the Youth Brigade Caucus, they changed their name to YELL when they became a full committee in late spring 1990.

Know/*SIDA: Lo Que TU Necesitas Saber*" to address the many questions and misconceptions students had about HIV/AIDS, providing explicit information about how to enjoy sex safely and empowering students to make their own choices about their bodies and their lives.[6]

By May 1990, they'd distributed pamphlets and condoms to over 25,000 eager students at sixteen schools across the city.[7] YELL had also won a spot on the Board of Education's AIDS Advisory Council, where they worked with other community advocates, including the Hetrick-Martin Institute,* helping newly appointed schools chancellor Joseph Fernandez draft a comprehensive AIDS education program that was "sex-positive, non-homophobic, and informatively explicit, focus[ed] on the realities of adolescent mentality and behavior rather than the moral ideals of parents and/or religious groups."[8] At the activists' urging, the new plan also included a condom distribution program, which drew immediate and angry opposition from the Catholic Church and other conservative groups.

Throughout the fall of 1990, YELL worked with supporters to stack public hearings and lobby board members to ensure the condom plan remained part of the proposed curriculum.[9] Among those speaking in favor of the proposal was Wayne Fischer, a thirty-three-year-old special education teacher at Martin Luther King Jr. High School in Manhattan. Wayne was a nice gay Jewish boy from Queens—identities fearlessly broadcast by his nasal Howard Beach bray, his Star of David earring, and the "Silence = Death" button perpetually affixed to his shirt. Far less apparent, given his buoyant attitude and physically robust appearance—Wayne often provided a welcome distraction on Monday nights in his low-cut tank tops and his tiny high-cut short-shorts—he was also HIV-positive.

Wayne announced his serostatus while testifying at a September Board of Ed meeting, becoming the city's first openly HIV-positive schoolteacher. The next day, he told his students, and soon thereafter, the entire city, via the front page of *Newsday*.[10] Wayne remained a magnet for print and TV coverage for the rest of his life, taking his AIDS workshops to classrooms around the city and chronicling his battles with the disease for a local news channel.†

---

*Founded by Dr. Emery Hetrick and Dr. Damien Martin in 1979 as the Institute for the Protection of Lesbian and Gay Youth, a counseling and drop-in center for vulnerable and at-risk LGBT youth. In 1985, they opened the Harvey Milk High School, the country's first high school specifically for LGBT youth. Both men, who were partners in life as well as in work, died from AIDS-related complications, Hetrick in 1987, and Martin in 1991. *May their memories be for a blessing.*

†"AIDS: A Journal of Hope," with reporter Debby Feyerick, was filmed with Wayne's handheld camera and shown weekly on the cable station New York 1 News from July 1993

Nonetheless, opposition to the curriculum, and particularly the condom distribution plan, was fierce. Bowing to political pressure, the board twice postponed voting on the plan, until finally, on February 27, 1991, after five months of pitched protests, public testimony, and backroom vote wrangling, they approved the curriculum at an emotional and suspense-laden meeting by a vote of 4–3, including, and without amendment, the controversial condom distribution plan.

By March 1991, ACT UP's internal problems had become so pronounced, they'd taken on physical proportions.

The previous summer, we'd moved from the overheated crush of the Community Center to the cool confines of the Great Hall of Cooper Union, a formal auditorium designed more for oratory than dialogue, with a stage— which we tried our best not to use—and fixed amphitheater seating for nine hundred spread across three separate sections. Mimicking the divides in the group, Mark, Peter, and T+D had colonized the house right section of the auditorium, while the Costas, Latina/o Caucus, and Women's Committee squatted on house left. (For the record, I usually seated myself on either side on the center-left aisle.) The rest of the membership sat in the vast demilitarized zone in the middle; a passive audience to the bitter infighting that plagued our Monday night meetings.

ACT UP's current internal battle concerned ACTG 076, an AIDS Clinical Trial Group protocol designed to test AZT in pregnant HIV-positive women to see if it would prevent perinatal transmission of the virus from mother to child during pregnancy.[11] It was a decidedly odd flashpoint, as everyone in ACT UP agreed there was no real scientific rationale for the trial (the results of earlier AZT trials that had enrolled women had yet to be analyzed, while early animal studies offered little hope for potential success); it was poorly designed (placebo trials for AZT made little sense, as they were easily unblinded); and worse, coercive and unethical (women were not told of the potential risks for vaginal tumors, their eligibility to receive AZT outside of the trial, or that 70–80 percent of babies born to HIV-positive women were not even HIV-positive).[12] All this would present a major concern for any

---

through the final episode on March 3, 1997, which chronicled his death the previous day. He was thirty-nine years old. *May his memory be for a blessing.*

clinical trial, let alone one expected to enroll the largest number of women and people of color in ACTG history.

Then there was the larger question of why the ACTG's biggest women-enrolling trial was solely concerned with the health of the baby and not the mother. The protocol even instructed that the infant would be followed for 78 weeks post-birth, while the mother would be dropped from the trial after just 6 weeks. As a further insult, the mother was required to get the "father's" consent in order to participate.*

ACT UP was not alone in questioning the trial's value. Members of the Community Constituency Group (CCG) were planning to express their own concerns during a dedicated ACTG 076 Team meeting on March 10 (part of the larger 11th ACTG Meeting, March 10–13); but the investigators' presentation was disrupted when members of a joint ACT UP NY/DC 076 working group† stormed the meeting, shouting the text of their fact sheet decrying the myriad problems with the trial and their demands for the creation of "scientifically and ethically sound [trials] for all women."[13] This would have been fine, as most of the attendees probably agreed with their critique, but the protesters inexplicably insisted on reading through their fact sheet a second time, preventing the researchers from responding to their concerns and prompting Dan Hoth to shut the meeting down completely.[14] The protesters then blew their air horns as furious Black and Latina/o CCG members hurled accusations of racism at the mostly White demonstrators, who then lobbed their own charges of co-optation back at the community representatives.

Though right on the merits—even NIAID conceded that some of their suggestions were valid‡—what the 076 activists had failed (or perhaps refused) to recognize was while their group may have included women with

---

*While outdated and outrageous, it was, at the time, a standard requirement for all trials involving pregnant women, with certain exceptions that could be addressed at the local level.

†There was no indication on the fact sheet of who was responsible for the action, save the use of the phrase "Silence = Death." I have seen the participants referred to elsewhere as the Women's Caucus, though that was the name of a specific group within ACT UP/NY, or possibly the Women's Caucus of the ACT UP Network. It has also been referred to as the "Stop 076" group, and while that was commonly understood to be the goal of the group—and the demand is found on some related fact sheets—other members insist it was never the group's intent to shut down the trial, only to stop it until it could be improved.

‡NIAID agreed the revisions to the "informed consent" information given to potential participants were "reasonable," though they still refused to make the necessary changes, claiming it would unnecessarily delay the beginning of the trial. Fact sheet: Ad-hoc 076 Working Group, "Think Again . . . ," undated.

HIV/AIDS, that didn't make them the sole legitimate voice in the room.* There were other HIV-positive women present, as well as activists of color, all of whom had their own issues with 076 and did not appreciate ACT UP shutting down their right to pose questions or make their own decisions about a trial directly impacting their lives and their communities. Rather than recognizing the 076 demonstrators as activists trying to give voice to women with AIDS, they saw the action as yet another attempt by ACT UP to seize even more control of the AIDS agenda.

While the CCG caucused in a closed-door "people of color only" session, Mark Harrington, David Barr, and the other mostly White treatment activists from the "ACT UP diaspora"† met to commiserate and calibrate a response. To which group did they owe their strongest allegiance, ACT UP or the CCG? If they maintained a united front with the protesters, they risked sundering the CCG, which represented not only years of work but also their best hope for a PWA/activist voice inside the ACTG. But if they separated themselves from the protest and condemned the action, they would further exacerbate the ruptures within ACT UP and risk the organization's implosion.

As a compromise, they criticized the tactics but not the substance of the protest, restating their commitment to direct action "in all its forms," while calling out the protesters for their "racist suppression of free speech and dialogue."

When white activists refuse to let activists and physicians of color respond, they are behaving in a racist fashion. This is racism.

When activists refuse to let scientists respond, they are preventing the very dialogue which ACT UP fought for three years to develop. This is censorship.

When ACT UP members refuse to allow dissent on their tactics and goals within ACT UP, they are suppressing the very force which gave ACT UP its strength: its ability to articulate informed dissent.[15]

While I appreciated the delicacy of the treatment activists' situation, as well as their obvious schadenfreude after being subjected to months of attacks from the 076 activists, I found it interesting the same folks who so

---

*In this, they were hardly alone. Throughout its history, ACT UP had a myopic tendency to see itself as the sole legitimate activist voice for PWAs.

†These included activists from ACT UPs NY, DC, LA, Golden Gate, and Philadelphia. Mark Harrington, "11th AIDS Clinical Trials Group (ACTG) Meeting," March 10–13, 1991, Washington, DC.

proudly prevented Louis Sullivan from being heard were now criticizing others for stopping a free exchange of ideas. Nonetheless, their response was fairly muted compared to the statement distributed by the People of Color Caucus of the CCG.

> We will not allow ACT UP, primarily representative of white gay men and women, to dictate the agenda for the research that will affect men, women, and children of color—whether gay or not.
>
> The lines have been drawn, and we clearly see these actions as racist and genocidal. We will not allow ACT UP to lead us or NIH when ACT UP does not advocate for the protection of lives of communities of color. ˙
>
> The paternalistic audacity of taking an action that prohibits us from making an informed decision by hearing all sides of the story is racist and resembles tactics utilized by plantation overseers during the years of overt slavery. We are still enslaved . . . .
>
> We do not see ourselves as vessels for fetuses. We instead see ourselves as women, mothers, fathers, and the trustees of the future of our communities.
>
> We will not allow ACT UP racist tactics to continue to kill us. We will not allow ACT UP to speak for us. We will not allow ACT UP to monopolize the NIH research agenda.[16]

While no doubt shocked to find themselves branded as racist oppressors and, despite their arguments with T+D, still regarded as operating within ACT UP's bubble of White privilege,* the 076 activists continued their critique of the trial, attending meetings and refuting NIAID's responses to activist complaints with a resounding point-by-point takedown of the institute's claims.[17]

News of the clash quickly traveled back to the Floor of ACT UP with dueling reports from the 076 activists and T+D, followed by yet another volley of heated discussions, "TITA" postings, and "Open Letters to ACT UP." While some, including David Barr and Maxine Wolfe, attempted to tamp down the fires, Tracy Morgan fanned the flames. Calling 076 "racist science,"[18] she defended the demo, arguing the fight against institutional racism and sexism required our tactics to become even more confrontational,

---

*It was assumed by many CCG members that the two groups were working in cahoots, with the T+D gang providing cover for the protesters.

and anyone who disagreed was enabling the oppression of women and people of color.*

The controversy would mark a serious turning point for the organization. From this point forward, discussions of racism and sexism would no longer be seen as opportunities for consciousness raising but would instead be weaponized and deployed for self-righteous finger pointing and displays of "political correctness."†

You know things are shitty when even Larry Kramer complains about the angry and vindictive tone of ACT UP meetings.

> Never in our history have differences of opinions been the cause of such angry rhetoric, floor communications, and other acts and deeds. . . . A number of our actions and activities seem to be motivated more by revenge, vendetta, personal angers, than with ending the AIDS plague. A number of these actions and activities are way out of all proportion to the wrong that is being acted against.[19]

And then things got worse.

An informal group of activists from around the country, including members of our Women's Action Committee, had been discussing strategies for jolting the authorities into action on issues concerning women and AIDS. Despite all our efforts, we'd made little progress. It was time, they agreed, to try something new.

After weeks of rumors, Maxine came to the Floor in late March with their proposal: a six-month "moratorium on meetings" with the CDC and NIAID on all issues relating to women's health. For six months ACT UP's strategy "vis à vis women's issues" would be restricted solely to direct action.[20] We would only communicate with the CDC, NIAID, and their representatives through zaps, demonstrations, flyers, and fact sheets, and talk to them only through direct questions at public forums. The proposal, Max insisted,

---

*ACTG 076 remains to this day a flashpoint between certain activists, with heated exchanges on Facebook reminding us of how lucky we were that social media did not exist back in the day.

†"Politically correct" was a phrase that had become weaponized by the political right to attack and ridicule efforts to address biased (racist, sexist, homophobic) language or behavior, much like what has happened to the term "woke" more recently. There was, however, sometimes a performative nature to "PC behavior," which we would now call "virtue signaling," that when carried to extremes could lead to the reckless demonization of individuals, the policing of dialogue, and the shutting down of the exchange of ideas (think "cancel culture"). Yes, everything old is new again.

had "nothing to do with silence," nor should it be interpreted as a "blanket condemnation of dialogue with government officials as an activist strategy." Rather, it was a considered response to the "institutionalized sexism in the research and government bureaucracies [that] makes dialogue ineffective for women's issues at this time."

> To sum up, we are at a point with women's issues where what is needed is public pressure and public exposure of their intransigence. We need to create that pressure publicly from ACT UP and from others so that when they come to the table it is with concrete ways they are going to change things to save lives.[21]

The room quickly split along ideological and geographical lines—vociferously opposed by T+D and those sitting on the right, and enthusiastically embraced by the Women's Committee, the Costas, and others sitting on the left.

The proposal found particularly strong support from the Latina/o caucus, whose members included not only women with HIV/AIDS, but also members from Latin American countries whose more radical politics and warnings about co-optation reflected their experiences fighting oppressive regimes and dictatorships back home.*

> Most of our past experiences dealing with bureaucrats have resulted in them trying to co-opt us. . . . There should be no closed door meetings. Latina HIV+ women and women with AIDS should be present at any meeting dealing with women's issues in large numbers. We should remember that ACT UP-NY's model is one of participation, not of representation, and that ultimate decisions are taken by the floor. Bureaucrats are accustomed to a model of meetings with only a few. This has to change. We will continue to do what we have been doing: denouncing the bureaucrats that profit from AIDS in our community, and working within the community to end the crisis.[22]

---

*The caucus now included members from Chile, Peru, Colombia, Venezuela, Argentina, and Mexico, as well as native Chicanos and Puerto Ricans. Some caucus members had already formed an Argentina Working Group to address government repression against homosexuals and in particular the targeting of members of the Communidad Homosexual Argentina (CHA), the only gay advocacy group in the country and a major provider of AIDS education. (ACT UP internal document: "Propuesta: Accion Frente Al Consulado Argentino En Nueva York/Proposal: Action in front of the Argentine Consulate in New York City.") The group would soon expand its mission, forming ACT UP Americas "to foster relationships with individuals and groups fighting AIDS throughout the continent." ACT UP internal document: ACT UP Americas, May 13, 1991.

In the wake of Day of Desperation, the Latina/o Caucus had launched a contentious campaign against the Hispanic AIDS Forum (HAF), an admittedly ineffective community organization, which they attacked with a ferocity previously reserved for politicians, pharmaceutical companies, and larger government institutions. This was a decided break from past ACT UP practice. Despite our disagreements, we had yet to directly target any community organization for not following our vision of activism, not even GMHC. While several "community leaders" may have felt our sting, they were more often collateral damage in our pursuit of larger quarry.

Things had come to a head during a caucus presentation in late February, when Yolanda Serrano, a longtime ACT UP ally who'd worked with us on IVDU issues during the 1988 Nine Days of Rain and was also on the board of HAF, was permitted to address the Floor and read HAF's written response to the caucus's claims. Caucus members felt disrespected, charging she'd been allowed "to insult, discredit and put to question the tactics and issues we, as AIDS activists, have been raising for the past several months," and questioning whether the group would have allowed any of our other proposed targets to do the same.[23]

Further complicating matters was the less than quietly held suspicion that despite the legitimate issues surrounding HAF, the campaign had been instigated by the personal grievances of Joe Franco, a caucus leader who had recently been fired from the foundation. Joe was one of ACT UP's charismatic loose cannons; a frequently unreliable narrator who had previously gotten us tangled up in a short-lived boycott of the Gay Games after some perceived slight led him to charge that the organization was discriminating against PWAs.* As even one of his closest friends later admitted, "it was always Joe's story, and there was what really happened."[24]

However, suggesting the caucus's agenda might be driven by a personal vendetta was so unavoidably condescending that it only strengthened their belief that ACT UP's failure to support their campaign against HAF, along with the larger group's lack of participation in other caucus actions, came from a racist lack of respect for the caucus and its members. This mirrored the feelings of many of the moratorium supporters, who felt their efforts likewise disrespected by the larger organization and specifically by T+D.

---

*In October 1990, at Joe's passionate urging, ACT UP had voted to initiate an international boycott of Gay Games IV: Unity '94, claiming the group discriminated against people with HIV/AIDS and their needs, and that other groups (women, people of color, and the elderly) were underrepresented in their leadership. ACT UP would call off the boycott three weeks later, when the claims were largely disproven.

Regardless of its stated goal, and despite Max's assurances that the restrictions would apply only to women's issues, it was hard not to see the boycott as an attempt to rein in T+D and, potentially, a first step in dictating the terms of ACT UP's entire treatment agenda. (We found out later the group had debated whether to extend the ban to "all ACT UP meetings around other issues," before deciding "it would be restricted to women's issues at the national level with NIAID and CDC officials" only.)[25] Given the existing tensions in the room, it seemed an unnecessary provocation.

We were all too aware of the splits that had occurred with ACT UPs in Chicago and San Francisco, where conflicts between factions had riven the groups in two. Some members, like perpetual gadfly Michael Petrelis, had already encouraged T+D to leave and form a separate organization to "free itself from ACT UP and its helter-skelter approach to AIDS treatment issues," and prevent the committee's important work from being "held hostage to the ever changing politically correct winds that blow through ACT UP."[26] But not even the committee's harshest critics really wanted T+D to leave. They just wanted them suitably humbled and returned to the fold. We'd had too much success and there was too much at stake to risk blowing it all apart. Or at least that was the feeling from many of the longtime members, regardless of where they sat in the auditorium.

ACT UP debated the proposal for several weeks—on the Floor, in hushed conversations in the back of the room, in "TITA," and in myriad "Open Letters" stacked on the back table—until one Monday night during a Floor discussion, a woman on the far left side of the room stood up and stated that she supported the moratorium because, after all, "six months is not a lifetime."

The room contracted, then exploded.

Although the speaker immediately apologized, the damage was done. And the response was not long in coming.

HIV NEGATIVES LISTEN UP. ACT UP is not a game or a contest to see who can be the most PC. Many of you can waste time on these meaningless discussions because as one of you said last week "Six months is not a life time." But, guess what? For those of us with low T-cells, it certainly is. Either help us to fight for our lives or get the fuck out of our way.[27]*

---

*The author, Derek Link, would later admit that he'd fabricated his own HIV-positive status, along with much of his biography, deeply wounding many of his close friends in T+D and other ACT UP comrades. However, this in no way diminishes the remarkable work he did in the organization and the many lives he saved through his work as an AIDS activist.

The serostatus card had been thrown and the comforting fiction of "We Are All Living with AIDS" was forever shattered. There were Positives and there were Negatives. Serostatus now joined the other overlapping identities of race and gender jockeying for supremacy, like some high-stakes version of rock-paper-scissors—but did gender crush race, race cut serostatus, serostatus cover gender? Which identity had greater claim to our loyalty?

This not-so-quiet grumbling was given even greater currency by a front-page article in that summer's Gay Pride issue of the *Village Voice*, suggesting ACT UP was no longer interested in fighting for the lives of gay White men; that with the exception of T+D, our agenda had become so broad that the needs of people living with HIV/AIDS—meaning the gay White men who had long supported ACT UP with their bodies, time, and money—were no longer the group's concern.[28]

Or as Charlie Franchino, long a T+D stalwart, charged in "TITA":

> We are in danger of being taken over by an overzealous group who see AIDS as nothing more than one battle in a larger "war on injustice." This view contends we can lose the HIV battle but still win the "war." I believe their goal is to seize control of ACT UP and turn it into yet another blathering multi-focus left wing gang. Well-intentioned I'm sure but misguided and dangerous to all PWA's.[29]

But did it have to be a zero-sum game? Did fighting for the lives of women and people of color with AIDS, or even more controversially, daring to strategize for the long term, automatically mean abandoning HIV-positive gay White men?

I'd always understood "to end the AIDS crisis" meant pursuing an agenda beyond just drugs-into-bodies and looking instead at the host of issues that had helped turn AIDS into a crisis; one that was not going to be over anytime soon. And as someone who was Negative and would therefore be continuing the fight for many years, I also recognized the need to talk about long-term strategies. But how could we talk about next year when some of us didn't know if we'd still be alive by then? We were operating under two different clocks: I need this drug NOW to save my life NOW, versus Where do we want to be in a year, two years, five years? Both outlooks were important, both imperatives valid, but it was becoming more and more difficult to reconcile the two.

For many of those supporting the moratorium, AIDS was the symptom, not the disease; and it was only by addressing the root causes of racism, sexism, and homophobia that we would finally succeed in ending the AIDS crisis. While this was undeniably true, I still held to Vito's dictum: first, "kick the shit out of this disease, and *then* kick the shit out of the system that allowed it to happen." My allegiance, perhaps selfishly, was to the lives of the people I knew—the people in the room and my friends and comrades whose lives were in immediate danger.

Serostatus crushed race and gender.

But what was particularly troubling to me about the moratorium proposal was the notion that one group in ACT UP might be able to use the Floor to dictate strategies to other committees, in this case forbidding our meeting with NIAID and CDC officials. This seemed, both in concept and in selected target, an anathema to the principles of the organization. I agreed, not for the first or last time, with Jim Eigo, who countered that a moratorium on meetings with officials "would only make sense if we could command a parallel moratorium on AIDS-related disease & death."[30]

> An ACT UP that refuses to talk to with [sic] people who have the power to make changes that will help people with AIDS will be an ACT UP that has betrayed its mission. It will have put its own purity ahead of the lives of women & men with HIV disease, many of whom will surely die if those changes aren't made. It is an ACT UP that will have decided that the only acceptable form of direct action is an abstract deposit of its own understandable rage, for it's an ACT UP that will have abandoned its former ideal of chanelling [sic] its anger to putting an end to the AIDS crisis.[31]

We'd always allowed our members to pursue their activism with a certain latitude—if you thought some issue or area of work was important, if it was in some way AIDS-related and could get people to work on it with you, *gey gezunterheyt,* go in good health. We'd never demanded allegiance to an ideology or specific strategy or tactic, but the moratorium proposal had called all that into question.

There were also practical concerns—how would the moratorium be implemented, or worse, enforced? How would we define "women's issues" and how would we segregate them from the rest of our agenda? Would ACT UP members have to resign from ACTG committees and the CCG? What about NIH panels and advisory boards? And finally, would this moratorium just pertain to ACT UPs or would we try to enlist other community-based organizations to join our boycott—and what would be the consequences if they refused?

As the tide turned against the moratorium proposal, T+D thankfully took the issue of their potential departure off the table.

We feel that we are an integral part of the organization, and that any schism would damage both the ability of ACT UP New York and this committee to do important AIDS treatment activist work. We are committed to developing creative solutions to the current political debate in ACT UP, and encourage other committees and individuals in the organization to do the same. The single most radical thing we can do is work together.[32]

Maxine, too, softened her stance, admitting she was not necessarily in favor of the moratorium, but had only agreed to bring it up for discussion.

I personally feel that this issue should not be used to divide NY ACT UP. In that regard, if this proposal "passes" but there are substantial numbers of people who feel that it jeopardizes their work, I would rather see us work out a joint strategy that would serve us all.[33]

Although ACT UP overwhelmingly defeated the proposal, the undertow of distrust and the growing rift between Positives and Negatives had only grown more pronounced. There were other consequences as well. Some of our most important leaders had lost their luster. Maxine, who had always been regarded as a wise elder and mediator, was now unjustly caricatured as "Madame Mao," the unrelenting leader of the crusading left, much as Mark Harrington, whose ability to synthesize politics and science had propelled ACT UP to great success, was now mischaracterized as the symbol of elitist White male privilege.

I felt bad for them both—and even worse for ACT UP.

While ACT UP may have taken a step or two back from the precipice, we could all still see the long trip down. Yet another fissure opened in June, when longtime member Dan Keith Williams* came before the Floor with the stunning admission he'd "mishandled" over $16,000 in ACT UP funds as the Needle Exchange Committee's representative to Coordinating Committee.[34]

---

*Though at this point, Dan spelled his name all lowercase with the middle initial k, I'm going to stick with his current preferred spelling.

The idea one of us—a respected, trusted member, a founder of Majority Action, and leader in our needle exchange efforts—could take—no, steal—so much money from the organization, and worse, *from the cause*, was a stunning blow.

While most of the room reacted in anger and disbelief, there were others who argued his actions should be seen through the lens of addiction. Though they didn't condone what he did, they felt his coming before the group—admitting his wrongdoing, taking on the public shame, and promising to pay the money back—was a sufficient response. (Dan would later admit to a severe drinking problem—which was apparently well known to those he worked with—as well as a later discovery of being bipolar as key to his mishandling of the money entrusted to him.)[35]

Others, including me, saw it as betrayal and theft and were furious at the notion that somehow an addiction absolved Dan of wrongdoing. Surely copping to it was not enough. But what were our options? We couldn't press charges—no one wanted to see Dan in jail—and the last thing we needed was Lily Law (or the *Native*) sniffing around ACT UP any more than they already did; but this forgive-and-forget shit didn't seem right.

I couldn't help but notice, however, the angriest response was coming from White men like myself, which made me wonder whether there wasn't something else at play—some race- or class-based privilege in operation. ACT UP always had a rather cavalier relationship to money. Even when we had little, we spent it without hesitation and with the expectation that somehow there'd always be more. Certainly, our love/hate relationship with our Fundraising Committee and our banishing of most financial discussions to the distant precincts of the Coordinating Committee spoke to a background of privilege, financial comfort, and entitlement. I know that however bad my own financial situation, I'd never worried about losing my apartment or my insurance or not having the money to pay my bills.

ACT UP had already voted to spend four times the amount Dan had stolen to send thirty-two members to the AIDS conference in Florence later that summer.* While ACT UP had always at least partially subsidized expenses for out-of-town travel to ensure that financial status did not become a barrier to participation, I'm fairly certain not every waking moment in Florence would be spent on AIDS-related activities. And surely, there had been other, much smaller, examples of members playing fast and loose with

---

*Numbers are from an internal ACT UP document, "Proposal concerning the Florence AIDS Conference," though I assume the actual budget was less than that amount.

ACT UP funds—unnecessary taxi trips, "borrowed" office supplies, personal photocopying, faxing, and long-distance phone calls from the workspace.

So why was I so frigging angry?

Yes, it was a lot of money, money entrusted to us to fight AIDS, and I was furious that Dan had betrayed that trust. But it also meant we were capable of betraying one another. It was a further tear in the fabric of the organization, a real-world intrusion into the idealistic Kumbaya of we're all in this together. Or maybe it was a reminder we *were* all in this together, and together was far messier than we'd been willing to acknowledge. ACT UP had waved away a lot of bad behavior over the years, choosing to be blinded by the ennobling glow of our greater purpose. We'd deliberately structured ourselves in a way that allowed us to deflect responsibility when it was convenient as a leaderless group whose members often acted individually or in affinity groups without the official approval of ACT UP.

But this was money pledged to ACT UP and, in the end, it was our fault the money was gone. We had an ethical responsibility to our donors and the people who depended on us to replace that money, even if it meant reaching into our own pockets to do so.* But we didn't. Although Dan pledged to pay the money back, we never truly followed up and neither did he. Certainly, I didn't volunteer my own time or savings to make up for the money that was lost, so I'm in no position to cast stones. However, our collective failure to make good on the stolen funds pointed to an even larger problem facing the organization.

We were no longer the frisky young upstart activist group. We were an established and, dare I say, respected organization—community leaders with a budget of over $1 million a year. ACT UP was moving, painfully, from adolescence into adulthood, and would need to make some tough decisions and accept responsibility for our actions.

As would I.

Ben

After nine months of no-distance coupledom, I'd grown dissatisfied with my relationship with Ben.

---

*Jim Serafini made just such a proposal, advocating the Floor take full responsibility for replacing the stolen money through individual contributions. Once Dan repaid the money, members could choose to be reimbursed or forgive the debt. Jim Serafini, "Dan Williams—The Money—The Floor's Responsibility: The Only Clean Way Out," June 24, 1991.

Part of the problem was Ben hadn't really settled into a life in New York—or at least his own life, as opposed to mine. I seemed to be doing most of the providing—my friends, my finances, my bed, and my apartment—but I wasn't getting what I needed from him in return. Ben had some strange ideas about relationships. He pointed to Jane Wyman's selfless—some might say masochistic and enabling—devotion to an alcoholic Ray Milland in *Lost Weekend* as the epitome of true love. He also hated if I called him *honey* or *bubby* or *sweetie*—"It's something a waitress says to a customer when she doesn't know his name"—and was generally uncomfortable with physical affection, even in private.

The place where our relationship seemed to flourish was when we were a trio with my best friend, Neal. Something about being with Neal made Ben more relaxed and even more physically demonstrative. Suddenly it was okay to sit on the couch together with my arm around his shoulder, sneaking in an occasional snuggle. Meanwhile, the lack of affection, both physical and verbal, was creating an unbridgeable distance between us.

Then I met Tom.

Tom was part Latin, part Irish, and all hot and sexy. We had an immediate and overwhelming physical connection and could not keep our eyes or hands off each other. He was also, as I'd soon discover, "complicated," but for the moment that didn't matter. He went through me like a charge.

I began a tricky courtship dance with Tom, flirting with him at ACT UP meetings—Ben had long since begged off Monday nights as not his thing—without disrupting the status quo at home. Matters with Tom escalated quickly, coming to a head (ahem) just in time for Gay Pride. Pride had always been the one day when I felt at ease holding hands and being affectionate, even sexual, in public, and god knows I was starving for it. Tom was going to be marching with ACT UP, and more than anything I wanted to march with Tom, so when Ben asked if I minded if he skipped Pride, I quietly thanked the Goddess and tried not to look too pleased.

But on Pride morning, Ben suddenly decided to grab his camera and take some photographs of the march. Since the last thing I wanted was some *Blow-Up* moment with Ben discovering incriminating images as he developed his film in a dark room, I stayed away from Tom, keeping him within hungry eyeshot until Ben headed back uptown. From that point on, Tom and I were glued to one another.

As soon as we reached the end of the march, the two of us peeled away from the crowd and ran hand in hand down Hudson Street toward the sound of drums and salsa music. Turning up a hidden side street, we found ourselves on a cobblestone dance floor, and as a soft summer rain began to fall, Tom pulled me close, put his hand firmly on my lower back, and led me through a hip-grinding merengue.

Later that afternoon, with the sun breaking through the clouds, we returned to Christopher Street and the joyful crush of the Pier Dance. Surrounded by hundreds of sweaty queers, we danced shirtless into the night, shouting the lyrics of disco tunes as if they were great truths. Then shortly after watching the fireworks light up the sky over the Hudson, we went back to my apartment and made our own.

Tom and I met for dinner a few nights later and once again could not get enough of each another. We were safe, of course—at least in the medical sense. Tom had recently found out he was Positive. This had coincided with his equally recent "coming out" and subsequent end of his marriage— I *told* you he was complicated—but in my romantic/sexual daze, I was willing to take all of this on, including his young son, all for the sake of some passion.

Subterfuge was never my strong suit, so a few days later, I sat Ben down on a park bench and tried to wiggle out of our relationship. I told him I felt we'd grown increasingly distant—*didn't he think so, too?*—but I really liked him and thought we should go back to being just friends. Basically, I was trying to play the good guy while doing a really shitty thing. I did *not* mention Tom and, in fact, denied there was someone else.

Ben was blindsided, but still wanted to save the relationship. As it was the first he'd heard of these problems, he thought we should try to work things out between us. Being terrible at this sort of thing, I folded immediately. And, whaddaya know, things got better; Ben became more affectionate and communicative, so I told Tom that Ben and I were trying to make it work, which was fine with him since he didn't feel ready to get into a relationship anyway.

But deep down I knew this was only delaying the inevitable. Something fundamental was missing from my relationship with Ben. Not just passion, which I recognized could burn hot and quick, but something else; something I could feel, if not define.

A couple of weeks later, I attended a memorial for Terry Beirn. Terry had been the programs officer at AmFAR and lovers with my boss, Paul Corser. They'd always seemed an odd couple; while Terry had been a politically savvy, publicly out gay man who'd been instrumental in passing major AIDS legislation on Capitol Hill,[36] Paul was a shy science geek with little feel for politics or gay culture. During my time at AmFAR, I'd seen Terry woo Paul and bring him out both personally and professionally, but I'd left before their relationship had blossomed. So, while I was surprised to hear about what Terry had accomplished on the Hill, I was stunned to hear the story of his devotion to Paul.

Sometime over the past year, Paul had gotten very sick. He'd been rushed to the hospital, where he'd remained in a coma for several days. Even with access to the best medical care and a full flight of experimental treatments, no one was sure he was going to make it. Throughout this terrible time, Terry was constantly at Paul's bedside, and even though he knew Paul might never wake to see it, Terry had decorated his hospital room with photos of the two of them and hung a big banner across from his bed that read, "Terry Loves Paul."

I knew immediately I could never do that for Ben.

So, I ended it. I told Ben the truth. It wasn't pretty. In fact, it went about as badly as it could go. But I had to get out. The stakes were too high. I needed—and deserved—to be in love.

TERRY BEIRN (1952–1991)
PAUL CORSER (1961–1999)
May their memories be for a blessing.

Chapter 23

▟▛

Target Bush

Kennebunk! Kennebunk!
We're going to go by bus and car.
Because Kennebunk! Kennebunk!
Is where the Bushes are!
(To the tune of "Camelot")*

WITH MY PERSONAL life in an uproar, it was time to once again redouble my involvement with ACT UP, this time becoming one of the Monday night meeting facilitators. If other facilitators were more adept at corralling discussions, I had a talent for keeping things moving while maintaining a congenial atmosphere—no small achievement given the tensions still coursing through the group.

I also joined the "Target Bush" Committee, which was organizing a monthlong series of actions focusing on the president, beginning with a Labor Day weekend protest at the Bush vacation home in Kennebunkport, Maine. Our goal was to "create an 'excess' of attention" to Bush's "deliberate and murderous neglect"[1] and provoke the "self-proclaimed 'education president' [to] assume leadership and make the AIDS crisis the #1 priority of [his] domestic agenda."[2]

---

*From "Kennebunk," another song parody by yours truly, sung to the tune of "Camelot" by Frederick Loewe and Alan Jay Lerner, and performed by me at the ACT UP "pep rally" meeting Monday, August 26, 1991.

The idea for Target Bush came from the Marys*—née the Bloody Marys—who had become one of ACT UP's most prominent affinity groups. Fortunately, the Marys had not been involved in the 076 or moratorium battles, so they were able to get the support of the entire organization, recruiting volunteers from both sides of the room—from the Costas to T+D.

Acting as "general contacts" for the sprawling enterprise was the triumvirate of Tim Bailey, a tart, stylish, platinum-blond designer, who worked for downtown fashion doyenne Betsey Johnson; Joy Episalla, a gifted, fierce, no-nonsense visual artist; and James Baggett, a shaggy sheepdog of a guy who was a writer and editor at *Home and Garden*. Together, they shared a strong commitment to the cause, a campy sense of the ridiculous, and a several-pack-a-day cigarette habit. (Smoking seemed almost mandatory around the Marys.)

While there was much to admire in the epic scope and organization of Target Bush—at one point there were over fifty separate tasks listed on the Target Bush contact sheet—I was particularly impressed by their messaging. ACT UP had reached a difficult inflection point, battling both a growing public complacency and our own AIDS fatigue. After ten years of the epidemic, and despite our best efforts, the deaths were only coming faster, with no magic bullets on the horizon. If activism only occurred when there was hope, we were in real trouble.

And so, the Marys created some.

Adopting the aspirational rallying cry, "The AIDS Crisis CAN END!" they drafted a thirty-five-point "Plan to End the AIDS Crisis," providing actions and solutions to the full range of AIDS issues, beginning with a demand to appoint a cabinet-level AIDS czar "to lend direction to the government's AIDS policies and programs; to weed out duplicative and wasteful research projects; to broaden the definition of AIDS; and to make AIDS education, care, and research a national priority."[3]

But while promoting this optimistic message to the AIDS community, we also had to deliver a second message of continued urgency—"The AIDS Crisis is NOT Over"—to the president and the chattering classes. To drive this message home, Target Bush created "The Obituary Project," distributing

---

*The original Marys included James Baggett, Tim Bailey, Ken Bing, Anna Blume, Neil Broome, BC Craig, Michael Cunningham, Joy Episalla, Mark Lowe Fisher, Jon Greenberg, Bob Henry, Barbara Hughes, Dennis Kane, Stephen Machon, Laurie Weeks, and Carrie Yamaoka, though there were others over the years, like me and Jamie, who became "Honorary Marys," or just "Mary-adjacent." Personal message from Joy Episalla to author, March 20, 2022.

photocopies of the previous week's AIDS-related death notices for us to mail to the White House, pleading with the president and first lady to extend their calls for compassion for babies suffering from AIDS—the "innocent people that are hurt by this disease," according to the president[4]—to *all people with AIDS*, since *all* people who contract the disease are innocent."[5] These mailings took on a personal cast, as they often included the obituaries of friends and comrades—Jeff Gates, Rodger Pettyjohn, Iris de la Cruz, Phil Zwickler, Tom Hannan, David Lopez—*May their memories be for a blessing*—who were dying at an unfathomable pace.

But while our mailings merited little more than a thank-you-for-your-concern form letter from Barbara Bush, our plans to invade the Bush "ancestral home"[6] in Kennebunkport were greeted with great alarm. The president, who'd previously declared our actions "offensive" and "an excess of free speech,"[7] expressed concern about the "adverse effect"[8] our demonstration would have on the good people and businesses of Kennebunkport, while local police warned of our "outrageous, vulgar, profane and obscene"[9] tactics, claiming we threw fake blood at bystanders and "exhibit[ed] people in advanced stages of AIDS in order to shock."[10] We also drew the notice of the Secret Service, who visited the home of one local Maine activist and tried unsuccessfully to intimidate him into revealing our plans.[11]

In response, we sent a letter to the local merchants and newspapers, assuring them our protest would be nonviolent and explaining our intent was not to shut down their businesses, but to "bring the AIDS crisis home to George Bush . . . [who] has chosen to take a vacation from the AIDS epidemic for the past seven years."[12] Although some continued to voice their unhappiness, we found surprising pockets of sympathy throughout the community, particularly among the local editorial boards. "If Sunday's demonstration forces us to acknowledge this disease, forces us to think about the need for a national plan to combat it, forces us to think about the hatred for homosexuality that prevents gays and all other people with AIDS from getting the medical services and support they need, it will have done its job,"[13] said one; while a second counseled, "if we get angry, let it not [be] at the inconvenience of the protest, but at the lack of leadership coming from the White House."[14]

Meanwhile, the national media continued to smack their lips in anticipation of an epic clash of communities, the "tan, wealthy, lobster-fed boaters in green plaid Bermudas with matching pink shirts" versus the "feared New Yorkers,"[15] the latter a conglomeration of several thousand angry gays and lesbians, people of color, IV drug users, and the homeless.

What a story!

David

Elisabeth Kübler-Ross has told us there are five stages of grief: denial, anger, bargaining, depression, and acceptance. I don't know that I went through all of them with David—and if I did, certainly not in that order—but the summer of 1991 had been all about bargaining. I'm not sure what I promised in return, but all I wanted was just one last summer on the beach with David in good health, where we could hang out, cruise guys, and swap stories and movie dialogue in treasured normalcy.

David's regimen had grown to include not only the usual assortment of pills and prophylactic inhalers, but also intravenous DHPG and clarithromycin. Rather than installing the usual Hickman catheter in his chest, David opted for a PICC (peripherally inserted central catheter) line, which was inserted into a large vein in his right arm, leaving the connected tubing dangling from his forearm. Although the PICC line was more difficult to manage, it gave David greater freedom to live his life.

David loved the beach nearly as much as he loved the dance floor, so almost every weekend that summer, we'd meet at Penn Station to take the morning train out to Jones Beach. As soon as we took our seats, David would unwrap the ace bandage from around his forearm, open his knapsack, and put on a pair of thin latex gloves. He'd then take out his IV bag of medication, making sure not to dislodge the long clear tube attached at the bottom, and hang it from the coat hook over the window. Ripping open a small packet, he'd remove a sterilized gauze pad and wipe the catheter portal, remove the protective cover from the other end of the tubing, and stick the revealed spike through the rubber cap on the catheter tube.

Then we'd sit back, drink our coffee, munch on bagels, and read the *Times*.

By some miracle of modern science, David's IV drip was always completed by the time we hopped off the train for the final bus ride to Jones Beach. Once there, it was another hike east to the gay beach, where we'd drop our towels, strip down to our speedos, and slather on our Number 4 suntan lotion.

Even then, David continued to dazzle. He was still in great shape, give or take the fuzzy eyesight, the hidden catheter, and the handful of still angry *M. haemophilum* scars that pocked his body—explaining, when asked, that they were the result of an exploding car battery. And since David neither looked nor acted like someone who was sick, none of his admirers thought to question him.

But at the end of August, everything suddenly shifted. Just days before Kennebunkport, David and I had tickets with some friends to see the divine Lypsinka at the Ballroom. David arrived just minutes before the lights went down, chalk white and sweating profusely. He staggered toward our table as if the effort to propel himself across the floor took all his strength and concentration. The transformation was shocking.

Well, I thought, we'd made it through the summer. The bargain had been kept. No more denial. It was time for acceptance.

A Different Mark

David was among the dwindling number of the no-judgment, good-time "girlfriends" I'd palled around with in the '80s. We'd flirted, had sex, and, having decided we were a better fit as friends, been the perfect company for indulging in an occasional demi-debauch. And now all, except me, were Positive.

Among them was Mark Roberts. I'd met Mark the summer after I graduated college. He was working with one of my friends as a waiter at Pershing's, a nothing-fancy gay burger joint on Columbus Avenue, back when the Upper West Side was still kind of dodgy.

Mark was a New Orleans boy—sweet, sexy, and a little trashy—a smiling catfish with a wispy mustache and a big ole southern drawl. As I was working just down the block, I frequently stopped by for a burger, beer, and banter. Months later, when I ran into Mark at a friend's Christmas party, he asked if I wanted to come dancing with him later that night at the Saint.

Even though I was nowhere near an A-List Gay, I'd already heard the Saint referred to in the hushed tones usually reserved for religious revelation or the opera. The Saint was where the most beautiful men in the world danced to the planet's greatest DJs on the most spectacular dance floor in the universe. It more than lived up to its reputation. It was a magical night, a gay fairy tale with Mark as Prince Charming and me as Cinderfella—hot, beautiful, sexy, and joyous.

For the next few months, Mark and I carried on a sort of loose affair, which soon segued into a kind of sex-for-a-haircut barter system—Mark was a hairdresser by profession—until, after a while, I became just a friend and regular paying customer. Every six to eight weeks, I'd head downtown to Mark's Village apartment for a trim, a toke, a glass of wine, and some dish.

When Mark tested positive, our conversations grew to include the latest health updates and treatment information, but as we didn't stay in touch between appointments, I didn't know much about his day-to-day health struggles. I'd like to say this was because it would have been impossible for me to keep up with all the people I knew who were sick and still keep my job, do my activism, and maintain something of my life—and while that's certainly true, I'm ashamed to say it had become, and has remained, a pattern with me. I'm really good when there's a crisis—seriously, call me—but I tend to pull back once things calm down. Whether it's my basic nature or learned behavior—a survival mechanism I picked up to prevent me from getting too overwhelmed by all the sickness around me—I can't say.

As a result, I was surprised when Mark told me he'd be leaving New York at the end of August and heading back home. He'd had a few minor HIV-related flare-ups, nothing terribly sinister, but his T-cells were dropping precipitously, and he felt it was time to leave the stress of the city and head back to his family.

I'd never see or speak to Mark again.

MARK ROBERTS (195?–199?)
May his memory be for a blessing.

September 1, 1991: Kennebunkport

David's sudden illness had created an additional problem. I'd volunteered to wrangle the dozen or so buses traveling up to Kennebunkport for our demonstration on September 1, and David was supposed to be my second. But since he was going to be in bed at home, if not in hospital, I needed to find someone else to help me run the caravan that weekend.

Joe Chiplock was a young, clean-cut, straw-haired boy with bright blue eyes, whom I'd first noticed a few weeks earlier when he volunteered to be one of my bus captains. Joe had just finished a cross-country tour as the assistant company manager for the Bolshoi Ballet, so I figured if he could manage a couple of busloads of Russian divas, he could probably handle us. Besides, he was very cute, if not exactly my type, and well . . . it was August.

August was my "what-the-hell" month. Still recovering from my disastrous breakup with Ben and, not coincidentally, still waiting for a call from an increasingly elusive Tom, I was licking my wounds by indulging in a little affairlette with an adorable young college student who was interning that summer with ACT UP. Wide-eyed, over beer and pizza, he'd gushed about how he'd studied ACT UP at school and how amazing it was to come down to New York for a few weeks and be a part of it. I was flattered, of course, and kind of dazzled by all that youthful admiration, so, yeah, what the hell.

And so it was with a combination of practicality and hormones that I asked Joe to help me run the buses.

After sending off the first round of travelers late Saturday afternoon, Joe and I had a brief getting-to-know-you, I mean, *strategy* discussion at a nearby diner, then returned to Seventh Avenue and Thirteenth Street at 2 a.m. to shepherd the remaining nine busloads of protesters up to Kennebunkport.

While four hundred activists—including members of Housing Works, Emmaus House, ADAPT, and other AIDS-related groups—had somehow managed to show up in time for our scheduled 3 a.m. departure, not all our buses had. Using one of the suitcase-sized mobile phones we'd rented for the occasion, I called the bus company, who told me, *oh yeah*, one of our buses had broken down somewhere in the Lincoln Tunnel. We could wait for a replacement or try to jam everyone onto the remaining eight buses and hope for the best.

I grabbed David, who had miraculously recovered from whatever had enfeebled him just days before, and asked him to save a seat on our bus for Joe, who was supposed to captain what I quickly determined to be the now-missing bus. And while the buses were packed, everyone got a seat, including Joe who, thanks to David, was sitting at the front of the bus directly across the aisle from us and right next to Jeff Griglak, a mutual friend who, it turned out, was also a friend of Joe's. It's a small gay world after all. So small, that who should I spy with my little eye sitting right behind Joe, but long-lost Tom, who'd finally decided to declare himself available after weeks of ignoring my phone calls. Also seated on the same bus, several rows back, was my young college friend, still hoping for a further continuation of our brief dalliance.

The trip had all the makings of a Feydeau farce complete with slamming port-a-potty doors, but I was far too tired to play. Instead, I casually began to search for common ground with Joe. It didn't take long.

Prior to his time with the Bolshoi, Joe had been Twyla Tharp's assistant—*I LOVE Twyla Tharp!*—and we soon discovered a shared and rather inexplicable affection for the musical *Applause*. (Joe had even written a paper on it in high school!) It all seemed very promising, but rather than pushing, I leaned back and spent most of the six-hour-plus ride kibitzing and cackling with David, as he infused himself from his bags of medicine dangling from the jacket hook above the window.

By the time we arrived in Kennebunkport, the roads into town had already been blocked and the day's activities were well under way. The streets were overrun with activists—fifteen hundred demonstrators carrying tall, brightly colored heraldic banners—"like Cleopatra's entry into Rome," according to Avram, who'd helped design them[16]—emblazoned with messages like "**Drug Treatment on Demand**" and "**AIDS Kills Prisoners**" along with hundreds of foam core signs shouting, "**114,000 AIDS Deaths—It's Time for a National Plan George.**" Affinity groups were hanging photos and obituaries of PWAs from tree branches, taking swings at George Bush piñatas filled with condoms, and playing miniature golf in Barbara Bush drag on their portable "George's AIDS Crisis Putt-Putt" golf course.

The local police, who usually numbered no more than eleven, had been supplemented by some two hundred reinforcements, including state troopers and Secret Service.[17] Unsure of our plans, they stiffened as we dropped to the ground in Dock Square, the town's commercial hub, for our first die-in. But soon we were up and heading east. While there were several pockets of support—one antiques dealer served marchers water from in front of her store—others were less sympathetic. "They're holding our town hostage," complained one longtime resident, and another called us "the most shocking thing I've ever seen in Kennebunkport. . . . I don't see many normal people around here."[18]

Leaving the quaint shops and curios of downtown Kennebunkport for the well-tended lawns and fenced-in precincts of the local golf and yacht clubs, we serenaded a group of vacationers gaping at us from the safety of their terraced patio with chants of "*WE DIE: YOU Go SAILING!*" and "*OFF the verANDA! INto the STREETS!*" But our high spirits soon dissolved into determined quiet as we continued our long march toward Walker's Point and the Bush home.

As we approached the road to the guarded compound, we were greeted by a menacing wall of several dozen state police in heavy black winter gloves blocking our way.[19] We stopped our march and dropped to the ground for a second die-in. Then, accompanied only by the mournful beat of a single drum, a group of us began loading the fallen bodies onto old army surplus stretchers and carrying them to the foot of the police barricade. The stretchers, another of Peter Staley's hardware purchases, quickly proved impractical, so we began carrying the bodies ourselves—by their hands and feet or cradling them in our arms; staggering forward to gently set our friends down amid the growing jumble. Back and forth we'd go, each trip more exhausting and upsetting than the next, until there were several hundred bodies lying in piles, motionless in the hot summer sun. It looked like one of those horrible photos of wartime atrocities. Only this time, I knew the names of these victims and had felt the weight of their bodies in my arms.

The experience proved too much for Joe, who began to sob. I wrapped my arms around him and gave him a long consoling hug.

When the die-in was over, we all moved to the side of the road as the Marys unrolled a hand-lettered fifty-foot banner listing our Plan to End the AIDS Crisis. We looked down at the plan, and then up the road beyond the checkpoint. We raised our fists and jabbed our fingers over the heads of the police, toward the man who for so long had ignored our pleas and would, no doubt, ignore them still. "*SHAME! SHAME! SHAME! SHAME!*" We then turned and marched back to town.

Rather than follow the rest of the group, Joe and I veered off the road and sat for a while on a bluff overlooking the Atlantic Ocean. It was a perfect end-of-summer day—warm and clear, with only a few puffy clouds for decoration. Staring out at the water with only the sound of the waves below, we shared our thoughts and feelings about the day and the demonstration. Joe was still shaken by the protest, so I listened and did my best to comfort him. It felt nice to be able to take care of someone—to be *allowed* to take care of someone—and I was deeply moved by his emotional openness.

By the time we wandered back into town, uptight Kennebunkport had been transformed into a sort of P-Town-lite. Angry activists were picnicking on the Village Green and walking down the street eating ice cream and holding hands, politely saying thank you to the brave merchants who, having kept their doors open, were being rewarded with a brisk business. It was such an all-American scene—give or take the clothes, haircuts, piercings, and skin tones—that I wondered if anyone in that town would ever be able to see us as "other" again.

When the time came to board our buses back to New York, David slid quietly into the seat across the aisle, so Joe and I could sit and snuggle together for the long ride home. When the bus pulled over at a rest stop a few hours later, I quickly cornered Jeff. "Is he as sweet as he seems to be?" I asked.

Jeff nodded and assured me he was.

In early August, as we were planning our Kennebunkport action, we received news that the CDC had finally blinked.

Sort of.[20]

When last year's big demonstrations and follow-up meetings proved ineffective, the CDC Working Group, including activists from ACT UPs New York, DC, and Atlanta, changed tactics. Announcing the time for meetings was over, they bombarded the CDC's James Curran with over a thousand postcards demanding he expand the AIDS definition, support anonymous testing, stop stigmatizing people's identities, and study routes of transmission.

The working group then did the hard work of building a broad-based coalition to join with us and endorse our demands. They proved so successful that even the staid AMA eventually came on board.[21] They further supplemented their coalition-building efforts with a diligent and targeted direct-action strategy, alternating large-scale demonstrations with small affinity group actions at the local CDC office in New York.

In June, the committee had prodded New York congressman Ted Weiss to hold a hearing on the shortfalls of the CDC definition and its impact on disability and Social Security benefits. At the same time, they flooded the offices of CDC director William Roper and his colleagues with copies of medical journal articles indicating a relationship between cervical cancer and HIV—funding for such research being yet another victim of the institution's obstinacy.

But the CDC remained adamant. After all, it was far easier, and far less expensive, to let HIV-positive women die "asymptomatic" from cervical cancer rather than from AIDS.[22]

The activists also initiated a powerful public awareness campaign, beginning with a full-page Gran Fury–designed ad in the *New York Times* with the headline "Women Don't Get AIDS. They Just Die From It." They continued to apply pressure until finally, and with great fanfare, the CDC announced it would soon be issuing new guidelines expanding the AIDS definition to include anyone who tested positive for HIV infection and had a T-cell count of less than 200.

Unfortunately, the 200 T-cell cutoff was an imprecise marker, neither accurately indicating disability nor helping doctors diagnose patients with HIV disease. Many people succumbed to life-threatening illnesses with T-cell counts far greater than 200, while others below the threshold were often otherwise quite healthy. The new definition also did little to improve women's and IV drug users' chances for being correctly diagnosed with AIDS, since no one would get a T-cell count until they had tested positive, and doctors wouldn't know to test them for HIV since the CDC had once again refused to include their likely symptoms as indicators of infection.

At the time, some worried the true purpose of the T-cell criterion was to provide a backdoor approach for the CDC to begin its long-desired policy of mandatory and nonanonymous testing. Unlike HIV tests, T-cell tests were not conducted anonymously, nor were they covered by nondisclosure guarantees. The CDC had already endorsed the mandatory testing of immigrants and health care workers, the latter thanks to the unfortunate and now notorious case of a young woman named Kimberly Bergalis.

Kimberly Bergalis was only seventeen years old when she was unknowingly infected with HIV during a visit to her dentist in 1987. Unlike Ryan White or AIDS Commission appointee Belinda Mason—neither of whom, though infected through blood transfusions, ever sought to divide people by the way in which they acquired the virus—Bergalis angrily embraced the label of "innocent victim."

> Whom do I blame? Do I blame myself? I sure don't. I never used IV drugs, never slept with anyone and never had a blood transfusion. I blame Dr. Acer and every single one of you bastards. Anyone who knew Dr. Acer was infected and had full-blown AIDS and stood by not doing a damn thing about it. You are all just as guilty as he was.[23]

Although her case was an anomaly—there were no other recorded cases of someone infected by an HIV-positive doctor—Bergalis and her family strongly advocated for the mandatory testing of all health care professionals.[24] When Bergalis's rapid health decline catapulted her onto the front pages in 1991, the Senate passed two bills to respond to the tabloid-generated panic over doctors with HIV. The first, another Jesse Helms special, mandated that all doctors, nurses, and health professionals with AIDS disclose their diagnosis to patients before performing "invasive procedures"—a vague and undefined term—or face prison terms of up to ten years and a fine of $10,000. When challenged about the severity of his bill, Helms crowed, "I believe in horsewhipping," particularly when it comes to those "rogues in the medical community who have knowingly and callously exposed hundreds upon hundreds of innocent people to the AIDS virus."[25] The bill passed 81–18.

To counter the Helms measure, the Senate passed a second, bipartisan "leadership" bill, which included the notification requirement but traded

Helms's fines and prison sentences for threats of discipline by state licensing boards and the loss of federal health financing for any state refusing to adhere to the new regulations.[26] Both these bills were dangerous and discriminatory and had no basis in science. As health care experts knew, the way to prevent HIV transmission was not by determining the serostatus of the health care worker but by maintaining proper infection control procedures.

While everyone in the AIDS community objected to the Helms bill, the professional medical groups and major gay organizations were shockingly silent about the leadership bill, although it, too, required the mandatory testing of medical personnel. It would take a nationwide day of "Doctors in Chains" protests, organized by a grassroots coalition of labor unions, community health care groups, activists, and health care providers, to finally sound the alarm.

"Kimberly-mania"[27] would peak in late September, when a frail Bergalis was wheeled into a congressional hearing room to testify at the behest of Rep. William Dannemeyer (R-CA), who'd proposed a companion bill that not only required the mandatory testing of health care workers but also allowed doctors to secretly test patients without their consent.

Among those who spoke in opposition to the bill was David Barr. Out of 180,000 cases and 120,000 deaths, noted David, "No other case of AIDS has received more attention than that of Kimberly Bergalis." But rather than portraying her as an enemy, David spoke of what they had in common. They were both "dying from the same neglect" and shared the same anger, even if the targets of their rage were different.

> I am angry because of an inadequate research budget. I am angry because life-saving drugs are unavailable to those who need them most. I am angry because Congress determined that cities need disaster relief for AIDS, but refused to provide the funds.
>
> I am angry that our Government will criminalize health-care workers instead of allowing them to do their jobs. They will test patients instead of providing care. They will collect names instead of providing treatments that could save our lives, yours and mine.[28]

One week later, both houses of Congress passed a bill *suggesting*, but not requiring, doctors and health care workers get tested for HIV, and asking states to certify they had adopted CDC guidelines asking doctors who tested positive to refrain from conducting "exposure prone" procedures. New York State was the first to reject the guidelines, requiring instead that all health care professionals take formal courses in infection control techniques.[29] Other states soon followed suit, and the bill's suggestions were never enforced.*

Back in New York, the Catholic Church, still smarting from its defeat over the city's new AIDS curriculum, had pressured the Board of Education to consider adding an opt-out clause allowing parents to proactively prevent their children from participating in the much-loathed condom distribution program.

While the idea of parental opt-out might seem harmless, in practice it would require students to give their names in order to be cross-checked against the do-not-distribute lists, significantly reducing participation by sexually active students while doing nothing to lessen the likelihood of their having unprotected sex.[30] Widely regarded as the church's consolation prize, the provision was expected to sail through the Board of Education when it came up for a vote on September 11; but by then, ACT UP and YELL had recruited some new and powerful allies—the students themselves. And among them, Kate Barnhart.

At fifteen, Kate was already a movement veteran. She'd worked with Pete Seeger's environmental group, Clearwater, while still in junior high school,[31] and more recently had helped organize Students against the War (SAW), a citywide youth group opposed to the Gulf War,[32] as well as an HIV peer-counseling group with her best friend, John Won, at the academically elite Stuyvesant High School.

After participating with YELL in the "Golden is Silent" takeover of Brooklyn Borough president Howard Golden's office, protesting his silence on AIDS education in schools, they began recruiting their SAW colleagues to join ACT UP and YELL.[33] By the time of the September opt-out vote, Kate and her friends were fully engaged, packing the hall and silencing the room with their heartfelt testimony. With their help, and much to the surprise of everyone, the opt-out proposal was defeated by a vote of 4–3.

As even the *New York Times* pointed out,[34] the biggest losers in this battle were Cardinal O'Connor and the Catholic Church. Not only had they failed to defeat the condom distribution plan; they weren't even allowed the

---

*Ten weeks after giving her testimony, Kimberly Bergalis died at age twenty-three. *May her memory be for a blessing.*

face-saving gesture of the opt-out amendment. Part of it was simply a matter of politics—the Dinkins coalition didn't include White Catholic voters from the outer boroughs, and the mayor's personal relationship with the cardinal could best be described as frosty[35]—but ACT UP and YELL owned a piece of it as well. Whatever its faults, Stop the Church had helped knock the church off its morally superior altar. As long as you didn't crumble a communion wafer or lie down in the aisles, it was now okay to criticize the church or regard it as just one of the city's many political constituencies.

September 30, 1991: Target White House

George Bush had not reacted well to our Kennebunkport protest. Challenged at a press conference about whether he "got the message" from our demonstration, the president sputtered that the key to the AIDS crisis lay in "behavioral change."[36] "Here's a disease where you can control its spread by your own personal behavior," the president explained. "You can't do that with cancer."[37] Dismissing our demonstration as a publicity stunt, he then compared it unfavorably to a protest held a week earlier by a group of unemployed workers.* "That was the one I was concerned about. That one hit home, because when a family is out of work, that's one I care very much about."[38]

And once again, the president, in his own inarticulate way, had unwittingly revealed the truth. We were not now, nor would we ever be, regarded as full-fledged Americans, as people with families and friends, deserving of his time and sympathy. Whatever responsibility he felt toward us came from his patrician sense of obligation rather than from empathy. For all our appeals, all our keening and obituaries and pleas to recognize and value our lives, we would always be "other," "less-than," "not our class, dear."

And worse, no one even noticed.

Not one pundit or politician felt the president's statements warranted any sort of public rebuke—and I knew it was ridiculous to expect one. The idea that a public official would dare suggest the lives of a bunch of faggots and junkies were equal to those of "real Americans" was preposterous. You'd have thought I'd have learned this lesson by now, but each time it came as a fresh slap in the face.

---

*The president had signed a bill extending unemployment benefits for workers who had exhausted their initial twenty-six weeks of eligibility, but he then refused to make the $5.8 billion in funds available.

The only people who understood were those whose lives had been directly affected by the disease. People like Jeanne White, mother of the late Ryan White,* who joined us in Washington for a rally on the final day of our Target Bush campaign and stood by us, even as reporters asked her about demonstrators burning an American flag. "I totally support ACT UP. I know what they are going through," she proclaimed.[39] "I am here to represent moms all around America who are losing their sons and daughters to AIDS. If you want to call these people radical, then you can call me radical, too. We are tired of not seeing anything done."[40]

Additional support came from the National Commission on AIDS, which, spurred by the recent death of one of its members, Belinda Mason, had issued a scathing report condemning the government's paltry response to the epidemic.[41]

BELINDA MASON (1958–1991)
May her memory be for a blessing.

After our rally and press conference in front of the National Archives, we all marched up Pennsylvania Avenue to the White House. While most of the protesters assembled across the street in Lafayette Park, Joe and I joined a smaller group of eighty demonstrators for a legally permitted picket on the sidewalk directly in front of the White House. And when the air horns sounded, we chained ourselves to the White House fence.

Chained next to us, his face and white shirt smeared dramatically with stage blood, was Bob Rafsky. Nodding conspiratorially to a white van parked a block away, Bob whispered that he was being filmed by *60 Minutes* and wearing a body mike. When it was time for his arrest, he warned, he'd be kicking it up a notch for the cameras and invited us to do the same.

Despite his full-throated participation, I always got the impression Bob was embarrassed by the amped-up theatrics required for the media and found the whole idea of play-acting to dramatize such a serious life-and-death situation terribly undignified. But Bob was a realist. If that's what it took to grab the media's attention, that's what he'd do.

---

*Ryan White died April 8, 1990, at age eighteen. *May his memory be for a blessing.*

So when the police came with their bolt cutters, we all shouted and put on a show.* We knew the president wouldn't hear us—he was, no joke, attending a fundraiser at Disney World—so we screamed instead for the cameras, hoping someone else might.

The following day, ACT UP laid siege to the Capitol as part of a national health care action.

ACT UP had first addressed health care issues in 1988, when we protested the shortage of beds at the city's public and private hospitals. This was followed, in 1989, by the establishment of an Insurance (later Insurance and Access, and later yet Insurance and Healthcare Access) Committee, yet another of our small groups that, despite a lack of support from the Floor, somehow managed to move mountains. A lot of the credit belonged to the committee's chair, Karin Timour.†

With her prim Peter Pan–collared blouses and ankle-length skirts, Karin looked more like a schoolmarm than an AIDS activist—but woe to anyone who mistook her cheerful and unthreatening exterior as the measure of her fearlessness.

When Karin first came to ACT UP in 1989, she was working as an HIV coordinator at Phoenix House, an outpatient drug treatment center. She'd also been researching insurance issues on behalf of her brother, who'd recently been diagnosed with Marfan syndrome, an inherited connective tissue disease, leading her to join—and shortly thereafter run—our Insurance Committee.[42]

As Karin explained it, the insurance industry was built on a contradiction; it was a for-profit industry charged with providing a public good: access to health care. But these two imperatives were in constant opposition—the more an insurance company's customers took advantage of health care services, the smaller the company's profits. It was therefore in the company's interest—if not society's—to limit access to health care as much as possible. To do this, insurance companies instituted stringent eligibility requirements, denying payments for what they determined to be preexisting conditions

---

*And if you look closely at the *60 Minutes* footage, you can see me being hauled away from the fence in my blue jean jacket, upside down and screaming.

†As well as key members Ken Bing, John Goodman, Mark Hannay, Wayne Kawadler, and Barry Lapidus.

and calibrating levels of coverage based on demographics and classes of people.*

To further limit their exposure to HIV-related costs, insurance companies "redlined" geographic areas, businesses, and professions known to have a high concentration of gay men, drug users, and people with AIDS, to prevent them from purchasing insurance. Even if a person with HIV managed to obtain insurance, they were still faced with low reimbursement rates, pre-existing condition clauses, exclusions for experimental treatments, and spending caps that severely limited their coverage for AIDS-related conditions.

The one exception for New Yorkers with HIV and other serious illnesses was Empire Blue Cross/Blue Shield. Like the other "Blues" across the country, Empire was a private not-for-profit insurance provider. In return for indirect government subsidies, like hospital and physician fee discounts and tax-free status, Empire was able to insure otherwise uninsurable populations and offer lower premiums. With over ten million customers, they were the largest insurer in the metropolitan area, and more than one-third of all New York's PWAs were, or had been, Empire customers.[43]

However, Empire's success in providing its customers with access to medical care had seriously affected its bottom line. To make up for constant shortfalls, Empire had raised its rates 75 percent in just four years. At the same time, unscrupulous commercial insurers were cherry-picking Empire's healthier customers, luring them away with cheaper premiums, leaving Empire with no way to balance its caseload of increasingly sick customers.†

In July 1991, when Empire announced it was raising its premiums another 50 percent, after a 19.5 percent increase just six months earlier, Karin took to the phones, calling organizations representing people with other chronic illnesses and asking them to have their clients testify at an upcoming hearing before the New York State Department of Insurance. While some groups understood the stakes immediately, the big players, like the American Cancer Society and the Heart Association, had little interest in working in coalition with a group like ACT UP and stayed on the sidelines.[44]

---

*Before the Civil Rights Act of 1964, insurance companies maintained different actuarial tables for people of color, since they were likely to live shorter and less healthy lives, due to, among other societal inequities, the lack of access to health care perpetuated by these same discriminatory insurance practices. The industry still differentiated costs based on gender and had been a key player in defeating the Equal Rights Amendment, which would have required them to offer equal rates to both men and women.

†Empire's rates depended on community-rated pools, which spread risk across a large group of both healthy and sick customers.

The hearing on September 6 was unlike anything Empire or the Department of Insurance had ever seen. After running a gauntlet of rowdy protesters from ACT UP and community-minded seniors from the Brooklyn-Wide Interagency Council on Aging—"If you're a socialist when you're in your 20s and 30s, and then you become a senior, all you are is a slightly older socialist," explained Karin[45]—company representatives were forced to give their testimony sandwiched between an **"Insurance Discrimination KILLS People with AIDS"** banner stretched across the stage above them and a row of "Faceless Bureaucrats" standing below.

The latter were members of Action Tours in one of their more popular disguises—nondescript business drag topped off with white paper plate face masks with two cutout eyeholes and a rubber-stamped mouth that read "Faceless Bureaucrats." Rather than speaking, they'd hang signs around their necks filled with bland excuses like "Don't Ask Me, I Just Work Here" or "Just Doing My Job." Today, they bore the names of the four people testifying on behalf of Empire.

When the Department of Insurance put the proposed increase on hold, Karin and her committee, working as members of the newly formed New Yorkers for Accessible Health Coverage coalition, helped draft insurance reform legislation and successfully lobbied state legislators to pass the Open Enrollment Community Rating Law of 1992,[46] which gave Empire the improved rates it needed, enshrined the concepts of open enrollment and community ratings for New York State, and penalized commercial insurers who refused to participate.

But whatever our success in New York State, the real problem was our country's broken health care system. Health care costs had increased 42 percent over the previous five years. One out of every eight dollars spent in the US was being spent on health care. At the same time, over 40 million people in the US, 16.5 percent of the population under sixty-five, lacked any form of health insurance.[47]

We'd participated in our first large health care–focused action in April 1990, when we joined over seven hundred activists from around the country in Chicago for a series of demonstrations sponsored by ACT NOW, including a "twenty-four-hour encampment at the severely underfunded and understaffed Cook County Hospital"[48] and CD actions targeting the insurance industry and the American Medical Association. And in May 1991, our National Health Care Working Group helped organize a demonstration in Washington, DC, to coincide with the publication of a special "health care reform" issue of the *Journal of the American Medical Association.*

Although everyone acknowledged health care was an important issue, the question remained whether it was something ACT UP should take on in addition to its more AIDS-specific efforts; and if so, which of the many proposed solutions ACT UP should support. I marveled at the skill with which the committee parried these questions, navigating the many political crosscurrents roiling the Floor.

Looking right, they acknowledged health care was a long-term goal and "ACT UP isn't here to cure society but to fight AIDS."[49] However, since people would need to use the health care system to access whatever treatments were eventually coughed up by the drug pipeline, didn't that make fixing the system a priority issue? Looking left, they submitted that since "ACT UP has always taken the position called for by the circumstances, even if it's been politically unfeasible," didn't it make sense for ACT UP to develop its own list of requirements for a health care system that would meet the demands of people with HIV/AIDS, rather than buying into one of the plans already in play?* After all, "Working for what's practical is the job of lobbyists, not activists."[50]

On October 1, 450 protesters from ACT UP and a coalition of other like-minded organizations blocked traffic and shut down the Capitol Rotunda, while affinity groups poured red dye into the fountains outside the Supreme Court and set off stink bombs in the congressional subway. One protester, Brad Lengyel, even managed to disrupt a debate inside the Senate Chamber,[51] shouting from the public gallery, "We're suffering and we're going to die . . . and the government won't do anything to help,"[52] before being dragged off by Capitol police, joining the seventy-three other activists who'd been arrested in actions across the Capitol district.

But despite the successes and distractions of the past few months, the truce between ACT UP's warring factions remained precarious at best. We were all still walking on eggshells and whistling past graveyards, just one explosion away from disaster.

---

*Our demands included universal coverage by "a single uniform health care system"; comprehensive benefits ranging from prevention, diagnostics, and treatment to health-related social services including long-term and prenatal care, as well as coverage for pharmaceuticals and experimental and alternative treatments; financing by the federal government through progressive taxation; economic efficiency, cutting the more than 20 percent of costs now consumed by administrative fees; proper allocation of health resources; community input and control; and substantially increased funding for medical research. ACT UP internal document: "Restructuring the American Health Care System: Background Papers," undated.

Chapter 24

⁙

Strategies and Consequences

WHEN ACTG 175 first appeared in July 1991, the *Treatment and Data Digest* described it as "the antiviral trial to end all trials."[1]

> Begin with an increasingly hostile political environment, a dysfunctional bureaucracy and ever diminishing resources. Then take three mediocre and fairly toxic nucleoside analogues—one approved (**AZT**), one recommended for approval (**ddI**) and the third nearing hearing (**ddC**). Now find 2,500—no make it 3,000—no 3,500— unfortunate or unenlightened subjects. Give some of them only **AZT** plus two placebos. Give others **ddI** plus two placebos. Still others get **AZT** and **ddI** but a **ddC** placebo. Another group receives **AZT** and **ddC** but a **ddI** placebo. Liberally apply a lion's share of the entire research budget (and about 75% of all ACTG trial participants). Blend. Blind. Randomize. Then let sit for 2–3 years.[2]

But if 175 was bad news for PWAs, it proved an unexpected gift for ACT UP, allowing all our warring factions to unite in its opposition. Among its many crimes—which included a massive waste of time, money, and resources— the trial was clinically useless, designed only to confirm the widely held assumption that antivirals were more effective when used in combination, but without determining which combination worked best or at what dosage.

A firestorm of hostility from both activists and researchers quickly forced the trial investigators back to their labs to recalibrate. They emerged in September with a new streamlined protocol that was less expensive, required fewer patients, and better answered questions regarding the presumed advantages of combination therapy. Taking a page from the activists' handbook, they argued whatever the trial's shortcomings, it was still worthwhile, as it would provide continuing health care and access to treatments for the hundreds of patients whose antiviral trials were soon ending. Although you could continue to debate the merits—and god knows we did—it was, without question, a better-designed trial.

But this raised another set of issues.

When 175 was first brought to the Floor, we'd voted overwhelmingly to demand the trial be abandoned. Now, in an echo of what had happened with 076, it appeared T+D, and particularly Mark Harrington and David Barr, had worked behind the scenes not to stop the trial as instructed, but to improve it. Even those who supported the new protocol were infuriated by the self-appointed "experts" from T+D negotiating a deal against the express wishes of the larger organization. When confronted, Mark sheepishly replied he'd thought the Floor's mandate was only to make sure the trial did not proceed "as is," and not to shut it down completely. "Since it was clear that the ACTG was going to do a combination trial," he argued (and not unreasonably), "wasn't it more important that activists saw to it that the ACTG did the best combination trial rather than demanding that no trial be done?"[3]

Unfortunately, their actions provided further proof of T+D's growing arrogance and lack of accountability. The committee rarely asked for advice or input from the Floor, informing us only of actions already taken and decisions already made. Although they continued to publish and distribute their invaluable *Treatment and Data Digest*, information flowed only in one direction, an impression given additional credence by the behavior of Mark and other T+D leaders, who responded to even the most legitimate questions and critiques with prickly anger and eye-rolling condescension.

Doubts about T+D's future in ACT UP were reignited when Peter Staley launched his new AIDS activist group, the Treatment Activist Guerrillas (TAG), with a spectacular action: covering the Virginia home of Senator Jesse Helms with a huge inflatable condom. Even as Peter insisted TAG was only an affinity group, everyone understood it to be a potential alternative for frustrated T+D members, not to mention a possible source of competition for ACT UP, should the current situation grow untenable.*

---

*Peter would later admit that he'd already registered the name with New York State as a nonprofit corporation and set up a separate bank account so the group could "hit the ground

With Target Bush ended and T+D in flux, ACT UP felt rudderless. The Floor, which had always been at the center of the organization, was now a largely passive body—an audience displaying little collective will or enthusiasm—while our committees functioned more like independent affinity groups: self-sufficient and focused on their own agendas, requiring little from the larger organization.

To reenergize the Floor and provide some much-needed direction, Maxine Wolfe and Bob Lederer convened a new Strategies and Actions Working Group* to jump-start a reassessment of our overarching goals, tactics, and strategies. Ideally, it would function like a combination of our old Actions Committee, with its focus on strategies and tactics, and our seasonal "Where Are We Going?" sessions, where we'd discuss the core issues and problems we hadn't the time to address on Monday nights.

In its first attempt to reengage the Floor, Strategies proposed dedicating an hour at our Monday night meetings for substantive discussions on controversial topics. For two consecutive Monday nights, ACT UP hosted presentations by Strategies and T+D about ACTG 175, followed by an open discussion to see if we could reach some common understanding, if not consensus, around key issues. The conversations, though heated, were remarkably civil, and seemed to augur a potential way forward for us to remain together.

But attending the weekly Strategies meetings, I felt far less optimistic.

Although intended as a forum to discuss ACT UP's response to a full range of AIDS issues, the conversation kept circling back to the behavior of "the boys" of T+D and the perceived lack of respect and recognition given to the work of the Women's Action Committee. (While a few T+D backbenchers attended Strategies meetings, their marquee players were noticeably absent.) There was a startling viciousness to the discussions whenever the subject of T+D came up, as if they were the real enemy, the great boulder standing in the way of ACT UP's success. And while a certain amount of grousing was to be expected, the meetings often felt like particularly nasty gripe sessions.

---

running" if a split did happen. Peter Staley, *Never Silent: ACT UP and My Life in Activism* (Chicago: Chicago Review Press, 2022), 174.

*The group was called both "Strategy and Actions" and "Strategies and Actions" rather interchangeably, though "Strategies" for short, in either case.

And it wasn't just what was being said, but who was saying it.

I'd always looked up to Maxine (and still do) even when I disagreed with her, as I had over the moratorium issue. She was unquestionably one of the most venerated members of ACT UP, so I was shocked to hear her complain about a lack of respect and recognition for her work and to see her usually acute analysis replaced by petty if-you-don't-support-me-I-won't-support-you sniping. While she'd been viciously attacked during the moratorium fiasco, I'd always respected her ability to step back and take the larger view. But Max had apparently had enough and was now giving as good as she got.

The Strategies meetings grew increasingly uncomfortable for me as any talk of reconciliation or even working with T+D soon disappeared, with "they can stay or go as they please—fuck 'em!" becoming the overriding sentiment. The working group also seemed perilously close to becoming a parallel organization, a shadow ACT UP creating manifestos and hashing out structures and strategies that would then be brought before a highly malleable larger organization for its rubber stamp endorsement.

Desperately searching for a way to keep the window for reconciliation from closing, I also started attending T+D meetings. My first meeting, however, began with Mark abruptly declaring that the era of good—or at least less hostile—feelings generated by the Monday night 175 discussions was over, and that the time had come for T+D to formally discuss leaving ACT UP. Barely pausing for breath, Mark laid out his case.

T+D's work had become increasingly complicated. There was much they wanted to do—create a new treatment agenda, push for funding for basic AIDS research, develop new drug protocols—but instead, they were forced to beg for money and constantly defend themselves from the spurious attacks of activists who demanded fealty to an outdated "separatist ideology"[4] that decreed the one true role of an activist was to be "outside criticizing rather than on the inside lobbying and negotiating." While conceding that T+D was now functioning in a "gray area" inside the system where they could "do as much harm as any greedy researcher,"[5] he argued their good intentions and the great importance of their work should override any mistrust or misgivings. They deserved to work in an environment "where people working on complicated issues got support and advice, not criticism and carping"[6]—a courtesy, it was quickly noted, rarely extended to other T+D members by Mark and the committee's Star Chamber, who sat arrayed at the front of the meeting room, lecturing and cross-examining the other attendees like professors at a dissertation defense.

Though I sympathized with the challenges facing the members of T+D— they were doing complex work that often had a direct impact on their own lives—I found it difficult to excuse their lack of appreciation for the work the rest of us were doing. They seemed to view activism as a zero-sum game, with treatment activism the one true calling. Any other type of activism, with few exceptions—my work organizing demonstrations not among them— was a distraction to be measured in terms of work not being done on treatment issues. (The Strategies activists had a point here.) But what I found most galling was the notion, prevalent in both camps, that somehow it was *everyone else* who was impossible to work with, and given the importance of *their* work, they should be forgiven their shortcomings and excused from having to tolerate anyone else's bad behavior.

What surprised me most, however, was how deeply wounded everyone at T+D was by the Floor's criticisms. They had always come off as so aloof and self-assured, I hadn't fully understood how unsupported and even betrayed they felt.*

Speaking as an unaffiliated longtime member, I assured them they had far more support from the general membership than they imagined. Their opinions continued to hold great sway on the Floor, which, to my knowledge, had never once voted down a single T+D request for money or support; and rather than being disinterested in their work, most members would welcome more information and input from the committee. I also suggested their excuses of "not having enough time to explain their work" or it being "too specialized" for the rest of us to understand sounded suspiciously like the arguments we used to hear from the FDA and NIH.

I further argued that while the current hostilities were difficult for everyone, the cure of splitting off from ACT UP would be far worse than the dysfunction of staying together.[7] After all, ACT UP was not going to fold up and disappear if T+D stormed away; the same conflicts would remain. Would they rather do battle in the relative privacy of Monday nights, or in a more public forum where the damage would extend beyond egos to our work?

In an attempt to bridge the gap between T+D and the rest of ACT UP, a small group of us organized some much-needed treatment teach-ins for the Floor and began meeting to discuss ways of helping T+D develop some larger treatment-related actions. Despite my anxiety about science and my closer personal relationships and political alignment with Strategies, I found it easier to work from the T+D side. I think it was because it was still "the

---

*I'd always suspected both factions were suffering from a bad case of jealousy—Max and the Strategies crowd wanted the respect T+D was accorded by Fauci and the scientists, while Mark and the T+D crowd wanted the love and loyalty engendered by Max and the Strategies members from the Floor.

work" that seemed to matter most and, unlike Strategies, everyone here—even Mark—seemed gutted by the prospect of T+D's potential departure. It was also where I felt the stronger sense of urgency. They were still looking at the clock, not the calendar—a point brought home at that same meeting by the announcement that Jay Lipner had died.

Jay's AIDS activism had predated ACT UP, to his fight as a lawyer with Lambda Legal for disability coverage for PWAs and the early release of experimental AIDS treatments. "Whenever our discussions became divisive and fractious, Jay always reminded us who the real villains were. His insight and courage will be greatly missed."[8] And how.

JAY LIPNER (1945–1991)
May his memory be for a blessing.

Twenty-four hours later, AIDS became a sudden, we-interrupt-this-program, front-page news story when basketball superstar Magic Johnson announced he was HIV-positive.

Considered one of the best players in the game, Johnson was still in good health and had displayed neither telltale symptoms nor any diminution of his skills. He'd discovered he was Positive quite by accident, after taking a routine blood test for a life insurance policy.

The entire country was stunned. Now, everyone knew someone with HIV. And this was no artsy faggot or junkie living in New York or San Francisco, but a real live sports hero, one with a well-documented fondness for the ladies. "Even Me," shouted the front cover of *Newsweek*,[9] announcing an article that evoked the Kennedy assassination to express the where-were-you-when-you-heard-the-news magnitude of the story. The day of Magic's announcement, the National AIDS Hotline recorded forty thousand phone calls, over ten times their usual rate, and the CDC was flooded with over ten thousand AIDS-related calls in a single hour.[10]

To his credit, Johnson didn't hide in shame, nor did he attempt to claim the mantle of "innocent victim" like Kimberly Bergalis. Instead, he embraced his role as a powerful advocate and spokesperson. "We think, well, only gay people can get it—it's not going to happen to me. And here I am saying that it can happen to anybody."[11] The fact that Johnson was Black also served as a much-needed wake-up call for the African American community, which remained in deep denial over the disease's impact. It also momentarily roused the conscience of the president, who finally admitted he hadn't "done enough," about AIDS.[12]

And yet . . .

Thankful as we were that AIDS was finally getting some attention, it was hard not to feel a little rage. More than 125,000 Americans had already died, 200,000 were currently living with AIDS, and as many as 1.5 million were infected with HIV. The gay community had been battling the disease for ten years and ACT UP had been in the streets screaming about it almost daily for four and a half years. We'd lost so many people—friends, colleagues, lovers, family members—but somehow those lives, even when added together, had not merited this kind of attention or calls to action.

The following week, President Bush named Johnson to the National Commission on AIDS—the same commission that had faulted the president's leadership on AIDS in their report just one month earlier, and whose recommendations he'd again ignored. But maybe now things would be different. Maybe Magic was what we needed to force the president and the country to take action and make the fight for AIDS their own.

David

David Serko seemed to have located his own private stash of magic, celebrating his thirty-first birthday by introducing us to his new boyfriend, Eddie.

Dark-haired and compact, with soft, deep-set brown eyes, Eddie had a reserve and quiet calm that was very different from David's previous boyfriends. Eddie seemed content to hang back and not try to keep pace with the high-speed banter ricocheting across the long party table. Despite the freshness of the relationship, Eddie seemed sure of where he stood.

The rest of us, however, were less sure. Who was this guy and where did he come from? Obviously, he had to know about all of David's health issues—it was hard to avoid the infusions, the *M. haemophilum* scars, the pills, and the fading eyesight. Yet here he was, seemingly willing to take all of this on, as well as whatever lay ahead. It was a tribute to him and, of course, to David. Who else could find a sexy new boyfriend while going blind?

December 2–5, 1991: ACTG 13

The next confrontation between ACT UP's warring factions played out in public, just as I'd feared. The arena was, once again, an ACTG meeting, and while the issue at hand was ostensibly the rejiggered ACTG 175 trial, it was merely a placeholder for our internal squabbles.

Strategies and Actions had become increasingly aggressive in its efforts to challenge T+D's position as the voice of ACT UP's treatment activism. In mid-November, the group had distributed a five-page draft document prepared by Bob Lederer, proposing a National AIDS Treatment Action Campaign to change the direction of federal AIDS research.[13]

The problem at NIAID, it argued, went beyond the slow pace and the narrow band of drugs being studied; it went to the very understanding of how AIDS was caused, the "fixed assumptions about the role of HIV," and the lack of research on cofactors and competing theories. What was needed was a long-term campaign combining big demonstrations like the NIH and FDA actions with an expansive coalition-building component similar to the CDC campaign. Although T+D's successes were graciously acknowledged, the new plan and its proponents held the CDC approach to be the better model, due to its greater emphasis on outreach and raising community awareness.

The members of T+D greeted the proposal with understandable exasperation; noting that while they'd achieved so many of their goals and the CDC campaign so few, they were now criticized for not accomplishing them in the appropriate manner. But that depended on the intended goal—affecting incremental change within an institutional structure or building a grassroots movement to topple that structure completely.

The Strategies proposal, with its consensus letters, conference calls, and community outreach efforts, was textbook long-term movement-building strategy and, as such, an absolute ode to process. While I respected and admired the thoroughness of Bob's vision for creating a coordinated AIDS movement, it was not what ACT UP was designed to do. We were built for speed and action. Process is what we complained about in other organizations; we were about results. And for people who were dying, results were more important than process—assuming you came up with the right ones.

The face-off between Strategies and T+D, when it finally came, was surprisingly anticlimactic—a damp fizzle more than the widely feared explosion. In a testament to its tone-deafness, the ACTG had decided to hold an opening-day cocktail reception to celebrate its "great success," the unironically named "Social Hour to Acknowledge the Accomplishments of the ACTG."[14] For members of the Strategies group it proved too good a target to pass up. While Mark and his fellow treatment activists and CCG members shared drinks and canapés with Fauci, Hoth, and the other ACTG bigwigs, a group of fifteen ACT UP members dressed in lab coats burst into the party, passing out fact sheets and loudly proposing fanciful toasts satirizing the ACTG's self-congratulation for a job barely begun.

But unlike the disruption at the March ACTG meeting, which threatened to rupture the entire CCG-activist coalition, the Cocktail Party Action barely caused a ripple. "History repeats itself—the first time as tragedy, the second time as farce," deadpanned Mark, who actively ignored the protest, choosing to sip his wine and continue his friendly chat with Dan Hoth.[15] In his report to the Floor, Mark would later characterize the demo as "threadbare both dramatically and intellectually,"[16] dismissing ACT UP's Position Statement as "an innocuous collection of clichés—'motherhood and apple pie,' according to a top NIAID employee."[17] (To be fair, in order to gain approval from the Floor, a principle that still mattered to the Strategies group, they had been forced to tone down their criticism of the ACTG and switch out their specific demands for a more generalized set of goals.)

I can only imagine the delight and confusion of the many researchers, officials, and pharmaceutical representatives, as they watched their former adversaries ignore their own colleagues' protests.

The following Monday, Eric Sawyer solemnly stood before the Floor and announced that Mark Fotopoulos had died.

Mark's death hit me hard. I'd lost touch with him when he left New York that fall. I'd never followed up with him; never checked in or called. And because I hadn't done what a good friend should've done, I'd let that get in the way of reaching out to his lover, Robert, or his family. When I saw Robert on Fire Island the following summer, I felt too ashamed to go up to him and offer my condolences. It was a huge failure on my part, something I regret to this day.

Despite all my trumpeted courage and activism, I still felt like a coward and a phony, a fair-weather friend who wouldn't come through unless directly asked.

Mark deserved better. He was a personal hero and one of the reasons I wrote this book: a courageous, talented, vibrant young man who deserved more time and a kinder fate.

MARK FOTOPOULOS (1956–1991)
May his memory be for a blessing.

News of the ACTG demonstration, and of ACT UP zapping ACT UP, quickly spread from the Floor to the community at large, thanks to an article in the gay press prematurely titled "ACT UP Splits Over Drug Trial."[18] While the article was surprisingly civil, it was laced with bitter commentary and provocative comments from bomb-throwers on both sides. "I think researchers are beginning to realize that there are two kinds of folks in ACT UP," sniped one T+D activist: "those who work on issues and those who are among the emerging lunatic fringe."[19] To which another activist countered, "Once you call Anthony Fauci 'Tony' and have drinks with him, it's hard to knock his files off his desk and chain yourself to his chair,"[20] as if that were the goal of our activism.

Not surprisingly, the mood at our Monday night meetings grew increasingly funereal. No one said it out loud, but we all knew we'd passed the point of compromise. The split was now inevitable, and our future uncertain. The only question was, Would this be the beginning of a new chapter, or the end of our last?

Part VI

AIDS CAMPAIGN '92

Chapter 25

ACT UP / Petrelis

A TRAUMATIZED ACT UP began 1992 in a state of mourning. There was still, as always, plenty to be done. Our committees continued to work feverishly on their issues. The CDC Working Group and their allies had successfully forced the CDC to delay the implementation of its controversial new AIDS definition. And even T+D had begun to reconstitute itself, with Jim Eigo committed to remaining in ACT UP, Garance Franke-Ruta and Derek Link continuing their Countdown 18 Months campaign, and two former T+D "backbenchers," Theo Smart and George M. Carter, taking over the publication of the *Treatment and Data Digest*. Everyone was doing their best to put on their smiley faces and focus on the future.

But there was a hole at the center of the organization.

Every Monday night, we took silent attendance, looking over at the empty seats on the right side of the Great Hall, checking to see who was still with us. Even after the official formation of the renamed Treatment Action Group in late January, Mark Harrington, Peter Staley, David Barr, and Charlie Franchino continued to haunt our meetings, drifting in and out like restless ghosts reluctant to give up their previous home. But were they coming to participate or to observe? To see if we could still work together, or to mock our efforts and congratulate themselves on the wisdom of their departure?*

---

*While TAG was invitation-only—with Larry Kramer conspicuously absent from that invite list—there was no requirement to renounce membership in ACT UP, so several members would continue to work with both groups.

In early February, Peter returned to the Floor to report on an ongoing T+D initiative asking the major pharmaceutical companies to donate a combined $25 million over five years toward community-based research. Both Peter and the initiative were met with blistering hostility, as the campaign, though briefly mentioned in an August *Treatment and Data Digest*,[1] had never been approved or even discussed on the Floor. Whatever its merits, it was held as yet another stunning example of Peter's and T+D's arrogance, with some members gleefully speculating there *must* have been some sort of quid pro quo—perhaps a moratorium on ACT UP protests?—in order to entice the drug companies to participate.

Peter vehemently denied making any such promises and argued this kind of investment was exactly what ACT UP had always wanted—drugs into bodies through trials designed by and for PWAs—and wasn't the achievement more important than the method employed? The "discussion" continued for weeks with Peter and Maxine Wolfe as chief protagonists, volleying a series of increasingly snarky open letters and memos via the back table. The knockout blow, however, would come from Mark Harrington who, on the occasion of ACT UP's fifth anniversary, disgorged two years of pent-up anger and withering analysis in an eight-page letter to the Floor.

Mark laid the blame for ACT UP's current "paralysis and division" squarely at the feet of Maxine and her "small but indefatigable" coterie, who demand a lockstep adherence to outdated strategies and "whose major form of activism seems to be interference with and criticism of other AIDS activists."[2]

> I believe that ACT UP would be far better off if Maxine Wolfe and those who share her views on appropriate political strategies expended their not inconsiderable talents on targets outside the AIDS movement.
>
> If ACT UP is not to become a parody of its original self, it must take its direction from people with HIV, and not from lifelong activists whose primary stake is in political agitation, and for whom specific issues come and go.[3]

By the time Maxine penned her response to Mark's letter, it was too late. Mark—and TAG—had left the building for good.

But the departure of the T+D "boys" was not the triumphant moment the left side of the Floor had anticipated. Although the internal enemy may have been vanquished, Strategies and Actions was unable to assume their expected leadership role within ACT UP due to the tactical excesses of some of their more ideologically dogmatic members. The tipping point came when an affinity group, led by Tracy Morgan, Heidi Dorow, and some of their more-radical-than-thou colleagues, handcuffed themselves to a group of community representatives who had ignored the activists' demands to walk out of a meeting with the CDC to protest the lack of representation for women and people of color with HIV/AIDS. While the cause was just, the tactic crossed an unacceptable line. Further, by targeting members of our own community—all of whom agreed with the demands for greater representation—rather than the federal officials responsible, the action suggested not just misplaced priorities, but a kind of unyielding zealotry that could threaten ACT UP itself.

So, with Strategies unable to provide ACT UP with a larger agenda, we needed to find some issue or project that could fill the growing vacuum at the center of the organization and keep us moving forward as we reconstituted ourselves.

While the rest of the group was consumed with internal conflicts, Michael Petrelis was once again focused on the approaching presidential campaign. Loud, impulsive, and—as he was the first to admit—obnoxious, Michael had a talent for publicity and, not coincidentally, self-promotion. As he had four years earlier, Michael once again came to the Floor in early December with a proposal to set up an outpost in New Hampshire in time for the season's first primary campaign. Although it was always a gamble to give Michael permission to wreak havoc in ACT UP's name, it was worth the $500 just to get him out of town while we tried to keep the organization from imploding. Besides, the issue was an important one, and there was little doubt Michael would be able to raise a stink on the campaign trail.

It took him less than a week.

Archconservative Patrick Buchanan was scheduled to announce his candidacy at a December 10 rally in Concord, New Hampshire. Buchanan, who had famously proclaimed AIDS "God's vengeance" against homosexuals, got only ninety seconds into his speech before Michael pulled out a handwritten sign and began shouting. He was immediately tackled and dragged out of the rally by two Buchanan campaign officials[4] who warned, "Every time you come here, this is what you are going to get. Tell your friends."[5]

So, Michael told his friends—his friends in the media.

He faxed, he called, he wrote press releases and gave interviews. Film of Michael's brutal ejection from the rally made the local news and was reported nationally. A week later, when interest began to flag, Michael pressed assault charges, and the story went national all over again.[6]

For his next media gambit, Michael announced he and a small team of local activists would be distributing condoms and AIDS information packets at Manchester Central High School. As he'd anticipated, the campaign press corps ate it up. The story was given additional oxygen when ultraconservative New Hampshire state senator Gordon Humphrey introduced a bill in the state legislature that would make high school condom distributions illegal.[7]

All the while, Michael continued to hound the candidates, Democrats and Republicans, supplementing his public disruptions with visits to campaign offices demanding to see their AIDS position papers. When staffers at Bush/Quayle headquarters explained the president's paper was not yet available, Michael exploded. "This epidemic is now in its second decade, and Bush has been in and around the White House for more than 10 years. If not yet, when?"[8]

But position papers would get us only so far. We needed the candidates to actually talk about AIDS.

In early January, Michael invested $200 to create a TV commercial denouncing the candidates' silence. As the camera panned Gran Fury's "Kissing Doesn't Kill" poster, a riff on the then-popular Benetton diversity ad, but featuring photos of lesbian, gay, and interracial straight couples kissing,* the announcer intoned:

> The issue is AIDS. AIDS is killing our friends, neighbors and lovers. Over 130,000 Americans have died from AIDS. Thousands of Granite State residents test positive for HIV. Scientists don't expect a cure before the end of the century, and yet all of the Presidential candidates remain silent about their plans to end the AIDS epidemic. Nothing is said about the way homophobia, racism and sexism harm efforts to control the spread of AIDS. Health care is a right. ACT UP, FIGHT BACK, FIGHT AIDS.[9]

After initially being accepted for airing by a local ABC affiliate, the ad was abruptly rejected by the nervous station management.

Once again, Michael took his case to the media.

"Station Pulls AIDS Ad," read the headline in the *Wall Street Journal*. "The AIDS Coalition to Unleash Power is charging a Manchester, N.H. network affiliate with censorship over a paid public issue ad that the station

---

*Julie Tulentino and Lola Flash, Mark Simpson and Jose Fidelino, and Heidi Dorow and Robert Vázquez-Pacheco, respectively.

refused to air because of 'sexually explicit visuals.'"[10] While the Associated Press reported, "The state's biggest television station is behaving homophobically by refusing to air commercials meant to force Presidential hopefuls to deal with AIDS, the activist group ACT UP said yesterday."[11]

By the time the commercial finally debuted on station WCSH-TV in Portland, Maine—in the hour preceding Bush's State of the Union Address, no less—the controversy had even made it into the Business Section of the *New York Times*. Twice.[12]

To close his New Hampshire offensive, Michael vowed to unleash "an unprecedented display of anger by people with AIDS, lesbians, gay men and our supporters"[13] on the final weekend of the primary campaign. His proposed "March for an End to AIDS and Health Care for All" immediately sent Manchester into a frenzy. The local Holiday Inn abruptly canceled ACT UP's meeting room reservation "due to the political nature of the group"[14]— which was ridiculous, since everything in Manchester primary week was of a political nature—while the local police force requested that ACT UP pay $500 for the expected police overtime.[15]

Michael threatened the Holiday Inn with the ACLU and told the police to stay home—we'd be happy to run the demonstration ourselves.

I agreed with Michael. The election was going to be the biggest news story of the year. If AIDS was ever going to make the leap from "special interest" to national issue—and if ACT UP wanted to remain a player in the national dialogue around AIDS—it was crucial we take a high-profile role in the upcoming campaign.

In late January, Jamie Bauer and I announced the formation of a new ACT UP committee to promote AIDS as a national issue during the presidential campaign. We called it "AIDS Campaign '92."

Our strategy was simple: we would organize a parallel campaign running AIDS as our "candidate" for national issue. We'd use all the traditional campaign trappings—buttons, posters, slogans, and commercials—and piggyback our campaign onto those of the candidates, treating their events as our own, and using the media they generated to promote our issues. We'd neither court nor seek insider status with the candidates, but instead confront them on their records and push them to develop and publicly discuss specific plans for ending the AIDS crisis.

And Michael's demonstration in Manchester would serve as the perfect kickoff action.

February 15, 1992: New Hampshire

Having settled into steady ACT UP coupledom, Joe and I spent our first Valentine's Day much as we had our first date—on another long holiday weekend in a small New England town, marching with several hundred of our closest friends.

"RACIST! SEXIST! ANTI-GAY! Pat Buchanan—GO AWAY!"

Earlier in the day, a handful of protesters had staged an impromptu kiss-in in front of Buchanan headquarters, taunting his volunteers with chants of *"We're HERE! We're QUEER! GET USED to It!"* Surprised by the activists' bravado, the Buchananites responded with stunned silence, save one middle-aged woman who approached the demonstrators and snarled, "If I had been your mother, I would have killed you in the cradle, faggot."[16] (I guess abortion is wrong, but infanticide is A-OK!) When we returned in numbers that afternoon, the campaign workers opted to watch our protest from the safety of their second-floor office.

The Clinton volunteers who rushed out to meet us were equally surprised to be greeted with chants of *"Sodomy Laws in Arkansas—WHERE WAS BILL?"* Kerrey and Harkin headquarters fared no better, though Jerry Brown, who had at least acknowledged AIDS by wearing a red AIDS ribbon when he crossed our path, was granted safe passage.

Bush/Quayle headquarters was not so lucky. Blowing past our police escort, we surrounded the campaign's locked and empty offices and pounded our stickers and handbills onto the pristine storefront window until the plate glass gave way. When the police pushed us back into the street, we dropped to the frozen ground for a mass die-in.

"HUNdreds of THOUsands DEAD from AIDS—WHERE IS GEORGE?"

Our brief walking tour complete, affinity group members piled into waiting cars and vans and took off to engage with the candidates at their final weekend rallies.

Although security forces had successfully weeded out most of the protesters attempting to crash the Bush rally in nearby Derry, they missed Frank

Smithson. Covered in Bush/Quayle buttons, Frank had ingratiated himself with a group of Bush supporters, cheering loudly when Arnold Schwarzenegger fag-bashed the Democratic candidates as "a bunch of girly-men."[17] But when the president began his speech, Frank dropped his disguise, unfurled his "**AIDS Bush Flag**" (the ol' Stars and Stripes, with skulls and crossbones replacing the stars), and began to shout. As Frank was dragged away, Bush shook his head and sighed, "Because of their tactics, they hurt their own cause."[18] It was the only time he referred to AIDS during the entire New Hampshire campaign.

While Frank was disrupting the Bush rally, members of Action Tours challenged Bob Kerrey at his Rivier College event, demanding to know why his vaunted national health care proposal didn't even mention AIDS. "Shame on you, shame on you for asking," the senator scolded, claiming the activists should be rallying to his side rather than fighting against him.[19] But later, away from the crowd, Kerrey admitted to the activists that he had more work to do and asked their assistance in forming an AIDS plan.

When activists confronted Bill Clinton during his Nashua rally, he immediately pivoted, responding that America had dealt with AIDS "the same way that it has done with every serious problem over the last 10 years, which is deny, deny, deny, maybe it will go away," adding, "If it weren't for the bad luck of the draw and the personal courage of Magic Johnson, the President of the United States would still not be uttering the word AIDS."[20] Clinton then promised, if elected, to promote an aggressive education program, expand the AIDS definition to include the opportunistic infections found in women and IV drug users, and implement the recommendations of the AIDS Commission.

It was by far the most comprehensive statement made by any candidate thus far, and further proof of the importance of our maintaining a constant presence throughout the campaign.

Instead of heading off to the rallies, Joe and I stayed behind in Manchester, conducting our own follow-up tour of the candidates' offices. With few exceptions, the campaign workers were polite and small-town cordial, eagerly supplying us with information and apologizing for the lack of AIDS-related literature.

By the time we finished our rounds, Elm Street was dark and deserted, save for the bands of young volunteers holding up their placards and shouting their candidate's name at the occasional passing car. Sometimes, they'd just yell at one another, cheering and booing as if the election were nothing more than a crosstown football rivalry.

Heading toward our car, we ran into a roving pack of clean-cut Buchanan volunteers patrolling the sidewalks, jeering and tearing down the other candidates' posters. Just then, a Buchanan campaign van adorned with decorative silver missiles turned the corner, gunned its motor, and roared down the block to the cheers and raised fists of the rowdy young men.

Quickening our pace, we crossed into Veterans Memorial Park, the site of our pre-action rally. Though the park was empty, we were not alone. Dangling from red ribbons, like forgotten Christmas tree ornaments, were the xeroxed photos of our dead friends and colleagues, haunting the park and, hopefully, the conscience of the candidates.

David

Despite his infusions, David's eyesight had continued to worsen. He tried intraocular shots injecting antiviral drugs directly into his eyeball, as well as an experimental surgical procedure that attempted to implant a small packet of DHPG to constantly bathe his eye in the drug—but nothing worked.

On March 3, David returned to Lenox Hill to get the dreaded Hickman catheter. A tube was inserted into David's body through an incision in his neck, and then tunneled through to a second incision site in his chest, where it was held in place by a subcutaneous cuff just below the skin. The top half of the tube was then inserted into his superior vena cava, to ensure the infused medication had a direct path into David's bloodstream.[21] Although the new catheter made infusions easier, it presented its own risk, as it was a frequent site of dangerous bacterial infections.

David never told me how he felt about the catheter or his rapidly diminishing eyesight, but neither did it stop him from doing the things he enjoyed. He went to movies with Eddie, who'd whisper descriptions of what was happening on screen, and Joe and I would occasionally join them both for late night dancing at the Roxy, where David's sunglasses gave him an unapproachable yet sexy look, even as they masked the increasing milky blankness of his eyes.

I was happy and relieved David had Eddie—solid, stalwart, and loving—a true angel in America. And no less than what David deserved.

We'd organized AIDS Campaign '92 with the understanding we'd need to be self-sufficient: able to generate posters, actions, and media and to run a successful campaign without depending on the active support of the larger organization. Fortunately, we were able to recruit a robust committee— workhorses, without attitude, including a number of the Marys, as well as an enthusiastic and dedicated collection of experienced hands and relative newbies fully committed to the work ahead of us.*

I knew from the outset the image I wanted for our campaign logo: a map of the United States with the word "AIDS" stretched across it. I sketched it out, wrote the words "WHAT ABOUT" above it, and handed it to Richard Deagle, who turned my scribbling into a bold red-and-white "**WHAT ABOUT AIDS**" poster that functioned as both an act of witness and a provocation prompting the candidates and media to talk about AIDS issues.

Thanks to the Marys' Target Bush contact list, we were able to distribute our posters to a network of ACT UPs and activist organizations across the country, ensuring the candidates would be confronted by the same signs and demands at every campaign stop. It wouldn't matter if our signs were held by one demonstrator or several dozen; the impact was the same, particularly when captured in a photo plastered on the front page of a local paper or a video on a local newscast. It reminded everyone that AIDS was not just an issue in the big coastal cities—it was a national crisis, affecting people across all fifty states. It also helped raise ACT UP's profile, giving the impression of a well-coordinated grassroots organization with national reach, even as we continued to reel from our own internal struggles.

We used the same AIDS map on our campaign buttons, posters, and stickers, bracketed with the words "CAMPAIGN '92" above and the phrase "VOTE AS IF YOUR LIFE DEPENDED ON IT" below. For our "campaign platform," we streamlined the Target Bush thirty-five-point Plan to End the AIDS Crisis into a twenty-five-point plan that served as both our list of demands and an educational tool to help raise the level of campaign discourse from vague promises of "more money for AIDS" into specific actions and proposals.

As AIDS Campaign '92 plotted in New York, Michael Petrelis and Frank Smithson, joined by a small coterie of like-minded activists from other cities,

---

*The core committee included Jamie Bauer, Ellen Bay, Andrea Benzacar, Jack Ben-Levi, David Binder, George Catravas, Joe Chiplock, BC Craig, Alexis Danzig, Naomi Danzig, Richard Deagle, Ron Goldberg, Barbara Hughes, Brownie Johnson, Esther Kaplan, Steven Keith, Barry Lapidus, James Learned, Noel Madlansacay, Barry Paddock, and Allen Payne, among others.

including Wayne Turner, Steven J. Smith, and Steve Michael, hit the campaign trail, following the candidates as they crisscrossed the country to South Dakota, Michigan, and Washington State. Renamed the ACT UP/Presidential Project, they generated media coverage by relying on the same tactics that had proved so successful in New Hampshire—confronting the candidates at their campaign events and distributing condoms at high schools.*

While the Democrats were at least willing to express their concern, the Bush administration chose to ignore those most affected by the disease, unveiling an AIDS education campaign that warned of the disease spreading in small towns, among teens and heterosexuals, but with no mention of condoms, safe sex, clean needles, or any other AIDS prevention techniques. When challenged, Assistant Secretary of Health James Mason explained "there are certain areas which, when goals of science collide with moral and ethical judgment, science has to take a time out."[22] A spokesperson from Mason's office put it more bluntly, "When you're fighting a fire, you control it from the outside and let the center burn."[23]

Pat Buchanan was even worse. For him, gays were not just kindling. They were the enemy. In late February, Buchanan unveiled a TV commercial using clips from *Tongues Untied*, Marlon Riggs's award-winning documentary about gay men of African descent—*a twofer!*—to attack George Bush for supporting "pornographic and blasphemous art" through the National Endowment for the Arts. The commercial combined the images of leather-clad black men joyfully dancing—*the horror!*—with an apocalyptic voice-over: "This so-called art has glorified homosexuality, exploited children, and perverted the images of Jesus Christ."[24] While this commercial was shown without incident throughout Georgia during the state primary campaign, Michael's AIDS commercial was again judged "too dicey" and "controversial" to be aired by Atlanta TV stations.[25]

---

*In a related gambit, Steve Michael would enter the Washington State primary as a Republican candidate for president, running on a platform of AIDS, Queer rights, choice, and health care reform. (Press release: Queer Campaign '92, "Queer Activist to Challenge Bush in Republican Primary," April 14, 1992.) Though the primary had no bearing on the nomination itself, it allowed him, as a candidate for federal office, to circumvent potential censorship issues and run AIDS education commercials promoting safe sex. ACT UP internal document: Solicitation Packet: Queer Campaign '92, May 4, 1992.

By mid-March and the run-up to the New York primary, the Democratic field had narrowed to just two candidates—Bill Clinton and Jerry Brown. The Republicans weren't even competing in New York, as the state party had successfully kept Buchanan off the ballot. Nonetheless, for three long weeks, New York would be the center of the political universe. The candidates, advisers, pundits, and national media were all going to be playing in ACT UP's backyard. And we would be ready.

AIDS would become a full-fledged campaign issue in New York or not at all.

Chapter 26

The In-Your-Face Primary

One HIV infection every minute
One AIDS death every 7 minutes
One presidential election every 4 years
Time to make the candidates talk about AIDS[1]

JOE CHIPLOCK DIDN'T look like an AIDS activist. A boyish blond in a sweater and Gap khakis, he appeared the perfect Young Republican standing in line at Bloomingdale's waiting for Marilyn Quayle to sign his copy of her new thriller, the provocatively titled *Embrace the Serpent*. Stepping up to the autograph table, Joe politely welcomed Mrs. Quayle to New York and announced he'd brought her a few gifts.

In rapid succession, he presented the vice president's wife with a CAM-PAIGN '92 button, a copy of ACT UP's twenty-five-point plan, and three condoms "for your son Tucker." Mrs. Quayle smiled wanly. "So," she asked, "do you want me to sign your book?" "Yes," he responded. "Please make it out to Larry Kramer for his tireless efforts in fighting the AIDS crisis on behalf of the hundreds of thousands that have died needlessly at the hands of this administration." Mrs. Quayle stopped writing. Joe prodded helpfully, "That's L-A-R-R . . ." before being whisked away by the Secret Service.

AIDS Campaign '92 was officially under way.

The following day, on March 19, Marty Robinson, hero of gay liberation, perfecter of the "zap," and founding member of the Gay Activist Alliance, the Lavender Hill Mob, and ACT UP, died at age forty-nine.

MARTY ROBINSON (1942–1992)
May his memory be for a blessing.

For the next three weeks, and sometimes several times a day, whenever a rally, fundraiser, or photo op was scheduled, AIDS Campaign '92 would issue a call to our pool of volunteers and zap the candidates. Fortunately, the events were well publicized and open to the public, the candidates generally accessible, and the media "spun-out" and starved for a little spontaneity. All we needed to make a big impression was a couple of people who were willing to shout and hold up a sign. Sometimes even a single person could make a zap newsworthy, particularly if that person was Bob Rafsky.

After a few years of relatively good health, Bob had recently developed Kaposi's sarcoma. The purplish lesions that sprouted on his legs and back, combined with the chemotherapy treatments required to keep them from growing, may have weakened him physically, but they served as a crucible for his anger, burning away any sense of doubt or equivocation.

On March 26, Bob skirted our small picket, kited a check for the required $100 donation, and disappeared into the crowd of young professionals assembled at the chic Laura Belle nightclub for a Bill Clinton fundraiser. Standing quietly near the front of the hall, Bob waited until the candidate launched into his stump speech before shouting:

> This is the center of the AIDS epidemic, what are you going to do? Are you going to start a war on AIDS? Are you going to just go on and ignore it? Are you going to declare war on AIDS? Are you going to put somebody in charge? Are you going to do more than you did as Governor of Arkansas? We're dying in this state. What are you going to do about AIDS?[2]

Clinton stopped his speech and peered into the audience, searching for his interlocutor. First, he tried to quiet Bob with a display of sympathy. "I know how it hurts," Clinton said. "I've got friends who've died of AIDS." But Bob gave him no quarter. "We're not dying of AIDS," he countered.

"We're dying from 11 years of government neglect." "That's why I'm running for President," Clinton chimed in to ringing applause.[3]

Assuming he'd won the debate, Clinton cued up his standard AIDS response. But it was not enough for Bob. "You're not dying of AIDS," he countered. "You're dying of ambition."[4]

Maybe it was just one too many activist interruptions, or the months of relentless questions about his purported extramarital affair with Gennifer Flowers, his draft record, and his "Slick Willie" persona. Or perhaps it was a planned "spontaneous response," crafted to allow the candidate to appear forceful and combative after his surprising loss to Jerry Brown in the Connecticut primary two days earlier. Whatever it was, Clinton exploded.

> If I were dying of ambition, I wouldn't have stood up here and put up with all this crap I've put up with for the last six months. I'm fighting to change this country. . . . I feel your pain, I feel your pain, but if you want to attack me personally you're no better than Jerry Brown and all the rest of these people who say whatever sounds good at the moment.[5]

The Clinton-Rafsky confrontation was the lead story on all the evening news programs, and footage of the exchange ran throughout the following day and into the weekend. Although most of the media accounts focused on the newly combative Clinton rather than AIDS, Bob's comments were widely reported. But while the confrontation may have played out positively for Clinton, it also presented a problem. Shouting down a gay man with AIDS would not sit well with New York's highly politicized gay community. Clinton would have to mend some fences before the primary campaign was over.

A week later, an opportunity unexpectedly presented itself.

On a cool Thursday night, Jamie Bauer and George Catravas had stationed themselves outside a fashionable brownstone on East Ninety-First Street, where Clinton was holding a private fundraiser. The candidate ignored their chants when he arrived, and again when he departed an hour later, brushing past them for a quick photo op with some kids playing across the street.

"Hey Bill!" shouted Jamie. "Why don't you come over and shake hands with an HIV-positive person?"

And with cameras from CNN and ABC's *Nightline* program whirring, Clinton came over, shook their hands, and asked what he could do to make people believe he cared about AIDS. George, who was Positive, told the candidate that he had to talk to the American people about AIDS at every campaign stop and in front of every audience. Clinton asked if they thought it would help if he made a speech about AIDS. They said it would. And in front of God and Ted Koppel, he said that's what he'd do.

Let the fence-mending begin.

United for AIDS Action (UAA) was David Barr's baby—a coalition made up of AIDS service, advocacy, and activist organizations, all working together to bring AIDS issues to the forefront of the presidential campaign. David was convinced the upcoming convention provided an ideal opportunity "to bring service providers into doing demonstration work,"[6] and for these disparate groups to embrace the commonality of their goals.

The idea was a logical outgrowth of David's own experiences in the AIDS community, where he held a kind of dual citizenship as both an HIV-positive treatment activist with ACT UP and TAG, and an "AIDS Professional," first as a lawyer working on AIDS discrimination, immigration, and confidentiality issues with Lambda Legal Defense Fund,[7] and now as assistant director of public policy at GMHC. It wasn't always easy to bridge the divide. In this instance, however, he'd managed to push GMHC to step outside of its usual service-oriented role and take the lead in organizing and sponsoring UAA and its proposed demonstration during the Democratic Convention in New York that summer.

I attended the first few UAA meetings as ACT UP's official representative, sharing our information about the candidates' AIDS platforms as well as our upcoming plans for AIDS Campaign '92. While appreciative of our efforts, it was clear UAA was going its own way. ACT UP, which was reflexively suspicious of GMHC and coalitions in general, had its own concerns about being reined in by too close an alliance with UAA. We decided it was best to step back, remaining part of the UAA coalition, but resigned to pursuing a less active role. We had plenty of members directly involved who could keep us informed, and besides, a confrontational ACT UP would only make it more attractive for the candidates to engage with UAA.

David and UAA had been working for weeks to arrange a meeting with Clinton and Brown, only to have both candidates cancel a promised appearance at the group's press conference announcing its plans for a march and rally during the convention. But then, a week after Clinton's confrontation with Bob and the day after Clinton's televised run-in with Jamie and George, I received an emergency fax announcing Clinton had agreed to a last-minute meeting with the UAA coalition late the following evening. Coincidence? Maybe.

But maybe not.

Although I desperately wanted to attend the meeting with Clinton, I first offered the invitation to Jamie. While I told myself it was because I felt I should step back to let a woman represent ACT UP, I think it was also tied to my continuing hesitancy about presenting myself as a leader.

For the most part, I'd always taken on roles that kept me at a slight remove—marshaling demonstrations, facilitating meetings, organizing actions—important, even vital, but just outside of full-throttle participation. And because of that, and because I was Negative and still daunted by the political savvy of some of my fellow activists, I felt unqualified to put myself forward as a representative of the organization.

But Campaign '92 was different. It was my idea and my strategy; the accumulation of everything I'd learned in my five years as an activist. I'd earned this opportunity and deserved to be at that meeting—so I called Jamie and asked if I could go instead. And Jamie, who was always a leader, shrugged and said, "Sure."

April 4, 1992: Meeting the Candidate

So, what does one wear to meet the potential future president?

The Nice Jewish Boy in me knew the right answer was a shirt and tie, but as I was representing ACT UP, I decided to go with a clean pair of jeans and a "Silence = Death" T-shirt. I wanted to make it clear that we pain-in-the-ass street radicals were part of this united AIDS community. If Clinton was serious about addressing AIDS issues, he would have to deal with us.

My wardrobe selection proved prescient.

With twenty-one UAA members in attendance and only a half-hour scheduled for our meeting, not everyone was going to have the opportunity to speak. We'd slashed our list of twenty-eight questions to less than a dozen and assigned them based on expertise and the communities represented. When I volunteered to talk about experimental drugs—an issue clearly in ACT UP's wheelhouse, if not mine—David Barr curtly replied the issue should be handled by someone who was HIV-positive.

Although he was absolutely right, his response still stung. What was I doing in that room, pretending to be an activist?

Thankfully, I got some of my activist mojo back when two gay members of Clinton's team, Bob Hattoy, his environmental adviser, and Marty Rouse, his New York gay liaison, both thanked me profusely for ACT UP's persistence in pressuring Clinton to address gay and AIDS issues—"We wouldn't be here otherwise."*

Our conversation was interrupted by a flurry of activity as the candidate walked through the door, surrounded by a group of familiar faces, including Congressman Barney Frank, longtime gay Friend-of-Bill David Mixner, and—surprise, surprise—Ann Northrup, who'd been drafted at the last minute to help Clinton prep for the meeting. Although he was hoarse and bleary-eyed, Clinton's presence galvanized the room.

Moving effortlessly down our informal reception line, Clinton smiled, shook hands, and exchanged brief pleasantries. But as he reached for my hand, his eyes fastened on my "Silence = Death" T-shirt. He then looked up and stared at me blankly, as if waiting for me to start shouting.

Mission accomplished. Presence duly noted.

After an uncomfortable photo op with the candidate, Barney Frank made a few introductory remarks about the historic nature of the event—the first ever sit-down meeting between a presidential candidate and members of the AIDS community. David Barr then introduced the coalition and presented Clinton with a few coins of the realm (condoms), which he received with practiced good humor.

The kabuki of the greeting ceremony completed; we began our presentations.[8]

Everyone was polite but insistent, stating their case without a hint of apology. Whether talking about the need for more drug treatment programs to stem the spread of AIDS among IV drug users, the way being homeless impacts people's access to health care, or how the CDC's AIDS definition prevents women from claiming disability benefits; it was clear, we *were* the experts. We laid out the facts, shared our personal experiences, and explained what needed to be done. The only question was whether the candidate would join us.

---

*Hattoy had participated in ACT UP's New Hampshire demonstration, admitting to a reporter, "Like all of them [the candidates], Bill's afraid to talk about AIDS. He's driven by what he reads in the polls. Maybe this will wake him up." Glenn Thrush, "ACT UP Storms New Hampshire in Prelude to Primary," *NYQ*, March 1, 1992.

Clinton listened intently and quickly warmed to the conversation. He seemed to understand AIDS was both a medical and political crisis, and that his job would be to find those political solutions. He vowed to use the "bully pulpit" of the presidency to speak out on AIDS issues and hoped that by giving AIDS a prominent place in his campaign, he could make it politically unacceptable for Bush to continue to ignore the crisis while he remained in office. He vowed to fully fund the Ryan White CARE Act,* providing "disaster relief" monies to the localities hardest hit by AIDS, and reiterated his promise to make an AIDS policy speech during the primary campaign. He also quickly agreed to have a PWA address the Democratic Convention.

Despite his apparent spontaneity, I assumed these promises had been prearranged and were being proffered as a goodwill gesture. I was more impressed when he said no; rejecting our suggestion to mandate the expansion of Medicaid to cover all people with HIV who meet income eligibility standards or resisting our call for single-payer health care. Though I was disappointed by his answers, it made the meeting feel more like a genuine discussion, and not just an opportunity to pander to a potential voting bloc.

What was most striking was Clinton's ability to engage—to listen to our issues, connect the dots, and thoughtfully respond. When a PWA recounted the cost of a single year of AIDS medications, Clinton suggested placing government-imposed price controls on the pharmaceutical industry. When someone referred to the early success of Mayor Dinkins's community clinic program, he proposed expanding the network of community health care clinics throughout the US by establishing a National Health Service Corps.

Clinton remained focused throughout, even as we pushed past the allotted thirty minutes and continued peppering him with questions. Asked about AIDS discrimination, he promised to abandon mandatory HIV testing for the Foreign Service and the Job Corps, though not as a prerequisite for military service. And while he vowed to change the current HIV restrictions on travel and immigration, he never clearly stated whether he'd lift the present ban.

When the meeting finally ended, the members of UAA moved downstairs for a sparsely attended press conference. The scheduling of the meeting for late Saturday night guaranteed there'd be no press coverage—it was too late for the Sunday papers, Monday belonged to the polls and

---

*The Ryan White Comprehensive AIDS Resources Emergency (CARE) Act, named in honor of the young PWA and passed by Congress in August 1990, established the largest federally funded AIDS care program in the country.

last-day-before-the-primary stories, and by the time the weeklies were published, the candidates would have moved on to the next campaign.

Nevertheless, the meeting represented an important victory, and I left the Sheraton impressed by Clinton—his intelligence and easy charm, his grasp of detail, and his obvious political skill. More importantly, I sensed he'd come to understand AIDS was an issue he could work to his political advantage and, as with most politicians, I trusted his political instincts far more than his personal convictions.

Less than thirty-six hours later, ACT UP was once again in the streets, marching from Clinton's headquarters at Forty-Seventh Street and Broadway through midtown and east to Madison Avenue for a CD arrest at Bush headquarters. If it felt a bit anticlimactic, it was largely because our campaign had already been such a smashing success. We'd pushed AIDS into the campaign spotlight, forced the candidates to make significant on-the-record promises, and helped pressure the presumptive Democratic nominee into holding a face-to-face meeting with community representatives, further promoting the notion of the "AIDS Community" as an important and powerful national constituency.

We'd also made a big impression on the media. "ACT UP Seizes the Moment,"[9] read the headline in *New York Newsday*, while the *Times* commented that a confrontation with ACT UP was "by now nearly a ritual of welcome in New York politics."[10] We'd proven ACT UP could still spark a story or create a spontaneous news event.

From now on, they'd be looking for us.

Chapter 27

III

Unconventional Behavior

THE DEMOCRATIC NATIONAL Committee was holding its party platform hearing in Cleveland on May 18 and Robert Rygor was going to be there.

Neither artistic nor an accomplished strategist or orator, Robert wasn't gifted in any of the ways that usually elevated members of ACT UP to leadership positions. But Robert was diligent and dedicated, and once he set his mind to doing something, it got done.

Robert had been devoted to the Democratic Party ever since the 1976 election. Two years later, he ran as the first openly gay candidate for the New York State Assembly. When he ran again in 1990, Robert discovered he had AIDS. He ended his campaign, joined ACT UP, and soon took on the thankless job of managing the ACT UP Workspace.*

In the spring of 1992, Robert had volunteered to help members navigate the application process to appear before the platform committee. When no one responded, he submitted his own application and secured a coveted speaking slot. After our committee declined his request to organize a support

---

*We'd moved into our new ACT UP Workspace in September 1990. Located on the tenth floor of 135 West Twenty-Ninth Street, the Workspace was a hive of activity from late morning—we were not an early-morning crowd—till very late at night, bustling with the business of the organization, everything from committee meetings and poster parties to individuals creating fact sheets and flyers on our thrillingly new computers, or members just stopping by to help or hang out, accompanied at all times by the constant whir and snap of our industrial-sized copy machine.

demonstration in Cleveland, Robert flew to Ohio and drafted members from ACT UP/Oberlin to carry one out in our place.

"I was one of you once," Robert told the platform committee. "I worked for this Party and supported this Party and all I thought it stood for. Now, I must ask that you—I must demand—that you listen to me, that you keep faith with me, that you show me that my beliefs in this Party and in this country . . . were not wrong."[1]

While it's impossible to say what impact Robert's words might have had on the committee, they certainly affected me. While I still supported our decision not to plan an action in Cleveland, I regretted my cursory dismissal of Robert's request. Everyone had a story that deserved to be told and listened to. As for the party platform, it would include the following:

> We must be united in declaring war on AIDS, implement the recommendations of the National Commission on AIDS and fully fund the Ryan White Care Act; provide targeted and honest prevention campaigns; combat HIV-related discrimination; make drug treatment available for all addicts who seek it; guarantee access to quality care; expand clinical trials for treatments and vaccines; and speed up the FDA drug approval process.[2]

Campaign '92 didn't spend much time focusing on the independent third-party candidate, Texas billionaire H. Ross Perot. But when the popular but undeclared candidate announced he was not only opposed to gays in the military but would also refuse to appoint any homosexuals to his cabinet, fearing they would become a "point of controversy with the American people,"[3] Steve Michael and the ACT UP/Presidential Project "declared war" on the Perot campaign.[4]

One month later, the battle was joined when Steve and a small band of demonstrators seized the stage in front of thousands of Perot supporters at the still undeclared candidate's July 3 campaign rally on the steps of the state capitol in Olympia, Washington. Since the Perot campaign had failed to get a permit to hold the rally, they didn't have the right to remove the protesters. Instead, Perot was forced to meet with Steve and the other demonstrators for twenty minutes and would agree to talk more positively about gay issues.

One week later, Perot would reverse his stand on gays in the military.[5] The following week, he halted his campaign completely.*

July 11–15, 1992: The Democratic National Convention

The second week of July, the eyes of the country turned once again to New York City, site of the 1992 Democratic National Convention. Our friends on the Left, including many of our own members, were eagerly hoping ACT UP would enact its own version of the 1968 Chicago riots, complete with anarchic demonstrations and queer-straight culture clashes. Certainly, the media was expecting a show.

But the idea of a giant yawp of anger seemed both impractical and counterproductive. We did not have the numbers to sustain a massive demonstration, and any likely coalition members were already committed to the United for AIDS Action rally on "AIDS Tuesday." Logistically, we knew we'd get nowhere near Madison Square Garden and would instead be relegated to protest pens blocks away from the convention site, our demonstrations devolving into standoffs with police, which would then become the story rather than the AIDS policies we were protesting.

Besides, how do you disrupt a circus?

Instead of focusing on large media-grabbing demonstrations, Campaign '92 decided to organize a series of smaller zaps targeting convention attendees. If we could get the delegates to see AIDS as a local issue directly affecting people in their own states, and then motivate them to take action when they returned home, we'd have accomplished a great deal, regardless of whether the media or our fellow travelers approved of our activities.

We selected a "dirty dozen" states with the worst AIDS records in the country—Arkansas, Colorado, Georgia, Illinois, Kentucky, Michigan, New Jersey, New York, North Carolina, Oregon, Tennessee, and Texas—and organized small affinity groups to zap their state delegation parties the night before the convention. Each state delegation got its own targeted fact sheet highlighting the key AIDS issues affecting that state and actions to be taken.

When we explained our plans to members of the Democratic gay caucus, we were swarmed by queer delegates eager to help us infiltrate their delegations. A group from Arizona, disappointed they'd not made the cut, asked for an ACT UP banner to smuggle inside the convention hall instead.

---

*Perot would return to the campaign on October 1 and participate in the three presidential debates, but never regained his earlier strength and functioned, at most, as a spoiler, earning 15 percent of the vote.

That evening, small bands of activists in delegate drag crashed parties all over town. Bill Dobbs and Jon Nalley, both Michigan natives, boarded the bus carrying their home delegation to a reception at the Museum of the Moving Image in Queens and passed out a homemade flyer, "A Queer Dozen Things Michigan Delegates Must Do in Michigan." Texas-born Scott Sawyer snuck into a lavish reception at the New York State Theater in Lincoln Center, commandeered the microphone, and lectured his fellow Texans about their draconian AIDS policies. Georgia's queer delegate caucus, six members strong,[6] cornered an uncomfortable Senator Sam Nunn aboard a chartered ferry circling Manhattan, confronting him over his AIDS record and homophobic comments about gays in the military.

There was, however, another highly influential group of people descending upon New York who we felt could also benefit from a little direct action—the national press corps. If we wanted to change the public discourse around AIDS, we'd have to educate both the politicians and the people reporting on them.

But while the police may have initially prevented us from crashing the big media welcome party at Bryant Park, the party soon came to us as reporters stopped by our "protest pen" to check out our demonstration. A few even slipped us their invitations and party passes, which we promptly copied at a nearby Kinko's.

Stashing our signs and stuffing our flyers into our bags, we casually strolled into the party and soon thereafter began leafleting the crowd. Our flyers featured an updated version of former Carter press secretary Jody Powell's list of "AIDS buzzwords" to be avoided. These included phrases like "bodily fluids" or "intimate sexual contact," which lacked specificity and confused people about the risk of infection, and terms like "general population" or "innocent victim" that further stigmatized people with AIDS.[7] This was not a question of "political correctness," but rather an attempt to show how language is not neutral and the use of certain terms can affect public perception.

On the back of the flyer was a multiple-choice quiz, highlighting often-misquoted facts and some tasty quotes from the president and his administration, ending with this final bonus question:

The next time I report a story on AIDS, I will . . .

 A. Just copy a government press release.

 B. Call my friendly pharmaceutical company press representative.

 C. Write a story promoting AIDS hysteria to sell newspapers.

 D. Consult with people with AIDS and their advocates.

Answer:

D. It is vital that the media learn to question government pronouncements about AIDS and consult with people who are on the front lines of the AIDS crisis.[8]

Here's hoping.

July 14, 1992: "AIDS Tuesday"

The UAA rally was never going to be ACT UP's kind of event. Although we'd agreed to limit our involvement solely to participating as a contingent, tensions persisted between the two groups, especially once Aldyn McKean was abruptly dismissed as UAA's chief organizer in late May. Depending on who you believed, Aldyn was either too closely tied to ACT UP to be able to divorce our needs from his responsibilities to UAA, or he was the victim of interorganizational jealousies over ACT UP and his being yet another gay White male in charge of a diverse coalition event.*

We even came close to withdrawing from UAA completely, when Bill Dobbs and Michael Petrelis attacked the entire UAA enterprise the week before the rally for its lack of confrontational activist edge. Why, they demanded to know, had UAA invited Mayor Dinkins to welcome the crowd? Given his disappointing AIDS record, ACT UP should demand his removal from the speakers' roster. Longtime ally Dennis Rivera, head of the hospital workers union, might be good on health care and AIDS, but he was anti-choice and a friend of the cardinal. Why was he being allowed to speak? And while Jesse Jackson may talk a great deal about the rainbow, he was not as vocal about AIDS. He, too, should go.

Their argument was yet another example of the bewildering activist calculus by which public officials had more to gain by being associated with us than we did by having them publicly promote our cause; or that maintaining our political purity and outsider status was more important than working in coalition with any organization or official with whom we agreed less than 100 percent of the time.

After a brutal discussion on the Floor, where the usual suspects got to fling their radical bona fides at us, we managed to defeat Bill's proposal to officially withdraw from UAA and, instead, agreed to petition for an activist

---

*According to David Barr, it was simply the result of a personality conflict between Aldyn and a key member of the GMHC event team. David Barr, conversation with the author, December 3, 2021.

speaker to be added to the rally lineup. We also voted against zapping Mayor Dinkins during his speech, as appropriate as it might have been under other circumstances, because it would likely be interpreted as an attack on UAA and could potentially be viewed along racial lines. Displeased with the outcome, Michael confronted me in the back of the room, calling me a "pansy," and sneering I should "stop trying to be such a nice little faggot."

It would be deeply gratifying to say that ACT UP's concerns about UAA were unfounded and that the event proved a great moment of unity and triumph for everyone; but while the UAA rally was widely covered and, with over 20,000 participants representing 425 organizations and communities from around the country,[9] by far the largest demonstration of the convention, ACT UP's participation proved a fiasco.

The afternoon began honestly enough, with the Anonymous Queers distributing yet another of their thoughtful, if provocatively titled, flyers, "Fuck the United AIDS Action. But Please Stay."[10] Acknowledging the importance of the event, they asked activists to "ACT UP, don't act out . . . stay, but when you get to the rally, change it." They begged for someone with AIDS to "storm the stage, grab the microphone and take it over," and cautioned those who were new to the fight—"now that it is okay to march *en masse*, wear red ribbons, produce star-studded prime time TV specials and devise party platforms about AIDS"—not to forget the epidemic's queer roots and the many sacrifices made by our community.

> The path to the future for straight HIV Positives has been paved over the bones, brains and guts of lesbians and gay men who have fought and died to provide them with hope. Shame on anyone, straight or gay, who forgets the brave queers who made it "safe" for us to be here today.[11]

Unfortunately, the day proved less "safe" than expected.

The police, in what felt like payback, isolated ACT UP from the rest of the marchers, diverting our contingent east onto Seventh Avenue as we approached Times Square, and penning us blocks away from the other groups. Hidden behind the TKTS booth, we couldn't see the stage or Jumbotron screens broadcasting the event, nor could anyone see us. After some tense negotiations, the police finally allowed us to begin moving closer, but then quickly slammed the barricades shut, splitting our contingent in two. When we demanded our group be reunited, they surrounded us with crash-helmeted, winter glove–wearing riot police.

As a further provocation, the cops ushered a group of Operation Rescue counterdemonstrators who'd been goading us with their photos of dead fetuses and shouts of "Faggots" and "Baby Killers" directly into our pen. When the inevitable fight broke out, the police violently hauled one of our members over the barricades and arrested him.[12] A handful of visiting activists from our Philadelphia chapter promptly took the bait and began taunting the police. When our marshals tried to defuse the situation, the visiting activists began hurling their abuse at us, yelling at the crowd to ignore the "good little gays" and take it to "the Pigs."

As we saw little advantage to our remaining and were concerned about having the entire group held hostage by a bunch of visiting anarchists looking for trouble (and a police force eager to give it to them), we decided to gather our posters and disband the "official" ACT UP contingent. People were welcome to stay as individuals—and thank you, Jamie Bauer° and the other committee members who agreed to remain and marshal "just in case"—but I was done.†

That night, Joe and I ordered in some Chinese take-out and watched the convention coverage from the air-conditioned calm of my bedroom. Although the "AIDS speeches" by Bob Hattoy and Elizabeth Glaser were deemed unworthy of network coverage, they'd be remembered as the emotional high

---

°Jamie et al. would have a busy afternoon, marshaling a breakaway group of two hundred protesters who marched out of the pens and attempted to reenter the rally further south, hoping to heckle Mayor Dinkins and Dennis Rivera, but were instead isolated on a side street, where their shouts and whistles disrupted a speech by Phyllis Sharpe, a Black PWA activist and ACT UP member, and were assumed to be a group of anti-AIDS demonstrators protesting the rally. Gregg Bordowitz, "By All Means Possible," *Village Voice*, July 28, 1992.

†I admit I still feel uneasy about my decision, wondering if, like the Costas at the CDC, I had abrogated my responsibilities as an organizer and abandoned my fellow demonstrators. On the other hand, at least we told everyone we were ending our official participation and, having reached the UAA rally, we had no further actions planned.

point of the convention. Hattoy, whom I'd met at our April UAA meeting with Clinton, spoke first.

> I am a gay man with AIDS and if there is any honor in having this disease, it's the honor of being part of the gay and lesbian community in America.
>
> We have watched our friends and lovers die, but we have not given up hope. Gay men and Lesbians created community health clinics, provided educational materials, opened food kitchens and held the hands of the dying in hospices. The Gay and Lesbian community is an American family in the best sense of the word.[13]

"We're a part of the American family," Hattoy continued. "And Mr. President, your family has AIDS."

> We're dying and you are doing nothing about it. Listen, I don't want to die . . . But I don't want to live in an America where the president sees me as the enemy. I can face dying because of a disease, but not because of politics.

Echoing our Campaign '92 message, he then exhorted America to "vote as if our life depends on it," ending his speech with a call to "ACT UP! FIGHT BACK! FIGHT AIDS!"[14]

The crowd, already standing, roared and picked up the chant, as TV cameras panned the convention floor awash with our "**What About AIDS**" signs and NGLTF's "**Lesbian and Gay Rights NOW**" posters. After years of banging on the door, trying to awaken our nation to the AIDS crisis and the value of our lives, we were finally inside the hall, not as protesters, but as speakers and delegates.

Elizabeth Glaser, who spoke next, had contracted AIDS through a blood transfusion she received during childbirth. Tragically, she'd passed the virus on to her daughter through breast milk and to her son in utero. "Exactly four years ago," she told the hushed crowd, "my daughter died of AIDS, she did not survive the Reagan Administration. I am here because my son and I may not survive four more years of leaders who say they care, but do nothing. I am in a race with the clock."[15]

> I started out just a mom fighting for the life of her child. But along the way I learned how unfair America can be today. Not just for people with HIV, but for many, many people—poor people, gay people, people of color, children. A strange spokesperson for such a group: a well-to-do white woman. But I have learned my lessons the

hard way, and I know that America has lost her path and is at risk for losing her soul.[16]

At the conclusion of her speech, the cameras once again scanned the convention floor, this time lingering on the tear-soaked faces of the delegates. Even the news commentators were, for a moment, unable to speak. Joe and I were wrecked. Maybe, just maybe, America had finally got the message.*

The following afternoon, ACT UP returned to Times Square for the free noontime "Broadway on Broadway" concert. Rather than disrupt the performance, we held up posters with enlarged photos of performers who had died from AIDS with a "**Not Appearing**" banner slapped across them, and on the reverse, the message "**Ribbons Are Not Enough—AIDS Action Now.**" We also distributed a leaflet detailing the tremendous losses sustained by theater and arts communities around the country, bordered by a painstakingly assembled list of over two hundred people from the entertainment industry who had died of AIDS—actors, writers, directors, designers, agents, publicists, and backstage personnel, the famous and the not-so-famous. The list included Mark Fotopoulos, and many other ACT UP members:

CHARLES BARBER, BRIAN DAMAGE, DENNIS KANE, DAVE LIEBHART, DONALD RUDDY, SCOTT SLUTSKY, DANIEL SOTOMAYER . . .
May their memories be for a blessing.

That evening Joe and I tuned in to watch the final coronation of Bill Clinton as the Democratic Party's candidate for president. Given the impact of UAA and the previous night's AIDS speeches, not to mention the ubiquity of the

---

*Elizabeth Glaser died on December 3, 1994, at age forty-seven. Bob Hattoy died on March 4, 2007, at age fifty-seven. *May their memories be for a blessing.* Glaser's son, Jake, is still alive.

112 out-and-proud lesbian and gay delegates, we couldn't wait to hear how Clinton would address our issues in his acceptance speech.

But when Ann Northrup scanned the press copy of the speech on the convention floor, she found no mention of gays or AIDS. As word spread, calls poured in to the Clinton people from delegations across the country, all pleading that, at the very least, Clinton should mention AIDS.[17]

In the end, wiser heads prevailed, and Clinton explicitly promised to implement the AIDS Commission recommendations and included "gays" on his laundry list of people that had been unfairly scapegoated by the Bush administration. But what this incident made clear, yet again, was that we'd need to stay on top of Clinton and his campaign right up to election day—and hopefully beyond—to make sure he followed through on his pretty promises.

August 17–22, 1992: The Republican National Convention

Whatever our problems with Clinton, UAA, or the NYPD, they paled in comparison to what lay in store for us the following month in Houston.

We'd long suspected lesbians and gays would be this year's "Willie Horton," the convicted killer whose furlough under Michael Dukakis had been cynically used by the Bush campaign to frighten White voters in a notoriously racist attack ad in 1988. This year, in place of lawless and violent Black men, American Civilization would be threatened by the specter of marauding gays spreading disease, flaunting their lifestyles, and demanding "special rights."

The Bush White House, forced by the unexpected popularity of the Buchanan campaign to make a hard right shift to shore up the party's conservative base, had been test-driving the heavily coded theme of "family values" since mid-May, when Vice President Dan Quayle attacked the popular sitcom character Murphy Brown as "mocking the importance of fathers" by choosing to have a baby as a single mother.* Quayle would later blame the "poverty of values" epitomized by Ms. Brown and encouraged by media elites for leading to "the breakdown of family structure, personal responsibility and social order" he claimed was responsible for Rodney King and the LA riots protesting police violence.[18]

The Bush campaign had conceded the party platform hearings to Buchanan's most rabid followers, who threw the leader of Republicans for Choice out of the hearing room and refused to allow gay Republicans to even address

---

*One can only imagine the outcry if Ms. Brown had instead followed in the footsteps of an earlier sitcom character, Maude Findlay, who chose to have an abortion.

the committee.* The resulting platform, the innocuously titled "The Vision Shared: Uniting Our Family, Our Country, Our World," supported a constitutional amendment banning abortion without exception; explicitly opposed civil rights protections for lesbians and gays, as well as any law recognizing same-sex marriages or allowing gay couples to adopt children or provide foster care; condemned the use of public funds to "subsidize obscenity and blasphemy masquerading as art"; and charged the Democratic Party with "waging a guerilla war against American values."[19] It further encouraged laws criminalizing the transmission of "the AIDS virus" and opposed the distribution of condoms and clean needles as AIDS prevention methods, advocating instead for AIDS education that promoted "marital fidelity, abstinence, and a drug-free lifestyle" as the best ways to curb the epidemic.[20]

None of this, however, prepared us for the virulence of the convention itself.

On the first night, Pat Buchanan stood on the stage of the Astrodome before an arena filled with frenzied delegates waving "**Family Rights Forever. Gay Rights Never**" signs and declared:

> There is a religious war going on in our country for the soul of America. It is a cultural war, as critical to the kind of nation we will one day be as was the Cold War itself. And in that struggle is the soul of America. Clinton & Clinton are on the other side, and George Bush is on our side.[21]

Things were even worse outside the Astrodome, where several hundred protesters were attacked by police on horseback and in full riot gear and driven into a dark, empty field where they were beaten, kicked, and clubbed.[22] Despite the many injuries—dozens were hurt and three protesters had to be hospitalized—and broadcast footage of a protester being violently knocked to the ground and set upon by cops, until a voice offscreen shouts, "Don't kick him when the lights are on,"[23] the local media largely supported the police over the demonstrators. Even after noting one activist was on crutches after being trampled by a horse and another suffered from blurred vision and vomiting after being clubbed in the head, the reporter from the *Houston Chronicle* assured her readers "none of the protestors . . . appeared seriously injured."[24] Meanwhile, the *Houston Post* heaved a sigh of relief: "The fracas

---

*There were only two out gay state delegates attending the convention, and the Log Cabin Republicans were not even allowed to host a welcome table inside the convention hall.

fell short of what the police dreaded most, a violent confrontation with hundreds of activists who could have been HIV positive."[25]

Clashes with convention delegates were just as dangerous as those with police, and the repercussions far more serious. When a small affinity group in "flawless Christian drag"[26] disrupted a speech by Jerry Falwell at a gathering of the Christian Action Network, they were brutally attacked by the good Christian delegates, who continued their beatings even as police dragged the activists away.[27] Three of the arrestees from ACT UP/New York were then held in jail for several days on trumped-up charges. James Learned, who'd been violently tackled by Falwell's son, was charged with resisting arrest and assault. Kim Edwards, who was African American, was charged with narcotics possession thanks to a loose yellow pill found in her purse, separated from the others, and transported to a jail several miles away. When the offending pill turned out to be an over-the-counter allergy medication, the drug charges were dropped and replaced with an equally false claim of assaulting a prison guard. While in custody, Kim was subjected to verbal abuse and strip searches, as well as regular questioning about her HIV status. "We are AIDS activists," she replied. "We are all living with AIDS."[28]

Things were even worse for Scott Sawyer, who was charged with aggravated assault and accused of biting an officer. When he, too, refused to reveal his HIV status, the police got a court order forcing him to take the test against his will. Even though the charges were false, Scott knew when his test results came back Positive, as he knew they would, he could quite possibly be facing attempted murder charges.*

For hours after their arrest, no one in Houston or New York knew the activists' whereabouts. The police refused to tell anyone where they were being held, what the charges were, or the amount of their bail. It wasn't until James used his one collect call to contact the ACT UP Workspace that we could even confirm they'd been arrested. We immediately hit the phones, calling our lawyers, contacting the press and the national gay organizations, reaching out to friends and relatives, and gathering the names and credit card numbers of people with high cash advance limits so we could wire money down to Houston once bail was set. The latter proved more complicated than expected, as Texas authorities kept changing the bail amounts,

---

*Texas had already convicted an HIV-positive inmate of attempted murder for just spitting at a prison guard.

each time demanding the exact payment through a bail bondsman, and keeping our friends incarcerated for days longer than expected.*

Wednesday night's convention theme was once again "family values," this time as defined by Pat Robertson, who praised Bush and the Republican Party as defenders of "God, strong families, freedom, individual initiative, and free enterprise," and castigated the Democrats as "carrier[s]" of "an insidious plague."[29]

The lone dissonant grace note came from Mary Fisher, a mother with AIDS and the daughter of a prominent Republican fundraiser, who'd been selected to give the Republican version of Elizabeth Glaser's PWA speech. Fisher seized her moment, challenging the delegates and the Republican Party to "set aside prejudice and politics to make room for compassion and sound policy."

> Tonight I represent an AIDS community whose members have been reluctantly drafted from every segment of American society. Though I am white and a mother, I am one with a black infant struggling with tubes in a Philadelphia hospital. Though I am female and contracted this disease in marriage and enjoy the warm support of my family, I am one with the lonely gay man sheltering a flickering candle from the cold wind of his family's rejection. . . . We may take refuge in our stereotypes but we cannot hide there long. Because HIV asks only one thing of those it attacks: Are you human?[30]

When the delegates rose to give Fisher a tearful standing ovation, it almost seemed possible to believe this woman had succeeded where hundreds of thousands of dead had failed. Maybe, even here, compassion would win out over hate.

But no sooner had Mary Fisher left the stage than actor Gerald McRainey, TV's "Major Dad," stepped to the podium and whined about his suffering with a deviated septum. Then on stormed Marilyn Quayle to reignite the Kulturkampf, declaring not everyone in her generation "demonstrated, dropped out, took drugs, joined in the sexual revolution or dodged the draft"[31] and that she'd gladly given up her job to take care of her family, because "most women do not wish to be liberated from their essential natures as women."[32]

---

*Kim Edwards was held for over forty-eight hours as we attempted to round up her $4,000 bail for a misdemeanor with a maximum fine of $500. It wasn't until she was released that she was informed of the second trumped-up charge of assaulting a jail attendant. Richard Brown, "ACT UP Interrupts Falwell," *Body Positive*, October 1992.

The evening mercifully came to a close with the entire Bush clan—children and grandchildren, nieces and nephews—assembling onstage and waving to the cheering crowds. And what music was chosen to accompany this picture of American Family Values? "The Best of Times Is Now" from *La Cage aux Folles,* a Broadway musical celebrating drag queens and the long-term "marriage" of two gay men.

Maybe there were gay Republicans at the convention after all.

David(s)

That weekend, Joe and I retreated to Fire Island for a much-needed vacation. While I'd always loved my occasional guest weekends on Fire Island, this summer marked my first summer share. I'd joined a house organized by David E. Kirschenbaum, ACT UP's former treasurer (and a brief romantic partner), and his lover, Gary Clare. But just before the season began, David E. unexpectedly became ill, even though it was Gary, not David, who had tested positive. But when David began having night sweats and severe diarrhea and rapidly losing weight, he was retested and diagnosed with full-blown AIDS, while Gary remained in relatively good health.

With David E. only well enough to come out to the house a few times that summer, Gary and my house-share roommate, Chris, generously offered to room together whenever David E. remained in town, allowing Joe to come out and stay with me. The other housemates were mostly AIDS and gay community activists, and we quickly became family—eating and preparing meals, setting up camp on the beach, and then skipping off to Tea (predinner cocktails), the bars, and most social activities together.

When a bedroom became available midweek during our August vacation, Joe and I invited David Serko and Eddie to join us for a couple of days. It would be the first time David and I had been on Fire Island together since our first trip to The Pines, almost ten years earlier. I assumed it would be our last.

After a yearlong struggle, David was completely blind. Being David, he took it as a challenge, enrolling in classes at the Lighthouse to learn how to read Braille and navigate the streets using a cane. Much to everyone's surprise, David had also become more spiritual, if not quite religious. He'd been befriended by the priest at his neighborhood church and made himself a favorite with the local women who volunteered there. I wasn't quite sure how David was squaring the circle with religion and being gay, but it didn't appear to be a problem with this particular priest or parish.

Even though David was on another path—living uptown, centering his life on his health and Eddie—I never felt left behind. We were still connected, and we'd learned to adjust to our changing circumstances. But in my eagerness to get David out to the beach one last time, I hadn't taken into account how grueling the trip would be. David arrived weak and haggard, his frailty and unsteadiness thrown into even greater relief by his unfamiliarity with his surroundings.

In my denial, or perhaps willful unknowing, I hadn't thought through any special accommodations that might be necessary or considered how his energy level might not be up to our usual Fire Island schedule of full beach days, late afternoon cocktails, and later dinners. To make matters worse, our house was not air-conditioned, the common rooms were up a flight of stairs, and we had no pool or an umbrellaed deck to lounge around once the beach and its uneven terrain proved impossible for David to navigate.

Despite my good intentions, the trip was a disaster, and David and Eddie left as soon as David was strong enough to make the journey home.

Chapter 28

▪▪▪

Vote as If Your Life
Depended on It

FOR THE BUSH campaign, the 1992 Republican National Convention had also proved a disaster. Unlike the Democrats, who'd seen a big postconvention bump following their exuberant, forward-looking convention, moderate and independent voters had been turned off by the angry rhetoric in Houston. Instead of using the convention to tack to the center for the general election, the president now found himself shackled to Pat Buchanan and the rabid right wing of the Republican Party.

ACT UP, recharged by the events in Houston, went after Bush and the Republicans with a fierce and reawakened purpose. When the president descended on New York to raise much-needed funds, we marched against him in the streets, chained ourselves to the doors of his campaign headquarters, and serenaded his private fundraising dinners, chanting: *"1-2-3-4: WHAT are FA-mily Values FOR? 5-6-7-8: Discrimin-A-tion, Fear, and HATE!"*

We were not alone in expressing our displeasure. On September 26, Magic Johnson announced he was quitting the AIDS Commission due to the Bush administration's "lack of support and even opposition" to the commission's recommendations. "I cannot in good conscience continue to serve on a commission whose important work is so utterly ignored by your Administration."[1]

But that didn't mean we were giving Bill Clinton a free pass.

Ever since the New York primary, we'd been patiently waiting for Clinton to deliver his promised AIDS policy speech. In May, he'd made a historic speech at a gay fundraiser in LA, welcoming our community and our issues into the mainstream of American politics. "I have a vision and you are a part of it," he proclaimed, restating his commitment to fighting AIDS and thanking us for our "courage," "commitment," and "service in the face of the terror of AIDS. . . . The nation owes you a debt of thanks for that, and I want to give you my thanks and respect for that struggle today."[2] Powerful stuff, but not the promised policy speech.

Friends inside the campaign reported Clinton was being advised to forget about the speech entirely. (The argument, I suspect, was that he'd already done his AIDS and gay thing, and given the competition, there was no reason to risk making a potentially controversial speech to shore up this particular constituency.) They asked us to apply a little outside pressure.

We began with a simple flyer faxed to his campaign offices asking, "Where's Clinton's AIDS Speech?" We then leafleted his fundraising events, distributing "An Open Letter to Governor Clinton" listing the candidate's many promises and asking about the speech and why, as a self-proclaimed gay ally, he'd remained silent about Republican gay bashing and declined to comment about Oregon's antigay Proposition 9 when he campaigned in Portland.*

> Governor Clinton, these are more than political issues. These are matters of life and death. **We will not stand silently by as our lives and our rights are sacrificed for the sake of political expediency.** We ask you to live up to your promises. We ask that you take a stand against hatred and ignorance and bigotry. We demand that you speak out about AIDS and homophobia.[3]

Soon another question loomed: Would Clinton visit the AIDS Quilt when it returned to Washington in October?

When the Quilt was first displayed in 1987, there were 1,920 panels; now, there were over 20,000.† While neither Reagan nor Bush had ever paid his

---

*Prop 9 would have prohibited the state from recognizing "sexual orientation" or "sexual preference" as a category deserving of minority status or civil rights; prevented the government from using monies or properties to "promote, encourage, or facilitate homosexuality, pedophilia, sadism or masochism" (nice grouping); and further required the government, including the public education system, to "assist in setting a standard for Oregon's youth that recognizes [these behaviors] as abnormal, wrong, unnatural, and perverse and to be discouraged and avoided." "1992 Oregon Ballot Measure 9," Wikipedia, last edited July 11, 2021, https://en.wikipedia.org /wiki/1992_Oregon_Ballot_Measure_9#cite_note-6, citing *Oregon Voters' Pamphlet*, November 3, 1992 (archived at the Benton County Elections website, https://www.co.benton.or.us/sites /default/files/fileattachments/elections/archive/3311/e92g_svp.pdf).

†As of 2022, the Quilt currently weighs over 54 tons, with approximately 50,000 panels, representing more than 110,000 individuals. "The History of the Quilt," National Aids Memorial, viewed April 6, 2022, https://www.aidsmemorial.org/quilt-history.

respects, for Clinton—whether as a smart campaign move or just because it was the right thing to do—it seemed a no-brainer. Many of his gay advisers agreed, and they once again asked us to provide some extra pressure.*

We created another fax flyer, this one featuring a mock *New York Times* front-page story with the screaming headline: "AIDS Activists Disrupt Clinton Press Conference—No-Show at AIDS Quilt Was 'Last Straw.'" The article described how activists, already angry with Clinton for failing to deliver his promised AIDS speech and now furious over his decision to forgo visiting the Quilt, were going to abandon their polite behind-the-scenes lobbying efforts and pursue a more aggressive strategy.

Despite our efforts, Clinton did not visit the Quilt, and instead sent Tipper Gore, the wife of vice presidential candidate Al Gore, to represent the ticket. Not that we cared that much about the Quilt. We had our own ideas of how to turn grief into action.

David Robinson, he of the dangling earrings, miniskirt, and ear-to-ear smile, had returned to ACT UP from San Francisco and announced he was planning to bring the ashes of his recently deceased lover, Warren Pierce, to Washington on the weekend of the October Quilt display and throw them onto the White House lawn. Did anyone want to join him?

On Sunday, October 11, ACT UP assembled at the foot of the Capitol and set off on a solemn march to the White House. At the front of the procession were over a dozen mourners carrying boxes, bottles, urns, and plastic bags filled with the cremated remains of friends, lovers, and family members. As a small corps of drummers beat out taps, the procession filed past the Quilt display chanting, *"Bringing the DEAD To Your DOOR! WE won't TAKE It ANY-MORE!"* gaining hundreds of new members as they marched by.

When they reached the White House, the mourners, protected by a moving wedge of activists, stormed the gates. Some angrily hurled their bags of ashes and bone chips over the White House fence, the contents exploding as they hit the ground; others climbed the wrought-iron fence and shook the ashes free, while still others flung what remained of their loved ones onto the lawn by the fistful. Clouds of gray and chalk-white dust

---

*ACT UP wasn't alone in pressuring Clinton to make his promised speech and visit the Quilt. UAA and other gay and AIDS groups were writing letters and using back-channel connections to persuade the candidate as well.

swirled around the demonstrators, getting in their mouths and muddying their tear-stained faces, as sounds of grief and keening filled the air.

The police tried to disperse the crowd by pushing in on horseback, but the protesters, remembering their CD training, bravely sat down in front of the advancing horses, knowing the animals wouldn't step where there was no open space.

What the mounted police couldn't accomplish, the darkening skies soon would. And as the protesters scattered, heaven wept.

WARREN PIERCE (1954–1992)
May his memory be for a blessing.

Joe and I weren't in Washington for the Ashes Action. Physically exhausted and emotionally spent, we instead took a final restorative weekend on the beach. Though we desperately needed the downtime, I soon regretted not pushing myself to make the trip. The following Monday night, many of the newer members spoke of the Ashes Action with reverent awe, a tone I recognized from years ago and my own early ACT UP experiences. The action itself had been organized not by one of the older hands, but by a recent recruit, a twenty-two-year-old classics major from Columbia University named Shane Butler. Older members, their voices catching, expressed both relief and gratitude that the torch of AIDS activism had been passed to this new generation, who'd be able to carry on until the battle against AIDS was finally won.

Astonishingly, the Ashes Action received very little press coverage, though AIDS got an unexpected callout at that weekend's presidential debate, when one of the moderators, noting the "tens of thousands of people [who had] paraded past the White House to demonstrate their concern about the disease AIDS" and the recent resignation of Magic Johnson, asked the president, "Where is this widespread feeling coming from that your Administration is not doing enough about AIDS?"

Bush blamed ACT UP.

And the other thing is part of AIDS—it's one of the few diseases where behavior matters. And I once called on somebody, "Well, change your behavior. Is the behavior you're using prone to cause AIDS? Change the behavior." Next thing I know, one of these ACT UP groups is out saying, "Bush should change his behavior. . . ." You can't talk about it rationally. The extremes are hurting the AIDS cause.[4]

Unlike Dukakis, who'd greeted a similar question four years earlier by agreeing with Bush that everything possible was already being done, Clinton proposed a different direction for this country's AIDS policy. No, it wasn't his AIDS speech, or even a turning point in the debate, but at least it was public acknowledgment the current policy wasn't working, and he wouldn't be afraid to change it.

It would take another three weeks for Clinton to finally give his long-promised speech. "[AIDS] is not vengeance or punishment or just deserts," he told his Jersey City audience. "It is an illness." His voice hoarse and failing, Clinton reiterated his earlier campaign promises and pledged that if he was elected, "no one will have to wage this fight alone."[5]

Many found Clinton's speech powerful and moving. Certainly, the media seemed to believe this was a brave and politically risky speech for the candidate to make so close to election day. But I was less impressed with what he said than the fact he'd made the speech at all. And what that said about the newfound clout of the gay and AIDS communities.

Two days later I received one of those all too familiar phone calls. Mark Fisher had died.

Mark was not an ACT UP "star," but one of the several dozen who for years had showed up every week and done the work. He'd acted as support for the Department of Health affinity group when they took over Stephen Joseph's office in 1988 and joined Wave 3 when they blocked traffic during Wall Street II. And just last year, he'd played an essential role helping the Marys plan and organize the Target Bush demonstrations in Kennebunkport and Washington.

But Mark's final protest was still to come.

For close to a year, the Marys had been actively exploring political funerals. They'd researched the restrictions on the public display of a dead body, the policies of funeral homes, and the formalities of last wills and testaments. Calling themselves the Stumpf/Kane Project, after John Stumpf and Dennis Kane, two recently deceased members of their affinity group, they'd placed ads and written articles soliciting PWAs who might be interested in having a political funeral.

Mark had recently written an article called "Bury Me Furiously," in which he invoked the late David Wojnarowicz's call to dump the lifeless bodies of friends and loved ones on the White House steps[6] to explain his own wishes for a political funeral.*

> I want to show the reality of my death, to display my body in public; I want the public to bear witness. We are not just spiraling statistics; we are people who have purpose, who have lovers, friends and families. . . . I want my death to be as strong a statement as my life continues to be. I want my own funeral to be fierce and defiant, to make the public statement that my death from AIDS is a form of political assassination.[7]

But no one had expected Mark to be the first.

By the rapidly shifting standards of PWA health, Mark had been in relatively good shape, and had taken a long-planned vacation with his close friend and Wave 3 colleague, Russell Pritchard. When Mark suddenly became ill in southern Italy, Russell rushed him back to the States, but Mark died in the air twenty minutes before his plane landed at JFK, with Russell sitting beside him, holding his hand.[8]

Four days after his death, on an appropriately cold and rainy Monday afternoon, over two hundred mourners gathered at Judson Memorial Church to say good-bye and to honor Mark's final wishes. After a brief memorial service, we assembled behind a stark black banner that read "**Mark Lowe Fisher 1953–1992 Dead From AIDS**" and waited for the six pallbearers shouldering Mark's open coffin to take their place at the front of the procession.

"MARK FISHER—DEAD from AIDS! WHERE IS GEORGE?"

The police wisely kept their distance as we took to the street, snaking around Washington Square Park and then onto Sixth Avenue, annexing two lanes of traffic as we marched Mark's body the thirty-five blocks uptown to Bush/Quayle headquarters. Maybe it was the weather, or perhaps our shrouding of the open coffin with umbrellas, but I was surprised by the lack of response or even curiosity from people on the street. Perhaps they assumed

---

*The Marys had previously honored David's wishes by organizing a memorial march in the East Village on July 29, 1992, shortly after his death. They then scattered his ashes on the White House lawn as part of ACT UP's Ashes Action.

we were carrying an empty coffin, or one containing a mannequin or stuffed dummy. People didn't go carting dead bodies around the streets of New York. At least not yet.

When we arrived at Bush/Quayle headquarters, the police closed off 43rd Street to traffic and lined up in front of the building to protect it from invasion. We transferred Mark and his coffin onto a gurney and draped him with our National Plan to End the AIDS Crisis—the same banner we'd taken to Kennebunkport. Last year we'd delivered it with a die-in. This year, with the body of our dead friend.

Though several people spoke, it was Bob Rafsky who gave full expression to both our sorrow and our anger.

Let everyone here know this is not a political funeral for Mark Fisher. Mark wouldn't let us burn or bury his courage and his love for us, any more than he would let the earth take his body until it was already in flight. He asked for this ceremony not so we could bury him, but so we could celebrate his undying anger. . . .

George Bush, we believe you'll be defeated tomorrow, because we believe there's still some justice left in the universe and some compassion left in the American people. But whether or not you are, here and now, standing by Mark's body, we put this curse on you: Mark's spirit will haunt you until the end of your days and in the moment of your death, you'll remember our deaths.[9]

Five years earlier, at my first ACT UP meeting, we'd rejected the idea of coffins and a reliance on death imagery as contrary to our message of PWA empowerment and people living with—not dying from—AIDS. Since then, we'd held hundreds of die-ins, hoisted cardboard tombstones at the FDA, and carted empty coffins through the streets during Day of Desperation. Now, within just three weeks' time, we'd hurled ashes at the White House and carried a dead body through midtown Manhattan.

How many more have to die?

MARK LOWE FISHER (1953–1992)
May his memory be for a blessing

November 3, 1992: Election Night

ACT UP had organized an election night party to watch the results and collectively hold our breath. The final polls had been promising and there was a strange excitement in the air, cautiously defined as "hope." However, like most good Democrats, I never underestimated our ability to snatch defeat from the jaws of victory.

Before heading over to Mr. Fuji's Tropicana for the evening's festivities, Joe and I stopped off to see our Fire Island housemates, Gary Clare and David E. Kirschenbaum. David had been in and out of St. Luke's-Roosevelt throughout the summer and fall. Even though I'd visited him in the hospital—frequently skipping across the hall to see Tim Bailey, another ACT UP friend—I was shaken by his appearance. Always skinny, David was now a living skeleton, a *Muselmann* out of my childhood nightmares. While we tried to keep the conversation light, all I wanted to do was run screaming from their apartment. David Serko may have lost his eyesight, but at least he still looked, acted, and functioned like himself. This David could barely get out of his chair and was in almost constant pain, unable to stop his body from consuming itself. I didn't know how he or Gary could stand it.

Things were much cheerier at Mr. Fuji's. There was a bar—*thank god!*—and a DJ and dance floor, but everyone was glued to the video screens, watching the results and greeting each new projected winner with shouts and screams as the electoral map turned to Clinton blue. Familiar, long-absent faces soon joined the crowd—Larry, Peter, Mark, Spencer, David Barr. It was the kind of night you wanted to share with family.

By 10:30, people were standing on chairs and sitting atop one another's shoulders. Just before 11 p.m., when the networks finally projected Bill Clinton the winner, chants of *"ACT UP! Fight BACK! FIGHT AIDS!"* filled the club, followed by shouts of *"BARbara: PACK the CHIna!"* It'd been a long time since I'd seen ACT UP so gleeful.

When Clinton appeared to make his acceptance speech, the room went silent. "My fellow Americans," he began, "on this day, with high hopes and brave hearts, in massive numbers, the American people have voted to make a new beginning."

> This election is a clarion call for our country to face the challenges of the end of the Cold War and the beginning of the next century, to restore growth to our country and opportunity to our people, to empower our own people so that they can take more responsibility for their own lives, to face problems too long ignored, from AIDS to the environment . . .[10]

I don't recall another word of his speech.

"AIDS." Without prompting from a disruptive activist or a well-placed sign. "AIDS." After years of begging for a president to even say the word, now we'd have one who said the word willingly to an entire nation. "AIDS." Not as a gay issue or a special interest, but as a national issue.

We'd waited so long for this moment. And even though I knew it was just one word, the first in a laundry list of problems, no doubt recited in alphabetical order, but I'd never felt so proud of anything in my entire life.

Four days later, David Serko checked back into Lenox Hill for the last time.

David

Like most of the AIDS floors I'd visited, the eighth floor of Lenox Hill had a particularly warm and familial feel—the rules more lax, the atmosphere more casual. People came and went as they pleased, staying long past visiting hours or even overnight, bringing in all sorts of food and treats with few restrictions. So, I was shocked when I was told by the attending nurse that before I could visit with David, I had to first put on a mask and gown. Who was responsible for these dehumanizing instructions? AIDS was not contagious, and I refused to suit up and make my friend feel like he was hazardous waste.

What I'd failed to understand in my righteous indignation was that this was not about protecting us from David, but rather protecting David, whose T-cell count might as well have been in negative numbers, from us.

Everyone, including David, knew this would be his final stay in hospital. David's family had come in—his parents from upstate, along with his older sister, Shirley, and her husband, and his two brothers, Peter, the oldest, and Jeff. David was particularly close to Peter, who'd been the first person David had told when he tested positive back in 1988. Peter had flown in from Seattle and was committed to staying in town for as long as necessary.

I was now working full-time as a legal secretary and would subway up to Lenox Hill every few days after work to visit for a couple of hours. Late one afternoon I stopped by just after the doctor had given David some sort of Demerol/morphine drip to make him more comfortable. Though David was feeling no pain, he was, he admitted, feeling a little dizzy. When the doctor asked him to describe what it felt like, David stopped for a moment and then answered sheepishly, "Well, this is going to sound really queer, but it's kinda like the beginning of *Family Affair*."

I burst out laughing, as did David, while the doctor and David's mom looked at us as if we'd lost our minds. As soon as I was able to catch my breath, I offered to translate: "He means that it's like a kaleidoscope, just like in the opening credits of the old TV show . . . you know . . . with Buffy, Jody, and Mr. French . . ." Not that my explanation made anything any clearer, other than David was, somehow, still David.

During one of my last visits, long after we'd dispensed with the gowns and masks, David waved me over to sit on the bed next to him. He had, he said, a favor to ask.

Would I be willing to write his obituary?

The favor, as David probably knew, was really a gift. It was his way of acknowledging the importance of our relationship. I was not family, his best friend, or his lover, but I had a place and he'd given me something important to do. Even as his life was ending, he went out of his way to take care of me, to make sure I felt special and valued. I was profoundly moved, and I remain, to this day, in awe of his grace and generosity.

As the vicissitudes of the calendar and the New York rental market would have it, at the same time as David's health was deteriorating, I was packing up my apartment after twelve years and moving into a new apartment with Joe.

After a year together, our relationship was surprisingly easy. We genuinely enjoyed each other's company and had great fun together, whether going to the theater or a museum, eating take-out and watching TV, or just relaxing on the beach collecting sea glass. Besides, having already been through so much together—the hospital visits, demonstrations, and deaths—we agreed on what was important and knew we could depend on each other when things really got rough, as we knew they would. And if we needed a further sign, both our leases were up on December 1, my birthday.*

Our plan had been to move during the weekend of November 21, so we'd be able to unpack and get settled over the Thanksgiving holiday. But as we were unloading the final boxes from Joe's apartment late Saturday morning, the phone rang.

David was going off his meds. It was time.

The eighth floor was packed with people. Everyone was stopping in to say good-bye—even the doctors and nurses were getting weepy. When it was my turn, I sat down on David's bed, gave him a hug and stroked his arm, which was unencumbered by needles and IV lines for the first time in weeks. He asked me how the move was going—*how the fuck could he even remember this?*—and wanted me to describe our new apartment.

It was not a complicated good-bye. There was nothing left unsaid or undone, nothing that needed to be explained. I told him he wasn't rid of me yet and took up residence in the hallway with Eddie and David's family, comforting friends who may not have seen David quite so recently or were dealing with their first death of a friend.

At dinnertime, when David's folks went down to the cafeteria for a break, a few of us piled back into David's room to hang out together one last time. The conversation was fast and furious, filled, as always, with movie and TV quotes. Though not participating, David seemed to enjoy the banter. We then said our "love-yous" and "see-you-tomorrows" and left.

I returned to the hospital Sunday morning. Even though David was barely conscious, I couldn't imagine being anywhere else. I got a couple more chances to visit—to talk to him, give him a kiss, and stroke his arm. I don't know if he heard me or even knew I was there, not that it mattered. I spent most of the day just sitting, pacing, and talking in brief quiet sentences with friends and with David's family.

Throughout his illness, David's family, and particularly his parents, had been extraordinary. They'd been so generous in letting us take care of David when he got sick, and that generosity had extended throughout these last

---

*Also, World AIDS Day. (I told you my life wasn't subtle.)

terrible days and hours. We were always welcome; there was never a sense of pulling rank, or "family only." We *were* family. And as much as I wanted to be there for David, I was glad I could be there for them as well.

Monday morning, as I was getting ready for work, the phone rang. It was David's best friend, Tim. David was gone. It was, he said, the most amazing thing he'd ever seen.

David had been having trouble breathing, and when he started to rattle, Eddie, Tim, Peter, and David's parents all huddled around his bed. Suddenly, David eyes flashed open, and he started to reach up toward the ceiling. Everyone grabbed hands and started chanting, "Go David, Go David! Go!" Then David fell back and died.

That morning, as I sat at my desk in the middle of a busy office, I typed out David's obituary:

> SERKO-David R., age 32, on November 23, 1992 of complications from AIDS. Broadway performer, AIDS activist, son, brother, lover, charmer and friend. As we mourn his loss we celebrate his great spirit, humor and tremendous courage. He is survived by his loving family, parents Nancy and Robert Serko of Endwell, NY, grandmother Anna Serko, brothers Pete and Jeff, sister Shirley, his beloved companion, Eddie Baez, and many devoted friends and relatives. Reposing at Frank E. Campbell Funeral Home, Madison Avenue and 81st Street, on Wednesday, November 25, 2–4 and 7–9 P.M. There will be a service at 8 P.M. Funeral in Endicott, NY on Saturday. Contributions should be made to the Actors Fund and to Broadway Cares/Equity Fights AIDS.

The *Times* would replace the word "lover" with "companion."

When I tried to explain to my coworkers what had happened, I heard myself saying that while I'd already lost several friends to AIDS, David was my first real close friend to die; as if there were some weird hierarchy of grief, like the others were sad and all, but somehow didn't count. Like there was "loss," and then there was "real loss."

That evening, I went to the ACT UP meeting to share the news and to be around people who would understand without my explaining. It was strange, announcing David's death on the Floor. Sadly, mine was not the only announcement that evening. Luis Salazar, a beloved young member of the Latina/o Caucus, had also died that weekend at the age of twenty-seven from leukemia.

LUIS SALAZAR (1965–1992)
May his memory be for a blessing.

David's viewing at Frank E. Campbell's two days later was surreal, like a particularly intense *This Is Your Life* episode. There were classmates and teachers I hadn't seen since college, colleagues from ACT UP, our New York and theater friends, Eddie's friends, and David's family. Aside from David, I was probably the only person who knew everyone there. However, I was in no condition to handle introductions, let alone small talk, and David was lying in an open casket in a well-lit corner of the room.

It took me a while to gather my courage to go over and look at him—and that's when things took a sort of black comedy turn. Now, I don't know how you're supposed to look in an open casket, but David was so heavily made-up, complete with "Light Egyptian" base and blue eye shadow, he looked like he was about to go onstage in a touring production of *Kismet*. Then the music, no doubt one of David's mixtapes, suddenly segued into the inappropriately bright party salsa of Peter Allen's "I Go to Rio," one of our dance class favorites. Somewhere between laughing and crying, I thought, *Oh god, David would have loved this!*

Two days later, on the Friday after Thanksgiving, I borrowed my parents' car to drive upstate for David's funeral. As Joe and I were about to leave, my mom gave me a bouquet of white roses to give to Mrs. Serko. Though she'd also known David, it was more an expression of sympathy from one mother to another. But for the luck of the draw, it could've easily been the other way around.

The following morning, we arrived at St. Mary's Orthodox Christian Church in Endicott just in time to help lift David's casket out of the hearse. Given the church's austere straw-bricked exterior, I was not prepared for the riot of color and gold leaf inside. Every inch of the sanctuary's walls and ceiling was covered with brightly painted portraits of saints and biblical characters.

I am never more acutely aware of being Jewish than when I'm sitting in a church. I have no idea what to do, only what NOT to do—no kneeling, no crossing, no Mary full of grace, and no talk of Jesus Christ as our savior. That morning, the feeling was compounded by the day's Bible selection, which focused rather relentlessly on the story of how the Jews were "inattentive" to Christ.

Despite the open casket and my pallbearer duties, I managed to keep it together until we were graveside and I saw David being lowered into the cold muddy ground. It was all so terribly wrong, so grossly unfair. I looked up and saw our college dance teacher standing by herself across the way. Our eyes caught and I was hurtled back to college—twelve years and a lifetime ago—to a random Saturday in her apartment; the three of us laughing, smoking a joint, and watching *The Muppet Show* before heading out to Lenny's, our local gay disco, for a night of drinking and dancing. Unable to push down my emotions any longer, I collapsed in her arms, heaving with sobs.

David's memorial service was scheduled for two weeks later at the Fort Washington Collegiate Church, where he'd found spiritual solace during his final few months. As was the fashion, it was to be a celebration of his life, with specifically requested songs performed by friends and stories told by the people who knew him best, sprinkled among some selected hymns and psalms.

David had asked me to be part of the planning committee with Eddie, Tim, and a couple of other friends. Although I wanted to be respectful of David's wishes, I found myself getting increasingly angry as the priest commandeered the conversation and sketched out an order of service. Suddenly I knew why David wanted me on the committee.

"No," I said curtly, squaring off with the priest. He was not going to lead a religious service. There'd be a place for the hymns and prayers David had requested, along with the other speakers and performances he'd asked for, but if we were going to celebrate David's life, we were going to celebrate *all* of it, and under no circumstances would anyone who knew and loved him be made to feel uncomfortable or unwelcome. While the priest was not happy with the changes or with me, everyone else seemed relieved.

The resulting event was, in the words of David B. Feinberg, "the Nicholas Nickleby of memorial services":[11] over three hours long, with a full church choir, eclectic song selections, and multiple eulogies.

I went first.

David was the bravest person I've ever known. I want to celebrate his bravery. His humor. His campiness. His gayness. His love of men. His talent. His chest and arms. His grace and charm, which grew from deep inside him.

I felt it deeply important to talk about his gay life: our evenings on the prowl at Uncle Charlie's, smoking real or imagined cigarettes, quoting movie and TV dialogue, and trashing everyone in sight. I talked about his attitude toward AIDS—"To live, to fight, to carry on with a minimum of complaining"—and shared stories of David infusing himself on the way to the beach and Kennebunkport and slapping "Silence = Death" stickers under the White House furniture when he performed *A Chorus Line* for the Reagans. And then I got angry.

We have all been living with AIDS for far too long. It has become commonplace. Another friend calls up and says that he's got night sweats and is losing weight and we switch into "social worker mode" and start suggesting this program or that medication or how to use "connections" to jump the lines at GMHC or the health project. It has become a part of an accepted cycle of events—the "grief thing." It is not part of any normal cycle of events. It is an outrage. . . . For those of us who have been living in the AIDS war for years—somehow, we must keep fighting. For those of you for whom David was the first bomb you heard dropping—please join the fight. Ribbons are a start, but there is more to do.

I closed with a benediction sent by a close college friend who had met David the very same day I did in late August 1978, on a trip to the Greene County Fair. It was from a new play he was rehearsing in Los Angeles.

This disease will be the end of many of us, but not nearly all, and the dead will be commemorated and will struggle on with the living, and we are not going away. We won't die secret deaths anymore. The world only spins forward. We will be citizens. The time has come.
Bye now.
You are fabulous creatures, each and every one.
And I bless you: *More Life*.
The Great Work Begins.[12]

DAVID SERKO (1960–1992)
May his memory be for a blessing.

If this were a play, the story would end here. (If it's good enough for Tony Kushner . . .) But life is not a script, and sadly the epidemic was only picking up speed.

Katrina Haslip, who bravely started the ACE program for women in prison with HIV, died December 2. Tom Cunningham, our former administrator and workspace manager—like David, only thirty-two years old—on December 9. Carl Sigmon died in January, as did Rudolf Nureyev. February brought the death of Arthur Ashe and my college friend, Tim Kivel, whom I failed once again, having lost track of him several months after he moved to Chicago. Then on February 20, Bob "Voice of the People" Rafsky, who raged and raged against the dying of the light, died at age forty-seven.

Sure, we had our share of victories. After years of intense prodding, the CDC finally expanded the AIDS definition to include invasive cervical cancer.[*] Terry McGovern won her class-action lawsuit forcing the Social Security Administration to revamp its disability regulations to include women-specific infections and people with a T-cell count lower than 200. And working with the AIDS Underground Railroad, ACT UP successfully helped relocate HIV-positive Haitian refugees from a detention camp at Guantanamo Bay into safe housing in New York City.

But mostly we were losing ground.

Conservative members of the Board of Education ousted Chancellor Joseph A. Fernandez for supporting the city's controversial AIDS curriculum. The House voted overwhelmingly to maintain the discriminatory HIV travel ban, while the Senate once again debated the sexual habits of gay men, this time in opposition to President Clinton's promise to allow gays and lesbians to serve openly in the military. In response, community leaders pushed AIDS to the sidelines and focused April's big LGBT March on Washington on Gays in the Military.

---

[*]Continuing pressure from activists and the AIDS community had forced the CDC to delay the adoption of the definition first proposed in August 1991 and finally agree to hold an open meeting on September 2, 1992. The resulting new AIDS definition, which went into effect on January 1, 1993, included pulmonary tuberculosis, recurrent pneumonia, and invasive cervical cancer, as well as HIV-positive individuals with less than 200 T-cells. "1993 Revised Classification System for HIV Infection and Expanded Surveillance Case Definition for AIDS among Adolescents and Adults," CDC, Morbidity and Mortality Weekly Report: Recommendations and Reports, December 18, 1992; https://www.cdc.gov/mmwr/preview/mmwrhtml/00018871.htm.

Things were even worse on the medical front. The results from the recently completed French-English Concorde study indicated little benefit in the early use of AZT. Not only did these findings contradict the current standard of care, they also threw the value of the entire class of similar drugs into question. Not one of the current antiretrovirals would stop the progression to disease and death. After twelve years of the known epidemic, we still didn't fully understand the fundamentals of how HIV worked, let alone how to stop it.

And while I continued to facilitate meetings, write fundraising letters, and organize demonstrations, I looked around the Floor on Monday nights with the sobering awareness that nothing I was doing would save the life of anyone in that room.

In May, my chanting buddy, the buoyant Robert Garcia, died at age thirty-one. When his death was announced on the Floor, over half the room had no idea who he was. After the usual desultory chanting of "*ACT UP! FIGHT BACK! FIGHT AIDS!*" I stopped the meeting, shouting, "Point of personal privilege" (whatever the hell that means), and demanded a few moments to talk about Robert, who he was and what he meant to the organization.

The summer, somehow, was even worse.

On July 1, a busload of activists drove down to Washington, DC, to march the body of Tim Bailey to the White House for a political funeral. But after an emotional three-hour standoff with police, including a violent tussle over the casket, the cops prevented us from leaving the Capitol parking lot. When the police arrested Tim's understandably distraught brother, Randy, Jim Aquino selflessly stepped forward to take the bust so he wouldn't go to jail alone.

We remained an honorable tribe.

Later that month, my Fire Island housemate and former ACT UP treasurer, David E. Kirschenbaum, died at age thirty. His partner, Gary Clare, asked me to help him make a mixtape of favorite songs he could copy and hand out to everyone attending the memorial. He also asked me to deliver a eulogy, with the caveat that David wanted his memorial to be celebration rather than a somber event. It's hard to celebrate someone dying at age thirty, but I did my best. One month later, Gary contracted the same disease that killed David and spent the fall shitting, vomiting, and withering away.

Jon Greenberg died the day after David, after refusing to go on Western medication. His body was carried through the streets of the East Village in a funeral march again organized by the Marys. Chris DeBlasio of T+D, and a promising classical composer, died a few days later, taking with him years of music we will never hear.

In the fall, during a brief pause between funerals, the Marys organized the "Clinton Pledge," vowing to greet the president with protests every time he came to New York until he took strong action to end the AIDS crisis. Meanwhile an ad hoc group, including Avram Finkelstein, Maxine Wolfe, Mark Milano, Bob Lederer, Enis Bengul, and Scott Sawyer, created the McClintock Project to Cure AIDS, a proposal for "an alternative AIDS research institute" dedicated solely to studying the pathogenesis of the disease.[13] Rep. Jerry Nadler (D-NY) agreed to put the project into legislative form and introduced it in Congress as H.R. 3310 in mid-October.

Things took another turn for the worse when Rudy Giuliani was elected mayor on November 2. Gary checked into St. Luke's-Roosevelt that same day, and the last of my goodtime girlfriends, Michael Irwin, reported to St. Vincent's a day later. By the time Thanksgiving rolled around, my erstwhile song partner Bradley Ball had joined Gary at St. Luke's, and I was alternating visits between the two hospitals. Given their respective conditions, I assumed Bradley, who was in a coma with a brain infection, would never make it out of the ICU; Gary would be released in a couple of weeks and then survive miserably for another few months; while Michael, who "only" had PCP, would recover.

I was angry with Michael. If he'd stayed on his meds, he wouldn't have contracted PCP, and with all my other friends fighting so hard to survive, I found it difficult to forgive him for appearing to give up. But after seeing the panic in his eyes as he gasped for air from underneath his oxygen mask—an image that haunts me to this day—I realized I had no right to judge him. I sat by his side as the nurses gave him a morphine drip to calm him down, and as he closed his eyes, I gave him a kiss on his forehead and, assured by the nurses there was no rush, told him I'd be back in a couple of days. I then headed across the street to our regular Monday night ACT UP meeting.

Wednesday, instead of visiting Michael, I went to see Bradley, who'd unexpectedly been moved out of ICU into the grimmest hospital room I'd ever seen. He looked a holy terror, like Lear on the heath, with wild staring eyes, long unkempt hair, and a scraggly beard. I couldn't imagine how he would come back from that, but somehow, he did. At least for a while.

Michael was not so lucky. I got the call Thursday afternoon at work.

Jamie Bauer and I rounded up what remained of our AIDS Campaign '92 gang and organized a big "welcome" for Mayor Giuliani on January 3, the first workday of his new administration. "Day One/Job One" was ACT

UP's largest demonstration in a year, with more than five hundred protesters. It felt good to be back on the streets.

On January 7, 1994, the FDA finally approved Bactrim and Septra as prophylaxis against PCP—only ten years and who knows how many deaths after doctors like Joseph Sonnabend had first started using those drugs to prevent PCP in their patients.

That weekend, I got the call that Gary, who'd been released from the hospital in early December, had decided to go off his meds. I should come to the apartment to say good-bye.

Gary looked better than he had in months, propped up comfortably in bed with his pillows and IV drips, surrounded by friends who'd come to take care of him till the end. I sat on the bed and we held hands, staring at one another. Finally, Gary said he loved me and that I'd been a good friend, but for some reason, I couldn't say "I love you" back. Yet, after he died, I was inconsolable; unexpectedly angry and bereft—more so than I'd been for David or Michael, or any of my other friends. Perhaps because it was the loss of a friendship that was only just beginning to bloom.

February was the cruelest month: Clint Wilding, David Roche, Michael Morrissey—no more Audrey Hepburn–themed Valentine's Day parties!—and Aldyn McKean died one after the other. So did AIDS reporter Randy Shilts.

Every conversation I had seemed to include the name of another person who had just died. I felt like the fucking Angel of Death.

We had a formidable enemy in Mayor Giuliani, who'd proposed eliminating the city's Department of AIDS services, and ACT UP spent much of the spring organizing zaps, CD protests, and coalition actions, including a huge march of 1,500 protesters across the Brooklyn Bridge. When Giuliani released his budget in May, AIDS funding remained intact, but with the help of his newly appointed Board of Education, he'd gutted the city's progressive AIDS curriculum.

In June, we celebrated the twenty-fifth anniversary of Stonewall. When Giuliani moved the march away from Fifth Avenue (and St. Patrick's Cathedral) to the less-trafficked First Avenue, ACT UP organized a simultaneous, inclusive, non-negotiated march up Fifth Avenue to the rally in Central Park with several thousand marchers.

But ACT UP was no longer the group I first joined. At age thirty-five, I'd become a crotchety *éminence grise*, dismissing proposals for zaps and actions, only to turn around and beg people to disagree with me, to tell me I was full of shit or didn't understand. Instead, they'd only nod and move on to the next item.

In October, while the Marys, who'd provided much of the muscle behind the Clinton Pledge and the new City Issues Committee, debated splitting off from ACT UP and forming a separate organization, Jamie Bauer and I tried to revive the Actions Committee to pass on our organizing skills, but few were interested.

The group received a body blow when long-trusted treasurer, Scott Sawyer, suddenly disappeared, leaving behind two sets of financial books and a seriously depleted ACT UP bank account. Since Scott could both deposit and write checks without a second signature, it was hard to determine just how much money was missing, though it was estimated to be somewhere between $50,000 and $80,000. It was left to Joe, Scott's co-treasurer, to try to explain what had happened. As angry as I was with Scott for his betrayal of ACT UP, I will never forgive him for his cruelty to Joe—robbing him of his rightful pride in his contributions to the organization. Though no one blamed Joe, it had happened on his watch, and I don't think he's ever gotten over his guilt that he'd somehow let the group down.

We both soldiered on through the winter and spring—Joe finishing up his term as treasurer; me, still facilitating Monday night meetings. And though we never made a decision to leave ACT UP, we began to drift away—skipping a meeting or two until it was summer and then vacation and Fire Island—until we just stopped going altogether.

While the day-to-day contours of my non–ACT UP life were still in place—a strong circle of pre–ACT UP friends, a supportive family, a steady and satisfying relationship with Joe, and a full-time job that paid for what had become my twice-a-week therapy sessions—the passionate organizing core of my life was missing. After seven years away, I couldn't call myself an actor, and now I wasn't an activist either. Then who, or what, was I?

I was a witness. And so, I began to write.

KATRINA, TOM, CARL, TIM, BOB, ROBERT, TIM, DAVID, JON, CHRIS, MICHAEL, GARY, CLINT, DAVID, MICHAEL, ALDYN...
May their memories be for a blessing.

AFTERWORD

WHILE I LOST many more of my friends and colleagues to AIDS, including Bradley Ball, Spencer Cox, George Catravas, Stephen Gendin, Billy Heekin, David B. Feinberg, Tony Malliaris, Tony Ortiz, Howie Pope, Tim Powers, Robert Rygor, Lee Schy, Rand Snyder, and Andy Valentin—*may their memories be for a blessing*—a remarkable number of my ACT UP comrades survived, including Eric, my first ACT UP boyfriend, thanks to protease inhibitors and the success of the drug "cocktail."

And thanks to ACT UP.

Through our protests, campaigns, and interventions, ACT UP helped save hundreds of thousands of lives. We successfully pressured the government to increase funding for AIDS research and support services. We forced the CDC to expand the AIDS definition to include the infections that affect women and IV drug users, earning them access to treatments and AIDS-related services. We refocused drug research and streamlined the drug approval process and created AIDS housing, education, and harm reduction programs. Along with these and other AIDS-specific victories, ACT UP provided a blueprint for successful patient advocacy and played an important role in changing the public's perception of LGBTQ+ people from just a "sexual preference" to a powerful, caring, and politically important community.

Over the last decade, ACT UP's reputation has grown. We've become the subject of books, films, and documentaries. While ACT UP and our legacy organizations, including TAG and Housing Works, continue to do important work, many of those who passed through the "ACT UP Finishing School" are now leaders in the world of AIDS and public health, or are important activists, writers, playwrights, actors, filmmakers, artists, and journalists.

But AIDS is still with us. Not just internationally, but here in America, where poverty, prejudice, lack of AIDS education, and unequal access to health care continue to keep infection rates at unacceptably high levels. Despite the availability of HIV medications and PEP and PreP prophylaxis treatments,* Blacks/African Americans, who represent only 13 percent of the population, comprise 44 percent of the new cases and Hispanics/Latinos 30 percent. Gay/Bisexual/Men who have Sex with Men (MSM) still make up the overwhelming majority of cases (69 percent), with Black MSM accounting for over one-third of that total. Meanwhile, Transgender people are among the few groups experiencing a rise in infection rates.[1]

AND THERE IS STILL NO CURE.

So, what happened?

Some point to the arrival of protease inhibitors and the drug cocktail, which miraculously stopped much of the dying, taking with it our sense of urgency. Others suggest ACT UP, though still active, simply fell victim to the natural life span of grassroots organizations, which tend to burn bright for only a few years. People can only act in crisis mode for so long. Add to that the years under a constant bombardment of sickness, death, and loss, which robbed us of our health, our friends, our family, lovers, colleagues, and leaders. The whole experience was so overwhelming, many of us, whether HIV-positive or not, had to finally back away for our own well-being.

When I left ACT UP in 1995, I felt stranded. I knew acting was no longer the answer. So much of what I'd hoped to find in the theater—a community, a purpose, a way to discover who I was and make a difference in the world—I

---

*Although HIV medication, when taken properly, can reduce viral counts to zero and eliminate risk of transmission, and PEP (postexposure prophylaxis) and PreP (preexposure prophylaxis) can prevent seroconversion, they are expensive treatments and require an often-unobtainable combination of money and/or insurance and regular access to health care to take full advantage of their benefits.

had found in "real life." Thanks to ACT UP, I was able to become the person I had hoped I'd be, if not the actor I had thought I'd be.

But having "saved the world" in my twenties and early thirties, what was I supposed to do for an encore? My peers were all well into their professional careers, acting or otherwise, while I was still working at my day job. And for some reason, helping lawyers make more money wasn't something I felt like embracing as my new life's work.

It took me a while, but ACT UP would once again help me find the answer. I became a community historian—writing, doing research, acting as a resource for other writers, talking to high school and college students, and sharing the lessons of AIDS activism with a new generation of activists, queers, and allies. Despite how much the world has changed—and how much it sadly hasn't—ACT UP still has much to offer as a model for people interested in activism on issues ranging from LGBTQ+ rights, health care, and abortion to income inequality, climate change, and racial justice.

I'm often asked what I learned from my experiences with ACT UP or what my advice might be to young people interested in activism. I usually rattle off some key strategies for planning successful actions—the importance of identifying achievable short-term goals, knowing your stuff, having a clear message, and understanding your role in the larger struggle. (Street activists don't ask for what's reasonable, they demand what's necessary.) And I always tell them how ACT UP is proof that a small group of individuals can make change happen.

And all of this is true.

But if I were to boil it all down, the first and most important step, whether as an activist or as a human being, is to just show up. Be there for your friends, your family, your community, and yourself. Even if you don't know what to do or what the answers are. Show up.

Take the leap. Make the call. Attend the meeting. Visit the hospital. Go to the demonstration. Show up.

The rest will follow.

February 28, 2020: A Parting Shot

In late February 2020, I joined a hundred other current and former ACT UP members for a photoshoot for *T: The New York Times Style Magazine*. The photo and accompanying article[2] would be part of an issue "celebrat[ing] various groups of creative people who, whether united by outlook or identity, happenstance or choice, built communities that have shaped the larger cultural landscape."

Yeah, okay, whatever.

There's still no love lost between ACT UP and the *Times*, despite its improved coverage of gay issues and retrospective appreciation of ACT UP (or at least the ACT UP of the '80s and '90s). There were multiple email exchanges and Facebook threads devoted to questions of how we could take control of the narrative or whether attending was to participate in a whitewashing of the *Times*'s role in the epidemic.

Like many, I went more for the reunion than the approbation. There remains a strong bond between us ACT UP vets, a shared sense of comradeship, love, and respect I imagine is close to what soldiers feel from wartime. Even though I often don't know people's histories or the specifics of their lives, I've seen their essence and know them deeply.

The gathering proved, in the words of Jamie Leo, "oddly and cringingly sublime."[3] While it was great to see so many familiar faces, I gasped when a photo of David Serko popped up unbidden on my Facebook thread as we waited for the photographer. It was a post of a shirtless David, his arms wrapped around an also shirtless Howie Pope. Judging from the ace bandage wrapped around his forearm, it was probably from Pride 1991. Both boys are young and beautiful; David smiling with his eyes shut and Howie staring out at the camera beaming. The love and joy of the photo took my breath away.

The last time I saw David was almost thirty years ago. By the time this book gets published, I'll have lived twice as long as he did.

As for the photoshoot, well, it was pretty strange, particularly when the photographer asked us to pose "in anger" and "chant something." (And you'd have thought the *Times* could at least have sprung for some coffee.)

Lest anyone think we'd mellowed with age, Jamie Bauer read a letter accusing the *Times* of having "blood on its hands, which it can never wash off, even though it is trying to 'work through' its lack of coverage of the AIDS crisis and AIDS activism," before the first shutter clicked.

> The *Times* continues, to this day, to ignore the activism of resistance, even while it prints opinion pieces calling for people to protest in the streets (e.g. David Leonhardt and Michele Goldberg). The *Times* does not cover organizing, does not cover resistance campaigns, and it does not cover demonstrations. It does not educate its readers about what demonstrations are coming up, who is organizing them, or why they should attend. It covers internecine bickering . . . which only drives people away. . . . The hypocrisy of the *Times* continues, celebrating what activists did thirty years ago, while ignoring what

activists are doing today. Despite your "good intentions," you are complicit.[4]

And then, for good luck, we chanted ***"FUCK the NEW YORK TIMES!"*** as the photographer took her shots from atop a crane.

We had no idea it would be our last mass gathering before COVID-19. Three weeks later, New York would shut down, with everyone but "essential workers" sheltering in place as the coronavirus cut its deadly swath through the city. (Nor would it escape our notice that, as with AIDS, the COVID epidemic would highlight the willful inaction of our government, the inequities of our health care system, and just whose lives were valued.)

It was also the last time we would see Larry. Wheeled into the gym by his husband, David, at the last possible moment, Larry took pride of place at the front of the group, weak but smiling gamely as he accepted hugs, greetings, and tributes in his black ACT UP cap. Three months later, Larry would be gone. It was hard to believe. It still is.

Larry was such a huge part of the landscape of my life. Of all our lives. Like many of us, I was surprised by how hard I took the news of his death. It reminded me of the shock of loss I'd get those first few months after 9/11, when I'd cross Sixth Avenue and automatically look downtown for the Twin Towers, only to realize once again that they were no longer there. Larry had been close to dying many times but had always bounced back. I figured he'd be around forever . . . like cockroaches and Cher.

LARRY KRAMER (1935–2020)
May his memory be for a blessing.

One final note. On March 20, 2020, just before everyone went into seclusion, and over twenty-eight years since our first "date" in Kennebunkport, Joe and I got married. We figured since we fell in love during one epidemic, it was only right we get married in another.

It was a small, quickly assembled, socially distanced ceremony, officiated by my college friend Joanne and witnessed by her husband, Mike, and my best friend, Neal.

And, no doubt, David.

May his memory,
and those of our many, many other friends
and comrades, both known and unknown,
who fought valiantly against this horrible disease,
be for a blessing.

Amen.

ACKNOWLEDGMENTS

AS THIS IS probably as close as I'll ever get to giving my Tony Award speech, this may take a while.

I've been very moved throughout my time working on this book by the generosity of the many people who've helped me out along the way. While it would be nice to think it was because I'm such a great guy, I know the real reason was because they all recognized the importance of getting this history recorded and shared. Everyone understood the mission behind this book. And for that I am deeply grateful.

A first big thank-you to Fred Nachbaur, who had the guts to option a 500-plus-page AIDS memoir and history from an unknown author, and to his team at Fordham University Press, including Richard Morrison, Eric Newman, Mark Lerner, Kate O'Brien-Nicholson, Katie Sweeney Parmiter, and the book's publicist, Michelle Blankenship. It was a shock when my manuscript went from "just something on my computer" to something in the real world, but they have gently and carefully helped coax it into existence. I thank them for their patience and kindness, not to mention their willingness to go with my original title as well as the photograph I first envisioned for the cover when I started writing this book twenty-eight years ago.

Speaking of photos, thank you to John Dominic Barbarino for that wonderful cover image,* and Joey Stamp for the beautiful author photo. Thank

---

*In return, John has asked that I highlight the remarkable work of God's Love We Deliver (glwd.org), which provides meals for people living with HIV/AIDS, cancer, and other illnesses.

you also to ACT UP's remarkable collection of photo and video activists including Donna Binder, Tracey Litt, Tom McKitterick, and Ellen Neipris, whose images, along with the personal photos of Gonzalo Aburto, Raymond Diskin Black, Joe Chiplock, and Tom Keane, have helped bring the history told in these pages to life.

I knew I was in good hands when my copy editor, Nancy Basmajian, noted that Deee-Lite had four *e*'s and that the record label of Robin Byrd's recording of "Baby Let Me Bang Your Box" did not have a comma after "Baby." I am grateful for her precision, her common sense, and her ability to tame my citations and adapt my New York Jewish syntax into *Chicago Manual* style.

There's a Yiddish word, *beshert*, that describes a lot of the energy around this book. It means "destined," or less pretentiously, "meant to be." For instance, why, in the fall of 1987, did I enroll in a writing for theater course with Leslie Avayzian? It was under Leslie's gentle prodding that I first began to write about my experiences with ACT UP and AIDS. I thought, at the time, I would turn it into some sort of performance piece. Thirty-five years later, some of that writing has found a home in this book.

Why did David France—who was, at best, an acquaintance—invite me to join his team at Sundance for the premiere of his film *How to Survive a Plague*? It was a trip that changed my life. Months later, David would hire me as his research associate for his book of the same name, giving me the opportunity to dive into the archives at the New York Public Library—heaven on earth—the LGBT Community Center and elsewhere, broadening my understanding of the early years of the AIDS epidemic, while at the same time letting me see firsthand how an experienced writer and journalist organizes and tames great masses of information into a coherent and gripping narrative. And as a bonus, I made a great friend.

David then gave my email address to Helene Dunbar, who was looking for someone to do a "sensitivity read" on her wonderful YA novel *We Are Lost and Found*. When she found herself, instead, dealing with this extremely opinionated 800-pound gorilla, she never complained (at least to me), but rather welcomed me into her creative world. If David helped me understand the journalistic side of writing, Helene helped me focus inward. She became a mentor, a writing guru, an enthusiastic early reader, and a great cheerleader for me and this book, as well as a dear, dear friend.

And it was Helene who introduced me to agent extraordinaire Lauren MacLeod, who fell in love with my book soon after discovering that her much-loathed step-grandmother was targeted by ACT UP when she was a member of Reagan's AIDS commission. In addition to being a tireless advocate and a bottomless fount of encouragement, Lauren, through some special agent-editor wizardry, helped me cut one-third of my original manuscript and then, as promised, found my book a home.

Throughout this process, I have been blessed by the enthusiasm and generosity of my early readers, beginning with Mitchell Ivers, who introduced me to my first agent, Jed Mattes (*may his memory be for a blessing*), who tried to find a publisher for this book back in the late 1990s, when it was little more than a sample chapter and summary.

Since then, Benjamin Dreyer, Brendan Mathews, Tim Murphy, and Ed Sikov have all shared their expertise and advice and have continued to advocate for me and this book in countless ways. A special thank-you to Debra Levine, an ACT UP comrade (and fellow AmFAR survivor), who made it through a couple of versions of this book and helped me understand that the best way to tell our collective story was to go deeper into my own. Also, a callout to Will Schwalbe, who, while gently declining to publish my book back when it was still in its adolescence, told me to not worry about its length. "If you're going to be a bear," he counseled, "be a grizzly."

Though I'm pretty sure I would have continued working on this book even if Larry Kramer had never called me, I don't know if I would ever have made it to that first ACT UP meeting without him. So, a deep bow and thank-you, *tante* Larry, for being such a mensch (and pain in the ass) as well as a most surprising and generous advocate, adviser, and supporter.

I am also deeply indebted—indeed, we all are—to Sarah Schulman, Jim Hubbard, and James Wentzy for the extraordinary ACT UP Oral History Project (www.actuporalhistory.org). While it proved a remarkable resource, helping me fill in missing pieces, faces, and stories, its greatest gift was how it allowed me to rediscover and fall in love again with the extraordinary people who were my comrades in the streets.

And to those comrades, both here and gone, I can only hope I've done you some small justice. I know I left a lot of you out of the book or only just mentioned you in a footnote, including a number of people who were very important to me personally (not to mention the history of ACT UP), including Andrea Benzacar, David Binder, Jay Blotcher, Steven Cordova, BC Craig, Joe Ferrari, Vincent Gagliostro, David Gipps, Gregg Gonsalves, Barbara Hughes, Wayne Kawadler, John Kelly, Tracey Litt, Tony Malliaris, Michael Marco, Andrew Miller, Allen Payne, Lee Raines, Herb Spiers (*may his memory be for a blessing*), John Voelcker, and Brian Zabcik—and I know I'm leaving even more of you out now. Please know that this in no way diminishes my appreciation of your courage, fierceness, love, and power. All our stories are important, and ACT UP wouldn't be what it is and was without your contribution. As a wise man once wrote, "It's the ripple, not the stream."°

I do need to single out, however, two ACT UP members who are more than mentioned. Back in the 1990s, when I tried to explain why I needed to write this book, I said it was so that future generations would know about Mark Fotopoulos. Thirty-five years after I saw him at my first demonstration, I am still in awe of his bravery.

The other member, not surprisingly, is David Serko. One of the bonuses of writing this book was that I got to be with David almost every day. Part of me thinks that when David asked me to write his obituary, what he meant was for me to write this book. He has remained a funny, warm, and infinitely generous presence in my life. And in another *beshert* moment, so has his family, particularly his older brother, Peter, who reached out to me ten years ago when he began working on his own writing project about David and has since become a close friend.

There were a number of people over the last twenty-eight years who "pulled me onto the raft," offering me jobs when I was unemployed, most notably Marianne Rosenberg, Nancy Donner (twice), and Paul DiDonato. Their support and their friendship made it possible for me to keep working on this book while simultaneously continuing to eat, and for that and more, I am deeply grateful.

Thank you also to Barbara Chiplock, Jennifer Griffiths, Linda and David Murray, Amy Potozkin, Jesse Rabinowitz, Peter Staley, Bobbie Wien (*may her memory be for a blessing*), and my colleagues at New York Institute of Technology, including Nada Anid (*may her memory be for a blessing*), Joe Boccagno, Kim Tucker Campo, Bobbie Dell'Aquilo, Ryan Gleason, Nicole Klein, Bessie Nestoras Knoblauch, Carolina Koutsoyannis, Libby Sullivan Roseman, and David Shaw, for their generosity and their belief in me and this project.

When my world was overwhelmed by AIDS and ACT UP, my friends were my ballast and kept me from going under. In the years since, they've never stopped giving me encouragement and support, while continuing to be the fastest, funniest, and most thoughtful people I know. I'm talking about you, Bob Bronzo, Benjamin Dreyer, Howie Cherpakov, Chris Christman and Mark Birchette, Nancy Donner and Gary Martin, Mitchell Ivers

---

°It's Stephen Sondheim, for those of you still playing, from "Someone in a Tree" from *Pacific Overtures*, and it posits that each actor, piece, or detail is of equal significance in the making of an event, experience, or object.

and Mark Swirsky, Neal Liebowitz, Neal Lerner, and Steven Lutvak. I'm lucky to have you all in my life.

And a special shout-out to my Fire Island housemates from 193 Beach Hill, 132 Beach Hill, 319 Sky, 277 Bay, 279 Bay, 96 Teal, and 623 Shore, for their years of friendship, laughs, delicious dinners, and strong cocktails, not to mention their patience and consideration as they tiptoed around me in the mornings while I sat typing away at my computer.

I owe a special debt of gratitude to my family, starting with my siblings, Joan and Bob Munch and Rick and Judith Goldberg, and my extended family of cousins—the Wiens, Munters, Murrays, Goldbergs, Fords, Bekers, and Nussbaums—and in-laws—Chiplocks, Pipinos, Gavins, and Malamuts—who somehow refrained from rolling their eyes every time I talked about "the book" year after year (after year) at Thanksgivings, Bar and Bat Mitzvahs, and other family gatherings. I am also relieved to say that my nieces and nephews—almost all of whom are younger than my first sample chapter—are now old enough to read this book without parental supervision.

Although my parents, Mel and Norma Goldberg, never got the chance to see my book in print—*may their memories be for a blessing*—they are present on every page. I am my parents' son. And it is their love and example that led me to ACT UP and to embrace the responsibility of recording this history.

Beshert also means "soulmate." And that is, without question, what I found when I met Joe Chiplock. Thirty-one years since our first "date" at Kennebunkport, we still make each other laugh every day. I will never forget his look of relief when he started reading the first draft of my book and realized it wasn't just 700-plus pages of "All work and no play makes Ronnie a dull boy." To say that I'd never have been able to write, let alone complete, this book without his tremendous generosity, understanding, love, and support, not to mention his excellent proofreading skills, would be a vast understatement. We don't have a dog. We don't have a child. Instead, we have a book. I love you.

NOTES

MOST OF THE documents cited here are from my own personal archive of original ACT UP documents and news clippings. The majority originally came from the information table at the back of the room at our weekly ACT UP meetings, so I expect that many of these documents can also be found in the ACT UP archive collection housed at the New York Public Library or as part of other personal collections of ACT UP members, some of which are housed in other institutions.

In addition to the online resources noted herein, the other major source of information has been the remarkable ACT UP Oral History Project (actuporalhistory.org), which includes videos and transcripts of interviews conducted with 188 former ACT UP members, as well as a cache of unedited contemporaneous videos of meetings and trainings and demonstrations by ACT UP's myriad videographers.

One additional resource I'd like to highlight is my own ACT UP Timeline (1987–95), which is available on my website (boywiththebullhorn.com). It tracks, by date, what was going on internally in ACT UP, as well as our zaps and demonstrations, key AIDS-related and "real-world" events, and the deaths of our members. While it is currently only in PDF form, it is my hope to eventually have it digitized so that it can link to original documents—flyers, posters, fact sheets, etc.—and, who knows, maybe someday, interviews, photos, news articles, and videos.

Preface

1. Martin Luther King Jr., "Letter from Birmingham Jail," April 16, 1963, https://www
.africa.upenn.edu/Articles_Gen/Letter_Birmingham.html.

1. Awakening

1. Marty Levine, "Fearing Fear Itself," *Gay Men's Health Crisis Newsletter*—New
York, no. 1, July 1982.

2. Larry Kramer, "1,112 and Counting," *New York Native*, March 14–27, 1983.

3. Larry Kramer, *The Normal Heart* (New York: New American Library, 1985), 19–22.

4. From "American Jewry during the Holocaust," prepared for the American Jewish
Commission on the Holocaust, 1984, edited by Seymour Maxwell Finger, as quoted in
Kramer, *The Normal Heart, 21–22.

5. Kramer, *The Normal Heart*, 32.

6. Pat Buchanan, syndicated column, *New York Post,* May 24, 1983, as quoted in Randy
Shilts, *And the Band Played On* (New York: St. Martin's, 1987), 311.

7. William F. Buckley Jr., "Crucial Steps in Combating the Aids Epidemic; Identify All
the Carriers," op-ed, *New York Times*, March 18, 1986.

8. Michael Callen and Richard Berkowitz, with Richard Dworkin, "We Know Who We
Are: Two Gay Men Declare War on Promiscuity," *New York Native*, November 8–21, 1982.

9. Richard Berkowitz and Michael Callen, *How to Have Sex in an Epidemic: One
Approach* (New York: Tower Press, May 1983).

10. ACT UP internal document: "The Rise of Militant AIDS Activism," undated.

11. Editorial, "Don't Panic, Yet, Over AIDS," *New York Times,* November 7, 1986.

12. Avram Finkelstein, interviewed by Sarah Schulman, ACT UP Oral History Project,
January 23, 2010, 21–22.

13. Mike Salinas, "Kramer, Mob, Others Call for Traffic Blockade, *New York Native,*
March 30, 1987.

14. Larry Kramer, "The Beginning of ACTing UP," in *Reports from the Holocaust:
The Making of an AIDS Activist* (New York: St. Martin's, 1989), 129–39.

15. Kramer, 129–39.

16. Kramer, 129–39.

17. Salinas, "Kramer, Mob, Others."

18. ACT UP internal document: "FACT UP ROUGH DRAFT," no date/author.

19. ACT UP internal document: "AIDS Coalition minutes," March 12, 1987.

20. Author interview with Bradley Ball, June 19, 1994.

21. Mike Salinas, "ACT UP Goes to Washington," *New York Native*, June 15, 1987, 13–15.

2. First Steps

1. Michael Savino, "ACT UP Protests Airline's Refusal to Fly PWAs," *New York Native*,
August 24, 1987.

2. Frank Jump, interviewed by Sarah Schulman, ACT UP Oral History Project,
November 1, 2003, 29.

3. "Presidential Commission on the Human Immunodeficiency Virus," Executive
Order 12601 of June 24, 1987.

4. Sandra G. Boodman, "Views of 4 U.S. AIDS Panelists Hit," *Washington Post*, August 26, 1987.

5. Boodman.

6. Mike Salinas, "President's AIDS Advisory Panel Is Filled with Non-Experts," *New York Native*, August 10, 1987.

7. Philip M. Boffey, "Hospital Official to Lead President's AIDS Panel," *New York Times*, June 26, 1987.

8. Boodman, "Views of 4 U.S. AIDS Panelists Hit."

9. Salinas, "President's AIDS Advisory Panel," quoting Senator Gordon Humphrey (R-NH).

10. Boodman, "Views of 4 U.S. AIDS Panelists Hit."

11. David Holmberg, "Reagan AIDS Panel Faces Its Critics," *Newsday*, September 10, 1987.

12. ACT UP fact sheet: "AIDS 25,000 Are Dead 300 Die Each Week One Every Hour," AIDS Commission Demo, Washington, DC, [ca. September 9, 1987].

13. ACT UP fact sheet: "AIDS 25,000 Are Dead."

14. Phil Zwickler, "AIDS Commission Meets in Washington," *New York Native*, September 21, 1987.

15. Zwickler.

16. "Test Drugs, Not People," quoting Rebecca Cole, Testimony before the Presidential Commission on the HIV Epidemic, Washington, DC, September 9, 1987, as reprinted in the *New York Native*, September 27, 1987, 16.

17. "Test Drugs, Not People," quoting Bill Bahlman, 14.

18. "Test Drugs, Not People," quoting Marty Robinson, 14–15.

19. "Test Drugs, Not People," quoting Henry Yeager, 15–16.

20. "Test Drugs, Not People," quoting Larry Kramer, 17.

21. Philip M. Boffey, "Doctors Who Shun AIDS Patients Are Assailed by Surgeon General," *New York Times*, September 10, 1987.

22. Philip M. Boffey, "AIDS Panel Marvels at Government's Efforts," *New York Times*, September 11, 1987.

23. AP, "Head of AIDS Commission Pledges Quick Reorganization of Panel," *New York Times*, October 11, 1987.

24. Randy Shilts, *And the Band Played On: People, Politics and the AIDS Epidemic* (New York: St. Martin's, 1987), xxii.

25. Michaeleen Ducleff, "Researchers Clear 'Patient Zero' from AIDS Origin Story," NPR, October 26, 2016, http://www.npr.org/sections/health-shots/2016/10/26/498876985 /mystery-solved-how-hiv-came-to-the-u-s.

26. Pamphlet: March on Washington Committee, "March on Washington for Lesbian & Gay Rights," 1987.

27. ACT UP fact sheet: "Silence = Death," March on Washington, [ca. October 11, 1987].

28. CDC, "AIDS Weekly Surveillance Report," December 28, 1987, CDC.gov, viewed December 16, 2018, https://www.cdc.gov/hiv/pdf/library/reports/surveillance/cdc-hiv -surveillance-report-1987.pdf.

29. "NAMES Project AIDS Memorial Quilt," Wikipedia, viewed December 16, 2018, https://en.wikipedia.org/wiki/NAMES_Project_AIDS_Memorial_Quilt.

30. ACT UP fact sheet: "Silence = Death."

31. Maxine Wolfe, interviewed by Jim Hubbard, ACT UP Oral History Project, February 19, 2004, 53–56.

32. AP, "Limit Voted on AIDS Funds," *New York Times*, October 15, 1987; see "The AIDS Crisis: A Documentary History," ed. Douglas A. Feldman and Julie Wang Miller, 190–93, for Helms speech, October 14, 1987, on congressional record.

33. Jill Lawrence, "Senate Says Federal AIDS Education Material Can't Promote Homosexuality," AP, October 14, 1987, https://apnews.com/article/65c596e0514c81b20 536d9cbf33c066f.

34. Congressional Record—Senate, October 14, 1987, p. 27754, viewed March 21, 2019, https://www.govinfo.gov/content/pkg/GPO-CRECB-1987-pt20/pdf/GPO-CRECB -1987-pt20-2-1.pdf.

35. Congressional Record—Senate, October 14, 1987, p. 27766.

36. ACT UP flyer: "While the U.S. plays politics on AIDS, 25,000 are dead. Don't join their silence," undated.

37. Banner front-page headline in the *New York Times:* "Stocks Plunge 508 Points, A Drop of 22.6%; 604 Million Volume Nearly Doubles Record," October 20, 1987.

3. Welcome to ACT UP

1. Ron Goldberg, "ACT UP's First Days," *POZ*, March 1997.

2. ACT UP internal document: Aldyn McKean, "ACT UP Facilitator's Guide," prepared October 10, 1990, revised February 14, 1991, 2.

3. Goldberg, "ACT UP's First Days."

4. McKean, "ACT UP Facilitator's Guide," 3.

5. ACT UP internal document: "Proposal to Create a Coordinating Committee," presented April 27, 1987, as amended May 4, 1987.

6. Author interview with Bradley Ball, June 19, 1994.

7. Avram Finkelstein, *After Silence: A History of AIDS through Its Images* (Berkeley: University of California Press, 2018), 77–82.

8. ACT UP internal document: Terry Riley and Mark Simpson, "Official Proposal re ACT UP Museum Project," October 13, 1987.

9. Douglas Crimp, "AIDS: Cultural Analysis/Cultural Activism," *October* 43 (Winter 1987): 3–16.

10. Gran Fury and Michael Cohen, curators, *Gran Fury: Read My Lips*, catalog from the exhibit at New York University's Steinhardt Gallery, January–March 2012 (New York: 80WSE Press, 2011).

11. Cover tease of article by Dr. Robert E. Gould, "Reassuring News about AIDS: A Doctor Tells Why *You* May Not Be at Risk," *Cosmopolitan*, January 1988.

12. ACT UP fact sheet: "Don't Go to Bed with Cosmo," [ca. January 15, 1988], quoting Gould, "Reassuring News about AIDS."

13. Sally Chew, "ACT UP Zaps Cosmo," *New York Native*, February 1, 1988.

14. Maxine Wolfe, "AIDS and Politics: Transformation of Our Movement," in *Women, AIDS, and Activism*, ed. ACT UP/New York Women and AIDS Book Group (Boston: South End, 1992), 233–37.

15. ACT UP fact sheet: "Don't Go to Bed with Cosmo."

16. ACT UP fact sheet: "Don't Go to Bed with Cosmo."

17. Page Six, "Cosmo Protest," *New York Post*, [ca. January 14, 1988].

18. Sally Chew, "ACT UP Zaps Cosmo."

19. Douglas Crimp with Adam Rolston, *AIDS Demo Graphics* (Seattle: Bay, 1990), 39–42.

20. Avram Finkelstein, interviewed by Sarah Schulman, ACT UP Oral History Project, January 23, 2010, 49–50.

21. Based on author's own contemporaneous notes and memory of Avram Finkelstein's eulogy for Steven Webb, delivered February 20, 1988, confirmed by Finkelstein in conversation with the author November 5, 2021.

22. Based on author's own contemporaneous notes and memory of Avram Finkelstein's eulogy for Steven Webb.

23. Finkelstein, interview, 49–50.

24. Based on author's own contemporaneous notes and memory of Avram Finkelstein's eulogy for Steven Webb.

25. Based on author's own contemporaneous notes and memories of Steve Webb's memorial, February 20, 1988.

4. We Are Family

1. Gene Sharp, *The Politics of Nonviolent Action*, 3 vols. (Boston: Porter Sargent, 1973).

2. Jamie Bauer, interviewed by Sarah Schulman, ACT UP Oral History Project, March 7, 2004, 16–17.

3. ACT UP fact sheet: "AIDS, POLITICS, & $$$$," Wall Street II, [ca. March 24, 1988].

4. Douglas Crimp with Adam Rolston, *AIDS Demo Graphics* (Seattle: Bay, 1990), 49–50.

5. Neil MacFarquhar, "AIDS Protest Jams Wall Street Traffic; 111 Are Arrested," *The Record* (AP), March 25, 1988.

6. Phil Zwickler, "ACT UP Marks First Anniversary with Massive Protest," *New York Native*, April 8, 1988.

7. From Herald Wire Services, "AIDS Protest near Wall St. Snarls Traffic," *Miami Herald*, March 25, 1988.

8. Phil Zwickler, "ACT UP Allegedly Roughed Up," *New York Native*, April 11, 1988.

9. The Flirtations, "Mr. Sandman" (YouTube), viewed April 2, 2022, https://www.youtube.com/watch?v=TaZrZpIqx_E.

5. ACT NOW and the Nine Days of Rain

1. AIDS Coalition To Network, Organize and Win, untitled press release, January 12, 1988.

2. Douglas Crimp with Adam Rolston, *AIDS Demo Graphics* (Seattle: Bay, 1990), 53.

3. ACT UP fact sheet: "Why We Kiss," [ca. April 29, 1988].

4. Reginald Roberts, "Group Protests Lack of Therapy in AIDS Cases," *Sunday Star-Ledger*, May 1, 1988.

5. Crimp and Ralston, *AIDS Demo Graphics*, 58–59; statistics from ACT UP fact sheet quoted from AIDS Discrimination Unit of the New York City Commission on Human Rights, *AIDS and People of Color: The Discriminatory Impact* (New York: Commission on Human Rights, 1987).

6. Kendall Thomas, interviewed by Sarah Schulman, ACT UP Oral History Project, May 3, 2003, 19.

7. Thomas, interview, 19.

8. Thomas, 14.

9. Gregg Bordowitz, "Fags and Junkies," *Gay Community News,* July 24–30, 1988.

10. ACT UP/ACT NOW, ADAPT fact sheet, "AIDS: Substance Abuse," [ca. May 2, 1988].

11. ACT UP fact sheet: "AIDS behind Bars," [ca. May 3, 1988].

12. ACT UP poster: Gran Fury, "AIDS behind Bars," 1988 (as cited in Crimp and Ralston, *AIDS Demo Graphics,* 61).

13. ACT UP fact sheet: "AIDS behind Bars."

14. Crimp and Ralston, *AIDS Demo Graphics,* 62–63.

15. ACT UP fact sheet: "AIDS IS NOT A BALLGAME!" [ca. May 4, 1988].

16. Crimp and Ralston, *AIDS Demo Graphics,* 62; also Thomas Morgan, "Mainstream Strategy for AIDS Group," *New York Times,* July 22, 1988.

17. Maxine Wolfe, interviewed by Jim Hubbard, ACT UP Oral History Project, 69–70.

18. ACT UP internal document: Issues Report, Action proposal, Meeting notes (Bradley Ball), April 18, 1988.

19. Vito Russo, *The Celluloid Closet* (New York: Harper and Row, 1981).

20. Toby Marotta, *The Politics of Homosexuality* (Boston: Houghton Mifflin, 1981), 295–97.

21. ACT UP internal document: Vito Russo, "Why We Fight," speech given in Albany, New York, May 7, 1988.

6. Taking Actions

1. "The Civil Rights Aspects of Public Health Policies and Initiatives to Control AIDS," US Commission on Civil Rights Project Proposal, CCR Form 401 Appendix 3, 1.

2. "Civil Rights Aspects," 3.

3. "Civil Rights Aspects," 3.

4. *School Bd. of Nassau County v. Arline,* 480 U.S. 273 (1987).

5. Letter to Clarence M. Pendleton Jr. from Sen. Edward M. Kennedy, Sen. Tom Harkin, Sen. Robert T. Stafford, Sen. Lowell P. Weicker Jr., January 29, 1988.

6. Letter to Sen. Edward M. Kennedy from Clarence M. Pendleton Jr., February 11, 1988.

7. AP, "Memo Urges Justice Department 'To Polarize Debate' on Key Issues," *New York Times,* February 26, 1988, quoting an internal memorandum sent earlier that week to Justice Department officials by William Bradford Reynolds, the assistant attorney general in charge of the Civil Rights Division.

8. AP, "Memo Urges Justice Department."

9. Opening Remarks by Clarence M. Pendleton, Jr., May 16, 1988, in United States Commission on Civil Rights, 3. This is the document I picked up at the hearing. It differs slightly from the published "Opening Statement by Clarence Pendleton, Jr.," in *AIDS, Hearing Held in Washington, D.C., May 16–18, 1988: Civil Rights Aspects of Public Health Policies and Initiatives to Control AIDS,* 3, but I've chosen the original because it better reflects the chairman's tone of condescension.

10. Sandra G. Boodman, "Protesters Interrupt AIDS Hearing," *Washington Post,* May 17, 1988.

11. Testimony of Alexander D. Langmuir, M.D., M.P.H., Department of Epidemiology, Johns Hopkins School of Hygiene, Baltimore, MD, in *AIDS, Hearing Held in Washington,*

D.C., May 16–18, 1988: Civil Rights Aspects of Public Health Policies and Initiatives to Control AIDS, 89.

12. Alexander D. Langmuir, M.D., M.P.H., "AIDS—Projections Reconsidered," prepared for a panel meeting of the US Commission on Civil Rights, Washington, DC, May 18, 1988. (While the remarks are dated for May 18, Dr. Langmuir appeared before the commission on Day One of the hearings, May 16, as confirmed by the meeting agenda.)

13. Langmuir, "AIDS," 7.

14. Testimony of Alexander D. Langmuir, 89.

15. Testimony of Alexander D. Langmuir, 90–91.

16. Testimony of Stanley K. Monteith, M.D., Santa Cruz, CA, in *AIDS, Hearing Held in Washington, D.C., May 16–18, 1988: Civil Rights Aspects of Public Health Policies and Initiatives to Control AIDS*, 94.

17. Philip M. Boffey, "Panel on AIDS Turns Voices of Criticism into Songs of Praise," *New York Times*, March 7, 1988.

18. Boffey.

19. ACT UP internal document: ACT UP meeting notes, February 22, 1988.

20. Julie Johnson, "Reagan, Spurning Tougher Move, Orders Anti-bias Rules on AIDS," *New York Times*, August 3, 1988.

21. Gerald M. Boyd, "Bush Backs Protection of AIDS Victim Rights," *New York Times*, June 29, 1988.

22. ACT UP fact sheet: "Let the Record Show," [ca. June 26, 1988].

7. Summer Awakening

1. Rex Wockner, "ACT UP Clashes with Atlanta Cops," *New York Native*, August 1, 1988.

2. Donna Minkowitz, "Lips That Touch Democrats," *Village Voice*, July 26, 1988.

3. Jim Newton and Bill Montgomery, "Police Move In to Control Protesters after Young's Pledge on Security," *Atlanta Journal and Constitution*, July 19, 1988.

4. Rex Wockner, "Riot Squad Turns Kiss-In into Bash-In in Atlanta," *Bay Area Reporter*, July 28, 1988.

5. Chris Duncan, "Viewpoint: ACT UP Adds to City Formula," *Southern Voice*, End of July Issue 1988.

6. Duncan.

7. Michel Marriott, "New York City Asks State and U.S. for AIDS Help," *New York Times*, May 17, 1988.

8. Bruce Lambert, "New York Called Unprepared on AIDS," *New York Times*, May 14, 1988.

9. Michael Specter, "AIDS Virus Likely Fatal to All Infected," *Washington Post*, June 3, 1988—based on Kung-Jong Lui, William W. Darrow, and George W. Rutherford III, "A Model-Based Estimate of the Mean Incubation Period for AIDS in Homosexual Men," *Science*, June 3, 1988.

10. Bruce Lambert, "Halving of Estimate on AIDS Is Raising Doubts in New York," *New York Times*, July 20, 1988.

11. Lambert.

12. Richard Dunne, "City Finds Virus—In California," *New York Newsday*, July 29, 1988.

13. Bruce Lambert, "Puzzling Questions Are Raised on Statistics on AIDS Epidemic," *New York Times*, July 22, 1988.

14. Lambert.

15. Bruce Lambert, "New York Again Revises Its AIDS Virus Estimates," *New York Times*, August 11, 1988.

16. Iris Long, interviewed by Sarah Schulman, ACT UP Oral History Project, May 16, 2003, 11–12.

17. Jim Eigo, interviewed by Sarah Schulman, ACT UP Oral History Project, March 5, 2004, 18.

18. Eigo, interview, 20.

19. "Proposal to Establish AIDS Treatment Registry (ATR) Computerized Database of AIDS Clinical Trials Underway in New York," May 1988.

20. Joe Ferson, "Angry Crowd Greets FDA Head at AIDS Session," *Boston Sunday Globe*, July 24, 1988.

21. Peter S. Arno and Karyn L. Feiden, *Against the Odds: The Story of AIDS Drug Development, Politics, and Profits* (New York: HarperPerennial, 1992), 72.

22. Peter Staley, interviewed by Sarah Schulman, ACT UP Oral History Project, December 9, 2006, 13.

23. Arno and Feiden, *Against the Odds*, 78–79.

24. Kathleen Conkey, Gregory Kolovakas, Rosemary Kuropat, and Darrell Yates-Rist, "Zapping the Mayor or Zapping Gays," letter to the editor, *New York Native*, July 4, 1988.

25. ACT UP fact sheet: "Missing: 200,000 New Yorkers," Numbers Demonstration at the NYC Department of Health, [ca. July 28, 1988].

26. Rick Shur, "ACT-UP Demands Joseph's Removal," *New York Native*, August 15, 1988.

27. Editorial, "A Lesson from the Political Conventions," *Windy City Times*, August 25, 1988.

28. Andrew Patner, "Gay Activists Unheard, Gay Delegates Unseen," *Windy City Times*, August 25, 1988.

29. Rex Wockner, "Outsiders in The Big Easy," *New York Native*, September 5, 1988.

30. Wockner.

31. Donna Minkowitz, "Bash in '88," *Village Voice*, August 23, 1988.

32. Minkowitz.

33. George Wittman, "I Was a Republican 'Bush-Hog,'" *New York Native*, September 5, 1988.

34. Wockner, "Outsiders in The Big Easy."

35. Wockner.

36. ACT UP internal document: Revised Proposal to ACT UP Coordinating Committee, June 28, 1988 (and voted on by Floor, July 5, 1988).

37. Neil Broome, interviewed by Sarah Schulman, ACT UP Oral History Project, April 25, 2004, 3–5.

38. Heidi Dorow, interviewed by Sarah Schulman, ACT UP Oral History Project, April 17, 2007, 20.

39. Rex Wockner, "Acting Up in Alabama, *New York Native*, August 29, 1988.

40. Wockner.

41. Gerri Wells, interviewed by Sarah Schulman, ACT UP Oral History Project, March 24, 2007, 41–43.

42. Rick Buck, "Gay Rights Protesters Given Escort," *Tampa Tribune,* August 26, 1988.

43. Buck.

44. Wells, interview, 41–43.

45. John T. McQuiston, "1,000 Protest Attacks Aimed at Homosexuals," *New York Times,* August 31, 1988.

46. Guy Trebay, "On the Bias," *Village Voice,* September 13, 1988.

47. SPREE, interviewed by Sarah Schulman, ACT UP Oral History Project, October 16, 2004, 31.

48. Maria Maggenti, interviewed by Sarah Schulman, ACT UP Oral History Project, January 20, 2003, 22.

49. Patner, "Gay Activists Unheard."

50. Donna Minkowitz, "D'Amato Acts Up," *Village Voice,* September 20, 1988; and Phil Zwickler, "Quayle Zapped," *New York Native,* September 19, 1988.

51. David Holmberg, "Commissioner Confronted by AIDS Activists," *Newsday,* August 4, 1988.

52. ACT UP internal document: Mark Harrington, "Actions Report," proposed article for ACT UP Newsletter, unpublished, August 22, 1988.

53. Joe Nicholson, "Secret City Memo Cuts AIDS Estimates," *New York Post,* August 5, 1988.

54. ACT UP internal document: Draft Letter from Jim Eigo to Stephen C. Joseph, M.D., M.P.H., August 1988.

55. ACT UP internal document: Transcription by Jim Eigo of Opening Statement by Stephen Joseph from Meeting between City Health Commissioner Stephen Joseph and ACT UP delegation, September 15, 1988 (as presented to Coordinating Committee, September 20, 1988).

56. ACT UP internal document: Jim Eigo, notes on the meeting with Stephen Joseph on September 15, 1988, presented to Coordinating Committee, September 20, 1988.

57. ACT UP internal document: Jim Eigo, notes on meeting with Stephen Joseph.

8. Seize Control of the FDA

1. ACT UP internal document: Mark Harrington, with Jim Eigo, David Z. Kirschenbaum, and Dr. Iris Long, "A Glossary of AIDS Drug Trials, Testing & Treatment Issues," July 5, 1988, 16.

2. Gregg Bordowitz, interviewed by Sarah Schulman, ACT UP Oral History Project, December 17, 2002, 27.

3. Harrington et al., "Glossary."

4. ACT UP internal document: Jim Eigo, Mark Harrington, Margaret McCarthy, Stephen Spinella, and Rick Sugden, "FDA Action Handbook," September 12, 1988, 16.

5. Michelangelo Signorile, interviewed by Sarah Schulman, ACT UP Oral History Project, September 20, 2003, 2.

6. Signorile, interview, 17–18.

7. Signorile, 19.

8. Signorile, 18–19.

9. Signorile, 18.

10. Transcript of the debate, *New York Times*, September 26, 1988.

11. Jeff Weinstein, "'A Map of Preventable Death': The Quilt Unfolds Again," *Village Voice*, October 18, 1988.

12. ACT UP flyer: "Show Your Anger to the People Who Helped Make the Quilt Possible: Our Government," [ca. October 8–10, 1988].

13. Kiki Mason, "FDA: The Demo of the Year," *New York Native*, October 24, 1988.

14. Mason.

15. Susan Okie, "AIDS Coalition Targets FDA for Demonstration," *Washington Post*, October 11, 1988.

16. Michelangelo Signorile, *Queer in America* (New York: Random House, 1993), 12–13.

17. Mason, "FDA: The Demo of the Year."

18. Another United Fruit Company leaflet: "Let's Play . . . Protocol," [ca. October 11, 1988].

19. Joyce Price, "AIDS Protest Closes FDA: 176 Arrested," *Washington Times*, October 12, 1988.

20. UPI, "175 Arrested in Protest of FDA Policy on AIDS," *Houston Chronicle*, October 12, 1988.

21. Signorile, *Queer in America*, 14.

22. Signorile, 14.

23. Signorile, 15.

24. Douglas Crimp with Adam Ralston, *AIDS Demo Graphics* (Seattle: Bay, 1990), 82.

25. Mason, "FDA: The Demo of the Year."

26. "The New Center for Drugs & Biologics: A History," a handout from *Rockville Is Burning*, a theatrical skit performed by Wave 3 at La Mama on January 12, 1988, as a benefit for ATR.

27. Signorile, *Queer in America*, 15.

28. Caption: "Hundreds Protest Government Policy on AIDS Medications," *New York Times*, October 12, 1988.

29. Philip J. Hilts, "How the AIDS Crisis Made Drug Regulators Speed Up," *New York Times*, September 24, 1989.

30. Photo: Impact Visuals/Marilyn Humphries.

31. Lawrence K. Altman, "Mainstream Medicine Joins Growing Debate about Drug Approval," *New York Times*, December 6, 1988 (quoting *JAMA* editorial, November 25, 1988).

32. Altman.

33. ACT UP internal document: Mark Harrington, "A Report to ACT-UP on the first meeting of NCRCPANDAC/the National Committee to Review Current Procedures for Approval of New Drugs for Aids and Cancer," January 4, 1989.

34. Laurie Garrett, "The Battle over FDA Drug Policy," *New York Newsday*, February 14, 1989.

35. Michael R. Kagay, "Poll Finds Antipathy toward Some AIDS Victims," *New York Times*, October 14, 1988.

36. Lisa Belkin, "Texas Judge Eases Sentence for Killer of 2 Homosexuals," *New York Times*, December 18, 1988.

37. Jim Whelan, "Joseph Walks out of Meeting," *New York Native*, December 5, 1988.

9. Targeting City Hall

1. Steve Lewis, "Five Easy Pieces: The Best Nightclubs in the History of New York City," Goodnight Mr. Lewis, *BlackBook*, August 26, 2009, http://www.blackbookmag.com /good-night-mr-lewis-1-109/five-easy-pieces-the-best-nightclubs-in-the-history-of-new -york-city/.

2. President Ronald Reagan on *Good Morning America*, January 2, 1984.

3. Partnership for the Homeless, *AIDS—The Cutting Edge of Homelessness in New York City*, January 1, 1989.

4. ACT UP fact sheet: "How's Ed Doing? 5,000 Homeless People with AIDS Can't Sleep in 62 Beds," [ca, November 1, 1988], with estimates from the Partnership for the Homeless (cited in Target City Hall teach-in guide *AIDS—The Cutting Edge of Homelessness in New York City*).

5. Gina Kolata, "Many with AIDS Said to Live in Shelters in New York City," *New York Times*, April 4, 1988—HRA policy requires PWAs to be referred to single-room occupancy hotels, apartments, or Bailey House.

6. Eric Sawyer, interviewed by Sarah Schulman, ACT UP Oral History Project, March 10, 2004, 13.

7. Michel Marriott, "Koch Picks 8 Sites in 3 Boroughs to House Homeless AIDS Patients," *New York Times*, October 31, 1988.

8. ACT UP handbook: Rich Jackman and Lei Chou, "Homeless People and AIDS," in Lei Chou et al., "Target City Hall: An AIDS Activist's Guide to New York City in 1989," March 20, 1989, 52.

9. Jackman and Chou, "Homeless People and AIDS," 58–59.

10. ACT UP handbook: Ray Navarro, Richard Elovich, and Mark Harrington, "Drug Use and AIDS," in Chou et al., "Target City Hall," 28, quoting statistics from "AIDS: New York's Response: A 5-Year Interagency Plan."

11. Navarro, Elovich, and Harrington, 28.

12. ACT UP handbook: "Broken Promises," in Chou et al., "Target City Hall," 29. Also, per press release from the AIDS Budget Working Group, "AIDS Group Charges Discrepancy between City Budget and 5-Year AIDS Plan," May 31, 1988.

13. ACT UP handbook: New York City Department of Health, "AIDS Surveillance Update," February 22, 1989, attached as Appendix A and as quoted in Chou et al., "Target City Hall."

14. "Ortez Alderson," Chicago LGBT Hall of Fame, viewed December 8, 2019, http:// chicagolgbthalloffame.org/alderson-ortez/.

15. Michael E. Howard, "A Tiger in the House," *Village Voice*, December 27, 1988.

16. ACT UP Majority Actions Committee, "Response to the 1988 CDC Conference on AIDS and People of Color," August 17, 1988, attached to Coordinating Committee minutes, August 23, 1988.

17. Ortez Alderson, "A Call to Action," attached to Coordinating Committee minutes, August 23, 1988.

18. Alderson.

19. ACT UP handbook: Ray Navarro, "People of Color and AIDS," in Chou et al., "Target City Hall," 15–21.

20. Howard W. French, "The Poor Overwhelm Hospitals in New York as They Seek Care," *New York Times*, December 4, 1988, quoting report from United Hospital Fund, "Poverty and Health in New York City."

21. Howard W. French, "Health Care in New York Is Not for All, Report Finds," *New York Times*, February 23, 1989.

22. French, "The Poor Overwhelm Hospitals" (quoting numbers from the Greater Hospital Association).

23. ACT UP handbook: Mark Harrington, "Health Care: Triage in the Streets?," in Chou et al., "Target City Hall," 42, citing Local 1199 fact sheet, "Understaffed, Overworked, Over-Stressed Health Care Workers in New York, Winter 1989, Albany Alert," March 1989.

24. Bruce Lambert, "AIDS Drives Jobs Away, Report Says," *New York Times*, March 7, 1989.

25. Lambert.

26. Ken Woodard, "Reason #2: 5,000 PEOPLE WITH AIDS DESERVE A BETTER PLACE TO LIVE THAN THE SIDEWALK YOU'RE STANDING ON," viewed March 25, 2020, https://digitalcollections.nypl.org/items/510d47e3-3eb6-a3d9-e040-e00a18064a99.

27. Douglas Crimp with Adam Rolston, *AIDS Demo Graphics* (Seattle: Bay, 1990), 92.

28. Crimp and Ralston, 93.

29. Scott Robbe, interviewed by Sarah Schulman, ACT UP Oral History Project, December 5, 2013, 14.

30. Richard Levine, "Koch, in Book with O'Connor, Traces a Conservative Shift," *New York Times*, May 7, 1989, 1, quoting *His Eminence and Hizzoner*.

31. ACT UP newspaper ad: Ken Woodard, "Invest in Marble and Granite," 1989, in Crimp and Rolston, *AIDS Demo Graphics*, 87.

32. James Harney, "Ed Finds Friends at AIDS Unit," *Daily News*, March 26, 1989.

33. Catherine Gund, ACT UP Meeting Prior to Target City Hall, NYPL Tape #01116-A, video, 00.09:39–00.11:11, viewed April 14, 2022, https://actuporalhistory.org/actions/target-city-hall.

34. James Wentzy, *Fight Back, Fight AIDS, ACT UP* (2002), video, 00:03:27–00:06:55. Most of my pre-action meeting "performance" is captured in this footage. Additional footage can be found on the two City Hall pre-action meeting videos on the ACT UP Oral History site, https://actuporalhistory.org/actions/target-city-hall.

35. "05.25.2010 Conversation: Wall Street," in *Gran Fury: Read My Lips*, catalog for exhibit curated by Gran Fury and Michael Cohen, New York University, Steinhardt Gallery, January–March 2012 (New York: 80WSE Press, 2011), 25–29.

36. Crimp and Rolston, *AIDS Demo Graphics*, 20.

37. Mark Harrington, "On March 28," *The Body Positive*, undated, 16–18.

38. Rita Giordano, "AIDS Protesters Strip-Searched," *Newsday*, April 3, 1989.

39. Robert D. McFadden, "30 Improper Strip-Searches Follow AIDS Rally Arrests," *New York Times*, April 2, 1989.

40. McFadden.

41. Kathryn Anastos and Carola Marte, "Women—The Missing Persons in the AIDS Epidemic," *Health/PAC Bulletin* 19, no. 4 (Winter 1989): 6–13.

10. Storming the Ivory Tower

1. Ron Goldberg, "Conference Call: When PWAs First Sat at the High Table," *POZ [Magazine]*, July 1998.

2. *The Montreal Manifesto/Le Manifeste de Montréal*, jointly issued by AIDS Action Now! Toronto, Canada, and ACT UP, New York, U.S.A., June 1989.

3. Lawrence K. Altman, "A New Therapy Approach: Cancer as a Model for AIDS," *New York Times,* June 13, 1989.

4. ACT UP/AIDS Action Now! press release: "AIDS Activists Steal the Show at Opening of Fifth International AIDS Conference," June 4, 1989.

5. Joe Nicholson, "Boos & Cheers for AIDS Plan," *New York Post,* June 5, 1989.

6. Jeffrey Goodell, "Stephen Joseph: Every Time the City's AIDS Chief Makes Some Progress, A Little Devil inside Him Acts Up," *Seven Days,* July 12, 1989.

7. "Remarks of Stephen C. Joseph, M.D., M.P.H., Commissioner of Health New York City at the V International Conference on AIDS Plenary Program, June 5, 1989, Montreal, Quebec."

8. Catherine Woodard, "Treatment: Logic Simple . . . Logistics Aren't," *Newsday,* June 18, 1989.

9. Woodard.

10. ACT UP, *A National AIDS Treatment Research Agenda,* V International Conference on AIDS, Montreal, June 1989, 2.

11. ACT UP, 3.

12. ACT UP, 2.

13. ACT UP, 16.

14. Irwin Block, "Men Who Don't Use Condoms Called Greatest AIDS Threat," *The Gazette, Montreal,* June 8, 1989, quoting Tracy Tief, a Toronto sex-trade worker.

15. "Beyond Compassion," remarks by Randy Shilts, National Correspondent, *San Francisco Chronicle,* V International Conference on AIDS, Montreal, June 9, 1989.

16. "A Call to Hold the International Conference on AIDS Only in Countries That Permit the Free Travel of HIV Infected People," cosponsored by AIDS Action Council (US), American Foundation for AIDS Research, Canada AIDS Society, Gay Men's Health Crisis (US), Mobilization Against AIDS (US), National Gay Rights Advocates (US), National Lesbian and Gay Task Force (US), San Francisco AIDS Foundation, Sixth International Conference on AIDS.

17. "A Call to Hold the International Conference on AIDS Only in Countries That Permit the Free Travel of HIV Infected People," motion proposed by Dr. Henry J. Yeager, ACT UP, New York, seconded by Ronald Goldberg, ACT UP, New York.

18. Michael Slocum, "Science Meets Activism," *Body Positive,* July–August 1989.

19. ACT UP internal document: Jim Eigo, "Treatment & Data Update 061989."

20. "Beyond Compassion," remarks by Randy Shilts.

21. ACT UP/AIDS Action Now! press release: "AIDS Activists Steal the Show" (quoting Tim Powers).

11. Remember Stonewall Was a Riot

1. ACT UP internal document: The Lesbian & Gay Activist History Project, *A His & Herstory of Queer Activism,* June 1989.

2. Kathleen Conkey, Gregory Kolovakas, Rosemary Kuropat, and Darrell Yates Rist, "Zapping the Mayor or Zapping Gays?," letter to the editor, *New York Native,* July 4, 1988.

3. Vito Russo, "Letters," *New York Native,* July 4, 1988.

4. Mike Salinas, "ACT UP Goes to Washington," *New York Native,* June 15, 1987.

5. Alisa Solomon, "The Demise of the 'Native'" (and sidebar article, "An Alter*Native*"), *Village Voice,* August 22, 1989.

6. Darrell Yates Rist, "The Deadly Costs of an Obsession," *The Nation*, February 13, 1989.

7. Martin Bauml Duberman, "Stonewall Place (1989)," in *About Time: Exploring the Gay Past*, expanded ed. (New York: Meridian Books, 1991), 424–27 (quotation on 426).

8. ACT UP flyer: "Why We March," [ca. June 24, 1989].

9. Radical Faerie flyer, "A Call for All Radical, Outsider, and Countercultural Lesbian and Gay People to Gather in New York City in June to Celebrate the Twentieth Anniversary of the Stonewall Riots," June 1989.

10. Radical Faerie flyer, "Stonewall What a Riot!," undated.

11. Radical Faerie flyer, "A Call."

12. C. Carr, "Queens and Knaves," *Village Voice*, July 4, 1989.

12. Parallel Tracks

1. ACT UP, *A National AIDS Treatment Research Agenda*, June 1989, 8. This is from the original document passed out in Montreal. A subsequent version, revised September 1989, is posted online at https://www.poz.com/pdfs/national-aids-treatment-research-agenda-1989.pdf.

2. Bruce Nussbaum, *Good Intentions: How Big Business and the Medical Establishment Are Corrupting the Fight against AIDS, Alzheimer's, Cancer, and More* (New York: Penguin Books, 1990), 286.

3. *Bracschi v. Stahl Associates*, 74 N.Y.2d 201,543 N.E.2d 49, 544 N.Y.S.2d 784, 1989 N.Y.

4. Philip S. Gutis, "New York Court Defines Family to Include Homosexual Couples," *New York Times*, July 7, 1989, quoting *Braschi v. Stahl Associates.*

5. "Giuliani Faults Koch on Bereavement Leave," *New York Times*, July 11, 1989.

6. Jennifer Preston, "Koch Says Rudy Is 'Gay-Bashing,'" *Newsday*, July 11, 1989.

7. Editorial, "What's a Family; Turning Landlords into Spies," *New York Times,* July 11, 1989.

8. David Shaw, "Coverage of AIDS Story: A Slow Start," *Los Angeles Times*, December 20, 1987.

9. David Shaw, "Hudson Brought AIDS Coverage out of the Closet," *Los Angeles Times,* December 21, 1987.

10. Shaw, "Coverage of AIDS Story" (quoting Dearing/Rogers USC Study).

11. "Why Make AIDS Worse Than It Is?," editorial, *New York Times*, June 29, 1989.

12. Sharon Wilkey, "Gay-March Sign Offends in P'town," *Cape Cod Times*, July 25, 1989.

13. Wilkey.

14. Peter Steele, "Complaints Issued over Gay Sign," *The Advocate,* July 27, 1989.

15. Wilkey, "Gay-March Sign Offends."

16. "Congressional Hearing on Parallel Track, July 20," *AIDS Treatment News*, no. 84, July 28, 1989.

17. Nussbaum, *Good Intentions,* 291–92.

18. Jim Eigo, excerpt from oral testimony to Congress representing ACT UP (July 20, 1989), ACT UP Reports, vol. 1, no. 5, September/October 1989.

19. Eigo.

20. ACT UP, Parallel Track Consensus Proposal, August 16, 1989.

21. Nussbaum, *Good Intentions,* 290.

22. Peter S. Arno and Karyn L. Feiden, *Against the Odds: The Story of AIDS Drug Development, Politics, and Profit* (New York: HarperPerennial, 1992), 183.

23. DF Transcript 20085 FDA_ACT UP_Parallel Track, 14.

24. DF Transcript 20085 FDA_ACT UP_Parallel Track, 14.

25. Marilyn Chase, "Shock Troops Activist Risk-Takers May Gain Legitimacy in the War on AIDS," *Wall Street Journal*, July 28, 1989; second quote is Jerome Groopman.

26. Marilyn Chase, "Pricing Battle: Burroughs Wellcome Reaps Profits, Outrage from Its AIDS Drug," *Wall Street Journal*, September 15, 1989.

27. ACT UP press release: "AIDS Activists Seize Office at Burroughs Wellcome, Demand Lower Prices and Cost Data on AZT, Subsidies for the Needy," April 25, 1989.

28. Chase, "Pricing Battle."

29. "AZT's Inhuman Cost," Opinion, *New York Times*, August 28, 1989.

30. Michelangelo Signorile, "AIDS Activists Storm Stock Exchange, Halting Trading," *OutWeek*, September 24, 1989.

31. Signorile.

32. Chase, "Pricing Battle."

33. Philip J. Hilts, "Wave of Protests Developing on Profits from AIDS Drug," *New York Times*, September 17, 1989.

13. Heading Inside

1. ACT UP fact sheet: "New York City AIDS Care: A Crime Giuliani Never Investigated," [ca. September 27, 1989].

2. ACT UP internal document: Jim Eigo, "No NIAID Funds for CRI: A Response," *Treatment & Data Update*, October 8, 1989.

3. ACT UP internal document: Jim Eigo, "No NIAID Funds for CRI: A Response."

4. "On the Right Track," *Pippin*, music and lyrics by Stephen Schwartz.

5. Mark Harrington (edited by Ken Fornataro, introduction by Jim Eigo), "A Critique of the AIDS Clinical Trials Group," ACT UP/New York, May 1, 1990, 22–23.

6. Bruce Nussbaum, *Good Intentions: How Big Business and the Medical Establishment Are Corrupting the Fight against AIDS, Alzheimer's, Cancer, and More* (New York: Penguin Books, 1990), 306.

7. ACT UP internal document: Mark Harrington, "7th AIDS Clinical Trials Group Meeting," November 6–8, 1989, quoting Dan Hoth.

8. ACT UP internal document: Jim Eigo, "ACTG: The Investigators Meet (Part 1)," *Treatment and Data Update*, November 13, 1989.

9. Gina Kolata, "Ignored AIDS Drug Shows Promise in Small Tests," *New York Times*, August 15, 1989.

10. Gina Kolata, "Critics Fault Secret Effort to Test AIDS Drug," *New York Times*, September 19, 1989.

11. Gina Kolata, "Innovative AIDS Drug Plan May Be Undermining Testing," *New York Times*, November 21, 1989.

12. Gina Kolata, "Physicians Rid a Man's Body of AIDS Virus in Experiment," *New York Times*, December 19, 1989.

13. Gina Kolata, "Doubt Voiced on Marrow Use against AIDS," *New York Times*, December 21, 1989.

14. Gina Kolata, "Federal Delay in Lowering Standard for Doses of AIDS Drug Is Assailed," December 27, 1989.

15. ACT UP internal document: Coordinating Committee Minutes, October 24, 1989.

16. Sean Strub, *Body Counts: A Memoir of Politics, Sex, AIDS, and Survival* (New York: Scribner, 2014), 219–25.

14. Stop the Church

1. Congregation for the Doctrine of the Faith, "Letter to the Bishops of the Catholic Church on the Pastoral Care of Homosexual Persons," October 1, 1986, Vatican website, viewed January 14, 2018, http://www.vatican.va/roman_curia/congregations/cfaith /documents/rc_con_cfaith_doc_19861001_homosexual-persons_en.html.

2. "The Many Faces of AIDS: A Gospel Response," US Conference of Catholic Bishops, November 14, 1987, http://www.usccb.org/issues-and-action/human-life-and -dignity/global-issues/statement-the-many-faces-of-aids-from-nccb-administrative-board -1987-11.cfm.

3. "The Many Faces of AIDS."

4. Ari L. Goldman, "Cardinal Won't Allow Instruction on Condoms in Programs on AIDS," *New York Times*, December 14, 1987, http://www.nytimes.com/1987/12/14/us /cardinal-won-t-allow-instruction-on-condoms-in-programs-on-aids.html.

5. B. D. Colen, "The Cardinal's Confusion on AIDS," *Newsday*, November 21, 1989.

6. Geraldine Baum, "Fight AIDS with Morality, Says the Pope," *Newsday*, November 16, 1989.

7. CNA Daily News, "Sisters of Life Mark 100th Birthday of Founder, Cardinal O'Connor," *Catholic News Report*, January 15, 2020, https://www.catholicworldreport .com/2020/01/15/sisters-of-life-mark-100th-birthday-of-founder-cardinal-oconnor/.

8. ACT UP/WHAM! fact sheet: "Welcome to Saint Patrick's Cathedral," December 10, 1989.

9. ACT UP/WHAM! flyer: "Dear Parishoners of Saint Patrick's Cathedral," December 3, 1989.

10. Emily Nahmanson, interviewed by Sarah Schulman, ACT UP Oral History Project, April 27, 2003, 11–12.

11. Jim Hubbard, *United in Anger: A History of ACT UP* (2012), video, 39:32–40:12.

12. Tom Keane, interviewed by Sarah Schulman, ACT UP Oral History Project, February 24, 2015, 20–23.

13. Esther Kaplan, "City Council Swallows the Wafer," *Village Voice*, January 9, 1990.

14. Manuel Perez-Rivas and Ji-Yeon Yuh, "Protest Siege at St. Pat's," *Newsday*, December 11, 1989.

15. Linda Stevens and Rocco Paarascandola, "Protests Rock St. Pat's," *New York Post*, December 11, 1989.

16. Charles King, Facebook post to ACT UP Alumni page, December 30, 2021.

17. Perez-Rivas and Yuh, "Protest Siege at St. Pat's."

18. Ellis Henican, "O'Connor Refuses to Back Down," *Newsday*, December 12, 1989.

19. "O'Connor Speaks," excerpts from the cardinal's remarks, *Newsday*, December 12, 1989.

20. ACT UP press release: "Position Statement," December 13, 1989.

21. Joel Benenson and Adam Nagourney, "Mass Protestors Not Sorry," *Daily News*, December 14, 1989.

22. Philip Nobile, "Body and Soul: New Allegations about the Secret Life of Father Ritter," *Village Voice*, January 24, 1990.

23. Robert Suro, "Vatican and the AIDS Fight: Amid Worry, Papal Reticence," *New York Times*, January 29, 1988.

24. Suro.

15. The Myers Mess

1. "Mayor Dinkins: A Pledge to All the People; Text of Dinkins Speech: 'We Are All Foot Soldiers on the March to Freedom,'" *New York Times*, January 2, 1990.

2. "Mayor Dinkins: A Pledge to All the People."

3. Catherine Woodard, "Ex-Heavyweight Takes a Shot at Health Commissioner Title," *Newsday*, January 14, 1990.

4. Heidi Evans, "Health Furor," *Daily News*, January 10, 1990.

5. Jeffrey Goodell, "Divided They Stand," *7 Days*, February 14, 1990.

6. Bruce Lambert with Dirk Johnson, "Health Post Candidate: 'Impressive' or 'Slick'?" *New York Times*, January 19, 1990.

7. Goodell, "Divided They Stand."

8. Garbriel Rotello, "Furor Erupts over Choice for Top NYC Health Post," *OutWeek*, January 21, 1990. (Despite the date, this issue was available January 15. It is industry practice for magazines to date their issues for the last day before their next issue is published in order to keep the current issue "fresh" on newsstands.)

9. Goodell, "Divided They Stand."

10. Richard Goldstein and Donna Minkowitz, "The Myers Mess," *Village Voice*, January 30, 1990.

11. Goldstein and Minkowitz.

12. Joe Nicholson, "Lock Up Some AIDS Carriers," *New York Post*, January 18, 1990.

13. Todd S. Purdum, "Leading Backers Turn from Applicant for Health Post," *New York Times*, January 19, 1990.

14. Purdum.

15. ACT UP internal document: "Mayor Dinkins to New Yorkers with AIDS: 'Drop Dead'"—undated, unsigned.

16. ACT UP internal document: Larry Kramer, "Letter to the ACT UP," January 22, 1990.

17. ACT UP Majority Action Committee, "Open Letter to NYC's AIDS Activist Community," undated.

18. ACT UP internal document: "Memo to ACT UP from the Majority Actions [*sic*] Committee, issue: cultural sensitivity and communication," no date.

19. Ray Navarro, "Woody or Wouldn't He? Toward a New Dialogue on the Health Commissioner," *OutWeek*, February 4, 1990.

20. Confirmed by Peter Staley in email to author dated October 20, 2021.

21. ACT UP internal document: Maxine Wolfe, "The CDC's AIDS Epidemiology and What's Wrong with It," November 6, 1990.

22. ACT UP, "Introduction and Overview," in *Treatment and Research Agenda for Women with HIV Infection*, undated, 3.

23. S. Chu et al., "Impact of the Human Immunodeficiency Virus Epidemic on Mortality in Women of Reproductive Age, United States," *Journal of the American*

Medical Association, July 11, 1990, 254(4): 225–29—as cited in ACT UP, "Introduction and Overview," *Treatment and Research Agenda for Women with HIV Infection*, 5.

24. 2010 Georgia Code, Title 16—Crimes and Offenses, Chapter 6—Sexual Offenses § 16-6-6—Bestiality, viewed April 17, 2022, https://law.justia.com/codes/georgia/2010/title-16/chapter-6/16-6-6.

25. 2010 Georgia Code, Title 16—Crimes and Offenses, Chapter 6—Sexual Offenses § 16-6-7—Bestiality, viewed April 17, 2022, https://law.justia.com/codes/georgia/2010/title-16/chapter-6/16-6-7.

26. Todd S. Purdum, "Dinkins to End Needle Plan for Drug Users," *New York Times*, February 14, 1990.

27. Nina Reyes, "Needling the Queer Nation," *OutWeek*, June 27, 1990.

28. ACT UP internal document: Richard Elovich, reused as draft for Day of Desperation, June 18, 1990.

29. ACT UP handbook: Richard Elovich, "Abstinence," in Lei Chou et al., "Target City Hall: An AIDS Activist's Guide to New York City in 1989," March 20, 1989, 35.

30. Catherine Woodard, "Needle Giveaway to Invite Arrest," *Newsday*, March 2, 1990.

31. Richard Elovich, press briefing on the effectiveness of education and bleach distribution programs in preventing the spread of HIV among IV drug users, May 10, 1990.

32. Purdum, "Dinkins to End Needle Plan."

33. Gregg Bordowitz, interviewed by Sarah Schulman, ACT UP Oral History Project, December 17, 2002, 39–46 (quote on 43).

34. Richard Elovich, interviewed by Sarah Schulman, ACT UP Oral History Project, May 14, 2007, 49.

35. Elovich, interview, 44.

36. Bordowitz, interview, 43.

16. Time's Up, Mario!

1. Catherine Woodard, "Cuomo Bares Plans for a War on AIDS," *Newsday*, February 16, 1989.

2. Bruce Lambert, "Cuomo Sets AIDS Plan, Admitting It Falls Short," *New York Times*, February 16, 1989.

3. Lambert.

4. Lambert.

5. Andrew Miller, "In a New York State of Mind," *OutWeek*, January 14, 1990.

6. Miller.

7. Miller.

8. ACT UP handbook: Eric Sawyer, Charles King, and Rand Snyder, "Housing for Homeless People with HIV/AIDS," in Heidi Dorow et al., *State of the State: AIDS Disaster Area, Albany Action Fact Book*, March 1990 (Heidi Dorow, Richard Elovich, IVDU Affinity Group, Wayne Kawadler, David Z. Kirschenbaum, Garry Kleinman, Margaret McCarthy, Madeleine Olnek, David Parrish, Cathy Potler, Robert Rygor, Eric Sawyer, Rand Snyder, Rod Sorge, Daniel Wolfe, Maxine Wolfe), 13–15.

9. ACT UP internal document: David Z. Kirschenbaum and John Chism, "ALBANY: 'It's Always Easy to Blame a Government Agency.'—Dr. David Axelrod," no date.

10. ACT UP fact sheet: "Cuomo's Budget Kills," [ca. March 28, 1990].

11. Kirschenbaum and Chism, "ALBANY," quoting statistics from Robert Greifinger, M.D., Deputy Commissioner of the NYS Department of Corrections.

12. Madeline Olnek and David Parrish, "AIDS Care and Prevention in the New York State Prisons," in Dorow et al., *State of the State*, 42.

13. Kirschenbaum and Chism, "ALBANY."

14. Olnek and Parrish, "AIDS Care and Prevention," 42.

15. William Bunch, "NY Cash Poor? It Doesn't Stop the Lobbyists," *LI Newsday*, February 13, 1990.

16. Dan Janison, "13 Arrested in AIDS Protest at State Office," *Albany Times Union*, February 14, 1990.

17. Guy Trebay, "In Mario's Face," *Village Voice*, March 10, 1990—conversation between Cuomo and Aurigemma.

18. Sam Howe Verhovek, "Albany Protest on AIDS Funds Brings Arrests," *New York Times*, March 29, 1990.

19. "A Costa Her/History," submitted to the Mulberry Group, March 2, 1991.

20. Tom Precious, "1,000 Rally at Capitol," *Albany Times Union*, March 29, 1990.

21. James Wagner, interviewed by Sarah Schulman, ACT UP Oral History Project, February 28, 2004, 14.

22. Catherine Woodard, "Activists ACT UP against AIDS Cuts," *Newsday*, March 29, 1990.

23. Philip J. Hilts, "Bush, in First Address on AIDS, Backs a Bill to Protect Its Victims," *New York Times*, March 30, 1990, https://www.nytimes.com/1990/03/30/us/bush-in-first-address-on-aids-backs-a-bill-to-protect-its-victims.html?searchResultPosition=1.

24. Lisa M. Keen, "Activists: Bush AIDS Budget Gives Distorted Picture," *Washington Blade*, February 2, 1990 (all figures/commentary).

25. Laurie Garrett, "Bush Gives First Speech on AIDS," *Newsday*, March 30, 1990.

26. Cliff O'Neill, "NGLTF Chief Heckles Bush at AIDS Speech," *OutWeek*, April 11, 1990.

17. Storm the NIH

1. Mark Harrington (edited by Ken Fornataro, introduction by Jim Eigo), "A Critique of the AIDS Clinical Trials Group," ACT UP/New York, May 1, 1990.

2. Mark Harrington, "Diary of a Mad Scientist," *OutWeek*, June 20, 2010.

3. Gina Kolata, "Advocates' Tactics on AIDS Issues Provoking Warnings of a Backlash," *New York Times*, March 11, 1990.

4. Gina Kolata, "Odd Surge in Deaths Found in Those Taking AIDS Drug," *New York Times*, March 12, 1990.

5. Marilyn Chase, "Report on the Experimental Drug DDI Prompts Concern from AIDS Patients," *Wall Street Journal*, March 13, 1990.

6. "Kolata's Hatchet," *Treatment and Data Digest*, no. 37, March 19, 1990.

7. Gina Kolata, "Many Doctors Recommend Disputed AIDS Drug," *New York Times*, March 19, 1990.

8. "On AIDS, Compassion and Confusion," editorial, *New York Times*, March 24, 1990.

9. "NIAID Responds to ACT UP Allegations and Demands," *NIAID AIDS Agenda*, May 1990, 1–5.

10. Chapin Wright, "AIDS Protesters 'ACT-UP' at Center," *Newsday*, May 22, 1990.

11. Linda Meredith, interviewed by Sarah Schulman, ACT UP Oral History Project, March 10, 2013, 32.

12. "Drug Development and Review Definitions," FDA, content current as of August 20, 2015, http://www.fda.gov/Drugs/DevelopmentApprovalProcess/HowDrugsare DevelopedandApproved/ApprovalApplications/InvestigationalNewDrugINDApplication /ucm176522.htm.

13. "The Ten Commandments Quotes," Rotten Tomatoes, http://www.rottentomatoes .com/m/1021015-ten_commandments/quotes/.

18. Inside or Out

1. Vincent Canby, "Manhattan's Privileged and the Plague of AIDS," New York Times, May 11, 1990.

2. "A Call to Hold the International Conference on AIDS Only in Countries That Permit the Free Travel of HIV Infected People," motion proposed by Dr. Henry J. Yeager, ACT UP, New York, seconded by Ronald Goldberg, ACT UP, New York.

3. "Red Cross Protest," Wall Street Journal, November 24, 1989.

4. Philip J. Hilts, "Agency to Use Dormant Law to Bar Homosexuals from U.S.," New York Times, March 3, 1990 (statute quoted).

5. Larry Kramer, "A Call to Riot," OutWeek, March 14, 1990.

6. Marilyn Chase, "Demonstrations and Boycott over Travel Curbs Threaten to Disrupt International AIDS Meeting," Wall Street Journal, May 8, 1990.

7. Michele DeRanleau, "Kramer Backs Off from Call to Riot," Sentinel, April 17, 1990.

8. Chase, "Demonstrations and Boycott."

9. ACT UP press release: "New York's ACT UP to Attend San Francisco AIDS Conference," June 8, 1990.

10. Robert M. Wachter, The Fragile Coalition (New York: St. Martin's, 1991), 198.

11. Wachter, 198.

12. Charles Petit, "AIDS Delegates Join in Immigration Protest," San Francisco Chronicle, June 21, 1990.

13. Wachter, Fragile Coalition, 200–201.

14. Peter Staley, Never Silent: ACT UP and My Life in Activism (Chicago: Chicago Review Press, 2022), 151.

15. Staley, 151.

16. Staley, 151.

17. Staley, 152.

18. ACT UP internal document: Peter Staley, internal memo to ACT UP, undated.

19. ACT UP press release: "ACT UP Protests at Opening of AIDS Conference," June 19, 1990.

20. ACT UP San Francisco press release: "AIDS Activists Target Sixth International Conference on AIDS," June 4, 1990.

21. Mervyn Silverman, "AIDS Care: The San Francisco Model," Journal of Ambulatory Care Management 11, no. 2 (May 1988): 14–18.

22. ACT UP background document: "The Crumbling 'San Francisco Model,'" undated.

23. ACT UP background document: "Women and AIDS," undated.

24. Rex Wockner, "ACT UP Dominates S.F. AIDS Conference, Science Shoved into Background," PGN, June 29–July 5, 1990.

25. David L. Kirp, "The Scientists from ACT UP," San Francisco Examiner, June 27, 1990.

26. ACT UP Treatment & Data Committee, New York, *AIDS Treatment Research Agenda*, June 1990, 3.

27. Treatment & Data Committee, *AIDS Treatment Research Agenda*, 26.

28. Wachter, *Fragile Coalition*, 219.

29. Kirp, "Scientists from ACT UP."

30. Wachter, *Fragile Coalition*, 219.

31. ACT UP flyer, "No More Words We Want Action," [ca. June 24, 1990].

32. Larry Leibert, "Sullivan Scolds AIDS Protesters for Politicizing S.F. Conference," *San Francisco Chronicle*, June 21, 1990.

33. Philip J. Hilts, "Jeers at AIDS Gathering Drown Out Health Chief," *New York Times*, June 25, 1990.

34. Robert W. Peterson and Chris Bull, "Fear and Loathing in San Francisco," *The Advocate*, July 31, 1990.

35. ACT UP press release: "ACT UP Prevents Louis Sullivan Address," June 24, 1990.

36. Deborah B. Gould, *Moving Politics* (Chicago: University of Chicago Press, 2009), 287.

37. "AIDS and Misdirected Rage," editorial, *New York Times*, June 26, 1990.

38. "Bush Should Have Come," editorial, *San Francisco Examiner*, June 26, 1990.

19. Can the Center Hold?

1. Cynthia Crossen, "AIDS Activist Group Harasses and Provokes to Make Its Point," *Wall Street Journal*, November 7, 1989.

2. ACT UP internal document: Bill Dobbs, "TITA," March 5, 1990.

3. Published Anonymously by Queers, "An Army of Lovers Cannot Lose," *Queers Read This*, [ca. June 24, 1990].

4. Published Anonymously by Queers, "When Anyone Assaults You for Being Queer, It Is a Queer Bashing, Right?," *Queers Read This*.

5. Jane Furse, "Bias Incidents Up 122% Nationwide," *New York Post*, June 18, 1990.

6. Confirmed by Darren Jurmé Allumiér in a private message to the author, April 15, 2022.

7. Kathy Ottersten, interviewed by Sarah Schulman, ACT UP Oral History Project, December 28, 2017, 31.

8. Confirmed by Jim Provenzano in a private email with the author, December 21, 2021.

9. "In Our Own Back Yard," *OutWeek*, July 11, 1990.

10. Published Anonymously by Queers, "I Hate Straights," *Queers Read This*.

11. Esther Kaplan, "A Queer Manifesto," *Village Voice*, August 14, 1990.

12. Martha Shelley, "Gay Is Good," in *Out of the Closets: Voices of Gay Liberation*, ed. Karla Jay and Allen Young (New York: Douglas Books, 1972), 31.

13. ACT UP internal document: David Robinson, "Letter to ACT UP/NY," May 2, 1990.

14. Ming-Yuen S. Ma, interviewed by Sarah Schulman, ACT UP Oral History Project, January 15, 2003, 16.

15. Ming-Yuen S. Ma, interview, 25.

16. Ming-Yuen S. Ma, 22.

17. Ming-Yuen S. Ma, 25–26.

18. Lei Chou, interviewed by Sarah Schulman, ACT UP Oral History Project, May 5, 2003, 23–24.

19. Ming-Yuen S. Ma, interview, 16.

20. Moisés Agosto, interviewed by Sarah Schulman, ACT UP Oral History Project, December 14, 2002, 6.

21. Deborah Ramirez, "Our AIDS Epidemic: Lack of Funding, Fear, Prejudice Threaten Patients," *San Juan Star*, May 27, 1990.

22. Miglisa Capo, "Clinical Drug Trials for AIDS Patients to Start Here," *San Juan Star*, August 23, 1990.

23. Juan Mendez, "Puerto Rico ACTs UP," special supplement to *ACT UP Reports*, Fall/Winter 1990.

24. Miglisa Capo, "AIDS Activists Claim Sullivan Offers Promises Not Action," *San Juan Star*," [ca. July 30, 1990].

25. Capo.

26. Mendez, "Puerto Rico ACTs UP."

27. Mendez.

28. Author interview with Gilbert Martinez, November 13, 1996.

29. Jorge Irizarry, ACT UP de Puerto Rico, "Our Point Was Made," special supplement to *ACT UP Reports,* Fall/Winter 1990.

30. ACT UP internal document: Kim Christensen, "Ableism on Parade," letter to the Floor, July 30, 1990; responding to a complaint in "TITA" that "reading *OutWeek, The Voice,* and *The Guardian* into a tape for PWA Ray Navarro, has nothing to do with ACT UP's 'real business,'" though the quote alludes to the dispute over the Community Center as well.

31. Paul Schwartzman and Leo Standora, "Bush 'Greeted' under Protest," *New York Post,* July 25, 1990.

32. Duncan Osborne, "Read My Coffin," *OutWeek*, August 8, 1990.

33. Eddie Borges and Don Gentile, "Activists Spring a Demo at Waldorf," *Daily News,* July 25, 1990.

34. Emily Nahamson, interviewed by Sarah Schulman, ACT UP Oral History Project, April 27, 2003, 9–10.

35. "A Costa Her/History" submitted to the Mulberry Group, March 2, 1991.

36. John Marzulli, "AIDS Activists Cry Foul," *Daily News,* July 27, 1990.

37. Charles Krauthammer, "AIDS: Getting More Than Its Share," *Time,* June 25, 1990.

38. Mona Charen, "Unsafe Sex Should Take AIDS Blame," *New York Newsday,* June 27, 1990.

39. Pete Hamill, "Confessions of a Heterosexual," *Esquire,* August 1990.

40. Michael Fumento, *The Myth of Heterosexual AIDS* (New York: New Republic/Basic Books, 1990).

41. Donna Minkowitz, "Death Sentences," *Village Voice,* January 30, 1990, quoting Fumento, *The Myth of Heterosexual AIDS*.

42. Dick Thompson, "The AIDS Political Machine," *Time,* January 22, 1990.

43. John S. James, "New Threats to AIDS Research Funding," *AIDS Treatment News,* no. 97, February 16, 1990.

44. Maxine Wolfe, "A Short Herstory of Women and AIDS Activism," *ACT UP Reports,* Fall/Winter 1990.

45. Wolfe.

46. Wolfe.

47. Wolfe.

48. ACT UP internal document: Risa Dennenberg, Heidi Dorow, Garance Franke-Ruta, and Maxine Wolfe, internal memo to ACT UP members dated August 7, 1990 (quoting Fauci from July 27 meeting).

49. Dennenberg et al., internal memo to ACT UP members.

50. *Harrigan 'n Hart, Playbill,* January 1985.

51. Mark Fotopoulos, "*Mark Fotopoulos: Alive Performance,*" unpublished, ©April 8, 1988.

52. Fotopoulos, 4.

53. Fotopoulos, 5.

54. Ned Rorem, "The Real John Simon," *New York Native,* May 6–19, 1985.

55. Fotopoulos, "*Mark Fotopoulos: Alive Performance,*" 5.

56. Fotopoulos, 5–6.

57. Bernard Gavzer, "Why Do Some People Survive AIDS?" *Parade,* September 18, 1988.

58. Gavzer.

59. Bernard Gavzer, "What We Can Learn from Those Who Survive AIDS," *Parade,* June 10, 1990.

60. Jim Fragale, "The AIDS Lady," *New York Native,* April 18, 1988.

61. Fragale.

62. Alan Bavley, "AIDS Activists Fight for Choice of Treatments," *Kansas City Star,* September 16, 1990.

63. ACT UP internal document: "Announcement: The Alternative Treatment Action Working Group," May 27, 1991.

64. Wade Richards, "Women, AIDS, and Alternative Therapies," in ACT UP, *Treatment and Research Agenda for Women with HIV Infection,* "A Work Still in Progress . . . ," 22.

65. ACT UP fact sheet: "Take the Blinders off AIDS Research," undated.

66. ACT UP internal document: "Proposal for Committee Status of Alternative and Holistic Treatments," undated.

67. ACT UP recruitment flyer: "Alternative & Holistic Treatment Committee of ACT UP New York," undated.

68. ACT UP internal document: Alternative and Holistic Treatment Committee, "Proposal for an ACT UP National Action against a Fraudulent Conference on 'Health Fraud,'" August 6, 1990.

69. J. D. Moore Jr., "AIDS Activists Protest Conference," *Kansas City Star,* September 17, 1990.

70. Bavley, "AIDS Activists Fight for Choice of Treatments."

71. Ethel Merman with George Eells, *Merman* (New York: Simon and Schuster, 1978), 229.

20. Bombs Are Dropping

1. *Treatment and Data Digest,* no. 58, August 27, 1990.

2. ACT UP press release: "Countdown 18 Months: Scientists to Be Given Deadline to Make AIDS O.I.s Treatment," November 12, 1990.

3. Treatment & Data Committee, ACT UP/NY, including Jason Childers, Chris DeBlasio, Garance Franke-Ruta, Jerry Jontz, Derek Link, Rich Lynn, Kim Powers, and Scott Slutsky, *The Countdown 18 Months Plan,* November 1990, 1.

4. Treatment & Data Committee, ACT UP/NY, 2.

5. Treatment & Data Committee, ACT UP/NY, 7.

6. ACT UP internal document: Mark Harrington, transcriber, "10th AIDS Clinical Trials Group (ACTG) Meeting," November 11–15, 1990.

7. Harrington.

8. Harrington.

9. Harrington.

10. ACT UP internal document: Mark Harrington, "9th AIDS Clinical Trials Group (ACTG) Meeting," July 10–13, 1990.

11. ACT UP fact sheet: "We Have Been Betrayed," [ca. November 6, 1990].

12. Larry Kramer, "Remembering Vito Russo—He Understood What Longings We Hold inside Us," *Village Voice*, November 20, 1990.

13. Arnie Kantrowitz and Larry Mass, "Remembering Vito Russo—He Had a Good Mouth on His Shoulders," *Village Voice*, November 20, 1990.

14. Debra Levine, "Another Kind of Love: A Performance of Prosthetic Politics," viewed March 9, 2022, http://hemi.nyu.edu/journal/2_2/pdf/levine.pdf.

15. Levine.

16. Kevin B. Smith, "An Open Love Letter to My Warrior Friends," ACT UP handout, also in his memorial notice.

17. ACT UP fact sheet: "The U.S. Department of Health and Human Service Routinely Denies Social Security Insurances and Benefits and Supplemental Security Income Disability Benefits to Women with AIDS," undated.

18. Terry McGovern, interviewed by Sarah Schulman, ACT UP Oral History Project, May 25, 2007, 11.

19. McGovern, interview, 13–15.

20. Mireya Navarro, "Conversations: Katrina Haslip; An AIDS Activist Who Helped Women Get Help Earlier," *New York Times*, November 15, 1992.

21. McGovern, interview, 18–19.

22. Nina Reyes, "Invisible Science: Lesbians and AIDS," *OutWeek*, January 9, 1991.

23. Kathryn Anastos and Carola Marte, "Women—The Missing Persons in the AIDS Epidemic," *Health/PAC Bulletin* 19, no. 4 (Winter 1989): 6–13.

24. ACT UP press release: "AIDS Activists Storm CDC at Two Locations Over 50 Occupy Executive Offices," December 3, 1990.

25. Jim Hubbard, *United in Anger: A History of ACT UP* (2012), video, 1:03:09–1:03:20.

26. Hubbard, 1:09:20–1:09:30.

27. "A Costa Her/History" submitted to the Mulberry Group, March 2, 1991.

28. Kramer, "Remembering Vito Russo."

29. Larry Kramer, "We Killed Vito," in Kramer, *Reports from the Holocaust: The Story of an AIDS Activist*, rev. ed. 1994 (New York: St. Martin's, 1997), 369.

30. "Ortez Alderson," Chicago LGBT Hall of Fame, viewed December 10, 2019, http://chicagolgbthalloffame.org/alderson-ortez/.

21. Desperate Measures

1. ACT UP internal document: Gay Wachman, "Needles for Woody," *"Newsletter,"* January 28, 1991.

2. Betty Williams, "ACT UP Town," *ACT UP Reports*, 1991, no. 1.

3. Gonzalo Aburto, interviewed by Sarah Schulman, ACT UP Oral History Project, August 26, 2008, 29–30.

4. Juan Mendez, "'Grito Latino': Latinas/os en el Dia de la Desperacion," *ACT UP Reports,* 1991, no.1.

5. ACT UP internal document: Latina/o Caucus, "The Naked Truth about the Hispanic AIDS Forum," undated.

6. ACT UP internal document: Anna Blume, "Alternatives for HHC," *"Newsletter,"* January 28, 1991.

7. ACT UP internal document: Tim Bailey, "Bones for Citicorp," *"Newsletter,"* January 28, 1991.

8. ACT UP internal document: Karin Timour, "VITOs Hit Insurers," *"Newsletter,"* February 4, 1991.

9. Aldyn McKean, "Getting Arrested." *ACT UP Reports,* 1991, no. 1.

10. Nina Reyes, "Cathedral Graffiti Leads to Three Arrests," *OutWeek,* February 20, 1991.

11. Letter to the editor from the Police Violence Working Group, ACT UP/Queer Nation re Nina Reyes's "When Bashers Wear Badges: Cops, Queers and the CCRB," *OutWeek,* April 24, 1991.

12. Emily Sachar, "Charges Dropped against Gay Activist," *New York Newsday,* October 1, 1991.

13. "Man Says Police Beat Him at Act-Up Rally," *New York Times,* February 20, 1991.

14. Nina Reyes, "ACT UP Lesbians Spooked by Threats and Harassing Calls," *OutWeek,* May 22, 1991.

15. Duncan Osborne, "Under Arrest," *OutWeek,* June 12, 1991.

16. Duncan Osborne, "ACT UP and the FBI," *The Advocate,* June 29, 1993.

17. Greg B. Smith, "FBI Eyeing AIDS Group," *Daily News,* May 15, 1995.

18. ACT UP, "Women's Treatment Agenda," in *Treatment and Research Agenda for Women with HIV Infection,* May 1991, 2.

19. Risa Dennenberg, "Women, AIDS, Lesbians and Politics," *OutWeek,* March 20, 1991.

20. *Treatment and Data Digest,* no. 71, November 26, 1990.

21. ACT UP internal document: Tracy Morgan, "TITA Pick of the Week," "TITA," no. 40, December 26, 1990.

22. Tracy Morgan, interviewed by Sarah Schulman, ACT UP Oral History Project, October 12, 2012, 52–53.

23. Morgan, interview, 58.

24. Letter from David Byar to ACT UP, undated.

25. Tracy Morgan response to David Byar letter, undated.

26. Morgan, interview, 61.

27. Morgan, 62.

28. Morgan, 60.

29. ACT UP internal document: Quinn Sellars—AIDS Project Social Worker, Coalition for the Homeless, "TITA," no. 42, January 14, 1991.

30. ACT UP internal document: "Town Meeting: Whither ACT UP?," *"Newsletter,"* January 14, 1991.

31. Peter Serko, *My Brother Kissed Mark Zuckerberg* (self-pub., Blurb Books, November 2017), 31.

22. Splitting Differences

1. ACT UP fact sheet: "Board of Ed: Look at the Facts—AIDS Education and Condom Availability Save Lives!," undated.

2. Center for Population Options, "Adolescents and Sexually Transmitted Diseases," April 1989, citing Lynda Madaras, *Lynda Madaras Talks to Teens about AIDS* (New York: Newmarket Press, 1988), 36.

3. Center for Population Options, citing Centers for Disease Control, *HIV/AIDS Surveillance Report*, March 1989.

4. Jeffrey Fennelly, "Writing on the Wall of Plato's Cave," *OutWeek*, June 27, 1990.

5. ACT UP internal document: "Y.E.L.L.," undated.

6. ACT UP pamphlet: "AIDS: What YOU Need to Know/*SIDA: Lo Que TU Necesitas Saber*," 1990–91.

7. ACT UP internal document: "Youth Brigade/Y.E.L.L. Fact Sheet," [ca. May 1990].

8. ACT UP internal document: "Y.E.L.L."

9. Samuel P. Helfrich, "YELL," *ACT UP Reports* 1991, no. 1.

10. Headline: "Teacher Tells Class: I Have AIDS Virus," *Newsday*, October 31, 1990.

11. NIAID Backgrounder: "ACTG Protocol 076—Questions and Answers," March 8, 1991.

12. Ad hoc 076 working group fact sheet: "ACTG 076 Is Bad Science and Is Unethical," [ca. March 10, 1991].

13. ACT UP fact sheet: "ACTG 076 Is Bad Science and Is Unethical."

14. Mark Harrington, "11th AIDS Clinical Trials Group (ACTG) Meeting," March 10–13, 1991, Washington, DC.

15. Untitled statement from AIDS Activists, March 10, 1991.

16. "A Statement of the People of Color Caucus of the Community Constituency Group," Washington, DC, March 11, 1991.

17. Ad hoc 076 working group fact sheet: "Think Again, ACTG 11," undated.

18. ACT UP internal document: Barbara Hughes, "Sidebar: 076 Discussion," "*Newsletter*," March 25, 1991.

19. ACT UP internal document: Larry Kramer, "To ACT UP on Its 4th Birthday," [ca. March 18, 1991].

20. ACT UP internal document: Maxine Wolfe, "A Proposal for an ACT UP Women's Issues Strategy vis à vis NIAID and the CDC," undated.

21. Wolfe, "A Proposal for an ACT UP Women's Issues Strategy."

22. ACT UP internal document: Latina/o AIDS Activists, no title, [ca. April 8, 1991].

23. ACT UP internal document: Activistas Latinas/os Contra El Side ACT UP Nueva York, "Compañeras y Compañeros de ACT UP/N.Y.," [ca. March 4, 1991].

24. Elias Guerrero, interviewed by Sarah Schulman, ACT UP Oral History Project, March 17, 2004, 24.

25. ACT UP internal document: Maxine Wolfe, "Of Meetings and Moritoria [*sic*]: Reality vs. Rumor—An Open Letter to NY ACT UP," undated.

26. Michael Petrelis, "An Open Letter to Jim Eigo & Mark Harrington," *Piss & Vinegar*, no. 7, February 1991.

27. ACT UP internal document: Derek Link, "HIV Negatives: Get Out of Our Way," undated.

28. Robin Hardy, "DIE HARDER—AIDS Activism Is Abandoning Gay Men," *Village Voice*, July 2, 1991.

29. ACT UP internal document: Charlie Franchino, "TITA," no. 52, April 1, 1991.

30. ACT UP internal document: Jim Eigo, "Of Meetings & Moratoria (An Open Letter to ACT UP)," undated.

31. Eigo.

32. ACT UP internal document: "Statement of the Treatment + Data Committee," April 1, 1991.

33. Wolfe, "A Proposal for an ACT UP Women's Issues Strategy."

34. ACT UP internal document: dan k. williams, "An Open Letter to ACT UP," June 10, 1991.

35. Dan Keith Williams, interviewed by Jim Hubbard, ACT UP Oral History Project, March 26, 2004, 36–43.

36. "HIV/AIDS: Snapshots of an Epidemic," amfAR, viewed April 26, 2015, http://www.amfar.org/thirty-years-of-hiv/aids-snapshots-of-an-epidemic/.

23. Target Bush

1. Follow-up Letter from the Target Bush Working Group to "AIDS Activists," undated.

2. "An Open Letter to George Bush," from the Target Bush 30 Days of Action packet, undated.

3. ACT UP/DC press release: "ACT UP Plans National Actions for Washington, D.C., September 28 through October 1," July 21, 1991.

4. Post Wire Service, "Bush Rips O'Connor's AIDS Foes," *New York Post,* April 20, 1991.

5. "Sample letter to the White House," part of the Target Bush information packet sent out to over 1,400 activist and community groups across all fifty states and Puerto Rico, asking them to participate in the campaign.

6. Andrew Rosenthal, "Bush Plays Down Protest on AIDS," *New York Times, September* 3, 1991.

7. AP, "Bush Assails Tactics Used by AIDS Lobby," *New York Times,* April 21, 1991, https://www.nytimes.com/1991/04/21/us/bush-assails-tactics-used-by-aids-lobby.html.

8. Maureen Dowd, "Bush Chides Protestors on 'Excesses,'" *New York Times,* August 17, 1991.

9. Susan Gilman, "Police Prepare for ACT UP," *York County Coast Star,* August 28, 1991, quoting Sgt. Ronan.

10. Gilman, "Police Prepare for ACT UP."

11. Tom Berg, "Acting Up: Activists' Tactics Reveal Anger," *Journal Tribune,* August 31, 1991.

12. ACT UP, letter to merchants of Kennebunkport, August 19, 1991.

13. "The AIDS Epidemic: Government Will Act When We Demand It," editorial, *Biddeford (ME) Journal Tribune,* August 31, 1991.

14. "Passion and Anger," editorial, *York County Coast Star,* August 28, 1991.

15. Susan Milligan, "Kennebunkport in a Storm," *New York Daily News,* August 30, 1991.

16. Avram Finkelstein, Facebook, viewed December 5, 2018, https://www.facebook.com/avram.finkelstein.

17. AP, "1,500 AIDS Demonstrators March near Bush's Estate," *Worcester (MA) Telegram & Gazette,* September 2, 1991.

18. Steve Campbell, "AIDS Activists Demand Attention," *Portland Press Herald,* September 2, 1991.

19. AP, "1,500 AIDS Demonstrators."

20. Mireya Navarro, "AIDS Definition Is Widened to Include Blood Cell Count," *New York Times,* August 8, 1991.

21. Letter to William Roper, MD, from M. Roy Schwarz, MD, May 29, 1991.

22. Tracy Morgan with Ed Ball and Kimberley Smith, "How Would It Change the World We Live In If We Were Told The Truth about the Real Numbers of People with AIDS? For Whose Benefit Is the Epidemic Being Statistically Suppressed and Artificially Deflated?"*ACT UP Reports,* 1991, no. 2.

23. Tim Golden, "Dental Patient Torn by AIDS Calls for Laws," *New York Times,* June 22, 1991.

24. Peter Applebome, "Dentist Dies of AIDS, Leaving Florida City Concerned but Calm," *New York Times,* September 8, 1990, http://www.nytimes.com/1990/09/08/us/dentist-dies-of-aids-leaving-florida-city-concerned-but-calm.html.

25. Martin Tolchin, "Senate Adopts Tough Measures on Health Workers with AIDS," *New York Times,* July 19, 1991, http://www.nytimes.com/1991/07/19/us/senate-adopts-tough-measures-on-health-workers-with-aids.html.

26. Tolchin.

27. Richard L. Berke, "AIDS Battle Reverting to 'Us against Them,'" *New York Times,* October 6, 1991.

28. Philip J. Hilts, "AIDS Patient Urges Congress to Pass Testing Bill," *New York Times,* September 27, 1991.

29. Kevin Sack, "Albany Plans to Allow Surgery by Doctors with the AIDS Virus," *New York Times,* October 9, 1991.

30. ACT UP internal document, "Arguments against Condom Availability/Arguments in Favor of Condom Availability," no date.

31. Kate Barnhart, interviewed by Sarah Schulman, ACT UP Oral History Project, March 21, 2004, 4–5.

32. Barnhart, interview, 10.

33. Barnhart, 11–13.

34. Joseph Burger, "The Region; In New York City, Catholic Clout Wanes," *New York Times,* September 22, 1991.

35. Burger.

36. Andrew Rosenthal, "Bush Plays Down Protest on AIDS," *New York Times,* September 3, 1991.

37. Susan Page, "Irked, Bush Defends His Policy on AIDS," *Newsday,* September 3, 1991.

38. Rosenthal, "Bush Plays Down Protest on AIDS."

39. Marcia Slacum Greene, "AIDS Activists March on the White House," *Washington Post,* October 1, 1991.

40. Melanie Howard, "AIDS Activists Are Arrested for Actions at White House," *Washington Times,* October 1, 1991.

41. Philip J. Hilts, "Panel Faults Leaders on AIDS Epidemic," *New York Times,* September 26, 1991, http://www.nytimes.com/1991/09/26/us/panel-faults-leaders-on-aids-epidemic.html.

42. Karin Timour, interviewed by Sarah Schulman, ACT UP Oral History Project, April 5, 2003, 8.

43. Barry Lapidus and Karin Timour, "Testimony by The Insurance and Healthcare Access Committee of ACT UP/New York on The Empire Blue Cross/Blue Shield Rate Proposal for October 1, 1991," August 5, 1991 (for hearing September 6, 1991).

44. Timour, interview, 24–25.

45. Timour, 27–30.

46. Timour, 39.

47. Mark Kostopoulos, "The American Medical Care Muddle," in *Universal Health Care: A Handbook for Activists*, ACT UP/Network Publication, October 1991.

48. Deborah B. Gould, *Moving Politics* (Chicago: University of Chicago Press, 2009), 406.

49. ACT UP internal document: "Healthcare Action" Report 4, March 1991.

50. ACT UP internal document: "Healthcare Action" Report 3, February 1991.

51. ACT UP press release: "ACT UP Continues 'Bloody' Assault on Washington Senate Disrupted by Demands for National Health Care," October 1, 1991.

52. AP, "74 Jailed as ACT-UP Storms Capitol," *New York Post*, October 2, 1991.

24. Strategies and Consequences

1. "ACTG #175: Nucleoside Ad Infinitum: Research Execs Feather Their Nests with Drug Industry Largesse—While Endlessly Scrutinizing Mediocrity," *Treatment and Data Digest*, no. 102, July 29, 1991.

2. "ACTG #175: Nucleoside Ad Infinitum."

3. "Mark's Travels," *Treatment and Data Digest*, no. 112, October 17, 1991.

4. "Whither T+D?" *Treatment and Data Digest,* no. 116, November 18, 1991. [Author's note: This issue may have been misdated, as there are two separate issues with the same date and number.]

5. Meeting transcript: Treatment and Data Committee meeting, November 6, 1991, 2. "A772 Mark Harrington, ACT UP (NYC) Treatment & Data group (+comments from Larry Kramer)" is the name of the transcript made by the team working for David France on *How to Survive a Plague*. The video time marking is 00:04:00.52.

6. "Whither T+D?"

7. "Whither T+D?"

8. "Jay Lipner," *Treatment and Data Digest,* no. 116, November 18, 1991. [Author's note: May be misdated, as there are two separate issues with the same date and number.]

9. Jerry Adler with Mary Hager, Jeanne Gordon, Emily Yoffe, Patricia King, and Lucille Beachy, "Magic's Message," *Newsweek*, November 17, 1991, https://www.newsweek.com/magics-message-202016.

10. Adler et al.

11. "Magic Johnson, as President," editorial, *New York Times,* November 9, 1991.

12. Deborah Orin, "Bush Hails Magic, Admits Neglect on AIDS," *New York Post*, November 9, 1991.

13. ACT UP internal document: Bob Lederer, "Some Suggested Concepts for a National AIDS Treatment Action Campaign," November 6, 1991.

14. ACT UP internal document: Mark Harrington, "A Fifth Anniversary Letter to ACT UP," March 5, 1992.

15. ACT UP internal document: Mark Harrington, "Brief Report—13th ACTG," December 1991.

16. Harrington.

17. Harrington.

18. Andrew Jacobs, "ACT UP Splits Over Drug Trial," *NYQ*, December 15, 1991.

19. Jacobs.

20. Jacobs.

25. ACT UP/Petrelis

1. *Treatment and Data Digest*, no. 103, August 5, 1991.

2. ACT UP internal document: Mark Harrington, "A Fifth Anniversary Letter to ACT UP, March 5, 1992."

3. Harrington.

4. Ann Northrup, "Elmer Fuddge," *NYQ*, January 26, 1992.

5. Adam Pertman, "Gay Activist Dragged from Buchanan Event," *Boston Globe*, December 11, 1991.

6. AP, "Assault Complaint Filed against Buchanan Workers," *New Hampshire Union Leader*, December 18, 1991.

7. Dolna Chiacu (AP), "Dogging the Candidates in New Hampshire," *Bay Windows* (Boston), January 9, 1992.

8. Chiacu.

9. ACT UP/New Hampshire press release: "Controversial ACT UP TV Commercial to Run during ABC's 'Nightline,'" January 8, 1992.

10. "Station Pulls AIDS Ad," *Wall Street Journal*, January 10, 1991.

11. AP, "WMUR Is Accused of Homophobia," *New Hampshire Union Leader*, January 10, 1992.

12. Stuart Elliot, "The Media Business: Advertising—Addenda; Miscellany," *New York Times*, January 13 and 31, 1992.

13. *ACT UP/New Hampshire press release:* "ACT UP Plans Massive Primary-Eve AIDS Demonstration in New Hampshire; Hundreds Expected for February 15 March and Rally," January 23, 1992.

14. *ACT UP/New Hampshire press release:* "Holiday Inn Hotel Cancels Agreement to Rent Meeting Room to ACT UP; Hotel Claims AIDS Group Is Too Political," January 28, 1992.

15. *ACT UP/New Hampshire internal document*: "Final Update for the February 15 Rally and March in Manchester," February 10, 1992.

16. Glenn Thrush, "ACT UP Storms New Hampshire in Prelude to Primary," *NYQ*, March 1, 1992.

17. Kevin Landrigan, "Hopefuls Storm New Hampshire," *Nashua (NH) Sunday Telegraph*, February 16, 1992.

18. Landrigan.

19. Christopher Williams, "Kerry Tags Bush as Being 'Monumentally Indifferent,'" *Nashua (NH) Sunday Telegraph*, February 16, 1992.

20. Dorothea Tsipopoulos, "Clinton Promises Change in Exchange for Chance," *Nashua (NH) Sunday Telegraph*, February 16, 1992.

21. "Hickman line," Wikipedia, accessed March 18, 2017, https://en.wikipedia.org/wiki/Hickman_line.

22. Janet Firshein, "Groups Pan New AIDS Commercials," *Faulkner & Gray's Medicine & Health* 46, no. 13, March 30, 1992.

23. Firshein.

24. Lisa M. Keen, "Buchanan Bashes Gays in New Television Commercial," *Washington Blade*, February 28, 1992.

25. Keen.

26. The In-Your-Face Primary

1. ACT UP fax zap flyer, "Time to Make the Candidates Talk about AIDS," [ca. March 1992].

2. "Heckler Stirs Clinton Anger: Excerpts from the Exchange," *New York Times*, March 28, 1992.

3. Timothy Clifford, "Heckler Razzes Clinton," *New York Newsday*, March 27, 1992.

4. Clifford.

5. "Heckler Stirs Clinton Anger."

6. David Barr, interviewed by Sarah Schulman, ACT UP Oral History Project, May 15, 2007, 77.

7. Barr, interview, 16.

8. Based on the notes of Aldyn McKean and my own handwritten notes from the April 4, 1992, meeting.

9. Catherine Woodard, "ACT UP 'Seizes the Moment,'" *New York Newsday*, March 28, 1992.

10. Michael Specter, "Treading a Mosaic of Nerve Endings," *New York Times*, March 28, 1992.

27. Unconventional Behavior

1. Testimony by Robert Rygor before the Democratic National Platform Committee in Cleveland, Ohio, Monday, May 18, 1992.

2. "1992 Democratic Party Platform," July 13, 1992, The American Presidency Project, https://www.presidency.ucsb.edu/node/273264.

3. Steven A. Holmes, "The 1992 Campaign: Undeclared Candidate; Perot in Wide-Ranging TV Interview," *New York Times*, May 29, 1992

4. ACT UP/Presidential Project internal fax release: "Urgent Fax/Phone Zap," May 29, 1992.

5. Michael Kelly, "Perot Shifts on Homosexuals in Military," *New York Times*, July 10, 1992.

6. Donna Minkowitz, "We Are Family," *Village Voice*, July 28, 1992.

7. Jody Powell, "You Can Do Something about AIDS," The Stop AIDS Project, Boston, MA, 1988.

8. ACT UP fact sheet: "Media: Beware—Your AIDS Reporting Is Killing Us," [ca. July 11, 1992].

9. UAA press release: "United for AIDS Action Statement on March & Rally Incidents between ACT UP and NYC Police," July 15, 1992, cites 20,000 participants and a coalition of over 425 organizations.

10. Anonymous Queers, "Fuck the United AIDS Action. But Please Stay," July 1992.

11. Anonymous Queers.

12. Letter from Ty Geltmaker and James Rosen to United for AIDS Action, July 16, 1992.

13. "Bob Hattoy's Speech to the 1992 Democratic National Convention," Towleroad, viewed July 10, 2016, http://www.towleroad.com/2007/03/bob_hattoys_spe/.

14. "Bob Hattoy's Speech."

15. Elizabeth Glaser, "1992 Democratic National Convention Address," American Rhetoric Top 100 Speeches, page updated July 21, 2021, http://www.americanrhetoric.com/speeches/elizabethglaser1992dnc.htm.

16. Sydney H. Schanberg, "AIDS Speeches Bring Rare Moments of Stillness," *Newsday*, July 17, 1992.

17. Minkowitz, "We Are Family."

18. Andrew Rosenthal, "After the Riots; Quayle Says Riots Sprang from Lack of Family Values," *New York Times*, May 20, 1992.

19. Excerpts from "The Vision Shared: Uniting Our Family, Our Country, Our World" as per "Excerpts from the Republican Party's Platform: A Call to Unity," *New York Times*, August 18, 1992.

20. "The 1992 Republican Party Platform," CNN, viewed June 23, 2019, http://www.cnn.com/ALLPOLITICS/1996/conventions/san.diego/facts/past.platforms/gop92/index.shtml#AIDS.

21. James Ridgeway, "Imperial Prudes" *Village Voice*, September 1, 1992.

22. Jack Ben-Levi, "Activists, Police Clash in Houston Streets," *QW*, August 30, 1992.

23. Tara Parker-Pope, "AIDS Activists Say Police Beat Them," *Houston Chronicle*, August 19, 1992.

24. Parker-Pope.

25. Matt Schwartz, "ACT UP Protest Turns Ugly," *Houston Post*, August 19, 1992.

26. Donna Minkowitz, "I Was the Antichrist at the Astrodome" (description of Falwell action, including quotes), *Village Voice*, September 1, 1992.

27. Minkowitz.

28. Richard Brown, "ACT UP Interrupts Falwell," *Body Positive*, October 1992.

29. Pat Robertson, "Speech: 1992 Republican Convention," Pat Robertson website, viewed May 1, 2016, http://www.patrobertson.com/Speeches/1992GOPConvention.asp.

30. Mary Fisher, "A Whisper of AIDS," Gifts of Speech, August 19, 1992, http://gos.sbc.edu/f/fisher.html.

31. "Voices: From the Floor, Words to Remember," *USA Today*, August 21, 1992.

32. Karen Houppert, "Close Your Eyes and Think of George Bush," *Village Voice*, September 1, 1992.

28. Vote as If Your Life Depended on It

1. Philip J. Hilts, "Magic Johnson Quits Panel on AIDS," *New York Times*, September 26, 1992.

2. Governor Bill Clinton, "Let Us Rise to the Challenge," speech at Palace Theater, May 18, 1992.

3. ACT UP flyer: "An Open Letter to Governor Clinton," undated.

4. "October 11, 1992, Second Half Debate Transcript," The Commission on Presidential Debates, viewed April 7, 2018, http://www.debates.org/index.php?page=october-11-1992-second-half-debate-transcript.

5. "Fighting the AIDS Crisis, Remarks by Governor Bill Clinton," Justice Brennan Courthouse, Jersey City, NJ, October 29, 1992.

6. David Wojnarowicz, *Close to the Knives: A Memoir of Disintegration* (New York: Vintage, 1991).

7. Mark Fisher, "Bury Me Furiously," viewed April 6, 2022, https://speakola.com/eulogy/fisher-rafsky-bury-me-furiously-1992.

8. Russell Pritchard, interviewed by Sarah Schulman, ACT UP Oral History Project, April 23, 2003, 33–34.

9. Bob Rafsky, "For Mark Fisher: 'We beg, we pray, we demand that this epidemic end!'," viewed April 6, 2022, https://speakola.com/eulogy/fisher-rafsky-bury-me-furiously-1992.

10. Transcript of Clinton victory speech, C-Span, viewed July 31, 2016, https://www.c-span.org/video/?34055-1/bill-clinton-victory-speech.

11. David B. Feinberg, "Memorials from Hell," in *Queer and Loathing: Rants and Raves of a Raging AIDS Clone* (New York: Viking, 1994), 162–68.

12. Tony Kushner, *Angels in America, Part Two: Perestroika* (New York: Theatre Communications Group, 1994), 148.

13. Avram Finkelstein, *After Silence: A History of AIDS through Its Images* (Berkeley: University of California Press, 2020), 202.

Afterword

1. "U.S. Statistics," HIV.gov, viewed January 6, 2022, https://www.hiv.gov/hiv-basics/overview/data-and-trends/statistics.

2. David France, "The Activists," *T: The New York Times Style Magazine*, April 19, 2020.

3. Email from Jamie Leo to John Weir et al. re "ACT UP Photo Shoot by T-Style Magazine on Feb 28," February 28, 2020.

4. Email from Jamie Bauer to John Weir et al. re "ACT UP Photo Shoot by T-Style Magazine on Feb 28," February 27, 2020.

INDEX

Ron Goldberg is a writer and activist. His articles have appeared in *OutWeek* and *POZ* magazines, *Central Park*, and *The Visual AIDS Blog*. Ron served as a research associate for filmmaker and journalist David France on his award-winning book, *How to Survive a Plague*, and enjoys speaking at high schools and colleges about the history of AIDS and the lessons and legacy of ACT UP.

Salvatore Basile, *Fifth Avenue Famous: The Extraordinary Story of Music at St. Patrick's Cathedral*. Foreword by Most Reverend Timothy M. Dolan, Archbishop of New York

Daniel Campo, *The Accidental Playground: Brooklyn Waterfront Narratives of the Undesigned and Unplanned*

Joseph B. Raskin, *The Routes Not Taken: A Trip Through New York City's Unbuilt Subway System*

Phillip Deery, *Red Apple: Communism and McCarthyism in Cold War New York*

North Brother Island: The Last Unknown Place in New York City. Photographs by Christopher Payne, A History by Randall Mason, Essay by Robert Sullivan

Kirsten Jensen and Bartholomew F. Bland (eds.), *Industrial Sublime: Modernism and the Transformation of New York's Rivers, 1900–1940*. Introduction by Katherine Manthorne

Stephen Miller, *Walking New York: Reflections of American Writers from Walt Whitman to Teju Cole*

Tom Glynn, *Reading Publics: New York City's Public Libraries, 1754–1911*

Craig Saper, *The Amazing Adventures of Bob Brown: A Real-Life Zelig Who Wrote His Way Through the 20th Century*

R. Scott Hanson, *City of Gods: Religious Freedom, Immigration, and Pluralism in Flushing, Queens*. Foreword by Martin E. Marty

Mark Naison and Bob Gumbs, *Before the Fires: An Oral History of African American Life in the Bronx from the 1930s to the 1960s*

Robert Weldon Whalen, *Murder, Inc., and the Moral Life: Gangsters and Gangbusters in La Guardia's New York*

Sharon Egretta Sutton, *When Ivory Towers Were Black: A Story about Race in America's Cities and Universities*

Britt Haas, *Fighting Authoritarianism: American Youth Activism in the 1930s*

David J. Goodwin, *Left Bank of the Hudson: Jersey City and the Artists of 111 1st Street*. Foreword by DW Gibson

Nandini Bagchee, *Counter Institution: Activist Estates of the Lower East Side*

Susan Celia Greenfield (ed.), *Sacred Shelter: Thirteen Journeys of Homelessness and Healing*

Elizabeth Macaulay-Lewis and Matthew M. McGowan (eds.), *Classical New York: Discovering Greece and Rome in Gotham*

For a complete list, visit www.fordhampress.com/empire-state-editions.